ENCYCLOPEDIA OF WAR CRIMES AND GENOCIDE

Revised Edition

VOLUME II

Leslie Alan Horvitz
and Christopher Catherwood

Facts On File
An Infobase Learning Company

Encyclopedia of War Crimes and Genocide, Revised Edition

Facts On File, Inc.
An imprint of Infobase Learning
132 West 31st Street
New York NY 10001

Library of Congress Cataloging-in-Publication Data

Horvitz, Leslie Alan.
Encyclopedia of war crimes and genocide / Leslie Alan Horvitz and Christopher Catherwood.—Rev. ed.
v. cm.
Includes bibliographical references and index.
ISBN 978-0-8160-8083-0 (hc : alk. paper) 1. Genocide—Encyclopedias. 2. War crimes—Encyclopedias. 3. Human rights—Encyclopedias. 4. Racism—Encyclopedias. 5. Geopolitics—Encyclopedias. I. Catherwood, Christopher. II. Title.
HV6322.7.H67 2011
364.1'3803—dc22   2010015771

You can find Facts On File on the World Wide Web at http://www.factsonfile.com

Text design by Joan M. McEvoy
Composition by Hermitage Publishing Services
Cover printed by Yurchak Printing, Inc., Landisville, Pa.
Book printed and bound by Yurchak Printing, Inc., Landisville, Pa.
Date printed: March 2011
Printed in the United States of America

10 9 8 7 6 5 4 3 2 1

This book is printed on acid-free paper.

Contents

M

MacBride, Sean (1904–1988) *human rights activist*
Dr. Sean MacBride was awarded the Nobel Peace Prize in 1974 and later the Lenin Prize from the Soviet Union and the American Medal of Justice for his work on behalf of human rights. His achievement is all the more remarkable in view of the fact that earlier in his life he was a nationalist who had fought against British rule of Ireland.

Born on January 26, 1904, MacBride was nurtured on the milk of Irish nationalism. His father, John MacBride, was executed by the British for participating in the Easter Rebellion in 1916; his mother, Maud Gonne MacBride, a fiery beauty and passionate nationalist in her own right, was immortalized in the poems of W. B. Yeats. MacBride spent his first years in France; upon returning home in 1918, he joined the Fianna, an Irish nationalist party. In 1921 he was involved in the negotiations with the British that resulted in the partition of Ireland. He continued to fight against British rule in the north of the country, and in 1936 he became chief of staff of the Irish Republican Army (IRA). After World War II, however, he abandoned militancy and began a political party, Clann na Poblachta, which won enough seats in the 1947 parliamentary elections to earn him a place in the government as minister for external affairs. In that capacity he was among the drafters of the EUROPEAN CONVENTION FOR THE PROTECTION OF HUMAN RIGHTS, which guaranteed international protection for human rights. As president of the Committee of Ministers of the Council of Europe from 1949 to 1950, MacBride was a driving force to gain acceptance of the convention, which was signed into law in Rome in November 1950. He devoted the rest of his life to the advocacy of the principles enshrined in the convention. A cofounder of AMNESTY INTERNATIONAL, he went on to serve as UN commissioner for Namibia (former South-West Africa) with the rank of assistant secretary general.

In awarding MacBride the Peace Prize in 1974, the Nobel Committee cited him for having "mobilized the conscience of the world in the fight against injustice." In 1979 he acted as a mediator in efforts to secure the release of American hostages being held in the U.S. embassy in Teheran. In addition to his other posts, he served as president of the International Board of Amnesty International, secretary general of the International Commission of Jurists, and chairperson and later president of the International Peace Bureau. He was also the author of what became known as the MacBride Principles, which were intended to ensure that U.S. companies operating in Northern Ireland comply with equal employment opportunities for Catholics. He died in Dublin on January 15, 1988.

Further Reading:

Steiner, Henry J., and Philip Alston. *International Human Rights in Context: Law, Politics, Morals.* Oxford: Oxford University Press, 2000.
Welch, Claude E., Jr. *Ngos and Human Rights: Promise and Performance.* Pennsylvania Studies in Human Rights. Philadelphia: University of Pennsylvania Press, 2000.

Macedonia, human rights violations in

A former Yugoslav republic, Macedonia emerged, largely unscathed, from the Balkan wars that broke out in the 1990s. However, the country has not managed to escape the violent ethnic conflict that sparked the conflict. Macedonia is divided along ethnic and religious lines: dominant Orthodox Christian Slavs (67 percent) and Albanian Muslims (25 percent). In 2001 Albanian insurgents rebelled in an effort to gain greater autonomy. The violence was precipitated by the war in neighboring Kosovo, which, while mostly populated by Albanians, was controlled by Slavic Serbia. Many Albanian Kosovar fighters and thousands of civilians fleeing the fighting took refuge in Macedonia, provoking a refugee crisis and fueling unrest among indigenous Albanians. After some initial successes on the battlefield, Macedonian forces were driven back by the

Albanian National Liberation Army (NLA), which seized territory in the north and west of the country. The fighting was brought to an end by the intervention of the European Union and NATO. A peace accord, known as the Ohrid agreement, granted Albanians more political rights in exchange for the rebels laying down their arms. Although the agreement was bitterly opposed by Macedonian nationalists, both parties to the conflict have upheld its terms.

During the rebellion, human rights groups observed abuses by both Macedonian security forces and the insurgent NLA. Macedonian forces illegally detained Albanian men fleeing the violence and subjected them to maltreatment intended to exact confessions, actions HUMAN RIGHTS WATCH described as tantamount to TORTURE. Police were charged with systematically beating Albanian male civilians, including teenagers and the elderly. Similar abuses were reported against some Macedonian Slavs. On the other hand, Albanian rebels were accused by human rights groups of torture, sexual abuse, and mutilation of Macedonian Slav civilians. The NLA was also implicated in a pattern of abductions and illegal detentions.

In 2007 Macedonia was ranked as a "flawed democracy" (72nd of the 167 countries ranked) according to the Democracy Index, an index created by *Economist* magazine intended to measure electoral process, civil liberties, political participation, and political culture. The human rights situation is still problematic; the International Helsinki Federation for Human Rights reported cases of police abuse; harassment of ethnic minorities, especially the ROM; and a culture of impunity and corruption among the police. Ethnic tensions stemming from the insurgency also persist between Macedonians and ethnic Albanians nearly a decade after the settlement ending hostilities, and human rights violations on both sides have been documented. Trafficking of women and girls for sex slavery remains a chronic problem.

See also KOSOVO, WAR CRIMES IN.

Majid, Ali Hassan al- (Chemical Ali) (1941–2010)
Iraqi war criminal

Ali Hassan al-Majid earned the sobriquet by which he is best known, "Chemical Ali," for ordering an attack in 1988 using outlawed CHEMICAL WEAPONS, which are believed to have killed up to 5,000 Kurds in northern Iraq. He was the king of spades in the famous deck of cards of the 55 most-wanted Iraqi officials following the U.S. invasion in 2003. A cousin of Saddam Hussein, al-Majid held several important positions in his regime, serving as a general and as a close presidential adviser, or as Saddam's "hatchet man," in the words of a HUMAN RIGHTS WATCH report. During the 2003 U.S. invasion, al-Majid disappeared from sight for several months, and at one point it was thought that he had died in an American bombing strike on his home. However, after U.S. forces took Baghdad, he was captured in August 2003.

As secretary general of the Northern Bureau of Iraq's Baath Party, Ali Hassan al-Majid was in charge of all state agencies in the Kurdish region in northern Iraq from March 1987 to April 1989, giving him control of the army's I and V Corps, the general security directorate, and military intelligence. In orders dated June 20, 1987, he directed army commanders "to carry out special bombardments [a reference to chemical weapon use] . . . to kill the largest number of persons present in . . . prohibited zones"— meaning the Kurds, whom Saddam considered *insurrectionists*. The operations against the Kurds were known as the Anfal campaign; the name was derived from a quranic verse that justified the pillaging of infidel property. The Anfal campaign was launched just as the 1980–88 Iraq-Iran war was coming to an end. Some 100,000 civilians were killed or "disappeared," and many Kurdish villages and farms destroyed as a result of the Anfal campaign. Iraqi intelligence documents confiscated by U.S. military authorities leave no doubt that the campaign was systematic and conducted under al-Majid's direct supervision. He proved so effective at suppressing the Kurds that he was put in charge of Iraq's military occupation of Kuwait in 1990. He subsequently had a principle role in the campaign against an uprising by Iraq's Marsh Arabs during the 1990s in which the marshes were drained and almost a quarter of a million people were displaced, annihilating a culture that had thrived in the region for centuries. Each of these campaigns was characterized by executions, arbitrary arrests, "disappearances," torture, and other atrocities.

In 2004, al-Majid was one of 12 Iraqi officials (including Saddam Hussein) who went before an Iraqi court to hear the charges against them. As expected, one of the principal charges against him was the gassing of Kurds. He was reported as expressing surprise that the charges against him weren't even more numerous.

In September 2008 an Iraqi appeals court upheld his death sentence, which was supposed to be carried out within 30 days. However, further legal delays resulted in a third trial before the nine-member Iraqi High Tribunal. The tribunal was established by the U.S. provisional government in 2003 to hear cases involving former officials of the Hussein regime. In March 2009 the tribunal again sentenced al-Majid to death for his role in carrying out the poison gas attacks against the Kurds. In February 2010 the sentence was carried out.

See also KURDISTAN (IRAQ), SUPPRESSION OF.

Further Reading:
Aburish, Said K., and Aburish Said. *Saddam Hussein*. London: Bloomsbury Publishing, 2001.

BBC.co.uk. "'Chemical Ali' Executed in Iraq after Halubja Ruling" (January 25, 2010). Available online. URL: http://news.bbc.co.uk/2/hi/8479115.stm. Accessed March 20, 2010.

Coughlin, Con. *Saddam: King of Terror*. New York: Ecco, 2002.

Dodge, Toby. *Inventing Iraq: The Failure of Nation-Building and a History Denied*. New York: Columbia University Press, 2003.

Malaysia, human rights violations in

Among the most prosperous countries in Asia, Malaysia is a multiethnic, multireligious country; the minority Chinese dominate the economy and constitute the wealthiest community whereas the indigenous Malays dominate the political landscape. Indians are among the poorest of the three. It is a constant challenge to the country's leadership to maintain harmony among the many groups that make up this nation of over 25 million.

Until recently Malaysia was ruled by the autocratic prime minister Mahathir bin Mohamad, who only stepped down in October 2003 after 22 years in power, making him Asia's longest-serving elected leader. His successor, Abdullah Ahmad Badawi, is a more self-effacing leader who, upon taking office, was forced to cope with a rising Islamic fundamentalist movement. In a significant departure from his predecessor, he released former deputy prime minister Anwar Ibrahim from prison. Freeing Malaysia's best-known opposition figure was considered a milestone in the struggle for human rights in Malaysia. Anwar had been arrested in September 1998 on charges of corruption and sodomy widely seen as politically motivated; until his arrest, he had been thought to be Mahathir's successor. Initially held under Malaysia's Internal Security Act, he was beaten by the national chief of police. After two separate trials in 1999 and 2000, he was sentenced to consecutive terms of six and nine years, respectively. Both trials were considered unfair by human rights groups; the prosecution frequently changed its charges, and government witnesses offered contradictory statements. The verdict was overturned by the nation's high court after Abdullah Badawi was elected. The sodomy conviction of a codefendant, Sukma Darmawan, was thrown out at the same time. Although Anwar's case is a "barometer" of Malaysia's commitment to freedom, HUMAN RIGHTS WATCH and other groups have called attention to about 100 lesser-known cases where detainees have been held under the Internal Security Act. Many of these are suspected militants who have remained in custody for up to three years without charges or trials. There have also been reports that these detainees have suffered from physical and psychological abuse. Some

were forced to stand seminaked for long periods and subjected to sexually humiliating interrogations. Human rights groups also expressed the hope that Anwar's release might signal greater judicial independence than was seen under Mahathir's administration. "At some point, the Malaysian courts will again be called upon to render justice in a politically charged case," said a representative of Human Rights Watch when Anwar's conviction was overturned. "They must be able to hear cases free of outside pressure. That didn't happen with Anwar until today."

Like many other countries, the Malaysian government has used the global war against terrorism instituted after the attacks of September 11, 2001, as a pretext to curtail its commitments to human rights. In 2003, 11 persons died in police custody. The government-sponsored Human Rights Commission of Malaysia (Suhakam) contended that in addition to deaths that occurred in police custody, it had received "numerous" complaints of police brutality and negligence. Although no constitutional provision or law specifically prohibits TORTURE, there are laws that prohibit "committing grievous hurt," which does encompass torture. When investigations are carried out by the government, however, it does not issue reports on its findings. The Bar Council has expressed its distress with the situation and called for an investigation of a "number" of allegations of police abuse.

The 2004 U.S. State Department *Country Report* on Malaysia, covering events of the previous year, gives Malaysia credit for adhering to human rights, though it said that some problems remained. The government itself has acknowledged that it restricts certain political and civil rights in order to maintain social harmony and preserve political stability. Limits have been placed on freedom of the press, freedom of association, and freedom of assembly. There is also some discrimination against nonethnic Malays. Because of its geographical location, Malaysia is both a source and destination for trafficking in women and girls for the purposes of prostitution.

Further Reading:
Crouch, Harold. *Government and Society in Malaysia*. Ithaca, N.Y.: Cornell University Press, 1996.

Gomez, Edmund Terence, and K. S. Jomo. *Malaysia's Political Economy: Politics, Patronage and Profits*. Cambridge: Cambridge University Press, 1997.

Manchuria, Japanese war crimes in

Japan's territorial ambitions in Manchuria in northern China extend back to the Russo-Japanese War (1904–05) from which Japan emerged victorious. Manchuria was a military prize because of its coal, iron, and other mineral resources. In 1931 Japan installed the last emperor of

China as the head of a puppet state called Manchukuo. However, the Japanese did not fully occupy Manchuria until 1937, when Japanese forces defied the League of Nations and invaded the region. Over the next several years the Japanese military proceeded to initiate a secret BIOLOGICAL WEAPONS program. The most notorious biological research facility, put into operation in 1939, was known as Unit 731 and based in Pingfan, Manchuria. The existence of Unit 731 and other similar units did not become known until nearly four decades after the war. The compound of 150 buildings housed a laboratory, an autopsy room, and a prison for the human subjects referred to as "logs," "monkeys," or "lumber." The prisoners were made up of criminals and political dissidents rounded up by the feared military police and other security forces.

Unit 731 was directed by a brilliant and flamboyant Japanese army microbiologist named Chujo Shiro Ishii. He called his work *Himitsu ni Himitsu*—"Secret of Secrets." An ultranationalist, he rose rapidly in the ranks of the military with the help of influential friends, eventually winning an assignment to Manchuria. His first command was code-named the "Togo Unit," where, in one of their first biological experiments, the Japanese introduced bubonic plague into China's eastern Zhejiang Province, killing 400 villagers in September 1942. Ishii later took over Unit 731, which was developing germ bombs that were intended to be dropped from warplanes on China. The unit was responsible for contaminating Manchuria's water supply with typhus. Every few days Ishii and his associates would draw 500 cc of blood from the prisoners until they became enfeebled from losing too much blood at which point he executed them by lethal injection. Ishii was particularly interested in developing biological weapons based on anthrax, glanders, and plague, all very contagious agents. He forced prisoners to consume drinks tainted with cholera, heroin, and castor oil seeds. After injecting prisoners with these agents, Ishii would carry out dissections rather than waiting for them to die. He did not confine his experiments to microbes; he also experimented with phosgene gas and potassium cyanide and used electricity to burn prisoners whom he later killed with poison. Frostbite experiments constituted another area of interest. Naked prisoners, male and female, were subjected to subfreezing temperatures; to ensure that the freezing was complete, the researchers pounded them with sticks until the impact produced a hollow sound. The prisoners were subsequently "defrosted" by a variety of means. Other experiments involved hanging prisoners upside down to determine how long it would take them to die.

A methodical record keeper, Ishii made certain to document these experiments in exhausting detail. As the war was coming to an end, he swore his officers to an oath of secrecy about their work at Unit 731. The facility itself was destroyed; so were most of the records of the experiments. Some of the dossiers survived, though, and came into the possession of Allied intelligence officials who were interested in learning about the research, fearing that the Americans had fallen too far behind the Japanese in the field of biological warfare. In 1948 the Allies offered Ishii and other top officials of Unit 731 immunity in exchange for their data, making it all but impossible for attorneys at the TOKYO TRIALS to prosecute them.

With characteristic bravado, Ishii delivered papers on the results of his research at distinguished scientific conferences. He never mentioned that the subjects of his research were human, but it was well known in Japanese scientific circles. He even went so far as to patent 200 of his discoveries, which earned him a considerable sum of money. At one point Ishii reportedly traveled to the United States after the war to give a talk. The role the United States played in cover-up of Unit 731 did not come to light until the publication of an article on the subject by John W. Powell, Jr., in the *Bulletin of Atomic Scientists*. But the American public did not really learn about the experiments and the deal the United States had reached with Ishii until 1992, when segments on Unit 731 were aired on CBS's *60 Minutes* and ABC's *20/20*.

In spite of the renewed attention, legal actions against the criminals of Unit 731 have made little progress; Japanese courts routinely reject lawsuits by victims of such experiments or their families, although appeals continue to be lodged. The Japanese government has also resisted calls to make financial restitution to survivors and their families. No Japanese government has ever acknowledged the guilt of physicians who participated in these experiments, although Japan had ratified the 1906 Hague Convention, which provides that "officers, soldiers, and other persons officially attached to armies, who are sick or wounded, shall be respected and cared for, without distinction of nationality, by the belligerent in whose power they are."

See also MATSUOKA YOSUKE.

Further Reading:
Daws, Gavin. *Prisoners of the Japanese: POWS of World War II in the Pacific.* New York: Perennial, 1996.

Harris, Sheldon. *Factories of Death: Japanese Biological Warfare 1932–45 and the American Cover-Up.* London: Routledge, 1995.

Li, Peter, ed. *Japanese War Crimes: The Search for Justice.* New Brunswick, N.J.: Transaction Publishers, 2003.

Maga, Timothy P. *Judgment at Tokyo: The Japanese War Crimes Trials.* Lexington: University Press of Kentucky, 2001.

Mendelsohn, John. *The Preservation of Japanese War Crimes Trials Records in the National Archives.* Washington, D.C.: National Archives and Records Administration, 1982.

Minear, Richard R. *Victors' Justice: The Tokyo War Crimes Trial.* Michigan Classics in Japanese Studies. Ann Arbor: University of Michigan Center for Japanese Studies, 2001.

Piccigallo, Philip R. *The Japanese on Trial: Allied War Crimes Operations in the East, 1945–1951.* Austin: University of Texas Press, 1980.

Rees, Laurence. *Horror in the East: Japan and the Atrocities of World War II.* New York: Da Capo Press, 2002.

Russell of Liverpool, Edward Frederick Langley Russell, Baron. *Knights of the Bushido: A Short History of Japanese War Crimes.* London: Greenhill Books, 2005.

Tanaka, Yuki. *Hidden Horrors: Japanese War Crimes in World War II.* Philadelphia: Westview Press, 1998.

Marri, Ali Saleh Kahlah al- (1966–) *Qatari terrorist*
Since the terrorist attacks on the United States of September 11, 2001, legal authorities have debated whether captured terrorists could be treated—and tried—as criminals or whether such persons should fall under the jurisdiction of special military tribunals. That dilemma was brought into sharp relief by the case of the AL-QAEDA operative Ali Saleh Kahlah al-Marri. An admitted sleeper agent, al-Marri, a U.S. citizen, trained at al-Qaeda camps and hid out at terrorist safe houses in Pakistan between 1998 and 2001. During that time, he learned how to handle weapons and how to communicate by phone and use coded e-mails. When he arrived in the United States on September 10, 2001, al-Marri was carrying an electronic device with phone numbers of other al-Qaeda agents. (Participants in the 9/11 attacks relied on a variety of rudimentary communications, including prepaid calling cards, public phones, and relatively simple codes.) Al-Marri also did research on cyanide gas on the Internet, suggesting that al-Qaeda might have been planning to use the gas on civilian populations. He was taken into custody in 2001 as a material witness in the FBI's probe of the 9/11 strike and initially charged with credit card fraud and other offenses. Then in June 2003, just before he was about to go on trial, the Justice Department reclassified al-Marri as an enemy combatant, and he was placed in solitary confinement in a U.S. Navy brig in Charleston, South Carolina. The American Civil Liberties Union (ACLU) challenged the reclassification, but before the case could be heard by the U.S. Supreme Court, the new Obama administration transferred al-Marri back to the criminal justice system. The about-face by the Justice Department

disappointed some civil libertarians who had hoped for a definitive ruling on the issue by the high court. Rather than go to trial, al-Marri entered a plea agreement in April 2009 that could cut his sentence in half to 15 years. (Since he had already served eight years in prison, it was possible that his actual sentence could turn out to be much shorter.) Legal experts agreed that the Justice Department's decision to cut a deal indicated that it would have had a difficult time convicting the al-Qaeda agent, possibly because he might have been subjected to harsh interrogation techniques sanctioned by the Bush administration that might have compromised the government's evidence against him. "If it went to trial," said Orin S. Kerr, a conservative law professor at George Washington University, "there would be all sorts of questions about the evidence: where it came from, how it was obtained, how it could be used." Stewart Baker, a former Homeland Security Department official, criticized the plea bargain, saying that it showed "some of the limitations of returning to the criminal enforcement model of antiterrorism." Not surprisingly, al-Marri's lawyer, Jonathan Hafetz disagreed, asserting that his client had been "finally given his day in court, consistent with the Constitution and the values that have long served the country." The case, while not resolving the issue, might have demonstrated that at least in some instances terrorists could receive a fair trial in the criminal justice system, but that the process would inevitably be slow and fraught with controversy. In June 2007, the U.S. Court of Appeals for the Fourth Circuit ruled in *al-Marri v. Wright* that the defendant was not deprived of his rights to challenge his accusers by being tried in a military proceeding, but nonetheless he would either have to be freed or remanded into the custody of U.S. civilian detention. In a rehearing of the ruling, the court ruled in July 2008 that al-Marri could be held indefinitely in military detention as an enemy combatant. In November 2008 al-Marri's lawyers petitioned the Supreme Court to overturn the lower court's ruling that allowed him to be held as an enemy combatant in spite of the fact that he was a U.S. citizen. The Supreme Court overturned the ruling of the circuit court, a decision that called into question the power of the executive to hold a U.S. citizen indefinitely in military detention, even though it was not a definitive ruling insofar as the high court failed to say whether such a detention was unconstitutional in all cases. Nor did the Supreme Court rule on the merits of the case itself, because al-Marri was no longer in military custody.

See also WAR ON TERROR.

Martens Clause

The Martens Clause is named for Professor Friedrich von Martens, the Russian delegate at the Hague Peace

Conferences of 1899. The clause is intended to address the issue of the status of civilians who take up arms against an OCCUPYING POWER. The larger states maintained that these civilians should be subject to execution, while the smaller states argued that they should be treated as lawful combatants who, if captured, should be treated as PRISONERS OF WAR. The Martens Clause states: "Until a more complete code of the laws of war is issued, the High Contracting Parties think it right to declare that in cases not included in the Regulations adopted by them, populations and belligerents remain under the protection and empire of the principles of international law, as they result from the usages established between civilized nations, from the laws of humanity and the requirements of the public conscience."

Ever since the clause's adoption, humanitarian lawyers have debated how its principles should be applied. For instance, some human rights advocates argue that the Martens Clause bans the use of nuclear weapons, a view that is rejected by the nuclear powers. The GENEVA CONVENTIONS of 1949 and the 1979 ADDITIONAL PROTOCOLS TO THE GENEVA CONVENTIONS have restated the Martens Clause. The International Law Commission has affirmed that the clause "provides that even in cases not covered by specific international agreements, civilians and combatants remain under the protection and authority of the principles of international law derived from established custom, from the principles of humanity and from the dictates of public conscience." That is to say, the clause is a part of CUSTOMARY LAW, which carries the force of law even when the protections in the clause are not cited in a particular treaty.

See also HAGUE CONVENTIONS.

Martić, Milan   *See* WAR CRIMINALS OF THE FORMER YUGOSLAVIA.

mass graves

Mass graves are often used to inter victims of atrocities during wartime. In recent years such graves have been uncovered in post-HUSSEIN Iraq, Argentina, Guatemala, El Salvador, Honduras, Ethiopia, Mexico, the former Yugoslavia, and Rwanda. Forensic examination of the remains in these graves can identify how the crimes were carried out and lead to the prosecution of those responsible. The discovery of mass graves also provides incontrovertible evidence of EXTRAJUDICIAL KILLINGS, TORTURE, and other crimes that in many cases the perpetrators denied had ever occurred. The discovery of mass graves in South America, for instance, has revealed the extent of the killings carried out by former military regimes against suspected dissidents during the "dirty wars" of the 1970s. After the U.S.-led invasion of Iraq in 2003, forensic investigators fanned out across Iraq to uncover mass graves. Early findings suggest that at least 400,000 people were killed and buried in such graves under the dictatorship of Saddam Hussein. Evidence gathered from these sites is expected to be used against the ousted strongman when he is brought to trial.

To establish a crime of GENOCIDE, it is necessary first to prove intent—for example, that individuals belonging to a particular religion, race, or ethnic group, were singled out for persecution, torture, or execution. To the extent that investigators can show that the victims discovered in a mass grave were all members of a particular class and were deliberately executed, the easier it is for prosecutors to determine a finding of genocide. Indeed, as Elizabeth Neuffer points out in an essay on the subject in the CRIMES OF WAR PROJECT, the very existence of mass graves can constitute a violation of INTERNATIONAL HUMANITARIAN LAW (IHL)—specifically, the Third and Fourth GENEVA CONVENTIONS and Additional Protocol I—which requires belligerents to comply with certain standards regarding the disposal of enemy dead. Deceased PRISONERS OF WAR or combatants must be buried in marked graves, their location mapped, and the INTERNATIONAL COMMITTEE OF THE RED CROSS notified of the death.

International law has not to date addressed the right to exhume mass graves. In 1973, however, the United Nations General Assembly adopted a resolution (3074) which calls on member states to cooperate with war crimes investigations. Additional Protocol I also requires parties to a conflict to conduct searches for missing persons after the end of hostilities. An individual state is not required to allow outside investigators to examine suspected mass graves. As Neuffer notes, not all mass graves can necessarily be considered evidence of atrocities; victims of a plague, for instance, may be buried hurriedly in a mass grave because of the danger of infection and the numbers of deaths involved. When they are crime scenes, though, mass graves must be protected from tampering.

To appreciate the difficulty that forensic anthropologists and other investigators confront when they investigate mass graves, one must take into consideration the fact that each human skeleton consists of about 200 bones and 32 teeth, any one of which can provide a knowledgeable researcher with evidence of a crime. Moreover, investigators need to collect evidence found with the remains—bullets, blindfolds, and binds, for instance, that were used by the perpetrators as well as clothing and personal possessions belonging to the victims that might help identify them and determine the circumstances under which they were executed. How the victim was killed is also difficult to resolve if a great deal of time has gone by since the execution was committed, depending on the state of decomposition. Dental records and DNA samples are often employed

A view of human remains found in a mass grave site near Mosul, Iraq, during Operation Iraqi Freedom *(Defense Imagery)*

in the absence of other evidence. In Rwanda identification of many of the victims has proven impossible because of the numbers of the victims and the lack of records which could be used to aid in identifying them.

See also ADDITIONAL PROTOCOLS TO THE GENEVA CONVENTIONS; PHYSICIANS FOR HUMAN RIGHTS.

Further Reading:
Cox, Margaret, and Jon Sterenberg. *Forensic Archaeology, Anthropology and the Investigation of Mass Graves.* London: CRC Press, 2006.
Ferllini, Roxana. *Silent Witness: How Forensic Anthropology Is Used to Solve the World's Toughest Crimes.* Buffalo, N.Y.: Firefly Books Ltd, 2002.
Gutman, Roy, ed. *Crimes of War: What the Public Should Know.* New York: W. W. Norton & Company, 1999.

Matsui Iwane (1880–1948) *Japanese general*
General Matsui Iwane was the Japanese commander largely responsible for the Nanjing (Nanking) massacre in 1937–38—also known to history as the Rape of Nanking

("Nanjing Datusha" in Chinese)—the worst single massacre of unarmed civilians by soldiers in 20th-century history. Between 200,000 and 350,000 Chinese civilians and soldiers who had laid down their arms were slaughtered by Japanese invaders over a period of less than two months. In addition, anywhere between 20,000 and 80,000 Chinese women and girls were raped, many of whom were later killed or forced to become sex slaves—one of the worst episodes of mass rape ever documented.

As commander of the Japanese expeditionary force, Matsui was given orders to "kill all captives" in Nanjing on December 5, 1937, after Chinese troops defending the city had refused to withdraw; Nanjing fell on December 13, and Matsui led the victorious Japanese into the city four days later. He remained for another week before being incapacitated by tuberculosis. During the time he was still in charge of the troops, he did nothing to stop the slaughter, which went on for the next six weeks. Matsui retired in 1938 and withdrew from active military duty at the war's end. However, he was considered one of the 14 Class A war criminals to be brought before the International Military Tribunal for the Far East established by the Allies, known as the TOKYO TRIALS. He was convicted for his role in the Nanjing massacre and executed. Even today, ultranationalists in Japan regard him as a martyr. He is buried at Yasukuni Shrine, which is dedicated to Japan's war dead and is also Japan's most revered Shinto temple.

See also NANJING (NANKING), MASSACRE IN.

Further Reading:
Honda, Katsuichi, and Frank Gibney, eds. *The Nanjing Massacre: A Japanese Journalist Confronts Japan's National Shame.* Studies of the Pacific Basin Institute. Armonk, N.Y.: East Gate Books, 1999.

Matsuoka Yosuke (1877–1946) *Japanese foreign minister and nationalist*

A former Japanese foreign minister during World War II, Matsuoka Yosuke was tried for war crimes after the end of World War II. Matsuoka stands out among other members of the Japanese military clique that exercised power in the 1930s and 1940s because he spent several years studying in the United States, graduating from Oregon University in 1900. He began his diplomatic career as consul in Shanghai. In 1927 he was appointed vice president of the Southern Manchuria Railway Company, an important position given Japan's territorial designs on the region. Matsuoka was an ardent supporter of annexing Manchuria to Japan; he espoused the view that mineral-rich Manchuria was "the Lifeline of Japan." In 1932 he was placed in charge of the Japanese delegation to the LEAGUE OF NATIONS. When the League strenuously protested Japan's invasion of Manchuria in 1937, he led the walkout of the Japanese delegation, an act that was widely applauded at home. His service was rewarded by an appointment to head the Southern Manchurian Railway Company.

In 1940 Matsuoka became minister of foreign affairs. In that capacity he promoted closer relations between Nazi Germany and Japan, advocating a policy known as the Greater East-Asian Co-prosperity Sphere, which served as a justification for Japanese dominance of the region. In a major diplomatic coup, Matsuoka brokered a neutrality accord with the Soviet Union in early 1941, although only a couple of months later he lobbied futilely for Japan to join Hitler's invasion of the Soviet Union. (The USSR only declared war against Japan a few weeks before the war ended.) Matsuoka was one of 27 Class A war criminals to be tried by the Allies, but he died of natural causes before he could be sentenced in 1946.

See also MANCHURIA, JAPANESE WAR CRIMES IN.

Further Reading:
Li, Peter, ed. *Japanese War Crimes: The Search for Justice.* Brunswick, N.J.: Transaction Publishers, 2003.

Maga, Timothy P. *Judgment at Tokyo: The Japanese War Crimes Trials.* Lexington: University Press of Kentucky, 2001.
Mendelsohn, John. *The Preservation of Japanese War Crimes Trials Records in the National Archives.* Washington, D.C.: National Archives and Records Administration, 1982.
Minear, Richard R. *Victors' Justice: The Tokyo War Crimes Trial.* Michigan Classics in Japanese Studies. Ann Arbor: University of Michigan, Center for Japanese Studies, 2001.
Piccigallo, Philip R. *The Japanese on Trial: Allied War Crimes Operations in the East, 1945–1951.* Austin: University of Texas Press, 1980.
Rees, Laurence. *Horror in the East: Japan and the Atrocities of World War II.* New York: Da Capo Press, 2002.
Russell, of Liverpool, Edward Frederick Langley Russell, Baron. *Knights of the Bushido: A Short History of Japanese War Crimes.* London: Greenhill Books, 2005.
Tanaka, Yuki. *Hidden Horrors: Japanese War Crimes in World War II.* Philadelphia: Westview Press, 1998.

Mau Mau uprising

The Mau Mau was an indigenous Kenyan insurgency directed against the British colonial power. Although it was crushed in the mid-1950s, it paved the way for eventual independence of the East African nation. The derivation of the phrase *Mau Mau* is in dispute. One theory holds that it comes from the mountain range bordering the western side of the Rift Valley, another that it is the cry of war of the Kikuyu, Kenya's largest tribe, and still another that it is an acronym for a Swahili phrase that means, "Let the white man go back abroad so the African can get his independence."

Known as the Movement or the Unifier, the Mau Mau rebellion was officially the creation of the Kikuyu Central Association (KCA). Initially the rebellion—which relied on a core of Kikuyu for its support though members of other tribes participated in it—targeted other Africans considered collaborators for working for the British. In one attack, Mau Mau guerrillas killed 93 Africans and as many as 1,800 altogether. But it was the attacks on white-owned farms—about 100 Europeans were killed—that terrorized European settlers, many of whom left the country. The British responded by imposing a brutal crackdown, and by 1953 the rebellion had virtually sputtered out, partly as a result of internal discord.

In 1955, of the 120,000 insurgents who had joined the Mau Mau, only about 15,000 were still alive and free. Official figures at the time put guerrilla losses at 11,000 and suspected African collaborators at 2,000. The British claimed that they had arrested another 30,000. Historians, however, have put the total deaths and detentions much higher: 14,000–30,000 guerrillas killed and from 80,000 to 100,000 arrested. The Mau Mau had accelerated the push for independence, which was finally achieved in 1963, but the legacy of the insurgency continues to haunt Kenya's former rulers. Five decades after the Mau Mau uprising, veterans of the movement took steps to reopen the books on alleged British abuses of Kenyans during the insurgency in the hope of gaining restitution from the British government. By 2003 lawyers had taken 6,000 depositions from Kenyans who reported that they had suffered from a variety of abuses, including rape, castration, TORTURE, whipping, indiscriminate killing, and theft of property. According to Caroline Elkins of Harvard University, who wrote a book about the alleged abuses, British security forces may have killed as many as 50,000 guerrillas, an estimate much higher than any previously given and a figure that has been disputed by other historians. The scale of abuses, if proven, would require the "rewriting of British imperial history" in the words of a BBC report.

See also KENYA, HUMAN RIGHTS VIOLATIONS IN.

Further Reading:
Elkins, Caroline. *Imperial Reckoning: The Untold Story of Britain's Gulag in Kenya.* New York: Henry Holt & Co., 2005.

Mauritania, human rights violations in

Bounded by the Atlantic Ocean and the Sahara Desert, Mauritania is a vast country with relatively few people; its population is fewer than 2 million. The country straddles a cultural divide that is also in part accountable for some of its most serious problems, since it links Arab Maghreb with western sub-Saharan Africa. Traditionally, the Arab-Berber north of the country has dominated the African south. Until the mid-1990s Mauritania was under one-party control. Opposition to the regime was suppressed, and arbitrary arrests and illegal detentions were frequent. Ethnic disputes often arose between the Arabs and African laborers and peasants who had migrated from neighboring Senegal seeking work. No matter how long they remained in the country, the Senegalese were not entitled to citizenship. These tensions flared into riots in 1989 in Mauritania and Senegal. The Mauritanian authorities reacted by deporting some 12,000 Senegalese back home. Black Mauritanians did not fare much better. In 1990 and 1991, 500 black Mauritanian soldiers were arrested on charges of plotting an uprising, and many were either arrested and deported without a trial or else killed.

In 1992 the government relaxed its grip on power and allowed political parties. Elections held in 1992 and 1993, however, were marred by accusations of fraud and boycotts by some opposition parties. A process of Arabization of the country appears to be under way. Arabic, for instance, is now compulsory in schools, and it is the only language taught in most of the schools over the objections of many black Mauritanians. According to human rights activists, the government restricts freedom of movement, especially involving travel by black Africans, and continues its practice of conducting arbitrary arrests and arbitrary detentions. In a new crackdown against dissidents, security forces rounded up dozens of religious leaders, opposition politicians, and human rights activists. Most were subsequently released but still faced charges of treason that many international watchdog agencies have denounced as groundless. "The government put forward no credible evidence that those arrested had been involved in any terrorist activities," charged the executive director of the Africa Division of HUMAN RIGHTS WATCH. "It seems that this is yet another example of a government opportunistically using the language of counter-terrorism to crack down on legitimate dissent."

Mauritania has also come under fire from international critics for condoning conditions that in most respects resemble SLAVERY. In a scathing report issued in 2002, the International Confederation of Free Trade Unions (ICFTU) condemned the government for the practiced of child labor and FORCED LABOR. Although Mauritania is a signatory to accords outlawing child labor, the report cites evidence that in 2000, 68,000 children ages 10–14 are working in agriculture and fishing and herding. Although "forced labor is not a widespread occurrence," the report said, "many workers remain in a situation tantamount to forced labor, as a consequence of established slavery." In fact, slavery is a shockingly recent phenomenon in Mauritania's history; it persisted until the early 1980s, when it was finally banned. International observers say that while the incidence of overt slavery has diminished significantly in the decades since then, the country is still haunted by its consequences, and many impoverished Mauritanians, mostly black African, remain in conditions that are almost indistinguishable from slavery. In spite of efforts by labor advocates to change government policy, forced labor practices continue unabated. "There has been no progress on this subject in recent years," the ICFTU report concluded. In August 2005 Mauritania's authoritarian leader Ould Taya was ousted in a military coup while he was out of the country, marking the end to 21 years of one-man rule. The Military Council for Justice and Democracy, as the junta was named, pledged a return to democracy, a promise that was greeted with skepticism. Nonetheless, some opposition leaders expressed hope that the military would keep its word.

Elections were held in 2009, but whether they represented a return to democracy was not so clear. Although international monitors judged the voting to be fair, the opposition denounced the elections as rigged, calling them an "electoral coup." Most observers believed that the newly elected president, Mohamed Ould Abdel Aziz, was unlikely to make any significant changes, pointing out that the 52-year-old victor was a retired general who retained close ties with the military. "We've gone backward to an era of dictatorship," said Boubacar Ould Messaoud, leader of an antislavery organization. "Aziz is no democrat. He is a soldier, and like all soldiers, he should stay in his barracks." Unsurprisingly, Aziz calls himself a defender of democracy and claims he launched the coup to bring an end to a tyrannical reign.

See also CHILDREN'S RIGHTS.

Further Reading:
Gerteiny, Alfred G. *Islamic Influences on Politics in Mauritania.* Boston: African Studies Center, Boston University, 1971.
Handloff, Robert L. *Mauritania: A Country Study.* Area Handbook Series. Washington, D.C.: Government Printing Office, 1990.
Morrow, James. *Mauritania.* Modern Middle East Nations and Their Strategic Place in the World. Philadelphia: Mason Crest Publishers, 2004.
Waltz, Susan Eileen. *Human Rights and Reform: Changing the Face of North African Politics.* Berkeley: University of California Press, 1995.

Meakić, Zeljko   *See* WAR CRIMINALS OF THE FORMER YUGOSLAVIA.

Médecins Sans Frontières   *See* DOCTORS WITHOUT BORDERS.

medical experiments
Nonconsensual medical experiments on human beings are crimes under international law and the laws of most nations. The GENEVA CONVENTIONS of 1949 defined medical experiments on PRISONERS OF WAR (POWs) and protected persons—civilians under the control of an OCCUPYING POWER—as a grave breach. The 1998 ROME STATUTE OF THE INTERNATIONAL CRIMINAL COURT stated that medical experiments are war crimes, whether they occur in an international armed conflict or an internal one. The statute defined the crime as: "Subjecting persons who are in the power of an adverse party to physical mutilation or to medical or scientific experiments of any kind which are neither justified by the medical, dental or hospital treatment of the person concerned nor carried out in his or her interest, and which cause death to or seriously endanger the health of such person or persons."

These legal prohibitions were seen as necessary to prevent a recurrence of the horrifying medical experiments that were conducted by both Nazi Germany and Japan during World War II. In what was called the DOCTORS' TRIAL (October 1946–April 1949), 24 Nazi physicians and other medical officials were charged with involvement in "medical experiments without the subjects' consent, upon civilians and members of the armed forces of nations then at war with the German Reich and who were in the custody of the German Reich . . . in the course of which experiments the defendants committed murders, brutalities, cruelties, tortures, atrocities, and other inhuman acts." Most of the subjects were inmates of CONCENTRATION CAMPS. In some experiments, subjects were placed in chambers meant to simulate high-altitude conditions; forced to remain in tanks of ice water for periods of three hours; injected with malaria, epidemic jaundice, spotted fever, streptococcus, gas gangrene, and tetanus; deliberately exposed to mustard gas; forced to endure transplants of bones, muscles, and nerves removed from other subjects; and sterilized by means of X-ray, surgery, and drugs. At the Buchenwald concentration camp, inmates were administered poison intravenously or shot with poison bullets. Most of these experiments resulted in death or severe injury. The Japanese, too, systematically carried out a program of medical experimentation on POWs and civilians in areas they occupied. Subjects were vivisected without anesthesia, infected with different pathogens, or used to demonstrate surgical techniques, after which they were liable to be shot. In some cases, tourniquets were applied to the arms and legs of American POWs for seven or eight hours, which could cause death once the tourniquets were removed. In June 1945, eight American airmen underwent vivisection at Kyushu Imperial University, one of Japan's most prestigious medical schools, lethal procedures in which doctors removed their lungs, hearts, livers, and stomachs. In Japanese-occupied Manchuria, the Japanese army established a special medical group—Unit 731—to carry out a series of barbaric medical experiments on captured Chinese civilians.

The crimes of Nazi and Japanese physicians led to the development of a Nuremberg Code governing medical experiments in war or in peacetime. The code declared that voluntary, informed consent from a human subject was necessary before any experiment could be undertaken. No deceit or coercion can be employed, and the subject must be apprised of all inconvenience and hazards to health that might result. The experiment must also be designed for the good of society. In addition, there must be no alternative to human experimentation such as animal experiments. All unnecessary physical and mental suffering and injury should be avoided, and any experiment that is likely to cause death or disabling injury should not take place at all.

Subjects should be able to withdraw their consent at any time; similarly, physicians or scientists conducting the experiments have an obligation to stop them if it appears likely that death, injury, or disability will result.

See also BRANDT, KARL; CLAUBERG, CARL; MAN-CHURIA, JAPANESE WAR CRIMES IN; MENGELE, JOSEF; OBERHEUSER, HERTA.

Further Reading:
Gutman, Roy, ed. *Crimes of War: What the Public Should Know.* New York: W. W. Norton & Company, 1999.
Harris, Sheldon. *Factories of Death: Japanese Biological Warfare 1932–45 and the American Cover-Up.* London: Routledge, 1995.
Lagnado, Lucette Matalon, and Sheila Cohn Dekel. *Children of the Flames: Dr. Josef Mengele and the Untold Story of the Twins of Auschwitz.* New York: Penguin Books, 1992.
Lifton, Robert. *The Nazi Doctors: Medical Killing and the Psychology of Genocide.* New York: Basic Books, 2000.
Rees, Laurence. *Horror in the East: Japan and the Atrocities of World War II.* New York: Da Capo Press, 2002.
Tanaka, Yuki. *Hidden Horrors: Japanese War Crimes in World War II.* Philadelphia: Westview Press, 1998.

medical personnel, protection of

Military attacks against medical personnel units are prohibited by the Fourth Geneva Convention of 1949. Article 20 of the convention states: "Persons regularly and solely engaged in the operation and administration of civilian hospitals . . . shall be respected and protected." The convention additionally forbids the destruction, closure (whether temporary or permanent), or interruption of the supply of food, water, medicines, or electricity to civilian hospitals and clinics. However, this prohibition can be waived if hospitals or medical units are put to use by a belligerent for military purposes, in which case they are liable to attack so long as the force used is proportionate to the military value of the facility. INTERNATIONAL HUMANI-TARIAN LAW (IHL) also confers protections on medical personnel—physicians, medics, nurses, ambulance drivers, etc.—but they must identify themselves as physicians or health-care workers, respect medical ethical principles, and provide treatment to all victims in need without discrimination. This means that a doctor, for example, cannot give priority to an injured soldier from his own side in preference to a more seriously injured enemy soldier. Medical personnel are also constrained from barring arms unless they are required for self-defense. IHL does not afford legal protections to physicians and health-care workers who act in a nonmedical capacity.

See also CIVILIAN IMMUNITY; GENEVA CONVENTIONS.

Further Reading:
Gutman, Roy, ed. *Crimes of War: What the Public Should Know.* New York: W. W. Norton & Company, 1999.

Memorial

Memorial is a Russian nongovernmental organization established to expose past political and civil human rights abuses in the former Soviet Union and advocate for human rights in present-day Russia. At the same time Memorial seeks "to introduce constructive proposals in government aimed at overcoming the totalitarian legacy and creating guarantees against its restoration." Memorial has created an information center and a map of the GULAG, the notorious system of labor camps where millions of people were imprisoned for years under JOSEPH STALIN. The organization has exposed atrocities committed by the MVD (former Soviet secret police) troops in Chechnya and restored a cemetery of an NKVD (the precursor of the KGB and MVD) camp, where prisoners from Poland, Germany, Italy, Romania, and Russia are buried. Plans are being made to erect memorials at other camp cemeteries. Memorial also organizes humanitarian aid to freed political prisoners who survived the camps. In an attempt to prevent a repetition of the past, Memorial representatives have conducted classes in human rights in secondary schools.

Further Reading:
Applebaum, Anne. *Gulag: A History.* New York: Doubleday, 2004.
Khlevnink, Oleg. *The History of the Gulag: From Collectivization to the Great Terror.* Translated by Vadim A. Staklo. Annals of Communism Series. New Haven: Yale University Press, 2004.
Kizny, Tomasz. *Gulag: Life and Death inside the Soviet Concentration Camps: 1917–1990.* London: Firefly Books Ltd., 2004.
Memorial. Available online. URL: http://www.memo.ru/eng/index.htm. Accessed March 20, 2010.
Solzhenitsyn, Aleksandr. *The Gulag Archipelago.* New York: HarperCollins, 1978.

Mengele, Josef (1911–1979) *Nazi medical experimenter and torturer*

Josef Mengele, the notorious doctor of Auschwitz, is known for good reason as the "Angel of Death." The son of a prosperous Bavarian industrialist, he was born on March 16, 1911. Those who knew him when he was growing up described him as a serious young man with ambition and intelligence. At the Frankfurt University Institute of Hereditary Biology and Racial Hygiene, Mengele chose to concentrate on physical anthropology and genetics. He pursued his medical studies at the Anthropological Institute at the University of Munich. His dissertation was entitled "Racial-Morphological Examination of the Anterior Portion of the Lower Jaw in Four Racial Groups." He published articles on twins and genetic abnormalities and the "irregular, dominant hereditary process." In retrospect, they hinted at the types of MEDICAL EXPERIMENTS he would later conduct on concentration camp inmates.

Although it seemed Mengele was preparing for a career in academia, he had other ambitions in mind. Attracted at a young age to fascism, he joined the SA, a Nazi paramilitary group, in 1923, and in 1937—four years after ADOLF HITLER came to power—he was accepted as a member of the Nazi Party, after which he applied for membership in the SS. In 1939 he served for six months with a mountain light-infantry regiment; beginning in 1940, as part of the reserve medical corps, he served three years with a Waffen SS unit. He was wounded in the Soviet Union and declared unfit for combat, but because of the

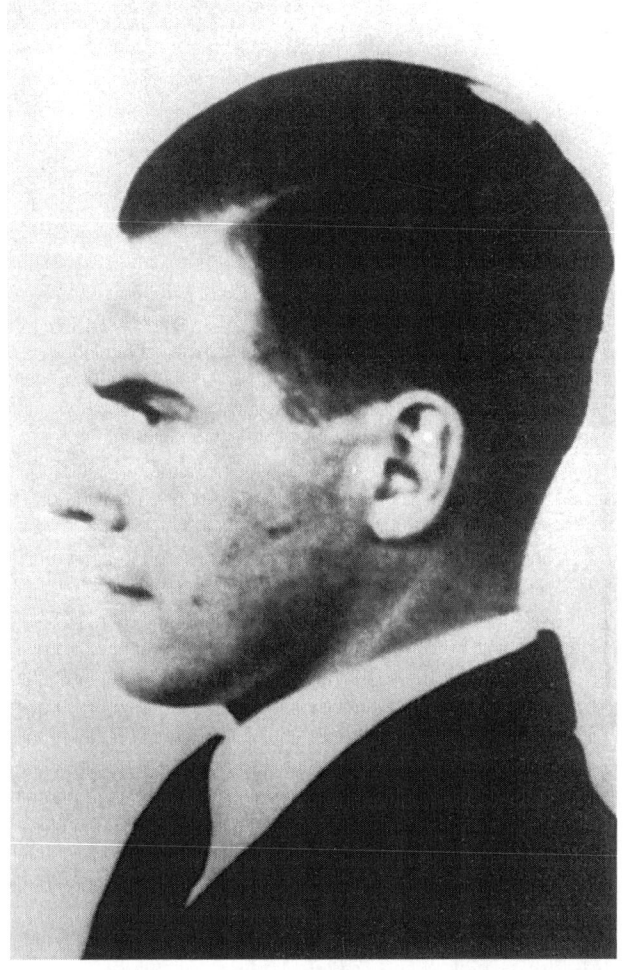

Former Nazi medical officer Josef Mengele (Bettmann/Corbis)

bravery he displayed on the battlefield, he was awarded the Iron Cross and promoted to captain.

In 1943 Mengele arrived at Auschwitz. Prisoners recall him as an attractive man, always well groomed and meticulously dressed, with an aristocratic bearing. There are credible reports that he would stand at the railway platforms and make decisions about the detraining detainees as to who would live and who would be sent to the gas chambers. At one point, informed that one block was infested with lice, he solved the problem by ordering the gassing of all 750 women quartered on the block. But his notoriety is mainly due to his unspeakable medical experiments on inmates. Mengele performed surgery without anesthesia, injected his subjects with lethal germs, undertook sex-change operations, and removed organs and limbs. He was also known to put chemicals into the eyes of children in an attempt to change their eye color.

But no group of subjects interested Mengele more than twins. He began his experiments on twins in 1944, placing them in a special barracks. About 1,500 sets of twins passed through Auschwitz during Mengele's tenure. One twin would be the "control" and the other the experimental subject. If one twin took sick and went to the infirmary, the other would disappear soon afterwards, executed with a shot of phenol. "Three times a week we were marched to Auschwitz to a big brick building, sort of like a big gymnasium," one of the surviving twins recounted. "We would have to sit naked . . . and people in white jackets would observe us and write down notes. They also would study every part of our bodies." On one occasion Mengele put 14 pairs of Rom (Gypsy) twins to sleep simultaneously, injected chloroform into their hearts, killing them instantly, after which he dissected them, meticulously noting each body part. He also sewed twins together to create Siamese twins. Nonetheless, a number of the twins recall Mengele as a gentle, kindly man who gave them chocolates. Others saw through his affable guise, but nearly all of them knew that it was important to keep on his good side.

Of the 3,000 children—twins and nontwins—Mengele had experimented on, only about 200 were alive when the camp was liberated by the Soviet army on January 27, 1945. Before then, though, Mengele managed to escape, disguised as a member of the regular German infantry. He was captured by the Allies but only remained in custody as a prisoner of war a brief time before being released because no one was aware of who he was. In 1949, using an Italian residency document with a false name, Mengele obtained a passport and received permission to enter Argentina. He had chosen that country because he felt he could count on the support of Nazi sympathizers, and his father had done business there in the past. After settling in Argentina, he divorced his wife Irene and in 1958 married his brother Karl's widow, Martha. He maintained a quasi-normal lifestyle as a man with a regular job. The world had not forgotten him, though. He was tried in absentia by a Frankfurt court, which charged him with "hideous crimes" committed alone or with others "willfully and with bloodlust." He was indicted for several CRIMES AGAINST HUMANITY, including making selections for the gas chambers, administering lethal injections, shooting and beating victims, and perpetrating other forms of deliberate killing.

In spite of many attempts to track him down and bring him to justice, Mengele succeeded in living undiscovered for 35 years under various aliases. He relocated from Argentina to Paraguay and then to Brazil, where he died in 1979. He suffered a stroke while swimming and died after he was dragged to shore. However, his death remained unknown to the world until the 1980s, when Nazi hunters located his grave, which was marked "Wolfgang Gerhard." His family acknowledged that he was buried there and turned over his diaries and letters to investigators. Even so, suspicion persisted that he was still alive and his death was a hoax. In 1992, however, DNA was extracted from the bones and matched with DNA in blood samples from Mengele's son, confirming his identity.

See also ROM (ROMA, ROMANY, GYPSIES), PERSECUTION OF.

Further Reading:

Goni, Uki. *The Real Odessa: How Peron Brought the Nazi War Criminals to Argentina.* London: Granta Books, 2003.

Lagnado, Lucette Matalon, and Sheila Cohn Dekel. *Children of the Flames: Dr. Josef Mengele and the Untold Story of the Twins of Auschwitz.* New York: Penguin Books, 1992.

Lifton, Robert. *The Nazi Doctors: Medical Killing and the Psychology of Genocide.* New York: Basic Books, 2000.

Posner, Gerald. *Mengele: The Complete Story.* New York: Cooper Square Press, 2000.

Rees, Laurence. *Auschwitz: A New History.* New York: Public Affairs, 2005.

Mengistu Haile Mariam (1937–   ) *Ethiopian despot*
The former Ethiopian dictator Colonel Mengistu Haile Mariam seized power in 1974 in a violent coup and proceeded to establish a brutal reign under a junta known as the Dergue, a committee made up of junior officers. There is little available information about Mariam's early life. It is known that he was born in 1937 in the southern Ethiopian district of Walayta. His father was a soldier and his mother a servant. According to some accounts, he moved to Addis Ababa with his mother at an early age and grew up in the household of a prominent nobleman. He joined the army when he was young and served briefly as a private before attending Ethiopia's Holeta Military Academy, graduating in 1966 with the rank of second lieutenant. Assigned to the logistical and ordnance section of the Ethiopian army, he fell under the sway of Marxism and regularly referred to his fellow junior officers as "comrades," in the Soviet style. He became one of the leading figures of the future Dergue, which was composed of some 108 officers.

After taking power in 1974, Mengistu initiated a bloody campaign in which officials of the ousted emperor Haile Selasse were executed by firing squad; later the emperor himself and the patriarch of the dominant Ethiopian Orthodox Church were secretly killed. (There are allegations that Mengistu himself strangled the emperor to death.) At the same time he moved to purge rivals within the Dergue, executing them as well. In 1976, to inaugurate what he called the Red Terror, he appeared before a crowd in the capital, Addis Ababa, and held up a bottle filled with red liquid, which he said contained the blood of his enemies—"imperialists" and "counterrevolutionaries." Mengistu then orchestrated a wave of killings, targeting students and members of outlawed political parties. Thousands of young men and women were killed by *kebeles,* neighborhood watch committees which insisted on debiting the families of the victims for the price of the bullets used to execute them.

As the Soviet Union's principal ally in Africa, Mengistu was guaranteed a steady flow of arms to carry out his so-called counterinsurgency campaigns, which are believed to have cost the lives of thousands of people. When famine struck in 1984, the Mengistu regime sought to keep it secret from the outside world. Two secessionist insurgencies broke out around the same time, spearheaded by the Tigray and Eritrean People's Liberation Fronts. Subsequently the Dergue forcibly evicted hundreds of thousands of villagers from northern Ethiopia, relocating them to the south, ostensibly because they would be assured of richer food sources. In fact, the Dergue was determined to empty villages in rebel-infested areas to deny insurgents support.

In 1991 the Dergue was ousted by the Ethiopian People's Revolutionary Democratic Front (EPRDF), a coalition of regional and ethnic rebel groups. It is believed that in its 17 years in power, the Dergue was responsible for a minimum of 150,000 and possibly as many as half a million civilian deaths. The new regime set up a Special Prosecutor's Office (SRO) to investigate the crimes committed during Mengistu's reign. Over the next six years the SRO brought charges against more than 70 leading Dergue figures; altogether 5,198 people were charged for GENOCIDE, war crimes, and CRIMES AGAINST HUMANITY, of whom 2,246 were already in detention and another 2,952 were charged in absentia. Mengistu himself managed to elude justice by fleeing to Zimbabwe after the Dergue was toppled; 19 years later he was still living in exile.

About 200 cases have been heard by the courts—each of them with multiple defendants—with most of the focus on high-level officials who had given the orders. Human rights advocates have criticized the justice system for lengthy pretrial detentions and excessive delays in the investigating the cases. Lawyers for the defendants have complained about a lack of due process and restrictions on their access to clients. In the meantime, evidence of crimes committed during the Dergue era continues to be uncovered. In one instance, the bodies of 87 students were found near a provincial city, all of whom had been executed without trial.

See also ERITREA, HUMAN RIGHTS VIOLATIONS IN.

Further Reading:
Marcus, Harold G. *A History of Ethiopia.* Updated ed. Berkeley: University of California Press, 2002.
Pausewang, Siegfried, Kjetil Tronvoll, and Lovise Aaeln, eds. *Ethiopia since the Derg: A Decade of Democratic Pretension and Performance.* London: Zed Books, 2003.

mercenaries

Mercenaries—soldiers for hire—have been employed for hundreds of years. In the 18th and 19th centuries the Swiss hired out battalions to other European countries; the British used Hessian mercenaries during the American Revolution. More recently, mercenaries have been widely used in many of the postcolonial conflicts in Africa. The 1989 United Nations Convention on the Recruitment, Use, Financing and Training of Mercenaries defines a mercenary as any person who "is specially recruited locally or abroad in order to fight in an armed conflict; is motivated to take part in the hostilities essentially by the desire for private gain and, in fact, is promised, by or on behalf of a party to the conflict, material compensation . . . ; is neither a national of a party to the conflict nor a resident of territory controlled by a party to the conflict; is not a member of the armed forces of a party to the conflict. . . ." The convention also considers a person a mercenary if he or she is specifically recruited to participate in an effort to overthrow a government, undermine a state, or threaten its territorial integrity and is neither a national of the state or a member of its armed forces.

In 1968 the United Nations General Assembly and the Organization for African Unity enacted laws against mercenaries, outlawing their use in wars of national liberation. In 1977 the Security Council adopted a resolution condemning the recruitment of mercenaries to overthrow governments of any member state. Additional Protocol I to the GENEVA CONVENTIONS denies mercenaries combatant status or the rights of prisoners of war if captured.

That means that mercenaries can be treated as common criminals. However, the increasing use of private security contractors in battlefield situations has made it more difficult to define a mercenary. Some critics contend that the UN definition is too subjective and depends too much on the motives of the fighter in making the determination. Moreover, the UN Charter gives states the right to individual or collective self-defense if attacked. If a state does come under armed attack and cannot depend on an outside force—such as the United Nations—to help it, the state may feel it has no choice but to hire mercenaries. The increasing reliance, too, on private security services has also made it difficult to ban the use of mercenaries outright.

Some critics of the UN ban suggest that mercenaries should enjoy combatant status under international law because that will make them more likely to abide by the Geneva Conventions and other treaties. In their view, private contractors hired to carry out military or security duties would become more accountable to the government that hires them. In 1999 the United Nations Human Rights Commission issued a "Report on the question of the use of mercenaries as a means of violating human rights and impeding the exercise of the right of peoples to self-determination" in which it stated that "mercenaries base their comparative advantage and greater efficiency on the fact that they do not regard themselves as being bound to respect human rights or the rules of INTERNATIONAL HUMANITARIAN LAW. . . . The participation of mercenaries in armed conflicts and in any other situation in which their services are unlawful may jeopardize the self-determination of peoples and always hampers the enjoyment of the human rights of those on whom their presence is inflicted." By relying on private military contractors (PMCs), the report said, the boundaries are blurred between combat and noncombat operations. For example, the DynCorp, a private security firm, provides bodyguards for Afghan president Hamid Karzai, and the Northrop Grumman Corporation has been paid $1.2 billion to fly planes that spray coca fields in Colombia and monitor smuggling. Although U.S. federal law bans American soldiers from participating in Colombia's war against a leftist insurgency and from training army units with ties to right-wing paramilitaries, these restrictions do not apply to PMCs.

The Pentagon has also used PMCs in Bosnia, Nigeria, Macedonia, and, most significantly, in Iraq. The *New York Times* called private military contractors the "new business face of war" because they provide "stand-ins for active soldiers." By 2004 the U.S. Defense Department had hired about 35 PMCs, including Kellogg Brown & Root, DynCorp, Vinnell, SAIC, ICI of Oregon, Logicon, and MPRI (Military Professionals Resources Inc.), which boasts of having "more generals per square foot than in the Pentagon." According to a July 2003 edition of *Soldier of Fortune* magazine (which covers the mercenary world), for-profit military companies do an estimated $100 billion in business worldwide annually.

The U.S. government's use of PMCs is grounded in the combined marque and reprisal and commerce clauses of the Constitution, which give Congress the power to regulate privateering, and the Arms Export Control Act, of 1979 which allowed Congress to delegate a large portion of its privateering power to the executive branch. Supreme Court rulings have also supported the government's ability to hire PMCs. Some members of Congress, though, are troubled by the Pentagon's use of PMCs. "Under a shroud of secrecy, the United States is carrying out military missions with people who don't have the same level of accountability," said Representative Jan Schakowsky (D-Ill.), "We have individuals who are not obligated to follow orders or follow the Military Code of Conduct. Their main obligation is to their employer, not to their country."

The Pentagon and State Department's reliance on security contractors has continued to grow in recent years. In the first nine months of the Obama administration, for example, the number of Defense Department armed security contractors registered increased by 236 percent—from 3,184 to 10,712. According to the Congressional Research Service, a quarter to nearly a third of the armed U.S. military force in Afghanistan—22 to 30 percent—was made up of security contractors. The total number of contractors of all kinds in Afghanistan in 2010 was more than 100,000, although the majority were Afghan nationals. Altogether, the United States employed more than 240,000 private contractors of all kinds in the wars in Iraq and Afghanistan. While Defense Department regulations forbid private contractors from participating in military activities, there have been some indications that these rules have been compromised. Contractors for Blackwater (later renamed Xe Services LLC) have engaged in firefights with the TALIBAN; in 2003 two Blackwater employees were killed in combat in Afghanistan in a battle with militants, and in 2006 12 Blackwater "tactical action operatives" took part in a secret raid into Pakistan—apparently targeting an al-Qaeda camp—conducted by the U.S. military's Joint Special Operations Command. In 2010 media outlets reported that Xe contractors were reportedly involved in secret operations to deploy drones—unmanned aircraft that carry out surveillance and missile strikes on militants in the tribal regions of Pakistan. The growing reliance on private contractors and their expanding role in U.S. wars have inevitably led to controversy. In the most notorious incident, Blackwater operatives opened fire at a crowded intersection in Baghdad in 2007, killing 14 people and wounding 20, even though there was no evidence that they were coming under assault. Charges of manslaughter against five contractors involved

in the incident were subsequently dropped when a federal judge ruled that the U.S. government's handling of the case violated the law. Although Blackwater (Xe) has compensated families of some of the victims, the Iraqi government expelled the company from the country, although other private contracting companies will be allowed to remain. Blackwater was by no means the only such company to become embroiled in controversy. In 1999 DynCorp employees were implicated in running a sex ring in Bosnia, trafficking in women and girls, some as young as 12 years old. In 2006 an employee for Triple Canopy reportedly opened fire on an innocent Iraqi in a pickup truck without provocation and later shot up a taxi, evidently for the sport of it. In Kabul another contractor providing security engaged in behavior that the media likened to "Animal House," characterized by hazing, sexual humiliation, and a climate of fear. Secretary of State Hillary Clinton denounced the contractor, the ArmorGroup, for a "pervasive breakdown in the chain of command and guard force discipline and morale."

See also AFGHANISTAN, HUMAN RIGHTS VIOLATIONS IN; IRAQ, HUMAN RIGHTS VIOLATIONS IN POST-SADDAM; UNITED NATIONS HUMAN RIGHTS COUNCIL; WAR ON TERROR.

Further Reading:
ABCnews.com. "Mercenaries? CIA Says Expanded Role for Contractors Legitimate." (December 11, 2009). Available online. URL: http://abcnews.go.com/Blotter/mercenaries-cia-expanded-role-contractors-legitimate/story?id=9302651. Accessed April 8, 2010.
CBSnews.com. "Shocking Hazing at U.S. Embassy in Kabul" (September 1, 2009). Available online. URL: http://www.cbsnews.com/stories/2009/09/01/evening-news/main5280465.shtml. Accessed April 10, 2010.
CNN.com. "High Pay—and High Risk—for Contractors in Iraq" (April 2, 2004). Available online. URL: http://www.cnn.com/2004/WORLD/meast/04/01/iraq.contractor/. Accessed April 8, 2010.
Scahill, Jeremy. *Blackwater: The Rise of the World's Most Powerful Mercenary Army.* New York: Nation Books, 2007.

Meron, Theodor (1930–) *international jurist*
Theodor Meron was the president of the International Criminal Tribunal for the Former Yugoslavia (ICTY) until 2005 and one of the few jurists to have personally experienced human rights violations: As a Jewish teenager he was held in a Nazi labor camp during World War II. Although he is reluctant to talk about his imprisonment, he does acknowledge that the ordeal influenced him to undertake a career in law in order to "explore the means to avoid mistreatment, to focus on ways to protect human dignity." In

an interview with the *New York Times*, he explained that his "hunger for learning" was heightened because of having been deprived of an education from the age of nine to 15.

Born in 1930 in Poland, Meron has steeped himself in the laws of war and is an enthusiast of Shakespeare, who had much to say about man's inhumanity to man. (Meron has written two books on Shakespeare—*Henry's Wars and Shakespeare's Laws* [1993] and *Bloody Constraint: War and Chivalry in Shakespeare* [1998].) Now a U.S. citizen, he was a professor of international law at New York University before being elected to his position on the tribunal. Meron believes that while crimes against humanity may not have diminished significantly over the years, there is at least a growing recognition on the part of the international community that the guilty should be brought to justice and their crimes exposed. Specifically, he has expressed hope that some of the cases still pending in connection to the Balkan wars of the 1990s could be tried in the countries where the war crimes took place—Serbia, Bosnia, and Croatia—rather than in a neutral country such as the Netherlands. In 2005 he declared that this goal was closer at hand thanks to initiatives taken by the countries involved. For instance, Bosnia and Herzegovina enacted legislation to formally establish a body known as the War Crimes Chamber to try suspected war criminals.

In March 2005 Meron paid an unprecedented visit to Serb authorities in Belgrade who in the past had shown little sign of cooperation with the tribunal. On this occasion, though, he praised the government for having facilitated the surrender of a number of individuals indicted by the ICTY, which he said had created a favorable climate for increased cooperation between Serbia and the tribunal. Nonetheless, he pointed out that the ICTY would not be satisfied until three of the most wanted men—Ratko Mladić, Radovan Karadžić, and Ante Gotovina—were brought to justice. Meron has also championed the role of the ICTY in lending its resources to the national tribunals being established in the region through various training programs, the transfer of documents, and expertise. That help will make it possible for courts in Bosnia, Serbia, and Croatia to continue the investigation and prosecution of war criminals once the ICTY's mandate expires in 2008. "We must remember," Meron said, "without this tribunal, what would have followed is impunity." Meron continues to take an active role in promoting human rights law. He leads the annual ICRC seminars for UN diplomats on international humanitarian law at New York University, where he is the Charles L. Denison Professor of Law Emeritus and Judicial Fellow.

See also Bosnia and Herzegovina, human rights violations in; Croatia, human rights violations in; Serbia, human rights violations in; Yugoslavia, war crimes in.

Further Reading:
Meron, Theodor. *Henry's Wars and Shakespeare's Laws.* Oxford: Oxford University Press, 1993.
———. *Human Rights and Humanitarian Norms as Customary Law.* Oxford: Oxford University Press, 1989.
———. *War Crimes Law Comes of Age: Essays.* Oxford: Oxford University Press, 1999.

Mexico, human rights violations in

Mexico suffered its most violent period in modern history during a dirty war that was seldom fought in the open and was characterized by rampant human rights violations. The war began in the late 1960s and continued until the 1980s. During that time government agents abducted, tortured, murdered, or "disappeared" hundreds of Mexicans; there are 350 documented cases according to the National Commission on Human Rights, a government agency, but doubtless many more have occurred that have not been exposed. Ostensibly, the dirty war pitted the government against leftist subversives and insurgents, but in fact many innocent civilians ended up being drawn into the conflict and sometimes paying with their lives. Although the administration of President Vicente Fox has made some progress investigating human rights violations by government police and security forces, abuses still occur, and it is debatable whether most of the worst offenders will ever be brought to justice.

The dirty war, which was carried on under the administrations of Presidents Luis Echeverría and José López Portillo, was one in which Mexican police forces routinely resorted to "systematic beatings, near drowning and electric shocks" in the words of an Amnesty International report. As in the case of other dirty wars in Latin America, notably in Uruguay, Argentina, and Chile, the government responded to leftist insurgencies by sweeping up many civilians in dragnets, even though their ties to guerrillas or subversive organizations were often either tenuous or nonexistent. Sometimes a blood relationship with a suspect was sufficient for the police to detain a person. There is some evidence that prisoners were executed after their torturers had extracted all the information from them that they could. Sometimes the killings took place out in the open, though. In 1968 troops opened fire on student protesters in the plaza at Tlatelolco. Human rights investigators say hundreds were killed in that incident, but the true number is unknown.

Even though the United States was aware of many of these abuses, Washington was slow to respond both for fear of jeopardizing relations with Mexico and because through the early 1970s, human rights was not given a high priority by the Nixon or Ford administrations. "Important point in Embassy's opinion, however," wrote the U.S. ambassador at the time, "is that GOM [Government of Mexico] . . . appears to be responding—however heavy-handedly—to legitimate and serious provocation by armed opponents who seek its overthrow and who in the last several years have come to constitute a genuine threat to public order in several parts of the country."

U.S. policy toward human rights abuses in Mexico underwent a dramatic shift during the Carter administration. In late 1978, after President Carter ordered a comprehensive review of relations between the two countries, the National Security Council (NSC) acknowledged in a secret annex to the report that grave abuses by the Mexican forces had taken place. The NSC singled out one paramilitary group in particular for some of the worst outrages known as the WHITE BRIGADES. Nonetheless, the United States was still reluctant to take concerted action to prod the Mexican government into improving its human rights record, believing that it would be "ill-advised and counterproductive." It was agreed that the White House would continue its old policy of "quiet diplomacy."

Human rights abuses persisted into the 1990s under the administration of President Carlos Salinas de Gortari. In May 1990, just as the United States, Mexico, and Canada were about to open negotiations on the creation of the North American Free Trade Agreement (NAFTA), a human rights advocate, Dr. Norma Corona Sapién, was slain by unidentified gunmen in Culiacán, capital of the Mexican state of Sinaloa. Her killing was linked by human rights organizations to her investigation of the TORTURE and killings of a Mexican lawyer and three Venezuelan University teachers reportedly carried out by judicial police officers. Sapién's death prompted a national outcry. Eager to burnish Mexico's human rights image, especially with such important trade talks looming, Salinas promised to crack down on abuses and punish the perpetrators. One tangible result was the creation of the National Human Rights Commission (CNDH). But new government agencies and well-intentioned pieces of legislation failed to put a halt to the abusive practices. On the contrary, Sapién's killing only seemed to mark the beginning of a campaign to silence human rights advocates. This campaign was not only limited to harassment, threats, or intimidation; sometimes it could become lethal. In June 1995 Dr. Abraham Polo Uscanga, a former judge, "disappeared." Two weeks later his body turned up—in his office. He had been killed with a single shot in the back of the head. A former member of the Federal District Supreme Court, which has jurisdiction over the Mexico City metropolitan area, he had been openly critical of corruption in the judiciary and had acquitted eight people falsely accused of terrorism, some of whom had undergone torture.

Even the clergy was not safe. Only weeks after Polo's killing, unknown gunmen opened fire on a car carrying Roman Catholic bishop Arturo Lona Reyes, a well-known human rights defender. The bishop survived, and five suspects were arrested. The authorities claimed that the attack was a robbery attempt, but the evidence indicated that the assailants had made no effort to stop the car in advance and had simply started shooting directly at the bishop. According to Amnesty International, the principal victims of rights abuses remain Indian or peasant activists who seek land reform. While an attack on a bishop will raise a hue and cry around the world, attempts to intimidate or kill people without a high profile will generally be overlooked.

The growing involvement of the Mexican military in maintaining public security is a source of concern to human rights organizations. Throughout the 1990s, the size and budget of the army increased in response to scattered insurgencies. On New Year's Day 1994 the country was taken unaware by an uprising in the southern state of Chiapas, an audacious action carried out by a hitherto unknown guerrilla group called the Zapatistas (or more officially the Zapatista National Liberation Army). The government first reacted by using excessive force against the rebels and their Indian supporters but later adopted a policy of containment. Many instances of abuses by the army in the Chiapas uprising have been exposed, but little has been done to investigate them. In one incident in 1994, 11 people were killed during the army occupation of a hospital. But HUMAN RIGHTS WATCH questioned the army's investigation and suggested that it really had no stomach for identifying or prosecuting the murderers. In an investigation of cases in Chiapas involving the alleged torture and rape of civilians by soldiers, the Inter-American Commission on Human Rights faulted the government for failing to do more to ensure the protection of the victims' legal rights and declared that its "investigation into the facts related to this case by the military courts [had been] completely inappropriate."

Two years after the Zapitista uprising, a guerrilla group called the Popular Revolutionary Army began one of their own in the southwestern state of Guerrero and in other states. As a result of continuing tensions in both areas of the country, the army has become a more dominant presence in the Mexican countryside.

The army has also been pressed into service in the war against drugs. Law enforcement officials consider Mexico the principal route through which drugs travel on their way to the United States from South America; more than 80 percent of the cocaine that feeds American drug habits passes through Mexico. But Mexico is more than a transshipment channel: It is also a major narcotics producer in its own right, supplying 29 percent of the heroin and 70 percent of the marijuana imported into the United States. In 1987 President Miguel de la Madrid declared drug trafficking to be a "national security problem." Nearly a decade later it was still a problem. In 1996 President

Ernesto Zedillo invited the country's top military leaders to join the National Public Security Council, giving the military an unprecedented role in establishing policy regarding public security. Five years later it was hard to see how much had changed. Drugs were still being produced and still flowing into the United States. In January 2001 President Vicente Fox declared his intention to fight a "war without quarter" against drug traffickers. More than 20,000 soldiers now take part in counternarcotics operations. However, it is possible to argue that the army is as much a part of the problem as it is the solution. Because officers usually rely on information from political allies about which suspects to target, they have become entangled in local power struggles. In Guerrero state, for instance, these invidious alliances have given caciques—local political bosses—the power to enlist the army to help their cause by the simple expedient of denouncing their enemies as either drug dealers or guerrillas. Evidence is trumped up, but because of an absence of outside monitors, these abuses become very hard to prove. The largest number of complaints about army abuses addressed to the National Human Rights Commission by civilians relates to its conduct while performing counternarcotics operations.

The ascension of President Vicente Fox to office in December 2000 was seen as a new beginning for Mexico. Finally the country had a president who was not from the PRI (Institutional Revolutionary Party), the party that had dominated Mexican political life for most of the 20th century. Individuals who had previously enjoyed immunity from prosecution for their crimes under the old regime might finally be forced to face their accusers. Crimes hushed up would soon be brought to light, or that was the hope anyway. Indeed, Fox vowed to bring an end to the climate of impunity and promised that his administration would resolve several high-profile human rights cases involving the army that until then had seemed to be going nowhere. However, although he secured the release of two prisoners who had been tortured while in custody, critics said that he had done little to curb human rights abuses halfway through his term in office. (Mexican presidents are only allowed to serve one six-year term.)

Efforts to come to terms with a lurid and bloody past have encountered a number of stumbling blocks, not the least the failure of high officials in the PRI regime to cooperate with investigators. Nonetheless, the release of once-secret documents has shed a good deal of light on the government's complicity in committing atrocities that it had long avoided responsibility for. Investigators have taken a special interest in identifying the perpetrators of a 1968 massacre of student protesters in Tlatelolco, in Mexico City. Some of the recently disclosed documents indicate that as many as 360 snipers under government command were involved. Among them was a secret battalion of police known as the Falcons, which undertook another attack on student protesters in 1971.

President Gustavo Díaz Ordaz had ordered Echeverría, then his interior secretary, to create the Falcons. He wanted a clandestine unit that could suppress student dissent in place of uniformed personnel, wishing to avoid a repetition of the controversy in the wake of the massacre of students at Tlatelolco, in Mexico City in 1968. Echeverría saw no reason to dissolve them when he became president. According to documents that only came to light in 2005, the Falcons were given false identification, code words, and nicknames. They were forbidden to talk about their real work, which was defined as being "dedicated . . . to committing crimes, with the intention of distracting the attention of public opinion." But the Falcons were by no means the only unit under government control; federal and city police as well as secret service agents were all present in and around the plaza where the massacre took place. At the time, the government claimed that it was the students who had opened fire on the police, an assertion contradicted by the documents.

The confrontation between students and police took place on October 2, 1968, only 10 days before the start of the Olympics in Mexico City. Estimates on the number of people killed range from 38 to several hundred. The true number will probably never be known. Echeverría denied having anything to do with the shootings, but the documents reveal that several of the snipers fired down on the crowd from an apartment owned by his sister-in-law. When he was called into the office of the special prosecutor Ignacio Carrillo in February 2005, Echeverría refused to talk, contending that he had a constitutional right as an ex-president to remain silent. He has ignored further attempts by the prosecutor's office to question him.

There is, however, some grounds for at least cautious optimism. As special prosecutor, Carrillo has taken some concrete steps to investigate past abuses, and the judiciary has shown some degree of independence. In November 2003 the Mexican Supreme Court ruled that former officials could be prosecuted in disappearance cases, saying that no statute of limitations could apply when no body had been found. Scarcely had the ink had time to dry on the decision than the former chief of Mexico's secret police, MIGUEL NAZAR HARO, was arrested in February 2004 on charges of kidnapping a leftist leader 29 years before whose body was never located. Nazar Haro thus became the first government official arrested for crimes committed during the dirty war. He had headed the Federal Security Directorate, which was both an intelligence agency and a secret police force. What is unclear is whether this arrest marks a renewed effort on the government's part to bring human rights violators to justice and investigate past abuses or whether it is simply an aberration.

In an especially bold move, the special prosecutor filed murder charges against former president Luis Echevarría and several former government officials and military officers in the killings of student protesters in 1971. Specifically, the charges related to the slayings of at least 25 protesters demanding reforms of the education system whom the Falcons had attacked with clubs and chains. Castillo said that Echevarría would face charges of GENOCIDE, defined in the Mexican penal code as "systematic crimes against the lives of members of any national group," including political dissidents. Human rights advocates, who had hailed the unprecedented initiative when it was announced in July 2004, had little time to savor their victory. The very next day an appeals court judge threw out the charges against the former president. That underscored the belief by human rights groups that the Fox administration had no interest in providing strong support to the special prosecutor, raising fears that the country's leader was backing away from his pledge to break with the past and bring about needed political and judicial reforms.

Nonetheless, in early February 2005 Carillo announced his intention to bring charges against two dozen former military and civilian officials for the 1968 student massacre at Tlatelolco. At the same time he also indicated that he would charge Echeverría in the new indictment even while the Mexican Supreme Court was reviewing the earlier decision to throw out the first indictment against the former president. The prosecutor also said that he would bring 30 additional indictments before the end of 2005.

A relentless wave of violence, largely driven by drug cartels and characterized by beheadings, kidnappings, the killings of police officers and municipal officials, especially in Tijuana and Ciudad Juárez, has led to increased human rights abuses by the Mexican army. There is no question that Mexico has been in the grip of a crisis. President Felipe Calderón (who assumed office in 2006) felt that he had no choice but to deploy the army to curb the power of the drug cartels because local and regional police forces were considered too corrupt or too ineffective to do the job. (The police are also outspent and outgunned by the cartels.) In 2008, at least 6,000 people lost their lives in the drug-fueled conflict, and the toll continued to rise in 2009. According to the State Department, the intensified war against drug trafficking has killed about 7,500 people in Mexico between the beginning of 2008 and the latter part of 2009. In total, as many as 28,000 people have been killed since Calderón launched his war on drug cartels.

Military officials have assumed command of many municipal police forces that have been tainted by corruption. According to Human Rights Watch, the army has been responsible for disappearances, the rape of indigenous women, the torture and arbitrary detention of environmental activists, and arbitrary detentions of dozens of people during public security operations. The organization noted that many victims of the abuses "had no connection to the drug trade or insurgencies." Military criminal investigations are either closed or appear intended to provide impunity for the accused. The U.S. State Department noted that human rights complaints against the military had multiplied sixfold—1,230, from 182—between 2006 and 2008. The Mexican government has taken few steps to punish the perpetrators. The majority of cases that do end up being investigated and prosecuted fall under the jurisdiction of the military, not the civil authorities. But according to Human Rights Watch, the military court system "is failing miserably to provide justice in cases involving military abuses against civilians." These abuses range from torture (21 complaints in 2008) to cruel or degrading treatment (580 complaints in 2008). Very few convictions have resulted. In response to an inquiry from the organization, Ministry of Defense officials could only cite one case of a prosecution of a soldier for human rights abuses, and that was a case that went back to 1998. While the State Department cited several examples of progress, including more mechanisms to make it easier for citizens to file complaints against the military, it was hardly a glowing endorsement. And a key Democratic senator said the report failed to adequately address the concerns about impunity within the Mexican military that led him to threaten to hold up millions of dollars in United States assistance.

In December 2009 Amnesty International issued a report accusing soldiers of torturing 25 police officers in Tijuana in March in an attempt to get the officers to confess to being involved with organized crime. Of five recent cases implicating soldiers engaged in the antidrug campaign, the army took responsibility for only one.

Violence only intensified in the first months of 2010. Drug gangs have even taken to stealing cars, burning thems and then abandoning them at major intersections, blocking traffic for hours, which they did in Monterrey in March. (The gangs were believed to be carrying out these disruptive actions in protest against the government's effort to stamp them out.) The slayings of employees of the U.S. consulate in Ciudad Juárez in the middle of the afternoon—apparently carried out by gangs—might represent an escalation of the drug war, raising fears that now U.S. officials are fair game. The war on drugs has also taken a disproportionate toll on journalists. Since Calderón launched the war on drug cartels in 2006, more than 30 journalists have been killed or have disappeared.

Further Reading:

Amnesty International. Mexico Human Rights. Available online. URL: http://www.amnesty.org/en/region/mexico. Accessed March 20, 2010.

Brysk, Alison, ed. *Globalization and Human Rights.* Berkeley: University of California Press, 2002.

Cartwright, William, ed. *Mexico: Facing the Challenges of Human Rights and Crime.* Jefferson, N.C.: Transnational Pub., 1999.

Human Rights Watch. Mexico Human Rights. Available online. URL: http://www.hrw.org/americas/mexico. Accessed March 20, 2010.

National Security Archive. *Archive Evidence of Mexico's Human Rights Crimes.* Available online. URL: http://www.gwu.edu/~nsarchiv/NSAEBB/NSAEBB307/index.htm. Accessed March 20, 2010.

military necessity

INTERNATIONAL HUMANITARIAN LAW (IHL) recognizes the legal concept of military necessity in view of the undeniable fact that belligerents wage a conflict with the intent of winning and that military actions are governed by that objective. That means that under certain circumstances in a conflict situation, military necessity may dictate attacks that cause loss of life to civilians or to civilian property. However, IHL imposes three fundamental constraints on the exercise of force because of military necessity, since humanitarian concerns do come into play. For one thing, an attack must be directed toward a military objective; if no military purpose is served, then IHL forbids an attack. An attack to terrorize or demoralize a civilian population, for instance, is banned. The second constraint involves the principle of proportionality: An attack on a military objective cannot be disproportionate to its military value. This principle is of particular concern when there is a likelihood of inflicting COLLATERAL DAMAGE, whether to civilians or to public property. Finally, military necessity can never be used as a pretext to violate other international humanitarian law—denying food or medical provisions to a civilian population under SIEGE, for instance.

Moreover, military necessity can only be used for military purposes and not as an instrument to bring about political goals. However, this determination is not so easily made, as Françoise Hampson points out in her essay on the subject for CRIMES OF WAR PROJECT. "Is persuading the enemy to surrender a military or political goal?" she asks. "Is 'persuading' the enemy to surrender by aerial bombardment a military or political goal?" It is possible that a belligerent will simply transform a political objective into a military one to justify its actions. The situation on the ground, which during a conflict is in constant flux, can also change the definition of what constitutes "military necessity." What may be justified at one point might not be justified at another because the circumstances have changed—for example, an area previously occupied by an enemy force becomes populated by civilians because of an influx of REFUGEES.

The use of weapons—in terms of both numbers and type—is also governed both by the immediate demands of military necessity and the constraints of IHL. Weapons are banned by IHL if they cause "superfluous injury or unnecessary suffering." However, opinion among legal experts is divided as to whether nuclear weapons, for instance, are outlawed under every circumstance. An advisory opinion by judges on the INTERNATIONAL COURT OF JUSTICE suggested that a state might be justified in using nuclear weapons if its very survival were at stake and no other recourse were available.

Hampson also points out that the judgment of what constitutes military necessity most often rests with a field commander; yet given the chaotic conditions prevailing on a battlefield, a commander may not be in a position to adequately assess the situation to be able to weigh military and humanitarian considerations. Under such circumstances, a finding of criminal culpability becomes more difficult. However, no ambiguity arises when a commander knows in advance that the orders he or she is giving are illegal on their face regardless of military necessity. IHL does take into account the assignment of legal responsibility by introducing the concept of "imperative military necessity" which, while not outlawing certain acts entirely, does presume that they are likely to be unlawful, thus putting "a significant burden of proof on those invoking the exception." That is to say, the commanders would be considered guilty until proven innocent. The Fourth Geneva Convention, for instance, permits an occupation force to deport or intern protected persons—civilians, medical personnel, sick or wounded combatants, and prisoners of war—for "imperative military necessity" as long as their protection, health, and safety is ensured. However, the occupier would have to establish that its actions were motivated by military necessity in order to avoid being held to account for a breach of international law. In sum, military necessity can be invoked only if the objective is vital to a military victory or if the survival of the belligerent's force is at risk.

See also CIVILIAN IMMUNITY; GENEVA CONVENTIONS; NUCLEAR ARMS AND INTERNATIONAL LAW; PROTECTED PERSONS; WILLFULL KILLING.

Further Reading:

Gutman, Roy, ed. *Crimes of War: What the Public Should Know.* New York: W. W. Norton & Company, 1999.

Milošević, Slobodan (1941–2006) *Yugoslav dictator*

The future Yugoslav president was born in 1941 in Serbia, then a part of the Kingdom of Yugoslavia, only months after the German invasion of the country. However, Slobodan

Milošević grew up in a new country known as the Socialist Federal People's Republic of Yugoslavia. While nominally a communist state, under the leadership of Josip Broz (Marshal Tito) it pursued an independent course rather than follow dictates from Moscow. The young Slobodan's early life was darkened by family tragedy: His father, a schoolteacher, committed suicide in 1962, and his mother followed suit 11 years later. Historians and psychologists have speculated for years on the influence that these events had on Milošević.

When Milošević decided to marry a high school classmate named Mirana Marković—she came from a family of Serbian communist activists—he was entering into a political collaboration as much as he was into a domestic partnership. She would become a forceful influence in the course of his rise to power. After joining the Communist Party in 1959, Milošević went on to earn a law degree from the University of Belgrade. Although he never put his degree to much practical use at the time—he served as a director of a major Belgrade bank instead—his knowledge of the subject would come in handy decades later when he chose to defend himself at his own war crimes trial.

April 24, 1987, marked a turning point in Milošević's life and, it could be said, in the turbulent history of Yugoslavia as well. On that day he appeared before a restive crowd of fellow Serbs who had laid siege to the town hall of Kosovo Polje. The crowd was protesting mistreatment at the hands of the Albanians who made up 90 percent of the population of the province. At the time Milošević was a minor Communist Party functionary, but he saw a chance to make a name for himself. "No one will ever beat you again!" he vowed to cheers and applause. His declaration of defiance almost instantly elevated him to national prominence as a defender of Serbian nationalism.

There is little question that Milošević would never have gained international fame—and so much opprobrium—were it not for the violent breakup of the former Yugoslavia in the 1980s. The republic that emerged in the rubble of World War II was practically the creation of Tito, the Yugoslav leader for 35 years, and it was Tito who held the country's disparate parts and ethnic groups together. (Serbia is mainly Eastern Orthodox, Croatia mainly Roman Catholic, Bosnia and Kosovo mainly Muslim.) It was a difficult task; the Balkans were so often engulfed in war and ethnic clashes that Winston Churchill once famously remarked that "the Balkans produce more history than they can consume." With Tito's death in 1980, though, efforts to maintain the unwieldy Federal Republic of Yugoslavia began to falter. Tito had effectively laid the seeds of the country's future dissolution. Seeking to reduce the concentration of Serbs and thereby reduce their political influence, he had seen to it that one-third of the Serbian population was scattered outside their own province. It was

Former Yugoslav president Slobodan Milošević during the war crimes tribunal at The Hague, 2004 *(Fred Ernst/Landov)*

a decision that would come back to haunt the country—and the world. With Tito gone, the Serbs began to demand their own homeland—but then so did the Croats, the Bosnian Muslims, the Slovenians, and the Albanians, all of whom had at one time called Yugoslavia home.

With the sudden collapse of the Soviet Union and the dismantling of its former Eastern bloc, Milošević was shrewd enough to exploit Serbian nationalism as a means to achieve the power he had sought as a rising communist star. Two years after rallying Serbs in front of the town hall in Kosovo, he fomented demonstrations that drove elected Albanian leaders out of office altogether. In December 1987 he ousted the president of Serbia, and two years later, with the aid of compliant Serbian parliament, he took the post for himself. His populist touch was undeniable: In Serbia's first post-Communist multiparty and direct presidential elections in 1990, he was reelected president by an overwhelming majority. But his increasing truculence stirred alarm among other nationalities who were not eager to become minorities in a Greater Serbia. Within two years of Milošević's ascension to power, Slovenia, Croatia, and Bosnia and Herzegovina all seceded, leaving behind only two republics: Serbia (including the province of Kosovo) and Montenegro. The divorce did not proceed peacefully. Serb minorities in Croatia and Bosnia and Herzegovina clamored for a Greater Serbia. (Slovenia escaped relatively unscathed because few Serbs lived in its territory.)

In 1991, encouraged by Serbia, the Serb minorities in Croatia and Bosnia openly rebelled. Yugoslav armed forces and Serbian militias came to the aid of their fellow Serbs, launching a campaign intended to uproot Bosnian and Croatian populations, killing those that they did not expel. The strategy to force peoples from their homelands came to be called ethnic cleansing, an especially sinister addition to the vocabulary of atrocity and GENOCIDE. At first the war went badly for the Bosnians and Croatians, who were overwhelmed by the far better-armed Serbian forces. In Bosnia, Serbs captured nearly 40 percent of the country. Sarajevo, only a few years earlier the host of the Winter Olympic Games, was turned into a horrific killing field as Serb artillery and snipers hidden in the surrounding hills indiscriminately rained fire down on the city's terrorized inhabitants.

The West was slow to react to the bloodiest conflict in Europe since 1945. But the daily carnage in Sarajevo carried live on television all over the world had its effect. NATO bombers were ordered to launch air strikes against Serb positions, which had the immediate effect of easing the stranglehold on Sarajevo. Meanwhile, on the ground, better-trained Croat and Bosnian troops began to beat back the Serbs, retaking much of the territory that they had yielded in the first months of the war. The reverses, coupled with the air strikes, forced Milošević to the bargaining table. The Clinton administration corralled the leaders of the three belligerents—Milošević, Bosnia's Alija Izetbegović, and Croatia's FRANJO TUDJMAN—at Wright-Patterson Air Force Base in Dayton, Ohio, keeping them there until they came to an agreement that was signed by the warring parties in December 1995 (known as the DAYTON ACCORDS).

The atrocities perpetrated on all sides during the four years of war were considered serious enough to establish a commission to investigate them and try those responsible. In March 1996 the United Nations International War Crimes Tribunal in The Hague quietly questioned Serbian soldiers about war crimes and issued arrest warrants for Bosnian Serb officers.

Although the United Nations lifted most of its sanctions, Yugoslavia's economy continued to erode, and with it so did Milošević's power. But the Yugoslav strongman moved quickly to crush any dissent. He continued to tighten his grip on the media and the reins of political power, annulling the results of municipal elections whose

results he did not like. In spite of the Dayton accords, he showed no sign of being chastened, and in 1998 he went to war again, this time over the Yugoslav province of Kosovo, where armed Albanian separatists threatened to mount open rebellion. The defeat of Serbs at the hands of the conquering Ottomans in the Battle of Kosovo in 1392 still rankled—Albanians were even branded as "Turks" because of their shared Muslim heritage—and the prospect of the province's loss inspired a new burst of Serbian nationalism. Once again the Balkans were plunged into war, and once again it was Milošević who was responsible. Yugoslav forces swept through Kosovo on the pretense of wiping out the armed separatists—the Kosovo Liberation Front (KLA)—but in the process killing hundreds of Albanian civilians and uprooting an estimated 780,000 from their homes. Pretending to buckle under diplomatic pressure, Milošević initially agreed to a partial troop withdrawal at a conference in Rambouillet, France, in March 1999, only to renege and resume fighting.

In late May the INTERNATIONAL CRIMINAL TRIBUNAL FOR THE FORMER YUGOSLAVIA (ICTY) unsealed an indictment accusing Milošević and four other senior Yugoslav officials of committing war crimes in Kosovo. Characteristically, Milošević shrugged off the charges. Losing patience, NATO responded with air strikes on Kosovo and, even more controversially, on military and industrial targets inside Serbia, including installations in Belgrade. Although NATO confined its attacks to the air—putting armed forces on the ground was thought too politically risky by the Clinton administration—the bombardment persuaded Milošević to withdraw his troops from the beleaguered province. UN peacekeepers then moved in to secure the region and supervise the return of Albanian refugees.

In spite of this latest defeat, Milošević continued to hold on to power, largely by playing the same nationalist card that had gotten him into power in the first place. He was so confident of his popularity, in fact, that he even went so far as to call for early elections for president in September 2000. But for the first time, his canny political instincts had deserted him. Exhausted by three wars and an economy that was in shambles, the Yugoslavs turned him out of office and elected a former constitutional law professor, Vojislav Koštunica, in his place. In a desperate attempt to cling to power, Milošević manipulated the courts into annulling the results. This time, though, he had overplayed his hand. Hundreds of thousands of demonstrators took to the streets, and, bowing to pressure, Milošević stepped down.

Now that Milošević had been shorn of power, the ICTY tried to convince Belgrade to arrest him and send him to The Hague to stand trial. The new Koštunica administration rebuffed the attempt, but the Serbia government acted on its own initiative and took him into custody in March 2001. Milošević was charged with embezzlement and abuse of power, but the Serb leaders had no wish to keep him. Three months later he was extradited to The Hague over the strenuous objections of the federal government and the Yugoslav Constitutional Court. Presumably the Serb government was motivated by the $1 billion in aid held out by Western Powers as an inducement.

Milošević has the dubious distinction of being the first head of state ever to be tried for war crimes. The tribunal has indicted him in three cases labeled simply Kosovo, Croatia, and Bosnia. As laid out in the formal indictment, it is alleged that:

1. Between 1 January 1999 and 20 June 1999, forces of the FRY [Federal Republic of Yugoslavia] and Serbia acting at the direction, with the encouragement, or with the support of the accused, executed a campaign of terror and violence directed at Kosovo Albanian civilians.
2. Milošević participated in a "joint criminal enterprise" between at least 1 August 1991 and June 1992. The purpose of this enterprise was the forcible removal of the majority of the Croat and other non-Serb population from approximately one-third of the territory of the Republic of Croatia, an area he planned to become part of a new Serb-dominated state.
3. Milošević exerted control over the elements of the Yugoslav People's Army ("JNA") and the Yugoslav Army ("VJ") which participated in the planning, preparation, facilitation and execution of the forcible removal of the majority of non-Serbs, principally Bosnian Muslims and Bosnian Croats, from large areas of Bosnia and Herzegovina.

Much to the surprise and chagrin of the presiding judges, Milošević rejected any legal help and insisted on defending himself. The first trial, which focused on his culpability in war crimes committed in Kosovo, began in February 2002 and concluded the following September. Later that month the prosecution began the presentation of its case regarding Milošević's alleged crimes in Croatia and Bosnia and Herzegovina. At no point in the trial, even when confronted with victims of the crimes he was charged with having perpetrated, has Milošević shown any hint of remorse or admitted any guilt. His trial was bedeviled by the defendant's recurring illness, the death of one of the presiding judges, and courtroom tactics by Milošević that seemed intended to bring the proceedings to a standstill. On March 11, 2006, with the trial still not concluded, the Balkan dictator died in his prison cell.

See also BOSNIA AND HERZEGOVINA, HUMAN RIGHTS VIOLATIONS IN; CROATIA, HUMAN RIGHTS VIOLATIONS IN; KOSOVO, WAR CRIMES IN; SARAJEVO, SIEGE OF; SER-BIA, HUMAN RIGHTS VIOLATIONS IN; SESELJ, VOJISLAV; SLOVENIA, HUMAN RIGHTS VIOLATIONS IN; YUGOSLAVIA, WAR CRIMES IN.

Further Reading:
Bassiouni, M. Cherif. *Sexual Violence: An Invisible Weapon of War in the Former Yugoslavia.* Chicago: International Human Rights Law Institute, DePaul University, 1996.

Clark, Wesley K. *Waging Modern War: Bosnia, Kosovo, and the Future of Combat.* New York: Public Affairs, 2001.

Glenny, Misha. *The Fall of Yugoslavia: The Third Balkan War.* New York: Penguin Books, 1996.

Hagan, John. *Justice in the Balkans: Prosecuting War Crimes in the Hague Tribunal.* Chicago Series in Law and Society. Chicago: University of Chicago Press, 2003.

Harris, Nathaniel. *The War in Former Yugoslavia.* London: Hodder & Stoughton, 1997.

Hazan, Pierre, and James Thomas Snyder. *Justice in a Time of War: The True Story behind the International Criminal Tribunal for the Former Yugoslavia.* Eugenia and Hugh M. Stewart Series on Eastern Europe. Austin: Texas A&M University Press, 2004.

Honig, Jan Willem, and Norbert Both. *Srebrenica: Record of a War Crime.* New York: Penguin Books, 1997.

ICTY. Milosevic Trial Public Archive. Available online. URL: http://hague.bard.edu/. Accessed March 20, 2010.

Kim, Julie. *War in the Former Yugoslavia: Chronology of Events August 16, 1992–May 30, 1993.* CRS Report for Congress. Washington, D.C.: Foreign Affairs and National Defense Division, Congressional Research Service, the Library of Congress, 1993.

Kipp, Jacob W. *International Ramifications of Yugoslavia's Serial Wars: The Challenge of Ethno-national conflicts for a Post-Cold-War, European Order.* Fort Leavenworth, Kans.: European Military Studies Office, 1993.

Mertus, Julie. *Former Yugoslavia: War Crimes Trials in the Former Yugoslavia.* Helsinki: Human Rights Watch/Helsinki, 1995.

Naimark, Norman, and Holly Case. *Yugoslavia and Its Historians: Understanding the Balkan Wars of the 1990s.* Stanford, Calif.: Stanford University Press, 2003.

Rhode, David. *Endgame: The Betrayal and Fall of Srebrenica.* New York: Farrar, Straus & Giroux, 1997.

Rogel, Carole. *The Breakup of Yugoslavia and the War in Bosnia.* Westport, Conn.: Greenwood Press, 1998.

Rossanet, Bertrand de. *War and Peace in the Former Yugoslavia.* Boston: Martinus Nijhoff, 1997.

Scharf, Michael P. *Balkan Justice: The Story behind the First International War Crimes Trial since Nuremberg.* Durham, N.C.: Carolina Academic Press, 1997.

Minami, Jiro *See* WAR CRIMINALS OF JAPAN.

Mladić, Ratko (1943–) *Serbian commander and indicted war criminal*

The onetime commander of Bosnian Serbian forces in the 1992–95 Bosnian war, Ratko Mladić remains a fugitive from justice, charged by the United Nations with war crimes relating to the siege of Sarajevo and the massacre of thousands of Muslim men and boys in the UN-protected enclave of Srebrenica, the worst atrocity in Europe since World War II. Mladić and RADOVAN KARADŽIĆ, the firebrand nationalist politician who was captured and tried by the United Nations on similar charges, captured and tried are considered the prime movers of a campaign of terror against Bosnian Muslim civilians.

In 1991 Mladić was appointed commander of the IX Corps of the Yugoslav People's Army in the Republic of Croatia (which had broken away from Yugoslavia) and subsequently was given command of the Bosnian Serb army. Like Karadžić, Mladić believed in the idea of a Greater Serbia that would unite minority Serb populations in Croatia and Bosnia and Herzegovina with what remained of Yugoslavia, where Serbs constituted the majority. In 1992 Mladić's forces occupied the heights over the Bosnian capital of Sarajevo, whose population by then had swelled with REFUGEES fleeing Serbian assaults elsewhere in the country. Over the next three and a half years Yugoslav regulars and Serbian paramilitary forces held the city hostage, killing an estimated 10,000 civilians, mostly Bosnian Muslims, with artillery and rocket fire.

In July 1995 Serb forces under Mladić's command shelled an enclave of Srebrenica that had previously been designated as a UN-protected area. Five days later the outmatched Dutch peacekeepers withdrew rather than attempt to defend the civilians who had taken refuge there. Mladić entered the town with Serb camera crews in tow to record his triumph for posterity. The following day the women and children were separated from the men and boys and taken away by buses. Mladić's troops then proceeded to execute more than 7,500 Muslim males ranging in age from 12 to 77.

When the DAYTON ACCORDS in November 1995 put an end to the Bosnian war, Mladić returned to Belgrade. For the next several years he continued to live openly in the Yugoslav capital, eating in expensive restaurants and attending soccer games with the assurance that he enjoyed government protection even though he was charged with war crimes and human rights violations by the INTERNATIONAL CRIMINAL TRIBUNAL FOR THE FORMER YUGOSLAVIA. The arrest of his patron, former Yugoslavian strongman president SLOBODAN MILOŠEVIĆ, in 2001 caused him to go underground. His present whereabouts are unknown, but in 2004 CARLA DEL PONTE, chief prosecutor for the tribunal, contended that he was still in Belgrade. The international warrant issued for his arrest declares that he is wanted for "assault, CRIMES AGAINST HUMANITY, crimes against life and health, grave breaches of the 1949 GENEVA CONVENTIONS, murder, plunder, violations of the laws or customs of war." In a somewhat gratuitous aside, the warrant also notes that Mladić "may be dangerous." After the capture of Karadžić in 2008, Mladić remains the most-wanted fugitive of the Balkan conflict. However, searches of suspected hiding places used by the former general have yielded some potentially significant finds. In one case, investigators discovered 18 notebooks containing his military diaries, 120 sound recordings, cell phone cards, computer memory sticks, and other documents. The thousands of pages, written in Cyrillic script, provided evidence of high-level coordination of the Bosnian Serbian Army and the Serbian government, an alliance that both parties had always denied. Although the documents omit any mention of Mladić's responsibility in the Srebrenica massacre, they are likely to help prosecutors in The Hague in several war crimes trials including Karadžić's.

See also BOSNIA AND HERZEGOVINA, HUMAN RIGHTS VIOLATIONS IN; CROATIA, HUMAN RIGHTS VIOLATIONS IN; SARAJEVO, SIEGE OF; SERBIA, HUMAN RIGHTS VIOLATIONS IN; SREBRENICA, MASSACRE IN.

Further Reading:
Bassiouni, M. Cherif. *Sexual Violence: An Invisible Weapon of War in the Former Yugoslavia.* Chicago: International Human Rights Law Institute, DePaul University, 1996.
Clark, Wesley K. *Waging Modern War: Bosnia, Kosovo, and the Future of Combat.* New York: Public Affairs, 2001.
Glenny, Misha. *The Fall of Yugoslavia: The Third Balkan War.* New York: Penguin Books, 1996.
Mertus, Julie. *Former Yugoslavia: War Crimes Trials in the Former Yugoslavia.* Helsinki: Human Rights Watch/Helsinki, 1995.

Mobutu Sese Seko (Joseph Desire Mobutu, Mobutu Sese Seko Ngbender wa za Banga) (1930–1997)
Congolese dictator

Mobutu Sese Seko was the dictator of Zaire (now the Democratic Republic of the Congo) for three decades, an era marked by repressive rule and such rampant corruption that his regime became widely known as a kleptocracy. Born Joseph Desire Mobutu on October 14, 1930, the future leader was raised in the northern village of Lisala in what was then the Belgian Congo. He was educated at a Catholic mission school and between 1949 and 1956 served in the Belgian colonial army, rising to the position of sergeant major, the highest rank open to an African.

In June 1960 Congo achieved its independence. The first prime minister, Patrice Lumumba, appointed the ambitious Mobutu as his private secretary and then as his chief of staff of the army. Within months the country was embroiled in civil war when Moise Tshombe, head of the mineral-rich province of Katanga, launched a secessionist rebellion. Lumumba sought help from the United Nations to restore order, and consequently the organization became caught up in the war. A month later, in September 1960, Mobutu, with the clandestine support of the CIA, participated in a military coup to oust Lumumba. As an avowed leftist and nationalist favoring a nonaligned policy, Lumumba was viewed as a threat to U.S. interests in the context of the cold war. Mobutu, on the other hand, was considered someone that Washington could work with. (Lumumba was executed a year later.) The war with Katanga continued, however. Evidence later emerged that Belgium was seeking to regain a foothold in the Congo—and secure its resources—by backing Tshombe. In the ensuing tumult, Tshombe even managed to become prime minister himself until he was forced out in 1964 after rigged elections.

Mobutu seized the opportunity to stage a second coup in November 1965. He put Tshombe on trial in absentia; the court condemned him to death. (Tshombe was later abducted to Algeria and died in a prison there in 1969.) Within two years of taking power, Mobutu declared a policy of "Africanization," and in October 1971 he changed the name of the country to Zaire, the name of the Congo River centuries before. In keeping with his African-roots policy, he also changed his own name, calling himself Mobutu Sese Seko Kuku Ngbendu wa za

Former leader of Zaire Mobutu Sese Seko *(Landov)*

Banga (officially translated as "the all-powerful warrior who, because of his endurance and inflexible will to win, will go from conquest to conquest leaving fire in his wake"). As a demonstration of his tribal roots, he took to wearing a leopard-skin hat, which became his sartorial signature. His obsession with names also manifested itself in a Nationality Law, which abolished the use of all European names for persons and places.

Mobutu consolidated his rule as a one-party state and seized European-owned businesses. Dissent was crushed and opponents jailed or executed. However, he did succeed—at least for a time—in fostering a sense of national unity among several tribal and ethnic groups. Because there was no official language—French, a legacy of the Belgian colonists, was the only common language—Mobutu promoted the widespread use of four local languages. At the same time he moved to shore up relations with the United States and Europe, cutting a number of deals with Western companies to exploit the country's valuable copper deposits. Because he positioned himself as a staunch anticommunist, he was looked upon by Washington as a vital ally in the region. Mobutu took advantage of his position to amass a fortune, estimated in the billions of dollars, most of which he evidently cached away in secret Swiss bank accounts. (The International Monetary Fund has estimated that his fortune reached its peak of about $4 billion in the 1980s.)

Although Mobutu made some moves toward democratic reform in the 1980s, allowing the formation of a political opposition party, he harassed and imprisoned its leaders. In the waning years of his regime, he confronted a number of uprisings, which he always managed to put down, twice with the assistance of French troops. Nonetheless, his hold on power steadily weakened. With the end of the cold war, Mobutu's value to the West diminished significantly, and the U.S. Congress cut off direct aid to protest his human rights abuses. A rebellion in eastern Zaire, led by a former Lumumba supporter named Laurent Kabila, gathered force, and the economy went into a tailspin. Meanwhile Mobutu's health was worsening—he suffered from prostate cancer—and he spent more and more time away from the capital of Kinshasa, preferring to stay on the Riviera or withdraw into the palatial splendor of his home in his native village of Gbadolite. Eventually Kabila's rebels succeeded in breaking out of their stronghold in the east and routing Mobutu's forces, which included a number of foreign MERCENARIES. Defiant until the end, Mobutu finally conceded power in May 1997 and went into exile. He died in Morocco in September of the same year. At the time of his death, Mobutu owned palaces and villas in Zaire, Morocco, South Africa, France, Belgium, Switzerland, Spain, and Portugal. He had also managed to assemble an impressive wine collection, worth an estimated $2.3 million, which he stored in his castle in Portugal.

See also CONGO, DEMOCRATIC REPUBLIC OF THE, WAR CRIMES IN; LEOPOLD II.

Further Reading:
Edgerton, Robert. *The Troubled Heart of Africa: A History of the Congo.* New York: St. Martin's Press, 2002.
Wrong, Michela. *In the Footsteps of Mr. Kurtz: Living on the Brink of Disaster in Mobutu's Congo.* New York: HarperCollins Publishers, 2001.

Monteneros *See* ARGENTINA, HUMAN RIGHTS VIOLATIONS IN.

Montesinos, Vladimiro Ilyich (1946–) *Peruvian spymaster*

Vladimiro Ilyich Montesinos was the security chief and intelligence head for Peruvian president ALBERTO FUJIMORI during a decade of authoritarian rule. A former army captain, Montesinos was second only to Fujimori in the power he wielded and was widely regarded—and reviled—as Fujimori's Rasputin. His parents were both communists, which explains why they named their son—born in 1946—after Vladimir Ilyich Lenin. Far from living up to his namesake, though, Montesinos developed into a committed rightist ideologue.

Montesinos joined the army in 1966, but he was cashiered and imprisoned in 1977 on the suspicion that he had sold state secrets to the CIA at a time when Peru was dominated by a leftist government and was a beneficiary of Soviet aid. In prison he studied law, and on his release he opened a practice defending people accused of tax fraud and drug trafficking. He soon acquired several new friends in the cocaine trade in addition to befriending corrupt army and police officials. When one general was accused of massacring civilians in an operation against insurgents, he turned to Montesinos to defend him; the case was dismissed. Montesinos also proved a valuable asset to the National Intelligence Service, known by its acronym SIN. In 1990 Fujimori sought Montesinos's help in resolving a tax-evasion case which might have jeopardized his bid for the presidency. Montesinos obligingly took care of the problem. There were also allegations that he had arranged for Colombia's drug baron Pablo Escobar to contribute $1 million to Fujimori's electoral campaign in exchange for allowing Escobar's agents the use of Peru's air space to transport cocaine. Nine years later Montesinos was thought to have orchestrated a "dirty tricks" campaign to influence Fujimori's victory for a third term in violation of the 1993 constitution, which limited a president to two terms.

Even as Montesinos was becoming more involved in extortion, drug trafficking, and illegal arms trading, Fujimori was publicly commending him for intercepting a consignment of arms from Jordan supposedly intended for the insurgent group Revolutionary Armed Forces of Colombia (FARC). The Jordanian government reacted angrily, insisting that the shipment had been sold to the Peruvian government. It later emerged that Montesinos himself was in the process of selling arms to FARC. In another suspect arms deal, the spymaster sold two shoddy MIG-29 fighters to Ecuador (which had just fought a brief border war with Peru), pocketing a sizable commission in the process. Montesinos has also been linked to a notorious death squad called La Colina, which might be implicated in the 1991 slaying of 15 civilians attending a party in a Lima slum who were apparently mistaken for a terrorist gathering.

In September 2000 a video was aired on Peruvian television that showed Montesinos bribing a member of the Peruvian Congress to influence his vote. The video scandalized the country, as much of the tape implicated Peru's most powerful figures. The tape, stolen from Montesinos's office safe, was only one of about a thousand that the spymaster had made for purposes of blackmail and as a kind of insurance policy to forestall any attempt to undermine him. In the uproar that ensued, Fujimori tried to put as much distance as he could between him and his former confidant and ordered his arrest. Montesinos fled the country immediately and, shortly after being denied asylum in Panama, dropped out of sight.

In November 2000 Switzerland announced that it was freezing about $50 million in five bank accounts that were linked to Montesinos, lending weight to the belief that he had laundered money through the accounts. Other suspect accounts were subsequently identified in the Cayman Islands, Uruguay, New York, and elsewhere, totaling $274 million. Much of these funds, investigators believed, came from his drug-trafficking and arms deals, but it still represents only about a third of the $800 million looted from Peru's treasury during the 10 years Fujimori had been in power. In November 2000 Fujimori took refuge in Japan, his parents' country of origin, and resigned from the presidency. (Peru has unsuccessfully tried to extradite him to stand trial for money laundering and other charges.) On June 23, 2001, the fugitive Montesinos was arrested in Venezuela and extradited to Peru. A year later he was tried and convicted of illegally controlling Peru's intelligence agency and received a sentence of nine years in prison. He was later given an additional sentence of eight years after standing trial on embezzlement charges. But it is likely that Montesinos will be returning to court several times in the near future; he still faces some 70 trials on various charges.

In 2006 Montesinos received a 20-year sentence for being involved in an illegal arms deal intended to funnel assault weapons to FARC. He later went on trial on charges of directing a death squad and plotting to burn down the National Bank headquarters in Lima in 2000 to discredit opponents of Fujimori.

See also COLOMBIA, HUMAN RIGHTS VIOLATIONS IN.

Morocco, human rights violations in

Morocco has made some progress in human rights especially since the ascension of King Mohamed VI, who assumed the throne in 1999 after the death of his father, Hassan II, who had held power since 1961. Although King Mohamed VI began to institute reforms when he came to power, the pace of liberalization has begun to slow because of the growing influence of Islamic radicalism. Power still remains concentrated in the monarchy, and while the government gives lip service to democratic ideals, human rights organizations are skeptical of a genuine commitment to implementing them in practice. Anxious to avoid the kind of violent discord that has taken place in ALGERIA next door, Moroccan officials speak of maintaining a proper balance between freedom and social cohesion. Coordinated attacks in May 2003 by AL-QAEDA in Casablanca, which killed 46 (including 12 suicide bombers) and injured about 100, led the government to implement a crackdown and set back democratization efforts. A terrorist law enacted in 2003 defined *terrorism* broadly to encompass any act that might arouse fear or jeopardize public safety. The act also extended by 10 days the time that a suspect can be held before charges must be filed. HUMAN RIGHTS WATCH called the antiterrorism law a "major regression" in efforts to create a civil society. After the act went into effect, security forces rounded up more than 2,000 people for suspected involvement with terrorist groups. As of 2009, Morocco's prisons were filled with about 1,000 people believed to be Islamic militants, although some were politicians. At least one was a reporter from the Hezbollah (Lebanon) television station. Most of the political prisoners have been accused of links to terrorist activities. Human Rights Watch has questioned the validity of the legal proceedings against five recently arrested politicians and the reporter, citing irregularities and the reliance of prosecutors on circumstantial evidence. Nonetheless, the militant threat is very real; the north of the country is regarded as a hotbed of extremism and the base from which many al-Qaeda operatives stage attacks. There is evidence, though, that the government's focus on terrorism and neutralizing Islamic influence has hobbled its efforts to liberalize laws for women's rights and reform the corrupt judiciary.

In spite of violations of civil liberties, the United States regards Morocco as a close ally in the war against terrorism and has provided Rabat with military and development assistance. It has also granted the country the status of "major non-NATO ally." However, human rights violations are rampant. While police usually arrest suspects in public,

they frequently fail to identify themselves or produce warrants. Several suspects have died in police custody, but no serious attempts have been made to investigate these cases. Because of the swelling prison population, it is difficult to ascertain the fates of many of the detainees. As a result, reports of politically motivated DISAPPEARANCES are impossible to verify. However, both the Moroccan Association for Human Rights (AMDH) and AMNESTY INTERNATIONAL contend that the practice of holding suspects incommunicado have amounted to "a period of disappearance." In such cases police are often in the habit of denying to families that they are holding the individuals. And while the Penal Code outlaws the use of TORTURE, human rights organizations have collected evidence indicating that security forces often ignore the law. The judiciary suffers from inefficiency and corruption and is subject to political influence. The government limits freedom of assembly and freedom of the press. About 1,000 Islamic candidates have been forced to withdraw from local elections because of their political beliefs. The government also imposes restrictions on labor unions and curtails the right to strike. The crackdown has failed to dampen enthusiasm for Islamic movements, though. On the contrary, they have become increasingly popular, not the least because they have established social welfare programs in areas where people consider the government's programs as inadequate.

Until the 2003 Casablanca bombings, the government was lauded by human rights organizations for releasing hundreds of political prisoners and easing restrictions on the press and political activity. King Mohamed VI even went so far as to establish the Justice and Reconciliation Commission to document abuses perpetrated under his father's regime and determine "the responsibility of state or other apparatuses in the violations and the incidents under investigation." This commission is supposed to investigate some 13,000 cases of alleged abuses prior to 1999 and arrange for out-of-court settlements in cases where proof of abuse is found. Although he was known as a "moderate" and pro-Western ruler, King Hassan had been responsible for a ruthless campaign to imprison or disappear thousands of suspected leftists, Islamists, and advocates of self-determination for Western Sahara, a region bitterly disputed by Morocco and Algeria. In the late 1980s, Hassan moved to liberalize society and pledged that incidences of forced disappearances would never recur. At that point 112 disappearances had been reported, some of which had taken place two decades previously. Human rights groups and families, however, maintain that there were many more disappearances besides these, many of them stemming from violence in the Western Sahara.

The Justice and Reconciliation Commission is subject to certain restrictions that might hamper its efforts. It cannot find any individuals culpable in cases of abuse. In addition, it has no power to compel testimony or obtain necessary documents. Its mandate specifies that it can investigate cases of "arbitrary detention" and "enforced disappearance," leaving open the question whether it can undertake any investigation of other types of abuses, including torture, sham trials, and the shooting of demonstrators. Nor is it clear whether the commission will have the right to probe any human rights violations that occurred after the May 2003 terrorist strikes in Casablanca.

See also BERBERS, HUMAN RIGHTS ABUSES OF.

Further Reading:

Amnesty International USA. Morocco and Western Sahara Human Rights. Available online. URL: http://www.amnestyusa.org/all-countries/morocco-and-western-sahara/page.do?id=1011203. Accessed March 20, 2010.

Araboo. *Morocco Human Rights and Liberties.* Available online. URL: http://www.araboo.com/dir/morocco-human-rights-liberties. Accessed March 20, 2010.

Howe, Marvine. *Morocco: The Islamist Awakening and Other Challenges.* New York: Oxford University Press, 2005.

McNamara, Ronald J. *Democracy and Human Rights in the Mediterranean Partner States of the Osce: Algeria, Egypt, Israel, Jordan, Morocco and Tunisia: Briefing of the Committee on Security and Cooperation in Europe.* Chicago: Diane Pub. Co., 2004.

Sherry, Virginia N. *Cleaning the Face of Morocco: Human Rights Abuses and Recent Developments/North Africa.* New York: Human Rights First, 1990.

Slyomovics, Susan. *The Performance of Human Rights in Morocco.* Pennsylvania Studies in Human Rights. Philadelphia: University of Pennsylvania Press, 2005.

Waltz, Susan Eileen. *Human Rights and Reform: Changing the Face of North African Politics.* Berkeley: University of California Press, 1995.

Mothers of the Plaza de Mayo (Grandmothers of the Plaza de Mayo)

The Mothers of the Plaza de Mayo (*Asociación Madres de Plaza de Mayo* in Spanish) is an association of women that has held demonstrations every Thursday at 3:30 P.M. in the famous Plaza de Mayo in Buenos Aires, Argentina, for over 20 years. (They are sometimes known as Grandmothers of the Plaza de Mayo.) They are mothers of children who were disappeared during the "dirty wars" of the 1970s. That tumultuous period was marked by a clandestine campaign by a succession of military juntas against leftist insurgents and suspected sympathizers. The women, dressed in black, march around a statue of liberty in front of the presidential palace. Many have used white handkerchiefs printed with the names of their vanished children or carry signs with their children's photographs.

For years the authorities denied all knowledge of the whereabouts or fate of the victims, who were often spirited away in unmarked cars in the dead of night. The mothers' weekly protest became the most vivid and powerful expression of resistance to the military regimes. After democracy was restored in 1982, the government proved more forthcoming with information. The military has acknowledged that more than 9,000 abductees are still unaccounted for; the Mothers of the Plaza de Mayo believe the number is closer to 30,000. The women recognize that most of their children have been tortured and are probably dead, yet they have refused any monetary compensation for their losses and continue to demand government accountability. Some of the mothers suffered the same fate as their children for opposing the military regimes, including the organization's founder, Azucena Villaflor de Vicenti. Sometime between December 8 and 10, 1977, along with 11 members and friends of the Mothers, she was kidnapped by Argentine government forces and never seen again. In December 2003 the president of Mothers of the Plaza de Mayo, Estela Barnes de Carlotto, was awarded a UN Human Rights Prize.

See also ARGENTINA, HUMAN RIGHTS VIOLATIONS IN.

Further Reading:

Arditti, Rita. *Searching for Life: The Grandmothers of the Plaza de Mayo and the Disappeared Children of Argentina.* Berkeley: University of California Press, 1999.

Davis, William Columbus. *Warnings from the Far South: Democracy versus Dictatorship in Uruguay, Argentina, and Chile.* New York: Praeger Publishers, 1995.

Goni, Uki. *The Real Odessa: How Peron Brought the Nazi War Criminals to Argentina.* London: Granta Books, 2003.

Lewis, Paul H. *Guerrillas and Generals: The Dirty War in Argentina.* New York: Praeger, 2001.

Moyano, Maria. *Argentina's Lost Patrol: Armed Struggle, 1969–1979.* New Haven, Conn.: Yale University Press, 1995.

Rombero, Luis Alberto. *A History of Argentina in the Twentieth Century.* University Park: Pennsylvania State University Press, 2002.

Mugabe, Robert   *See* ZIMBABWE, HUMAN RIGHTS VIOLATIONS IN.

Mullah Omar (Mohammed Omar) (1959–) *Taliban leader*

The onetime TALIBAN leader of Afghanistan, Mohammed Omar—better known as Mullah Omar—suddenly gained a high public profile after the September 11, 2001, attacks in New York and Washington, D.C. At the time, his regime was harboring Osama bin Laden, the mastermind of the terrorist strikes, but Mullah Omar refused to hand him over to Washington even at the cost of his regime. Within months the United States had invaded Afghanistan, toppling the Taliban and sending Mullah Omar into exile.

Reporters who met the reclusive Mullah while he was in power say that he loved to tell war stories. Presumably he had a lot of them to tell: He had been wounded four times in the jihad against Soviet forces, which had invaded the country in 1979; one of the battles had deprived him of an eye. Calling himself Commander of the Faithful, Omar followed a fundamentalist branch of Islam that is so strict that even the playing of music or flying a kite was made illegal. Born in 1959, the son of a peasant farmer, he claimed to have started the Taliban movement after a dream in which Allah asked him to lead the faithful. The core of the Taliban (from *talib*, meaning "one who seeks") consisted of young students of Islam, many of whom were driven into exile in neighboring Pakistan after the Soviets took over the country. Omar himself studied the Quran in a fundamentalist school, or madrassa, in Pakistan. Although he might have been motivated by a dream, he had other reasons to try to wrest control over his native country. After the withdrawal of Soviet troops in 1989, Afghanistan had plunged into chaos as various warlords fought among themselves for domination. Omar has told interviewers that he was appalled by the lawless atmosphere that prevailed but was provoked especially by one incident in which mujahideen (veterans of the resistance against the Soviets) went on a rampage, raping several women who lived near Kandahar, Omar's family home.

Initially accompanied by only 30 followers from his Pashtun tribe, Omar went to war. More fighters soon joined him, and he began to acquire a kind of cult status, which he did nothing to discourage. On the contrary, in 1996, accepting the title of *amirul momineen* (commander of the faithful), he appeared before cheering Taliban followers wrapped in a coat said to have been worn by the prophet Mohammed. (His title was not accepted by Muslims outside of Afghanistan.) By 1998 he had secured control over most of the country, although at no point did the Taliban ever extend its power over all Afghani territory. Anti-Taliban fighters, collectively known as the Northern Alliance, continued to hold out. Omar ruled from Kandahar, never visiting the capital, Kabul. In the first years of the Taliban regime, he would routinely appear in local mosques, but over time he became increasingly reclusive, preferring to ride around in armed convoys of Landcruisers. He increasingly fell under the influence of the radical Saudi exile Osama bin Laden, his deputy Ayman Zawahiri, and the Islamic jihad faithful that they had brought with them from Saudi Arabia and Egypt.

There were reports that the Taliban was divided about the course it should take, with some moderates favoring a more open policy. Nonetheless, it appeared that by late 2001 Omar was becoming increasingly beholden to bin Laden and reliant on his generous subsidies. After the United States had satisfied itself that bin Laden's AL-QAEDA group was behind the terrorist attacks on 9/11, Washington demanded that Omar turn over bin Laden or face an invasion. Omar was characteristically defiant. "America is very strong," he admitted in an interview with the Voice of America (VOA). But he went on to say that it would make no difference: "Even if it were twice as strong or twice that, it could not be strong enough to defeat us. We are confident that no one can harm us if God is with us." Asked by VOA if he would give up bin Laden, he said, "No. We cannot do that. If we did, it means we are not Muslims . . . that Islam is finished. If we were afraid of attack, we could have surrendered him the last time we were threatened and attacked. So America can hit us again, and this time we don't even have a friend." The United States did, as he predicted, hit him, and by November 2001 Omar, bin Laden, and other top Taliban officials were on the run, presumably taking refuge in the remote mountainous region on the border with Pakistan.

It is believed that Mullah Omar still directs the Taliban insurgency, which intensified in 2008 and 2009, prompting President Barack Obama to dispatch 30,000 additional U.S. forces to Afghanistan. According to intelligence reports, the command structure of the Taliban is based in the Pakistani city of Quetta. The Quetta Shura, as it is called, meets periodically to plan strategy. In spite of the arrests of several of Mullah Omar's top lieutenants in 2010, the Taliban remained an effective fighting force and a long-term threat to the stability of the Karzai government in Kabul. Efforts to buy off Taliban militants and integrate them into the Afghan army have had only limited success. However, there has been increasing recognition in Washington and Kabul, if not in Islamabad, that some form of political settlement would have to be reached with the Taliban because a definitive military victory over the group was considered unlikely. As of 2010 there was no sign of any serious negotiations taking place, nor was it clear whether Omar would engage in any talks intended to bring the Taliban into Karzai's government.

See also AFGHANISTAN, HUMAN RIGHTS VIOLATIONS IN; WAR ON TERROR.

Further Reading:
Anderson, J. L., and Thomas Dworzak. *Taliban.* London: Trolley, 2003.
Burke, Jason. *Al-Qaeda: Casting a Shadow of Terror.* London: I. B. Tauris, 2004.
———. *Al-Qaeda: The True Story of Radical Islam.* London: I. B. Tauris, 2004.

Ewans, Martin. *Afghanistan: A Short History of Its People and Politics.* New York: Perennial, 2002.

Micheletti, Eric. *Special Forces in Afghanistan 2001–2003: War against Terrorism.* Paris: Historie & Collections, 2003.

Rashid, Ahmed. *Jihad: The Rise of Militant Islam in Central Asia.* New York: Penguin Books, 2003.

———. *Taliban: Militant Islam, Oil and Fundamentalism in Central Asia.* New Haven, Conn.: Yale University Press, 2001.

Tanner, Stephen. *Afghanistan: A Military History from Alexander the Great to the Fall of the Taliban.* New York: Perseus Books Group, 2003.

Zayy-at, Montassor al-. *The Road to Al-Qaeda: The Story of bin Laden's Right-Hand Man.* Critical Studies on Islam. Translated by Ahmed Fekry. Edited by Sara Nionis. Ann Arbor, Mich.: Pluto Press, 2004.

Müller, Heinrich (1900–?) *Gestapo chief*

Heinrich Müller (also spelled Mueller) was the chief of the GESTAPO from 1939 until the end of World War II in 1945. Although he remained in the shadows, he wielded immense power over the lives of hundreds of millions of people in parts of Europe occupied by the German army. For decades the German Office of Investigation of Nazis considered him its most wanted war criminal.

Born in Munich on April 28, 1900, Müller served as a pilot in World War I. After the war he joined the police in his native Munich, where he became known for pursuing communists. Although he proved to be an able investigator, he was indifferent to the norms of legal procedure. His reputation for getting results, however, attracted the interest of HEINRICH HIMMLER and REINHARD HEYDRICH, who headed the SS, the Nazi elite police. After ADOLF HITLER came to power in 1933, Himmler and Heydrich formed a national political police which they called the Geheime Staatspolizei (Gestapo). The following year Müller joined the SS. He won succeeding promotions until he was appointed chief of the Gestapo, known formally as Reich Main Security Office (RSHA) Amt IV. In his new position, Müller undertook to implement Nazi policies designed to crush Jews and other enemies of the state. One of his most trusted subordinates was ADOLF EICHMANN, who ran the Gestapo's Office of Resettlement and then its Office of Jewish Affairs. Müller subsequently put Eichmann in charge of the deportation and extermination of the several million Jews in occupied Europe.

Müller was also behind a plot to blame Poland for starting World War II in 1939 by staging a phony Polish attack against a German radio station. In March 1944 he signed the "Bullet Order," which authorized the killings of escaped PRISONERS OF WAR. A committed Hitler loyalist, he earned a military decoration for his role in rounding up and torturing the participants in the July 20, 1944, plot to kill Hitler. As head of the Gestapo, he also masterminded counterespionage operations against the French Resistance and a Soviet spy network known as the Rote Kapelle (Red Orchestra). He organized the kidnapping of British intelligence officials and even plotted to abduct the duke of Windsor, a scheme that was never executed. As the war turned increasingly in favor of the Allies, he used his spy network to try to cause a rift between the Soviets and the United States and Great Britain.

After the war, some high-placed Nazi officials told their American captors that Müller might have been a Soviet agent, but most SS officers who were close to him asserted that such an accusation was absurd. According to witnesses later interviewed by West German police, Müller was last seen alive on May 1, 1945. At the time he refused to try to escape with other Nazi officials gathered at Hitler's Chancellery building. "We know the Russian methods exactly," Müller was reported to have said. "I haven't the faintest intention of . . . being taken prisoner by the Russians." While the search for Müller has continued intermittently over ensuing decades, it is not known whether he is alive or dead.

Further Reading:

Browder, George C. *Hitler's Enforcers: The Gestapo and the SS Security Service in the Nazi Revolution.* Oxford: Oxford University Press, 1996.

Butler, Rupert. *The Gestapo: A History of Hitler's Secret Police 1933–45.* Havertown, Pa.: Casemate Publishers and Book Distributors, 2004.

Douglas, Gregory. *Gestapo Chief: The 1948 Interrogation of Heinrich Muller.* Vol. 3. San Jose, Calif.: R. James Bender Pub., 1998.

Hohne, Heinz Zollen. *The Order of the Death's Head: Story of Hitler's SS.* New York: Penguin, 2001.

Myanmar, human rights violations in

Myanmar (formerly Burma) has been ruled by a succession of military dictatorships since 1962. Dissent has been ruthlessly suppressed, and Myanmar's most prominent political opposition leader, AUNG SAN SUU KYI, winner of the Nobel Peace Prize, was under house arrest intermittently until November 2010. There is little question that she would be the country's president if democracy were restored. Her party, the National League for Democracy (NLD), gained a majority in parliament in elections in 1990, but rather than concede defeat, the military annulled the election. Since then security forces have rounded up and arrested members of the opposition; those that remain free are kept on a tight leash. AMNESTY INTERNATIONAL estimated that more than a thousand political prisoners were still being detained in early 2003. In spite of periodic negotiations between the army and San Suu Kyi, there are few signs that the military has any intention of voluntarily relinquishing power.

Myanmar also confronts serious ethnic problems, perhaps not surprising given the fact that the population is made up of 135 different ethnic groups. (The Burman is the largest, accounting for around 55 percent of the population.) Ethnic tensions have led to a number of insurgencies. Members of the Karen, for instance, have been fighting the government for more than 50 years. In its attempt to quell ethnic rebellions, the Myanmar army has become increasingly aggressive. According to human rights groups, the army has committed numerous human rights violations, including forced relocation, razing of villages, rape, TORTURE, and summary executions. The army has also made widespread use of conscription, forcing local villagers to work without pay growing food for soldiers, performing road maintenance, or serving as porters in military camps.

Myanmar has the dubious distinction of having more child soldiers than any other country in the world, accounting for approximately one-fourth of the 300,000 children currently believed to be involved in armed conflicts around the world. The United Nations secretary-general has placed Myanmar on a list of violators that flout international laws prohibiting the recruitment and use of children as soldiers. A 2002 investigation by HUMAN RIGHTS WATCH found that as many as 70,000 children under the age of 18 may be serving in the army. Another 6,000–7,000 serve in Myanmar's armed ethnic opposition groups; about 20 percent of the Karen insurgent army is composed of children under the age of 18. Army recruiters force boys as young as 11 into the army and regularly haul children off the street. Child soldiers are forced to commit human rights abuses against civilians. Children have rounded up villagers for FORCED LABOR, burned villages, and carried out executions. In an account reported by Human Rights International, a 14-year-old soldier reported that his unit had killed 15 women and children in operations in Shan State. The women were blindfolded, the boy said, and "then six of the corporals loaded their guns and shot them. They fired on auto. The women had no time to shout. I felt very bad because there were all these people in front of me, and they killed them all. After the mothers were killed they killed the babies. They swung them by their legs and smashed them against a rock."

In 2007 and 2008 Myanmar underwent three tumultuous events: a violent crackdown against mass demonstrations led by Buddhist monks, a constitutional referendum that seemed intended to ratify the junta's continued hold on power, and a devastating cyclone that resulted in thousands of deaths and called into question the regime's ability to provide urgently needed assistance to its own people.

The demonstrations began in the former capital of Yangon (Rangoon) in late August, sparked by a rise in gas

Red Cross workers speaking with a detainee in a Myanmar prison *(J. P. Moret/ICRC)*

prices—a 66 percent increase that occurred literally overnight—imposing an onerous burden on an impoverished population. As many as 100,000 people may have taken part in the demonstrations in August and September 2007, led by 30,000 monks and nuns who had not previously been in the forefront of any protests. As protests grew, the demonstrators began to call for sweeping reforms. Security forces reacted violently, suppressing the demonstrators with clubs and tear gas and conducting raids on their homes without troubling to obtain search or arrest warrants. Although the exact numbers may never be known, some reports say that up to 100 people were shot to death in the turmoil. (UN Special Rapporteur Paulo Sergio Pinheiro said that at least 31 persons had died as a result of the crackdown, including the 15 individuals accounted for by the Myanmar government.) Several hundred people were arrested; Amnesty International estimates that after the crackdown the regime doubled the number of political prisoners it was holding to more than 2,100. Hundreds more were arrested in 2008 in spite of assurances provided by the government to the UN Special Adviser Ibrahim Gambari in November 2007 that the arrests had ceased. Most of the demonstrators taken into custody were charged under Law 5/96, which allows up to 20-year prison sentences for anyone who is found guilty of expressing opinions that disrupt the stability of the state, or "undermine, belittle and make people misunderstand the functions being carried out by the National Convention."

On May 3, 2008, the southern portion of Myanmar was struck by Cyclone Nargis. The Irawaddy Delta and Yangon were especially hard hit, with the death toll rising into the tens of thousands. Many thousands more were displaced. For the most part, the junta rebuffed efforts by other nations (including the United States) or international aid organizations to provide assistance, partly out of unwarranted fears of a covert invasion under the cover of rendering assistance, partly out of fear of being seen as ineffectual. (A year later restrictions were eased, and nongovernmental organizations could function more freely in helping the affected region to recover.) Undaunted by the natural disaster, the regime went ahead with a constitutional referendum that effectively ratified its grip on power. The regime announced that the referendum was passed with 90 percent of the vote, although it was widely denounced as unfair by the opposition. Citing the adoption of the new constitution as a "critical first step," Prime Minister General Thein Sein maintained that his government was committed to a program of "democratization and reconciliation." Although the regime insists that it will hold elections in the near future to establish a "genuine multiparty democracy," it has demonstrated little inclination to make good on its promise of democratic reform. In 2009, Aung San Suu Kyi was put on trial for supposedly violating the terms of her house arrest. (She was accused of harboring an intruder who had evaded her security patrol by gaining access to her home by swimming across a nearby lake.) Observers believed that the junta was looking for any pretext to extend Suu Kyi's imprisonment, because the term of her house arrest was about to expire. The military government appeared determined to sideline her prior to the upcoming election campaign. In August 2009 she was convicted of sheltering an uninvited guest and violating the terms of her house arrest and returned to house arrest for 18 months. (She has, however, been permitted rare meetings with foreign emissaries.) In a possible sign that the military may be easing its iron grip in response to tentative overtures by the international community (the Obama administration in particular), the government allowed a meeting between Aung San Suu Kyi and top levels of her party in December 2009.

As Myanmar's military government prepared to adopt a new and disputed constitution in 2010, a fragile patchwork of cease-fire agreements between the central government and more than a dozen armed ethnic groups was showing signs of fraying. Several conflicts between government forces and various rebel groups have led to a humanitarian crisis, especially in eastern Myanmar, where the Myanmar army, known as the *tatmadaw,* has been pressing an offensive against ethnic Karen civilians in Kayin (Karen) State and Bago (Pegu) Division. The conflict has caused what human rights organizations call "widespread and systematic violation of international human rights and humanitarian law." It is estimated that 66,000 people from these ethnic minority communities have been displaced as a result of the recent violence; altogether, at least 451,000 people have

been reported to be internally displaced in the rural areas of eastern Myanmar since the military campaign began in November 2005. Civilians caught up in the conflict have been victims of unlawful killings, torture, disappearances, arbitrary arrests, forced labor, and forced recruitment into the army. Villages have been razed and crops and food stocks destroyed, all forms of collective punishment banned by international law. Civilians are being targeted simply because they are members of the Kayin ethnic group or because they reside in Karen areas. The new constitution calls for autonomy for the Kayins and other ethnic groups, but only if the groups disarm, something that these groups are reluctant to do, not only because they remain suspicious of the regime's intentions and resent Burman domination, but also because in many of these areas they control a lucrative trade in timber, jade, gems, and even drugs.

In August the central government confronted ethnic groups in the northern highlands—the Wa, the Kokang and the Kachin—which, according to the UNITED NATIONS HIGH COMMISSIONER FOR REFUGEES, uprooted 10,000 to 30,000 people who took temporary refuge in neighboring China. Nonetheless, the inroads the government has made against the Karen, the ethnic group that has posed the gravest threat to extending its authority, has allowed it to consolidate more territory than any time in recent memory. The people in these disputed areas have suffered disproportionately. The Karen Human Rights Group estimates that nearly 5,000 villagers from Karen territory have sought refuge in Thailand. In recent years thousands of an ethnic Muslim group called the Rohingya have also fled the country, seeking refuge in neighboring Thailand as well as Indonesia and India. It is believed that 20,000 Rohingyas have taken refuge in Thailand alone, piling into crowded refugee camps that hold more than 120,000 people. But their status in exile is illegal, and as a result they are often mistreated by security forces in these countries. Any Rohingya who is caught in Thailand is deported to Myanmar.

On November 7, 2010, the military regime finally held its long-promised elections for a 665-member, two-chamber national parliament and 14 regional parliaments. Not surprisingly, the two opposition parties were badly beaten by the Union Solidarity and Development Party, the party backed by the military government. Although the elections were intended to lead to the first civilian government since a military coup in 1962, most observers agreed that they were mainly a sham intended to provide the regime with a veneer of legitimacy (especially in the view of neighbors like Thailand, which might be induced to ease some economic sanctions as a result). The personnel changes were likely to be minimal because many of the same senior military officials previously in charge were set to head key ministries, such as Interior, Defense, and Border Affairs, wearing civilian clothes rather than uniforms. The international community was not impressed by the show. "You look at Burma holding flawed elections today that once again expose the abuses of the military junta," said U.S. secretary of state Hillary Clinton. "It's heartbreaking because the people of Burma deserve so much better." About a week after the disputed election, the government freed Daw Aung San Suu Kyi. On November 13th she emerged from her home to a tumultuous welcome from supporters. Her lawyer insisted that she would not accept any restrictions on her freedom and would "resume active politics and make organizing tours around the country." That might set up conditions for yet another confrontation with the military-backed regime, even as it assumes a civilian guise.

See also CHILDREN'S RIGHTS.

Further Reading:

Amnesty International USA. Myanmar (Burma) Human Rights. Available online. URL: http://www.amnesty-usa.org/all-countries/myanmar-burma/page.do?id=1011205. Accessed March 20, 2010.

Clements, Alan. *The Voice of Hope.* New York: Seven Stories Press, 2008.

Derechos. Human Rights in Burma. Available online. URL: http://www.derechos.org/human-rights/seasia/burma.html. Accessed March 20, 2010.

Diller, Janelle M. *The National Convention in Burma (Myanmar): An Impediment to the Restoration of Democracy: a Report.* New York: International League for Human Rights, 1996.

Ross, James D. *Human Rights in Burma (Myanmar) since the May 1990 National Election.* New York: Lawyers Committee for Human Rights, 1991.

Suu Kyi, Aung San. *Letters from Burma.* New York: Penguin, 1998.

My Lai massacre

On March 16, 1968, the South Vietnamese village of My Lai became the site of the most infamous atrocity committed by U.S. forces in the Vietnam War. News of the massacre of civilians shocked the American public and led to intense questioning about the wisdom of the war. The village was located in the heavily infiltrated Vietcong (VC) district of Son My. A number of U.S. troops with Charlie Company conducting operations in the area had been wounded or killed in previous weeks by VC communist insurgents. Under the command of Lieutenant William Calley, members of Charlie Company were ordered to conduct a "search and destroy" mission. Although there was no evidence of the village having harbored Vietcong, the soldiers entered the village firing without encountering opposing fire. In the ensuing massacre, as many as 500 unarmed villagers were killed. Eyewitnesses gave accounts of elderly men being bayoneted and praying women and children being shot in the back of the head. Calley reportedly rounded up several villagers personally, ordered them into a ditch, and then proceeded to slaughter them with machine-gun fire.

Initially the incident was portrayed by the Pentagon as a battle and the killings attributed to combat casualties. A secret military investigation was instituted, and consequently Calley was charged with murder in September 1969. An unemployed college dropout in civilian life, Calley claimed at his trial that he had been ordered by his superior, Captain Ernest Medina, to kill the village population, but his defense failed. The evidence gathered against him was too compelling, and he was found guilty and sentenced to life. (He was released in 1974 and, after being dishonorably discharged from the army, found work in the insurance business.) No one else in Charlie Company was ever tried for participating in the massacre.

In spite of the military proceedings, the official cover-up continued, and the massacre did not become public knowledge until November 1969, when journalist Seymour Hersh published a story about the incident based on conversations with a Vietnam veteran named Ron Ridenhour, who had heard of the massacre from members of Charlie Company. A military commission was established to conduct a sweeping investigation of conditions among the armed forces serving in Vietnam; it found endemic failures in leadership, discipline, and morale, especially among draftees. The uproar over the massacres also had the effect of pushing the administration of President Richard M. Nixon into accelerating its efforts to withdraw U.S. troops from the region, which were finally completed in 1973.

See also TAYLOR, TELFORD; TIGER FORCE; VIETNAM, HUMAN RIGHTS VIOLATIONS IN.

Further Reading:

Bilton, Michael, and Kevin Sim. *Four Hours in My Lai.* New York: Penguin Books, 1993.

Hersh, Seymour. *My Lai 4: A Report on the Massacre and Its Aftermath.* New York: Random House Trade, 1970.

Olson, James S., and Randy Roberts, eds. *My Lai: A Brief History with Documents.* "The Bedford Series in History and Culture." Sydney, Australia: Palgrave Macmillan, 1998.

Taylor, Telford. *Nuremberg and Vietnam: An American Tragedy.* New York: Times Books, 1970.

Vietnam Veterans against the War. *The Winter Soldier Investigation: An Inquiry into American War Crimes.* Boston: Beacon Press, 1972.

N

Nagano, Osami   *See* WAR CRIMINALS OF JAPAN.

Nanjing (Nanking), massacre in

In November 1937, Nanjing (previously known as Nanking), the provisional capital of the Republic of China, came under siege by the Japanese Imperial Army. When the city fell in early December, the Japanese carried out a massacre that became known to history as the Rape of Nanking. It was the worst single massacre of unarmed civilians by soldiers in the 20th century.

After launching their assault in July 1937, the Japanese had successively driven Chinese forces under President Chiang Kai-shek (Jiang Jieshi) from Beijing, Tianjin, and Shanghai. The Chinese retreated to Nanjing, where they held out for several weeks. When they initially rejected demands for surrender, the Japanese commander MATSUI Iwane was given orders not to take any prisoners alive. Before Nanjing fell, about half a million inhabitants—half the population—managed to escape. When the city finally capitulated on December 13, the Japanese troops laid it to waste and went on a rampage that continued for the next seven weeks. By the time the massacre was over, anywhere between 100,000 and 350,000 people—civilians and Chinese soldiers who had surrendered—had been killed; in addition, some 20,000 women and girls were raped, the second-largest mass rape recorded. Many were later killed, and still other women were forced to become sex slaves. Japanese soldiers engaged in killing contests to see who could kill the fastest. Victims were slaughtered in a variety of ways. Some were buried alive or nailed to wooden boards and then run over by tanks; others were crucified on trees or electric posts, flayed, and used for bayonet practice. There were reports of men having their eyes gouged out and noses and ears hacked off before being set ablaze and babies being bayoneted and flung into vats of boiling water. The rate of killings per day was in excess of 8,000.

In 1946, even as the International Military Tribunal for the Far East was conducting trials of war criminals in Japan, better known as the TOKYO TRIALS, China held a war-crimes trial of its own under the supervision of the United States. More than 1,000 eyewitnesses came forward to testify about the atrocities in Nanjing. Bringing to justice the many potential defendants was almost impossible given the lack of investigators and the chaotic conditions prevailing in postwar China. Nonetheless, 148 Japanese officers and soldiers—including the general in charge of Nanjing—received death sentences, and another 83 were sentenced to time in prison. In contrast to Germany, Japan has been slow to acknowledge its culpability for war crimes like the Nanjing massacres, a source of continual friction between China and Japan over half a century later.

See also RAPE AS A TACTIC OF WAR.

Further Reading:
Chang, Iris. *The Rape of Nanking: The Forgotten Holocaust of World War II.* New York: Penguin, 1998.
Honda, Katsuichi, and Frank Gibney, eds. *The Nanjing Massacre: A Japanese Journalist Confronts Japan's National Shame.* Studies of the Pacific Basin Institute. Armonk, N.Y.: East Gate Books, 1999.

National Intelligence Directorate (DINA)

DINA is the acronym for *Departamento de Inteligencia Nacional* (Department of National Intelligence, or National Intelligence Directorate), the Chilean secret police agency under the military dictatorship of General AUGUSTO PINOCHET. Officially established in a decree in 1973, two years after Pinochet seized power in a coup, DINA became a "state within a state"; all other intelligence agencies were subordinated to it.

DINA had two principal objectives: instilling terror in the population to ensure political security and gaining intelligence about enemies of the regime. In early 1974 its agents carried out the arrests of up to 250 people a week, most of whom had not been formally charged. The arrests were conducted secretly by men who arrived at the homes of the accused after curfew, wearing civilian clothes and refusing to identify themselves. They would blindfold the victims and take them away in unmarked pickup trucks. DINA agents were given unlimited power to arrest suspects without charges and to raid and search houses without warrants.

All authority in DINA was concentrated in its head, General MANUEL CONTRERAS, who answered only to Pinochet himself. The core of the network was the General Command, a cadre of 30–40 men who were personally loyal to Contreras. The elite units of DINA were known as the Brigades of Arrests and Interrogation. These operated in squads of five or six persons under the command of a captain or major and used the names of Chile's traditional Indian tribes, such as Antumapu, Pehuenche, and Peldehue. Special safe houses were set up where interrogations could take place. Those detainees regarded as "incapable of rehabilitation" were tortured, sometimes for months, before being executed. The authorities, meanwhile, continued to deny any knowledge of the victims' whereabouts to desperate family members and friends. DINA issued no warrants and maintained no official arrest records; no bodies were ever taken to a morgue nor were death certificates filed.

DINA's largest and most secret divisions were known as the Government Service and Internal sections, which were given the responsibility for identifying and suppressing dissent within the government and in the civilian population as a whole. Operating out of a large complex of offices in downtown Santiago, DINA ran a vast network of spies and as many as 20,000–30,000 informants called *soplones,* or whisperers. With so many informants, people were naturally fearful of saying anything that could be considered seditious. In the early years of the Pinochet regime, DINA concentrated on leftists who had gone underground and taken up arms. Later, however, Contreras moved against socialists, communists, and other leftist supporters of former socialist president Salvador Allende. In 1975 he extended his dragnet to include members of the opposition Christian Democrats and even suspected opponents in the Catholic Church. Contreras retired from DINA in 1978, and the organization was disbanded after Pinochet gave up power in 1990.

See also CHILE, HUMAN RIGHTS VIOLATIONS IN.

Further Reading:
Constable, Pamela. *A Nation of Enemies: Chile under Pinochet.* New York: W. W. Norton & Company, 1993.
Dinges, John. *The Condor Years: How Pinochet and His Allies Brought Terrorism to Three Continents.* New York: New Press, 2004.
Dorfman, Ariel. *Exorcising Terror: The Incredible Unending Trial of Augusto Pinochet.* New York: Seven Stories Press, 2002.
Kornbluh, Peter. *The Pinochet File: A Declassified Dossier on Atrocity and Accountability.* A National Security Archive Book. New York: New Press, 2003.
Politzer, Patricia, and Diane Wachtel. *Fear in Chile: Lives under Pinochet.* New York: New Press, 2001.

Nazar Haro, Miguel (1927–) *Mexican police chief*
In February 2004 justice finally caught up with Miguel Nazar Haro, the former head of the Mexican secret police. At the age of 79, Nazar Haro was probably under the impression that he could live out his retirement in peace since no official of his prominence had ever been prosecuted for human rights abuses committed in the so-called dirty war between government security forces and suspected leftist sympathizers. At the height of the dirty war, during the late 1970s and early 1980s, Nazar Haro had headed the Federal Security Directorate, which served as both an intelligence agency and a secret police force. (The directorate was shut down in 1985.) In this position, Nazar Haro was able to cultivate important friends, including the CIA, to which he supplied information about leftists throughout Latin America. His work as a liaison for the U.S. Intelligence agency was considered so critical that even after he left his post, the CIA reportedly blocked his indictment in 1982 by a San Diego grand jury on charges of running an auto-theft ring. (He was alleged to have stolen hundreds of cars in California and resold them in Mexico.)

In 2004 Nazar Haro was charged in connection with the disappearance of Jesús Piedra Ibarra, the leader of a small guerrilla group called the 23rd of September League. Ibarra had been arrested in 1975, beaten, tortured, transported to a military camp in Mexico City, and held in secret for years. He was last seen alive in 1984; his body has never been found. For years the absence of a body made it difficult to bring charges against officials accused of having arranged the disappearance of the victim. But that changed in November 2003 when the Mexican Supreme Court ruled that an individual could be indicted for a disappearance even if no body was found, declaring that such a crime was not covered by any statute of limitations. Nazar Haro's arrest on a Mexico City freeway was the first case in which the high court's ruling was put into effect. The arrest was also seen as a triumph for the special federal prosecutor appointed by President Vincente Fox to investigate past human rights crimes attributed to security forces and the military during the dirty war and afterwards. Luis de la Barreda Moreno, Nazar Haro's predecessor as secret police chief, faces similar charges and remains a fugitive. Celebration of Nazar Haro's capture was premature. In May 2006 the prosecution of Nazar Haro and other former security officials accused of the enforced disappearance of Piedra Ibarra was halted. In September of that year a judge ordered the end of Nazar Haro's house arrest when the other case against him for human rights violations committed during the 1970s collapsed.

See also MEXICO, HUMAN RIGHTS VIOLATIONS IN.

Nazi Party, Leadership Corps of

The Leadership Corps was the governing elite of the Nazi Party (National Socialist Party; NSDAP) with ADOLF HITLER as its head. Membership at all levels was voluntary. According to Nazi doctrine, the Leadership Corps was "responsible for the complete penetration of the German Nation with the National Socialist spirit." The corps was placed in control of the German state, as Hitler bluntly made clear when he addressed a Nazi Party Congress in 1935: "It is not the State which gives orders to us, it is we who give orders to the State." In effect, the Nazi Party was seen as embodying the will of the German people. Thus, the NSDAP was not a party that simply occupied power and filled government positions with its members. Far from being under the rule of law, carrying out "single tasks of public administration," the NSDAP was supposed to be the "bearer of the German state-idea" in all areas of life. Under this doctrine, the distinction between party and state was virtually abolished, and the Nazi Party was also given the right to destroy all opponents.

In 1945 the Leadership Corps was indicted as a criminal organization by the International Military Tribunal conducted by the Allies at the NUREMBERG TRIALS. The indictment stated: "All the defendants, with divers other persons, during a period years preceding 8 May, 1945, participated as leaders, organizers, instigators or accomplices in the formulation or execution of a common plan or conspiracy to commit, or which involved the commission of, Crimes against Peace, War crimes, and CRIMES AGAINST HUMANITY, as defined in the Charter of this Tribunal, and, in accordance with the provisions of the charter, are individually responsible for their own acts and for all acts committed by any persons in the execution of such [a] plan or conspiracy."

The verdicts of the trial were announced on September 30 and on October 1, 1946; 12 defendants were sentenced to death by hanging, seven were sentenced to life imprisonment or to lesser terms, and three were acquitted. The last defendant convicted, RUDOLF HESS, committed suicide in prison in August 1987.

Further Reading:

Buscher, Frank. M. The U.S. War Crimes Trial Program in Germany, 1946–1955. Contributions in Military Studies. Westport, Conn.: Greenwood Press, 1989.

Nesbit, Roy Conyers. The Flight of Rudolf Hess: Myths and Reality. New York: Sutton Publishing, 2003.

Padfield, Peter. Hess: The Fuhrer's Disciple. London: Cassell, 2001.

Russell of Liverpool, Edward Frederick Langley Russell, Baron. The Scourge of the Swastika: A Short History of Nazi War Crimes. London: Greenhill Books/Lionel Leventhal, 2002.

Weindling, Paul Julian. Nazi Medicine and the Nuremberg Trials: From Medical War Crimes to Informed Consent. Sydney, Australia: Palgrave Macmillan, 2005.

Nazi war crimes

See CIA WAR CRIMES ARCHIVE; FINAL SOLUTION; NUREMBERG TRIALS; WANNSEE CONFERENCE.

Nepal, human rights violations in

Since 1996 civil war has created a grave human rights crisis in the tiny Himalayan nation of Nepal. Up to 10,000 Nepalese, mostly civilians, have perished during the conflict. The war was sparked by a rebellion by Maoist insurgents that began in the remote countryside but now reaches into the capital of Katmandu. The rebels, who assert that they are fighting a "People's War," have gained sufficient strength to blockade Katmandu for days at a time, threatening the city's fuel and food supplies. Civilians are caught between the Maoists and security forces. They must choose between cooperating with the military or with the rebels, risking reprisals from one side or the other. According to human rights organizations, civilians are regularly executed, abducted, and tortured by both parties to the conflict. The government has announced a policy to "break the backbone" of the rebellion, which has led to EXTRAJUDICIAL KILLINGS and DISAPPEARANCES. The Maoists are, if anything, more culpable; villagers deemed supporters of the regime are classified as "class enemies" and put to death.

Although the Royal Nepal Army has expanded its ranks—by 2004 it was able to muster 72,000 men—it still has proven incapable of defeating the insurgents even though it is believed to have no more than 4,000 core members and some 15,000 militia supporters. The insurgents have also pressed children—about 8,000 in 2004 alone—into service. The army has largely been confined to the capital. Approximately two-thirds of the country has been abandoned by the police, allowing the Maoists to move freely and exert power over a large segment of the population. The fear of being swallowed up in the conflict has driven thousands of Nepalese to take refuge in India.

Vulnerable villagers are also subjected to intimidation and extortion. The insurgents are in the habit of imposing a "tax" on civilians. They have also recruited children as messengers or porters or as spies, clear violations of international conventions against the conscription of children in armed conflicts. Soldiers, too, have also been known to use extortion and blackmail or isolate whole villages in an effort to deny food and shelter to the rebels. "Rampant abuses have created a climate of intense fear in Nepal's villages," said a HUMAN RIGHTS WATCH representative. "Because of Nepal's geography and poverty, Nepalis under attack or threat usually have nowhere to turn to for protection or redress."

Human rights organizations as well as lawyers and journalists have come under fire from the government, which tends to brand them as Maoist sympathizers. There is little indication that the government intends to honor its public commitments to human rights. By the same token, Maoists have executed local activists whom they view as adversaries. When challenged by human rights organizations, the insurgents contend that their victims had stood in the way of liberating the country from oppressive rule. Both sides, however, maintain that they support the creation of a Human Rights Accord, which would pave the way for the deployment of impartial monitors to prevent future abuses.

The insurgency was fueled by the country's endemic and widespread poverty. According to the World Bank, 42 percent of the Nepalese live below the poverty line. The nation is also 85 percent rural. The country is run more like a feudal fiefdom than the parliamentary democracy the government claims it to be. In many respects, because of its misguided policies, the government is to blame for the insurgency's success. Most notably, Katmandu failed to institute land reform legislation once representative government was restored in 1990. Peasants began to protest against the excessive rents they were forced to pay to use the land. In response, the government sent military forces into the countryside—Operation Romeo and Operation Kilo Sera II—but far from suppressing peasant agitation, they only succeeded in winning recruits for the Communist Party of Nepal (Maoist), or CPNM. By abolishing the elected parliament, King Gyanendra marginalized other political factions. Students have grown increasingly vocal in protesting the monarchy and the government's policies. In April 2004 more than 1,000 people demonstrated for restoration of democracy. Police plunged into the crowd, injuring 150 protesters with truncheons, rubber bullets, and tear gas. As many as 25,000 protesters turned out subsequently in defiance of a ban on demonstrations. Nonetheless, the government postponed elections, and efforts at reconciliation have all but collapsed.

Deteriorating conditions in Nepal have caused increasing alarm in foreign capitals. The Bush administration warned that the country was in danger of becoming a "failed state" and placed the CPNM on the State Depart-

ment's Watch List, labeling it a terrorist organization. The United States, India, Britain, and other countries have provided military aid to the government to support the counterinsurgency. In addition, the United States has sent in military advisers. Human rights organizations have charged that the addition of 8,400 American M-16 submachine guns, Belgian FAL submachine guns, high-tech night-fighting equipment, and British helicopters has only succeeded in intensifying the conflict. According to the Nepal human rights group, Informal Sector Service Centre, 800 of the 1,100 deaths since the end of a seven-month ceasefire in August 2003 were inflicted by government forces. AMNESTY INTERNATIONAL issued a statement at the end of 2004, saying that the killings are occurring in "the context of a severe human rights crisis and a breakdown in the rule of law." According to statistics compiled by the group, the number of killings by both security forces and Maoist rebels increased significantly in 2004.

The Maoist insurgency and lack of democracy are not the only human rights crises facing Nepal. Ethnic tensions have also bedeviled the country. The Dalit ethnic group in particular has suffered grievous human rights abuses. These abuses stem from a caste-based system that has encouraged discrimination against the Dalits, who number 4.5 million, or 21 percent, of Nepal's population. While the Dalits have suffered from persecution for centuries, the Maoist insurgency has put them at further risk. Security forces tend to view them as supporters of the insurgents, and violence against the Dalits is seldom investigated by the police.

In January 2005, in what amounted to a coup, King Gyanendra suspended the government, imposed a state of emergency, and clamped down on civil liberties, including the right of assembly and freedom of speech. He also cut off communication with the outside world by phone or Internet and placed political opposition leaders under arrest. He declared that his decision was necessary because the politicians had failed to resolve the country's political crisis and said that instead he would govern for three years. Only in this way, he said, could the army effectively deal with the Maoist insurgency. Leaders of several governments, especially Nepal's neighbor India, denounced the king's move. Human rights groups warned that the coup represented a step backward after a 15-year experiment with democracy, and also pointed out that if the army—now 86,000 strong—was needed in the fight against the Maoists, then they should be put to better use than patrolling TV and newspaper offices to ensure that the media said nothing critical about the king. By September 2005 the king had lifted emergency rule but parliament remained suspended. Mounting pressure forced an end to direct rule by King Gyanendra in April 2006, at which time the Maoists entered talks with the newly restored parliamentary government concerning how the war could be brought to an end. Those talks concluded with an accord in November, although the rebels pressed for abolition of the monarchy. The Constituent Assembly—Nepal's parliament—agreed to this demand in December 2007. After elections the following April, the Maoists had the largest parliamentary majority. In May the monarchy was ended after 239 years, and Prachanda, who headed the Maoists, became prime minister.

The peace agreement, brokered and monitored by the United Nations, also called for 19,000 former Maoist insurgents to remain confined to their barracks. It was that provision that was at the root cause of a crisis that erupted a year later. Prachanda insisted on the integration of his former fighters into the army, a position that the army chief opposed. The prime minister then tried to fire the army chief, only to be thwarted by the president, Rookmangud Katawal. The rift caused the dissolution of the ruling coalition as the Communist Party (UML) pulled out while accusing the Maoists of acting unilaterally. Prachanda then quit. By the end of 2009 the tenuous peace agreement seemed in danger of becoming unraveled as thousands of Maoist protesters took to the streets and went on a general nationwide strike. Police used batons and tear gas to break up protesters, arresting 70.

A year later the country's major political parties still had not been able to resolve the crisis. Maoists called a general strike in May 2010, which ended after six days without their demands being met. In November Nepal's parliament voted and failed for the 15th time to elect a prime minister. Nor was there any sign that the process of integrating and rehabilitating 19,000 Maoist combatants would begin in the foreseeable future.

Further Reading:

Amnesty International. Nepal Human Rights. Available online. URL: http://www.amnestyusa.org/all-countries/nepal/page.do?id=1011207. Accessed March 20, 2010.

Gregson, Jonathan. *Massacre at the Palace: The Doomed Royal Dynasty of Nepal.* New York: Miramax Books, 2002.

Hutt, Michael, ed. *Himalayan People's War: Nepal's Maoist Rebellion.* Bloomington: Indiana University Press, 2004.

NepalHumanRightsNews.com. Available online. URL: http://nepalhumanrightsnews.com/. Accessed March 20, 2010.

NHRCNepal.org. National Human Rights Commission, Nepal. Available online. URL: http://www.nhrcnepal.org/. Accessed March 20, 2010.

Onesto, Li. *Dispatches from the People's War in Nepal.* Ann Arbor, Mich.: Pluto Press, 2005.

Neurath, Konstantin von (1873–1956) *German diplomat*

The German diplomat Konstantin von Neurath was already in the German government when ADOLF HITLER came to power in 1933. However, Hitler initially kept him on because he was such a staunch advocate of Nazi foreign policy. His participation in the Nazi regime led to his being convicted for crimes against peace at the NUREMBERG TRIALS after World War II.

Born in Württemberg, Germany, in 1873, the son of a minor aristocrat, Neurath went on to study law in Tübingen and Berlin. In 1901, after briefly practicing law, he joined the civil service and worked for the Foreign Office, representing Germany in London and Constantinople. He enlisted in the army as an infantry officer in World War I; badly wounded in 1914, he was awarded the Iron Cross. On recovering, he returned to the diplomatic service. He was assigned to the embassy in Rome in 1921 and remained there for a decade during Benito Mussolini's ascent to power as head of a fascist government. (Neurath was not very impressed with the Italian brand of fascism.) In 1932, after a brief posting in London, he was recalled to Germany to become minister of foreign affairs under FRANZ VON PAPEN. In 1938, five years after Hitler had come to power, Neurath was dismissed in favor of JOACHIM VON RIBBENTROP. However, after Germany seized Czechoslovakia, he was appointed reich protector of Bohemia and Moravia in 1939. In that capacity he was responsible for dissolving the Czech parliament and its political parties as well as suppressing freedom of the press and imposing the racist NUREMBERG LAWS. He did not remain long in that position, because the Nazi regime felt that he had treated the Czechs too leniently, and he was replaced by the far more reliably brutal REINHARD HEYDRICH in 1941. Neurath concluded his career in the Nazi regime as a general in the SS.

Tried before the International Military Tribunal of War Criminals in Nuremberg, Neurath was found guilty of conspiracy, crimes against peace, war crimes, and CRIMES AGAINST HUMANITY. The charges were based on his having served the Third Reich as foreign minister and reich protector of Bohemia and Moravia in addition to other positions. The court ruled that he had committed crimes against peace by carrying out a foreign policy intended to break international treaties and having willingly acceded to Hitler's war plans. In his position as reich protector, the tribunal declared, he must have known "that war crimes and crimes against humanity were being committed under his authority." In 1946 he was sentenced to 15 years in prison, but he was released for reasons of ill health in 1954. He died two years later at the age of 83.

Further Reading:

Gilbert, G. M. *Nuremberg Diary.* New York: Da Capo Press, 1995.

Goldensohn, Leon, and Robert Gellately, eds. *The Nuremberg Interviews*. New York: Knopf, 2004.

Marrus, Robert, and Michael R. Marrus. *The Nuremberg War Crimes Trial of 1945–46: A Documentary History*. Bedford Series in History and Culture. Sidney, Australia: Palgrave Macmillan, 1997.

Maser, Werner. *Nuremberg: A Nation on Trial*. New York: Scribner, 1979.

Persico, Joseph. *Nuremberg: Infamy on Trial*. New York: Penguin Books, 1995.

Rice, Earle. *The Nuremberg Trials*. Famous Trials Series. San Diego, Calif.: Lucent Books, 1997.

Taylor, Telford. *The Anatomy of the Nuremberg Trials: A Personal Memoir*. New York: Little, Brown & Co, 1993.

Ngugi wa Thiong'o (1938–) *Kenyan human rights advocate and writer*

Ngugi wa Thiong'o is Kenya's best-known novelist and a leading human rights advocate who spent 22 years in exile for espousing his political views. Although he was a supporter of an indigenous insurgency against British rule in the 1940s, he subsequently attacked the country's postcolonial leaders for perpetrating a culture of inequality and injustice. In 1977 he wrote two works critical of the government: a novel entitled *Petals of Blood* and a play called *I Will Marry When I Want*. President Jomo Kenyatta was so infuriated that he not only jailed Ngugi but also ordered the destruction of the theater where the play had been performed. Even in prison, Ngugi refused to stop his attacks on an increasingly repressive regime, using toilet paper to write a play, *Devil on the Cross*, and a memoir, *Detained: A Writer's Prison Diary*. The government refused to allow him to return to his position teaching at the University of Nairobi upon his release.

On a visit to London in 1982, Ngugi learned that an order for his arrest had been issued by Kenyatta's successor, President Daniel arap Moi, and he decided to remain abroad. Although in exile, he continued to write and make his influence felt in his homeland. In a novel called *Matigari*, he depicted a character who roamed the countryside seeking justice. The government was so convinced that such a man actually existed that it ordered an arrest warrant for the character. In 2004 Ngugi returned home after a new government replaced Moi's regime in democratic elections. However, no sooner had he received a tumultuous welcome than he and his wife were assaulted by intruders while they slept in their hotel room. Ngugi was repeatedly burned with a lit cigarette, and his wife was raped. Although the incident was blamed on criminals, there were rumors that the attack—perpetrated on the very night of his homecoming—was not a coincidence but was actually an attack by political opponents.

In 2006 Ngugi published a critically acclaimed novel, *Wizard of the Crow*. He continues to teach and edit literary journals and frequently gives talks at universities around the world.

See also KENYA, HUMAN RIGHTS VIOLATIONS IN.

Nicaragua, human rights violations in   *See* SOMOZA DEBAYLE, ANASTASIO; SOMOZA GARCÍA, ANASTASIO.

Nigeria, human rights violations in

Since the death in 1999 of the country's strongman, Sani Abacha, Nigeria has begun to enjoy some of the benefits of freedom. Nonetheless, serious human problems remain, and ethnic and religious tensions hamper progress in many regions. Even though Nigeria's democratic leader, President Olusegun Obasanjo, has vowed to fight abuses and corruption, there are still reports of EXTRAJUDICIAL KILLINGS, deaths in custody, TORTURE, and cruel and inhuman or degrading treatment in police detention centers throughout the country. Many of these violations occurred in the course of anticrime operations. The lawless climate is aggravated by the proliferation of armed vigilante groups, especially in the south and southeast; these groups are blamed for torture, inhumane treatment, and DISAPPEARANCES of suspected criminals. In some cases the vigilante groups appear to be operating with the backing of state governments that have effectively "outsourced" law enforcement. In its 2003 annual report, for instance, AMNESTY INTERNATIONAL (AI) noted the extrajudicial killings of dozens of people in Anambra State by a vigilante group officially endorsed by a law passed in 2000 by the Anambra State House of Assembly. Police found that the vigilantes had set up five secret detention centers; at least 100 members of the group were arrested but released without charges.

According to AI, state-sanctioned vigilante groups in two other states were also responsible for extrajudicial executions, torture, and unlawful detention. Moreover, reports cited by AI indicate that politically motivated killings and "acts of harassment and intimidation" that have taken place throughout the country may be linked to officials in state and local governments as well as to political parties. At the same time the authorities have shown no willingness to bring to justice perpetrators of human rights violations. These violations include two incidents in which large groups of civilians were killed by the army in recent years—over 250 unarmed civilians in the town of Odi, Bayelsa State, in 1999 and more than 200 civilians in Benue State in 2001. The 10-member Judicial Commission of Inquiry has since been created by the federal government to investigate the causes of intercommunal violence in Benue and three other states, but its mandate did not include a probe of the massacre.

In a July 2005 report on police abuses, HUMAN RIGHTS WATCH said that the number of people the police claimed as "killed in combat" had grown from 834 to 3,100 between 2000 and 2003. Many suspects taken into police custody were beaten, subjected to electric shocks, and raped, according to witnesses interviewed for the report. During the same period, however, the police force has more than doubled because of the rising threat of crime. But police receive poor training and often lack the technical facilities or tools to perform fingerprinting, for example, or conduct autopsies. The situation has gotten so dire that the United Nations appointed an official to investigate allegations of unlawful killings. There are some signs, however, that the government is finally taking action to curb the abuses. In the fall of 2005 the government convened an unprecedented commission of inquiry in response to the slayings of six people in the capital of Abuja. The police initially claimed that the six were robbers and tried to bury the bodies before they could be identified. It turned out that they were young people celebrating an engagement, and, in the course of a roadside dispute, the police had executed them. They then proceeded to plant guns and knives in the victims' bullet-riddled car and positioned the corpses around the vehicle to take photographs to support their case. Five of the seven officers involved have been charged; one vanished under mysterious circumstances and the other decided to cooperate with the commission. Nigerians hope that the investigation will become a precedent and not an aberration.

Ethnic and religious tensions have grown in the north of the country where twelve states with large Muslim populations have adopted strict Islamic law (sharia). These courts have handed down sentences of death and corporal punishments that include amputations of hands (for thievery and armed robbery) and flogging (for fornication, drinking alcohol, and other offenses). Premarital consensual sexual relations, for instance, is a crime punishable by 100 lashes. No case tried by these Islamic courts has stirred more international opprobrium than that of Amina Lawal, who was convicted of adultery and sentenced to death by stoning. (The man involved was not charged.) The judges were not swayed by the fact that as a result of her "crime" she had become the mother of a baby girl. When she appealed her conviction, however, she received significant support from a team of pro bono attorneys and international human rights organizations. Her acquittal in 2003 was greeted with widespread relief, but there is little evidence to indicate that the satisfactory resolution of her case has tempered verdicts in other Islamic court proceedings.

In recent years Nigeria has been wracked by ethnic and religious clashes that have left hundreds dead and thousands displaced. But religious and ethnic differences tell only part of the story and may actually camouflage the true source of the disputes, which often involve a fight over resources. In the central highlands, for example, the farmers are mostly Christian and herders are mostly Muslim. Tensions have been building for years between those who consider themselves indigenous to the area—mainly Christian tribes—and those whom they consider interlopers—namely, the herders, ethnic Fulani, and Hausa. In September 2001 what began as a political dispute in the Yelwa state capital of Jos degenerated into violence. The ensuing riots took the lives of a 1,000 Christians and Muslims in four days. The rift between the two communities, which had once lived in relative peace, was irreparable: Intermarriage was banned, and even the city's market was divided along religious and ethnic lines. The riots in Jos ignited violence in nearby villages, causing families to flee their homes and turning what was once Nigeria's breadbasket into a wasteland. Yelwa witnessed more pogroms over the next few months. In February 2002 Muslims burned Christians to death inside a Yelwa church; in May, Christian militias killed several Muslims, setting off a wave of revenge killings and leading to the declaration of a state of emergency by the national government.

The election of President Umaru Musa Yar'Adua in a disputed election in April 2007 did little to improve the human rights situation in the country. In a 2009 report released by the U.S. State Department, the Yar'Adua administration was taken to task for perpetuating the practice of extrajudicial killings, torture, ill-treatment, arbitrary arrests, extortion, and other violations of law. All legal institutions—the police, the judicial system and elected officials—were held responsible for a human rights record the report characterized as "poor and deplorable." Elections, including the one that brought Yar'Adua to power, have been tarnished by fraud, political violence, and vote rigging. Although the report conceded that no political killings were carried out under the new administration, security forces were charged with using excessive force in pursuit of criminals or to disperse protesters. The UN Special Rapporteur on Torture accused Nigerian police of routinely torturing suspects during investigations and deplored the crowded and unsanitary prison conditions common throughout Nigeria. AI reported that in some cases police secretly executed suspects. Although the government has promised reforms, a culture of impunity persists, and there are few instances of police being held accountable for extrajudicial killings or for the use of deadly force against suspects in custody. In one case, in February 2009, in the town of Ogaminana, "police killed approximately 50 persons, burnt nearly 100 homes, and destroyed more than 150 market stalls." In another case, when ethnic fighting between Muslim and Christian gangs in the central Nigerian city of Jos broke out in November 2008, security forces were implicated in the deaths of at least 90 of the 400 people killed in the violence. While the gangs were responsible for burning churches and mosques and destroying homes and businesses, Human Rights Watch documented the killings of 46 men and boys, mostly Muslim, who were slain by police acting under shoot-to-kill orders given by the state governor. Witnesses reported police hunting down victims and shooting them at close range. The government has also come under fire for the forcible eviction of more than 2 million people from their homes in different parts of Nigeria in the decade since 2000. Those uprooted receive inadequate or no compensation and are often subject to beating and other forms of abuse. In 2006 the Geneva-based Centre on Housing Rights and Evictions named Nigeria one of the three worst violators of housing rights.

In an attempt to end strife in the Niger Delta region the government introduced an amnesty for insurgents on the condition that they lay down their arms. The amnesty was a turnabout for the government, coming only a short time after a military offensive in May 2009 that took the lives of hundreds. The Delta is one of the most impoverished areas of the country, in spite of the fact that it provides much of Nigeria's oil output. However, the population of the region has never shared more than a small fraction of the revenue from the oil. Unrest sparked by political and economic demands ultimately created a climate of violence and fear. Pipelines have been sabotaged, oil workers have been kidnapped, and drilling operations shut down. It has become harder to distinguish between insurgents and criminal gangs. Civilians have been caught up in clashes between the military, insurgents, vigilantes, and thugs. The government of President Yar'Adua promised insurgents cash and jobs for putting down their weapons and offered to invest in the region's infrastructure by building schools and hospitals and repairing roads, but several months later many of these promises were unmet, and those insurgents who took advantage of the amnesty began to complain. In some cases they have rioted and gone on rampages, terrifying civilians and looting stores. Some residents of Port Harcourt, the Delta's major city, believe that they were actually safer before the amnesty. By early 2010 there were indications that the peace accord was breaking down when the Movement for the Emancipation of the Niger Delta, the largest rebel group, issued a statement calling off the cease-fire, charging that the government had acted "like a victor over a conquered people" and promising more attacks against foreign-owned pipelines. Meanwhile, more ethnic violence between Muslims and Christians erupted around the central Nigerian city of Jos, with considerable loss of life. The winter of 2010 saw two bloody tit-for-tat massacres in which at least 200 Muslims were killed in January and as many as 500 Christians were slain in March. Approximately 2,000 people in the region have lost their lives in these spasms of violence since the beginning of the decade. The government was also hobbled by the absence of President Yar'Adua, who had sought medical treatment in Saudi Arabia. As months went by without any indication of what was wrong with him or how long he would be gone, Yar'Adua's vice president, Goodluck Jonathan, was temporarily appointed to serve in his place. Yar'Adua returned to Nigeria in February 2010 but died three months later. Goodluck Ebele Jonathan was sworn in as president on May 6, 2010.

See also BIAFRA, WAR CRIMES IN; SOYINKA, WOLE.

Further Reading:
Achebe, Chinua. *The Trouble with Nigeria*. London: Heinemann, 1984.
Amnesty International USA. Nigeria Human Rights. Available online. URL: http://www.amnestyusa.org/all-countries/nigeria/page.do?id=1011212. Accessed March 20, 2010.
Derechos.org. Human Rights in Nigeria. Available online. URL: http://www.derechos.org/human-rights/afr/nigeria/. Accessed March 20, 2010.
Kashi, Ed. *Curse of the Black Gold: 50 Years of Oil in the Niger Delta*. Brooklyn: powerHouse Books, 2008.
Maier, Karl. *This House Has Fallen: Nigeria in Crisis*. Philadelphia: Westview Press, 2003.
National Human Rights Commission of Nigeria. Available online. URL: http://www.nigeriarights.gov.ng/. Accessed March 20, 2010.
Okonta, Ike. *Where Vultures Feast: Shell, Human Rights and Oil*. New York: Verso, 2003.
Osaghae, Eghosa E. *Crippled Giant: Nigeria since Independence*. Bloomington: Indiana University Press, 1998.

Nikolić, Ivan   *See* WAR CRIMINALS OF THE FORMER YUGOSLAVIA.

Niyazov, Separmurat   *See* TURKMENISTAN, HUMAN RIGHTS VIOLATIONS IN.

No Gun Ri (Korea), massacre in
Until 2001, the 1950 massacre of civilian REFUGEES in No Gun Ri during the Korean War was unknown to the American public. An investigation initiated by the Associated Press (AP) news agency in that year found that U.S. soldiers had opened fire on the refugees at a railway bridge on

July 26, 1950. According to the AP investigation, which was confirmed by 12 former soldiers who had witnessed the event, American troops machine-gunned as many as 300 civilians. They had taken shelter under the bridge in an attempt to escape strafing by U.S. warplanes that had already killed about 100 people. This was at a time when American troops were retreating in the face of a North Korean onslaught. U.S. commanders feared that North Korean soldiers were infiltrating disguised as civilians and hiding out among the refugees. The officers gave orders to all units to "shoot civilians" as a precautionary measure. Six former members of the 1st Cavalry Division later admitted firing on the refugees under the bridge at No Gun Ri. One soldier described the event as "wholesale slaughter." Some soldiers, however, refused to obey the orders. The shooting went on for three nights.

The massacre of No Gun Ri was not the only attack on civilians in which U.S. forces were involved during the Korean War. In another incident, American aircraft reportedly firebombed 300 civilians trapped in a cave, even though some pilots voiced misgivings that they might be targeting innocent people. According to eyewitnesses and U.S. military documents, two strategic bridges used by refugees fleeing the Communist advance were ordered destroyed by American army officers in August 1950, killing hundreds of civilians. There are reports that the South Korean Defense Ministry had become aware of 40 cases where civilians were killed by U.S. forces during the war. South Korean soldiers and police, too, are thought to have executed more than 2,000 political prisoners without trial in the early weeks of the conflict. After the AP reports were published, the Clinton administration issued a formal apology for the No Gun Ri massacre, although in South Korea there were calls for a fuller investigation.

In November 2009 South Korea's Truth and Reconciliation Commission announced that the military and police had executed at least 4,900 civilians in the opening months of the Korean War because of their suspected Communist sympathies. The commission, established in 2005 by South Korea's parliament, has been charged with investigating several possible civilian massacres at the hands of South Korean authorities. The number of victims who were summarily executed is probably much greater than the figure the commission released. Nonetheless, the commission's announcement was the first time that any state institution had acknowledged what has become known as "the National Guidance League Incident." The league had been set up by the regime of President Syngman Rhee before the war broke out in June 1950, ostensibly for the purpose of reeducating former Communist sympathizers. But thousands of suspected Communists were arrested in the belief that they might aid North Korean forces, and many of them subsequently vanished and were presumed to have been

executed. Although many of the victims were civilians, South Korean officials classified them as "enemy personnel." Some observers believe that the number of dead might reach the tens of thousands. In the years after the war, families were prevented by authorities from trying to dig up mass graves in an attempt to find the bodies of their relatives and punished for committing "treason." It was only in the late 1990s, with the strengthening of democracy, that the country began to come to terms with these war crimes. The commission has no power to compel testimony, prosecute suspects, or award compensation to victims' families. Nonetheless, since its inception, it has confirmed more than 50 mass killings of civilians, out of 1,222 reported by victims' relatives, and it has also located 168 mass graves. As of late 2009, however, only 13 of the graves had been excavated. The Republic of Korea Truth and Reconciliation Commission, charged with investigating wartime atrocities, has found that U.S. troops killed groups of South Korean civilians on 138 separate occasions during the Korean War. When the commission's mandate had expired in June 2010, it recommended that Seoul try to obtain compensation from Washington for eight cases that it had determined were unlawful. But the commission decided not to seek charges or compensation in about 130 cases because either the evidence was lacking or the killings were considered militarily justified. "They were more like cases of negligence than of liability or war crimes," said one of the commission members. In the cases judged "unlawful," the commission found that U.S. pilots had indiscriminately struck refugee groups with machine-gun fire, missiles, and napalm. In these attacks, 855 refugees were killed, including 100 people gathered on a beach and another 200 who had sought shelter in a cave and were then suffocated by fires triggered by the air strikes. The commission also found evidence implicating North Korean troops and South Korean leftists in the massacre of Korean rightists during the war.

Further Reading:

Bateman, Robert. *No Gun Ri: A Military History of the Korean War.* Mechanicsburg, Pa.: Stackpole Books, 2002.

Chinnery, Philip D. *Korean Atrocity!: Forgotten War Crimes, 1950–1953.* Annapolis, Md.: United States Naval Institute, 2001.

Hanley, Charles. *The Bridge at No Gun Ri: A Hidden Nightmare from the Korean War.* New York: Holt Paperbacks, 2002.

Nokmin (Avengers)

The Nokmin (Avengers) were established by Jewish survivors of the Holocaust to assist the illegal immigration of

Jews to Palestine. However, the Nokmin expanded their mission to hunt down Nazi war criminals who had evaded justice after the war. The group was reportedly founded by three men: Israel Carmi, Chaim Laskov (later Israel Defense Forces chief of staff), and Abba Kovner. Disguised as British soldiers, they scoured Europe, even infiltrating prisoner-of-war camps run by British and American forces, summarily executing men identified as war criminals, including hundreds of SS soldiers involved in running the Nazi CONCENTRATION CAMPS. Initially they had handed over the men they captured to the Allied authorities, but in the chaotic aftermath of the war, many of the SS managed to escape, causing the Nokmin to change their tactics and simply kill the former Nazis they found. By some estimates the Nokmin assassinated as many as 1,000 war criminals before disbanding.

noncombatants *See* CIVILIAN IMMUNITY; JOURNALISTS, PROTECTION OF; MEDICAL PERSONNEL, PROTECTION OF; PROTECTED PERSONS.

nondefended localities

Nondefended localities are places identified under Article 59 of the 1949 GENEVA CONVENTIONS that may not be attacked. In the overall context of the conventions, these are primarily civilian locales but also places without weapons. Such locations are places where:

(a) all combatants, as well as mobile weapons and mobile military equipment, must have been evacuated;

(b) no hostile use shall be made of fixed military installations or establishments;

(c) no acts of hostility shall be committed by the authorities to the population; and

(d) no activities in support of military operations shall be undertaken.

Police forces do not count as military personnel under Article 59.

The 1995 massacre at Srebrenica is a clear example of a flagrant breach of the convention, since the local people and UN peacekeeping forces had clearly surrendered and made apparent that they would not be taking hostile action against the Serb forces who were moving in to occupy the city. Any attack upon such a locality can thus be regarded as a war crime.

Further Reading:
Gutman, Roy, ed. *Crimes of War: What the Public Should Know.* New York: W. W. Norton & Company, 1999.

Jackson, Nyamuya Maogoto. *War Crimes and Realpolitik: International Justice from World War I to the 21st Century.* Boulder, Colo.: Lynne Rienner Publishers, 2004.

Jokie, Aleksander. *War Crimes and Collective Wrongdoing: A Reader.* London: Blackwell Publishers, 2001.

Noriega, Manuel (1938–) *Panamanian dictator*
General Manuel Noriega, former Panamanian strongman, is best known for provoking an invasion of his country by U.S. forces in 1989. He was subsequently tried and convicted on drug-trafficking charges and sentenced to 40-years in prison. Earlier in his colorful career, though, Noriega had enjoyed a close relationship with the United States and had reportedly collected $100,000 a year working for the CIA.

Born in Panama City, Noriega won a scholarship to study at the Chorrios Military Academy in Lima, Peru. On his return to Panama, he received a commission as a sub-lieutenant in the National Guard, where he became a close ally with the future Panamanian leader Omar Torrijos Herrera. Under Torrijos's patronage, Noriega's career prospered, and after Torrijos took power in a coup in 1968, Noriega was appointed chief of military intelligence. After Torrijos's death in an airplane crash in 1981, Noriega became chief of staff to the head of the National Guard. Two years later he promoted himself to general, a position that allowed him to effectively take control of the government, although he never assumed the office of president. Under Noriega's dictatorial rule, the military increased its power and its size, corruption became rampant, and political dissent was curbed. Noriega was widely suspected of being implicated in the killing in 1985 of a leading critic of the military, Hugo Spadafora. When President Nicolás Ardito Barletta tried to investigate, Noriega had him thrown out of office.

Throughout much of this period, Noriega acted as a CIA asset. In 1976 he met with then-CIA director George Bush (later the 41st president of the United States) for the first time and apparently remained on a friendly basis with him for some years afterward. Initially Noriega provided help to the U.S. effort to support the contras in Nicaragua who were seeking to topple the leftist Sandinista regime; he allowed Panama to be used by the United States as a transshipment point for the CIA to fly in weapons to the contras. Eventually, though, he balked at further cooperation with the United States. In 1986 reports surfaced in the news that Noriega was involved in drug trafficking, money laundering, and serving as a double agent for both the CIA and Cuba's intelligence agency. For agents of the U.S. Drug Enforcement Agency (DEA), allegations of Noriega's involvement in illegal drugs were nothing new; the DEA

General Manuel Noriega is escorted onto a U.S. Air Force aircraft by U.S. Drug Enforcement Agency agents. The former Panamanian leader was flown back to the United States to stand trial on drug charges. *(Defense Imagery)*

had been investigating him for trafficking as early as 1975, though nothing had come of it.

Noriega became increasingly repressive, prompting increased protests and violence. In 1987 the U.S. Senate demanded that the Panamanian government oust him and investigate his activities. The United States suspended all aid to Panama. A year later a U.S. grand jury in Florida indicted Noriega on charges of racketeering, violating drug laws, and money laundering. U.S. officials charged that he had amassed as much as $200–$300 million from his illegal activities. He was said to have acquired an apartment in Paris, a helicopter, three Lear jets, and three yachts. Conveniently, he also had a bank of his own in Panama City.

As the United States ratcheted up its diplomatic pressure on Panama. Noriega stubbornly resisted calls for him to go. In fall 1989 he "annulled" the elections and declared himself head of state. After putting down an attempted coup by disaffected elements of the Panamanian Defense Forces, he accused the United States of "aggression . . . against the tranquility of our country." In December 1989 President George Bush authorized an invasion of Panama to oust

Noriega. A contingent of 16,000 American soldiers took control of the country within a few days, though at the cost of 1,000 Panamanian lives. Noriega was arrested a month later and sent to stand trial in Miami. At his 1991 trial, Noriega's attorneys argued that his fortune came not from drug dealing but from the CIA and that many of the witnesses against him were involved in illegal activities themselves and were hardly credible. Nonetheless, Noriega was found guilty of cocaine trafficking, racketeering, and money laundering; he received a sentence of 40 years in prison. It was the first time that a foreign head of state was found guilty of criminal charges by a U.S. court. In Panama he was later convicted in absentia for ordering the murder of Spadafora, his former critic, as well as for the killing of an army officer. He was sentenced to 20 years in prison for each crime.

In January 2010 the Supreme Court turned down a plea by Noriega's attorneys seeking to prevent his extradition to France, where he had been implicated in laundering drug money through the French banking system. Noriega had hoped to be returned to Panama, where chances of his receiving an early release might have been better. In July

2010 Noriega was found guilty of laundering almost $3 million worth of drug profits through French banks and was sentenced by a French court to seven years in prison.

Further Reading:

Albert, Steve. *The Case against the General: Manuel Noriega and the Politics of American Justice.* New York: Scribner, 1994.

Dinges, John. *Our Man in Panama: How General Noriega Used the United States—and Made Millions in Drugs and Arms.* New York: Random House, 1990.

Eisner, Peter. *America's Prisoner: The Memoirs of Manuel Noriega.* New York: Random House, 1997.

North Korea, human rights violations in

Arguably the most isolated country in the world, the Democratic Republic of Korea has a deplorable human rights record. North Korean citizens are deprived of nearly all fundamental rights: freedom of speech, freedom of the press, freedom of religion, freedom of assembly, and even freedom of residence. Radios, for instance, are manufactured so that they can only be tuned into state-run stations; it is a violation of the law to tinker with the radio to receive other broadcasts.

Communist North Korea has had only two leaders since its founding after World War II: the late KIM IL SUNG, known as "Great Leader," and his son KIM JONG IL, known as "Dear Leader." According to HUMAN RIGHTS WATCH, the population is divided into three groups: the core group, made up of the elite (28 percent); the "unstable," or "wavering" (45 percent); and the "hostile" (27 percent). These three groups are further subdivided into 51 classifications based on their loyalty to the Korean Workers Party (KWP). These classifications determine the access an individual has to employment, residence, food, and medical care as well as privileges including the right to patronize certain businesses and stores. For those who are suspected of disloyalty, the punishment may be execution or consignment to one of 12 camps reserved for political prisoners. These camps are now thought to hold about 200,000 people, or about 1 percent of the population. Families of dissidents may also be sent off to labor camps, where they frequently perish from starvation, exposure, or maltreatment.

Defectors and REFUGEES report that the regime executes political prisoners and other opponents, including repatriated defectors, suspected spies, and people accused of being involved in plots against the leadership. The death penalty is mandatory for activities "in collusion with imperialists" aimed at "suppressing the national liberation struggle." According to the 2003 U.S. State Department *Country Report,* people have been condemned to death for such ill-

defined "crimes" as "ideological divergence," "opposing socialism," and the ambiguously classified "counterrevolutionary crimes." In some cases, executions were carried out at public gatherings of workers, students, and even schoolchildren. Border guards operate on shoot-to-kill orders, and there are reports that members of underground churches have been executed for practicing their faiths against the law.

Although funds and privileges are lavished on the military to maintain their loyalty, there are signs of dissension even in the army. In 1998 there were uncorroborated reports of a purge of several thousand members of the army—many of whom were killed—after a failed coup attempt. Agence France-Presse, the French press agency, said that in 1997 a four-star general who ran the Political Bureau of the Korean People's Army was executed along with several top officials before a crowd of thousands. The government, however, has insisted to AMNESTY INTERNATIONAL that only a handful of executions had taken place since 1985. The North Korean authorities do not limit their depredations to their own citizens; there were numerous abductions of Japanese citizens by North Korean agents between 1977 and 1983. Some of these abductees were later repatriated although only after spending years as prisoners in North Korea. There are also reports of kidnappings of South Koreans.

Until a tentative rapprochement between the two Koreas in the early 2000s, North Korea regularly staged confrontations with South Korea that sometimes led to violent clashes. The loss of economic assistance from the USSR after the collapse of communism there has only added to North Korea's woes. Starvation is probably the worst crisis facing the country. The forced collectivization of North Korea, coupled with drought, has resulted in recurrent famines that are estimated to have taken the lives of as many as 2 million people, with children bearing the brunt. Increasingly desperate North Koreans are willing to risk arrest and imprisonment by fleeing to China. (Because the border with South Korea is so well guarded, it is almost impossible to flee in the other direction.) Since 1994, when famine first broke out, thousands have defied the law to find sanctuary in China. The Chinese authorities have made it clear, though, that they do not welcome the influx of refugees and have frequently sent them back in violation of international law. China is a party to the 1951 UN Convention on the Status of Refugees and its 1967 Protocol, the Refugee Convention, which forbid states to push back migrants "to the frontiers of territories where [their] life or freedom would be threatened on account of . . . race, religion, nationality, membership of a particular social group or political opinion." Even those North Koreans who do manage to slip into China are forced to live underground for fear of exposure, eking out a living and risking exploitation.

In spite of the regime's adherence to the doctrine of *juche* (self-reliance), North Korea has been compelled to seek aid from international relief agencies to feed its population, but its suspicion of foreigners has made it difficult for the agencies to ensure that the food is properly distributed. Pyongyang has begun to relax its iron grip at least to some degree; in recent years, initiating diplomatic relations with 19 countries, including Britain and several European nations. It has also invited foreign investment: South Korean firms are engaged in several major projects in the North, among them a multimillion dollar industrial complex in the southwest of the country. This cautious economic liberalization has not, however, been matched by a similar political opening. Nor has the expanded diplomatic effort lessened suspicion that North Korea is pursuing a weapons-development program with an eye to producing nuclear weapons. Indeed, far from discouraging such suspicions, Pyongyang has periodically boasted that it already has a nuclear capacity. It is unknown whether North Korea is playing a game of brinkmanship for the purpose of extorting more aid in exchange for halting its nuclear program or the program is being pursued out of the regime's paranoia that only by acquiring nuclear weapons will it be able to stave off an attack by the United States.

In what has become an annual tradition, the United Nations renewed its resolution in 2009 urging North Korea to improve its human rights conditions. The resolution had the support of 99 countries, including South Korea, and 20 others, including China (North Korea's closest neighbor and grudging ally), were against it, with 20 abstentions. The vote marks the fifth year in a row in which the resolution was approved. While not legally binding, it stated that members had "very serious concerns at the persistence of continuing reports of systemic, widespread, and grave violations of civil, political, economic, social and cultural rights." The resolution also noted that torture, public executions, forced labor, and other inhumane punishments remained rampant. In spite of reports that Kim Jung Il was stricken with a serious illness, he still seemed able to exercise uncontested power. However, possibly in acknowledgment of his own mortality, he has apparently put plans in place to elevate his third-born son, Kim Jong Un, to power after his death. Some analysts, however, question whether a third Kim will be acceptable to the military and security elite. Tensions that might have been connected to the succession struggle continued to run high throughout the first half of 2010. In March, a South Korean warship, the *Cheonan*, was sunk under mysterious circumstances, killing 48 sailors. After conducting an inquiry, South Korean authorities declared that the ship had been deliberately targeted by a North Korean submarine, a charge that Pyong-

yang adamantly denied. Nonetheless, the UN Security Council condemned the act, although its statement did not specifically mention North Korea as the culprit because of Chinese objections.

Further Reading:
Amnesty International USA. North Korea Human Rights. Available online. URL: http://www.amnestyusa.org/all-countries/north-korea/page.do?id=1011213. Accessed March 20, 2010.
Breen, Michael. *Kim Jong-Il: North Korea's Dear Leader.* New York: John Wiley & Sons, 2004.
Harrold, Michael. *Comrades and Strangers: Behind the Closed Doors of North Korea.* New York: John Wiley & Sons, 2004.
HRNK.org. The Committee for Human Rights in North Korea. Available online. URL: http://www.hrnk.org/. Accessed March 20, 2010.
Martin, Bradley K. *Under the Loving Care of the Fatherly Leader: North Korea and the Kim Dynasty.* New York: Thomas Dunne Books, 2004.
Vollertsen, Norbert. *Inside North Korea.* London: Encounter Books, 2005.

nuclear arms and international law

The legality of the use of nuclear arms remains in dispute. Several treaties, most of them dating back to the cold war, limit the production, stockpiling, and testing of nuclear weapons as well as their proliferation. In a 1997 advisory opinion, the INTERNATIONAL COURT OF JUSTICE (ICJ; more popularly known as the World Court), the principal judicial organ of the United Nations, concluded that the use of nuclear weapons would generally be contrary to the principles and rules of INTERNATIONAL HUMANITARIAN LAW. Even "in an extreme circumstance of self-defense," the ICJ said, humanitarian law should hold priority. At the same time the court rejected the argument that small targeted nuclear weapons—so-called bunker busters for their ability to penetrate hardened defenses deep underground—were legal under international law, either. Even so the ICJ refused to make a definitive determination, saying that "in view of the current state of international law, and of the elements of fact at its disposal, the Court cannot conclude definitively whether the threat or use of nuclear weapons would be lawful or unlawful in an extreme circumstance of self-defence, in which the very survival of a State would be at stake." The court did, however, find that if indeed there were circumstances in which using nuclear weapons would ever be legal, then they were limited only under "an extreme circumstance of self-defense, in which the very survival of a State would be at stake." The president of the court, Judge Bedjaoui, hastened to add, lest there be any misconceptions, that the ICJ's opinion could "in no way be interpreted as a partially-opened door through which it recognizes the legality of the threat or use of nuclear weapons." Nuclear weapons, the judge pointed out, were "blind weapons" that "destabilize, by their very nature, humanitarian law, the law of distinguishing in the use of weapons." Further, he argued that they represented "absolute evil" and have the effect of destabilizing humanitarian law "which radically exclude each other, the existence of one necessarily supposing the nonexistence of the other." The court unanimously found that: "There exists an obligation to pursue in good faith and bring to a conclusion negotiations leading to nuclear disarmament in all its aspects under strict and effective international control." (The ICJ also took up a question raised by the World Health Organization, or WHO, which was whether the use of nuclear weapons by a state in war or other armed conflict would be in breach of its obligations under international law "in view of the health and environmental effects." The ICJ declined to respond to the WHO query because it was beyond the scope of the United Nations' jurisdiction.)

Some experts cite the HAGUE CONVENTIONS of 1907 as precedent for the ICJ's view. The conventions set forth the distinction between civilian and military objectives, specifying that belligerents must take measures to protect the former as much as possible even while targeting the latter. The Hague Draft Rules stated: "Aerial bombardment for the purpose of terrorizing civilian population, of destroying or damaging private property not of military character, or of injuring noncombatants is prohibited." One reading of this stipulation has led some legal scholars to contend that dropping the atomic bombs on Hiroshima and Nagasaki was illegal because the greatest impact was felt among a civilian population, notwithstanding any military objectives that the Allies sought to destroy. However, there is no comprehensive or universal prohibition against the use of nuclear weapons today, nor has any state with nuclear weapons (whether acknowledged or not) indicated any change in nuclear policy to take into account the ICJ's advisory opinion. Some legal scholars refer back to the principles of the NUREMBERG CHARTER, which formed the basis for the prosecution of Nazi war criminals at the end of World War II. These principles declared that individuals could not escape responsibility for their actions simply by asserting that they were only obeying orders. Nor, in this view, does the fact that no national law exists outlawing the use of nuclear weapons necessarily immunize a head of state or other government officials from being found culpable of ordering a nuclear strike if the Nuremberg Principles—promulgated by the United Nations in 1950—were to be applied.

See also NUREMBERG TRIALS; WEAPONS IN THE CONDUCT OF WAR; WEAPONS OF MASS DESTRUCTION.

Further Reading:
Feaver, Peter. *Guarding the Guardians: Civilian Control of Nuclear Weapons in the United States.* Cornell Studies in Security Affairs. Ithaca, N.Y.: Cornell University Press, 1992.

Krepon, Michael. *Strategic Stalemate: Nuclear Weapons and Arms Control in American Politics.* Sydney, Australia: Palgrave Macmillan, 1986.

Nichols, Gary W., and Milton L. Boykin, eds. *Arms Control and Nuclear Weapons: U.S. Policies and the National Interest.* Contributions in Military Studies. Westport, Conn.: Greenwood Press, 1987.

Nuon Chea (1928–   ) *Khmer Rouge leader*
Nuon Chea was Brother Number Two in the leadership of the Khmer Rouge and the brother-in-law of Brother Number One, POL POT. Born into a wealthy Chinese-Cambodian family and educated in Thailand, Nuon Chea became Pol Pot's comrade—and brother-in-law—in the 1950s. As second in command of the radical Maoist group that held power in Cambodia from 1975 to 1979, he was in charge of the security forces that hunted down traitors to the regime. Researchers and historians believe that as the movement's ideologue, Nuon Chea was responsible for Khmer Rouge policies that led to the genocidal campaign that was supposed to create a self-reliant agrarian utopia. Instead it led to the deaths of almost 2 million people and ushered in a reign of terror.

After the collapse of the Khmer Rouge in 1998, Nuon Chea settled on the outskirts of Pailin, a town that was once a Khmer Rouge stronghold. Pailin also had the advantage of being rich in gems and timber, making it a source of revenue for the insurgents. Nuon Chea took up residence in a modest bungalow with his wife. In interviews with the press, he claims to have begun to practice Buddhism. Nuon Chea has declared that he would "gladly appear" before a UN-backed tribunal, but it seems that he does not think he would be found guilty. He admitted that he made "mistakes" but denied that he was guilty of GENOCIDE, even rejecting the idea that millions of people had perished because of the Khmer Rouge's brutal despotism. "People died but there were so many causes of their deaths. We have to know the situation, what the situation was like." He tried to excuse himself by appealing to his youthful idealism. "But I had my ideology," he stated. "I wanted to free my country. I wanted people to have well-being." Nevertheless, he also insisted that he failed to "use wisdom to find the truth of what was going on, to check who was doing wrong and who was doing right. I accept that error." In a 2002 interview with PBS's *Frontline*, when he was 77, Nuon Chea even went so far as to contend that the Khmer Rouge deserved some credit for its accomplishments "A person's not always wrong and not always right. Like the leaders—we did some wrong, but we also did some right. Just because you're wrong doesn't mean you're a bad person. If you do anything, you're going to make mistakes."

Nuon Chea's claims of innocence are dismissed by many analysts and historians of the Khmer Rouge era. "Nuon Chea, in my view, is more guilty of CRIME AGAINST HUMANITY—war crimes, TORTURE and mass murder—than any other single Cambodian," asserted Nate Thayer, a journalist who covered the Khmer Rouge for years. "We have far more documentary evidence against Nuon Chea than we do against Pol Pot." Some of that evidence was collected from the notorious detention center of Tuol Sleng, where 20,000 political prisoners were tortured and executed. Documents maintained by the authorities of the center indicate that Nuon Chea was responsible for ordering the arrests and approving the executions. "For every single person who came through Tuol Sleng, Nuon Chea was given a copy of the briefing of the torture and remarked on when it was appropriate to have them killed. We have overwhelming evidence he was involved at least in those 14,000 murders personally, that he personally ordered them." In September 2007 Nuon Chea was arrested and brought before the Cambodia Tribunal to face charges of crimes against humanity and war crimes.

In September 2007 Nuon Chea was arrested on a warrant from the Cambodia Tribunal and charged with war crimes and crimes against humanity. He was held in detention in Phnom Penh, but it was unclear when his trial would begin.

See also CAMBODIA, WAR CRIMES IN.

Further Reading:
Chandler, David. *A History of Cambodia.* Philadelphia: Westview Press. 2000.
———. *The Tragedy of Cambodian History: Politics, War, and Revolution since 1945.* New Haven, Conn.: Yale University Press, 1993.
Gottesman, Evan. *Cambodia after the Khmer Rouge: Inside the Politics of Nation Building.* New Haven, Conn.: Yale University Press, 2004.
Hinton, Alexander Laban, and Robert Jay Lifton. *Why Did They Kill?: Cambodia in the Shadow of Genocide.* California Series in Public Anthropology, Vol. 11. Berkeley: University of California Press, 2004.
Kiernan, Ben. *How Pol Pot Came to Power: Colonialism, Nationalism, and Communism in Cambodia, 1930–1975.* New Haven, Conn.: Yale University Press, 2004.
———. *The Pol Pot Regime: Race, Power, and Genocide in Cambodia under the Khmer Rouge, 1975–79.* New Haven, Conn.: Yale University Press, 2002.
Pran, Dith, comp. *Children of Cambodia's Killing Fields: Memoirs by Survivors.* Edited by Kim De Paul. New Haven, Conn.: Yale University Press, 1999.
Short, Philip. *Pol Pot: Anatomy of a Nightmare.* New York: Holt Rinehart, 2005.
Ung, Loung. *First They Killed My Father: A Daughter of Cambodia Remembers.* New York: Perennial, 2001.

Nuremberg Charter (Agreement for the Prosecution and Punishment of the Major War Criminals of the European Axis and Charter of the International Military Tribunal; London Charter)

The Nuremberg Charter, agreed upon in 1945 by the victorious Allies the United States, the Soviet Union, Great Britain, and France after World War II, established the principles that would be applied in bringing Nazi war criminals to justice. Formally known as the Agreement for the Prosecution and Punishment of the Major War Criminals of the European Axis and Charter of the International Military Tribunal (IMT), the Nuremberg Charter introduced the concept of CRIMES AGAINST HUMANITY in Article 6C. Crimes against humanity included "murder, extermination, enslavement, deportation, and other inhumane acts committed against civilian populations, before or during the war; or persecutions on political, racial or religious grounds in execution of or in connection with any crime within the jurisdiction of the Tribunal, whether or not in violation of the domestic law of the country where perpetrated."

Until the Nuremberg Charter, there was no separate crime in international law that addressed crimes committed by a state against its own civilian population (in contrast to war crimes and crimes against peace or wars of aggression). The charter is also significant because it affirmed that individuals were responsible for their own actions and could not use the defense that they were only obeying orders. The United States and its allies hoped that the charter would make war an international crime except when carried out in self-defense. The notion that wars of aggression should be considered crimes was such a break with precedent that a French delegate to the conference deliberating the terms of the Charter described it as "shocking," contending that it would amount to "ex post facto legislation"—that is, it would question the legality of past wars, even those fought by the Allies.

A second objective of the charter was to ensure that henceforth civilians received protections against brutal treatment regardless of whether the perpetrator was an invader or their own government. Third, the charter was meant to enshrine the principle that crimes were to be answered by justice and not by acts of revenge. Thus, the Nazi war criminals were to be tried in accordance with accepted norms of jurisprudence—the right to counsel, the right to mount a defense and appeal a verdict, and so forth—even though they never accorded the same rights to suspects when they were in power. Nonetheless, some critics still saw the NUREMBERG TRIALS as "victors' justice" since only the defeated were subject to trial. Of the 21 major Nazi war criminals tried, 18 were convicted, mostly of crimes against peace.

In spite of the Allied hopes, legal attempts to outlaw war have not met with much success and there have been few prosecutions for crimes against humanity. However, this category of crimes has been included in the statutes of the INTERNATIONAL CRIMINAL TRIBUNAL FOR THE FORMER YUGOSLAVIA (ICTY) and the INTERNATIONAL CRIMINAL TRIBUNAL FOR RWANDA (ICTR), both of which were established by the United Nations, and appears as well as in the statute of the INTERNATIONAL CRIMINAL COURT (ICC). Altogether there are no fewer than 11 international texts in which crimes against humanity are recognized, although their definition differs slightly both in terms of what constitutes a crime against humanity and its legal ramifications. Nonetheless, they all have certain elements in common insofar as (1) they refer to specific acts of violence against persons regardless of his or her citizenship or whether the acts were committed in wartime or peacetime, and (2) that these acts are motivated by a deliberate persecution of a particular group on the basis of its nationality, race, ethnicity, or culture.

Further Reading:

Bosch, William J. *Judgment on Nuremberg: American Attitudes toward the Major German War-Crime Trials.* Durham: University of North Carolina Press, 1970.
Gilbert, G. M. *Nuremberg Diary.* New York: Da Capo Press, 1995.
Goldensohn, Leon, and Robert Gellately, eds. *The Nuremberg Interviews.* New York: Knopf, 2004.
Maser, Werner. *Nuremberg: A Nation on Trial.* New York: Scribner, 1979.
Marrus, Robert, and Michael R. Marrus. *The Nuremberg War Crimes Trial of 1945–46: A Documentary History.* Bedford Series in History and Culture. Sidney, Australia: Palgrave Macmillan, 1997.
Persico, Joseph. *Nuremberg: Infamy on Trial.* New York: Penguin Books, 1995.
Rice, Earle. *The Nuremberg Trials.* Famous Trials Series. San Diego, Calif.: Lucent Books, 1997.
Taylor, Telford. *The Anatomy of the Nuremberg Trials: A Personal Memoir.* New York: Little, Brown & Co, 1993.
———. *Nuremberg Trials: War Crimes and International Law.* New York: Carnegie Endowment for International Peace, 1949.
Tusa, Ann, and John Tusa. *The Nuremberg Trials.* New York: Cooper Square Publishers, 2003.

Nuremberg Laws (Nuremberg Decrees)

The Nuremberg Laws, enacted in 1935 by the Congress of the National Socialist German Workers Party (NSDAP, or Nazi Party), were designed to clarify who could be considered a German citizen while segregating Jews from society and depriving them of economic, political, and other rights. The laws were intended to ensure the purity of German blood and honor as conceived by the Nazis. The laws, passed on September 15, 1935, in Nuremberg, were supplemented by other laws that imposed additional restrictions on the Jews in Germany, depriving them of political rights.

Not all the delegates to the congress gathering in August 1935 were in favor of the state-sponsored discrimination against Jews, especially in the economic sphere. The economics minister, for instance, while offering no moral condemnation of limiting Jewish rights, nonetheless suggested that the Third Reich could benefit by using Jewish entrepreneurial talent that would henceforth be kept out of the labor market. The Nuremberg Laws, which were publicly announced at the annual rally of the Nazi Party, were improvised and hastily written—so quickly, in fact, that the drafters ran out of paper and had to resort to menu cards. So-called Jewish advisers were flown from Berlin to Nuremberg to offer their input. The first law—the Law for the Protection of German Blood and German Honor—banned marriages and extramarital intercourse between Jews and Germans or those of "related blood." Jewish households could not hire German females under age 45. It stated:

1. A citizen of the Reich is that subject only who is of German or kindred blood and who, through his conduct, shows that he is both desirous and fit to serve the German people and Reich faithfully.
2. The right to citizenship is acquired by the granting of Reich citizenship papers.
3. Only the citizen of the Reich enjoys full political rights in accordance with the provision of the laws.

The second law, called the Reich Citizenship Law, stripped Jews of their German citizenship and introduced a new distinction between "Reich citizens" and "nationals."

It is important to note that these racial purity laws did not classify a Jew by his or her religious affiliation; instead a Jew was a person with three or four Jewish grandparents, irrespective of whether that person followed the Jewish faith. That meant that many Jews who regarded themselves as secular German citizens were officially classified as Jews and stripped of their rights. Even Christian converts were defined as Jews. The Nuremberg Laws simply made official a policy of persecution that was already being applied. However, the Nazi regime was sensitive enough to international opinion that it moderated the enforcement of some of the laws in the weeks before the 1936 Olympic Games in Berlin, and signs prohibiting Jews from public venues were taken down.

Once the Olympics were over (no German Jews had been allowed to participate), the persecution of Jews was renewed on a larger scale than before. Over the next two years Jews were forced to register their property as a first step to driving them into destitution. The Germans proceeded to "Aryanize" Jewish businesses, turning them over to German managers and workers and throwing Jewish employees out of work. Jewish doctors and Jewish lawyers were forbidden to practice. Jews were also required to carry identity cards with a red J stamped on them. (Later Jews were forced to wear yellow stars.) If a Jew did not have a readily identifiable "Jewish" name, the Nazis assigned Jewish middle names: "Israel" for males, "Sara" for females. These discriminatory measures, as it turned out, only represented an initial phase in what became a systematic campaign to empty Europe of its entire Jewish population, first by forced migration and then by execution.

See also FRICK, WILHELM; STUCKART, WILHELM; WANNSEE CONFERENCE.

Further Reading:

Bloxham, Donald. *Genocide on Trial: War Crimes Trials and the Formation of Holocaust History and Memory.* Oxford: Oxford University Press, 2003.

Dawidowicz, Lucy. *A Holocaust Reader.* Library of Jewish Studies. Chicago: Behrman House Publishing, 1976.

Dwork, Deborah, and Robert Jan Van Pelt. *Holocaust: A History.* New York: W. W. Norton & Company, 2003.

Giblin, James Cross. *The Life and Death of Adolf Hitler.* New York: Clarion Books, 2002.

Gilbert, Martin. *The Holocaust: A History of the Jews of Europe during the Second World War.* New York: Owl Books, 1987.

Roseman, Mark. *The Wannsee Conference and the Final Solution: A Reconsideration.* New York: Metropolitan Books, 2002.

Nuremberg Medical Trial   *See* DOCTORS' TRIAL.

Nuremberg Trials (International Military Tribunal)

The trials of Nazi war criminals in the immediate aftermath of World War II at Nuremberg, Germany, stands out as a major achievement in the development of INTERNATIONAL HUMANITARIAN LAW. For one, it represented a commitment on the part of the victorious Allies to try individuals implicated in war crimes and GENOCIDE in a court of law. The objective was to see justice done rather than to seek revenge. For another, the trials led to the creation of a large body of international law designed to prevent similar abuses from recurring and establish mechanisms to punish offenders. Nuremberg also established the principle of individual responsibility: A defendant could no longer claim that he was not culpable of a crime because he was only following orders from a superior or a government.

The first indictments, announced on October 18, 1945, charged 24 individuals with a variety of crimes and atrocities, including the deliberate instigation of aggressive wars; extermination of racial and religious groups; murder and mistreatment of PRISONERS OF WAR; and the murder, mistreatment, enslavement, and deportation of hundreds of thousands of inhabitants of countries occupied by Germany during the war. The initial group of defendants was made up of some of the most powerful officials in the hierarchy of the Third Reich, most of whom were in the custody of one of the four prosecuting nations: the United States, the Soviet Union, Great Britain, and France. The choice of these defendants was based more on their prominence than on the evidence that had been gathered against them. Some were included because of the demands of one of the prosecuting nations. For example, HANS FRITZSCHE, a relatively minor official who had served in the propaganda ministry, was put on trial at the insistence of the Soviet Union. But most of the defendants were in fact major figures who had wielded vast power under ADOLF HITLER: HERMANN GÖRING, RUDOLF HESS, JOACHIM VON RIBBENTROP, Field Marshal WILHELM KEITEL, Grand Admiral ERICH RAEDER, and 18 other military leaders and civilian officials, in addition to the munitions maker GUSTAV VON BOHLEN KRUPP. Three of the accused individuals avoided trial: ROBERT LEY, the Nazi labor leader, hanged himself before the trial could begin; Krupp was found too weak to stand trial; and Hitler's powerful deputy, MARTIN BORMANN, had vanished. (Bormann was convicted and sentenced to death in absentia; his fate is unknown.) In addition, several institutions that formed part of the basic structure of the Nazi government were indicted as criminal organizations, including the SS (Schutzstaffel, or Defense Corps), the GESTAPO (Geheime Staatspolizei, or Secret State Police), the SA (Sturmabteilung, or Storm Troops), the Reich Cabinet (Reichsregierung), the Corps of the Political Leaders of the Nazi Party, and the general staff and high command of the German armed forces.

The groundwork for the Nuremberg Trials was established the previous August in London when the British, French, Americans, and Soviets signed the agreement known as the London Charter, also known as the NUREM-

Courtroom of the Nuremberg Trials, 1945–46 *(Library of Congress)*

BERG CHARTER, which created the Nuremberg court, officially the International Military Tribunal. The charter described the types of crimes that the tribunal would hear. While the Allies decided as well to try organizations like the SS and SA, they made no attempt to define what was meant by the term *criminal organizations.* Nonetheless, by indicting these organizations, the Allies intended to implicate by association thousands of their members, even if it was impossible to bring them all to trial.

The trial rules for the tribunal were based on a combination of Anglo-American jurisprudence and continental civil law derived from the Napoleonic Code. The hybrid legal framework that resulted differed in significant respects from the legal system in place in the United States. In an American court, for instance, prosecutors must present sufficient evidence to indict an individual, whereas the tribunal did not require prosecutors to offer all the proof

against defendants at the time they unsealed their indictments. In addition, hearsay evidence was allowed at Nuremberg in the form of testimony from individuals who would not be called upon as witnesses, whereas in most instances hearsay evidence cannot be admitted in an American court. The tribunal also allowed evidence to be admitted if it were only "probative," a lower standard than in U.S. courts, and did not allow defendants to confront or question their accusers, which is a right guaranteed by the U.S. Constitution. The defendants would have no right to a jury trial, and all decisions made by the judges were final and could not be appealed, although the defendants were entitled to ask the Control Council of Germany—the Allied occupation government—to reduce or change their sentences. Defendants could, however, select an attorney of their choice or else represent themselves if they wished. In a novel legal strategy, Lieutenant Colonel Murray Bernays, an attorney in the U.S. War Department, proposed an approach whereby the defendants would be tried as conspirators in planning and waging a war of aggression (which, among other things, entailed breaking international treaties). His proposal was eventually incorporated into the Nuremberg Charter.

The trial of the individual defendants was to take place first; only then would legal proceedings begin against the indicted criminal organizations. The Allies agreed to divide up the prosecution, with each power taking turns. The United States was given the most difficult task, proving Count One, the conspiracy charge. There were four counts altogether:

Count One: Conspiracy to Wage Aggressive War
The conspiracy charge was designed to circumvent the problem of how to find the defendants guilty of acts they had committed before the war. It was one of the most controversial aspects of the trial—the concept of conspiracy is not recognized in continental law—because to some historians, it sought to find a coherent policy (or organized plot) that might exist only in the minds of prosecutors. Moreover, pursuing conspiracy charges allowed lawyers for the defendants to argue that they had never participated in any conspiracy or at least known in advance that the scheme would lead to any serious criminal acts.

Count Two: Waging Aggressive War, or "Crimes against Peace"
The Nuremberg Charter defined this count as "the planning, preparation, initiation, and waging of wars of aggression, which were also wars in violation of international treaties, agreements, and assurances." The prosecution of this charge was put in the hands of the British. The prosecution was handicapped to some degree. On the one hand, there was no doubt that Nazi Germany had waged aggressive war or that it had broken international treaties, particularly the Kellogg-Briand Pact of 1928, which renounced war as an instrument of national policy (which was distinguished from a defensive war); however, the pact failed both to define "aggressive war" or to prescribe any penalties for violators. Moreover, in two cases—the Anschluss (the merger of Germany and Austria) and the invasion of Czechoslovakia—the charge could not be applied since Hitler had orchestrated events so as to accomplish his aims without force of arms. Moreover, the Soviet Union had violated the Kellogg-Briand Pact itself by invading Finland, Poland, and the Baltics and had in addition signed a nonaggression pact with Hitler to divide up Poland.

Count Three: War Crimes
The Nuremberg Charter defined war crimes as "murder, ill treatment or deportation to slave labor or for any other purpose of civilian population or in occupied territory, murder or ill-treatment of prisoners-of-war or persons on the seas, killing of hostages, plunder of public or private property, wanton destruction of cities, towns, or villages or devastation not justified by military necessity." The Soviet and French prosecutors, who were given this part of the case, had more precedent to rely upon than their American and British prosecutors had. Much of this precedent had been established in a series of treaties governing treatment of prisoners of war (POWs), setting the rules for the conduct of warfare, and banning certain types of armaments (dumdum bullets, poisonous gas, etc.), including the GENEVA CONVENTIONS of 1864 and 1906 and the HAGUE CONVENTIONS of 1899 and 1907.

Count Four: Crimes against Humanity
War crimes were defined by the Nuremberg Charter as "murder, extermination, enslavement, deportation, and other inhumane acts committed against any civilian population before or during the war, or persecutions on political, racial, or religious grounds in execution of or in connection with any crimes within the jurisdiction of the International Military Tribunal, whether or not in violation of domestic law of the country where perpetrated." This was the charge applied to defendants who had organized and run the CONCENTRATION CAMPS and death camps and participated in Nazi death squads in Eastern Europe and the Soviet Union. The prosecution for this count was conducted by the French and Soviets. Until the Nuremberg Charter, there had been some debate as to whether CRIMES AGAINST HUMANITY referred exclusively to crimes committed by a state against its own people or whether it could apply to international conflicts. The Nuremberg Charter decided the issue in favor of the latter, establishing an important precedent for international humanitarian law.

The first trial began on November 20, 1945, and judgments were handed down on September 30–October 1, 1946. In announcing the verdicts, the tribunal rejected two major claims by the defense: (1) that the defendants' rights had been violated because crimes of aggression had not previously been defined as crimes under international law, and (2) that they were not legally responsible for committing any crimes because they were acting under orders. The tribunal stated that "the true test . . . is not the existence of the order but whether moral choice [in executing it] was in fact possible." The evidence, said the tribunal, overwhelmingly proved that most of the defendants were guilty of systematic atrocities—including the extermination of 6 million Jews and thousands of Rom (Gypsies) and the forcible DEPORTATIONS of 5 million people from their homes in occupied Europe to serve as slave laborers in Germany.

Twelve defendants were sentenced to death by hanging, seven received prison terms ranging from 10 years to life, and three were acquitted, including FRANZ VON PAPEN, the German diplomat, and HJALMAR HORACE GREELEY SCHACHT, the president of the German Central Bank. The convicted defendants sought clemency from the Control Council, but their appeals were rejected. The Allies acted quickly to carry out the death sentences, hanging 10 condemned to death on October 16, 1946. Only Göring escaped his punishment by committing suicide in prison a few hours before he was to be executed.

With the first trial over, the International Military Tribunal turned to the trial of the indicted criminal organizations. After the monthlong trial, the tribunal found three of the organizations guilty: the SS, the Gestapo, and the Corps of the Political Leaders of the Nazi Party. Three others were acquitted: the SA (whose power had vastly diminished before the war), the Reich Cabinet, and the general staff and high command of the German Armed Forces. In the case of the cabinet and the general staff, the judges determined that relatively few members were responsible for criminal acts and that these could be better prosecuted individually. The prosecution of criminal organizations was controversial because it raised the prospect of guilt by association, although no individual member was ever punished on the basis of the tribunal's convictions. (The Allied occupation authorities did, however, hold de-Nazification trials of individual members of these organization.)

Between 1946 and 1950, the Allies held 12 more trials of accused Nazi officials and supporters under the authority of Control Council Law No. 10, which was modeled on the Nuremberg Charter but provided for prosecuting the trials in each of the four zones of occupied Germany. Some 185 individuals were indicted in the 12 cases, including SS officials who had supervised concentration camps and participated in the extermination of Jews and other groups, doctors who had carried out immoral MEDICAL EXPERIMENTS on concentration camp inmates and POWs, judges who had used the color of law to murder, high military and civilian officials who had actively participated in Nazi criminal acts, and industrialists accused of looting and using slave labor. Several doctors and SS leaders were condemned to death by hanging, and approximately 120 other defendants were given prison sentences of various durations; 35 defendants were acquitted. Although war-crimes charges were leveled against about 5,000 other Nazis, including concentration camp guards and soldiers, many of them managed to escape. Still others were arrested later and tried in courts of individual countries under national laws.

A similar tribunal set up to try Japanese war criminals became known as the TOKYO TRIALS. The International Military Tribunal for the Far East, as it was known, was made up of judges from 11 of the Allied nations, who sentenced seven of the 28 defendants to death and handed down prison sentences to the rest.

The legacy of the Nuremberg Trials is a mixed one. Until Nuremberg, jurisdiction over war crimes generally fell under national military courts. Nuremberg also established a precedent in which the concepts of conspiracy and collective guilt were introduced as prosecutable offenses. The Nuremberg and Tokyo trials represented the first organized attempt to apply principles of international law that often had scant legal precedent, if any. Although the fact that prosecutors had to improvise and face charges of using ex post facto law—trying crimes for which no law existed at the time that they were committed—the Nuremberg verdicts won widespread acceptance internationally. In 1950 the United Nations promulgated the so-called Nuremberg Principles—among them the concept that individuals cannot avoid responsibility for their actions by claiming they were acting under orders—which many countries have since adopted into the legal systems of most countries.

The Nuremberg Trials fulfilled another important function as well: providing what remains the most comprehensive account of the Nazi era, from Hitler's coming to power to the planning for war to the crimes committed in the prosecution of that war. There were bound to be misgivings on the part of some legal experts. The defendants, critics contended, were selected arbitrarily and implicated for violations of international law, which was binding on nations but not on individuals. Moreover, some detractors believed that an accused individual should only be tried under the laws of his or her own nation, not under a new regime and new laws that came about after the war. Proponents of the trials acknowledge that perfect justice could never be achieved under the circumstances but that the trials represented the best alternative available and were in any case far preferable to simply summarily executing Nazi war criminals without troubling with any legal formalities—an idea that even JOSEPH STALIN and Winston Churchill had entertained. (In 1944 Churchill had said that Nazi war criminals should be "hunted down and shot.") The promise of the Nuremberg Trials—that they might deter others from perpetrating atrocities or waging aggressive war—was short-lived. Atrocities on an alarming scale continued to occur—in Cambodia, Liberia, Rwanda, the former Yugoslavia, and Darfur, among other places—and yet the international community has yet to find a reliable means of intervening to stop them or providing a permanent means to punish their perpetrators.

See also BRANDT, KARL; DOCTORS' TRIAL; DÖNITZ, KARL; EINSATZGRUPPEN; FRANK, HANS; FRICK, WIL-

HELM; FUNK, WALTHER; JACKSON, ROBERT; JODL, ALFRED; KALTENBRUNNER, ERNST; KRAMER, JOSEF; NAZI PARTY, LEADERSHIP CORPS OF; NEURATH, KONSTANTIN VON; POHL, OSWALD; ROSENBERG, ALFRED; SAUCKEL, FRITZ; SCHELLENBERG, WALTER; SCHIRACH, BALDUR VON; SEYSS-INQUART, ARTHUR; SPEER, ALBERT; SS; STREICHER, JULIUS; TAYLOR, TELFORD.

Further Reading:

Bosch, William J. *Judgment on Nuremberg: American Attitudes toward the Major German War-Crime Trials.* Durham: University of North Carolina Press, 1970.

Gilbert, G. M. *Nuremberg Diary.* New York: Da Capo Press, 1995.

Goldensohn, Leon, and Robert Gellately, eds. *The Nuremberg Interviews.* New York: Knopf, 2004.

Maser, Werner. *Nuremberg: A Nation on Trial.* New York: Scribner, 1979.

Marrus, Robert, and Michael R. Marrus. *The Nuremberg War Crimes Trial of 1945–46: A Documentary History.* Bedford Series in History and Culture. Sidney, Australia: Palgrave Macmillan, 1997.

Persico, Joseph. *Nuremberg: Infamy on Trial.* New York: Penguin Books, 1995.

Rice, Earle. *The Nuremberg Trials. Famous Trials Series.* Farmington Hills: Lucent Books, 1997.

Taylor, Telford. *The Anatomy of the Nuremberg Trials: A Personal Memoir.* New York: Little, Brown & Co, 1993.

———. *Nuremberg Trials: War Crimes and International Law.* New York: Carnegie Endowment for International Peace, 1949.

Tusa, Ann, and John Tusa. *The Nuremberg Trials.* New York: Cooper Square Publishers, 2003.

Nzapali, Sebastian (1951–) *Congolese war criminal*
Sebastian Nzapali, a former Congolese military officer, became the first person convicted under a new Dutch law permitting the prosecution of CRIMES AGAINST HUMANITY that were committed in another country. The Dutch law is based on the 1984 United Nations CONVENTION AGAINST TORTURE. Nzapali's case was considered exceptional because few countries actually apply laws that flow from the convention. (France and Switzerland have both held foreigners suspected of committing TORTURE in other countries, but the suspects were never tried, because they were either released for lack of evidence or managed to escape.) Nzapali had arrived in the Netherlands in 1998 seeking political asylum, but he was recognized and denounced by some of his victims. The Dutch dispatched investigators to the Congo to determine whether the allegations had any basis in fact. When they were convinced that Nzapali was implicated in torture, they placed him under arrest. Nzapali contended that he was persecuted himself and denied charges that he had tortured and raped people in 1996 when the Congo (then known as Zaire) was ruled by the late dictator MOBUTU SESE SEKO. Prosecutors established, however, that Nzapali had in fact committed torture and that he had acquired his nickname "The King of the Beasts" because he had treated prisoners like animals. In April 2004 the 51-year-old Nzapali was found guilty of torture (though not of rape) and sentenced to 30 months in prison.

See also CONGO, DEMOCRATIC REPUBLIC OF THE, WAR CRIMES IN.

Further Reading:

Edgerton, Robert. *The Troubled Heart of Africa: A History of the Congo.* New York: St. Martin's Press, 2002.

Wrong, Michela. *In the Footsteps of Mr. Kurtz: Living on the Brink of Disaster in Mobutu's Congo.* New York: HarperCollins Publishers, 2001.

Oberheuser, Herta (1911–1978) *Nazi doctor*

Dr. Herta Oberheuser was the only female defendant to be charged with crimes based on MEDICAL EXPERIMENTS in CONCENTRATION CAMPS in the DOCTORS' TRIAL part of the NUREMBERG TRIALS. She was implicated in the murder of children by injecting them with oil and other substances; once they were dead, she would then amputate their limbs and remove their vital organs. Usually it took only three to five minutes for the injections to kill their victims, who were conscious almost until the last moment. She was also known to have inflicted wounds on her unwilling victims—to simulate the wounds German soldiers might sustain—and then to aggravate the resulting infections by rubbing in foreign objects, such as wood, rusty nails, crushed glass, dirt, or sawdust. She was sentenced to 20 years in prison but released after only a few years in 1952. She went back to medicine, becoming a family doctor in a small town until her medical license was revoked in 1958.

Further Reading:
Lifton, Robert. *The Nazi Doctors: Medical Killing and the Psychology of Genocide.* New York: Basic Books, 2000.

Obote, Milton (Apollo Milton Obote) (1924–2005) *Ugandan dictator*

Milton Obote was twice president of Uganda; his corrupt and dictatorial policies ultimately led to his ouster and exile—twice. Born on December 28, 1924, Obote became active in Ugandan politics when the country was still under British rule. After founding the Ugandan People's Congress, he took part in a coalition that took over the government of Uganda after it won its independence in 1963. Soon thereafter he became the country's second president. By keeping the military placated, Obote strengthened his control over Uganda, suppressing the opposition. He came to rely more and more on an illiterate soldier named IDI AMIN to advance his own ends, elevating Amin to positions of ever greater authority.

When Amin was implicated by Parliament in a gold and ivory smuggling scheme, Obote reacted by snubbing the legislators, convinced that he and Amin were above the law. However, when Parliament brought down his government with a vote of no confidence, he called upon Amin to launch a coup against his own government, had himself declared president, and passed a new constitution. Martial law was imposed to forestall any resistance. Over the next few years, though, Obote began to fear for his position—he escaped a number of assassination attempts—and became increasingly fearful of Amin. He formed an elite security unit to protect him and gave orders to arrest Amin on charges of financial malfeasance. Amin got wind of the order and seized the capital of Kampala, executing Obote's supporters. Obote fled to Tanzania, where he bided his time in exile while Uganda was plunged into chaos under Amin's bloody regime. Tensions between Tanzania and Uganda erupted into open warfare in 1978. Tanzanian troops moved into Uganda, toppled Amin (who went into exile in Saudi Arabia), and reinstalled Obote as the head of an interim government.

In 1980 Uganda held its first democratic elections in 18 years. When the vote did not favor Obote's party, as expected, Obote simply had the votes recounted to make him president. Obote's efforts to consolidate power antagonized a top military official, Colonel Yoweri Museveni, who launched a guerrilla war. As it became apparent that Museveni enjoyed popular support, Obote resorted to ever more brutal methods. He was accused of perpetrating massacres and carrying out a scorched earth policy, forcing as many as 20,000 civilians from their homes in areas with high levels of support for Museveni. The U.S. State Department claimed that his forces killed up to 200,000 in its campaign. (It is believed that some 300,000 people were killed altogether in the conflict.) And even briefly considered the idea of accepting military aid from North Korea. Obote, who seemed to have learned nothing from history, became increasingly concerned about the loyalty of his own supporters, and while he was out of the country, he ordered the arrest of his top military advisers. The military struck first and took over Kampala, driving Obote into exile a second time—to Tanzania and then Zambia, but not before he looted much of Uganda's treasury. A year later Museveni assumed power. It is estimated that the war between Obote's and Museveni's forces cost as many as 300,000 lives. Obote remained exiled in Zambia for the remainder of his life. He died, however, in a hospital in South Africa while waiting for medical treatment from a series of strokes. He was 80 years old.

See also UGANDA, HUMAN RIGHTS VIOLATIONS IN.

Further Reading:
Allen, John. *Idi Amin.* History's Villains. San Diego: Blackbirch Press, 2003.
Allen, Peter A. P. *Interesting Times: Life in Uganda under Idi Amin.* London: Book Guild, Limited, 2000.
Mutibwa, Phares. *Uganda since Independence: A Story of Unfulfilled Hopes.* London: Africa World Press, 1992.

occupying power

International law—in particular Section III of the Fourth Geneva Convention of 1949—establishes basic principles an occupying power should abide by in its treatment of populations that come under its control. A foreign territory is considered occupied only if the belligerent actually controls it. The obligations of an occupying belligerent do not forbid it from suspending or repealing local laws that are seen as a threat to its security or are in violation of the convention; however, with minor exceptions penal laws of the territory must remain in place. The earlier Hague Regulations Concerning the Law and Customs of War on Land also forbid altering local law.

An occupying power may take measures that it believes necessary to protect its security or communication system. Individuals resisting the occupier are liable to arrest and punishment; however, the Geneva Convention requires the occupying power to meet certain conditions: The detainee is entitled to a trial and has the right to seek counsel, summon witnesses in his or her defense, and appeal a verdict. If an occupier employs military courts, they must be nonpolitical judicial bodies and sit in the occupied territory rather than be employed simply as instruments of punishment to persecute resistors. If a death penalty is imposed, the convention calls for a six-month delay before it can be carried out; moreover, a third party—typically a government of an outside country charged with protecting civilians under occupation—must be notified. In addition, the convention bars TORTURE, murder, corporeal punishment, mutilation, and "any other measures of brutality." The convention also specifies that an occupying power may not "alter the status of public officials or judges in the occupied territories . . . should they abstain from fulfilling their functions for reasons of conscience."

How, though, are the limitations enshrined in the Fourth Convention to be reconciled in cases such as occupied Iraq? The U.S.-led coalition that took over the country in 2003 has made it clear that it seeks to overhaul Iraq's political, judicial, and other state institutions that had previously served the dictatorship of SADDAM HUSSEIN. It is possible to argue that the coalition is not, in fact, an occupying power—which would make the question moot—but in the absence of any alternative source of governance, it is difficult to imagine what other role the coalition has assumed for itself. In a 2003 essay on the subject, Thomas D. Grant, a public international lawyer and fellow of Wolfson College in Britain, writes: "The coalition in Iraq presents a case distinct from certain past cases of occupation, in the sense that, though the Iraqi state continues to hold all rights to its territory, there remains now no governmental organ that can exercise those rights—apart from the coalition itself." The Fourth Convention, he points out, does allow an occupying authority to make certain changes in laws to ensure good governance during the occupation. It should be kept in mind that an occupying power can make certain changes to ensure its own security. Because occupation was seen as temporary, however, the occupying power is not free to change laws to bring them into accord with its own judicial conceptions. Grant takes the view that it is possible to "carve out" from the Hague Resolu-

Iraqi prime minister Ayad Allawi (left), U.S. Ambassador to Iraq L. Paul Bremer (center), and Iraqi president Sheikh Ghazi Ajil al-Yawar (right) after a ceremony celebrating the transfer of governmental authority to the Iraqi Interim Government on June 28, 2004 *(Defense Imagery)*

tions and Fourth Convention the authority to overhaul laws of the occupied territory, which could be achieved by a United Nations Security Council resolution. Precedent has already been established during the transition to independence of East Timor (formerly a part of Indonesia) or in the creation of an autonomous Kosovo (formerly ruled by Serb-dominated Yugoslavia). In both instances, with UN sanction, existing laws were swept aside in the interests of reform, democracy, and political stability.

See also EAST TIMOR, WAR CRIMES IN; GENEVA CONVENTIONS; HAGUE CONVENTIONS; IRAQ, HUMAN RIGHTS VIOLATIONS IN POST-SADDAM; KOSOVO, WAR CRIMES IN.

Further Reading:
Falk, Richard A. *Crimes of War: A Legal, Political-Documentary, and Psychological Inquiry into the Responsibility of Leaders, Citizens, and Soldiers for Criminal Acts in Wars.* New York: Random House, 1971.
Gutman, Roy, ed. *Crimes of War: What the Public Should Know.* New York: W. W. Norton & Company, 1999.
Jackson, Nyamuya Maogoto. *War Crimes and Realpolitik: International Justice from World War I to the 21st Century.* Boulder, Colo.: Lynne Rienner Publishers, 2004.
Jokie, Aleksander. *War Crimes and Collective Wrongdoing: A Reader.* London: Blackwell Publishers, 2001.

Office of Special Investigations

The Office of Special Investigations (OSI), which operates within the U.S. Department of Justice, was established to uncover individuals involved in war crimes before and during World War II who might have slipped into the United States illegally or fraudulently. The OSI has helped deport nearly 100 former concentration-camp guards who worked for the Nazis since its inception. At the same time it has prevented 170 war-crimes suspects from entering the United States. It has also the responsibility for tracking down gold, jewelry, and money that the Nazis stole from victims of the Holocaust. Once a suspect is located, the OSI seeks to take appropriate legal action, which can entail exclusion, denaturalization, or deportation.

The OSI was formed in 1979 in response to reports that thousands of Nazi war criminals were living in the United States. Since then it has conducted hundreds of investigations and filed complaints against more than 70 Nazi war criminals, most of whom were Lithuanian, Latvian, or Ukrainian nationals who had collaborated with the Nazis. These criminals fall into several categories: Some were responsible for giving the orders for atrocities, while others were members of local police or administrators who carried out executions of Jews and others singled out for persecution. Additional cases involve individuals who had spread racist and inflammatory propaganda as well as German scientists who participated in unethical MEDICAL EXPERIMENTS on concentration-camp inmates. The OSI has pursued several important cases, including those of Andrija Artuković, minister of the interior of Croatia; Feodor Federenko, a Ukrainian guard at the Treblinka death camp; JOHN DEMJANJUK, the Ukrainian operator of the gas chambers at Treblinka; Valerian Trifa, leader of an Iron Guard (fascist) student group in Romania; and Arthur Rudolph, a Nazi rocket scientist involved in slave labor at the Dora-Mittelbau camp. Several of these men were expelled from the United States. The OSI also undertook the investigation of two special cases at the request of the U.S. government: KLAUS BARBIE, "the Butcher of Lyon," and the notorious Dr. JOSEF MENGELE.

In addition to tracking down war criminals, the OSI has also sponsored research on fascist movements in Eastern Europe and the role played by local collaborators in Nazi war crimes. The OSI has come in for criticism, especially from European émigré groups who have protested against the use of newly opened Soviet archives to investigate cases, contending that the evidence is tainted and that the individuals named were targeted not because they were Nazis but because they were anticommunists. Critics also say that the OSI has concentrated too much on lower-level war criminals.

In recent years the OSI's workload has increased because of new information about suspects that has been disclosed by the opening of archives in the former Soviet Union and East-bloc countries. In 2005 its mandate was shifted to take into account the reality that fewer Nazi war criminals still remained alive to hunt down. As a result of legislation overhauling U.S. intelligence agencies, the OSI has been given a new mission to locate and prosecute individuals suspected of war crimes in current conflicts around the world, including the Balkans, Rwanda, and Cambodia, many of whom have come to the United States masquerading as REFUGEES. "For the first time since Nuremberg, the world is really getting serious about these kinds of cases," said Eli M. Rosenbaum, head of the OSI, when the changes were announced.

The new mission, included as part of the broad intelligence restructuring package recently passed by Congress and signed by President Bush, has Justice officials scrambling to assemble an operating plan and proposed budget for the tiny office. Currently, the OSI has 28 employees and $5 million in annual expenses. The expansion of the office was a reflection of growing worldwide concern over the fate of suspected war criminals from the Balkans, Cambodia, and elsewhere, many of whom have escaped prosecution by blending in with immigrant populations in the United States.

The passage of time would seem to argue for the abolition of the OSI, as more and more suspected Nazi war criminals die of old age. Nonetheless, the OSI's longtime director, Eli M. Rosenbaum, told an interviewer in 2009 that he does not intend to give up. "There is still time to bring some of these people to justice, and we ought not fail to do that." Moreover, the Office's role has been expanded as a result of a 2004 law that allows it to investigate contemporary war criminals. The OSI's principal mission remains identifying war-crimes suspects living in the United States; if they are located, they are prosecuted under immigration law and deported. Rosenbaum believes that as of 2009 there were about 30 people in the United States who may have a Nazi past and possibly 80 individuals linked to more recent war crimes. In the last few years, the OSI devoted about half of its time to John Demjanjuk, who, after years of litigation, was deported to Germany. (He went on trial in late 2009 in Munich.) In its pursuit of modern war criminals, the OSI has had to take a new approach; instead of relying on documentation, as it customarily did in the case of suspected Nazi war criminals, it is now much more dependent on witnesses' testimony to bring cases.

In November 2010 the *New York Times* revealed sensational details of a 600-page report describing the successes and failures of the OSI in handling Nazi cases over the three decades of its existence. The U.S. Justice Department had tried to keep the report secret for four years and only released it (and then in a redacted version) because of a law suit brought under the Freedom of Information Act. (The *Times*, however, obtained a complete copy.) The Justice Department maintains that the report was incomplete and contained factual errors, although it declined to say just what those errors were. According to the report, in many instances the U.S. government actively helped Nazi war criminals resettle in the United States. The rationale was that these criminals had valuable intelligence useful in the struggle against the Soviet Union. "America, which prided itself on being a safe haven for the persecuted, became—in some small measure—a safe haven for persecutors as well," the report said, noting, however, that the actual number of war criminals admitted to the United States was lower than the 10,000 figure sometimes cited by government officials. (Since the OSI's founding in 1979, about 300 Nazi war criminals have been deported from the United States, stripped of citizenship or barred from entry.) Otto Von Bolschwing was one of the more notorious Nazis to have found refuge in the United States, thanks to the cooperation of the CIA. An associate of ADOLF EICHMANN, he was involved in the initial planning "to purge Germany of the Jews." The Justice Department belatedly sought to deport him in 1981 once it learned of his past, but he died before the legal proceedings could be completed. Another case cited in the report involved Arthur L. Rudolph, a Nazi scientist, brought to the United States because of his knowledge of rocket manufacturing. Rudolph had run a munitions factory for Nazi Germany that relied on slave labor. Some U.S. intelligence officials objected when the Justice Department tried to deport him in 1983. On the other hand, the Justice Department sometimes went to considerable lengths to conceal the identities of Nazi war criminals hiding in the United States.

The report also disclosed that Switzerland had bought gold from the Nazis pilfered from Jewish victims of the Holocaust. Among the more grisly details disclosed in the report was a reference to a piece of scalp apparently belonging to the notorious Nazi doctor Josef Mengele that was kept in the desk of an OSI manager in the hope that DNA extracted from it could help establish his identity if he were ever found, alive or dead. The report indicated that the piece of scalp did in fact turn out to be a critical piece of evidence in establishing that remains found in Brazil were those of Mengele, who was believed to have died in or about 1979.

Further Reading:
Office of Special Investigations. Available online. URL: http://www.justice.gov/criminal/osi/. Accessed March 20, 2010.

Okawa Shumei (1886–1957) *Japanese militarist*
Okawa Shumei, a staunch nationalist, political theorist, and propagandist, was indicted by the International Military Tribunal for the Far East (better known as the TOKYO TRIALS) for war crimes. An ultranationalist who had served as chief of the East Asian Economic Survey Bureau, he was actively involved in two rightist coups in 1931, and in 1932 he was imprisoned for the assassination of Premier Tsuyoshi Inukai. Okawa advocated a political philosophy known as "Asia for the Asians," which had a great deal of influence on the Kodoha, or "Imperial Way Faction," a right-wing association of mostly junior Imperial Army officers who saw Western influences as poisonous, opposed the dominance of the government by political powers, and sought to "restore" the emperor as an absolute ruler, with the army serving as the protector of Japanese values. The Kodoha movement was dismantled after a failed coup in 1936, but by then its ideas had gained currency in higher echelons of the government, and many of its adherents had acquired positions of power. The rightists who decided to carry out the war against the Allies were putting into practice policies that Okawa had espoused. Though he was not involved in the war itself, he was implicated for his role in inflaming the Japanese against the Allies and promoting a war to establish Japanese hegemony in Asia.

On the first day of his trial, at the reading of the indictments, Okawa went mad and began to beat the head of codefendant HIDEKI TOJO, the former prime minister. All charges against him were dropped, and he was committed to a psychiatric hospital, never to be tried. He was discharged in 1948 and died nine years later.

Olivera Castillo, Jorge (1961–) *Cuban dissident*
Jorge Olivera Castillo, head of an independent Havana news agency, is a well-known political dissident in Cuba who has

been imprisoned for his activities on behalf of greater freedom. He was among 76 noted dissidents arrested in March 2003 and sentenced to several years imprisonment. However, he was released in late 2004 after serving about 20 months of his sentence. Olivera Castillo was accused of maintaining links with subversive press groups from 1991 on, particularly with Radio Martí, a U.S.-based radio outlet broadcasting in Cuba, as well as for having "an illegal email account." In addition, he was charged with possession of a typewriter and a Super-8 video camera that he had reportedly received from U.S. diplomats to help him with his work.

Born in 1961, Olivera Castillo was the director and editor of the independent, non-state-controlled news agency Habana Press. Previously he had worked for the state-controlled Cuban Institute of Radio and Television before being fired in 1992 for reportedly collaborating with dissident movements. Accustomed to being harassed and arrested for his political activities, he was detained for trying to escape from Cuba on a raft and at one point was evicted from his house by a neighborhood vigilante group and forced to sleep on park benches. He was held under house arrest in 1999 and denounced by name by Fidel Castro (also in 1999) as a threat to the security of the forthcoming Ibero-American Summit in Havana.

In the six years since his release, Olivera Castillo has lived under surveillance, according to PEN, the international writers' organization, and he and his family have been barred from leaving Havana. However, these restrictions have not prevented him from continuing to write poetry and short stories.

See also CUBA, HUMAN RIGHTS VIOLATIONS IN.

Omar, Mullah   *See* MULLAH OMAR.

Operation Condor

Operation Condor was a clandestine campaign of terror in the mid-1970s supported by an alliance of rightist regimes in six Southern Cone nations: Argentina, Bolivia, Brazil, Chile, Paraguay, and Uruguay. Spearheaded by President AUGUSTO PINOCHET, who had seized power in Chile in 1973, and launched that same year, it principally targeted leftist insurgents and political dissidents. In a period of seven years, under the pretext of keeping communism at bay, agents working for Operation Condor are believed to have killed between 15,000 and 30,000 people considered as subversive. In fact, the operation was designed to maintain several dictatorships in power.

On one level—Phase I—Condor was set up to carry out abductions, DISAPPEARANCES, interrogations, and TORTURE; on another level—Phase II—it was designed to facilitate mutual cooperation among military intelligence

services, which involved the coordination of political surveillance and exchange of information across borders. But its most clandestine activities—Phase III—were intended to crush prominent political dissidents in exile who might have the capacity to mobilize opposition against the military regimes. To carry this out, special commando teams were formed and sent on missions in South America, Europe, and the United States. In 1976 the CIA reported that it had received information that Condor intended to undertake "executive action" outside of the Southern Cone. That same year, on September 21, agents of Condor brazenly carried out the assassination of former Chilean ambassador and Pinochet opponent Orlando Letelier and his aide in the heart of Washington, D.C. The killings were perpetrated by a U.S. expatriate with ties to the Chilean intelligence agency DINA (NATIONAL INTELLIGENCE DIRECTORATE) acting under orders of the spymaster MANUEL CONTRERAS. Condor assassins also targeted then-New York congressman Ed Koch (later New York's mayor), though the plot was never carried out. Condor was responsible for the slayings of Chilean Christian Democrat leader Bernardo Leighton and his wife in Rome and General Carlos Prats, former commander in chief of the Chilean army, in Buenos Aires. Other victims of Condor included the ex-president of Bolivia, Juan José Torres, and two Uruguayan legislators known for their opposition to the military regime in their country.

Operation Condor is noteworthy not only because of its clandestine nature and its violent excesses, but because it embraced a transnational ideology that trumped sovereignty. Many of those who championed Condor believed that they were engaged in a Third World War and that any means was permitted to defeat the enemy. Leftists were not the only victims: Labor activists and peasant leaders, priests and nuns, intellectuals, journalists, students, and teachers also fell afoul of the military juntas. Substantial evidence has emerged from declassified documents that the United States supported Condor as a legitimate counterterror organization and that the CIA worked closely with some of the security forces involved in its operation. The former chief of staff of Paraguay's armed forces claimed that the United States had made an arrangement with South American intelligence chiefs involved in Condor to "keep in touch with one another through a U.S. communications installation in the Panama Canal Zone which covers all of Latin America," to allow them "to co-ordinate intelligence information among the southern cone countries."

Operation Condor eventually collapsed in the late 1970s as a result of internal tensions. Moreover, the dictatorships that had backed it had begun to crumble, and by the early 1990s none of the participating governments were still in power. But it took some time before the world learned about Operation Condor and longer still before at least some of the perpetrators of the crimes committed on behalf of Condor were brought to justice. Condor first came to light in December 1992 when a Paraguayan judge uncovered what was named a "terror archive"—dossiers on hundreds, perhaps thousands of men and women who had been abducted, tortured, and killed by the security forces of the six member states. Some of these archives have been used to prosecute the offenders. In September 2009 a Chilean judge issued arrest warrants for 129 former security officials who were accused of killings of political opponents and other human rights violations during the Pinochet reign from 1973 to 1990. The warrants came after nearly a decade of investigations by Chilean judges into Operation Condor and other secret operations. Not all of those indicted were top officials or high-ranking officers; some were chauffeurs. The operations involved surreptitious collaboration between Chilean secret police and secret police services in Argentina, Uruguay, and Paraguay that were undertaken to identify leftists, track them down, and kidnap, torture, and disappear them. In a number of cases, the secret security services were directly involved in assassinations of dissidents in Latin America, Europe, and even the United States.

See also ARGENTINA, HUMAN RIGHTS VIOLATIONS IN; BOLIVIA, HUMAN RIGHTS VIOLATIONS IN; BRAZIL, HUMAN RIGHTS VIOLATIONS IN; CHILE, HUMAN RIGHTS VIOLATIONS IN; URUGUAY, HUMAN RIGHTS VIOLATIONS IN.

Further Reading:
Constable, Pamela. *A Nation of Enemies: Chile under Pinochet.* New York: W. W. Norton & Company, 1993.
Crimes of War Project. Operation Condor: Deciphering the US Role. (July 6, 2001). Available online. URL: http://www.crimesofwar.org/special/condor.html. Accessed March 20, 2010.
Davis, William Columbus. *Warnings from the Far South: Democracy versus Dictatorship in Uruguay, Argentina, and Chile.* New York: Praeger Publishers, 1995.
Dinges, John. *The Condor Years: How Pinochet and His Allies Brought Terrorism to Three Continents.* New York: New Press, 2004.
Dorfman, Ariel. *Exorcising Terror: The Incredible Unending Trial of Augusto Pinochet.* New York: Seven Stories Press, 2002.
Kornbluh, Peter. *The Pinochet File: A Declassified Dossier on Atrocity and Accountability.* A National Security Archive Book. New York: New Press, 2003.
Politzer, Patricia, and Diane Wachtel. *Fear in Chile: Lives under Pinochet.* New York: New Press, 2001.

Oradour, massacre in

Oradour-sur-Glane was the site of the worst atrocity that occurred on French soil in World War II. In early June 1944 an order was issued to the OKW (High Command of the Armed Forces of Germany) to the effect that henceforth active members of the French Resistance were to be treated as guerrillas who represented a "danger to the rear of our fighting troops." The danger was not exaggerated. In the town of Tulle in southern Normandy, the 2nd Waffen-SS Division *Das Reich* found 62 mutilated bodies of German soldiers who had surrendered to the Resistance. In reprisal, the SS, with the aid of the local prefect and the mayor, rounded up all the males in town. Twenty-one were released because of their youth; the remaining 99 were hanged. Then reports reached the German High Command that a German general had been captured by armed citizens in the town of Oradour who were threatening to burn him in public. The SS occupied the town on June 10—four days after D-Day—and rounded up the population. The men were separated from the women and children, locked in garages and barns, and shot. The women and children were imprisoned in a church that was burned to the ground; all but two women died in the blaze. There is some dispute whether the SS deliberately set the church afire or whether fires burning in neighboring houses spread to that building. (According to some accounts, the Resistance maintained an arsenal in the belfry, which exploded.)

The death toll from the massacre was compiled only after the war. It is estimated that 393 residents of the town, 167 people from the surrounding countryside, 33 people from Limoges, and 55 from other areas were killed during this rampage. The German casualty rate was far lower: one SS member killed, one SS wounded.

No official action was taken by the German authorities against the atrocities' perpetrators, who were judged to be guilty of no more than an "excess of zeal," while the dead were officially classified as the "enemy." In early 1953 a trial was held in Bordeaux to prosecute some of the individuals involved in the massacres. Most of those accused were Alsatian French. Because Alsace had a large German population—Alsace had been under German control at various point in history—and is the most Protestant province in France, the case had stirred a good deal of unease. Anxious to avoid antagonizing a region that the government hoped to reintegrate into France, the judges handed down relatively light sentences to the defendants. Moreover, many of the accused had served with the French colonial forces fighting in Indochina, and so there was little motivation to call them into account for the atrocities in either Oradour or Tulle. By 1958 those defendants who had been sentenced to prison were freed. Then General Charles de Gaulle (who would later become president) ordered a 100-year embargo on all files relating to the massacres. With improving relations between France and Germany, neither government had any wish to reopen the case.

Further Reading:
Browder, George C. *Hitler's Enforcers: The Gestapo and the SS Security Service in the Nazi Revolution.* Oxford: Oxford University Press, 1996.

Hohne, Heinz Zollen. *The Order of the Death's Head: The Story of Hitler's SS.* Classic Military History. New York: Penguin, 2001.

Organization for Security and Cooperation in Europe (OSCE)

The Organization for Security and Cooperation in Europe (OSCE) is the largest regional security organization in the world. It evolved from the Conference on Security and Cooperation in Europe, which resulted in the Final Act, a politically binding accord (though not a formal treaty), signed in Helsinki, Finland, in 1975 by the European nations (except Albania), Turkey, the United States, Canada, and the Soviet Union. In its earlier incarnation as the Conference on Security and Cooperation in Europe (CSCE), it served as a forum for a series of meetings and conferences to expand and review the commitments of participants in carrying out the HELSINKI ACCORDS. But with the end of the cold war in 1990, the organization began to play a greater role in shaping Europe. Henceforth the CSCE—and later the OSCE—would acquire permanent institutions and operational capabilities.

The OSCE is a cooperative body in which all 55 participating nations (based in Europe, North America, and central Asia) have equal rights. Its major focus is the maintenance of security in all its aspects: political, military, humanitarian, economic, and environmental. In fulfilling its mandate, the OSCE specializes in conflict resolution and crisis management, which requires it to deal with a wide range of issues, including arms control; confidence and security building; and policing, disarmament, counter-terrorism, and economic and environmental activities. Decisions are reached by consensus but are not politically binding on members. Several treaties have come into force in recent years that seek to ensure security on the continent: the Treaty on Conventional Armed Forces in Europe (CFE), the Treaty on Open Skies, and the Document on Small Arms and Light Weapons. The OSCE is headquartered in Vienna, Austria, with regional offices in Copenhagen, Geneva, The Hague, Prague, and Warsaw.

Organization of American States (OAS)

The Organization of American States (OAS) is made up of 34 nations in the Western Hemisphere with democratically elected governments. The organization was founded in 1948 by 21 nations whose representatives signed the OAS Charter, which set out common goals while affirming each nation's sovereignty. The concept of the OAS actually dates back much further: The great Latin American liberator Simón Bolívar conceived of just such a hemispheric alliance "united in heart" in the 1820s. In the 1890s several

nations in the region formed the Commercial Bureau of American Republics, which evolved into the Pan American Union, the precursor of the OAS. The Pan American Union subsequently expanded to include nations of the English-speaking Caribbean and Canada.

The formation of the OAS was accompanied by the adoption of the American Declaration of the Rights and Duties of Man, the first international statement of its kind. This declaration was based on the principle that individuals have certain essential rights that are derived not from their nationality or place of residence but rather from their very status as human beings. The OAS Charter begins the main body of the text with a ringing affirmation: "All men are born free and equal, in dignity and in rights, and, being endowed by nature with reason and conscience, they should conduct themselves as brothers one to another." But with rights come duties: "The fulfillment of duty by each individual is a prerequisite to the rights of all. Rights and duties are interrelated in every social and political activity of man. While rights exalt individual liberty, duties express the dignity of that liberty." Among the duties the Declaration cites are "duties of a juridical nature" that "presuppose others of a moral nature which support them in principle and constitute their basis."

The OAS defines its mission in the Inter-American Democratic Charter, adopted in 2002: "The peoples of the Americas have a right to democracy and their governments have an obligation to promote and defend it." The OAS seeks to promote democracy and good governance, strengthen human rights, foster peace and security, and expand trade. In addition, the OAS tries to encourage decentralization of governments, modernization of political parties, and the increasing role of civic society; and it seeks to ensure peace and security in the region. In this role it is committed to combating terrorism and resolving territorial disputes between members. Regional peace is seen as inseparable from the issue of human rights. The Declaration on Security in the Americas, issued in 2001, states: "Peace is a value and a principle in itself, based on democracy, justice, respect for human rights, solidarity, security, and respect for international law."

The OAS has established two principal mechanisms to address human rights: the Inter-American Commission on Human Rights, based in Washington, D.C., and the INTER-AMERICAN COURT OF HUMAN RIGHTS, located in San José, Costa Rica. Individuals who believe they are unable to find justice for human rights violations in their own countries have the right to appeal to the Inter-American Commission, which can recommend to the member state involved ways to redress the problem. The commission can also recommend that the case be heard by the Inter-American Court for a binding decision, but only if the member state accepts its jurisdiction. The commission also dispatches representatives to make on-site visits to analyze and report on human rights conditions, but they must be invited by the state. In June 2009 foreign ministers meeting in HONDURAS voted to lift CUBA's suspension from the organization, a move that became possible after President Barack Obama indicated that the United States would not oppose Cuba's regaining its membership. But a month later, in an ironic twist, the OAS suspended Honduras after the military launched a coup and toppled President Manuel Zelaya, the first time that the OAS had suspended any country since Cuba in 1962.

Further Reading:

Fawcett, Louise, and Andrew Hurrell, eds. *Regionalism in World Politics: Regional Organization and International Order.* Oxford: Oxford University Press, 1996.

Guillermoprieto, Alma. *Looking for History: Dispatches from Latin America.* New York: Vintage, 2002.

Organization of American States. Available online. URL: http://www.oas.org/en/default.asp. Accessed March 20, 2010.

Skidmore, Thomas F., and Peter H. Smith. *Modern Latin America.* Oxford: Oxford University Press, 2000.

Williamson, Edwin. *The Penguin History of Latin America.* New York: Penguin Books, 1993.

Oxfam

Oxfam is a nongovernmental organization dedicated to tackling problems associated with poverty and providing famine relief to devastated regions of the developing world. Oxfam began life during the Second World War to deal with the famine in Nazi-occupied Greece that resulted from an Allied blockade. Several famine-relief committees sprang up in Britain to persuade the government there to allow essential supplies to reach the civilian population. One of these committees, the Oxford Committee for Famine Relief, met for the first time on October 5, 1942. Among its founders were Canon T. R. Milford of the University Church and Gilbert Murray, a former professor of Greek at Oxford University. Unlike other famine committees that dissolved after the war, the Oxford Committee expanded its mandate to include "the relief of suffering in consequence of the war." The committee worked to bring food and clothing to Europeans recovering from the war and then, in 1949, expanded its activities to provide "the relief of suffering arising as a result of wars or of other causes in any part of the world." The Oxford Committee became formally known as Oxfam in 1965.

Oxfam sought to portray the peoples in the developing world as human beings, not faceless abstractions, and to educate the peoples of the developed world about the root causes of poverty. In Oxfam's view, the globe had sufficient resources to ensure adequate food and shelter for the worldwide population; what was lacking was political will to get them where they were most needed. In the 1960s Oxfam initiated several self-help programs to encourage Third World communities to improve their water, farming practices, and health care. Oxfam has also tried to prod governments and international bodies to respond to problems of trade imbalances, hunger, and endemic poverty. To raise funds, Oxfam relies on donors and some 22,000 volunteers in the United Kingdom who sell donated items and handicrafts from overseas. In the 1980s Oxfam concentrated most of its relief efforts on the Horn of Africa, devoting half of its budget to relief of the famine that was then laying waste to the region.

With a growth in income from donations, Oxfam has been able to dedicate its resources to "policy, research, and campaigning work to address the structural causes of poverty in the South, such as crippling debt burdens, unfair terms of trade, and inappropriate agriculture policies." Oxfam has been involved in providing emergency humanitarian aid to parts of the former Soviet Union and the former Yugoslavia, but its largest response to a humanitarian disaster to date has been in the Great Lakes region of central Africa (which encompasses eastern Zaire, Burundi, and Rwanda) in the mid-1990s. Oxfam recognized, though, that merely offering aid could only do so much given the political, economic, and social problems that ignited the crisis. For this reason the organization mounted an international lobbying campaign meant to galvanize the United Nations, the Organization of African Unity, and powerful governments into taking concerted action to bring peace to the region.

Further Reading:

Aall, Pamela R., Daniel Miltenberger, and George Weiss. *IGOs, NGOs, and the Military in Peace and Relief Operations.* Washington, D.C.: United States Institute of Peace Press, 2000.

Byman, Daniel, Ian Lesser, Bruce Pirnie, Cheryl Benard, and Matthew Waxman. *Strengthening the Partnership: Improving Military Coordination with Relief Agencies and Allies in Humanitarian Operations.* Santa Monica, Calif.: Rand Corporation (NBN), 2000.

Erskins, Toni. *Can Institutions Have Responsibilities: Collective Moral Agency and International Relations.* Global Issues Series. Sydney, Australia: Palgrave Macmillan, 2004.

Oxfam. Available online. URL: http://www.oxfam.org/. Accessed March 20, 2010.

Rieff, David. *A Bed for the Night: Humanitarianism in Crisis.* New York: Simon & Schuster, 2002.

Vaux, Anthony. *The Selfish Altruist: Relief Work in Famine and War.* London: Earthscan Publications, 2001.

P

★

Padilla, Jose (1972–) *American al-Qaeda supporter*
Jose Padilla, an American citizen, came to international attention when he was arrested on May 8, 2002, at Chicago's O'Hare Airport on suspicion that he had plotted to detonate a "dirty bomb" (one that could spread radiation) and use natural gas to blow up apartment buildings in Washington, D.C., New York, and Florida. (No bomb or bomb-making components were found in his possession at the time of his arrest.) The U.S. government declared him to be an "enemy combatant" and had him transferred from civilian to military custody. He was held incommunicado in a South Carolina military brig without access to a lawyer from June 2002 until March 2004, when the Justice Department bowed to outside pressure and allowed a lawyer to see him.

The United States viewed Padilla as an enemy combatant taken in the war on terrorism that was launched in response to the September 11, 2001, attacks by AL-QAEDA; as such, the Bush administration contended that he was not entitled to the constitutional protections accorded to other American citizens charged with a crime. In fact, Padilla was not formally charged with any crime at all. Specifically, the government contended that Padilla was "closely associated with al-Qaeda"; that he had engaged in "war-like acts, including conduct in preparation for acts of international terrorism"; that he had intelligence that could help the United States prevent future terrorist attacks; and that he was a continuing threat to U.S. security. Nonetheless, the government did not allege that Padilla was actually a member of al-Qaeda. According to a Justice Department report issued spring 2004, Padilla had admitted that he had attended al-Qaeda training camps where the plot to blow up apartment buildings was discussed. Because no lawyer was permitted to represent Padilla during his interrogation, any evidence gained at that time would not have been admissible in court. Nor was Padilla in a position to challenge an indictment since there was none.

In its report, the Justice Department stated that Padilla had not been mistreated but refused to confirm that the interrogation had complied with the Geneva Convention. There was no means to determine what had transpired during the interrogations since his appointed lawyer was under a gag order. A footnote in the report did shed some light on Padilla's defense: He contended that while he was in an al-Qaeda camp he had never sworn allegiance to the group and any talk of a plot was only a pretext so that he could leave Afghanistan and avoid having to fight.

The case began to make its way through the federal justice system. A panel of the second U.S. Circuit Court of Appeals issued a 2-1 ruling barring the president from declaring a U.S. citizen an "enemy combatant" without congressional authorization. The court ordered Padilla freed from military custody in 30 days, leaving open the option that he could be held pending a criminal trial in civilian courts. The Justice Department appealed, and the case—*Padilla v. Rumsfeld*—was argued before the U.S. Supreme Court. On June 28, 2004, the High Court ruled on narrow technical grounds that the Padilla case should be heard in a federal court in South Carolina rather than by a federal court in New York, where the suit had originally been filed. In its decision the court also said that Padilla had improperly named Secretary of Defense Donald Rumsfeld as the respondent, instead of the warden of the military brig where Padilla was held. On the same day the Supreme Court ruled more emphatically in a case related to another U.S. citizen, YASER ESAM HAMDI, who, unlike Padilla, had been captured in Afghanistan.

Padilla's case came before the federal district court in South Carolina in early 2005. Although the decision was technical and did not rule on the merits of the case, many legal observers believed that it left the government with the choice of either charging him or freeing him. In March 2005 a federal district judge in South Carolina ruled that the government should release Padilla from the military brig where he was being held within 45 days, saying that the Bush administration was not entitled to detain an American citizen for three years without bringing charges. In his opinion Judge Henry Floyd wrote, "The court finds that the president has no power, neither express nor implied, neither constitutional nor statutory, to hold petitioner as an enemy combatant." In September 2005 a Federal Circuit Court overturned an earlier decision by a U.S. District Court judge in South Carolina, where Mr. Padilla was imprisoned, in favor of the Bush administration. In the South Carolina decision, the judge held that the president had no authority to detain an American citizen arrested in the United States as an enemy combatant. The District Court ruled that Padilla must be treated no differently from any criminal suspect even if he was an al-Qaeda terrorist. The Fourth Circuit Court, however, maintained that since Congress had authorized the use of force against al-Qaeda, and since the Supreme Court had approved Congress's action, the Bush administration did have the authority to detain or to kill the enemy. Although it had not been proven in court that Padilla wa, in fact, a terrorist the Federal Court ruled that his detention was legal. The ruling was appealed to the Supreme Court. In late 2005 the Bush administration moved to transfer Padilla for trial in a civilian court without waiving its right to charge him again as an unlawful combatant. After being tried in the U.S. District Court for the Southern District of Florida, Padilla was found guilty of having conspired to kill people in a jihad in Afghanistan and of funding and supporting overseas terrorism. He was, not, however, convicted of trying to build a "dirty bomb," which was one of the accusations made against him at the time of his arrest. He was sentenced on January 22, 2008, to 17 years and four months in prison.

Further Reading:

Danner, Mark. *Torture and Truth: America, Abu Ghraib, and the War on Terror.* New York: New York Review Books, 2004.

Hersh, Seymour M. *Chain of Command: The Road from 9/11 to Abu Ghraib.* New York: HarperCollins, 2004.

Human Rights First. In the Courts Jose Padilla, US Citizen. Available online. URL: http://www.humanrights first.org/us_law/inthecourts/supreme_court_padilla. aspx. Accessed March 20, 2010.

Pakistan, human rights violations in

The political turmoil that has engulfed Pakistan in recent years has only made the human rights situation worse. Pakistan has been buffeted by a relentless succession of terrorist attacks by a variety of Islamic militant groups that have taken hundreds of lives in Lahore, Peshawar, Islamabad,

and Karachi. In addition to elements of AL-QAEDA and TALIBAN that have taken refuge in Pakistan following the U.S. invasion of Afghanistan in 2001, there are several other Islamic groups that share a similarly radical Islamic ideology. Many of these groups have remained hidden for years in the lawless North West Frontier Province, which has never been effectively controlled by the central government. The main power base of the Afghan Taliban under MULLAH OMAR appears to function with relative impunity out of Quetta (it is called the Quetta Shura), underscoring the ambivalent attitude toward many of these Islamic militant groups on the part of the military and Directorate for Inter-Services Intelligence (ISI), which continues to regard India as the principal enemy. Several militant groups that have waged a guerrilla campaign to wrest KASHMIR from Indian control still appear to enjoy at least covert support from some elements in the military and intelligence. These groups have all committed serious human rights abuses, including direct attacks on civilians, abduction, and hostage-taking, torture, and killings. Women and girls are frequently victims of militants, especially if they are perceived as violating strict Islamic law. There is also an ongoing insurgency seeking autonomy or independence in the province of Balochistan that shows no signs of being adequately addressed by Islamabad. The government of President Asif Ali Zardari, who took the reins of power in September 2008, is widely considered ineffectual, and many experts believe that real power resides in the military. Zardari, the widower of the former president Benazir Bhutto, who was assassinated in Karachi in 2007, could only run for office after corruption cases were dropped under terms of an amnesty in the same year. Known as "Mr. Ten Percent" for the commissions he was alleged to have taken on various business projects, Zardari is one of the country's richest men, with an estimated wealth approaching 1 billion dollars. At the end of 2009 the Pakistani Supreme Court declared that the amnesty was illegal, which could potentially put thousands of officials at risk of indictment, including Zardari. There was no immediate prospect that Zardari would be ousted, because his office guaranteed him immunity from prosecution, but the Supreme Court was said to be looking into the possibility that he might not have been eligible to run for office to begin with.

In the last few years, arbitrary detention, torture, deaths in custody, forced disappearances, and extrajudicial execution have become more rampant, according to AMNESTY INTERNATIONAL. The government has proven incapable of protecting the human rights of individuals, particularly women, religious minorities, and children. Security agencies have detained many people on charges of being linked with "terrorist" organizations and denied them access to lawyers. Hundreds of people have been disappeared, especially in connection with the Balochistan insurgency;

the Supreme Court in 2009 agreed to resume hearings of disappearance cases (which were curtailed under the former ruler, President Musharif) in an attempt to hold accountable the security and intelligence agencies that might have abducted the missing individuals. These cases were hobbled by the government's continued intransigence in handing over any information. According to the Defence of Human Rights, a Pakistani organization that represents relatives of the disappeared, 195 cases out of 416 enforced disappearance cases filed in the Supreme Court since 2005 remained pending as of 2009. By any measure, the legal system is a mess. According to the Human Rights Commission of Pakistan, the number of pending cases had reached 1.6 million by August 2009. As a result, thousands of potentially innocent people languish in prisons because of long delays in rulings on bail hearings.

Pakistani authorities have also been criticized for their handling of antiterrorist operations, which have caused the displacement of about 2 million people from North West Frontier Province, the Swat Valley, and Waziristan. Unknown numbers of civilians have also been killed and injured in these operations. In mid-2009 the Pakistani army retook control of the Swat Valley, once a scenic tourist site, from Taliban militants after the breakdown of a peace accord between the government and militants. The government was criticized by human rights groups for failing to provide adequate shelter and humanitarian aid to the hundreds of thousands of refugees who were forcibly evacuated. Although many civilians expressed gratitude to be relieved of the heavy hand of Taliban rule, they had reason to fear the army too. In the months following the Taliban eviction, hundreds of bodies turned up. Human rights groups suspected that the military had carried out a series of extrajudicial executions of suspected Taliban militants or supporters, although it is likely many of the victims were innocent of association with any armed group. Victims have been found with signs of torture and with bullet wounds in their neck or head. A number of people have also disappeared. The Pakistani army insists that it had nothing to do with the killings. The exact number of victims may never be known. An attempt by the INTERNATIONAL COMMITTEE OF THE RED CROSS to conduct an investigation was thwarted by the government. Evidence of extrajudicial killings by Pakistani soldiers surfaced in October 2010 in a video recording, apparently taken by a cell phone, which showed them executing six men suspected of having ties with militants. Once the video began to circulate on the Internet, the Pakistani high command acknowledged its authenticity, and an investigation was ordered to identify the perpetrators and bring them to justice.

The increasing influence of Islamic militancy in the country has only heightened religious and ethnic tensions that were already present before the fall of the Afghan Tal-

iban in 2001. Violence regularly flares up between adherents of Shiite and Sunni factions, with hundreds of people having been attacked and killed. (Pakistan is predominantly Sunni.) Although Musharraf had made some efforts to quell the sectarian violence and rein in militant groups, HUMAN RIGHTS WATCH and other human rights advocates contend that his rule had been marked by a rise in extremist activity and an increase in religious killings, partly because he had marginalized mainstream political groups and stifled political dissent. Opposition leaders and legislators have been harassed, beaten, subjected to blackmail, and arrested. Nor is there any sign of political liberalization. In December 2004 police disrupted a rally held by the Pakistan People's Party (PPP), arresting hundreds, including several legislators. The president of another opposition party, the Alliance for the Restoration of Democracy, was sentenced to 23 years in prison for reading an anti-Musharraf letter to journalists. The former speaker of the National Assembly was jailed for 10 years on charges of corruption. Human rights groups have criticized the judiciary, which Human Rights Watch has characterized as "emasculated."

The country has become increasingly militarized, a trend benefiting religious parties that have traditionally enjoyed close relations with the army. On the other hand, women and religious minorities have suffered. The laws pertaining to rape and honor killings of women are weak or seldom enforced, creating a climate of impunity for the perpetrators. According to government figures, about 1,000 women are victims of honor killings every year, usually committed by members of their families. At the same time, penalties for violating blasphemy laws have been stiffened, resulting in long prison terms and even the imposition of death sentences for Muslims who have questioned a strict interpretation of the Quran.

According to Human Rights Watch, Pakistan's collaboration with the United States in pursuing al-Qaeda and other Islamic militants has been "exemplified by a disregard for DUE PROCESS," as demonstrated by the number of arbitrary arrests and detentions. Concerns about military actions have also been raised by the Human Rights Commission of Pakistan (HRCP), the country's most prominent human rights group, which has criticized the government's reliance on security forces to deal with social and civil conflicts. The group charged that, in addition, the private sector was falling under military control, with officers being appointed to head large and small businesses. Two tribal regions, South Waziristan and Balochistan, have experienced a much deeper involvement of the military than in the past. In spring 2004, for example, some 25,000 troops moved into South Waziristan, a region where 200,000 Afghans had taken refuge, as part of a campaign to root out al-Qaeda terrorists. In the course of counterterrorism operations, the army displaced some 25,000 refugees, forcing them back over the border. Some of the refugees were only given two hours notice to pack up and leave. The incursions also took the lives of tribes living in the area, which resulted in violent clashes. (Most of the troops were later withdrawn from the area.)

The military has also committed abuses in Punjab, the country's breadbasket, where army and paramilitary forces allied with the army have killed and tortured farmers who refuse to cede land rights to them. These forces have even resorted to torturing children of farmers and have suppressed a farmers' movement. Punjab is considered especially important to the army because it draws more recruits from the province than anywhere else. Because the military claims on farmland—the most fertile in the country—have virtually no legal basis, the army has undertaken a campaign of murder, arbitrary detention, and TORTURE to force farmers into submission. According to Human Rights Watch, on two occasions the army laid siege to villages, depriving their inhabitants of food and water. Most of the abuses have been attributed to the Pakistan Rangers, a paramilitary unit that has set up detention centers—known as "torture cells"—to hold farmers until they sign agreements giving up title to their land. Musharraf's efforts to burnish Pakistan's reputation in the eyes of the world suffered a grave setback in September 2005 while he was attending the world summit at the United Nations. In comments to the press, which he subsequently denied making, he dismissed complaints about persistent abuse and rape of women in his country. Claiming rape, he told a *Washington Post* correspondent, had become a "moneymaking concern"; he added, "A lot of people say if you want to go abroad and get a visa for Canada or citizenship and be a millionaire, get yourself raped." Predictably his comment caused outrage among women's groups and human rights organizations. Musharraf was reacting specifically to recent reports of two high-profile cases that had attracted worldwide notoriety: one involved Mukhtar Mai, who was allegedly gang-raped in 2002 on orders of a village council, and the other Shazia Khalid, a physician apparently attacked inside a government hospital quarters in Balochistan Province in 2005. In both cases the perpetrators received light sentences or were acquitted, or else were never apprehended at all. When Mai tried to go abroad to speak about the lack of rights for women in her country, Musharraf denied her permission (he later backed down under pressure from Washington), saying, "I don't want to project the bad image of Pakistan." Khalid, for her part, said that she was forced to leave Pakistan because of death threats. When a government-sponsored conference on "violence against women" then-president Musharraf decried nongovernmental organizations for participating and said that Pakistan should not be singled out since rape was a global problem.

See also AFGANISTAN, HUMAN RIGHTS VIOLATIONS IN; COLLECTIVE PUNISHMENT; RELIGIOUS PERSECUTION.

Further Reading:

Abbas, Hassan. *Pakistan's Drift into Extremism: Allah, the Army, and America's War on Terror.* Armonk, N.Y.: M. E. Sharpe, 2004.

Abou, Mariam, and Olivier Roy. *The Afghan-Pakistan Connection.* The CERI Series in Comparative Politics and International Studies. New York: Columbia University Press, 2007.

Amnesty International USA. *Pakistan Human Rights.* Available online. URL: http://www.amnestyusa.org/all-countries/pakistan/page.do?id=1011216. Accessed March 20, 2010.

Burke, Jason. *Al-Qaeda: Casting a Shadow of Terror.* London: I. B. Tauris, 2004.

———. *Al-Qaeda: The True Story of Radical Islam.* London: I. B. Tauris, 2004.

Gunaratna, Rohan. *Inside al-Qaeda: Global Network of Terror.* New York: Berkley Publishing Group, 2003.

Haqqani, Husain. *Pakistan: Between Mosque and Military.* Washington, D.C.: Carnegie Endowment for International Peace, 2005.

Human Rights Commission of Pakistan. Available online. URL: http://www.hrcp-web.org/default.asp. Accessed March 20, 2010.

Human Rights Watch. Human Rights in Pakistan. Available online. URL: http://www.hrw.org/asia/pakistan. Accessed March 20, 2010.

Hussain, Zahid. *Frontline Pakistan: The Struggle with Militant Islam.* New York: Columbia University Press, 2008.

Weaver, Mary Anne. *Pakistan: In the Shadow of Jihad and Afghanistan.* New York: Farrar, Straus & Giroux, 2003.

Zayyat, Montasser al-. *The Road to Al-Qaeda: The Story of bin Laden's Right-Hand Man.* Critical Studies on Islam. Translated by Ahmed Fekry. Edited by Sara Nimis. Ann Arbor, Mich.: Pluto Press, 2004.

Ziring, Lawrence. *Pakistan: At the Crosscurrent of History.* Oneworld Beginners' Guides. Oxford, U.K.: Oneworld Publications, 2005.

Palestine, human rights violations in

Palestine entered a new era with the death of Yasser Arafat, longtime leader of the Palestinians, in 2004. He was succeeded in early 2005 by Mahmoud Abbas (known also by the nom de guerre Abu Mazen). Within months of his assuming power, talks began between Abbas and the Israeli prime minister Ariel Sharon. But subsequent attempts to negotiate a two-state settlement reached a virtual standstill four years after Abbas's election. Several factors have contributed to the impasse. Sharon was felled by a stroke that left him comatose. His successor, Ehud Olmert, was forced to step down amid allegations of corruption. While both men (members of the newly formed centrist Kadima Party) were open to a two-state solution, Benjamin Netanyahu of the rightist Likud Party, elected as prime minister in 2009 (for the second time), only grudgingly acknowledged the prospect of an independent Palestinian state. But the question remained: Which Palestinian state was he referring to? In 2007 the Islamic group Hamas seized control over the GAZA Strip, ousting the Fatah leadership, which was widely regarded as corrupt. As a result, Fatah could claim authority only over the occupied West Bank (and its writ extends only so far, because Israel enjoys almost complete control). By 2009, in spite of mediation efforts by Egypt and Saudi Arabia, Hamas and Fatah remained at loggerheads. Israel attempted to bolster Abbas's Palestinian Authority by easing some restrictions and facilitating the training of Palestinian security forces, an initiative aided by the United States. At the same time, Jerusalem has tried to drain support from Hamas by putting curbs on imports to Gaza apart from humanitarian aid (and even that has been restricted from time to time). Even concrete for much needed repairs is forbidden because it could possibly be used for military purposes. (The population mainly relies on tunnels between Gaza and Egypt for supplies and arms.) Hamas refused to recognize Israel's right to exist (unlike the Palestinian Authority), although it holds out the possibility of a long-term cessation of hostilities. (There are reported to be some differences in strategy toward Israel between Hamas officials in Gaza and Khaled Mashaal, the senior Hamas leader in exile in Damascus.) Since the Hamas takeover of Gaza, tensions have been rising between Gaza and Israel. Hamas and other militant groups routinely launched Qassam rockets into Israeli territory, putting at risk civilian populations. Hamas claimed that because of the virtual blockade that Israel had thrown up around Gaza, they were acting in self-defense. While most of these rockets were rudimentary, they caused a great disruption to Israeli communities within striking range as well as some fatalities. After Hamas declared the end of a six-month cease-fire and rocket attacks resumed, the Olmert government, then in its last months in power, responded by going to war. Although Israel announced that its objective was to stop the rocket attacks, most observers believed that its actual goal was to topple Hamas. The war began in December 2008 and ended with both sides declaring a unilateral cease-fire three weeks later. About 1,500 people were killed, the vast majority of them Palestinians; how many were civilians and how many were combatants was a subject of dispute. Israel pronounced the campaign a success, but its actions aroused an international outcry and a UN inquiry that found Israel and Hamas culpable of war crimes, a conclusion repudiated by both parties. Although the Hamas leadership survived the conflict, it sustained a serious blow. The war also represented a grave setback to

efforts by the U.S. to jump-start negotiations. And while Netanyahu announced that all new Jewish settlement building would cease on the West Bank (excluding ongoing construction and Jewish settlements in Jerusalem) the Palestinian Authority reacted coolly, adopting an all or nothing position. The Palestinians believed that the Israeli move was more of a gesture to the Obama administration, which had demanded an end to all settlement activity, which Washington viewed as an obstacle to concluding a peace, than as a serious commitment to ending the occupation.

Until Israel occupied the West Bank and Gaza in the Six-Day War of 1967, the West Bank had been part of Jordan and Gaza had been under the rule of Egypt. However, growing sentiment for an independent Palestinian state led to violent resistance that initially took the form of stone-throwing against Israeli forces. The first intifada (Arab for "uprising") began in 1987 and lasted until 1993; by the time it ended with the signing of the Oslo accords, which called for the creation of an independent Palestinian state, 1,162 Palestinians and 160 Israelis had been killed. The second and more violent intifada broke out in September 2000 and continued until the death of longtime Palestinian leader Yasser Arafat in 2005.

Throughout the four years of the intifada Palestinian militant groups maintained that any violence carried out against Israel was justified as a form of resistance to foreign occupation. This view received wide support from the Palestinian population. A number of militant organizations conducted suicide bombings and mortar attacks against Israeli civilians, with considerable loss of life. Three militant groups in particular—Hamas, Islamic Jihad, and the Al Aksa Brigades—took responsibility for most of these terrorist strikes. Israel retaliated by closing off West Bank cities and towns, invading refugee camps, and rounding up hundreds of young men suspected of links with the militants. In addition, Israel has used tactics that have been widely condemned by other governments and the United Nations, including targeted assassinations meant to decapitate the leadership of the militant groups. Israel has also engaged in practices such as demolishing the homes of families of suicide bombers—over 200 Palestinian homes in 2002 and 2003 alone—even in the absence of evidence that the families were aware of or supported the actions of the bombers. About 2,500 houses have been destroyed in this way, leaving more than 4,300 people homeless. The demolitions have been decried as COLLECTIVE PUNISHMENT, which is banned under INTERNATIONAL HUMANITARIAN LAW. In 2005 a special commission set up by the IDF concluded that demolitions should stop because they were only causing more resentment and doing little to deter future attacks.

American publications have documented that during the 2000–2004 period of the intifada, nearly 3,000 Palestinians were killed, 534 of them being children under 18.

According to the *Journal of Palestinian Studies,* 119 people alone were killed in an IDF attack on the West Bank city Nablus in April 2002, and 600 between 2000 and 2004. The U.S. government also estimates that in the IDF's "targeted killings" of known Palestinian terrorists, 47 innocent civilian bystanders also lost their lives. Attacks by the IDF in response to terrorist attacks have resulted in the injuries of some 40,000 Palestinians; at least 2,500 have been left with permanent disabilities. More than 300 schools have been destroyed; 30 of them were converted into military posts. The U.S. government reckons that there are over 5,000 prisoners held by Israel, although several hundred were released as a goodwill gesture in the weeks following Abbas's election.

Neutral sources such as the U.S. State Department make clear that during the Second Intifada, which began in 2000, the security forces of *both* sides—the Israeli Defense Forces and the Palestinian Authority—"committed numerous, serious human rights abuses." The violence had a profoundly disruptive effect on the Palestinian economy. The U.S. Agency for International Development (USAID) stated that up to 44 percent of Palestinian children were

A Palestinian throws a stone at an Israeli armored vehicle in the northern West Bank, 2006. *(Getty Images)*

anemic, and other sources found that 60 percent of the Palestinians were living below the poverty level (of $2-a-day income), with a 43 percent unemployment rate. In response to attacks by Palestinian militants, the Israelis have imposed serious restrictions on the movements of Palestinian civilians and have often carried out mass arbitrary arrests. Israel forces established over 700 checkpoints, most of which were located on the West Bank (occupied by Israel since the Six-Day War in 1967), and around 60 in Gaza. (The Sharon government announced that it intended to withdraw from Gaza and tear down settlements that have been home to about 8,000 Israeli settlers; this process began in August 2005.) To prevent the infiltration of suicide bombers, the Israeli government began a Security Wall, which is intended to separate Palestinian population centers from Israel. In an advisory opinion, the INTERNATIONAL COURT OF JUSTICE ruled in 2004 that the wall was illegal because its route would enclose large parcels of Palestinian-owned land on the Israeli side. Israel's Supreme Court has ordered the government to relocate segments of the wall to take into account some Palestinian claims. Although the wall appears to represent a unilaterally drawn border—which carves out a significant amount of the West Bank beyond the pre-1967 border known as the Green Line—the Israeli authorities insist that its purpose is only to safeguard its citizens and is not meant to be permanent.

Although Yasser Arafat routinely criticized terrorist strikes on Israeli civilians, there is little evidence that he took any steps to rein in the militants who carried out the attacks. Moreover, with over a dozen different security forces under the Palestinian Authority and other groups, such as Hamas, acting autonomously, Israel contended that the situation was close to anarchy and that it had no partner with whom to negotiate. In the four years of the Second Intifada, Palestinians became disenchanted with a state of continual war, which has also brought economic devastation, corruption, and an upsurge in crime. Signaling their readiness to try another course, the Palestinian electorate gave Abbas almost 60 percent of the vote after he had renounced violent resistance against Israel. Indeed, shortly after he met Sharon in a summit hosted by Egypt in February 2005, he pronounced the intifada to be over.

In fact, there has been no third intifada. Palestinian security forces have demonstrated that they can effectively maintain order. In spite of the anger that swept the West Bank over the Israeli incursion into Gaza, their presence put a break on any outbreak of violence. But tensions between Jewish settlers and their Arab neighbors run high. In December 2009 a mosque was vandalized, presumably by Jewish extremists. There have also been attacks on Palestinian villagers by settlers. Sporadic attacks by Palestinians on Israelis on the West Bank and within the 1967 borders (the so-called green line) have also taken place, but suicide bombings of the kind seen only three or four years earlier seldom occur. Israelis credit the drop in bombings to the security wall that they have been building between the two populations. However, Palestinians accuse the Israelis of using the wall to illegally confiscate their property, because the security wall intrudes into the Occupied Territories. According to UN Resolutions 242 and 338, Israeli occupation of the West Bank and East Jerusalem is illegal, which makes all settlement activity illegal. But neither the 1993 Oslo agreement between Israel and the Palestinians or the Road Map of 2003, put forward by the Bush administration, has brought any resolution to the land dispute. Although the International Court of Justice has ruled that the security wall (also known as a security fence) is illegal, Israel showed no indication that it would cease its construction. On assuming office President Obama announced that he was making a priority of getting a peace deal between the Israelis and Palestinians and named former senator George Mitchell as a special diplomat to mediate. While Mitchell had success in brokering the Good Friday Agreement, which brought peace to Northern Ireland, he was finding it much tougher going in the Middle East.

Further Reading:

Finkelstein, Norman G. *Image and Reality of the Israel-Palestine Conflict.* New York: W. W. Norton & Company, 2003.

Human Rights Watch. Palestine and the Occupied Territories. Available online. URL: http://www.hrw.org/middle-eastn-africa/israel-and-occupied-territories. Accessed March 20, 2010.

Palestinian Centre for Human Rights. Available online. URL: http://www.pchrgaza.org/portal/en/. Accessed March 20, 2010.

Palestinian Human Rights Monitoring Group. Available online. URL: http://www.phrmg.org/. Accessed March 20, 2010.

Roraback, Amanda. *Israel-Palestine in a Nutshell.* Santa Monica, Calif.: Enisen Publishing, 2004.

Said, Edward W. *The Question of Palestine.* New York: Vintage, 1992.

Smith, Charles D. *Palestine and the Arab-Israeli Conflict.* New York: Bedford/St. Martin's, 2004.

Papen, Franz von (1879–1969) *German diplomat*
As a former chancellor of Germany, Franz von Papen lent his prestige and support to the Nazis and helped them gain power. He was tried by the Allies after World War II and acquitted, though a German court subsequently convicted him as "a major offender" during the war. Unlike most Nazi officials, Papen could boast of an aristocratic lineage: He

was born into an old Westphalian noble family on October 19, 1879, the son of a wealthy landowner. Papen joined the German army before the outbreak of World War I and was sent to Washington to serve as a military attaché. He was expelled a year later for initiating an illegal arrangement with a company in Bridgeport, Connecticut, to produce armaments for Germany, a violation of the U.S. Neutrality Act. After the war he became a leading figure in the Catholic Center Party (BVP) and in 1921 was elected to the Reichstag (parliament). He gained further influence by purchasing a controlling share of the party newspaper, the *Germania*, which he tried to use—unsuccessfully—to impose his reactionary views on the BVP. He was named chancellor by President Paul von Hindenburg in 1932 but opposition to his ultraconservative policies forced his ouster within months. Still, during his brief tenure he managed to do the Nazis several favors, lifting the ban on the SA (Sturmabteilung), the Nazi security police, and ousting Prussia's Social Democratic government.

Once out of power, Papen looked to ADOLF HITLER to revive his political prospects. He used his connections with such industrialists as HJALMAR SCHACHT, Fritz Thyseen, and GUSTAV KRUPP and his son Arthur to convince Hindenburg to appoint Hitler as chancellor. The lobbying effort succeeded, and Hitler rewarded Papen by naming him vice chancellor. Papen assured Hindenburg that he would temper Hitler's more extremist policies, a promise that he could not possibly have kept even if he were sincere. Papen later served Hitler as ambassador to Austria, a position he held from 1934 to 1939. As ambassador, he was involved in plans to implement the Anschluss—the union of Germany and Austria under Nazi rule. From 1939 until 1944, Papen represented the Third Reich as ambassador to Turkey. Before the war ended, he retired to his native Westphalia, where he was arrested by Allied forces on April 10, 1945.

Papen was tried at the NUREMBERG TRIALS on charges of conspiring to start World War II and found not guilty. However, the new West German government put him on trial as a "major offender" for aiding the Nazi regime and sentenced him to eight years' imprisonment. Like many wealthy supporters of Hitler, he was forgiven within a short time and released in January 1949; all of his property and wealth, confiscated as part of his punishment, was returned to him, although he was forced to sacrifice his pension and deprived of a driver's license. Papen died on May 2, 1969.

Further Reading:

Goldensohn, Leon, and Robert Gellately, eds. *The Nuremberg Interviews.* New York: Knopf, 2004.

Marrus, Robert, and Michael R. Marrus. *The Nuremberg War Crimes Trial of 1945–46: A Documentary History.* Bedford Series in History and Culture. Sidney, Australia: Palgrave Macmillan, 1997.

Maser, Werner. *Nuremberg: A Nation on Trial.* New York: Scribner, 1979.

Rice, Earle. *The Nuremberg Trials.* Famous Trials Series. San Diego, Calif.: Lucent Books, 1997.

Taylor, Telford. *The Anatomy of the Nuremberg Trials: A Personal Memoir.* New York: Little, Brown & Co, 1993.

———. *Nuremberg Trials: War Crimes and International Law.* New York: Carnegie Endowment for International Peace, 1949.

Papon, Maurice (1910–2007) *French Nazi collaborator*
As head of the southwestern Gironde region of Vichy France during World War II, Maurice Papon was responsible for the DEPORTATIONS of as many as 1,500 Jews to CONCENTRATION CAMPS. But he managed to avoid having to answer for his crimes for several years, succeeding in masquerading as a member of the French Resistance after the war. His skill in covering his tracks was such that he was decorated by General Charles de Gaulle and even managed to become a cabinet minister.

Born in 1910, Papon entered public service at the age of 20. His advancement through the ranks of the civil service was not hampered by the Nazi occupation of France in 1940, and at the age of 31 he was appointed general secretary of the prefecture of the Gironde region. However, when he realized that the Germans were losing the war, he switched sides, informing on his former allies to the French Resistance, an act that later won him the Carte d'Ancien Combattant de la Résistance, a coveted decoration for fighting the German occupation. Under de Gaulle's government, Papon became prefet de police in Paris, a post he held until 1968. He then entered politics, becoming budget minister in the government of President Valéry Giscard d'Estaing in the 1970s.

In 1981 Papon's cover was blown when old documents were uncovered by accident in the Bordeaux town hall, including the deportation orders he had signed. Shortly after the papers were published in a popular magazine, charges were brought against him, but in 1987 they were dropped because of legal technicalities. The following year, new charges were brought, accusing him of CRIMES AGAINST HUMANITY (later changed to complicity in crimes against humanity). After spending years trying to stop the legal process from going forward, Papon was finally compelled to stand trial in October 1997. At that point he was the highest-ranking former Vichy official to be put in the dock. Specifically, he was charged with ordering the arrest and internment of hundreds of Jews, some of whom were eventually sent to their deaths in Auschwitz. (There were allegations by human rights advocates that the French government had deliberately delayed the legal proceedings out of fear that putting Papon on trial would bring to light the extent of French collaboration with the German occupiers during the war.) At his trial, Papon contended that he was a victim of mistaken identity and in any case, the meaning of the 50-year-old documents was subject to misinterpretation. In addition, he claimed to have no idea of what became of the Jews whose deportations he had ordered. He reminded the court that he had aided the Resistance and in this capacity had actually helped save Jews. His trial, which lasted six months, was the longest in French history.

On April 2, 1998, Papon, then 87, was found guilty, although the jury acquitted him on the most serious counts, agreeing with his defense attorney that he was unaware of the ultimate fate of the Jews whose deportation orders he had signed. He was sentenced to 10 years' imprisonment as well as 10 years' privation of his civic, civil, and family rights. He was also stripped of all decorations and ordered to pay a fine equivalent to nearly $800,000. Papon's trial assumed a larger importance because it forced the French public to come to terms with the fact that collaboration with the Nazis was hardly an aberrant phenomenon and that many thousands—some in important positions, such as the late president François Mitterrand—had not acquitted themselves honorably during the war. Papon was released in 2002 due to poor health, much to the consternation of his critics. He died in 2007 at the age of 96.

Papua, New Guinea, human rights violations in
See INDONESIA, HUMAN RIGHTS VIOLATIONS IN.

Party of God *See* UGANDA, HUMAN RIGHTS VIOLATIONS IN.

Pavelić, Ante (1889–1959) *Croatian Nazi collaborator*
Ante Pavelić—known as the Butcher of the Balkans—was the fascist dictator of the Nazi puppet state of Croatia during World War II and one of the founders of the Croatian fascist movement, the USTACHE (also Ustasha and Ustaše). He is responsible for instigating the mass murder of 80,000 Jews, 30,000 Rom (Gypsies), and over 500,000 Serbs. Nonetheless, he was never brought to justice for his crimes.

Born in Bosnia and Herzegovina on July 14, 1889, Pavelić studied law in Zagreb, Croatia's capital. As a young man he joined a nationalist party called the Pure Party of Rights, eventually becoming the party secretary. In 1927 he began his political career by running for the Zagreb city council. In 1929 he cofounded the Ustache and then fled to Italy to avoid arrest for subversive activities. When the Yugoslav king Alexander was assassinated, Pavelić and other members of the Ustache were arrested on charges of conspiring to kill him. Pavelić was extradited to Yugoslavia but soon released.

In 1941 the Germans invaded Yugoslavia and installed Pavelić as *poglavnik* (leader) of the Independent State of Croatia. As the head of Croatia he ordered, orchestrated, and instituted a campaign of terror against Serbs, Jews, Rom, and communist Croats. Although there was no legal definition of GENOCIDE at the time—the word itself did not come into general use until after World War II—Pavelić can be accused of committing genocide against the Serbs since the Ustache under his command was targeting a whole people on the basis of their ethnicity. Serbs were exterminated, expelled from Croatia, or else forced to convert to Catholicism. (Serbs are largely Eastern Orthodox.) Pavelić enriched himself by plundering the wealth confiscated from concentration-camp inmates, Orthodox Christian churches, and Jewish synagogues as well as the property seized from Serbs, Rom, and Jews. All the same he had powerful allies in the Vatican and Franciscan Order and was personally received by Pope Pius XII.

As the war was coming to an end, Pavelić managed to slip away. Assisted by high-placed connections in the Vatican, he was spirited off to South America along with hundreds of other fugitive Nazis and Ustache members. He took up residence in Argentina, where he became a security adviser to President Juan and Eva Perón before retiring to Spain, another hospitable country then under the rule of Francisco Franco. He died peacefully in Spain in 1959. Some nationalist Croatians still regard Pavelić as a hero of Croatian independence in spite of his atrocities and seek the return of his body to Croatia. In 1998 a class action lawsuit was filed in San Francisco against the Vatican bank, the Order of the Franciscans, and surviving members of Ustache, demanding an account of the loot that Pavelić plundered.

See also CROATIA, HUMAN RIGHTS VIOLATIONS IN; ROM (ROMA, ROMANY, GYPSIES), PERSECUTION OF.

Further Reading:
Goldstein, Ivo. *Croatia: A History.* Montreal: McGill-Queen's University Press, 2000.
Muñoz, Antonio J. *For Croatia and Christ: The Croatian Army in World War II, 1941–1945.* Bayside, N.Y.: Europa Books Inc., 2004.
Tanner, Marcus. *Croatia: A Nation Forged in War.* New Haven, Conn.: Yale University Press, 2001.

Perisić, Momcilo   *See* WAR CRIMINALS OF THE FORMER YUGOSLAVIA.

Peru, human rights violations in   *See* FUJIMORI, ALBERTO; MONTESINOS, VLADIMIRO ILYICH; SHINING PATH.

Philippines, human rights violations in

The Philippines, while a democratic country since 1984, confronts serious political and economic problems, most of them stemming from inequality in the distribution of wealth and entrenched poverty. Even maintaining a democratically elected government is fraught with difficulties. The run-up to elections can often be a period characterized by a surge in violence. The police reported that 64 people were killed during the 1998 elections. In the 2001 midterm elections, the price in blood was even worse: 132 people were killed. The trend has shown no sign of abating. Political violence poses a particular risk to ensuring that human rights are upheld. Human rights violations are especially rampant in rural areas of the country that have been wracked by Muslim and communist separatist insurgencies for several years.

The Philippines has also become a frontline country in the U.S.-backed war on terrorism because its territory has been used by Muslim extremists who appear to have at least ideological, if not logistical, links to other militant Islamic groups in the region. Elements of the security services are blamed for arbitrary, unlawful, and occasionally EXTRAJUDICIAL KILLINGS, as well as DISAPPEARANCES, TORTURE, and arbitrary arrest and detention. The Philippine National Police (PNP) have been blamed for some of the worst abuses of human rights of any government institution, according to the constitutionally mandated Commission on Human Rights (CHR). Extrajudicial killings by police and vigilantes authorized by local officials have been employed "as expedient means of fighting crime and terrorism" in the words of the 2004 U.S. State Department *Country Report*. These summary executions of suspects are known as "salvaging." Police and military spokesmen often try to explain away suspicious deaths of suspects as the "unavoidable" consequence of shoot-outs or an effort to stop them from escaping police custody. In rural areas, extralegal executions serve political ends as local officials rely on assassinations (some perpetrated by elements of the police or the military) to assassinate political rivals or members of their families.

According to the Task Force for Detainees of the Philippines (TFDP), a human rights activist group, torture of suspects is "ingrained" in the arrest and detention process. Detainees are routinely struck or threatened with guns; beatings were more common at the beginning of interrogations. Police often practice arbitrary arrests and detentions in spite of constitutional guarantees requiring a judicial determination of probable cause before an arrest warrant can be issued and a prohibition against holding prisoners incommunicado or in secret places of detention. In the first six months of 2003, the CHR investigated 72 cases of illegal arrest and detention—an increase of 24 percent from the number recorded during the same period in 2002. Many of those taken into custody are political detainees, although they are often charged for ordinary crimes; the TFDP and the Philippine Human Rights Information Center (Philrights, a nongovernmental organization) both estimated the total number of political prisoners in the country was approximately 200 by the end of 2003.

The legal system is ill prepared to redress the violations of human rights: Because they are underpaid, judges and prosecutors are susceptible to corruption and the influence of the powerful. There have been attempts to reform the judiciary and institute fairer and speedier trials, but even so, most Filipinos appear to believe that they have little hope of obtaining justice. Human rights activists, too, have a hard time making headway since they are often subject to harassment by the military and police. Although the Philippines has a free press, journalists are at grave risk if their reporting threatens powerful political or criminal interests; more journalists were killed as a result of deliberate assassinations in the Philippines in 2004 than in any other country but war-torn Iraq; nearly 50 have been killed since 1984, the year that democracy was restored.

Two significant insurgencies have also contributed to grave human rights abuses. The largest is led by the Philippine Communist Party (CPP) and its well-funded military wing, the New People's Army (NPA), which is active in various regions of the country. The NPA has been fighting the army for almost three decades. AMNESTY INTERNATIONAL (AI) has called attention to several reported extrajudicial executions that "appear to have taken place within the context of military anti-insurgency operations" against the NPA, which the group says are likely to have been carried out by Armed Forces of the Philippines (AFP). AI points to what it terms "a pattern of killings and 'disappearances' of left-wing opposition activists and human rights defenders." The military has also alarmed human rights groups by labeling members of legitimate political parties as belonging to "front organizations" for the NPA. Once such individuals are stigmatized, AI says, they are more likely to be targets of military action.

The other major insurgency is being spearheaded by the smaller Abu Sayyaf Group (ASG), which is seeking an Iranian-style Islamic state in Mindanao, an island in the southern Philippines inhabited by a large Muslim population. Abu Sayyaf, whose name means "Bearer of the Sword," broke with the less-extremist Moro National Liberation Front in 1991. Various Moro factions had been waging a separatist war with Manila throughout the 1970s, but in January 1987 the larger groups eventually reached peace agreements that allowed for greater autonomy for Mindanao. Some groups such as Abu Sayyaf, which operates almost exclusively in the southern islands, have never accepted the accord. Abu Sayyaf, which is said to number several hundred young Islamic radicals, has become a par-

ticular cause for concern for U.S. policymakers after the September 11, 2001, terrorist attacks since it maintains ties to a number of Islamic fundamentalist organizations around the world, including Osama bin Laden's AL-QAEDA. It is thought that Ramzi Yousef, who was convicted of organizing the 1993 bombing of the World Trade Center in New York, also had some connection to the guerrilla group.

Fighting has broken out between the ASG and other Muslim insurgents, which has resulted in the displacement of about 350,000 persons from Mindanao in 2003 alone, according to the Department of Social Welfare and Development. There are credible reports of widespread human rights violations by the government forces as well as the ASG. The CHR investigated almost 100 killings in the first half of 2003 that had been committed by both insurgents and the army (the same number as 2002 for the same period). Terrorists carried out kidnappings and killings, including political assassinations and summary beheadings of hostages and local residents. Six summary executions of civilians by government forces were documented by the TFDP between January and June in 2003. The army has been charged by some groups with illegally detaining citizens, torching houses, uprooting residents from their homes, and even shelling villages suspected of being ASG strongholds. Both sides have used children as fighters.

The abduction in 2009 of an American activist, a 31-year-old woman, and two companions by military agents underscored the persistent scourge of enforced disappearances. The woman, Melissa Roxas, had been doing volunteer health work for a nongovernmental organization called Bayan in a province north of Manila. She was the first U.S. citizen to have been kidnapped under such circumstances. Human rights groups expressed alarm that human rights abuses were rising to levels not seen since the Marcos years (1965–86). According to the human rights group Karapatan, more than 200 Filipino activists have been kidnapped and never heard from since 2001 when President Gloria Macapagal Arroyo took office. Still other activists have turned up dead, with many showing signs of torture. HUMAN RIGHTS WATCH and other human rights organizations contend that the disappearances and killings of activists have been a deliberate part of an anti-leftist counterinsurgency campaign by Philippine military and security forces. A UN special rapporteur, Philip Alston, urged Arroyo to institute reforms within the military and to investigate "credible allegations" of abuses by the military. Arroyo's government denied the charges and accused Alston of holding a leftist bias. Human Rights Watch has also accused security forces of being responsible for the extrajudicial killings of hundreds of Filipinos suspected of committing petty crimes, many of them drug dealers, gang members, and street children. The group also charged local authorities of turning a blind eye to these crimes. The death squads operate in "state-protected impunity," according to the human rights organization; as many as 124 such killings took place in 2008. In Davao, the largest city in the southern region of Mindanao, 814 people were killed by death squads from August 1998 to February 2009. "The continued death squad operation reflects an official mindset in which the ends are seen as justifying the means," Human Rights Watch said in a report released in April 2009. "The motive appears to be simple expedience: courts are viewed as slow or inept. The murder of criminal suspects is seen as easier and faster than proper law enforcement." The organization contends that the death squad in Davao is made up of thugs and former rebels who rely on the police to supply them with the names and photos of their victims. "Police stations are then notified to ensure that police officers are slow to respond, enabling the death squad members to escape the crime scene, even when they commit killings near a police station," the report said. The Arroyo administration promised to cooperate with the UN in investigating the murders, but it remains to be seen whether the killings will be curbed or whether any perpetrators will be brought to justice.

The military has come under intense criticism for violating human rights of people who are suspected of being Communist or Muslim insurgent sympathizers. According to Karapatan, the largest human rights group in the Philippines, more than 1,000 activists, peasants, and civilians have died, and thousands more have been tortured or abducted between 2001 and 2009. Human Rights Watch accused the government of conducting a "dirty war" against leftists similar to the "dirty war" Latin American dictators engaged in during the 1970s. The UN Human Rights Council has also weighed in, asserting that the military's counterinsurgency policy called Operation Freedom Watch makes no distinction between Communist combatants and peaceful activists. Nonetheless, the UN noted some progress, citing a 70 percent decline in the number of killings in the two and a half years beginning in early 2007, partly as a result of wider publicity given to human rights abuses. However, in the first half of 2009, the Philippine Human Rights Reporting Project recorded the murders of 36 activists. In May 2009 the UN Committee against Torture said that it was "deeply concerned about the numerous, ongoing, credible and consistent allegations, corroborated by a number of Filipino and international sources, of routine and widespread use of torture and ill-treatment of suspects in police custody." The Philippine government has reaffirmed its commitment to respecting human rights and insists that it does not condone torture or mistreatment of prisoners.

In February 2009 the country saw the 100th killing of a journalist since 1986, making the Philippines one of the most lethal places for the practice of reporting anywhere in the world. That dubious milestone was exceeded only eight months later when 30 more journalists were killed in a massacre in Maguindanao Province that claimed the lives of more than 50 people, an incident precipitated by a bitter political feud between two rival families in the region. The election dispute that prompted the massacre, for which the province's governor was blamed, is hardly unusual. Politics is a lethal sport in the Philippines. In the 2007 mid-term elections, for example, about 60 candidates for various offices were killed.

In May 2010 Benigno Simeon Cojuangco Aquino III, better known as NoyNoy Aquino, was elected president of the Philippines. NoyNoy won support not only because of his reputation for probity but also because of his political pedigree. His late mother was Corazon Aquino, the first president after the overthrow of Ferdinand Marcos in the so-called People Power Revolution of 1986, and his father, a senator, had been a leading opponent of the Marcos dictatorship before his assassination in 1983.

Further Reading:
Barreveld, Dirk J. *Terrorism in the Philippines: The Bloody Trail of Abu Sayyaf, bin Laden's East Asian Connection.* New York: Writers Club Press, 2001.
Commission on Human Rights of the Philippines. Available online. URL: http://www.chr.gov.ph/. Accessed March 20, 2010.
Derechos.org. Human Rights in the Philippines. Available online. URL: http://www.derechos.org/human-rights/seasia/phil.html. Accessed March 20, 2010.
Human Rights Watch. Philippines Human Rights. Available online. URL: http://www.hrw.org/asia/-philippines. Accessed March 20, 2010.
Schirmer, Daniel B., and Stephen Shalom. *The Philippines Reader: A History of Colonialism, Neocolonialism, Dictatorship, and Resistance.* Boston: South End Press, 1987.

Phoenix program

The Phoenix program (Ké Hoạch Phung Hoàng in Vietnamese) was a covert intelligence operation run by the CIA during the Vietnam War from 1968 to 1972. The secret operation, which was assisted by the South Vietnamese, was intended to curb communist Vietcong (VC) infiltration in the south and eliminate its base of support. Many of the suspected VC sympathizers were killed in what one former Phoenix officer, testifying before Congress, called "a sterile depersonalized murder program," which he compared to "Nazi atrocities."

Some of the Phoenix operations involved intelligence gathering, while others were military in nature—for example, interdicting Vietcong assassination squads. As part of the program, Provincial Interrogation Centers (PICs) were established in South Vietnam's 44 provinces; South Vietnamese, North Vietnamese defectors as well as mercenaries from Cambodia and China were recruited to staff them. Overall administration, however, was handled by the CIA, with assistance from Green Berets and Naval SEALs (sea, air, and land teams). Later the program was taken over by the U.S. Army and armed forces of the Republic of Vietnam as part of the "Vietnamization" policy promoted by President Richard Nixon to expedite withdrawal of U.S. forces from the region. In congressional testimony, the U.S. ambassador to Vietnam, William Colby (later director of CIA), described the program as a vital part of a long-term strategy. "Since this is a sophisticated and experienced enemy," he said, "experts are also needed to combat it. Thus, the Phoenix program started in mid-1968 to bring together the police, military, and the other government organizations to contribute knowledge and act against this enemy infrastructure. It secures information about the enemy organization, identifies the individuals who make it up, and conducts operations against them." He cited an example: "These operations might consist of two policemen walking down the street to arrest an individual revealed as a member of the enemy apparatus or they might involve a three-battalion attack on a jungle hideout of a district or province committee." As a result of Phoenix, he went on to say, communists were captured, turned themselves in, or were killed in firefights. "Our own government provides advisory assistance and support to this internal security program through the police, the administration, the information services and the intelligence services."

The Phoenix program was intended to meet a growing insurgency by the Vietcong (formally known as the National Liberation Front). The apparatus Colby referred to was responsible for killing more than 6,000 people in terrorist attacks, including some 1,200 targeted assassinations of village chiefs and officials in 1969 alone. The program, however, began to be used by the South Vietnamese government to eliminate political opponents, whether or not they were affiliated with the Vietcong. Corruption became rife as South Vietnamese officials working with the program demanded protection money to avoid arrest or released suspects in exchange for bribes. The program was also characterized by CIA-sanctioned assassinations in contravention to the GENEVA CONVENTIONS. U.S. military officials' "Body counts" of Vietcong cadres killed were notoriously unreliable, and many of those who were killed were labeled VC posthumously. Provincial chiefs also sought to meet quotas of VC killed or captured by resorting to schemes such as arresting the same person several times or asserting that soldiers killed in combat were eliminated as a result of the Phoenix program. The program was ultimately judged a failure, not least because of widespread abuse, corruption, and EXTRAJUDICIAL KILLINGS.

See also TIGER FORCE; VIETNAM, HUMAN RIGHTS VIOLATIONS IN.

Further Reading:
Taylor, Telford. *Nuremberg and Vietnam: An American Tragedy.* New York: Times Books, 1970.
Vietnam Veterans against the War. *The Winter Soldier Investigation: An Inquiry into American War Crimes.* Boston: Beacon Press, 1972.

Physicians for Human Rights

Physicians for Human Rights (PHR) is a nongovernmental advocacy group whose guiding philosophy is based on the belief that health is inseparable from human rights. In 1997 the group shared the Nobel Peace Prize with the International Campaign to Ban Landmines. PHR uses medical and scientific methods to investigate and expose violations of human rights throughout the world and tries to put a stop to them. The organization also supports a wide-ranging educational campaign for health professionals and nursing students to get them involved in human rights work. Since 1996 PHR has been active in seeking to prevent TORTURE, DISAPPEARANCES, and EXTRAJUDICIAL KILLINGS as well as working to improve health and sanitary conditions in prisons and detention centers. While supporting the idea of medical neutrality in conflict situations, PHR also works to ensure that physicians and other health-care workers do not participate in torture. Among its other activities, PHR lends its services to investigations of MASS GRAVES to recover the dead, determine the cause and manner of death, identify the remains, and gather evidence that might prove valuable in bringing perpetrators of massacres and other war crimes to justice.

Further Reading:
Aall, Pamela R., Daniel Miltenberger, and George Weiss. *IGOs, NGOs, and the Military in Peace and Relief Operations.* Washington, D.C.: United States Institute of Peace Press, 2000.
Byman, Daniel, Ian Lesser, Bruce Pirnie, Cheryl Benard, and Matthew Waxman. *Strengthening the Partnership: Improving Military Coordination with Relief Agencies and Allies in Humanitarian Operations.* Santa Monica, Calif.: Rand Corporation (NBN), 2000.
Erskins, Toni. *Can Institutions Have Responsibilities: Collective Moral Agency and International Relations.* Global Issues Series. Sydney, Australia: Palgrave Macmillan, 2004.
PHR.org. *Physicians for Human Rights.* Available online. URL: http://physiciansforhumanrights.org/. Accessed March 20, 2010.
Rieff, David. *A Bed for the Night: Humanitarianism in Crisis.* New York: Simon & Schuster, 2002.

Vaux, Anthony. *The Selfish Altruist: Relief Work in Famine and War.* London: Earthscan Publications, 2001.

pillage

Pillage—the act of looting or plundering property—has long been associated as a justifiable reward for victory and compensation for assuming the risks of combat. Pillage is banned under international law. The Hague Convention of 1907 declared: "The pillage of a town or place, even when taken by assault, is prohibited." The GENEVA CONVENTIONS of 1949 reaffirmed the ban on pillage in the most succinct and emphatic way possible: "Pillage is prohibited."

During World War II the Nazis carried out a campaign of pillage possibly unrivaled in history, looting the patrimony of the nations they conquered and making off with thousands of artistic treasures from Europe's great museums. Even American troops were not immune from the temptation of pillage. It was only in 2004 that the U.S. government agreed to settle a lawsuit brought by Hungarian Jews over the looting of their valuables by American soldiers during World War II. The pillaged property included gold, silver, paintings, and furs, originally stolen from Jews by the Nazis before the end of the war. U.S. forces intercepted a train shipment of the goods but refused to turn it over to the original owners, who had survived the CONCENTRATION CAMPS, on the grounds that the property and valuables were "unidentifiable." Some of the items were appropriated by the U.S. Army and sold to soldiers, according to a 1999 report by the Presidential Advisory Commission on Holocaust Assets in the United States. In 2005 the U.S. government reached a settlement with the victims of the theft for $25 million.

International law distinguishes between *pillage*, which is defined as looting or plunder, and *requisitioning*, which is defined as the taking of "necessities" from a population for the use of an army of occupation. Until canning was invented, allowing armies to preserve and carry their food, armies would frequently seize food and provisions from the conquered populations. However, requisitioning has become more limited now that armies are better able to bring their own supplies with them. The Geneva Conventions specify that an army is legitimately entitled to requisition food or medical supplies but under two conditions: (1) the provisions must be intended only for the use of occupation forces—that is, the goods cannot be acquired for enrichment or profit, and (2) requisitioning can take place "only if the requirements of the civilian population have been taken into account." Fair value must be paid for the goods, in cash if possible. Nonetheless, international law does recognize that goods may be taken by an army "subject to the laws and customs of war," which can be interpreted as a justified basis under certain circumstances for seizing booty.

In spite of international laws outlawing pillage, the practice has continued: Iraqi forces pillaged Kuwait just before they were forced to withdraw by coalition forces in 1991, and Serb forces and militia groups pillaged Bosnia and Herzegovina and Croatia during the Bosnian War in the early 1990s as well as Kosovo during the 1999 war in that breakaway province.

Further Reading:

Gutman, Roy, ed. *Crimes of War: What the Public Should Know.* New York: W. W. Norton & Company, 1999.
Jackson, Nyamuya Maogoto. *War Crimes and Realpolitik: International Justice from World War I to the 21st Century.* Boulder, Colo.: Lynne Rienner Publishers, 2004.
Jokie, Aleksander. *War Crimes and Collective Wrongdoing: A Reader.* London: Blackwell Publishers, 2001.

Pinochet, Augusto (Augusto Pinochet Ugarte)
(1915–2006) *Chilean dictator*

The former dictator of Chile, General Augusto Pinochet Ugarte, came to power in a coup in 1973 and held power for the next 17 years. His rule was marked by brutality and a campaign of intimidation and terror designed to quash all dissent. It is believed that over 3,000 people were killed by his security forces, hundreds of thousands were tortured, and almost a million were driven into exile by fear and threats.

The future dictator was born into a middle-class family on November 26, 1915, in the Pacific coastal port of Valparaiso, Chile. He attended military school and graduated in 1936 as a sublieutenant in the infantry. Rising quickly in the

Chilean dictator Augusto Pinochet (left) with Salvador Allende, the president he overthrew in a violent military coup *(Landov)*

ranks, he was a major by 1953, and that year he was made commander of a detention camp during a military crackdown on the Communist Party. It was an indication of things to come. At the beginning of 1972, he was appointed general chief of staff of the army, an elevation that came during a turbulent time. Protests were growing against the leftist government of Salvador Allende, who had been elected two years previously and whose socialist policies had wreaked havoc on the economy. Allende's government was also coming under pressure from the Nixon administration, which feared that Allende would turn Chile into another pro-Soviet Cuba. Plans were put in motion to destabilize the Allende government, and contacts were initiated between the Chilean military and U.S. intelligence agencies.

Unsuspecting, Allende sought to quell unrest in his armed forces by appointing Pinochet commander in chief of the army in late August 1973. On September 11, 1973— only weeks later—the military staged a coup d'état. Allende reportedly committed suicide while defending himself in the besieged palace, and many of his top aides were arrested and subsequently put to death. The following day the four heads of the military services and the police designated Pinochet as president, a position he was to hold until 1990. Pinochet has stated in his memoirs that he was the mastermind of the coup, although other military officials have disputed this assertion, contending that he was more or less dragged into the plot just a few days before the coup actually took place. But there is no question that once in power he was quick to consolidate his rule and launch a campaign of terror to crush any opposition. At the same time he instituted a new economic regime, reversing the socialist policies of his ousted predecessor, returning nationalized businesses and industries to their owners, and lowering barriers to free trade. Inflation was brought under control, and the country acquired a reputation as a flourishing model of capitalism in Latin America, in contrast to the statist economies of many of its neighbors. But prosperity came at a high price. In 1988 Pinochet took a major gamble and announced a plebiscite in which the Chileans could vote whether to extend his presidency an additional eight years. He evidently believed that he would have no trouble winning, but instead he lost. In 1990 he agreed to step down as president but only on the condition that he remain commander in chief of the army and that he serve as senator for life, a position that would confer immunity on him for any crimes committed while he held the presidency. With support from much of the military, Pinochet had little reason to think that he would ever have to stand trial. He was mistaken.

Pinochet had drawn the attention of the Spanish judge Manuel García-Castellon, who had earned a reputation for pursuing perpetrators of human rights abuses during the "dirty war" in Argentina (1976–83). Like his more famous colleague, Balthasar Garzón, García-Castellon had pursued the fate of Spanish citizens who had been disappeared and presumably murdered by security forces. (In Spain judges also have a prosecutorial role in that they can bring charges as well as hear trials.) Just as Garzón investigated the 320 Spaniards who were killed in Argentina, García-Castellon wanted to find out what happened to 100 Spaniards who were disappeared in Chile during Pinochet's military rule. He was particularly interested in clandestine alliances that had been formed between military juntas in Argentina, Uruguay, and Chile. In an effort to exterminate political opposition in these countries, agents would be sent across borders to carry out assassinations of political dissidents in what was known as Operation Condor.

In 1998 García-Castellon went to Washington in hope of obtaining secret files about Operation Condor from the FBI. He based his request on a 1990 legal assistance treaty that requires the exchange of information on legal cases between U.S. and Spanish law enforcement officials. Most of the material in FBI files concerned the 1976 car-bomb assassination of Orlando Letelier, a former Chilean diplomat who had been killed by Chilean agents in Washington D.C. Although García-Castellon reported that the FBI had offered its "full cooperation," he failed to obtain more information about the clandestine operation than was already known. Nor did the judge obtain much information about relevant files that might reside in other U.S. agencies, particularly the CIA, which had worked closely in the mid-1970s with DINA (National Intelligence Directorate), the Chilean secret police. García-Castellon did, however, meet with two DINA agents implicated in the Letalier assassination: Michael Townley (who was in a federal witness protection program) and DINA chief Manuel Contreras, who was convicted in Chile in 1997 for masterminding the assassination plot. Contreras told García-Castellon that his actions had been sanctioned by Pinochet's government and insisted that the Chilean courts had had no right to try him.

It was from these interviews and the intelligence records he had gathered during his Washington visit that García-Castellon determined there was sufficient evidence to justify the interrogation of Pinochet. Pinochet, however, was adamant that no Spanish court could try him because of an amnesty program that he had implemented himself before giving up power in 1990. Recognizing that he did not have sufficient clout to pursue a case as controversial and charged as Pinochet's, García-Castellon handed off the prosecution to Garzón—who proved equal to the task.

In 1998 while in London, where he had gone to seek medical treatment, Pinochet was served with a warrant issued by Garzón and placed under house arrest. The charges included 94 counts of TORTURE and one count of conspiracy to commit torture that had occurred in the last 14 months of his rule. The time limit was dictated by a legal technicality: Britain had only signed the CONVENTION

AGAINST TORTURE in 1988. Human rights advocates seized upon Pinochet's detention as a watershed, a sign that war criminals, no matter how powerful, could indeed be brought to justice. The Chilean government, fearing a military reaction, contended that Pinochet should only be tried in Chile. Others decried the arrest altogether, including former British prime minister Margaret Thatcher. There was also concern about Pinochet's age—he was 82 at the time—and his health. In the first legal action the lord chief justice, Lord Bingham, ruled that Pinochet was "entitled to immunity as a former sovereign from the criminal and civil process of the English courts."

Pinochet's case then went to the House of Lords, which in November 1998 ruled 3-2 that state immunity applied only to acts that were consonant with international law. Torture and abductions clearly were not legal functions of a sovereign, and thus Lord Bingham's justification was flawed. It began to look as though Pinochet would be extradited to Spain to stand trial, but only on torture charges relating to the period after December 8, 1988, the date on which Britain had ratified the torture convention. However, the British home secretary decided against extraditing Pinochet on humanitarian grounds.

On his return to Chile, the former dictator was greeted warmly by supporters when he stepped down from the plane, prompting the government to insist that he make no further public appearances. Chile was not the same country Pinochet had left two years before. He was no longer a dreaded or a powerful figure, and efforts began to bring him to justice on several fronts, including in Argentina, which sought his extradition for orchestrating the assassination of a political opponent in Buenos Aires. Several suits were filed in Chilean courts against him as well, his senatorial immunity was removed, and he was once more placed under house arrest. In July 2002 the Chilean Supreme Court, by a vote of 2-1, dismissed all the cases against him for medical reasons (moderate vascular dementia). The decision drew harsh criticism from many legal experts who believed that Pinochet was sufficiently in command of his faculties to defend himself.

Convinced that he would never have to be tried for his crimes, Pinochet retired to his estate in the countryside. Even after the bloody years of his dictatorship, Pinochet still had many supporters in Chile convinced that he had rescued the country from communism and paved the way for a dynamic economy regarded as one of the most prosperous in Latin America. For those who suffered from the repression or whose friends and relatives were tortured or killed, the failure to bring him to justice was a wound that would never heal. Pinochet's legal problems, though, were only beginning.

In May 2004 a Santiago court ruled that the former dictator could in fact be sued by families of the victims for his part in the repression of the 1970s and 1980s. This action occurred after Pinochet gave a television interview in which he appeared lucid, calling into question the Supreme Court's rulings that he was unfit for trial. One of the prosecution lawyers called the new ruling "a miracle." The Supreme Court was once again forced to decide whether Pinochet could be forced to stand trial. Chilean investigators reportedly began gathering evidence tying Pinochet to the 1974 assassination of General Carlos Prats, Pinochet's predecessor as commander of the Chilean army, and the 1976 Letelier assassination.

Before going to prison for 12 years in another case, Pinochet's former security chief, Manuel Contreras, threatened to expose misdeeds that he had personal knowledge of, saying, "General Pinochet needs to assume his responsibility." At the time the family of Charles Horman, an American journalist who was abducted and presumably killed by Chilean secret police shortly after the coup, announced their intention to pursue Pinochet in the courts. Even some supporters of Pinochet grew disenchanted with him when it was revealed that while in power he had secreted over $16 million in Chilean and foreign banks under five different aliases, belying the image of the austere, incorruptible general that he had tried to foster. In 2006 Pinochet was indicted for kidnappings and torture at a detention center, among other crimes, including assassination. In November, on his 91st birthday, his wife read a letter he had written to supporters in which he declared that he had assumed "the political responsibility of all that has been done." Two days later he was ordered to submit to house arrest for the kidnapping and murder of two bodyguards of Allende who were executed after the coup. Pinochet never had to stand trial; he died on December 10, 2006.

See also CHILE, HUMAN RIGHTS VIOLATIONS IN; UNIVERSAL JURISDICTION.

Further Reading:

Constable, Pamela. *A Nation of Enemies: Chile under Pinochet.* New York: W. W. Norton & Company, 1993.

Davis, William Columbus. *Warnings from the Far South: Democracy versus Dictatorship in Uruguay, Argentina, and Chile.* New York: Praeger Publishers, 1995.

Dinges, John. *The Condor Years: How Pinochet and His Allies Brought Terrorism to Three Continents.* New York: New Press, 2004.

Dorfman, Ariel. *Exorcising Terror: The Incredible Unending Trial of Augusto Pinochet.* New York: Seven Stories Press, 2002.

Kornbluh, Peter. *The Pinochet File: A Declassified Dossier on Atrocity and Accountability.* A National Security Archive Book. New York: New Press, 2003.

Politzer, Patricia, and Diane Wachtel. *Fear in Chile: Lives under Pinochet.* New York: New Press, 2001.

piracy and international law

Piracy continues to flourish in spite of sporadic efforts to quell it. If anything, maritime shipping has become even more at risk of pirates in recent years, especially in such hotspots as the Straits of Malacca and the waters off INDONESIA; NIGERIA; Chittagong, BANGLADESH, and Santos, Brazil. However, in 2008–09, pirates from SOMALIA garnered the lion's share of attention for their daring and well-publicized attacks on international shipping. Ironically, piracy attacks had actually been declining in the past several years and seemed to have bottomed out in 2007 at around 240 attacks, according to the International Maritime Bureau. In November 2009 the International Maritime Bureau reported 359 attacks or attempts to attack since the beginning of the year. Somalia was far and away the record setter; in 2009 alone Somali pirates were responsible for 214 attacks and 47 hijackings. By the end of the year, they were still holding a dozen ships and 263 crew members for ransom.

Moreover, Somali pirates began to stage attacks farther out in the Indian Ocean and along the African coast from Somalia toward the Mozambique Channel, tending to avoid the Gulf of Aden, which had become better patrolled. By the end of 2009, pirates were believed to be holding more than a dozen ships, including a Saudi oil tanker and nearly 300 crew members.

The Somali pirates flourish because of the anarchic conditions prevailing in their homeland. With no central authority in charge, they are free to come and go as they choose, and indeed the local economies of many coastal towns and villages are prospering thanks to the infusion of cash they provide. In most cases, governments and shipping companies prefer to negotiate with the pirates and pay ransom for the release of their ships and crews than take the risk that the pirates might pillage their shipments and injure or kill crew. Estimates of ransom paid in 2008 alone range from $40 million to $100 million. Economic losses are not only confined to ransom. Shipping companies also incur higher costs in more expensive insurance premiums or in the expense of rerouting freighters to avoid pirate-infested waters. Many countries have dispatched military vessels and spotter planes to the area to protect shipping. Even China, which seldom contributes to international peacekeeping initiatives, has decided to participate in such patrols because its own shipping is at risk. Surprisingly, bringing pirates to justice is not a clear-cut matter, even leaving aside issues of practicality. (Once the pirates take refuge on Somali territory, it is difficult to apprehend them.) The Geneva Convention of the High Seas, adopted in 1958, established a definition of piracy for the first time in the postwar era. According to this definition, piracy consists of (1) illegal acts committed on the high seas (2) for private ends (3) by the crew or passengers of one ship against the crew, passengers, or property onboard another ship. It is the second component of the definition—that piracy must be motivated "by private ends" that has complicated the process of bringing pirates to account, because it neglects the possibility that piracy might be committed for political ends. And it is only a criminal act committed for political reasons that falls under the doctrine of UNIVERSAL JURISDICTION, which basically states that a country with a fair judicial system has the right to prosecute a suspected criminal for human rights violations or genocide that he or she might have carried out in another country that either cannot or will not try the suspect. Even a UN accord governing piracy (the UN Convention on the Law of the Sea, or UNCLOS) failed to cover violent crimes as was most vividly demonstrated by the 1985 hijacking of the Italian cruise liner *Achille Lauro*, by Palestinian terrorists. Because the attack was politically motivated, took place in Egyptian waters, and originated from the target ship (the hijackers were stowaways) rather than from a separate ship, UNCLOS did not cover the act and neither, presumably, did universal jurisdiction. The United States, ISRAEL, and other countries that might have wanted to prosecute the hijackers had no legal recourse under existing law (codified or common) to do so. Moreover, UNCLOS defined piracy in such a way that it could only take place "on the high seas" or "outside the jurisdiction of any state," which excludes the coastal areas of Somalia, where piracy is especially virulent. To address the glaring loophole, the UN (through the International Maritime Organization, or IMO), adopted the Convention for the Suppression of Unlawful Acts against the Safety of Maritime Navigation in Rome in 1988, which made it a crime to seize or take control of a ship by force or the threat of force or to commit violence on board, interfere with navigation, or destroy cargo. Any state that is party to the convention had a right to take jurisdiction over the case if either the perpetrator or victim had strong ties to the state (citizenship or habitual residence) or if the piracy was carried out to threaten or extort the state (to release prisoners that it was holding, for example). But for the most part, nations that have mobilized to meet the Somali threat have relied on UN Security Council resolutions that allow states with the consent of Somalia's transitional government to "enter the territorial waters of Somalia for the purpose of repressing acts of piracy and armed robbery at sea" and to "use . . . in a manner consistent with the action permitted on the high seas with respect to piracy under relevant international law, all necessary means to repress acts of piracy and armed robbery." Once again, though, the legal definition carries some important caveats because "action permitted on the high seas" does not permit pursuing and boarding a pirate vessel or arresting the pirates. To do that would require the sanction of the transitional government, a problematic criterion because the government exercises virtually no authority over the coun-

Members of the U.S. Navy capture a ship in the Gulf of Aden suspected of being involved in pirate activity, 2009. *(Defense Imagery)*

try. Using laws against terrorism enacted after the 9/11 attacks apparently does not work, either. "We have to look at compliance issues to make sure nobody is committing an offence under the Terrorism Act," a leading piracy lawyer in Britain said. "There is nothing illegal under English law about making a ransom payment in itself. But we have to make sure the money is going to pirates who are just trying to raise funds, and not to terrorists." That raises the question as to whether Somali pirates are criminals or a paramilitary force. The Somali pirates themselves have professed that they are serving as a kind of surrogate coast guard in the absence of a viable government, but few doubt that their primary motivation is profit. The same confusion has bedeviled attempts to interdict pirate vessels in the Gulf of Aden, where several ships have been seized by pirates. However, navies patrolling the gulf have been stymied in their efforts to intervene, because their mandate restricts them to attacking only ships captured by terrorists. Further complicating the issue, few countries are eager to put pirates on trial because of the huge expense involved. On the other hand, if a shipper is aware that there is little

prospect of a military rescue being mounted to retrieve his or her ship and crew, he or she is more likely to pay a ransom, which, of course, only encourages other pirates. Some observers argue that the international community can easily cut the Gordian knot. In a commentary written for the op ed page of the *New York Times,* Douglas R. Burgess, Jr., the author of a book on piracy, took the position that the United States and the international community could "adopt a new, shared legal definition that would recognize the link between piracy and terrorism." This could take the form of an act that called for "a new jurisdiction for piracy and terrorism cases at the International Criminal Court." He pointed out that airline hijacking by terrorists in the 1970s led to a UN accord defining the practice as "aerial piracy." Alternatively, international jurists could simply scrap the term *piracy* entirely and call the crime *maritime terrorism,* which would then, presumably, allow states to prosecute the pirates under exiting antiterrorism statutes. Moreover, Burgess contends, such a redefinition will give countries reluctant to prosecute pirates a convenient out, as they can always turn to the INTERNATIONAL CRIMINAL

COURT in The Hague to essentially do their dirty work for them. "If pirates are recognized under their traditional international legal status—as neither ordinary criminals nor combatants, but enemies of the human race—states will have a much freer hand in capturing them."

The capture of a U.S. cargo ship in April 2009 in the Indian Ocean highlighted the difficulty of curbing the piratical depredations, even though the incident proved disastrous to the invaders. The pirates were thwarted when the crew disabled the ship. The pirates then abducted the captain, who was subsequently rescued by U.S. military after snipers killed three of his four captors. The fourth, a Somali teenager, was brought to the U.S. to face piracy charges in a federal courthouse in New York, the first time that such charges had been brought against anyone in more than a century. "We are expecting this to be a very long proceeding," said Omar Jamal, director of the Somali Justice Advocacy Center in Minneapolis, Minnesota, at the time. "How long has it been since the United States tried a pirate? They must dig through the books for precedents." The teenage pirate later pleaded guilty. By the end of 2010 Somali pirates were believed to be holding as many as 25 vessels and about 500 hostages.

Further Reading:

Burgess, Douglas R., Jr. *The Pirates' Pact: The Secret Alliances between History's Most Notorious Buccaneers and Colonial America.* New York: International Marine/Ragged Mountain Press, 2008.

Guardian.co.uk. Piracy at Sea. Available online. URL: http://www.guardian.co.uk/world/piracy. Accessed March 22, 2010.

Lehr, Peter. *Violence at Sea: Piracy in the Age of Global Terrorism.* New York: Routledge, 2006.

pogrom

A pogrom is an organized, often state-sanctioned massacre or persecution of a minority group, especially Jews. The word is derived from the Russian *pogromit,* which is variously translated as "outrage," "havoc," and "riot." As its etymology implies, the first pogroms took place in Russia in the late 19th and early 20th centuries, but their number—and intensity—increased after the assassination of Czar Alexander II in 1881. In 1903 crowds went on a three-day pogrom in Chișinău (now the capital of Moldova), resulting in the death of 45 Jews. Anti-Semitism was by no means new to Russia. What distinguished pogroms was their organization and direct or indirect government sponsorship. These pogroms played upon and exacerbated resentment against Jews and were frequently used to divert attention from political or economic problems. The abortive anti-czarist revolution of 1905, for example, precipitated a wave of violent pogroms, as the government tried to restore its credibility. If the czarist regimes did not actively encourage these attacks, they took few steps to put a stop to them. Soldiers and police looked the other way when inflamed crowds descended on the Jewish quarters or ghettoes. In some cases, they actively participated in the beatings, killings, looting, and arson. The pogroms hastened the migration of hundreds of thousands of Jews, who found sanctuary in the United States in the late 19th and early 20th century. Pogroms came to an end in Russia only with the 1917 revolution that brought the Bolsheviks to power. Pogroms continued to be carried elsewhere out, though. On November 9 and 10, 1938, the Nazis organized a nationwide pogrom—Kristallnacht (Night of the Broken Glass)—encouraging crowds to loot Jewish businesses and burn synagogues, setting the stage for a systematic campaign to eliminate the Jews from public and commercial life in Germany. There is evidence that the Soviet dictator Joseph STALIN intended to revive the pogrom in the USSR against Jews, just before he died in 1953.

Further Reading:

Klier, John Doyle, and Sholomo Lambroza, eds. *Pogroms: Anti-Jewish Violence in Modern Russian History.* Cambridge: Cambridge University Press, 1992.

Rubenstein, Joshua, Vladimir Naumov, and Laura E. Wolfson, eds. *Stalin's Secret Pogrom: The Postwar Inquisition of the Jewish Anti-Fascist Committee (Annals of Communism).* New Haven, Conn.: Yale University Press, 2001.

Pohl, Oswald (1892–1951) *Nazi economic czar*
Obergruppenführer Oswald Pohl was the head of the economic empire established by the SS (Schutzstaffel), the principal Nazi security force. Pohl was born in Duisburg, Germany, on May 30, 1892. Trained as a navy purser, he joined the NSDAP (National Socialist German Workers Party, later the Nazis) in 1926. He soon attracted the attention of SS chief HEINRICH HIMMLER, who advanced his career. In 1942 Himmler appointed Pohl the chair of the SS Economic and Administrative Department (Wirtschaftsverwaltungshauptamt). This department consisted of five administrative divisions that handled the SS's financial and legal affairs, such as procurement and management of equipment, which included uniforms, buildings, and crematoria; the management of businesses run by the SS; and the Death's Head units (Totenkopfverbdnde), which administered the CONCENTRATION CAMPS. The Death's Head units routinely confiscated the possessions of Jews when they entered the camps, including watches, valuables, jewelry, money, and even hair and gold fillings. Pohl

was also responsible for farming out slave labor to SS-affiliated companies such as I. G. Farben and Krupp.

Pohl was arrested in 1945 at the end of World War II and brought to trial by the Allies at Nuremberg. Together with 16 other SS officials, he was tried for crimes against concentration camp inmates and for exploitation of slave labor. Convicted and sentenced to death in November 1947, he was only executed in June 1951.

See also NUREMBERG TRIALS.

Further Reading:

Browder, George C. *Hitler's Enforcers: The Gestapo and the SS Security Service in the Nazi Revolution.* Oxford: Oxford University Press, 1996.

Hohne, Heinz Zollen. *The Order of the Death's Head: The Story of Hitler's SS.* Classic Military History. New York: Penguin, 2001.

Pol Pot **(Saloth Sar)** (1925–1998) *Khmer Rouge leader*
As "Brother Number One," the leader of the Maoist Khmer Rouge movement, Pol Pot orchestrated a genocidal campaign in Cambodia that in a five-year period (1975–79) accounted for as many as 1.7 million deaths. Pol Pot was born Saloth Sar in 1925 (though experts have not completely agreed on his actual birth date) into a relatively prosperous farming family in central Cambodia. (The country was then under French colonial rule.) One of his brothers, Saloth Neap, recalled Pol Pot as a gentle and kind child, although he admitted that he had lost track of him until he spotted a poster of him identifying him as Brother Number One many years later. As a young boy, Pol Pot was sent to the capital of Phnom Penh, where he was raised by a cousin. He spent six years in a Buddhist monastery and became a monk for two years. Buddhism evidently lost its allure for him because he went on to study carpentry at a technical school. He still had time to become involved in politics and participated in the anti-French resistance. In 1946 he joined the Cambodian Communist Party.

Pol Pot earned a scholarship to study radio electronics in Paris, where his experiences reinforced his Marxist leanings. He hosted a series of communist cell meetings with other like-minded Cambodian students in his apartment in the Latin Quarter. His political activism might have proven too much of a distraction from his studies, because he failed his exams and lost his scholarship. By 1953 he was back in Phnom Penh. There he found a job teaching at a private school, a position he kept until 1963, but all during that time he was active in the underground Cambodian Communist Party, rising in its ranks and ultimately assuming its highest post in 1962 as secretary-general.

In 1963 Pol Pot and several of his confederates were forced to flee into the jungles in eastern Cambodia to avoid arrest. While in hiding he established a base in Kampong Thom, where he began to assemble a guerrilla force and plot a communist takeover of the country. It was in Kampong Thom, that the radical Khmer Rouge was born. There is some indication that he was influenced by the self-sufficient lifestyle of the hill tribes in the region. What struck Pol Pot was that they did not need to rely on help from outsiders, were "untainted" by Buddhism, and conducted all their transactions without using money.

In 1970 a military coup backed by the United States overthrew Cambodia's leader, Prince Norodom Sihanouk. The Khmer Rouge began an offensive aimed at toppling the military regime, a war that played out against the backdrop of the Vietnam War, which had begun to engulf neighboring Cambodia as well. The Khmer Rouge gradually captured most of the country and by April 1975 stood at the gates of Phnom Penh. Once in power, the Khmer Rouge launched a radical utopian experiment intended to

This photograph of Khmer Rouge leader Pol Pot hangs in the Tuol Sleng Museum. *(Pablo San Juan/Corbis)*

remake Cambodia into a completely self-reliant agrarian society. Although Pol Pot served as prime minister, the Khmer Rouge leadership maintained a chilling anonymity. As many as 3 million people were expelled from the cities and forced to farm in what became known as the "killing fields." Estimates of casualties vary, but most analysts believe that in the five years the Khmer Rouge ruled the country, nearly 2 million people were either killed outright for infractions as trivial as wearing glasses or speaking French (evidence that they were "intellectuals") or perished as a result of starvation and disease. Although Pol Pot seldom appeared in public, he is believed to have given the orders for the killings.

In 1979 increasing tensions between Cambodia and Vietnam led to war. Less than two weeks after its troops had crossed the Cambodian border, the Vietnamese took Phnom Penh, putting an end to the Khmer Rouge's five-year reign of terror. Pol Pot reconstituted his forces near the Thai border. No longer self-reliant, the Khmer Rouge now relied on China for arms and financial aid. It also retained diplomatic recognition from many Asian nations and the United States, which still considered the Khmer Rouge the legitimate government and the Vietnamese illegal occupiers.

Pol Pot retained his leadership position throughout the 1980s and early 1990s, but the exact nature of his authority is murky: In 1985 he was reportedly removed from military and political leadership and given an ill-defined defense position instead. Nonetheless, he is believed to have used his influence to bring the Khmer Rouge to the negotiating table in 1991, an action that was intended to lead to UN-sponsored elections. In 1992 Prince Sihanouk, who had once supported the Khmer Rouge, turned on them and gave his backing to the Hun Sen government installed by Vietnam. The Khmer Rouge withdrew from the peace process, boycotted the elections, and resumed fighting. But the guerrillas failed to make much headway, and dissension broke out in the Khmer Rouge ranks as to which direction it should take. The Hun Sen regime made it clear that it would not negotiate with the Khmer Rouge as long as Pol Pot was still in authority. In 1996 the Khmer Rouge split apart, and its moderate faction in the north, led by IENG SARY, defected to the government. But hard-liners remained in their stronghold near the Thai border. In 1997 leaders of the hard-line faction mutinied against Pol Pot and arrested him. He was tried by a "people's tribunal" made up of his former comrades and sentenced to life imprisonment. Two months later, under house arrest in his jungle redoubt, he was permitted to give an interview to the press in which he declared, "My conscience is clear."

Certainly the "people's tribunal" was not the trial that Pol Pot's victims or human rights organizations wished for. Until this point, the United States had opposed a trial of Pol Pot for war crimes. "There's certainly a major American responsibility for this whole situation," asserted Cambodia scholar Stephen Heder in an interview with the *New York Times:* "A war-crimes trial could have posed a problem for the US because it could have raised questions about US bombing [in Cambodia] from 1969 through 1973."

Pol Pot would never have to face a war crimes trial, though. He died at 72—apparently of a heart attack—on April 15, 1998. According to one witness, his body was "burned like old rubbish."

See also CAMBODIA, WAR CRIMES IN.

Further Reading:
Chandler, David. *A History of Cambodia.* Philadelphia: Westview Press, 2000.
Coates, Karen J. *Cambodia Now: Life in the Wake of War.* Jefferson, N.C.: McFarland & Company, 2005.
Gottesman, Evan. *Cambodia after the Khmer Rouge: Inside the Politics of Nation Building.* New Haven, Conn.: Yale University Press, 2004.
Hinton, Alexander Laban, and Robert Jay Lifton. *Why Did They Kill?: Cambodia in the Shadow of Genocide.* California Series in Public Anthropology, Vol. 11. Berkeley: University of California Press, 2004.
Kiernan, Ben. *How Pol Pot Came to Power: Colonialism, Nationalism, and Communism in Cambodia, 1930–1975.* New Haven, Conn.: Yale University Press, 2004.
———. *The Pol Pot Regime: Race, Power, and Genocide in Cambodia under the Khmer Rouge, 1975–79.* New Haven, Conn.: Yale University Press, 2002.
Pran, Dith, comp. *Children of Cambodia's Killing Fields: Memoirs by Survivors.* Edited by Kim DePaul. New Haven, Conn.: Yale University Press, 1999.
Short, Philip. *Pol Pot: Anatomy of a Nightmare.* New York: Holt Rinehart, 2005.
Ung, Loung. *First They Killed My Father: A Daughter of Cambodia Remembers.* New York: Perennial, 2001.

Prabhakaran, Vellupillai (1954–2009) *Tamil Tiger leader*

Until his slaying by Sri Lankan forces, Vellupillai Prabhakaran had led one of the most effective and brutal insurgent movements in the world: the TAMIL TIGERS (formally, the Liberation Tigers of Tamil Eelam, or LTFE). The Tigers carried out a ruthless campaign of massacres, suicide bombings, and assassinations, targeting Sinhalese officials, soldiers, and civilians, as well as moderate Tamils. For more than a quarter-century the Tigers fought for an independent Tamil state in northern and eastern SRI LANKA in an area known as Eelam. (The mostly Buddhist Sinhalese are the dominant ethnic group in a population of 21 million, and the Tamils, with about 12 percent of the population, are mostly Hindu.) At one point during the war, the

Tigers fielded a small air force and even a navy equipped with homemade submarines. The Black Tigers, an elite squad created by Prabhakaran, was responsible for many of its most sensational assassinations, kidnappings, and terrorist attacks. The Tigers were the first insurgent group to introduce suicide bombings into the modern terrorist arsenal. The reclusive Prabhakaran who founded the Tigers encouraged a cult of personality, recruiting women (who made up 40 percent of the Black Tigers) and children. He ordered his followers to abstain from sex and sever all ties with their families. Born to a middle-class family in the Tamil heartland of Jaffna on November 26, 1954, he dropped out of school and went underground in 1972. He emerged three years later in a spectacular manner by shooting the governor of Jaffna at point-blank range. (Prabhakaran loved to watch shoot-outs in westerns and liked to imitate his cinematic heroes.) Chubby, boasting a thick mustache, he did not look like anyone's idea of a romantic insurgent leader, nor did he act much like one. "The quietest man I have come across," reported an Indian journalist, who also said that Prabhakaran was so soft-spoken he was barely audible. "My first impression was that of utter disappointment," remarked another journalist. "He looked stunningly ordinary." Nonetheless, this "stunningly ordinary" man acquired a reputation for concealment, eluding capture, and daring escapes. Analysts believe that without him, the insurgency, which was finally brought to a bloody end in May 2009, might have ended much sooner. Prabhakaran adamantly opposed any peace talks. In November 2008 he gave an address in which he declared: "No sane voice is being raised either to abandon war or to seek a peaceful solution to the conflict." His supporters were unapologetic about their tactics and high-profile assassinations that took the lives of Indian prime minister Rajiv Gandhi in 1991 and Sri Lankan president Ranasinghe Premadasa in 1993. "Our methods of warfare are unacceptable to various people," stated S. Subramaniam, a longtime associate of Mr. Prabhakaran. "But Prabhakaran as well as our movement have survived precisely because of them." However, Prabhakaran's refusal even to consider compromise might have been his undoing. The Sri Lankan army launched a military campaign in 2008 that within a matter of months squeezed the Tigers into a small spit of territory, closing all means of escape. In May 2009 Prabhakaran was caught and killed by a rocket strike while trying to escape using an ambulance. His uncanny talent for evasion had deserted him at last.

Further Reading:

Clarance, William. *Ethnic Warfare in Sri Lanka and the U.N. Crisis.* London: Pluto Press, 2006.

Tambiah, Stanley Jeyaraja. *Ethnic Fratricide and the Dismantling of Democracy.* Chicago: University of Chicago Press, 1991.

Time.com. "Prabhakaran: The Death of a Tiger." Available online. URL: http://www.time.com/time/world/article/0,8599,1899590,00.html. Accessed March 20, 2010.

Priebke, Erich (1913–   ) *Nazi war criminal*

SS Hauptsturmführer Erich Priebke is a convicted war criminal who was tried for his responsibility for the March 1944 Ardeatine caves massacre in which German soldiers executed 335 Italian civilians in revenge for a bomb attack by a partisan communist group that had killed 33 German soldiers. Among the victims were 75 Jews, which made the massacre the largest single episode of the Holocaust in Italy during World War II. However, Priebke is believed to have been responsible previously for deporting 6,000–7,000 Italian Jews to Auschwitz and to have tortured political prisoners.

After Germany's defeat, Priebke was captured by the British and held in a prison camp, but he succeeded in escaping and fleeing to Argentina before he could be tried for his participation in the massacre. He remained in exile for the next 50 years without any attempt being made to bring him to justice. Then, in 1994, he decided it was safe enough for him to speak publicly about his role in the massacre, which brought renewed attention to an incident largely forgotten by the world. His interview on ABC television eventually led to a trial that would last for four years. In the interview with Sam Donaldson, Priebke maintained that he had only been following the orders of the GESTAPO chief in Rome, Lieutenant-Colonel Herbert Kappler. (Kappler was convicted in 1948 and sentenced to life in prison, but he managed to escape in 1977, only to die a few months later of cancer.) Priebke further asserted that in any case, the victims (ranging from 14-year-old boys to men in their 70s) were terrorists. Nonetheless, he did acknowledge that he had compiled the lists of those marked for death.

The interview stirred outrage among people who wondered how an unrepentant Nazi war criminal could have lived openly in Argentina for half a century. The Argentine authorities responded by placing him under house arrest, citing his advanced age and poor health to explain why they had not put him in prison. After 17 months of legal wrangling, the Argentine Supreme Court ordered Priebke extradited to Italy to stand trial. Priebke pleaded not guilty. While not denying his responsibility, he nonetheless insisted that the Italians who had attacked the German soldiers were to blame and that their execution should be considered a legitimate punishment. At the trial it emerged that Priebke had personally shot two of the victims, but the court found him not guilty because the statute of limitations made it impossible to convict him. He was not freed, however, since he faced trial in Germany as well. While Italian prosecutors appealed, Germany requested that he remain in prison until his extradition could be finalized. Then the Italian Supreme Court weighed in by repudiating the competence of the lower court that had acquitted him, although it declined to extradite him on the grounds that he was going to be tried for the same crime in an Italian court.

In his second Italian trial, Priebke was convicted and sentenced to 15 years in prison (with 10 years subtracted because of time already served in Italy and Argentina.) In 2004 some Italian demonstrators took to the streets to demand his release because of his advanced age. The demonstration stirred anger among Italian Jewish groups and city officials who had no wish to see him released. Priebke appealed, but the appellate court ruled that by committing first-degree murder, he should be imprisoned for the rest of his life. He showed no signs of contrition: "I gave Argentina 50 years of my life, and they don't want me. I fought for Germany during the war, now they want me put to trial for obeying orders." Still in jail in 2010, the 97-year-old Priebke is the oldest prisoner in Europe.

prisoners of conscience

The term *prisoners of conscience* is used by AMNESTY INTERNATIONAL (AI), a human rights organization, to refer to people who have been arrested or detained because of their political views or because they have been singled out on the basis of their race, religion, or ethnicity. According to AI, prisoners of conscience are those "who have not used, or encouraged the use of, violence; have not openly supported or recommended hatred for racial, religious or similar reasons to provoke people to discriminate, or to be hostile or violent; are detained or imprisoned because of their political, religious or other beliefs, or their ethnic origin, sex, color or similar reasons." Among those who fall into this category are individuals who have been arrested because they tried to hold a political demonstration or form a political party in a country where the exercise of democratic rights is banned. AI makes a distinction between prisoners of conscience and political prisoners. Under AI's definition, political prisoners are those who have been imprisoned because of their political background, which "may include being a member of a forbidden political party, or being involved in armed struggle against the government, or being victims of other kinds of systematic discrimination based on sex, race or other reasons." The principal difference, of course, is that a political prisoner, unlike a prisoner of conscience, "may have used or encouraged the use of violence."

Further Reading:

Benenson, Peter. *Persecution.* London: Penguin Books, 1961.
Winner, David. *Peter Benenson: Taking a Stand against Injustice—Amnesty International.* Milwaukee: Gareth Stevens Pub., 1992.

prisoners of war (POWs)

The treatment of prisoners of war (POWs) has long been a major concern of INTERNATIONAL HUMANITARIAN LAW (IHL). Although captured soldiers obviously lose their freedom, they do not lose their military status according to the Third Geneva Convention Relative to the Treatment of Prisoners of War. POWs, for instance, are expected to salute captor officers of a higher rank. Of paramount concern in IHL is the principle that POWs are entitled to humane treatment; the INTERNATIONAL COMMITTEE OF THE RED CROSS (ICRC) is mandated under Article 126 of the Geneva Convention to guarantee that POWs receive all the protections to which they are entitled. Although the ICRC has the obligation to visit POW camps to assess conditions under which POWs are being held, the convention also allows visits by other outside parties such as journalists and humanitarian aid workers. The convention also specifies that POWs must be placed in camps that do not jeopardize their health and safety; in other words, the camps cannot be located in areas where the inmates are exposed to conflict or aerial bombardment. Prisoners must also be housed in humanitarian conditions that should meet the standards of the living quarters of the captor forces. They must be adequately fed and provided with competent medical care if they need it. The convention obliges the captor to ensure that the POWs are properly

Japanese prisoners of war being guarded by U.S. soldiers during World War II *(Library of Congress)*

clothed, usually in their own uniforms. POWs also are guaranteed the ability to communicate with the outside world; under Article 71 they can correspond with families and are permitted to receive shipments of food, clothing, and other necessities.

There are provisions in the convention covering the use of force to impose discipline and prevent or punish escape attempts. Article 42 provides that the use of weapons against POWs is "an extreme measure" and that their use "shall always be preceded by warnings appropriate to the circumstances." Once hostilities cease, the Geneva Convention and Additional Protocol I of 1977 call for the immediate release and repatriation of all POWs. The protocol states that any "unjustifiable delay in the repatriation of prisoners of war or civilians" is a grave breach of international humanitarian law. There is no excuse to delay the release of POWs until a formal treaty is signed. However, a captor is not required to release or repatriate prisoners of war when there is a justifiable reason to believe that hostilities have not in fact ended—when, for example, a cease-fire is likely to be only temporary. Moreover, there are cases where POWs may not wish to be repatriated, as happened after the end of World War II, when many Soviet soldiers held in German POW camps balked against being returned to the Soviet Union. (Their resistance to repatriation was justified since thousands of returning POWs were labeled as traitors for having allowed themselves to be captured and shipped off to Siberian labor camps.) According to the ICRC, international law gives prisoners the right to refuse forcible repatriation.

See also ADDITIONAL PROTOCOLS TO THE GENEVA CONVENTIONS; GENEVA CONVENTIONS; GUANTÁNAMO DETAINEES.

Further Reading:

Berry, Nicholas O. *War and the Red Cross: The Unspoken Mission.* New York: St. Martin's Press, 1997.

Dormann, Knut, and Louise Doswald-Beck. *Elements of War Crimes under the Rome Statute of the International Criminal Court: Sources and Commentary.* Cambridge: Cambridge University Press, 2003.

Falk, Richard A. *Crimes of War: A Legal, Political-Documentary, and Psychological Inquiry into the Responsibility of Leaders, Citizens, and Soldiers for Criminal Acts in Wars.* New York: Random House, 1971.

Gutman, Roy, ed. *Crimes of War: What the Public Should Know.* New York: W. W. Norton & Company, 1999.

Jackson, Nyamuya Maogoto. *War Crimes and Realpolitik: International Justice from World War I to the 21st Century.* Boulder, Colo.: Lynne Rienner Publishers, 2004.

Moorehead, Caroline. *Dunant's Dream: War, Switzerland and the History of the Red Cross.* New York: Carroll & Graf Publishers, 1999.

private military contractors   *See* MERCENARIES.

prostitution, enforced   *See* TRAFFICKING IN PERSONS.

protected persons

INTERNATIONAL HUMANITARIAN LAW recognizes several different categories of individuals in conflict situations as "protected." Under certain circumstances, both combatants and noncombatants are entitled to protected status. The first three GENEVA CONVENTIONS of 1949 set forth standards for protection of combatants in international armed conflicts. *Combatants* are defined as members of an armed force who are also legitimate military targets. In addition to combatants, the conventions also protect associated military personnel including those who are HORS DE COMBAT—no longer able to fight; wounded and sick in the field; wounded, sick, and shipwrecked at sea; and prisoners of war.

The Fourth Geneva Convention of 1949 refers specifically to the protection of civilians. Whether combatants or civilians, the Fourth Convention states that all protected persons "shall in all circumstances be treated humanely, without any adverse distinction founded on race, color, religion or faith, sex, birth or wealth, or any other similar criteria." Protected persons must not be subjected to "violence to life and person, in particular murder of all kinds, mutilation, cruel treatment and TORTURE; taking of HOSTAGES; outrages upon personal dignity, in particular, humiliating and degrading treatment; the passing of sentences and the carrying out of executions without previous judgment pronounced by a regularly constituted court, affording all the judicial guarantees which are recognized as indispensable by civilized peoples."

Protected persons may not be killed, tortured, coerced, used as human shields, collectively punished or employed as subjects of MEDICAL EXPERIMENTS. The 1998 Rome Statute, which established the INTERNATIONAL CRIMINAL COURT, classified medical experiments as war crimes, whether they occur in an international armed conflict or an internal one. Protected persons cannot be forcibly transferred or deported from occupied territory, although there are exceptions in cases of emergencies or security concerns. Women must be "treated with all the regard due to their sex" and female prisoners of war are to be treated no differently from male prisoners of war. The Fourth Geneva Convention further prohibits "rape, enforced prostitution, or any form of indecent assault" directed against women. The wounded and sick, expectant mothers, the aged, children, clerics, and medical personnel are also entitled to special consideration.

The Fourth Geneva Convention classifies civilians into three categories: aliens in a territory that is engaged in an international conflict, persons residing in an occupied territory, and internees. Although the protected status of each of these groups differs to some extent, members of all groups are entitled to be treated with respect and given humanitarian treatment under all circumstances. Additional Protocol I of 1977 affirms the right of civilians to be protected against INDISCRIMINATE ATTACKS that fail to distinguish between combatants and noncombatants. Thus, any attack on a military objective is prohibited if it is known that it will also result in widespread civilian casualties disproportionate to the objective being targeted. Additional Protocol I also states that civilians under occupation are entitled to adequate food and medical supplies vital to its survival. Additional Protocol II applies the protections in Protocol I to internal conflicts, proscribing making civilians—as individuals or as a group—targets of attack. Attacks are banned against facilities—such as electric plants, dams, dikes, etc.—that are essential for the survival of the civilian population. Additional Protocol II (which technically is binding only on signatories) also calls upon military units to protect civilians and, when conducting operations, to distinguish between civilians and combatants.

See also CIVILIAN IMMUNITY; MEDICAL PERSONNEL, PROTECTION OF; ROME STATUTE OF THE INTERNATIONAL CRIMINAL COURT.

Further Reading:
Dormann, Knut, and Louise Doswald-Beck. *Elements of War Crimes under the Rome Statute of the International Criminal Court: Sources and Commentary.* Cambridge: Cambridge University Press, 2003.

Gutman, Roy, ed. *Crimes of War: What the Public Should Know.* New York: W. W. Norton & Company, 1999.

International Committee of the Red Cross. *International Law Concerning the Conduct of Hostilities: Collection of Hague Conventions and Some Other Treaties.* Geneva, Switzerland: International Committee of the Red Cross, 1989.

Protocol on Prohibitions or Restrictions on the Use of Mines, Booby-Traps and Other Devices

The Protocol on Prohibitions . . . emerged from the Anti-Personnel (AP) Mine Ban Convention (September 1995–May 1996) and was an outgrowth of the 1981 CONVENTION ON PROHIBITIONS OR RESTRICTIONS ON THE USE OF CERTAIN CONVENTIONAL WEAPONS Which May be Deemed to be Excessively Injurious or to Have Indiscriminate Effects. The AP Mine Ban Convention, which banned blinding lasers, fragments, and incendiary devices as well as the use of mines against civilians, defined an antipersonnel mine (APM) as "a mine designed to be exploded by the presence, proximity or contact of a person and that will incapacitate, injure or kill one or more persons." (Mines that are designed to be detonated by the presence, proximity, or contact of a vehicle rather than a person are not considered APMs.) By comparison, a booby trap is defined as a device "designed, constructed or adapted to kill or injure, and which functions unexpectedly when a person disturbs or approaches an apparently harmless object or performs an apparently safe act." "Other devices" are defined as "manually-emplaced munitions and devices including improvised explosive devices designed to kill, injure or damage and which are activated manually, by remote control or automatically after a lapse of time."

The AP II, as the protocol is known, makes each state party responsible for all mines, booby traps, or other devices it uses and obliges the state party to clear, remove, destroy, or maintain all mines, booby traps, and other devices in accordance with the protocol. Banned is any device falling into these categories that causes "superfluous injury or unnecessary suffering," and is intended against civilians or civilian "objects." The protocol mandates that mines should only be used for military purposes and against military objectives and, like bombs, should not be delivered by "indiscriminate means" or placed in such a manner as to inflict "excessive impact" on civilians disproportionate to the significance of the military objective being targeted. Warnings should be given whenever possible to civilians to protect them from being endangered by mines.

In December 1997 a more comprehensive effort was made at the Anti-Personnel Mine Ban Convention (also known as the Mine Ban Treaty, or Ottawa Convention), which sought to destroy or ensure the destruction of all APMs. The convention, which entered into force on March 1, 1999, became known as the CONVENTION ON THE PROHIBITION OF THE USE, STOCKPILING, PRODUCTION AND TRANSFER OF ANTI-PERSONNEL MINES AND ON THEIR DESTRUCTION.

Further Reading:
Cornish, Paul. *Anti-personnel Mines: Controlling the Plague of "Butterflies."* London: Royal Institute of International Affairs, 1994.

Harpviken, Kristian Berg, ed. *The Future of Humanitarian Mine Action.* Third Worlds. Sydney, Australia: Palgrave Macmillan, 2004.

Prokosch, Eric. *The Technology of Killing: A Military and Political History of Anti-personnel Weapons.* London: Zed Books, 1995.

U.S. Congressional Budget Office. *Convention on Prohibitions or Restrictions on the Use of Certain Conventional Weapons.* Report to Accompany Treaty Doc. 103–25. Washington, D.C.: U.S. Government Printing Office, 1995.

Protocol to the Hague Convention of 1954 for the Protection of Cultural Property in the Event of Armed Conflict, Second

The Second Protocol to the Hague Convention of 1954 for the Protection of Cultural Property in the Event of an Armed Conflict, adopted on March 26, 1999, affirms and elaborates on the 1954 Hague Convention, which sought to protect valuable cultural property in times of international conflict. The convention was drafted in response to the destruction of entire cities during World War II and set forth the standard that cultural property could be attacked only in case of "imperative military necessity." It suffered from a failure to define what was meant by "military necessity." In 1977 Additional Protocol I to the GENEVA CONVENTIONS took the position that only narrowly defined military objectives could be subject to attack, which meant that except in rare exceptions—for example, when a church or museum is used for military purposes by a belligerent and when no alternative to attacking the site is available—cultural property is immunized. The Second Protocol to the HAGUE CONVENTIONS took into account the enhanced protections offered by the Additional Protocols. The Second Protocol accords valuable cultural property additional protections so long as it is adequately protected under local law and is not used for military purposes or to shield military installations; these properties are placed on the List of Cultural Property under Enhanced Protection. Decisions as to which properties are entitled to inclusion on the list are made by the Committee for the Protection of Cultural Property in the Event of Armed Conflict, an intergovernmental committee established under the protocol. The protocol also criminalizes acts that violate the protections of cultural property conferred by the protocol and applies equally to international and internal conflicts.

See also ADDITIONAL PROTOCOLS TO THE GENEVA CONVENTIONS; CULTURAL PROPERTY, PROTECTION OF.

Further Reading:

Gutman, Roy, ed. *Crimes of War: What the Public Should Know.* New York: W. W. Norton & Company, 1999.
International Committee of the Red Cross. *International Law Concerning the Conduct of Hostilities: Collection of Hague Conventions and Some Other Treaties.* Geneva, Switzerland: International Committee of the Red Cross, 1989.

public property, protection of

INTERNATIONAL HUMANITARIAN LAW outlaws the destruction of public property during armed conflict with certain important exceptions. The limited prohibition is found in Article 52 of the 1977 Additional Protocol I to the GENEVA CONVENTIONS. The protocol affirms that "civilian objects shall not be the object of attack or reprisals, and objects or installations ordinarily of civilian use are presumed to be civilian unless determined to be otherwise." However, the protocol does allow the destruction of "those objects which by their nature, location, purpose or use make an effective contribution to military action and whose total or partial destruction, capture or neutralization, in the circumstances ruling at the time, offers a definite military advantage." There are also exceptions for COLLATERAL DAMAGE—that is, unavoidable damage caused to property in the vicinity of a legitimate military objective. However, destruction cannot be wanton or indiscriminate.

The 1998 Rome Statute, which established the INTERNATIONAL CRIMINAL COURT, describes "extensive destruction and appropriation of property, not justified by military necessity and carried out unlawfully and wantonly" as a crime liable to be prosecuted. The Fourth Geneva Convention of 1949 prohibits the destruction of public property by an occupation force. Under those circumstances, the Fourth Convention states, the "extensive destruction and appropriation of property, not justified by military necessity and carried out unlawfully and wantonly" is a violation of international law. International law exempts public property from complete immunity if that property is appropriated for military purposes—for example, if a museum is used as a command post. But even in such cases, the damage inflicted on the property must be proportionate to its importance as a military objective. Again, the damage cannot be wanton—destroyed simply for the sake of destruction or a desire for revenge. This principle was put forward as early as the 1907 Hague Convention, which specified that destruction or seizure of property is prohibited unless it is "imperatively demanded by the necessities of war."

In practice, of course, it is often difficult to determine whether damage was proportional or wanton, since neutral observers are seldom present when an attack on property takes place. Only an assessment of the attack's military context of the attack would enable an outsider to determine whether a war crime has been committed or not. The bombed-out ruins of a church or a mosque, for instance, might be seen as evidence of a crime, but culpability might not be found if it turned out that the religious institution had been used by a belligerent to stage an ambush. In an opinion issued in 1994, the INTERNATIONAL COMMITTEE OF THE RED CROSS (ICRC) declared that belligerents "do not have an unlimited right regarding the choice of methods and means of warfare," adding that they are obliged to make "a clear distinction . . . between civilians and civilian objects on the one hand and combatants and military objectives on the other." Attacks on civilian property designed to spread terror in a civilian population are prohibited. The ICRC also emphasizes the concept of proportionality, declaring that "all attacks directed indiscriminately at military and civilian objectives and those which may be expected to cause incidental loss of human life, injury to civilians or damage to civilian objects which would be excessive in relation to the concrete and direct military advantage anticipated." International law has long called for the protection of "hospitals, ambulances, and any other object bearing the Red Cross," which are not to attacked or used for military purposes under any circumstances.

See also ADDITIONAL PROTOCOLS TO THE GENEVA CONVENTIONS; CIVILIAN IMMUNITY; MEDICAL PERSONNEL, PROTECTION OF; ROME STATUTE OF THE INTERNATIONAL CRIMINAL COURT.

Further Reading:
Falk, Richard A. *Crimes of War: A Legal, Political-Documentary, and Psychological Inquiry into the Responsibility of Leaders, Citizens, and Soldiers for Criminal Acts in Wars.* New York: Random House, 1971.

Goldstone, Richard. *For Humanity: Reflections of a War Crimes Investigator.* Castle Lectures Series. New Haven, Conn.: Yale University Press, 2000.

Gutman, Roy, ed. *Crimes of War: What the Public Should Know.* New York: W. W. Norton & Company, 1999.

Jackson, Nyamuya Maogoto. *War Crimes and Realpolitik: International Justice from World War I to the 21st Century.* Boulder, Colo.: Lynne Rienner Publishers, 2004.

Jokie, Aleksander. *War Crimes and Collective Wrongdoing: A Reader.* London: Blackwell Publishers, 2001.

Meron, Theodor. *War Crimes Law Comes of Age: Essays.* Oxford: Oxford University Press, 1999.

Q

Qaeda, al-

The most infamous terrorist organization of modern times, al-Qaeda was responsible for the 9/11 (2001) terrorist attacks on the World Trade Center and the Pentagon, which accounted for over 3,000 deaths. But while it was unknown to most of the world prior to those strikes, the movement had been conducting terrorist acts for many years. Al-Qaeda—whose name means "the base" or "the foundation" in Arabic—was founded in Peshawar, PAKISTAN, in 1988. Popular use of the name is credited by some to U.S. intelligence officials who found a reference to the al-Qaeda-al-Jihad ("the base of the jihad," or holy war) and assumed that al-Qaeda was the name of the group. (The leading figures of al-Qaeda do not refer to it as such.) Its ideology can be traced back to the Muslim Brotherhood, which arose in Egypt. Most of al-Qaeda's members subscribe to a strict Wahabi interpretation of Islam that is practiced in Saudi Arabia. Over the years al-Qaeda has expanded its list of grievances; whereas at first it claimed to be fighting to rid Saudi Arabia—home to Mecca, Islam's holiest site—of the American military presence established after the Persian Gulf War in 1991, it later promoted a jihad to combat Western influence throughout the Muslim world. In a broader sense, some historians believe that al-Qaeda seeks to restore the caliphate, hearkening back to the 13th century, when Muslim hegemony extended throughout much of Asia and much of Europe. To achieve this goal al-Qaeda has vowed to overthrow authoritarian regimes in Egypt, Saudi Arabia, and Pakistan that have received strong support from the West. Israel is especially seen as an alien presence in the Middle East that must be eliminated.

The founder of al-Qaeda, Osama bin Laden, a wealthy Saudi, is undoubtedly the most wanted man in the world. He received his military training in the war against the Soviets in AFGHANISTAN during the 1980s. Bin Laden was among the mujahideen (holy warriors) who formed a paramilitary group called the Office of Services under Sheikh Abdullah Azzam. Ironically, like many other mujahideen,

he had benefited from arms and financial assistance from the Central Intelligence Agency (CIA) and the Pakistani intelligence agencies, which had a common goal in seeing the Red Army driven out of Afghanistan after a decade of occupation. Just before the Soviet withdrawal in 1989, bin Laden and Azzam parted company, reportedly because bin Laden wanted to extend the conflict beyond Afghanistan. Over the next few years, bin Laden devoted himself to building a financial and organizational structure for the group. In 1991 he was invited to establish a base in Sudan, which had come under the rule of an Islamic regime. For the next several years, al-Qaeda set up several businesses—trading companies, farms, construction firms, and diamond-smuggling enterprises—to build up its financial resources. The group also ran training camps where followers learned how to use weapons and plant explosives.

When al-Qaeda was linked to an attempted assassination of Egyptian president Hosni Mubarak in Addis Ababa, Ethiopia, Sudan expelled bin Laden, but not before first offering to hand him over to the United States. However, at the time the Clinton administration had no legal basis to take him into custody. In 1996 bin Laden returned to Afghanistan, where he entered into an alliance with the new TALIBAN regime there under MULLAH OMAR. The Taliban, which also followed a fundamentalist form of Islam, provided al-Qaeda with funds, arms, and—most importantly—protection. Al-Qaeda opened several training camps in its new home, recruiting militants from India, Chechnya, the Philippines, Kosovo, YEMEN, SOMALIA, and Uzbekistan, as well as the Arab nations. Some recruits even found their way to Afghanistan from the United Kingdom and the United States. Bin Laden's principal deputy, Ayman al-Zawahiri, an Egyptian doctor, announced a fatwa (an Islamic decree) under the banner of "the World Islamic Front for Jihad Against the Jews and Crusaders," in which he declared that "to kill Americans and their allies, civilians, and military is an individual duty of every Muslim who is able." Zawahiri, who was implicated in the assassination

Poster depicting Osama bin Laden *(Getty Images)*

of Egyptian president Anwar Sadat, is considered the organizational genius of al-Qaeda; as of early 2005 he, like bin Laden, has managed to avoid capture.

Al-Qaeda announced its debut on the world stage with a series of spectacular attacks, including a boat attack on the American naval vessel USS *Cole* in Yemen; the simultaneous bombings of the American embassies in Nairobi and Tanzania, which took over 300 lives in 1998; and the bombings of aircraft and movie theaters in the Philippines. In 1993 an attempt to blow up the World Trade Center in New York, which killed five people, made Americans aware of the terrorist threat from Islamic militants for the first time. Al-Qaeda is also blamed for the 1996 bombing of the Khobar Towers, which killed several U.S. military personnel, in Dhahran, Saudi Arabia. Al-Qaeda adherents volunteered for service in the war in Bosnia in the early 1990s and in the war in Chechnya between separatists and the Russian army.

After the 9/11 attacks, U.S. intelligence officials quickly identified al-Qaeda as the perpetrator, and Washington demanded that the Taliban surrender bin Laden. Mullah Omar's refusal led to war in the fall of 2001. Within a matter of months, the Taliban and its al-Qaeda allies had been routed and largely driven out of the country. Both Mullah Omar and bin Laden went into hiding, presumably in the isolated mountainous border region on the Afghan-Pakistani border. By the beginning of 2005 the two men

were still at large in spite of the fact that the United States had placed a large price on their heads.

Although several top leaders of al-Qaeda have been captured or killed in the war on terrorism, as Washington has called it, most experts believe that the organization has metastasized, spawning several offshoots. Terrorist cells have sprung up in several countries, including Algeria, Morocco, Turkey, Egypt, Syria, Uzbekistan, Tajikistan, Iraq, Saudi Arabia, Kuwait, Indonesia, Kenya, and Tanzania. Cells have also been identified in France, the Netherlands, Germany, Britain, and Spain, finding sanctuary among supporters in Muslim émigré communities. According to *Jane's*, the respected British military journal, al-Qaeda has informal ties with at least 24 other terrorist groups, including the Egyptian Islamic Jihad, Abu Sayyaf, Jemaah Islamiyah, Hezbollah, Hesb' I Islami, Ansar al Islam, and the Islamic Group. Political observers also believe that many autonomous terrorist groups with no connection to al-Qaeda nonetheless claim an affiliation because it offers added prestige in the eyes of many disaffected people in the Arab world.

There is some debate as to how directly al-Qaeda can be linked to many of the terrorist acts that have occurred since the organization lost its base in Afghanistan, but there is some evidence that its adherents have been involved in bombings, kidnappings, and killings of Westerners in Indonesia, Morocco, Saudi Arabia, and Western Europe. Jemaah Islamiah, for instance, which is closely aligned with al-Qaeda, is believed to have been behind the nightclub bombing in Bali that killed over 200 mostly Australian youths in 2002. An al-Qaeda-affiliated Moroccan cell was implicated in the commuter train bombings in Madrid in March 2004 that killed 200 people. There is also considerable evidence to indicate that al-Qaeda militants have exploited the chaos in Iraq during the U.S. occupation there, carrying out roadside bombings, abductions, beheadings, and executions of Iraqis, Americans, and other foreigners. Al-Qaeda was also involved in the assassination of U.S. diplomat Laurence Foley in Jordan; a terrorist car bombing in Kenya; an abortive missile attack on an Israeli aircraft in November 2002; bombings of a foreign compound in Riyadh, Saudi Arabia; and the bombing of a synagogue in Istanbul in 2003. Whether bin Laden has ordered all or some of these attacks, or whether he is aware of them in advance, is unknown. Many political observers believe that, as a fugitive, he is too isolated to be intimately involved in planning terrorist attacks but rather serves as an inspirational figure and advocate for those who do. Despite initial reports that he had been killed or was critically ill (he is said to have kidney disease) after he fled Afghanistan, bin Laden subsequently resurfaced in a number of videos and audiotapes in which he exhorts his followers to continue the jihad and reminds the world that he hasn't gone away.

In recent years al-Qaeda seems to have metastasized in two significant respects. A small number of al-Qaeda followers have left their sanctuary in the tribal areas of Pakistan and traveled to Somalia and Yemen. (At the end of 2010, U.S. officials estimated that there were fewer than 100 al-Qaeda members in Afghanistan.) But al-Qaeda has also become a brand that has been appropriated by many other militant groups, such as al-Qaeda in Mesopotamia (a homegrown Iraqi terrorist group), which have little or no connections with the original al-Qaeda. The movement of al-Qaeda operatives into Somalia and Yemen is attributed partly to an intensification of U.S. unmanned drone attacks that have killed several top al-Qaeda leaders in Pakistan. At the same time, terrorists are free to plot and conduct operations in a failed state such as Somalia rather than in a country with an effective central government. In addition, much of Somalia has fallen under the control of a radical Islamic group, the Shabab, which shares many of al-Qaeda's radical goals. Although Yemen is not a failed state, its government is weak, and al-Qaeda enjoys considerable support from certain segments of its population. (Yemen was once Osama bin Laden's home.) U.S. intelligence officials believe that al-Qaeda members in all three countries (Pakistan, Somalia, and Yemen) are in regular communication with one another. U.S. military and intelligence operations have been bolstered in Somalia and in North Africa in response to the growing Islamic militant threat.

If there is one trend that characterizes the persistent threat of al-Qaeda it lies in its ability to adapt and metastasize. Two back-to-back bombing attacks in UGANDA in July 2010, which killed 74, were carried out by Islamic militants affiliated with al-Shabab, a Somali insurgent group closely linked to al-Qaeda. Other militant groups associated with al-Qaeda have launched attacks against Western interests and taken hostages elsewhere in Africa, including MAURITANIA and Niger. Al-Qaeda has been particularly active in Yemen, exploiting the tribal and political conflicts that have made large parts of the country virtually ungovernable. On Christmas Day, 2009, a Nigerian national, trained in bomb making in Yemen, tried to blow up a Detroit-bound plane (he was subdued by passengers before he could detonate his explosive device). Then in October 2010 authorities found and defused on U.S.-bound cargo planes explosive packages whose origin was also traced to al-Qaeda agents in Yemen. Intelligence officials believed that al-Qaeda might only have been testing for breaches in the security regime of cargo transport, which is not as restrictive as it is on passenger flights. At the same time, al-Qaeda has ramped up its recruitment of foreigners, mostly young men. Several second-generation Somalis from the Detroit area have joined al-Shabab in Somalia and participated in fighting. In October 2010 five German nationals apparently being trained by Islamic militants in the lawless tribal areas of Pakistan were killed in a U.S. drone attack. Al-Qaeda and allied groups are especially interested in recruiting foreigners because they can escape scrutiny more easily and act as sleeper agents in their home countries.

See also SAUDI ARABIA, HUMAN RIGHTS VIOLATIONS IN; WAR ON TERROR.

Further Reading:
Atwan, Abdel Bari. *The Secret History of al Qaeda.* Berkeley: University of California Press, 2008.
Burke, Jason. *Al-Qaeda: Casting a Shadow of Terror.* London: I. B. Tauris, 2004.
———. *Al-Qaeda: The True Story of Radical Islam.* London: I. B. Tauris, 2004.
Council on Foreign Relations [U.S.]. *Backgrounder: al-Qaeda.* Available online. URL: http://www.cfr.org/publication/9126/. Accessed March 20, 2010.
FAS.org. Intelligence Resource Program. *Al-Qa'ida (The Base).* Available online. URL: http://www.fas.org/irp/world/para/ladin.htm. Accessed March 20, 2010.
Gunaratna, Rohan. *Inside Al Qaeda: Global Network of Terror.* New York: Berkley Publishing Group, 2003.
Raymond, Ibrahim. *The Al-Qaeda Reader.* New York: Broadway, 2007.
Reidal, Bruce. *The Search for Al Qaeda: Its Leadership, Ideology and Future.* Washington, D.C.: Brookings Institution Press, 2008.
Scheuer, Michael. *Imperial Hubris: Why the West Is Losing the War on Terror.* Washington, D.C.: Potomac Books, 2004.
Zayy-at, Montassar al-. *The Road to Al-Qaeda: The Story of bin Laden's Right-Hand Man.* Critical Studies on Islam. Translated by Ahmed Fekry. Edited by Sarah Nimis. Ann Arbor, Mich.: Pluto Press, 2004.

Qahtani, Mohammed al- (1979–) *Saudi suspected terrorist*

Mohammed AL-Qahtani, a detainee held in the federal detention facility at Guantánamo in Cuba since 2002, is widely believed to be the "20th hijacker"—the al-Qaeda operative who was set to join his four comrades on board United Airlines Flight 93, which crashed in Pennsylvania on September 11, 2001. (The three other airlines involved in the attacks of 9/11 were hijacked by teams of five.) Evidently, al-Qahtani was unable to participate in the terrorist plot because he had been refused entry to the United States due to immigration problems a month before the attacks. He was subsequently captured in AFGHANISTAN. Allegations that he was subjected to harsh and illegal treatment at the hands of his interrogators might make it impossible to ever assure him of a fair trial. Al-Qahtani admitted that he had been chosen as a hijacker by Khaled Sheik Mohammed, architect of the 9/11 attacks, and that he had met Osama bin Laden and other senior members of AL-QAEDA on several occasions. He also confessed to having received training at al-Qaeda camps in Afghanistan. He later repudiated many of his statements, asserting that he had made them under duress. In addition, he informed on 30 other detainees, providing Pentagon lawyers with intelligence to justify their detention as "enemy combatants" in cases before special military tribunals established by the Bush administration. Al-Qahtani's court-appointed lawyer, Gitanjali S. Gutierrez of the Center for Constitutional Rights, filed a challenge in federal court to al-Qahtani's detention. After visiting him in December 2005, Gutierrez described al-Qahtani as a broken man who claimed to have endured "months of isolation, torture and abuse, during which he was nearly killed, before making false statements to please his interrogators." Military documents confirm many of these charges; between 2002 and 2003 al-Qahtani was subjected to prolonged isolation, sleep deprivation,

forced nudity, and exposure to cold. He was also forced to dance with a male interrogator and to respond to commands like "stay" and "bark." While the Pentagon denied that he had been mistreated, Susan J. Crawford, the senior Pentagon official in the Bush administration's system for prosecuting detainees, determined that he had in fact been tortured. Her ruling in January 2009 meant that no trial could take place. (She had previously dismissed charges against him without explanation.) Military prosecutors had expected to ask for the death penalty. Al-Qahtani's lawyers believe that it is possible that he will never be tried. Whether he will remain in a legal limbo for the rest of his life is also uncertain.

See also GUANTÁNAMO DETAINEES; WAR ON TERROR.

R

Raeder, Erich (1876–1960) *Nazi naval commander*

Erich Raeder, German supreme naval commander from 1928 to 1943, was among the war criminals put on trial in Nuremberg at the end of World War II. The son of a headmaster, he was born in Schleswig-Holstein on April 24, 1876. He joined the Imperial Navy in 1894 and quickly rose in the ranks. In 1928 he was promoted to admiral and head of the German navy. While not a strong supporter of the Nazi Party, which took power in 1933, he backed ADOLF HITLER's efforts to rebuild the navy and make Germany a great military power once again. In 1936, just before Raeder's 60th birthday, Hitler rewarded him with the title grand admiral.

In October 1939, shortly after the invasion of Poland, Raeder proposed to Hitler that the Germans invade Norway and Denmark, pointing out that without establishing naval bases in those countries, it would be impossible for Germany to successfully mount an attack against Great Britain. At the same time, Raeder advocated a policy of deploying greater numbers of U-boats and small surface vessels while establishing a strong German presence in North Africa and the Middle East that would allow Germany to dominate the Mediterranean. In Raeder's view, the planned assault on Britain—known as Operation Sea Lion—would also require the German air force, the Luftwaffe, commanded by Raeder's rival HERMANN GÖRING, to gain air supremacy over Britain's Royal Air Force. However, the Luftwaffe's failure to meet this goal forced Hitler to cancel an invasion of the British Isles.

With the loss of the Battle of Britain, Hitler diverted his resources to an invasion of the Soviet Union (Operation Barbarossa), which Raeder opposed. As the German navy began to sustain a series of setbacks, Hitler became disillusioned with Raeder's performance and accused him of incompetence for failing to stop a large Allied convoy from reaching Europe. Raeder was subsequently demoted to the rank of admiral inspector of the German navy in January 1943. He resigned the following May and was succeeded as commander of the navy by KARL DÖNITZ, who was later appointed Hitler's designated successor just before the latter committed suicide in 1945, as the Allies were tightening their noose around Berlin. At the NUREMBERG TRIALS, Raeder was found guilty of conspiring to wage a "war of aggression" for promoting the remilitarization of the German navy and sentenced to life imprisonment. However, because of ill health his sentence was reduced, and he was released in 1955. He went on to write a memoir entitled *Mein Leben*. He died on November 6, 1960.

rape as a tactic of war

Rape and other forms of sexual violence have been used as a tactic of terror in many wars throughout history. The Nazis raped Jewish women on Kristallnacht (Night of Broken Glass) in November 1938 at the start of the pogrom against Jews. Soldiers of the Red Army raped thousands of German women in the waning days of the Second World War as they pushed into Berlin in revenge for German atrocities committed on Soviet territory. The Japanese raped Chinese women during the massacre of NANJING, and during Japan's colonial rule of Korea, Japanese soldiers exploited between 100,000 and 200,000 Korean women, turning them into sexual slaves called COMFORT WOMEN. The Pakistani army was implicated in rape that occurred during the nine-month war of Bangladeshi independence in 1971. According to International Planned Parenthood, an estimated 250,000–400,000 women in Bangladesh were raped in the war, resulting in an estimated 25,000 pregnancies. Some U.S. troops in the Vietnam War raped Vietnamese women, who suffered further violence after the war as thousands of boat people attempting to flee communist rule in frail boats were set upon by pirates. The UNITED NATIONS HIGH COMMISSIONER FOR REFUGEES reported that 39 percent of Vietnamese boat women between the ages of 11 and 40 were abducted or raped at sea in 1985. More recently, rape was employed as a deliberate strategy of terror in the 1980s and 1990s in Liberia, Uganda, Ethiopia, Rwanda, Myanmar (Burma), and the former Yugoslavia. In Bosnia and Herzegovina, Muslim and Croat refugees uprooted by Serb forces in the Bosnian War reported that women were raped in public as part of a campaign of "ETHNIC CLEANSING," forcing families to flee their villages.

Rape is not only a crime directed against an individual but also targets the victim's family and community. In many cultures a woman who has been raped is stigmatized and considered a pariah; a child born to a woman who becomes pregnant by rape is especially at risk of being shunned by family and community. In that sense, rape is used to tear apart the bonds of family and society at large. Rape is also used as a manifestation of ethnic or nationalistic hatred. It has the additional effect of humiliating and shaming male members of the victim's family, since acts of sexual violence against women demonstrate the men's inability to protect their women. As a result, an enemy can traumatize a large number of people by targeting only a relatively few victims.

In spite of the frequency of its use as a tool of war, rape has been underreported and often overlooked by law-enforcement agencies. Nonetheless, rape has been considered a war crime for several centuries; as far back as 1474, Sir Peter von Hagenbach, an emissary of Charles the Bold of Burgundy, was convicted on charges of rape as well as murder and PILLAGE, tactics he used to subdue the Austrian town of Breisach. The LIEBER CODE, drafted by Francis Lieber at the request of Abraham Lincoln, made rape a capital crime for Union troops during the American Civil War. Article 46 of the regulations annexed to the 1907 Hague Convention calls for respect for "family honor and rights"; this provision was applied in the prosecution of Japanese officers for thousands of rapes committed by Japanese troops in Nanjing.

Although evidence of rape was introduced at the NUREMBERG TRIALS, none of the convicted Nazi war criminals was ever found guilty of that crime. The first time that rape was specifically cited as a war crime was at the TOKYO TRIALS of Japanese war criminals who were charged with violation of the laws and customs of war. Several Japanese officers were found guilty of allowing troops under their command to rape women in areas they conquered. Many legal experts contend that rape could be considered GENOCIDE if it is directed systematically at victims who belong to a particular race, ethnic or national group, as was the case in Rwanda and the former Yugoslavia. In January 1993, after a UN investigation revealed the prevalence of rape in the Bosnian War, the UNITED NATIONS HUMAN RIGHTS COMMISSION passed a resolution that identified rape as a war crime for the first time and called for an international tribunal to prosecute these crimes. As envisioned, this tribunal could try officers for ordering and committing

rape; individuals who are in a position to stop rape and do not could also be held liable.

The most recent effort to make rape a crime under international law is found in the Rome Statute of 1998, adopted by delegates to a UN conference, which established the permanent INTERNATIONAL CRIMINAL COURT. The statute listed forced pregnancy as a war crime for the first time: "The unlawful confinement, of a woman forcibly made pregnant, with the intent of affecting the ethnic composition of any population or carrying out other grave violations of international law." The court's statutes also consider sexual slavery, enforced prostitution, and enforced sterilization treat to be CRIMES AGAINST HUMANITY as well as rape, whether they are committed in war or peacetime, as long as the acts are widespread or systematic in nature. If committed in an international conflict, these crimes may constitute a grave breach of Article 27 of the Fourth Geneva Convention of 1949, which states that women shall be protected against any attack on their honor, including rape, enforced prostitution, or any form of indecent assault. In addition, sexual violence can be considered an action willfully causing great suffering or serious injury to body or health, which is a grave breach under Article 147 of the Fourth Geneva Convention. If, on the other hand, these acts are committed during an internal conflict, it may be a serious violation of ARTICLE 3 COMMON TO THE GENEVA CONVENTIONS.

Women are not the only victims of rape. The INTERNATIONAL CRIMINAL TRIBUNAL FOR THE FORMER YUGOSLAVIA (ICTY) convicted Dusko Tadić, a Bosnian Serb, for violating Common Article 3, as incorporated into the statute of the Yugoslav tribunal, for forcing one detainee at Omarska camp, where he was a commanding officer, to bite off the testicle of another. A Bosnian Croat paramilitary chief named Anto Furundzija was found guilty by the ICTY for allowing a subordinate to rape a Bosnian Muslim woman. Furundzija's case was the first time a UN war crimes tribunal tried a case where rape was the major crime charged against a defendant. In its description of the crime, the tribunal chose to use the gender-neutral term *victim* in defining any person who had been raped or subjected to other forms of sexual violence.

No country on earth rivals the Democratic Republic of the CONGO in the use of rape as a means of terrorizing civilians in wartime. The incidence of rape, perpetrated by rebel groups and government forces alike, has reached epidemic proportions in Congo. In 15 years of war tens of thousands of women and girls, and some men as well, have been raped, brutalized, and kidnapped. While most abuses are concentrated in the eastern Congo, the site of ongoing ethnic conflict exacerbated by the spillover from the Rwandan genocide of 1994, gang rapes have occurred elsewhere in the country, including a mass rape of as many as 600 illegal Congolese immigrant women expelled from neighboring Angola in October 2010. "We spend a lot of time in the bush," one Congolese soldier said, "and when we meet a woman and she doesn't want us we take her by force."

See also BANGLADESH, HUMAN RIGHTS VIOLATIONS IN; BOSNIA AND HERZEGOVINA, HUMAN RIGHTS VIOLATIONS IN; CONGO, DEMOCRATIC REPUBLIC OF THE, WAR CRIMES IN; ETHIOPIA, HUMAN RIGHTS VIOLATIONS IN; GENEVA CONVENTIONS; HAGUE CONVENTIONS; LIBERIA, HUMAN RIGHTS VIOLATIONS IN; MYANMAR, HUMAN RIGHTS VIOLATIONS IN; NANJING, MASSACRE IN; ROME STATUTE OF THE INTERNATIONAL CRIMINAL COURT; RWANDA, GENOCIDE IN; UGANDA, HUMAN RIGHTS VIOLATIONS IN; WOMEN'S RIGHTS, VIOLATIONS OF; YUGOSLAVIA, WAR CRIMES IN.

Further Reading:

Bloxham, Donald. *Genocide on Trial: War Crimes Trials and the Formation of Holocaust History and Memory*. Oxford: Oxford University Press, 2003.

Cooper, Belinda, and Richard Goldstone. *War Crimes: The Legacy of Nuremberg*. New York: TV Books Inc., 1999.

Dormann, Knut, and Louise Doswald-Beck. *Elements of War Crimes under the Rome Statute of the International Criminal Court: Sources and Commentary*. Cambridge: Cambridge University Press, 2003.

Falk, Richard A. *Crimes of War: A Legal, Political-Documentary, and Psychological Inquiry into the Responsibility of Leaders, Citizens, and Soldiers for Criminal Acts in Wars*. New York: Random House, 1971.

Goldstone, Richard. *For Humanity: Reflections of a War Crimes Investigator*. Castle Lectures Series. New Haven, Conn.: Yale University Press, 2000.

Gutman, Roy, ed. *Crimes of War: What the Public Should Know*. New York: W. W. Norton & Company, 1999.

Jackson, Nyamuya Maogoto. *War Crimes and Realpolitik: International Justice from World War I to the 21st Century*. Boulder, Colo.: Lynne Rienner Publishers, 2004.

Jokie, Aleksander. *War Crimes and Collective Wrongdoing: A Reader*. London: Blackwell Publishers, 2001.

Rapp, Stephen (1949–) *American jurist and ambassador*

A former U.S. attorney who served as chief prosecutor of the SPECIAL COURT FOR SIERRA LEONE, Stephen Rapp was appointed by the Obama administration as ambassador at large for war crimes issues in late 2009. The ambassador at large, who works for the State Department, is responsible for coordinating U.S. policy on legal issues related to violations of international human rights law and to international courts and tribunals. "I think we've learned that contrary to fears, holding people accountable for atrocities does not make the problem worse," Rapp told *Time* magazine, "it makes it better. When Milošević was indicted for ethnic cleansing in Kosovo, people were convinced that they would never have peace and he would be worse than ever. Within a short time he was charged and jailed in his own country." Although Rapp said that he did not believe that the United States was likely to recognize the INTERNATIONAL CRIMINAL COURT (ICC) any time soon, he expressed his support of the mission of the ICC, a stance at odds with that of the Bush administration. "If the people who were worried [when the United States was one of seven nations not in favor of the ICC] would pay attention to what the court is actually doing, they would be relieved," he said. "The ICC just indicted Joseph Kony [head of the Lord's Resistance Army in Uganda]. Darfur is a case Americans feel strongly about. We want to send a signal that the US is prepared to exercise leadership."

See also KONY, JOSEPH.

Raznatovíc, Željko   *See* ARKAN.

Red Cross   *See* INTERNATIONAL COMMITTEE OF THE RED CROSS.

refoulement

Refoulement is a term that describes the involuntary return to their homelands of REFUGEES who have a legitimate fear of facing persecution. People who can legally claim refugee status are protected by international law from refoulement. This protection is found in the United Nations Convention Relating to the Status of Refugees and its 1967 Additional Protocol. Only when a person no longer claim refugee status is the prohibition against refoulement lifted.

Voluntary return is distinguished from refoulement by the absence of what are known as "push factors"—those influences that push a person to repatriate (go home). One push factor is coercion or force. Another push factor is denying a refugee the right to seek the advice or protection of a neutral body such as the INTERNATIONAL COMMITTEE OF THE RED CROSS. Reducing or denying essential services in the host country so as to force refugees to return would also be considered a push factor. However, refoulement can also be said to occur if a person claiming refugee status is kept in ignorance or is misinformed as to the actual conditions in his homeland and is convinced to return. The UNITED NATIONS HIGH COMMISSIONER FOR REFUGEES (UNHCR) has stated in the Repatriation Handbook that "[o]nly an informed decision can be a voluntary decision." Some human rights advocates have charged that Australia was wrong to try to repatriate detainees from Afghanistan temporarily settled on the Pacific island of Nauru both because the Afghanis were given no choice and because they had no access to objective and reliable information about what conditions obtained in Afghanistan. However, questions have been raised about exactly which persons should be considered immune from refoulement and who is entitled to claim refugee status. Would illegal aliens, for instance, have the same rights as those who are legally admitted to another country? In addition, the nature of many regional conflicts has made it more difficult, if not impossible, to distinguish between those who are legitimate refugees and those who are pretending to be refugees to escape punishment for crimes committed in the territory they have fled. This situation arose when hundreds of thousands of Hutus made their way across the border of then Zaire (now Democratic Republic of the Congo) after the 1994 genocide in neighboring RWANDA. Most of those who sought sanctuary were civilians but among them were Hutu militants responsible for many of the killings of Tutsi civilians in their native land. In the chaos the UNHCR officials had little way of knowing which people had committed crimes and which were should be guaranteed protection from refoulement because they had a legitimate fear of persecution if forced to return to Rwanda. The UNHCR decided to confer protected status on all the Hutus without making an effort to separate out the killers for fear of sending innocent refugees back. Two years later, though the Tutsi-led Rwandan army pushed into eastern Zaire and forced most of the refugees back anyway.

See also AFGANISTAN, HUMAN RIGHTS VIOLATIONS IN; CONGO, DEMOCRATIC REPUBLIC OF THE, WAR CRIMES IN; RWANDA, GENOCIDE IN.

Further Reading:
Fritz, Mark. *Lost on Earth: Nomads of the New World.* New York: Routledge, 2000.
Groenewold, Julia, and Doctors Without Borders. *World in Crisis: The Politics of Survival at the End of the Twentieth Century.* London: Routledge, 1996.
Gutman, Roy, ed. *Crimes of War: What the Public Should Know.* New York: W. W. Norton & Company, 1999.
Helton, Arthur C. *The Price of Indifference: Refugees and Humanitarian Action in the New Century.* A Council on Foreign Relations Book. Oxford: Oxford University Press, 2002.
Hyndman, Jennifer. *Managing Displacement: Refugees and the Politics of Humanitarianism.* Minneapolis: University of Minnesota Press, 2000.
Ingleby, David, ed. *Forced Migration and Mental Health: Rethinking the Care of Refugees and Displaced Persons.* International and Cultural Psychology: Topics, Issues, and Directions. New York: Plenum US, 2004.
Lischer, Sarah Kenyon. *Dangerous Sanctuaries: Refugee Camps, Civil War, and the Dilemmas of Humanitarian Aid.* Cornell Studies in Security Affairs. Ithaca, N.Y.: Cornell University Press, 2005.
Moorehead, Caroline. *Human Cargo: A Journey among Refugees.* New York: Henry Holt and Co., 2005.
Ogata, Sadako, and Kofi Annan. *The Turbulent Decade: Confronting the Refugee Crises of the 1990s.* New York: W. W. Norton & Company, 2005.

refugees

Refugees are defined as people who are forced to leave their homes in order to seek safety or refuge elsewhere. Many factors can lead to a person becoming a refugee, but conflict, persecution, economic deprivation, natural disaster, and harsh living and working conditions are among the major causes. The United Nations defines the term *refugees* more narrowly as "persons who are outside their country and cannot return owing to a well-founded fear of persecution because of their race, religion, nationality, political opinion, or membership in a particular social group."

By 2008 the number of refugees had swelled to 15.2 million—about 3 million more than just six years previously and nearly double the 10 million refugees worldwide estimated in 1981. According to REFUGEES INTERNATIONAL, a nongovernmental organization, 80 percent of refugees are women and children. The UN Refugee Agency reported that those countries of origin that accounted for the highest number of refugees in 2007 were Afghanistan (2.8 million), Iraq (1.9 million), Somalia (561,000), Sudan (419,000), and Colombia (374,000). Refugees are accorded certain protections under international law that are not granted to INTERNALLY DISPLACED PERSONS (IDPs) who have not crossed international borders. (Internally displaced persons are described by the UN as "persons who have been forced or obliged to flee or to leave their homes or places of habitual residence, in particular, as a result of, or in order to avoid the effects of, armed conflict, situations of generalized violence, violations of human rights, or natural or human-made disasters, and who have not crossed an internationally recognized state border." There are an estimated 20–25 million IDPs in the world, far greater than the number of refugees.) International law requires governments to grant asylum to refugees who have a legitimate fear of persecution if they are returned to their homelands. In principle, states are obliged to provide shelter, food, and other vital resources to refugees and are prohibited from repatriating them so long as conditions remain unsafe in their countries of origin.

For all intents and purposes, many refugees have become permanent inhabitants of their host countries; thousands of Afghans, for instance, remain in refugee

Lebanese refugees in Beirut, 1978 *(United Nations)*

camps in Pakistan, having taken refuge there in the 1980s after the Soviet invasion of their country. There are thought to be over 3.5 million Afghan refugees living abroad—the largest refugee population in the world—although some have begun to return since the overthrow of the TALIBAN regime in 2001. New refugee populations have been created (or else prevented from returning home) in recent years due to conflicts in Afghanistan, Iraq, Angola, Sudan, the Democratic Republic of the Congo, Burundi, and Bosnia and Herzegovina. Each of these conflict areas has added another 400,000 refugees to the total. A potential refugee crisis is brewing as a result of economic and political instability in Communist North Korea; many desperate North Koreans have tried to find refuge in China and Russia in the hope of eventually finding asylum in South Korea, the United States, or elsewhere. The Western Hemisphere

has seen large influxes of refugees fleeing political oppression and destitution in Cuba and Haiti. The emergence of a refugee problem is often the first signal the world has of political dislocation in the country from which refugees are fleeing. Europe has also begun to grapple with a tide of African and central Asian refugees who risk their lives to make the treacherous sea crossing.

Like the United States, European countries have become increasingly restrictive and more discriminating about according refugee status. Ideas have been floated to "outsource" the refugee problem by establishing temporary havens outside of Europe for asylum seekers; one such zone, for instance, was proposed for Libya to prevent refugees from sub-Saharan countries from reaching European shores. In the United States, refugees from Haiti are at risk of being repatriated because they are deemed to be economic refugees seeking jobs rather than people who fear political violence. Cuban refugees, on the other hand, are granted refugee status under a program called humanitarian parole. The UN High Commissioner for Refugees, the leading international agency for refugee issues, has promoted three ways to protect refugees: voluntary repatriation, settlement in the host country, and third-country resettlement.

One particularly vivid example of the intractability of the refugee problem is the refugee camp of Dadaab, located in Kenya 50 miles from the Somali border. The camp, which has become one of Kenya's largest cities, was established in 1990 and is now home to 300,000 people (including 100,000 children), most of them Somali refugees. It is now the largest such camp in the world. Although it can now boast of grocery stores, cinemas, and hotels, it is lacking in schools, health centers, and water stations. Given the continuing strife in Somalia, the camp, nominally under UN supervision, is unlikely to disappear any time soon. Dadaab has also become a recruiting center for both the Somali army and al-Shabab, the Islamic insurgent group trying to overthrow the fragile Somali government. Each side has resorted to the illegal use of child soldiers. "There is a tendency to see refugee camps as warehouses for storing unused people; we need to treat them as normal people," said a senior coordinator for the UN in Dadaab. The persistent existence of such a camp raises a difficult question for the international community: How does it respond to a refugee problem that simply won't go away?

See also ASYLUM, POLITICAL; DISPLACED PERSON CAMPS; REFOULEMENT; RELIGIOUS PERSECUTION.

Further Reading:
Fritz, Mark. *Lost on Earth: Nomads of the New World.* New York: Routledge, 2000.
Groenewold, Julia, and Doctors Without Borders. *World in Crisis: The Politics of Survival at the End of the Twentieth Century.* London: Routledge, 1996.
Gutman, Roy, ed. *Crimes of War: What the Public Should Know.* New York: W. W. Norton & Company, 1999.
Helton, Arthur C. *The Price of Indifference: Refugees and Humanitarian Action in the New Century.* A Council on Foreign Relations Book. Oxford: Oxford University Press, 2002.
Hyndman, Jennifer. *Managing Displacement: Refugees and the Politics of Humanitarianism.* Minneapolis: University of Minnesota Press, 2000.
Ingleby, David, ed. *Forced Migration and Mental Health: Rethinking the Care of Refugees and Displaced Persons.* International and Cultural Psychology: Topics, Issues, and Directions. New York: Plenum US, 2004.
Lischer, Sarah Kenyon. *Dangerous Sanctuaries: Refugee Camps, Civil War, and the Dilemmas of Humanitarian Aid.* Cornell Studies in Security Affairs. Ithaca, N.Y.: Cornell University Press, 2005.
Moorehead, Caroline. *Human Cargo: A Journey among Refugees.* New York: Henry Holt and Co., 2005.
Ogata, Sadako, and Kofi Annan. *The Turbulent Decade: Confronting the Refugee Crises of the 1990s.* New York: W. W. Norton & Company, 2005.
Refugees International. Available online. URL: http://www.refugeesinternational.org/. Accessed March 20, 2010.
UN.org. United Nations High Commissioner for Refugees. Available online. URL: http://www.unhcr.org/cgi-bin/texis/vtx/home. Accessed March 22, 2010.

Refugees International

A nongovernmental organization (NGO) established in 1979, Refugees International (RI) describes its mission as generating "lifesaving humanitarian assistance and protection for displaced people around the world" while working to put an end to conditions that create displacement in the first place. RI states that its foremost role is to act as "a witness to the suffering of the displaced." Representatives of the organization spend time in the field, gathering information from people affected by war as well as from NGOs and relevant agencies. Based in Washington, D.C., RI regularly sends representatives on assessment missions to regions where war-affected populations have been forgotten by the rest of the world. In 2004 RI was involved in 20 countries where displacement is a critical problem, including the Darfur region of Sudan, Ethiopia, Bangladesh, Liberia, Haiti, Uganda, and Cambodia. RI seeks to identify the most urgent needs of REFUGEES and the internally displaced and then find solutions for them. To do this, the organization conducts advocacy campaigns intended to influence various governments and the United Nations. It is funded by individuals, foundations, and corporations.

The concept of RI originated with Sue Mortan, an American expatriate living in Asia. In 1979 she became aware of the problem of displaced people when she witnessed some 40,000 Cambodians being forced back into their war-torn country after taking refuge on the Thai border in 1979. She envisioned Refugees International as a "global voice for the world's dispossessed." She later joined a handful of protesters in front of the White House, calling for the protection of Indonesian refugees. President Jimmy Carter subsequently ordered U.S. naval vessels to rescue "boat people" fleeing Vietnam in fragile fishing boats. RI grew out of that initial effort.

See also DISPLACED PERSON CAMPS.

Further Reading:
Aall, Pamela R., Daniel Miltenberger, and George Weiss. *IGOs, NGOs, and the Military in Peace and Relief*

Operations. Washington, D.C.: United States Institute of Peace Press, 2000.

Byman, Daniel, Ian Lesser, Bruce Pirnie, Cheryl Benard, and Matthew Waxman. *Strengthening the Partnership: Improving Military Coordination with Relief Agencies and Allies in Humanitarian Operations.* Santa Monica, Calif.: Rand Corporation (NBN), 2000.

Erskins, Toni. *Can Institutions Have Responsibilities: Collective Moral Agency and International Relations.* Global Issues Series. Sydney, Australia: Palgrave Macmillan, 2004.

Lischer, Sarah Kenyon. *Dangerous Sanctuaries: Refugee Camps, Civil War, and the Dilemmas of Humanitarian Aid.* Cornell Studies in Security Affairs. Ithaca, N.Y.: Cornell University Press, 2005.

Ogata, Sadako, and Kofi Annan. *The Turbulent Decade: Confronting the Refugee Crises of the 1990s.* New York: W. W. Norton & Company, 2005.

Rieff, David. *A Bed for the Night: Humanitarianism in Crisis.* New York: Simon & Schuster, 2002.

Refugees International. Available online. URL: http://www.refugeesinternational.org/. Accessed March 20, 2010.

Vaux, Anthony. *The Selfish Altruist: Relief Work in Famine and War.* London: Earthscan Publications, 2001.

religious persecution

As a phenomenon, religious persecution has been going on since antiquity. It has probably accounted for more bloodshed than wars over ideology or resources. In many cases religious persecution is used as a cover for political or territorial objectives. In the Bosnian War of the early 1990s, for instance, Bosnian Muslims were targeted by Serbs because they had declared their independence (political), stood in the way of a greater Serbia (territorial), and subscribed to a faith that was introduced to the Balkans by Turkish invaders in the 14th century (religious). During the war, mosques were vandalized and sacked just as they were during the 1999 war in Kosovo, a separatist province with a majority Albanian Muslim population. Religious persecution is not always lethal, of course, but it almost always seeks to deprive a person practicing a certain faith of a number of rights, including the right to have an education, to work, or to own property.

Religious persecution became a focus of INTERNATIONAL HUMANITARIAN LAW (IHL) after World War II, during which millions of people had been slaughtered simply because they were Jewish. Freedom of religion was guaranteed in Article 13 of the United Nations Charter (1945), which declared: "The General Assembly shall initiate studies and make recommendations for the purpose of . . . promoting international cooperation in the economic, social, cultural, educational and health fields, and assisting

in the realization of human rights and fundamental freedoms for all without distinction as to race, sex, language or religion." The right to practice one's faith without fear of persecution was also enshrined in the 1948 UNIVERSAL DECLARATION OF HUMAN RIGHTS. Article 18 of the declaration states: "Everyone has the right to freedom of thought, conscience and religion; this right includes freedom to change his religion or belief, and freedom, either alone or in community with others and in public or private, to manifest his religion or belief in teaching, practice worship and observance." In 1966 the UN General Assembly adopted two covenants that recognized a right to freedom of religion, including both freedom of belief and practice. In 1981 the United Nations expanded upon these protections by adopting the Declaration on the Elimination of All Forms of Intolerance Based on Religion or Belief, and by the subsequent creation of a special rapporteur on religious intolerance.

It is rare for the United Nations to intervene in a humanitarian crisis solely on the basis of religious persecution, although the organization has intervened in situations posing a threat to peace and security where religious rivalry or persecution was also taking place. The UN Truce Supervision Organization in Jerusalem (UNTSO) was deployed in 1948 to monitor the truce between Israelis, the majority of whom were Jews, and Arabs, the majority of whom were Palestinian Muslims. In 1949 the UN Military Observer Group (UNMOGIP) was deployed to maintain a cease-fire between India (predominantly Hindu) and Pakistan (predominantly Muslim). More recently, the United Nations intervened in East Timor, which is mainly populated by Christians and had been in the process of gaining its independence from Indonesia, which has the largest Muslim population of any country in the world.

Attempts to deter and prevent religious persecution are hardly limited to the United Nations. Many intra- and interreligious coalitions have brought together Christians, Jews, Muslims, Sikhs, Buddhists, and representatives of other religions. Such a coalition brought pressure on the U.S. Congress in the late 1990s to address religious repression in other countries. In October 1998 Congress unanimously passed the International Religious Freedom Act (IRFA), establishing an Office of International Religious Freedom in the State Department, which is responsible for producing an annual report on religious freedom and persecution in all foreign countries. The reports are intended for use in identifying countries that have "systematic, ongoing and egregious" violations of religious freedom. The reports are also to be used by the U.S. government in determining policies toward nations that practice or condone religious persecution. In recent years the renewed attention on religious persecution has put a spotlight on Chinese repression of Tibetan Buddhists, Christians, and followers of the Falun Gung and Russian persecution of certain groups, such as Jehovah's Witnesses, which do not have official state recognition. Efforts by the United States to mediate the 20-year civil war between the Muslim north and Christian south in the Sudan were also influenced by American Christian organizations.

Religious tensions are rising in many regions throughout the world, often fueled by economic deprivation, illegal emigration, and political discord. In recent years, for example, Western Europe has begun to experience a surge in violence against Muslim immigrants because of their perceived failure to adapt to the culture of their new homes. At the same time, some Muslim radicals have called for violence against Christians and Jews. Attempts by governments to neutralize religion as a factor in civil society often arouse as many passions as they are meant to allay. France, for instance, imposed a hotly debated policy banning the display of any religion by students in public schools, such as crucifixes, Jewish stars, or head scarves for Muslim girls. Some critics contend that these measures, however well intentioned, can also be seen as a form of religious persecution.

See also BOSNIA AND HERZEGOVINA, HUMAN RIGHTS VIOLATIONS IN; CHINA, HUMAN RIGHTS VIOLATIONS IN; EAST TIMOR, HUMAN RIGHTS VIOLATIONS IN; INDIA, HUMAN RIGHTS VIOLATIONS IN; KOSOVO, WAR CRIMES IN; PAKISTAN, HUMAN RIGHTS VIOLATIONS IN; RUSSIA, HUMAN RIGHTS VIOLATIONS IN; SUDAN, HUMAN RIGHTS VIOLATIONS IN.

Further Reading:
Buergenthal, Thomas. *Religious Fundamentalisms and the Human Rights of Women.* Sidney, Australia: Palgrave Macmillan, 1999.
Mayer, Ann Elizabeth. *Islam and Human Rights: Tradition and Politics.* Philadelphia: Westview Press, 1998.
Vyver, Johan D. van der, and John Witte, Jr., eds. *Religious Human Rights in Global Perspective: Legal Perspectives.* Grand Rapids, Mich.: Wm. B. Eerdmans Publishing Company, 2000.

reparations
After the end of a war, reparations usually take the form of financial compensation paid by a defeated nation to the victors. Until the Thirty Years War of the 17th century, conquering armies generally took compensation in the form of booty, but monetary damages became more common during the Napoleonic Wars of 1803–15. In 1871, after the Franco-Prussian War, the Prussians demanded that the defeated French pay about $1 billion in reparations (in today's dollars). After World War I, U.S. president Woodrow Wilson and the heads of France and Great Britain insisted on reparations from Germany that proved crip-

pling: After making an initial payment of $250 million, Germany defaulted. Historians believe that the Allies made a grave mistake by demanding excessive reparations, which are thought to be one of the major contributing factors that led Germany to remilitarize and go to war again. After initially agreeing on a reparations policy for Germany after the Second World War, the Allies eventually went their separate ways. The Soviets obtained their reparations from East Germany, while West Germany (the Federal Republic of Germany) undertook to pay reparations to groups that had suffered egregiously from Nazi persecution, providing more than $700 million to Israel and to Jews who had survived the CONCENTRATION CAMPS or to their families elsewhere in the world. Japan and other Axis powers paid about $1.4 billion in reparations as well.

While there is established precedent for war reparations, the situation is more complicated when it comes to reparations as a remedy for human rights violations. Debate periodically flares up in the United States, for instance, about whether the U.S. government should pay reparations to descendants of African-American slaves. Many indigenous peoples have also asserted their rights to reparations, among them the Aboriginals of Australia. There is no question that indigenous peoples—a category that numbers about 600 million worldwide—have suffered from abuse, exploitation, and persecution at the hands of governments and corporations without receiving adequate compensation. Campaigns to obtain reparations, however, usually have met with limited success, if any. Most nations do not carry laws on their books obliging them to remedy human rights injustices or racial discrimination. The ability of victims to obtain compensation is constrained by statutes of limitation, the imposition of AMNESTY laws granting immunity to officials implicated in human rights violations, a failure on the part of the government concerned to acknowledge that an injustice was done, and the failure of the victims to forcefully make their cases or find sufficient funding to press their causes.

Although there is still no universally applicable code of laws pertaining to reparations, the UNITED NATIONS HUMAN RIGHTS COMMISSION has put forth a set of principles to assist victims of human rights violations; they are formally known as "The Draft Basic Principles and Guidelines on the Right to Remedy and Reparation for Victims of Violations of International Human Rights and Humanitarian Law." The Draft Basic Principles underscore the need for defined standards for the right to reparations in international law that "are amenable to universal application by all states, reflecting the various legal cultures and traditions of the world." The draft states further: "Having a single body of international principles and guidelines is the only way to guarantee the ultimate goal of reparation: the non-repetition of the act." But these principles are only recommendations and have no force in law.

See also ABORIGINALS (AUSTRALIA), MISTREATMENT OF.

Further Reading:

Cose, Ellis. *Bone to Pick: Of Forgiveness, Reconciliation, Reparation, and Revenge.* New York: Atria, 2004.

Gutman, Roy, ed. *Crimes of War: What the Public Should Know.* New York: W. W. Norton & Company, 1999.

Salzberger, Ronald P. *Reparations for Slavery: A Reader.* Evanston, Ill.: Rowman & Littlefield Publishers, Inc., 2004.

reprisal

Reprisal is a legal term in INTERNATIONAL HUMANITARIAN LAW (IHL) that refers to a particular kind of retaliation. It differs from retaliation, however, in that it is considered a self-enforcement mechanism rather than a form of punishment. Under IHL a reprisal can only be undertaken to force a belligerent to cease its violation of an international law, which has brought harm to the other party. If the same action were undertaken without a breach of international law already having been committed, it would simply be a breach of international law itself.

Reprisal must be a response, not an initiative. It can take the form of an equal injury to the offending party—effectively violating the same laws that the first party has broken already—or it can be disproportionate to the initial harm and conducted with few if any constraints. The former type of reprisal is known as "in kind" and the latter as "not in kind." In general, reprisal by a belligerent for harm done by an adversary is in violation of international law. However, CUSTOMARY LAW has established some precedents allowing a "right of reprisal" as long as some basic "rules" are complied with. The right of reprisal requires subsidiarity (the failure to find redress by any other means), notice (official warning that retaliatory action is intended), and proportionality (the injury and suffering inflicted on the adversary cannot exceed that leveled by the enemy). The act of reprisal should also be temporary, lasting only as long as is necessary to cause the enemy to cease its violation.

As Frits Kalshoven points out in an essay for the CRIMES OF WAR PROJECT, the major problem with reprisals is that they are almost invariably directed against people who had nothing to do with the original violation that prompted the reprisal. Moreover, reprisals are seldom seen as justified by the party that is on the receiving end and can often lead to further reprisals by the other side. That is why for the most part international law has sought to ban reprisals as much as possible. Reprisal was explicitly cited in the 1929 Geneva Convention, which outlawed the practice against PRISONERS OF WAR. Subsequent treaties further limited the potential targets of reprisals. The GENEVA CONVENTIONS of 1949 broadened the protections against reprisals already in place for prisoners of war by prohibiting reprisals against civilians and objects (which would include vital installations such as dams and electric plants or cultural property). The prohibition is further elaborated on in Articles 51–55 of Additional Protocol 1 of 1977, although it is not mentioned in Additional Protocol II. Not all states that ratified Additional Protocol 1 have accepted a blanket ban against reprisals. The United Kingdom, for example, has taken the position that it would have the right to undertake "in kind" reprisals under certain circumstances. Reprisal has almost vanished from IHL, with one possible exception in which illegal methods of warfare are used against combatants.

See also ADDITIONAL PROTOCOLS TO THE GENEVA CONVENTIONS.

Further Reading:

Gutman, Roy, ed. *Crimes of War: What the Public Should Know.* New York: W. W. Norton & Company, 1999.

Jackson, Nyamuya Maogoto. *War Crimes and Realpolitik: International Justice from World War I to the 21st Century.* Boulder, Colo.: Lynne Rienner Publishers, 2004.

Jokie, Aleksander. *War Crimes and Collective Wrongdoing: A Reader.* London: Blackwell Publishers, 2001.

Responsibility to Protect

The doctrine of responsibility to protect, or R2P, is an attempt to formulate a principle regarding when members of the United Nations (UN) should intervene to stop genocide, war crimes, crimes against humanity, and ethnic cleansing. Ban Ki-moon, the UN secretary-general, has emphasized that the UN is in a unique position to prevent such genocidal campaigns such as the one in 1994 in RWANDA that took 800,000 lives. "It is high time to turn the promise of the responsibility to protect into practice," he said. "Resist those who try to change the subject or turn our common effort to curb the worst atrocities in human history into a struggle over ideology, geography or economics." The doctrine is very controversial, however. Many developing countries suspect that R2P could be used as a pretext to justify intervention by Western powers and interference in their internal affairs. Skeptics point to the U.S. invasion of IRAQ, France's attempt to use military force to distribute aid to victims of Cyclone Nargis in MYANMAR, and RUSSIA's incursion into South Ossetia in the war against GEORGIA. In each case, the government concerned claimed it wanted to intervene abroad for humanitarian purposes. The doctrine of R2P rests on three basic pillars: that all states must protect their populations from atrocities, that the UN and other institutions can help do so in countries that fail to live up to this commitment, and that the international community must respond when a large number of civilians are at risk and, if necessary, intervene militarily. It is the third pillar that has generated the most furor. The Bush administration opposed the doctrine, but the Obama administration is generally favorable to it. While acknowledging that R2P has been abused in conflicts such as Iraq, the U.S. ambassador to the UN, Susan Rice, said that it was incumbent on the world body "to respond to the worst outrages."

Further Reading:

International Coalition for the Responsibility to Protect. Available online. URL: http://www.responsibilitytoprotect.org/. Accessed March 20, 2010.
The Responsibility to Protect. Available online. URL: http://www.iciss.ca/menu-en.asp. Accessed March 20, 2010.

Ribbentrop, Joachim von (1893–1946) *German foreign minister*

Joachim von Ribbentrop, foreign minister of the Third Reich, was instrumental in forging a short-lived nonaggression pact with the Soviet Union in 1940. In spite of his claims that he was unaware of Nazi atrocities during World War II, he was found guilty of war crimes by the Allies at the NUREMBERG TRIALS and sentenced to death.

The son of a German army officer, Ribbentrop was born in Wesel, Germany, on April 30, 1893. He was educated at a Swiss boarding school and spent time in France and England, where he began working as a clerk with a German importing firm. He then moved to Canada to take up a job as a timekeeper on the Quebec Bridge and the Canadian Pacific Railroad. He continued his peripatetic existence, working as a journalist in New York and Boston, but when World War I erupted, he returned to Germany to join the army. In 1917, having sustained a war wound and acquired an Iron Cross for bravery, he entered the War Ministry; two years later he served as a delegate to the Paris Peace Conference to negotiate an end to the war. He spent the next several years making a considerable fortune in the wine business.

Although he joined the National Socialist German Workers Party (NSDAP) in 1921, Ribbentrop did not gain prominence in the Nazi hierarchy until 1933, when he became ADOLF HITLER's foreign affairs adviser. In August 1936 Hitler named him ambassador to London. Ribbentrop's principal mission was to persuade the British to stay out of the war and make common cause with Germany against the Communist Soviet Union. He did not succeed in either objective, nor did he endear himself to the British public by posting SS guards in front of the German embassy or giving the Hitler salute to King George VI when he presented his credentials.

In 1938 Hitler appointed Ribbentrop as foreign minister, replacing KONSTANTIN VON NEURATH. In August 1938 he was deeply involved in negotiations with England and France to secure the annexation of Czechoslovakia. Hitler then called on Ribbentrop's diplomatic skills to forge a military alliance with Japan and Italy, which collectively became known as the Axis powers. In a deft bit of diplomatic maneuvering, Ribbentrop sent a telegram to Vyacheslav Molotov, the Soviet foreign minister, informing him about the pact and assuring him that the new alliance had no designs on his country, which, he said, was actually directed against the United States. (As it turned out, Molotov was already aware that the alliance had been formed, thanks to one of his spies.) Although Hitler intended to invade the Soviet Union, he realized that he needed a delaying action to give him time to advance his military buildup. Ribbentrop and Molotov met in Moscow to work out a nonaggression pact, which was signed on August 23, 1939. The pact remained in force until Germany launched its invasion of the Soviet Union in June 1941. The pact also contained a secret appendix that carved up Estonia, Latvia, Lithuania, and Poland between the two powers.

Ribbentrop played a comparatively minor role for the duration of the war. He was arrested in June 1945 by British troops and put on trial by the Allies at Nuremberg, charged with conspiring and waging aggressive war, war crimes, and CRIMES AGAINST HUMANITY. Although he maintained that he did not know about the CONCENTRATION CAMPS or the Nazi extermination program, the judges were not persuaded. He was convicted and hanged in 1946.

Further Reading:

Bloch, Michael. *Ribbentrop: A Biography.* New York: Crown, 1993.
Goldensohn, Leon, and Robert Gellately, eds. *The Nuremberg Interviews.* New York: Knopf, 2004.
Maser, Werner. *Nuremberg: A Nation on Trial.* New York: Scribner, 1979.
Marrus, Robert, and Michael R. Marrus. *The Nuremberg War Crimes Trial of 1945–46: A Documentary History.* Bedford Series in History and Culture Sidney, Australia: Palgrave Macmillan, 1997.
Weitz, John. *Joachim von Ribbentrop: Hitler's Diplomat.* London: Weidenfeld and Nicolson, 1992.

Ríos Montt, José Efraín (1926–) *Guatemalan dictator*

General Efraín Ríos Montt headed Guatemala from March 1982 to August 1983, a turbulent period during which the military conducted a brutal war against a leftist insurgency.

A born-again evangelical Protestant, Ríos Montt was once quoted as saying that "a Christian has to walk around with his Bible and his machine gun." In 1954 he was involved in the CIA-backed ouster of leftist-leaning President Jacob Arbenz, declaring that Arbenz was holding the country "in the grip of a Russian-controlled dictatorship." After nearly three decades of successive dictatorships, Ríos Montt assumed power in a 1982 coup. In 2001 The Asociación para la Justicia y Reconciliación, a Guatemalan organization set up to investigate abuses committed in the Guatemalan civil war, charged that Ríos Montt had promoted what amounted to a genocidal policy to destroy ethnic Maya communities that were seen by the military as providing a base for the insurgents. According to the association, the policy of eliminating leftist sympathizers led to attacks—directed at both Maya and non-Maya peoples—that "included inhumane killings, exterminations, extrajudicial executions, forced DISAPPEARANCES, TORTURE, rape, cruel treatment, mutilations, and persecution on such a massive scale that they constitute CRIMES AGAINST HUMANITY." This policy, said the association, resulted in mass murder and mass displacement of the targeted communities "which forced them into sub-human conditions." It is not clear whether Ríos Montt directed these attacks, but it is reasonable to assume that he had some knowledge of them. Nonetheless, after Ríos Montt came to power, the U.S. ambassador at the time declared that Guatemala "has come out of the darkness and into the light." President Reagan later maintained that Ríos Montt had been given "a bum rap" by human rights groups and was actually only cleaning up the mess left by his predecessor, General Fernando Romeo Lucas García. Ríos Montt attempted a political resurrection in 2003 when he tried to run for president, but the effort failed when he came in third—much to the relief of human rights advocates.

Because it seemed unlikely that Ríos Montt would ever be prosecuted in Guatemala, the Nobel Peace Prize winner Rigoberta Menchú brought charges against him in Spain in 1999, accusing the former strongman of torture, genocide, illegal detention, and state-sponsored terrorism. In September 2005 Spain's Constitutional Court ruled that Ríos Montt and four other former Guatemalan generals (two of them ex-presidents), as well as three nonmilitary high-ranking officials who had served in the government between 1978 and 1982, could be tried in Spanish courts. Arrest warrants were issued against Ríos Montt and two ex-presidents (one of whom died) and for a former minister of interior and two ex-chiefs of police. At a press conference in 2006 Ríos Montt acknowledged that the army had committed "excesses" during his tenure but also insisted that he was not culpable of them. However, documents from the national archives that came to light as a result of the case in Spain revealed that contrary to Ríos Montt's protestations of innocence, he had orchestrated a campaign in the summer of 1982 called Operation Sofia that resulted in the massacre of thousands of innocent indigenous Mayan civilians. Far from lying low, however, Ríos Montt ran for and won a seat in the Guatemalan Congress in 2007.

See also GUATEMALA, HUMAN RIGHTS VIOLATIONS IN.

Further Reading:
Archdiocese of Guatemala. *Guatemala: Never Again!* Maryknoll, N.Y.: Orbis Books, 1999.
O'Kane, Trish. *Guatemala: A Guide to the People, Politics, and Culture.* London: Latin America Bureau, 1999.
Wilkinson, Daniel. *Silence on the Mountain: Stories of Terror, Betrayal, and Forgetting in Guatemala.* Boston: Houghton Mifflin, 2002.

Rom (Roma, Romany, Gypsies), persecution of

The Rom, also known as Roma or Romany and commonly misidentified as Gypsies, settled in Europe as early as the 14th century after migrating from the Indian subcontinent. They have long suffered from persecution, and never more so than under German occupation during World War II. It is estimated that as many as 1.5 million Rom perished between 1935 and 1945 at the hands of the Nazis. Even today, though, Rom face discrimination and harassment that contribute to high rates of poverty and unemployment. When he came to power in Germany in 1933, ADOLF HITLER did not need to introduce new laws directed against the Rom; he only built upon so-called "anti-Gypsy" laws that had originated in the Middle Ages. However, he was confronted with an ideological dilemma: His well-known antagonism toward the Jews was based on the fact that they were non-Aryan, but because of their descent from Indians—the quintessential Aryans—the same could not be said about the Rom. The Nazis resolved this particular conundrum by simply denying the truth and insisting that the Rom were not of Aryan origin at all but were instead "subhuman beings" and members of a "lower race."

In September 1935 the Nazis enacted the racist NUREMBERG LAWS, which were intended to remove Jews from the political, social, and economic life of the country. Two years later the laws were applied to the Rom as well. Under these laws, the Rom were also forbidden to intermarry people who were classified as Aryans. An individual was classified as a Rom if two grandparents had Romany blood. Like Jews, the Rom were placed in CONCENTRATION CAMPS—initially at Dachau, Dieselstrasse, Mahrzan, and Vennhausen—as early as 1937. Subsequently Rom were imprisoned at Buchenwald, where thousands were worked to death, tortured, shot, or hanged. Rom were frequently sterilized, a practice that began as early as 1933. When the Nazis determined on the Entlösung, or FINAL SOLUTION, only two groups were singled out for complete destruction: Jews and Rom. After 1938, Rom were deported from many parts of occupied Europe, including the Baltic states, Poland, Austria, Czechoslovakia, France, Italy, and Hungary and sent to concentration camps for extermination. But some Rom still remained at large, prompting the Nazis to conduct roundups of Rom in February 1943. As a result of these dragnets, over 10,000 Rom were placed in Sachsenhausen, and 16,000 were sent to Auschwitz. At both camps the Rom were brutalized and killed in a variety of ways and were also sent to the gas chambers for the first time.

Notwithstanding the systematic campaign to annihilate the Rom, their plight was ignored by Allied prosecutors at the Nuremberg Trials. In fact, no war crime tribunals after the war ever investigated the atrocities that led to the deaths of so many Rom. This is not to say that there has not been official recognition of Rom suffering during the war; the U.S. Holocaust Memorial Council, for instance, has acknowledged that, like the Jews, the Rom were victims of a genocidal campaign by the Nazis. The distinguished writer Elie Wiesel, a Jewish survivor of Auschwitz, spoke about the Rom when he accepted the 1986 Nobel Peace Prize: "We have not done enough to make other people listen to your voice of sadness. I can promise you we shall do whatever we can from now on to listen better."

Nonetheless, persecution of the Rom persists in Europe, often fostered by neo-Nazis and other right-wing extremists. In the 1990s, for instance, neo-Nazis claimed responsibility for planting a pipe bomb in an Austrian village that killed four Rom. In another incident, racists attacked a hostel housing Rom asylum seekers in Rostock, Germany. The Rom have also found themselves in the middle of the ethnic conflicts in the former Yugoslavia; in 1994 they were persecuted by Serbs during the Bosnian conflict; then in 1999 they were persecuted by ethnic Albanians in the breakaway province of Kosovo because some of them were accused of taking sides with the ethnic Serbs.

The Rom have been especially embattled in Hungary in recent years. Between 2008 and mid-2009, seven Rom were killed and Rom homes were damaged by at least 30 firebomb attacks. In one case, in February 2009, a Rom man and his four-year-old son were murdered as they sought to flee their burning house. Hungarian investigators speculate that veterans of the Balkan wars and Hungarian members of the French foreign legion might be behind some of the attacks. Exploiting the economic turmoil and rising unemployment, rightist nationalist parties in the former Communist Eastern bloc have been stirring up xenophobic fervor against Rom. The leader of a hard-line Hungarian party has warned of a scourge of what he termed "gypsy crime." In the Czech Republic, demonstrators were forcibly prevented from marching through Rom neighborhoods by police. "We are living in fear, all the Roma people

are," lamented one woman who lost both her son and grandson to extremist violence. The Rom also suffer from routine discrimination and are often barred from restaurants, swimming pools, and discotheques. When Rom attempt to flee from countries where they face persecution, they may find themselves subjected to restrictive asylum policies that prevent them from finding refuge.

In spite of violence directed against the Rom, the United Nations did not formally address the issue until a resolution was adopted in 1991 that acknowledged, "in many countries, various obstacles exist to the full realization by persons belonging to the Rom community of their civil, political, economic, social and cultural rights and that such obstacles constitute discrimination directed specifically against that community, rendering it particularly vulnerable." A subsequent resolution entitled "Protection of Roma (Gypsies)," adopted the same year, urged the special rapporteur on minorities to give special attention to conditions in Rom communities. In the mid-1990s, as part of this effort, the Office of the United Nations High Commissioner for Refugees (UNHCR) conducted a survey of Rom communities in Europe. The results were alarming: UN investigators found that persecution against the Rom in central and eastern Europe had the potential of becoming "one of the greatest destabilizing factors in Europe since the 1920s and 1930s." They identified three factors contributing to the problems afflicting the Rom: "increasing economic deprivation, increasing social instability, and the surfacing of long-suppressed ethnic hostilities . . . fuelled by the 'skinhead' syndrome that has made its way from Western Europe."

The plight of the Rom attracted worldwide attention when France began to accelerate the deportation of Romanian and Bulgarian Rom in 2010. Although France had deported thousands of Rom from those countries in the past, the latest wave drew intense criticism at home and elsewhere in Europe. European justice commissioner Viviane Reding caused a firestorm when she seemed to compare France's policy to the Nazi deportations of Rom during World War II. French president Nicolas Sarkozy reacted with such fury to the accusation that Reding later backed down. As of 2010 the Council of Europe estimated that the Rom population in France ranged from 100,000 to 500,000. The highest concentrations of Rom populations—over 1 million in each country—are found in Romania and Turkey.

See also Kosovo, war crimes in; Yugoslavia, war crimes in.

Further Reading:
Bancroft, Angus. *Roma and Gypsy—Travellers in Europe: Modernity, Race, Space and Exclusion.* Research in Migration and Ethnic Relations. Aldershot, U.K.: Ashgate, 2005.

European Roma Human Rights Centre. Available online. URL: http://www.errc.org/. Accessed March 20, 2010.

Lieseois, J. *Roma Gypsies: A European Minority.* Minority Rights Group Reports. London: Minority Rights, 1995.

NGO Roma Together. Available online. URL: http://www.romatogether.org/. Accessed March 20, 2010.

OSCE.org. Office for Democratic Institutions and Human Rights Roma and Sinti. Available online. URL: http://www.osce.org/odihr/18148.html. Accessed March 20, 2010.

Rome Statute of the International Criminal Court

The INTERNATIONAL CRIMINAL COURT (ICC), described as "the first ever permanent, treaty based, international criminal court established to promote the rule of law and ensure that the gravest international crimes do not go unpunished," was established by the Rome Statute on July 17, 1998. It was adopted by delegates of 120 countries participating in the United Nations Diplomatic Conference of Plenipotentiaries on the Establishment of an International Criminal Court. The statute set out the ICC jurisdiction, structure, and functions. It entered into force on July 1, 2002, after being ratified by 60 nations. Any individual implicated in a crime under the statute after that date became liable to being brought before the ICC, which sits in the Hague in the Netherlands. It should be noted that the ICC is separate from two ad hoc UN tribunals—the INTERNATIONAL CRIMINAL TRIBUNAL FOR THE FORMER YUGOSLAVIA and the INTERNATIONAL CRIMINAL TRIBUNAL FOR RWANDA.

See also WAR CRIMES, CATEGORIZATION OF.

Further Reading:

Dormann, Knut, and Louise Doswald-Beck. *Elements of War Crimes under the Rome Statute of the International Criminal Court: Sources and Commentary.* Cambridge: Cambridge University Press, 2003.

International Criminal Court. Available online. URL: http://www.icc-cpi.int/Menus/ICC. Accessed March 20, 2010.

Romano, Cesare, Andre Nollkaemper, and Jann K. Kleffner, eds. *Internationalized Criminal Courts and Tribunals: Sierra Leone, East Timor, Kosovo, and Cambodia.* International Courts and Tribunals Series. Oxford: Oxford University Press, 2004.

Rosenberg, Alfred (1893–1946) *Nazi ideologue*

Alfred Rosenberg was the official National Socialist ideologist who was charged by the tribunal at the NUREMBERG TRIALS after the war with being "an essential part of the conspirator's program for seizure of power and prepara-

tion for aggressive war." A rabid anti-Semite, he also provided the Nazis with a philosophical basis for some of their most pernicious policies, including the theory of racism, lebensraum (the removal of non-Aryan people from German-occupied territory), the abolition of the Versailles Treaty, and persecution of the Jews and of Christian churches. As early as 1918, he gave a speech about the "Jewish problem," which represented his first foray into politics. "For Germany the Jewish Question is only then solved when the Last Jew has left the Greater German space," he wrote years later when Germany was already at war. "Since Germany with its blood and its nationalism has now broken for always this Jewish dictatorship for all Europe and has seen to it that Europe as a whole will become free from the Jewish parasitism once more, we may, I believe, also say for all Europeans: For Europe the Jewish question is only then solved when the last Jew has left the European continent."

Rosenberg was born to ethnic German parents in Tallinn, Russia (now Estonia), on January 12, 1893. As a student of architecture at the Riga Technical Institute, he joined a pro-German student group. A supporter of the Whites—the anti-Bolshevik forces—during the Russian Civil War, he fled to France when the Communists came to power. In 1918 he relocated to Germany, where he joined the nascent National Socialist German Workers Party (NSDAP) in January 1919—nine months before ADOLF HITLER—becoming editor of the party newspaper *Voelkischer Beobachter* (National observer). His first publication in 1922 was entitled "Nature, Basic Principles, and Aims of the NSDAP," which set forth Nazi political objectives. He befriended Hitler and visited the future führer when he was imprisoned after the Beer Hall Putsch, an abortive coup attempt in 1923 against the government of Bavaria. Some biographers believe that Rosenberg helped Hitler write his memoir, *Mein Kampf (My Struggle).* While Hitler remained in prison, Rosenberg briefly served as head of the Nazi Party. Although Rosenberg was flattered by his appointment, there is some indication that Hitler chose him because he believed Rosenberg had a weak character and thus could pose no threat to his leadership once he was freed.

In 1929 Rosenberg founded the Militant League for German Culture. When the Nazis came to power in 1933, he hoped to become foreign minister but was passed over in favor of JOACHIM VON RIBBENTROP. Instead he became the Nazi's chief ideologue when, in January 1934, Hitler made him responsible for the spiritual and philosophical education of the Nazis and allied groups. In 1940 he became head of the Hohe Schule (literally "high school"), the Center of National Socialist Ideological and Educational Research. When Operation Barbarossa—the code name for the German invasion of the Soviet Union—

appeared to be going well, he received an additional appointment as minister for the eastern territories (though he had to share his responsibilities with HERMANN GÖRING, HEINRICH HIMMLER, and ERICH KOCH). Nonetheless, he took advantage of his position to plunder money and valuables from Jews in Poland and occupied parts of the USSR. In advocating the policy of lebensraum, Rosenberg wrote, "The understanding that the German nation, if it is not to perish in the truest sense of the word, needs ground and soil for itself and its future generations, and the second sober perception that this soil can no more be conquered in Africa, but in Europe and first of all in the East-these organically determine the German foreign policy for centuries." He also sought to substitute a pagan-oriented mythology in place of Christianity: "Today, a new faith is awakening—the Myth of the Blood, the belief that the divine being of mankind generally is to be defended with the blood. The faith embodied by the fullest realization, that the Nordic blood constitutes that mystery which has supplanted and overwhelmed the old sacraments." By the same token, he advocated the persecution of Christian churches: "We now realize that the central supreme values of the Roman and the Protestant Churches, being a negative Christianity, do not respond to our soul, that they hinder the organic powers of the peoples determined by their Nordic race, that they must give way to them, that they will have to be remodeled to conform to a Germanic Christendom."

But no issue obsessed Rosenberg as much as the "Jewish Question." He sent representatives to the WANNSEE CONFERENCE to determine how the FINAL SOLUTION was to be carried out, a policy that had as its aim the destruction of the entire Jewish population of Europe. He also proposed an Anti-Jewish Congress, to be held in June 1944, but it was cancelled because of the war. At one point, when 100 Frenchmen were about to be executed in REPRISAL for attacks on German soldiers, Rosenberg proposed instead that 100 Jewish bankers be substituted for the purpose of "awakening the anti-Jewish sentiment," in the words of the Nuremberg Tribunal indictment.

At the end of the war Rosenberg was captured by Allied troops. He was charged by the Nuremberg Tribunal with "conspiracy to commit crimes against peace; planning, initiating and waging wars of aggression; war-crimes; CRIMES AGAINST HUMANITY." Found guilty on these charges, he was sentenced to death and executed with several other codefendants on October 16, 1946.

Further Reading:

Dawidowicz, Lucy. *A Holocaust Reader.* Library of Jewish Studies. Chicago: Behrman House Publishing, 1976.
Dwork, Deborah, and Robert Jan Van Pelt. *Holocaust: A History.* New York: W. W. Norton & Company, 2003.
Gilbert, Martin. *The Holocaust: A History of the Jews of Europe during the Second World War.* New York: Owl Books, 1987.
Roseman, Mark. *The Wannsee Conference and the Final Solution: A Reconsideration.* New York: Metropolitan Books, 2002.

Russia, human rights violations in

In Russia, as Vladimir Putin secured his grip on power, first as president and then as prime minister, human rights protections have continued to deteriorate. A 2009 HUMAN RIGHTS WATCH report called on the European Union to reassess "Russia's commitment to the shared values articulated in the EU-Russia Partnership and Cooperation Agreement"—then under renegotiation—in light of murders and attacks against human rights activists; the failure to implement European Court of Human Rights judgments on cases from Chechnya; abuses in the North Caucuses, "including extrajudicial executions, torture, and illegal detentions, and continued impunity for these abuses"; as well as for persistent harassment and other abuses against migrant workers. An AMNESTY INTERNATIONAL report in 2009 criticized Putin for consolidating power by eliminating the election of regional governors in favor of Kremlin appointments. The group also noted a trend toward increasing domestic violence and racial hate crimes that was exacerbated by worsening economic conditions in 2008 because of the global recession. (Although Russia has benefited from higher prices for oil, its dependency on its petroleum resources is a potential vulnerability if prices fall precipitously, as they have in the past.) One of the most disturbing trends in recent years has been a spate of killings of journalists. The COMMITTEE TO PROTECT JOURNALISTS cited Russian authorities for failure to solve the murders of 16 journalists killed between 2000 and 2009. At the time of the report, the committee declared that Russia was third in the number of journalists slain, after IRAQ and ALGERIA (although it is possible that the PHILIPPINES may vie for inclusion in the top three). The committee concluded that critical and investigative journalism in Russia was almost "extinct" and that the government was imposing its message by tightening control over media outlets, especially television. (Print media are under fewer constraints, but fewer Russians get their news from such sources.)

The report said "systematic failures have created a devastating record of injustice," describing a situation in which investigative reporters were "isolated, undervalued and vulnerable to attack." The slain journalists worked for both broadcast and print media as reporters, editors, photographers, and columnists, but they all tackled sensitive subjects involving abuses by the government and law enforcement agencies as well as corrupt practices by businesses and the infiltration of public institutions by criminal organizations. The committee noted that if the people killed had been ordinary citizens, their murderers would have been brought to justice, but the cases against suspects in the slayings of journalists are frequently compromised; evidence is concealed, bogus charges are brought, or juries are intimidated. The government may not be directly responsible for the killings, but human rights organizations hold it responsible for failing to properly investigate or punish those who are guilty, fostering a climate of impunity for the perpetrators while intimidating others who would follow in the paths of the murdered journalists. The most prominent journalist to be killed was Anna Polikovskaya, who was shot to death in the elevator of her building in October 2006. The newspaper she worked for, *Novaya Gazeta*, which is known for its investigative stories, has been repeatedly targeted, most recently in January 2009 when a masked gunman burst into its editorial office and fatally shot a lawyer and a young reporter. That made a total of five journalists working for the paper who were slain under violent or suspicious circumstances since 2000. The editor subsequently put two of his reporters under armed guard and instituted a policy that obliged reporters with sensitive information to publish it immediately to avoid the possibility of being killed to silence them. Assaults on journalists have only increased. In one week in November 2010 alone, three journalists were brutally attacked and badly injured. Whether the victims were singled out because of their criticism of the government or because their articles offended prominent business interests was unclear. The beating of a 30-year-old journalist, Oleg Kashin, who worked for the *Kommersant* newspaper, drew special attention because it was recorded on surveillance video cameras, prompting President Dmitry Medvedev to call for an investigation. Many observers doubted that Medvedev's interest in the case will make much of a difference, because practically every attack on journalists in recent years, including the slaying of Politkovskaya, have gone unsolved. In such a political climate, it is not surprising to find that Russia's human rights record has worsened in many areas, but nowhere more than in Chechnya, where Russia has fought two wars since the early 1990s to end a separatist insurgency. Sporadic efforts to resolve the conflict have, however, failed. The war continues to account for atrocities, DISAPPEARANCES, and other forms of abuse in which both sides are complicit. The violence has spread from Chechnya to other parts of Russia, including Moscow, which has suffered from a number of terrorist attacks, most of them connected to the war. Security forces have engaged in TORTURE and violence, and the Federal Security Service (FSB), the successor of the KGB, operates with only limited oversight by the Procurator (chief prosecutor) and the

courts. According to the Observatory for the Protection of Human Rights Defenders, a human rights nongovernmental organization (NGO), Putin's policy of "controlled democracy"—creating a strong centralized state—is being justified by the need to combat terrorism in Chechnya.

Security forces, which previously were charged with maintaining civil order, are becoming increasingly militarized as they are called upon to take part in conflicts like the one in Chechnya. Although the Code of Criminal Procedure bans arbitrary arrests or protracted detentions, abuses persist. Security forces continue to infringe on citizens' privacy rights. In general, the government has taken step to circumscribe rights that citizens had only begun to enjoy since the fall of communism in 1990. In July 2003, for instance, a new law was passed by the Duma that imposed several new limits on demonstrations, banning them altogether near government buildings, although some of the more stringent restrictions were subsequently modified. Regional and local authorities have shown even more of a disregard for human rights than the Kremlin, in some cases suppressing freedom of assembly and imposing restrictions on select religious groups, such as Jehovah's Witnesses, that do not have official recognition. (The Russian Orthodox Church is the dominant faith.) Members of certain ethnic groups have been singled out for persecution and attack by racists, resulting in beatings and killings. Victims of bigotry are more likely to be dark-skinned; those people who are Rom (Gypsies) or come from the Caucasus, central Asia, or Africa are particularly at risk. In many instances officials not only condone persecution of ethnic minorities but practice it themselves. People from the Caucasus are routinely harassed by security forces and often detained at checkpoints near the border with Chechnya. Chechen men are regularly the victims of targeted security operations known as night raids. Activities of NGOs—especially human rights groups trying to gain access to Chechnya—also suffer from harassment and restrictions. But human rights activists elsewhere in the country come under pressure as well, particularly in St. Petersburg, where legal proceedings have been instituted against NGOs as a means of shutting them down.

Political opposition figures have been assassinated, but there is little evidence that the government has seriously tried to identify, much less pursue, the perpetrators. The constitution bans the use of torture, violence, or other types of mistreatment of suspects by police, but human rights groups report that torture and beatings by police and other security forces continue nonetheless. The authorities have been slow to punish the guilty, in part because neither the criminal code nor the constitution offers a definition of torture, making it more difficult to bring charges. Human rights activists are also concerned about the confinement of individuals in psychiatric hospitals because of their political or religious beliefs, a practice that was common in the Soviet era as well. At one point, according to the Independent Psychiatric Association of Russia, 10 Jehovah's Witnesses were incarcerated in a psychiatric hospital where doctors purportedly tried to "return to them their mental health."

As an institution, the military is rife with abuse; there is almost an epidemic of violent hazing—called *dedovshchina*—of new recruits that have resulted in deaths and severe injuries. In 2001 the chief military prosecutor announced that approximately 2,000 hazing incidents had been reported in the first half of the year. Threats of beatings have been used to extort money from recruits.

See also CHECHNYA, WAR CRIMES IN; RELIGIOUS PERSECUTION; ROM (ROMA, ROMANY, GYPSIES), PERSECUTION OF.

Further Reading:

Amnesty International USA. Russian Federation Human Rights. Available online. URL: http://www.amnesty-usa.org/all-countries/russian-federation/page.do?id=1011228. Accessed March 20, 2010.

Billington, James H. *Russia in Search of Itself.* Washington, D.C.: Woodrow Wilson Center Press, 2004.

Campbell, Ben Nighthorse, ed. *Troubling Trends: Human Rights in Russia Hearing before the Commission on Security and Cooperation in Europe.* Chicago: Diane Pub. Co., 2003.

Hoffman, David E. *The Oligarchs: Wealth and Power in the New Russia.* New York: PublicAffairs, 2003.

Human Rights Watch. Russia Human Rights. Available online. URL: http://www.hrw.org/europecentral-asia/russia. Accessed March 20, 2010.

Klebnikov, Paul. *Godfather of the Kremlin: The Decline of Russia in the Age of Gangster Capitalism.* New York: Harvest Books, 2001.

Meier, Andrew. *Chechnya: To the Heart of a Conflict.* New York: W. W. Norton & Company, 2004.

Memorial. Available online. URL: http://www.memo.ru/eng/index.htm. Accessed March 18, 2010.

Orr, Michael. *Russia's Wars with Chechnya 1994–2003.* Essential Histories. London: Osprey Publishing, 2005.

Politkovskaya, Anna. *Putin's Russia: Life in a Failing Democracy.* Translated by Arch Tait. New York: Holt Paperbacks, 2007.

———. *A Small Corner of Hell: Dispatches from Chechnya.* Chicago: University of Chicago Press, 2003.

Tishkov, Valery, and Mikhail Gorbachev. *Chechnya: Life in a War-Torn Society.* California Series in Public Anthropology. Berkeley: University of California Press, 2004.

U.S. Department of State. *2008 Human Rights Report: Russia.* Available online. URL: http://www.state.gov/g/drl/rls/hrrpt/2008/eur/119101.htm. Accessed March 20, 2010.

Weiler, Jonathan. *Human Rights in Russia: A Darker Side of Reform.* Boulder, Colo.: Lynne Rienner Publishers, 2004.

Witte, John, and Michael Bourdeaux. *Proselytism and Orthodoxy in Russia: The New War for Souls.* Religion & Human Rights Series. Maryknoll, N.Y.: Orbis Books, 1999.

Rwanda, genocide in

In 100 days in 1994, some 800,000 people, mainly members of the Tutsi ethnic group, were slaughtered in the East African nation of Rwanda, making it one of the worst atrocities in the bloody history of the 20th century. (Estimates of deaths range from approximately 800,000 to 1 million, or one in every 16 people living in Rwanda at the time.) The violence came about as a result of simmering tensions between the majority Hutus, who make up 85 percent of Rwanda's population of 7.2 million (as of 1994), and the Tutsis, who had traditionally enjoyed elite status. The Belgian colonial rulers contributed to the problem by rewarding the Tutsis with privileges and a Western education while denying political and economic power to the Hutus. The Belgians issued identity cards to distinguish the two groups, an act that would have chilling ramifications nearly a century later.

In the 1950s Hutu resentment against the Tutsis burst into violence; by 1963, after Rwanda had become independent, the Hutus were firmly in control of the country. Tutsis were massacred and subjected to discrimination and persecution. Many Tutsis went into exile in neighboring Uganda, where they formed the Rwandan Patriotic Front (RPF). In the early 1990s the RPF invaded the country, setting off a civil war lasting six months that ended only with a cease-fire—formally called the Arusha Accords—in 1991. In spite of the agreement, animosities between the ethnic groups only deepened: By early 1994 the situation had deteriorated to such an extent that humanitarian agencies began to evacuate their employees. The commander of the United Nations peacekeeping force, deployed in the country to supervise the Arusha Accords, recognized the danger and requested authorization from UN headquarters in New York to take action to prevent the conflict from exploding. But the United Nations failed to respond in any meaningful way.

The event that precipitated the subsequent GENOCIDE occurred on April 6, 1994, when the plane carrying President Habyariman, a moderate Hutu, and his Burundian counterpart was brought down by a rocket under mysterious circumstances. Habyarimana had been involved in negotiations to reach an accord that would have diminished the political influence of Hutu extremists, leading to suspicion that they were responsible for the attack. In any case, the assassination served as a pretext to launch a massacre by Hutu militants that had been planned far in advance. For months Hutu propagandists had made wide use of radio and television broadcasts to incite violence against Tutsis. In late 1993 and early 1994, two Hutu radical political parties—the National Republican Movement for Democracy (MRND) and the Coalition for the Defense of the Republic (CDR)—had aggressively recruited unemployed young men to fill the ranks of their militias. At the same time the militias acted to procure arms from South Africa and Egypt and sought advisory assistance from the French military mission. (The French were longtime allies of the Hutus.) In February 1994 Hutu militants assassinated a moderate Hutu minister and killed several of his supporters.

Once the genocidal campaign was launched, checkpoints were set up throughout the capital of Kigali, and Rwandan army soldiers went from house to house killing Tutsis and moderate Hutus. Acting together with the Presidential Guard the militias succeeded in killing an estimated 20,000 people in the capital and its immediate environs within a week. No sooner had a group of Hutu politicians close to the late president formed a new government than the Tutsi-backed RPF in exile resumed the civil war. Two weeks into the massacres, the interim prime minister was assassinated, in addition to the 12 Belgian soldiers guarding him. The UN peacekeeping mission proved ineffective to forestall the atrocities. After Belgium announced the withdrawal of its 400-man peacekeeping contingent, the Hutu extremists decided to extend their genocidal campaign beyond the capital to the east and the southwest. Militias fanned out into the countryside to continue their killings; if local Hutus refused to collaborate in the bloodbath they, too, were killed. Local Hutu officials and broadcasters, however, often volunteered to help, directing the militias to Tutsi homes or to churches and schools where Tutsis had taken refuge. Survivors were frequently set upon and killed with machetes. In some localities, thousands were massacred within a matter of hours.

The militias would generally begin their "work" at eight in the morning and finish their slaughter by four in the afternoon and then resume the following day until all Tutsis in the community were killed. The objective was ethnic extinction. Those who tried to flee the targeted communities were stopped at barricades set up in the roads where soldiers or militiamen would demand to see their identity papers. If people were found to be registered as Tutsis, they would be killed immediately. Rape was widely employed as a means of warfare; many Tutsi women were gang-raped, sometimes for weeks at a time by men who had murdered their families. As many as 7,300 rape victims later died from AIDS; it is estimated that as many as 14,000 women have

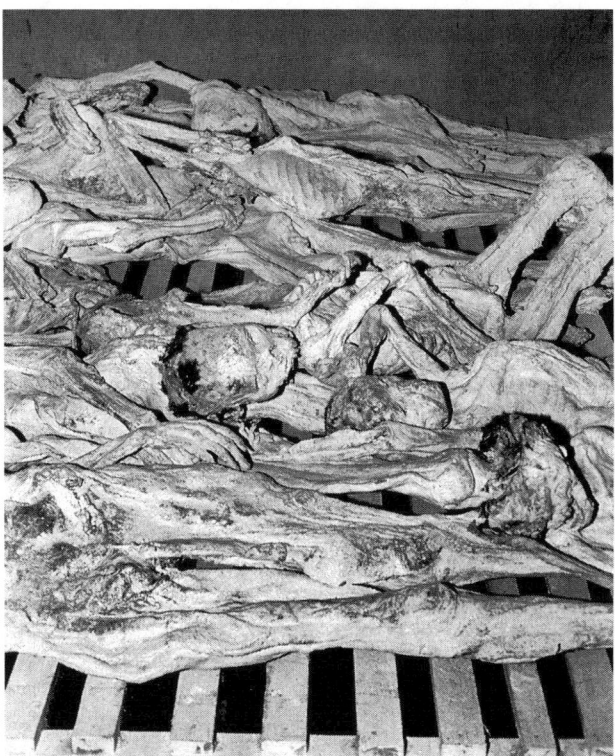

The remains of victims of the Hutu-Tutsi massacre, Rwanda (*Exile Images*)

been infected. (A total of 500,000 people, or nearly 9 percent of the adult population of Rwanda, is HIV-positive.)

By mid-May 1994 Hutu militia leaders were exhorting their forces to finish "cleaning up" those Tutsis and moderate Hutus who had managed to survive the first wave of attacks. Catholic priests and nuns were not spared (though some of them actually took part in the massacres). The most widely listened-to Hutu radio station, RTLM, even went so far as to remind the extremists that Tutsi children, too, should be targeted. There were, to be sure, some Hutu officials and military commanders who refused to participate in the slaughter or tried—even at risk of their own lives—to protect Tutsi civilians. But their efforts, heroic as they were, were not enough to impede the savagery.

As the massacres continued, forces of the RPF were beginning to make significant gains on the battlefield against the Rwandan Hutu army. Attempts to broker a cease-fire came to naught, and by July 4 the RPF, under the command of Paul Kagame, had taken control of Kigali, spurring a mass exodus of almost 2 million Hutu soldiers and civilians into neighboring Zaire (now the Democratic Republic of the Congo), Burundi, and Tanzania. Hundreds of thousands of Hutu REFUGEES were crowded into squalid camps, dying in large numbers from disease, starvation, or lack of water. The same Hutu leaders who had instituted the genocide in the first place asserted control over the camps, supervising the distribution of food, water, and medical supplies to ensure their power. At the same time they announced their intention to return to Rwanda to complete their "work" of slaughtering Tutsis.

Although the UN Security Council had adopted a resolution on April 30, 1994, shortly after the massacres began, condemning the killings, the word *genocide* never appeared in it. Nearly three weeks later the Security Council authorized the deployment of a peacekeeping mission of 6,800 soldiers, called United Nations Assistance Mission in Rwanda (UNAMIR II). It was not until late June, however, after a great deal of bureaucratic wrangling, that a contingent of French troops actually reached Rwanda and established a so-called safe zone in the southwestern region of the country. Even then they were not permitted to use force. The United States remained on the sidelines, and the Clinton administration refused to publicly characterize the violence as genocide, even though the word was used in internal State Department documents that were later declassified.

Three years later, on July 1, 1997, the UN Security Council voted to establish a commission of experts to consider the idea of setting up an international tribunal to try those accused of perpetrating atrocities. Ironically, Rwanda, now led by a Tutsi government, voted against the resolution on the grounds that the proposed tribunal would not be able to use the death penalty; Rwanda did, however, agree to cooperate with the tribunal. Resolution 955, setting up the INTERNATIONAL CRIMINAL TRIBUNAL FOR RWANDA, was passed on November 8, 1994. The course of justice, though, has been painfully slow; after eight years the tribunal, based in Arusha, Tanzania, had only convicted 18 defendants. On their own the Rwandan authorities have arrested 120,000 individuals suspected of participating in the atrocities, but it lacks the capacity to put them on trial. For that matter, there is hardly any room to hold so many prisoners. Recognizing that it would take about a century to process all the accused, the government has released thousands of suspects, angering humanitarian groups. Some 5,000 have been rearrested on more serious charges than those originally leveled against them. To try to bring as many to justice as possible, the government has resorted to mass trials. In the biggest one, 105 were convicted and 37 acquitted.

Rwanda has implemented an innovative policy of reconciliation, which, while controversial, is widely accepted by the country's population, mostly because of a lack of plausible alternatives. The policy is based on what are known as *gacaca,* or community, courts (usually held outdoors), convened to hear cases of genocide. There are some 12,000 of these courts, and by 2009 more than a million cases had been heard. The proceedings bear a resemblance to the truth and reconciliation trials that were held in South Africa to investigate abuses committed under the white APARTHIED regime. A defendant who willingly confesses to his or her role in the genocide may receive a light sentence or be given credit for time served. While there is no question that some individuals have been convicted on the basis of false evidence, there have also been a surprising number of acquittals. No one has been sentenced to death; the death penalty has been abolished. From most accounts, the victims and their families do not believe that the *gacaca* courts serve the cause of justice, but at the same time they are resigned to their necessity. The courts represent the centerpiece of the policy instituted by President Paul Kagame to restore normalcy to Rwanda a decade and a half after the genocide. Even though he has largely succeeded in doing so in his own country the conflict between Hutus and Tutsis has never come to an end just over the border in the Congo. During the late 1990s, Hutus driven into exile by Rwandan forces plotted their return to power. The Hutus enjoyed some support from then President Laurent Kabila of Congo and later from his son, Joseph Kabila, who took over the presidency after his father's assassination. In 2001 an estimated 12,000 Hutu combatants in Congo formed the FDLR (Forces Démocratiques de Liberation du Rwanda). However, they sustained significant losses at the hands of the Rwandan army, which took up positions inside eastern Congo. Several hundred members of the FDLR were captured, but instead of being executed, as they anticipated, they were allowed to go free after demobilizing. Some were offered positions in the same Rwandan army that they had been fighting against for years. Ironically, ex-Hutu fighters receive more benefits from the state than their victims, in the belief that the Hutus could still pose a potential risk while there is no threat from the victims. Although Kagame withdrew his forces from Congo in 2002 under an accord with Joseph Kabila, the Hutu militancy did not come to an end, nor did Kabila show any sign that he was cutting his ties with the FDLR. Warfare intensified in eastern Congo after an insurgent leader, General Laurent Nkunda, initiated a rebellion he claimed was intended to protect Congolese Tutsis from Hutus and their Congolese army allies. Although Rwandan president Kagame repeatedly declared that he was not sponsoring Nkunda, many international observers believed that Nkunda was acting as a proxy for Rwanda. There is no question that his aims and Rwanda's coincide—curbing the threat of Hutu militants—but there is also no question that Nkunda's forces were guilty of committing atrocities in their efforts. (Congolese soldiers were also implicated in human rights abuses.) It was only when Nkunda's rebels were on the verge of seizing the principal eastern Congolese city of Goma that Kagame intervened to halt his advance. An uneasy cease-fire took hold, and a new peace accord was hammered out between Kabile and Kagame, easing tensions between the two adversaries. Rwandan forces withdrew a short time later. Nkunda was arrested by Rwanda but gave no indication whether he would be turned over to Congolese authorities. In spite of the international opprobrium Kagame suffered as a result of his intervention in Congo, the Rwandan president maintained that the successive wars in eastern Congo that were meant to cripple the power of Hutu militants were necessary if he was to pursue his policy of reconciliation at home. But the government's overture to its opponents had its limits. In the run-up to parliamentary elections in August 2010, members of the political opposition and journalists came under intense pressure. In a June 2010 report, Human Rights Watch noted that insecurity and political repression had intensified. Several opposition political leaders have been targeted. In one especially macabre case, the body of the leader of the Democratic Green Party was found nearly beheaded. In June, an attempt was made on the life of a general and a former ally of Kagame who had broken with the regime and taken refuge in South Africa. A few weeks later, a prominent journalist for a newspaper that had linked the Kagame government with the assassination attempt was gunned down in front of his home. Several opposition leaders were detained by police, and some political parties, including the Democratic Green Party, have been prevented from taking part in the elections. Political protests have been broken up and demonstrators arrested. The result of this crackdown, said Human Rights Watch, was to ensure "that opposition parties are unable to function and are excluded from the political process."

In August 2010, a controversial UN report called into question Rwanda's role in the Congo in the aftermath of the genocide. The report, which focused on 600 serious atrocities, reviewed the history of Rwanda's intervention in the eastern region of the Congo. About a million Hutus, most of them civilians, had sought refuge in what was then known as Zaire. Until recently, it was widely believed that Rwandan forces, along with their Zairian rebel allies, were principally targeting Rwandan Hutu militia forces (the Interahamwe) and former Hutu army forces responsible for the 1994 genocide. According to the UN report, however, the Rwandan army made little or no distinction between soldiers and civilians but instead had a "tendency to put all Hutu people together and 'tar them with the same brush.'" The report asserts that the killings of civilians—the majority of whom were "children, women, elderly people and the sick, who were often undernourished"—could not be attributed to "the hazards of war or seen as equating to collateral damage." Many of the victims were also Congolese Hutus. In 1996, for example, the report said that the Rwandan forces and Zairian militia under the command of Laurent Kabila (who later became the president of the Democratic Republic of the Congo) broke up Hutu refugee camps and then chased hundreds of thousands of fleeing Hutu refugees across the countryside. In another case, cited by the report, Rwandan and Zairian troops lured Hutu refugees by promising to repatriate them and then massacred 500 to 800 of them. The Rwandan government has taken sharp issue with the report and denounced its findings. Kagame threat to end any cooperation with the UN apparently caused a delay in the report's release. Whether Rwandan forces did engage in genocide or other war crimes cannot be determined unless and until an international court rules on the cases in question.

See also ARMS, TRAFFICKING IN AND CONTROL MECHANISMS; RAPE AS A TACTIC OF WAR; UGANDA, HUMAN RIGHTS VIOLATIONS IN.

Further Reading:
allAfrica.com. Rwanda Links. Available online. URL: http://allafrica.com/rwanda/. Accessed March 20, 2010.
BBC.co.uk. "Rwanda: How the Genocide Happened." (December 18, 2008). Available online. URL: http://news.bbc.co.uk/2/hi/1288230.stm. Accessed March 20, 2010.
Barnett, Michael. *Eyewitness to a Genocide: The United Nations and Rwanda.* Ithaca, N.Y.: Cornell University Press, 2003.
Gourevich, Philip. *We Wish to Inform You That Tomorrow We Will Be Killed with Our Families: Stories from Rwanda.* New York: Picador, 1999.
Dallaire, Romeo, and Brent Beardsley. *Shake Hands with the Devil: The Failure of Humanity in Rwanda.* New York: Carroll & Graf, 2004.
Mamdani, Mahmood. *When Victims Become Killers: Colonialism, Nativism, and the Genocide in Rwanda.* Princeton, N.J.: Princeton University Press, 2002.
Melvern, Linda. *A People Betrayed: The Role of the West in Rwanda's Genocide.* London: Zed Books, 2000.
Peterson, Scott. *Me against My Brother: At War in Somalia, Sudan and Rwanda.* London: Routledge, 2001.
Straus, Scott. *The Order of Genocide: Race, Power, and War in Rwanda.* Ithaca, N.Y.: Cornell University Press, 2008.
Temple-Rason, Dina. *Justice on the Grass: Three Rwandan Journalists, Their Trial for War Crimes, and a Nation's Quest for Redemption.* New York: Free Press, 2005.

Rwandan human rights violators

Although it is well known that the 1994 atrocities in Rwanda took the lives of some 800,000 ethnic Tutsis and moderate Hutus, few people would recognize the names of the murderers. The United Nations–sponsored tribunal established in Arusha, Tanzania, to try suspects implicated in the genocidal campaign has convicted several individuals, but the caseload far outstrips its ability to bring to justice many of the worst offenders. Thousands more still await trial inside Rwanda, but the court system there is unequal to the task of giving the multitudes of defendants a fair trial. Nonetheless, a number of the perpetrators have been brought to justice, and it is instructive to make note of three of the cases because of the light they shed on the crimes that were carried out and the reasoning that underlay the court's judgments.

Akayesu, Jean-Paul

Jean-Paul Akayesu, a former official in Rwanda, had the dubious distinction of being the first suspect to stand trial for war crimes under the auspices of the newly formed INTERNATIONAL CRIMINAL TRIBUNAL FOR RWANDA (ICTR). More importantly, though, his conviction was an acknowledgment that sexual violence against women was a war crime. The ruling was the first time that an international court punished sexual violence in a civil war and the first time that it was determined that rape was used as an act of GENOCIDE as well as an act of TORTURE.

Born in 1953, Akayesu, a Hutu, was a teacher and school inspector before becoming a burgomaster, or mayor, of the commune of Taba, a position he was holding in April 1994 when genocidal warfare broke out in Rwanda, mainly perpetrated by Hutu extremists against the minority Tutu population. As mayor, Akayesu was responsible for maintaining law and public order in his commune, but instead he stood by as at least 2,000 Tutsis were killed in Taba between April 7 and the end of June. Many of the victims were fleeing killings elsewhere. Women were raped and threatened; those who were allowed to live suffered emotional and physical trauma. The killings were so widespread and so flagrant that there is no question of his not being aware of them.

Akayesu was arrested in Zambia in 1996 on a warrant issued by the United Nations, which had established the criminal court to prosecute war crimes. During his initial nine-hour interrogation, he insisted on his innocence. Nonetheless, the court had sufficient evidence to charge him with 12 counts of genocide, CRIMES AGAINST HUMANITY, and violations of ARTICLE 3 COMMON TO THE GENEVA CONVENTIONS, governing a state's treatment of civilians. It was only later that the indictment was amended to include rape charges as well and then only as a result of concerted pressure by nongovernmental organizations.

The trial lasted from January to May 1997, during which over 30 witnesses testified about the mass killing in Taba while Akayesu was in power. Four witnesses appeared to testify about sexual violence, reporting incidents of gang rape and murder. They agreed that Akayesu had done nothing to stop the rapes or killings of women. At one point a witness recalled him saying to the rapists, "Don't complain to me now that you don't know what a Tutsi woman tastes like."

Although rape is a violation of the 1949 GENEVA CONVENTIONS, the 1948 GENOCIDE CONVENTION, the 1984 CONVENTION AGAINST TORTURE, and it is considered a crime against humanity under international CUSTOMARY LAW, military or political authorities often have dismissed the gravity of the offense, labeling it an aberrant act of individual soldiers rather than as a willful pattern of terror. Akayesu mounted a vigorous defense, calling several witnesses and even taking the stand himself, but on October 2, 1998, the ICTR found him guilty and sentenced him to three life sentences for genocide and crimes against humanity and to 80 years for other violations, including rape and encouraging widespread sexual violence.

Bagaragaza, Michel

In 2009 Michel Bagaragaza, a former tea industry official from Rwanda, was sentenced by the ICTR to eight years in prison for ordering subordinates to kill hundreds of Tutsis hiding in a church. He received a relatively short sentence because he had cooperated with the tribunal and expressed contrition over his actions.

Bagosora, Theoneste

Theoneste Bagosora, a colonel in the Rwandan army, was sentenced in December 2008 to life imprisonment for war crimes by the ICTR, which called him the "mastermind" of the Rwandan genocide. He became the highest ranking official to be tried and convicted by the tribunal. His conviction was the culmination of a long trial, begun in 2002, during which the tribunal heard 242 witnesses—82 for the prosecution and 160 for the defense. Bagosora was sentenced with two other officers convicted of war crimes: Major Aloys Ntabakuze and Lieutenant Colonel Anatole Nsengiyumva. The tribunal accused Bagosora of laying plans for the genocide and later ordering Hutu militias to carry them out. A year before the outbreak of violence, Bagosora had announced his opposition to any concessions made by his government to Tutsi rebels at 1993 peace talks in Tanzania. When he walked out of negotiations, he said that he was returning to Rwanda to "prepare the apocalypse." The apocalypse was not long in coming. Shortly after the April 6, 1994, surface-to-air attack on a plane that killed the presidents of Rwanda and Burundi (an incident still shrouded in mystery), Bagosora gave orders for the army to take over Rwanda, bypassing the prime minister, Agathe Uwilingiyimana, who was later arrested and killed by officers in the army, along with 10 Belgian peacekeepers assigned to protect her. As head of political and military affairs, Bagosora effectively took over the country during the genocide. Troops under his command moved swiftly against opposition leaders, including the president of the constitutional court and government ministers who were detained and killed. "Bagosora was the highest authority in the Ministry of Defense and exercised effective control of the Rwandan army and gendarmerie," said presiding judge Erik Mose. "He's therefore responsible for the murder of the prime minister, the four opposition politicians, the 10 Belgian peacekeepers, as well as the extensive military involvement in the killing of civilians during this period." According to an ICTR prosecutor, Bagosora and the two other convicted officers "prepared, planned, ordered, directed, incited, encouraged and approved the murder of innocent civilian Tutsis."

Bazaramba, François

In 2009 Bazaramba, a former Rwandan Baptist pastor, went on trial in Finland, where he had sought asylum six years earlier. He has been implicated in orchestrating the slaughter of 5,000 Tutsis. He has denied the charges. If convicted, he could face a sentence of life in prison (which in Finland can mean as little as 12 years).

Bikindi, Simon

Simon Bikindi stands out among other individuals convicted by the ICTR in that he is a musician and not an official or a soldier. In fact, he was Rwanda's most famous musician in 1994 when the genocide occurred. In December 2008, the tribunal found him guilty of incitement to genocide and sentenced him to 15 years in prison. Specifically, he was convicted for putting his talent to use on behalf of repellent objectives; three of his popular rap songs were featured in a propaganda campaign to debase the Tutsi population prior to the outbreak of violence. Mobs of raging Hutus would sing his lyrics as they hunted down their victims. In addition, Bikindi also employed a public-address system along Rwandan roads to exhort fellow Hutus to slay Tutsis. His sentence would probably have been longer, but the tribunal was not able to link his music directly to any attacks or murders. Bikindi, 54 at the time of his conviction, earned the dubious distinction of becoming the first entertainer to be found guilty of genocide.

Gacumbitsi, Sylvestre

Former Rwandan mayor Sylvestre Gacumbitsi is one of several suspects implicated and tried for the 1994 genocide in his country. A Hutu, Gacumbitsi was tried by the ICTR and found guilty of organizing the killings of 20,000 people (though not of genocide), mostly ethnic Tutsis. He was sentenced to 30 years' imprisonment. According to the indictment, he lured his victims into a church, at Nyarubuye

parish on April 5th 1994, where he promised them that they would be safe from marauding Hutu militants. He then proceeded to distribute weapons and urged Hutus to kill and rape Tutsis who had lived together as neighbors for years. He also was responsible for using rape as a weapon of war: He went around announcing through a megaphone that all Tutsi women were to be raped and "sexually degraded." Apparently he felt he should set an example. One witness testified that Gacumbitsi had raped her. After the genocide ended, leaving 800,000 Tutsis and moderate Hutus dead, he sought refuge in Tanzania, where he was identified by a television news crew. He was arrested shortly afterward in June 2001. In June 2004 Gacumbitsi was found guilty of genocide, extermination, and rape by the International Criminal Tribunal for Rwanda in Tanzania.

Habyarimana, Agathe

The widow of Juvenal Habyarimana, the Rwandan president whose plane was shot down in 1994 (an act which precipitated the genocide), Habyarimana was arrested in France in early 2010. She had been living in exile in the country but had failed to obtain political asylum after a French court found that as a major figure in the Hutu regime that carried out the genocide she was not eligible. Whether she would be extradited to stand trial in Rwanda was unclear.

Kalimanzira, Callixte

In June 2009 Callixte Kalimanzira, former interior minister, was sentenced to 30 years in prison for deceiving thousands of Tutsi refugees into taking refuge in an area where they were certain to be slaughtered by Hutu militants. The International Criminal Tribunal for Rwanda found the 56-year-old Kalimanzira guilty of two counts of genocide and direct and public incitement to genocide.

Kambanda, Jean

Jean Kambanda, the former prime minister of Rwanda, became the first leader of a government to be convicted of genocide. He was sentenced by the ICTR in September 1998 for crimes committed during the genocidal campaign by Hutu extremists four years earlier in which about 800,000 people were killed. Initially he had pleaded guilty and was sentenced to life imprisonment in 1999. In his appeal Kambanda claimed that he had been forced into pleading guilty, a defense the appeals court rejected in upholding the verdict.

Munyaneza, Désiré

The conviction of Désiré Munyaneza in 2009 for war crimes, crimes against humanity, and genocide in the 1994. Genocide was the first under a Canadian war crimes law. Munyaneza, a Hutu from a middle-class family, was accused of participating in murders, rape, and pillaging against

Tutsis in the Butare region of Rwanda. "The accused's criminal intent was demonstrated beyond a reasonable doubt, as was his culpable violence," wrote Justice André Denis in his decision. "The educated son of an important bourgeois family in Butare, Désiré Munyaneza was at the forefront of the genocidal movement." One witness described a killing spree that went on for an entire day, as Hutu militants dragged their victims out of three religious institutions where they had sought refuge—a mosque, a Roman Catholic church, and an Adventist church—and then proceeded to kill them. Another witness testified that Munyaneza had led a group of men who had repeatedly raped her and other women over a period of several days.

Murwanashyaka, Ignace
The former leader of a Rwandan Hutu rebel group known as the FDLR (Forces Démocratiques de Liberation du Rwanda) was arrested in November 2009 in Germany on suspicion of committing war crimes and crimes against humanity during the 1994 genocide. He had been hiding out in eastern Congo since the Hutu perpetrators of the genocide were driven out of Rwanda.

Ndahimana, Grégoire
Ndahimana was a mayor during the genocide when, according to the ICC, he helped organize the massacre of 2,000 Tutsis who had taken refuge in a church. He was arrested in August 2009 in eastern Congo, where he had spent 15 years fighting with the Forces Démocratiques de Liberation du Rwanda, or FDLR, whose ranks were filled with Hutu militants who had fled Rwanda in 1994. Rwanda's justice minister, Tharcisse Karugarama, called him "one of the big ones." The ICC considers him as a Category 1 suspect, designating him as one of the planners and executioners of the genocide.

Nizeyimana, Idelphonse
Nizeyimana was one of the most wanted fugitives sought for crimes committed in the 1994 genocide when he was caught in October 2009 in Uganda. The former intelligence officer in the former Rwandan army and commander of an elite military school was under indictment by the International Criminal Tribunal for Rwanda (ICTR) for crimes against humanity and offenses related to genocide, including the massacre of civilians. He has also been accused of the abduction and slaying of a ceremonial Tutsi queen who was in her 80s at the time of her death. After the militant Hutus were forced to flee Rwanda, Nizeyimana was a commander of the Forces Démocratiques de Liberation du Rwanda, or FDLR, which carried out an insurgency in eastern Congo. He has been accused of launching several attacks in the Congo. "This guy was causing terror in Congo, and he was a

threat to the region," stated a Rwandan police spokesman. The ICTR listed him as one of the four top fugitives wanted for crimes related to the genocidal campaign.

Nkezabera, Ephraim
Nkezabera, a former Rwandan bank director, was sentenced to 30 years in prison by a Belgian court in 2009, which found him guilty of war crimes, including murder, attempted murder, and rape during the 1994 genocide. The banker had admitted to inciting violence, threatening Tutsis with genocide, and arming Hutu militias but denied being responsible for the rapes with which he had originally been charged.

Renzaho, Tharcisse
In July 2009 Tharcisse Renzaho, a former governor, was sentenced to life for his role in the genocide by the International Criminal Tribunal for Rwanda. He was found guilty on five charges including rape, assassination, and genocide. He had served as the head of the police and local militia and supervised the construction of roadblocks set up to ambush and kill Tutsis.

Rukundo, Emmanuel
Emmanuel Rukundo, a Roman Catholic priest and former military chaplain, was convicted in 2009 and sentenced to 25 years in prison for genocide by the International Criminal Tribunal for Rwanda. A Hutu extremist, he was found guilty of betraying Tutsi refugees who had taken refuge in a seminary on no less than four occasions, sending them to their deaths at the hands of Hutu militants. Rukundo was 50 years old at the time of his sentencing.

See also RAPE AS A TACTIC OF WAR; RWANDA, GENOCIDE IN.

Further Reading:
Barnett, Michael. *Eyewitness to a Genocide: The United Nations and Rwanda.* Ithaca, N.Y.: Cornell University Press, 2003.
Dallaire, Romeo, and Brent Beardsley. *Shake Hands with the Devil: The Failure of Humanity in Rwanda.* New York: Carroll & Graf, 2004.
Gourevich, Philip. *We Wish to Inform You That Tomorrow We Will Be Killed with Our Families: Stories from Rwanda.* New York: Picador, 1999.
Mamdani, Mahmood. *When Victims Become Killers: Colonialism, Nativism, and the Genocide in Rwanda.* Princeton, N.J.: Princeton University Press, 2002.
Melvern, Linda. *A People Betrayed: The Role of the West in Rwanda's Genocide.* London: Zed Books, 2000.
Peterson, Scott. *Me against My Brother: At War in Somalia, Sudan and Rwanda.* London: Routledge, 2001.

S

Sabra and Shatilla, massacre in

In June 1982 Israel's prime minister Menachem Begin ordered an invasion of Lebanon, which had increasingly fallen under the influence of the Palestine Liberation Organization (PLO), then regarded as the greatest threat to Israel's security. Begin, together with Defense Minister Ariel Sharon (later prime minister), believed that intervention would allow Israel to manipulate events in its favor by eliminating the PLO's base of operations—it was recruiting more members from Palestinian refugee camps in the country—while installing a sympathetic regime that would make peace with Israel. At the time, Lebanon was embroiled in a civil war that divided the country largely along ethnic lines. Israel, however, looked on the Maronite Christians as their allies and proxies who still wielded considerable economic and political power, although they were outnumbered by Muslims.

On June 6, 1982, the Israel Defense Forces (IDF) pushed over the border and moved all the way to the capital of Beirut, laying siege to the PLO stronghold in West Beirut for two months. The United States devised a plan to evacuate the PLO fighters from Lebanon, and a multinational force was dispatched to carry the evacuation out in August. Under the plan, the PLO, led by Yasser Arafat, left Lebanon for more hospitable quarters in Tunisia. Proclaiming that it had accomplished its mission, the force pulled out in September. Nonetheless, Israel contended that 2,000 PLO guerrillas remained in refugee camps and applied pressure to Lebanon's new president, Bashir Gemayel, a Maronite Christian, to send his forces into the camps to root them out.

On September 14, 1982, Gemayel was killed when a powerful bomb went off, destroying the headquarters of his Phalangist Party in East Beirut, a district largely under Christian control. The next day the IDF violated the evacuation agreement and entered Muslim West Beirut. The IDF provided military protection for members of Gemayel's Lebanese Forces, a Phalangist militia, and Saad Had-

dad's South Lebanon Army. These troops proceeded to enter the Sabra and Shatilla refugee camps, which housed 30,000 Palestinians and some Lebanese; Israeli tanks surrounded the camps, cutting off all access. Beginning on September 16, for the next 38 hours the militia carried out a massacre that, according to the INTERNATIONAL COMMITTEE OF THE RED CROSS (ICRC), left 2,400 dead. Some analysts believe that the figure might be higher; Palestinian sources put the number at closer to 3000. Nor is there any way to be certain how many, if any, of the victims were PLO fighters.

Although Israeli forces had not done any of the killings, Israel was widely criticized for failing to take any action to stop the Phalangists even when it was clear what was happening within the camps. Indeed, there is some evidence to indicate that the IDF was closely collaborating with the militias. An Israeli commission of inquiry was established which concluded that several leading figures, including Begin, Sharon, and IDF generals, bore "indirect responsibility" for the massacres, based on the fact that Israeli troops had not directly participated in the killings.

See also WALLEYN, LUC.

safe havens

The term *safe haven* applies to an area that is designated off-limits for military targeting. The term does not have specific legal standing, but the Fourth Geneva Convention of 1949 concerning the Protection of Civilian Persons in Times of War and Additional Protocol I do provide for three types of protected areas: hospital zones, neutralized zones, and demilitarized zones. For demilitarization to take place, however, the belligerents must agree to set aside such a zone. Article 14 states that the parties concerned may "conclude agreements on mutual recognition of the zones and localities they have created." The convention does not indicate how these agreements are to be made, leaving it up to the belligerents. Article 15 states that any party to a conflict may propose to establish "neutralized zones intended to shelter from the effects of war" the "wounded and sick combatants or non-combatants" and "civilian persons who take no part in hostilities." Articles 23 and 59 state that parties shall permit "the free passage of all consignments of essential foodstuffs, medical supplies, and clothing to these zones."

The treatment of REFUGEES was specifically addressed by the 1951 United Nations Refugee Convention, which establishes the obligation of states toward refugees and describes the rights they enjoy; the treaty was a formal recognition that states could take in refugees fleeing persecution in their home countries. Until World War II the body of international law protected civilians only in situations where they were threatened by forces of a belligerent state. Article 33 of the convention states that "no Contracting State shall expel or return a refugee in any manner whatsoever to the frontiers of a territory where his life or freedom would be threatened on account of his race, religion, nationality, membership of a particular social group or political opinion."

The concept of safe havens—also known as corridors of tranquility, humanitarian corridors, neutral zones, security zones, and safety zones predates the 1949 Geneva Convention and the 1951 Refugee Convention. A safe haven was established in Shanghai in the 1930s, for instance, while war was waging between China and Japan. Both belligerents agreed to the protected area, which eventually offered sanctuary to about 1 million Chinese. The UN Security Council and other bodies have attempted to establish safe havens in many recent conflicts as well. The principal reason for such safe havens is to protect refugees and INTERNALLY DISPLACED PERSONS. Another reason is to prevent refugees from seeking sanctuary across an international border. During the GENOCIDE in Rwanda, for instance, safe havens, called *zones humanitaires sûres* (safe humanitarian zones) were set up in southwestern Rwanda to prevent potential refugees from fleeing to Zaire.

In principle, these safe havens are to remain free of military occupation. The Kurdish area of northern Iraq is a good example of a successful safe haven. Established after the 1991 Persian Gulf War and protected from Iraqi incursion by U.S. and British warplanes, the area enjoyed relative peace and autonomy until the fall of SADDAM HUSSEIN in 2003. It also afforded sanctuary for approximately 400,000 Kurdish refugees who had fled over the border to Turkey to escape Saddam's forces in the aftermath of a failed Kurdish uprising.

Many safe havens have proven to be tragic deceptions. In 1993 during the Bosnian War, the UN Security Council designated six safe havens in Bosnia and Herzegovina that were intended to shelter Muslim civilians from depredations of Serb forces. However, there was no attempt to define the borders of these safe havens or to ensure the protection of refugees in these areas. In July 1995 UN troops, mainly composed of Dutch soldiers, abandoned designated safe havens in Srebrinca and Zepa rather than defend them against Serb forces and paramilitary units. The Serbs proceeded to expel the Muslim women and children before killing nearly 7,000 youths and adult men. It was the worst atrocity in Europe since World War II and underscored the problems of setting up a safe haven without also providing the means with which to protect it.

See also ADDITIONAL PROTOCOLS TO THE GENEVA CONVENTIONS; BOSNIA AND HERZEGOVINA, HUMAN RIGHTS VIOLATIONS IN; GENEVA CONVENTIONS; KURDISTAN (IRAQ), SUPPRESSION OF.

Further Reading:

Feller, Erika, Volker Turk, and Frances Nicholson, eds. *Refugee Protection in International Law: UNHCR's Global Consultations on International Protection.* Cambridge: Cambridge University Press, 2003.

Fritz, Mark. *Lost on Earth: Nomads of the New World.* New York: Routledge, 2000.

Groenewold, Julia, and Doctors Without Borders. *World in Crisis: The Politics of Survival at the End of the Twentieth Century.* London: Routledge, 1996.

Helton, Arthur C. *The Price of Indifference: Refugees and Humanitarian Action in the New Century.* A Council on Foreign Relations Book. Oxford: Oxford University Press, 2002.

Hyndman, Jennifer. *Managing Displacement: Refugees and the Politics of Humanitarianism.* Minneapolis: University of Minnesota Press, 2000.

Ingleby, David, ed. *Forced Migration and Mental Health: Rethinking the Care of Refugees and Displaced Persons.* New York: Plenum US, 2004.

Lischer, Sarah Kenyon. *Dangerous Sanctuaries: Refugee Camps, Civil War, and the Dilemmas of Humanitarian Aid.* Cornell Studies in Security Affairs. Ithaca, N.Y.: Cornell University Press, 2005.

Moorehead, Caroline. *Human Cargo: A Journey among Refugees.* New York: Henry Holt and Co., 2005.

Ogata, Sadako, and Kofi Annan. *The Turbulent Decade: Confronting the Refugee Crises of the 1990s.* New York: W. W. Norton & Company, 2005.

Sakai Takashi (1887–1946) *Japanese war criminal*
Sakai Takashi served as a Japanese military commander in China first during Sino-Japanese hostilities that erupted in 1931 and then during World War II. After the war he was tried for war crimes and CRIMES AGAINST HUMANITY as well as crimes in violation of Chinese law. Sakai was also governor-general of Hong Kong for the occupation

authorities. Born in 1887, he was among the high officials in the Japanese military who promoted Japan's aggression against China. In 1931, after the Mukden incident (a staged provocation that provided the pretext for Japan's attack on Manchuria), he formed a terrorist group to foment disorder in Beijing (then Peking) and Tianjin (then Tientsin); the group carried out assassinations of various Chinese officials, politicians, and newspaper reporters.

In May 1934 Sakai threatened to attack Beijing using artillery and air forces, and he demanded the dismissal of the heads of the local Chinese authorities in the province of Hopei as well as the withdrawal of all Chinese troops from the province. As a commander of the Japanese Twenty-third Army operating in South China, he organized a puppet government and formed a so-called Peace Army in an effort to overthrow the Chinese government. Later, as regimental commander of the 29th Infantry Brigade in China, he was involved directly or indirectly in acts of atrocity, including the massacre of over 100 civilians in Guangdong (Kwangtung) and Hainan by shooting, bayoneting, and drowning. Women were raped and mutilated, their bodies fed to dogs. Troops under Sakai's command forcibly evicted civilians from their homes, plundered their produce and animals, and burned down their houses. Sakai also allegedly ordered the execution of more than 100 PRISONERS OF WAR, many of whom were already wounded. In December 1941 he ordered the execution of 20 members of a British medical unit; seven nurses were raped and mutilated as well.

Following the war, Sakai was tried in China under the Chinese Rules governing the Trial of War Criminals that were in force at the time. While he initially pleaded not guilty, he later asked for the charges to be amended, acknowledging that while he might have been guilty of having taken part in a war of aggression and had committed a crime against peace, he contended that he had acted under orders of his government. He also asserted that he had no knowledge of any atrocities, which he attributed to subordinates. Nonetheless, his pleas to have the charges changed were rejected, and he was found guilty "of participating in the war of aggression" and "of inciting or permitting his subordinates to murder prisoners of war, wounded soldiers and non-combatants; to rape, plunder and deport civilians; to indulge in cruel punishment and torture; and to cause destruction of property." He was also found guilty of participation in a war of aggression, a crime against peace, war crimes, and crimes against humanity. Sakai was sentenced to death and executed in 1946.

See also MANCHURIA, JAPANESE WAR CRIMES IN.

Further Reading:
Daws, Gavin. *Prisoners of the Japanese: POWs of World War II in the Pacific.* New York: Perennial, 1996.
Li, Peter, ed. *Japanese War Crimes: The Search for Justice.* New Brunswick, N.J.: Transaction Publishers, 2003.
Maga, Timothy P. *Judgment at Tokyo: The Japanese War Crimes Trials.* Lexington: University Press of Kentucky, 2001.
Mendelsohn, John. *The Preservation of Japanese War Crimes Trials Records in the National Archives.* Washington, D.C.: National Archives and Records Administration, 1982.
Minear, Richard R. *Victors' Justice: The Tokyo War Crimes Trial.* Michigan Classics in Japanese Studies. Ann Arbor: University of Michigan, Center for Japanese Studies, 2001.
Piccigallo, Philip R. *The Japanese on Trial: Allied War Crimes Operations in the East, 1945–1951.* Austin: University of Texas Press, 1980.
Rees, Laurence. *Horror in the East: Japan and the Atrocities of World War II.* New York: Da Capo Press, 2002.
Russell, of Liverpool, Edward Frederick Langley Russell, Baron. *Knights of the Bushido: A Short History of Japanese War Crimes.* London: Greenhill Books, 2005.
Tanaka, Yuki. *Hidden Horrors: Japanese War Crimes in World War II.* Boulder, Colo.: Westview Press, 1998.

sanctions

Sanctions, which are often (though not always) economic in nature, are a controversial weapon to force a law-breaking state to abide by international law or punish it for past violations. Many political analysts are convinced that they are ineffective at achieving their purpose and, in addition, impose unjustified suffering on civilian populations in the affected countries. The use of economic sanctions gained worldwide attention after the 1991 Persian Gulf War. Until the 2003 U.S.-backed invasion, sanctions had been imposed on Iraq as punishment for its earlier invasion of Kuwait. It is debatable whether those sanctions accomplished the objectives members of the United Nations Security Council envisioned in light of the ease with which the Saddam HUSSEIN regime was able to violate them.

In addition to economic sanctions—a trade embargo, for example—sanctions can take the form of diplomacy—for example, diplomatic relations are suspended or officials in the government of an outlaw state may be denied the right to travel outside of their country. In recent years the Security Council has imposed some form of trade sanctions on Angola, Haiti, Liberia, Libya, Rwanda, Somalia, and the countries of the former Yugoslavia as well as Iraq. The Security Council can act under Chapter VII of the UN Charter to decide whether any threat to the peace, breach of the peace, or act of aggression warrants the imposition of mandatory sanctions to force a state to alter its behavior. In certain cases military force can be employed to enforce sanctions. Economic sanctions often take a long time to prove effective, and states can evade them by smuggling and resorting to black markets. Nonetheless, in some instances they have proven effective; both Serbia and Libya significantly changed policies inimical to the international community under the pressure of economic sanctions. Countries such as Myanmar, which are poor and isolated to begin with and thus are less reliant on trade, are less susceptible to sanctions.

There is also a legal basis for sanctions in Article 41 of the UN Charter that provides for economic and other kinds of nonmilitary measures for maintaining or restoring international peace and security. It should be noted, however, that the term *sanctions* is not mentioned in the text. Once the United Nations agrees on the imposition of sanctions on a country, all member states are bound to comply with them.

Sanctions may be partial or comprehensive. Even the most stringent sanctions make allowances, and exceptions are usually made for humanitarian purposes—for instance, ensuring that medicines and food are delivered to states under sanction. In the case of Iraq, an "oil for food program" was instituted in which the United Nations allowed the oil-rich country to sell a certain amount of oil each year—approximately $2 billion worth—in exchange for food. (The program was later revealed to be riddled by massive corruption.) Even the United States did not abide by the embargo of Iraq, turning a blind eye to oil smuggling by its allies Turkey and Jordan.

Not all sanctions enjoy UN approval. Some states may unilaterally impose sanctions on another state, which is the case with the United States' long-standing embargo of Cuba. Although the world leader has maintained its sanctions against the Castro regime for decades, other countries—including Canada, members of the European Union, and most states in Latin America—continue to do business with Cuba. Some legal scholars believe that sanctions impose what amounts to COLLECTIVE PUNISHMENT (which is otherwise outlawed by international law) since the civilian population of a sanctioned state is deprived of its economic lifeblood because of actions committed by a government over which it has little or no control. In an essay on the subject, Dr. Hans Köchler points out what he perceives is a contradiction between two lofty goals advocated by the United Nations: maintaining international peace and security on the one hand and human rights on the other. Sanctions aimed at the former, he maintains, come at the price of the latter.

Economic sanctions are often viewed as a preliminary step before taking military action, as provided for in Article 42. It is up to the UN Security Council, however, to determine whether military action is required based on its assessment that a threat to peace, a breach of peace, or an act of aggression exists. Where force is contemplated, the Security Council authorizes its member states to "use all necessary means to restore international peace and security." Humanitarian considerations are not cited. Moreover, Köchler says, the decision of what violations require sanctions is left in the hands of powerful member states that sit on the Security Council: China, France, Russia, the United Kingdom, and the United States. In 2003 the United States argued—unsuccessfully—that Iraq was in breach of the sanctions because it was developing weapons of mass destruction, and therefore military force was required to enforce the sanctions.

Some governments may be involved in egregious violations of human rights but avoid sanctions, whereas other governments may be less culpable in this regard and come under a sanctions regime. Governments that perpetrate grave human rights abuses on civilians do not always represent a threat to international peace or security, after all. Other forms of sanctions also exist that are not quite so extreme. International organizations have established procedures for applying pressure on states that do not comply with their human rights obligations. Many international treaties require member states to report on their compliance, and if they are found in violation they may be suspended from the organization and come under fire in the media. Shame can also be used to enforce sanctions, even if they do not have the force of law. Regimes may suffer a blow to prestige and a severe loss of business because of human rights campaigns, for instance, even in the absence of formal sanctions.

Further Reading:
Arnove, Anthony, ed. *Iraq under Siege, Updated Edition: The Deadly Impact of Sanctions and War.* Boston: South End Press, 2002.
Collins, Joseph J., and Gabrielle D. Bowdoin. *Beyond Unilateral Economic Sanctions: Better Alternatives for U.S. Foreign Policy (Csis Report).* Washington, D.C.: Center for Strategic and International Studies, 1999.
Gutman, Roy, ed. *Crimes of War: What the Public Should Know.* New York: W. W. Norton & Company, 1999.

Sankoh, Foday (1937–2003) *Sierra Leone guerrilla leader*

A firebrand and polarizing political figure, Foday Sankoh brought terror to his home country of Sierra Leone on an unparalleled scale in the 1990s. Adjectives such as *charismatic* and *ebullient* were regularly used to describe him. One reporter called him a "tubby leader," a characterization that made him sound more like a lovable clown than a murderous thug.

In the 1970s Sankoh began making a name for himself as a student leader in the small West African nation. He served as an army corporal and later as a TV cameraman before briefly being imprisoned for antigovernment activities. He then went into exile in Libya, where he befriended other political dissidents. At the time Libya, under Colonel Muammar al-Gadhafi, was a hotbed of revolutionary fervor, a refuge for exiles from all over West Africa. Sankoh's fellow revolutionaries looked up to him because he was a decade older than most of them; they called him Papei (Papa).

In 1987 Sankoh returned to Sierra Leone. After receiving military training he slipped into the bordering country of Liberia. There he befriended CHARLES GHANKAY TAYLOR, a like-minded Liberian revolutionary with no more moral scruples than he had. Taylor was plotting his own ascent to power in Liberia and was happy to lend a helping hand to Sankoh in his effort to seize power in Sierra Leone. It would take Taylor eight years—and a vicious campaign of terror—to achieve his ambition: the presidency of Liberia. In 1991, under Taylor's patronage, Sankoh formed the Revolutionary United Front (RUF) in Sierra Leone. If initially Sankoh railed against corruption among Sierra Leone's elite, he soon dropped all pretense of revolutionary reform. All that truly interested him was seizing power and wealth—in the form of diamonds. He launched his campaign in the countryside, initially focusing his efforts on the eastern districts where the diamond mines were located. His forces abducted and raped children; there are reports that some even engaged in cannibalism when food ran short. But if there was one horrifying practice that distinguished Sankoh's depredations, it was the amputation of limbs. Sankoh persisted in denying that these atrocities were sanctioned or indeed that they were taking place at all. Critics who dared to cross Sankoh by telling the truth sometimes paid with their lives. The brutal campaign met with success, and Sankoh was able to consolidate control over the diamond-producing areas, providing him with a base from which to threaten the capital of Freetown. Meanwhile government forces bottled up in Freetown were on the verge of collapse. In 1992 a young army officer, Valentine Strasser, took power in a coup backed by mercenaries. But Taylor continued to support the RUF, using the diamond wealth to subsidize its ragtag, drug-addled army.

Sierra Leone enjoyed a brief fling with democracy with the election of Ahmed Tejan Kabbah, who had the backing of Nigeria, but he, too, was soon overthrown in yet another military coup. A Nigerian peacekeeping mission restored Kabbah to power, but their presence failed to quell the civil war, which was further complicated by other factions and militia groups with agendas of their own. Sankoh's luck appeared to run out when he was captured and sentenced to death. After he announced that he had rediscovered God, his fortunes took another turn when a peace accord, brokered by the United States, was struck between the government and the RUF in 1999. Instead of being put to

death, he was elevated to a high-ranking position in a coalition government. Under the terms of the Lome accord, as the peace agreement was called, RUF soldiers were to be integrated with the regular army. Sankoh was even allowed to regain control over the diamond mines. The fragile peace did not last very long, however, as RUF forces challenged the United Nations, capturing 500 peacekeepers. As the former colonial power, Great Britain felt a special responsibility for Sierra Leone and dispatched troops to rescue the trapped UN soldiers. In the chaos, Sankoh tried to escape Freetown but was recognized and captured. Gradually the United Nations asserted control over Freetown and portions of the countryside. A disarmament program was instituted, and by 2002 nearly 50,000 RUF fighters had laid down their arms. A SPECIAL COURT FOR SIERRA LEONE was established under UN auspices to try the worst offenders on all sides. However, Foday Sankoh, the man most responsible for the carnage of the last decade, escaped justice one last time, dying in prison of natural causes in July 2003.

See also CONFLICT DIAMONDS; LIBERIA, HUMAN RIGHTS VIOLATIONS IN; SIERRA LEONE, HUMAN RIGHTS VIOLATIONS IN.

Further Reading:
Ferme, Mariane C. *The Underneath of Things: Violence, History, and the Everyday in Sierra Leone.* Berkeley: University of California Press, 2001.
Jackson, Michael. *In Sierra Leone.* Durham, N.C.: Duke University Press, 2004.
Richards, Paul. *Fighting for the Rain Forest: War, Youth, and Resources in Sierra Leone.* African Issues Series. London: Heinemann, 1996.
Romano, Cesare, Andre Nollkaemper, and Jann K. Kleffner, eds. *Internationalized Criminal Courts and Tribunals: Sierra Leone, East Timor, Kosovo, and Cambodia.* International Courts and Tribunals Series. Oxford: Oxford University Press, 2004.
Voeten, Teun. *How de Body? One Man's Terrifying Journey through an African War.* New York: Thomas Dunne Books, 2002.

Sant'Anna di Stazzema, massacre in

The Tuscan village of Sant'Anna di Stazzema was the site of a massacre of 560 people—mostly women, children, and the elderly—by Nazi SS forces during World War II. The killings took place on August 12, 1944, shortly after Italian dictator Benito Mussolini had been deposed. The SS rounded up civilians in nearby villages to prevent them from lending support to the partisans who were harassing the retreating German forces. Feeling they were likely to be arrested and killed, the men in Sant'Anna di Stazzema decided to flee under the mistaken assumption that the SS would leave the women and children alone. An inquiry conducted by the U.S. Army in October 1944 turned up evidence of charred remains in houses that had been burned, but the SS officers involved were never pursued. Further investigation was hampered for political reasons. The Allies had determined only to try higher-ranking Nazi officials, and Italy, eager to establish close relations with West Germany, had no motivation to risk opening old wounds. Therefore, although the victims were memorialized, no serious attempts were made to bring the perpetrators to justice until 2004, when Italian military prosecutors decided to reopen the case by charging seven former SS officers for their involvement in the atrocity. The trial of the first three defendants began in absentia in spring 2004. In June 2005, after a yearlong trial, 10 former members of the Nazi SS accused of taking part in the massacre were found guilty in absentia and sentenced to life in prison. All the defendants, now in their eighties, remained in Germany, which, as a matter of principle, will not extradite its own citizens. However, a court in Stuttgart was conducting its own investigation of the event in preparation for a possible trial in Germany.

Further Reading:

Browder, George C. *Hitler's Enforcers: The Gestapo and the SS Security Service in the Nazi Revolution.* Oxford: Oxford University Press, 1996.

Hohne, Heinz Zollen. *The Order of the Death's Head: The Story of Hitler's SS.* Classic Military History. New York: Penguin, 2001.

Sarajevo, siege of

Until 1992 Sarajevo, now the capital of Bosnia and Herzegovina, was a lively cosmopolitan city where Muslims, Christians, and Jews lived together in peace. In 1984 it played host to the Winter Olympics. Founded in the 15th century, Sarajevo takes its name from the Turkish word *serai*, which means "palace." On June 28, 1914, the archduke of Austria, Francis Ferdinand, was assassinated by a Serbian nationalist, an event that triggered the outbreak of World War I. Violence again struck the city in spring 1992 when Bosnia and Herzegovina declared its independence from Yugoslavia, setting off another war. Serbs opposed the independence of Bosnia and neighboring Croatia because it would make the Serb populations a minority in both those republics. (Serbs enjoyed a majority status only in Serbia proper.) The conflict was worsened by religious and ethnic rifts: The Serbs belonged to the Eastern Orthodox Church whereas most of the Bosnians were Muslims. While the Muslims were predominantly secular, many Serbs regarded them as descendants of the reviled Turks

whose armies had pushed into the Balkans in the 14th century.

At the start of the conflict, Serbian forces, aided by Bosnian Serb paramilitary units, attacked the Bosnian army. Initially the Serbs enjoyed considerable success on the battlefield, seizing nearly all Bosnian towns except for Sarajevo. Then, on April 6, 1992, Serb militants opened fire on peace demonstrators, killing five and injuring 30. On May 1 Serb mortars delivered the opening salvo of a SIEGE that would last for four years. That the United Nations had declared Sarajevo a safe haven made no difference. The Bosnian Serb Romanija Corps, under the command of General Stanislav Galić, proceeded to besiege the city, blockading all roads and shutting down the airport to deny Sarajevo's approximately half a million residents food, medicine, water, and electricity. Red Cross trucks given clearance to enter Sarajevo were often seized or destroyed. The Serbs set up artillery on the mountains surrounding the city, allowing them to shell it at will.

During the siege Sarajevo was pounded with an average of 329 shells a day, reaching a high of 3,777 shell impacts. It was only the reopening of the airport in June 1993 and a United Nations airlift that kept the inhabitants from starving to death. But the killings continued unabated, and the most routine actions became perilous. For example, on June 1–15, 1992, 15 people had been killed and another 80 wounded in a mortar attack during a soccer game. But a year later, 12 people were killed while waiting in line to get water. But the incident that caused the most outrage throughout the world occurred on February 5, 1994, when a mortar shell killed 66 and wounded 140 others in the Sarajevo marketplace. Even maternity wards were not spared. By the time the siege ended on February 29, 1996, after a cease-fire had been put into place, an estimated 10,000–12,000 people had been killed and another 50,000 wounded. Hardly a single structure had escaped damage or destruction. Today the population is about 220,000, less than half of what it was before the war.

See also BOSNIA AND HERZEGOVINA, HUMAN RIGHTS VIOLATIONS IN; YUGOSLAVIA, WAR CRIMES IN.

Further Reading:

Clark, Wesley K. *Waging Modern War: Bosnia, Kosovo, and the Future of Combat.* New York: Public Affairs, 2001.

Glenny, Misha. *The Fall of Yugoslavia: The Third Balkan War.* New York: Penguin Books, 1996.

Hagan, John. *Justice in the Balkans: Prosecuting War Crimes in the Hague Tribunal.* Chicago Series in Law and Society. Chicago: University of Chicago Press, 2003.

Harris, Nathaniel. *The War in Former Yugoslavia.* London: Hodder & Stoughton, 1997.

Mertus, Julie. *Former Yugoslavia: War Crimes Trials in the Former Yugoslavia.* Helsinki: Human Rights Watch/Helsinki, 1995.

Rossanet, Bertrand de. *War and Peace in the Former Yugoslavia.* Boston: Martinus Nijhoff, 1997.

Saravia, Álvaro (1946–) *alleged Salvadoran assassin*

Álvaro Saravia, a Salvadoran national, was named in a civil suit as the man who participated in the assassination of Archbishop Óscar Romero in 1980 while the cleric was celebrating mass in San Salvador, the capital of El Salvador. Romero, an outspoken opponent of the right-wing death squads and their political allies then in power, was killed to silence his voice. His slaying had been ordered by the founder of El Salvador's rightist party, ROBERTO D'AUBUISSON, who died in 1992. No Salvadoran court has ever conducted an investigation into Romero's death. (An AMNESTY law makes prosecutions of war criminals all but impossible and has effectively nullified the findings of a UN-sponsored truth commission, which had implicated D'Aubuisson and Saravia.)

The effort to bring Saravia to justice took place in 2004 in an unlikely venue—Fresno, California—under the Alien Tort Claims Act of 1789, which allows nationals of a foreign country to bring a civil suit against another foreign national for certain types of crimes committed elsewhere in the world. The suit asserted that the former Salvadoran air force captain had actively abetted the assassination by obtaining the gun, arranging for the killer's transportation to the chapel, and paying him off. The suit, which was filed by the Center for Justice and Accountability, a human rights organization, on behalf of a relative of the archbishop, sought damages for EXTRAJUDICIAL KILLINGS and CRIMES AGAINST HUMANITY. Because it was a civil trial, the defendant could only be punished by being fined. Saravia was found guilty, although it was difficult to say when, if ever, the monetary damages assessed could be collected. A legal U.S. resident, Saravia had gone into hiding before the trial had begun. According to declassified State Department and CIA documents, the U.S. administration was aware of his alleged involvement in the Romero slaying shortly after it occurred, raising questions as to why he had been permitted to settle in the United States.

In 2006 Saravia gave an interview published in the *Miami Herald* acknowledging his role in Romero's killing. He claimed to be writing a book in which he said he would name others responsible in the assassination plot, including the shooter. He was still a fugitive in early 2010.

See also EL SALVADOR, WAR CRIMES IN.

Further Reading:
Armstrong, Robert. *El Salvador: The Face of Revolution.* Boston: South End Press, 1982.

Wood, Elisabeth Jean, Peter Lange, et al., eds. *Insurgent Collective Action and Civil War in El Salvador.* Cambridge Studies in Comparative Politics. Cambridge: Cambridge University Press, 2003.

Sauckel, Fritz (1894–1946) *Nazi war criminal*

As Nazi plenipotentiary general for labor mobilization from 1942 to 1945, Fritz Sauckel was responsible for mobilizing the slave labor force to sustain the military and industrial power of the Third Reich during World War II. He was tried by the victorious Allies at the NUREMBERG TRIALS and convicted as a war criminal.

Born in Hassfurt am Main on October 27, 1894, Sauckel worked as a young man on Norwegian and Swedish merchant ships. During World War I he was captured and interned in a French prisoner-of-war camp. He was an early adherent of the Nazis, joining the party shortly after its inception in 1921. After the Nazis took power in Germany in 1933, Sauckel was made governor of Thuringia; he also held the rank of honorary general in the elite Nazi paramilitary units, the SA and the SS. In 1942 he was put in charge of the labor mobilization effort, and in this capacity he organized the deportation of 5 million people from occupied European territories to work as slave labor in Germany. He gave specific orders that they were to be exploited "to the highest degree possible at the lowest conceivable degree of expenditure." Special protection squads were used to press-gang laborers into SLAVERY. Sauckel was also responsible for the executions of thousands of Polish Jews.

At his trial before the International Military Tribunal at Nuremberg, Sauckel maintained his innocence and denied any knowledge of the CONCENTRATION CAMPS. He expressed his shock at learning of the widespread atrocities carried out by the Nazis. In spite of his profession of innocence, he was found guilty and hanged on October 16, 1946.

Further Reading:
Ferencz, Benjamin B., and Telford Taylor. *Less Than Slaves: Jewish Forced Labor and the Quest for Compensation.* Bloomington: Indiana University Press, 2002.

Jaskof, Paul B. *The Architecture of Oppression: The SS, Forced Labor and the Nazi Monumental Building Economy.* London: Routledge, 2000.

Saudi Arabia, human rights violations in

Saudi Arabia is a recent country that came into being in 1932 as the result of the conquests of King Abdul Aziz Al Saud, better known in the West as Ibn Saud. It is one of the most repressive regimes on earth, and U.S. State Department reports describe its human rights record as poor, despite close American-Saudi ties. The home of 15 out of the 19 of the 9/11 (2001) bombers and of AL-QAEDA founder Osama bin Laden, Saudi Arabia is a monarchical dictatorship and the most restrictive of all Islamic countries.

In the 18th century the Al Saud clan, then rulers of the Najd region of central Arabia, came together with the Islamic religious reformer Al-Wahhab. Wahhab followed the hard-line Hanbali school of Islam, the severest of the four main schools of Sunni Islam (the version of that faith followed by 85 percent of Muslims worldwide). In the early 20th century, the Al Saud family and the Wahhabi sect of Hanbali Islam again combined, with Ibn Saud leading campaigns of conquest that resulted in his capture of most of the Arabian peninsula by 1924. This context is important, since the majority of Muslims outside of Arabia do not follow the austere Hanbali/Wahhabi interpretation of that faith, and would therefore reject the radical, often extreme, version that prevails in Saudi Arabia. (Leading moderate Islamic thinkers such as Akbar Ahmed have argued that much of Saudi Islam is in fact more cultural than strictly Islamic, especially in the treatment of women and of religious minorities.)

As well as being a dictatorship, ruled by the Al Saud family, Saudi Arabia is highly repressive religiously. Islamic law, sharia, is rigidly enforced, and all the ancient punishments are still enforced. For example, there was enormous controversy 20 years ago when a Saudi princess was executed for committing adultery, a crime that still carries the death penalty. Thieves often have their right hand and left foot amputated. Beheading is not infrequent, and Islam is the only religion permitted in the country. Even the Shiite minority (the sect of Islam prevalent in Iran and predominant in Iraq) is harassed, even though—or perhaps because—Shiites live primarily in the oil-producing provinces. In the closed-court justice system, most defendants are not entitled to legal representation. The U.S. government's human rights reports on Saudi Arabia also note that the jails are mainly unsanitary. Furthermore, in legal proceedings the testimony of a woman is half the value of that of a man. While other Muslim countries often use sharia law for family issues, in Saudi Arabia it is the sole legal code for the country.

Limited local elections were allowed for the first time ever in 2005, but, unlike several Persian Gulf states and Iran, where women may vote, no woman was permitted to vote. While many Islamic countries permit women to go alone outdoors and wear a head scarf without facial covering, in Saudi Arabia women are not allowed out alone without a male relative, and they may not drive. They also have to cover their faces entirely when in public. Except for the brief time of TALIBAN rule in Afghanistan, the Saudi regime is drastically more restrictive than any other Islamic country. The U.S. State Department human rights reports point out that spousal violence against women is common and that persecuted women are not allowed by law to leave the country, even if they are fleeing their abusive husbands.

While many Middle Eastern countries have secret police to crush political dissent, Saudi Arabia also has a unique police force, which is charged with the zealous enforcement of the Hanbali/Wahhabi code of Islam. The *mutawwa'in*—police for the repression of vice—ensure obedience to the religious observances, from the absolute prohibition on alcohol to the subjection of women. In a notorious recent case, girl pupils fleeing a burning school were forced back into the flames by these police so that they would not be seen in public without head and face coverings. Several girls died as a result, and an embarrassed Saudi regime was then obliged to transfer the supervision of girls' schools from the religious authorities to the education ministry.

The security forces, however repressive, have been unable to stop terrorist attacks by Islamic militants who have targeted foreigners in Riyadh, Jidda, and elsewhere. Several Saudis have lost their lives in the attacks as well. Many of the attacks appear designed to scare off foreign investment and damage the oil industry, which is dependent on foreign workers and provides the major source of revenue for the country. While Osama bin Laden has vowed the destruction of the Saudi monarchy, it is unknown whether the terrorist groups implicated in these attacks are directly connected to al-Qaeda or are merely claiming an affiliation. For several years wealthy Saudis provided funding for the jihadis—holy warriors—who fought the Soviets in Afghanistan and subsidized the madrassas (religious Islamic schools) in Pakistan and elsewhere, fostering Islamic militancy in the belief that they were buying immunity for themselves. But that illusion has been shattered now that the terrorists have shown their willingness to strike on Saudi soil.

In August 2005 King Fahd died after a long illness. He was succeeded by his more reform-minded half brother, Crown Prince Abdullah. King Abdullah's efforts to bring reform to the kingdom have met with only modest success, and most human rights organizations agree that its human rights record has not significantly improved. If anything, executions have increased. According to Amnesty International, Saudi Arabia was third in the number of people executed in the world in 2008 (after China and Iran). Approximately half of the 1,695 people known to have been executed in the past 23 years (as of 2007) were foreigners, mostly workers from such developing countries as Somalia, Egypt, India, the Philippines, Bangladesh, and Sudan who lacked the influential ties that might earn them a pardon. Foreign workers have practically no legal protections whatsoever. Amnesty's report on the kingdom's human rights record noted that proportionately, more people were executed in recent years for crimes such as drug violations, apostasy, adultery, and "rebellion and highway robbery," a term for violent criminal acts against people or property, than for murder. Unsettled security conditions—a result of sporadic terrorist attacks on foreigners, oil installations, and urban centers—have only exacerbated the human rights problem. Thousands of people have been detained as part of antiterrorist sweeps and held for years without charges being brought against them or access to lawyers or translators. Security forces still carry out occasional extrajudicial killings and torture, protracted detention and unfair trials persist. Human rights groups maintain that the kingdom holds scores of political prisoners. Many detainees are punished with flogging and amputations. Calls for more equality for women have yet to yield substantial results; women are not free to move around, marry, or study without authorization from a male relative or husband, a policy more regressive than that of Saudi Arabia's neighboring states in the Gulf. Children, too, do not enjoy legal protections and in a number of cases have been condemned to prison, sometimes for life, for crimes committed at age 12. "The laws are valid but they are not applied." stated Ibrahim al-Mugaiteeb, a Saudi representative of the U.S.-based NGO Human Rights First, "Ever since 2003, we have a penal code that says that a person cannot be detained more than five days without having access to a judge. But we have detainees in our prisons who have been there more than 5, 8, 10 years without meeting an attorney."

Further Reading:

AbuKhalil, As'ad. *The Battle for Saudi Arabia: Royalty, Fundamentalism, and Global Power.* New York: Seven Stories Press, 2004.

Amnesty International USA. Saudi Arabia Human Rights. Available online. URL: http://www.amnestyusa.org/all-countries/saudi-arabia/page.do?id=1011230. Accessed March 20, 2010.

Bradley, John R. *Saudi Arabia Exposed: Inside a Kingdom in Crisis.* Sidney, Australia: Palgrave Macmillan, 2005.

Center for Democracy and Human Rights in Saudi Arabia. Available online. URL: http://www.cdhr.info/. Accessed March 20, 2010.

Human Rights First Society. 2010 Archives (Saudi Arabia). Available online. URL: http://hrfssaudiarabia.org/?page_id=750. Accessed March 20, 2010.

Lacey, Robert. *Inside the Kingdom.* New York: Viking, 2009.

Long, David E. *The Kingdom of Saudi Arabia.* Tallahassee: University Press of Florida, 1998.

Weston, Mark. *Prophets and Princes: Saudi Arabia from Muhammad to the Present.* Hoboken, N.J.: Wiley, 2008.

Sawoniuk, Anthony (1921–2005) *Nazi war criminal*
Anthony Sawoniuk was the first of 376 suspected war criminals tried in Britain for war crimes in World War II under the 1991 War Crimes Act. In 1999 Sawoniuk, then 78, was found guilty of killing one unnamed Jewish woman. A former railway ticket collector and pensioner, Sawoniak said that he was innocent of any wrongdoing and claimed to be the victim of a conspiracy. He contended that the murders he was implicated for were the Germans' responsibility. His trial is significant because it was the first time that a British jury had traveled abroad to view a crime scene (in Belarus) and because the defendant was the first U.K. citizen accused of war crimes to speak in his own defense in a criminal court.

Sawoniuk was identified as a suspect in 1988 as a result of information turned over to the British government by the former Soviet government. An inquiry into his conduct during the war did not begin, however, until 1994. He was ultimately charged with war crimes that had taken place in 1942 in the village of Domachevo in Belarus, a former Soviet republic, when Belarus was occupied by the Nazis. A witness said that he had seen Sawoniuk, known then as "Andrusha," order three Jews—two men and a woman—to undress in front of an open grave before shooting them in the back of the head. There was testimony that he might have killed as many as 15 Jews at the time, using a submachine gun. The prosecution alleged that Sawoniuk had led "search and kill" police squads, which hunted down Jews trying to escape the Nazis. He was "not only prepared to do the Nazis' bidding," the lead prosecutor said, "but carried out their genocidal policy with enthusiasm." Sawoniuk died in Norwich Prison at age 84.

Schacht, Hjalmar Horace Greeley (1877–1970)
German banker
Hjalmar Schacht was a leading German financier who served as minister of economics under ADOLF HITLER before falling out of favor with the führer. He was exonerated on war crime charges by the tribunal at the NUREMBERG TRIALS after the war, although he was later found guilty for other offenses by a German court.

Born on January 22, 1877, the son of a salesman who had lived in the United States, Schacht was named for the fiery American journalist Horace Greeley, who had campaigned against slavery before the Civil War. Schacht studied medicine, philology, and political science before turning to economics and went on to hold a number of executive positions in the banking industry, becoming director of the German National Bank in 1916. His advancement continued after the end of World War I; in 1923 he became Reich currency commissioner at a time when hyperinflation was threatening the stability of the Weimar Republic. As a reward for bringing inflation under control, he was appointed president of the Reichsbank, though he resigned in 1930 because of his opposition to ruinous REPARATIONS to the Allies that Germany had agreed to pay under the Versailles treaty. His conversion to National Socialism (Nazism) occurred after reading Hitler's memoir, *Mein Kampf*.

In early 1931 Schacht was introduced to Hitler, who persuaded him to raise funds for the Nazis, using his contacts with prominent industrialists like Albert Voegler of the United Steel Works and the arms manufacturers GUSTAV KRUPP and Alfried Krupp. Schacht did not confine his support to fund raising. In 1932 he collected the signatures of industrialists for a letter addressed to Chancellor Paul von Hindenburg, requesting that he appoint Hitler as chancellor. After Hitler's ascension to power, Schacht organized the Association of German Industrialists, which put up 3 million marks for the Nazi election campaign. On Hitler's behalf he traveled to the United States, making over 40 speeches in public and on the radio in which he reassured his listeners that Hitler was committed to restoring democracy to Germany. He even succeeded in meeting President Franklin Roosevelt, who thought the banker was "extremely arrogant."

In 1934 Hitler made Schacht his minister of economics. Schacht's economic views were shaped more by the seminal British economist John Maynard Keynes and the tenets of Roosevelt's New Deal than by Nazi ideology. He convinced Hitler to support a massive public-works program that resulted in the construction of the *Autobahnen*, Germany's famous highway system. Schacht shared the anti-Semitism of the other Nazi officials; in one speech he maintained that "the Jews must realize that their influence in Germany has disappeared for all time." However, unlike many Nazis, he was opposed to violent means to solve "the Jewish problem." Instead he worked out an arrangement with the World Zionist Organization to allow Jews to emigrate to Palestine (then under British mandate) in exchange for 15,000 reichmarks each. Some 170,000 Jews ultimately left for Palestine as part of the deal, which allowed them to escape the CONCENTRATION CAMPS. Schacht also repudiated the rabid anti-Semitic articles in *Der Stürmer*, published by Nazi propagandist JULIUS STREICHER, condemning what he termed "unlawful activities" against Jews. He pointed out that many Jews had fought bravely for Germany during the First World War and ought to be treated fairly.

Although Schacht negotiated bartering agreements with countries in the Balkans and Middle East to provide Germany with raw materials to rebuild its military strength, he harbored misgivings about the vast sums of money being spent on Germany's remilitarization. He cautioned Hitler that the expenditures on arms posed a risk of reigniting inflation. His words fell on deaf ears. Hitler's trusted deputy, HERMANN GÖRING, who ran the economy (and was nominally Schacht's superior), supported Germany's rearmament. He told Schacht, "If the Führer wishes it then two times two are five." In 1937 Schacht resigned as minister of economics over disagreements about rearmament but remained in Hitler's government as minister without portfolio. In 1944, however, he was arrested and placed in Dachau concentration camp on suspicion of participating in the failed attempt on Hitler's life in July 1944. Two of the conspirators had, in fact, approached Schacht, hoping to enlist him in the plot, but he had rebuffed their overtures.

Schacht survived the war, after which he fell into the custody of the Allies and was put on trial at Nuremberg, charged with CRIMES AGAINST HUMANITY. Acquitted, he was nonetheless subsequently rearrested on other charges and convicted by a German court. He was sentenced to eight years' imprisonment but was freed in 1948. In 1953 he established a private bank in Düsseldorf and went on to write an autobiography, *Confessions of the Old Wizard*. He also served as an economic adviser to a number of foreign governments including, that of President Gamal Nasser in Egypt. Schacht died in Munich on June 4, 1970.

Schellenberg, Walter (1910–1952) *Nazi official*

Walter Schellenberg was deputy director of the SS (security police) during the Third Reich and later became actively involved in counterintelligence activities. In contrast to other top Nazi officials tried at the NUREMBERG TRIALS for war crimes, he testified against the regime that he had served, sparing himself a long prison sentence.

Born on January 16, 1910, in Saarbruecken, Germany, Schellenberg studied medicine and law at the University of Bonn. In 1933, shortly after ADOLF HITLER had come to power, Schellenberg decided to join the SS, the elite Nazi security police, motivated more by ambition than by ideology. Clever and intelligent, he cultivated friendships with powerful Nazi officials, including SS head HEINRICH HIMMLER and Admiral Wilhelm Canaris, chief of the Abwehr (military intelligence). After the Germans occupied Czechoslovakia, Schellenberg became allied with REINHARD HEYDRICH, deputy chief of the GESTAPO and protector of Bohemia and Moravia. As a counterintelligence officer, he was involved in the planning of a plot to kidnap King Edward VIII of England—a plan that was never carried out. He was more successful in penetrating the fabled Soviet spy ring called the Red Orchestra. After the failure of the assassination attempt on Hitler's life on July 20, 1944, Schellenberg was given orders to arrest his old friend Admiral Canaris, who was suspected of involvement in the plot. (Canaris was subsequently released, only to be arrested again by the Allies.)

In 1944, recognizing that the Third Reich would shortly collapse, Schellenberg sought to ingratiate himself with the Allies by traveling to Stockholm, where he tried to start peace negotiations on behalf of Himmler, who was his superior. The negotiations went nowhere, and in June 1945 he was arrested by the Allies and subsequently tried at Nuremberg for war crimes. However, by testifying against his former associates, he received a sentence of only six years. Released in 1950, he went on to write his memoirs, in which he contended that his spy network had managed to penetrate England, unaware that all his spies had been turned by MI5, the British secret service. Schellenberg died in Turin, Italy, on March 31, 1952.

Further Reading:

Whiting, Charles. *Heydrich: Henchman of Death.* Barnsley, S. Yorkshire, U.K.: Leo Cooper, 1999.

Schirach, Baldur von (1907–1974) *Nazi youth leader*
Baldur von Schirach served as youth leader of the Nazi Party and later as gauleiter of Vienna. He was charged with and convicted of war crimes at the NUREMBERG TRIALS, although he was one of the few Nazi officials to repudiate Hitler. Schirach was born in Berlin on March 9, 1907. At the age of 10 he became a member of the Young Germans' League, where he developed the racist views that would guide him throughout his life. In 1925 he joined the National Socialist German Workers Party (NSDAP), and only a year later he was introduced to the party's head, ADOLF HITLER. Hitler took Schirach under his wing and in 1929 appointed him head of the Nazi Students' Union, later promoting him to the head of the Hitler Youth in 1933. As the youth leader Schirach composed prayers in praise of the führer that had to be recited by members of Nazi youth organizations before their meals. In 1940 he joined the German army and won an Iron Cross fighting in France. That same year Hitler made him gauletier (district leader) of Vienna; in that capacity he supervised the deportation of Jews from the Austrian capital to death camps in Poland.

After his capture by Allied troops at the end of the war, Schirach claimed that he was unaware of the purpose of the CONCENTRATION CAMPS and so could not have known that he was sending Jews off to be exterminated. He even presented evidence that he had lodged a protest with MARTIN BORMANN, Hitler's influential deputy, regarding the brutal treatment of Austrian Jews. Nonetheless, he was convicted and sentenced to 20 years in prison. He died on August 8, 1974.

scorched earth

Scorched earth is a military tactic used to destroy resources in an attempt to deprive an enemy force of its ability to wage war. The term is derived from the practice of burning crops—e.g., scorching the earth—to deny an opponent from living off the land. But the term is equally applicable to the destruction of industrial infrastructure and communication or transportation networks and facilities. A scorched earth policy is by no means limited to invading forces; defenders have been known to destroy their own resources to prevent them from falling into the hands of the enemy. This tactic was famously employed by the Russians during the Napoleonic invasion of 1812; rather than allow the French to seize the capital, the czarist armies burned Moscow to the ground. Denied booty and food, the French troops were forced to retreat. The Russian forces stood by while a bitter Russian winter took its toll. Weaker forces often rely on scorched earth tactics to undermine a more powerful enemy. For example, Spanish guerrillas carried out scorched earth tactics in the Peninsular War (1808–14), allowing them to overcome the much larger French army. General Sherman's March to the Sea in the American Civil War is another well-known example; it was during that campaign that Atlanta was burned to the ground by Union forces. In the Sino-Japanese War (1937–45), the Chinese destroyed dams and levees, flooding their own territory to forestall the advance of Japanese forces. German forces used similar tactics at the end of World War II, destroying rail networks in Europe as they retreated before the Allied advance. In the two-decades-old civil war in Sudan, both government and guerrilla forces in the south of the country looted livestock and destroyed houses, clearing out civilian populations to ensure access to oil resources in violation of the GENEVA CONVENTIONS. Arab militias in the DARFUR region of western Sudan have also carried out a scorched earth policy to drive out an indigenous black African population.

Further Reading:

Carell, Paul. *Scorched Earth: The Russian-German War 1943–1944.* Atglen, Pa.: Schiffer Publishing, 1994.
Power, Samantha. *"A Problem from Hell": America and the Age of Genocide.* New York: HarperPerennial, 2003.
Prunier, Gerard. *Darfur: The Ambiguous Genocide.* Ithaca, N.Y.: Cornell University Press, 2005.
Zamoyski, Adam. *Moscow 1812: Napoleon's Fatal March.* New York: HarperCollins, 2004.

Serbia, human rights violations in

Serbia is a constitutional republic and a former part of the Federal Socialist Republic of Yugoslavia. Serbia is still recovering from the Balkan wars of the 1990s and the authoritarian regime of the former president SLOBODAN MILOŠEVIĆ, and its political stability remains at risk. In March 2003 the assassination of Prime Minister Zoran Djindjić prompted the government to impose a 42-day state of emergency. Although the government has generally reined in security forces, there are still maverick elements of the police that commit human rights abuses, which increased during the emergency. Abuses encompassed beatings, arbitrary arrests, detentions, and TORTURE, reported forms of which included asphyxiation with a plastic bag, electric shock, and mock executions. During the security sweeps, more than 10,000 individuals were detained; approximately 2,000 remained in custody by the end of the year. Djindjić's assassination, carried out by a group of nationalist paramilitaries and organized criminals, was viewed as a botched attempt to topple the government. Suspects were quickly rounded up, and the conspirators went on trial in December 2003.

The justice system is susceptible to political influence, and defendants face the prospect of lengthy trials. In a marked departure from the Milošević era, the parliament has enacted legislation to establish a special domestic war-crimes court and appoint a special prosecutor. Until recently the Serbian government failed to investigate or prosecute suspected war criminals who were involved in the Bosnian War or the Kosovo War. The parliament has also demonstrated greater willingness to cooperate with the INTERNATIONAL CRIMINAL TRIBUNAL FOR THE FORMER YUGOSLAVIA (ICTY), which resulted in four voluntary surrenders of indicted officials and paved the way for the arrest and transfer of another five to The Hague, where the court sits. In addition, the government handed over documents to the ICTY relevant to the prosecution of former Serb officials and permitted witnesses to testify. Even so, the ICTY has expressed misgivings about the willingness of Serbian authorities to bring the worst offenders to justice, noting that one of the most notorious individuals indicted by the tribunal—General RATKO MLADIĆ—has been at large in Serbia for almost a decade. Meanwhile, the government continues to make progress in identifying exhumed bodies of victims killed during the war. In 2001, for instance, Serb authorities discovered hundreds of bodies of ethnic Albanians in a mass grave; it is assumed that the victims were killed in Kosovo during a secessionist war in 1999 and then transferred to Serbia to conceal evidence of the slayings. Almost 200 bodies were identified by the Serbian government, in cooperation with international organizations and the International Commission on Missing Persons (ICMP), and repatriated to Kosovo.

After Milošević's ouster in 2000, Serb authorities have taken steps to investigate several high-profile political killings that appear to have a criminal dimension. Two former police officers and five accomplices went on trial for the 2002 killing of former Belgrade police chief Bosko Buha. During the trial a Belgrade police inspector offered sensational disclosures implicating other members of the police in other crimes. A former official was also sentenced to seven years imprisonment for the attempted murder of

Vuk Drašković, a political opposition leader during the Milošević era.

In June 2006, after a referendum in Montenegro favored independence, Serbia's National Assembly acknowledged that the former "State Union of Serbia and Montenegro" would be known as the "Republic of Serbia." Serbia also applied for membership in the European Union (EU) in 2009 with the intention of accessing to it by 2014. Serbia's attempt to integrate with Europe has meant putting a distance from its past, and its government has taken some significant steps to do so. In March 2010, for instance, Serbian war crimes prosecutors announced that they were investigating 26 former paramilitary and police officers suspected of committing crimes—including killing 41 people in one village—against Albanians in Kosovo in 1999. In addition, police arrested nine people in Serbia for the robbing and killing of more than 200 Albanians in the Kosovo conflict. When former Bosnian vice president Ejup Ganić was arrested in London in March on a Serb warrant based on alleged war crimes, the Serb government indicated that it would be willing to allow Bosnian authorities to try him. (Ganić was charged with being responsible for killing Yugoslav troops in Bosnia during their retreat from Sarajevo in 1992.) A few years ago the Serbs would never have held out such a prospect, given the suspicion and animosity between Belgrade and Sarajevo.

See also BOSNIA AND HERZEGOVINA, HUMAN RIGHTS VIOLATIONS IN; KOSOVO, WAR CRIMES IN; YUGOSLAVIA, WAR CRIMES IN.

Further Reading:

Hagan, John. *Justice in the Balkans: Prosecuting War Crimes in the Hague Tribunal.* Chicago Series in Law and Society. Chicago: University of Chicago Press, 2003.

Hazan, Pierre, and James Thomas Snyder. *Justice in a Time of War: The True Story behind the International Criminal Tribunal for the Former Yugoslavia.* Eugenia and Hugh M. Stewart Series on Eastern Europe. Austin: Texas A&M University Press, 2004.

Mertus, Julie. *Former Yugoslavia: War Crimes Trials in the Former Yugoslavia.* Helsinki: Human Rights Watch/ Helsinki, 1995.

Rossanet, Bertrand de. *War and Peace in the Former Yugoslavia.* Boston: Martinus Nijhoff, 1997.

Seselj, Vojislav (1954–) *Serbian paramilitary commander*

Vojislav Seselj (pronounced SHESH-el), a former Serbian officer, was indicted by the INTERNATIONAL CRIMINAL TRIBUNAL FOR THE FORMER YUGOSLAVIA (ICTY) in The Hague on war crimes charges relating to the Slovenian, Bosnian, and Croatian wars of the 1990s. Under Seselj's direction, several paramilitary groups known as Seselj's Men and the White Eagles carried out persecutions, plunder, and killings of non-Serbian civilians. Although these groups had the support of the then Yugoslav leader SLOBODAN MILOŠEVIĆ, the two were bitter political rivals. If anything, Seselj was more intemperate than Milošević. He once threatened to blow up a nuclear power plant in the breakaway province of Slovenia (now an independent state) and warned that the Serbs would launch missile strikes in Italy, Austria, and Croatia in retaliation for NATO air strikes on Belgrade, the Yugoslav capital. While he has denied any complicity in the crimes of which he stands accused, he voluntarily turned himself into The Hague.

Born in 1954 in eastern Herzegovina (then a part of Yugoslavia), Seselj had a brilliant academic career: He was the youngest student ever to earn a Ph.D. in Yugoslavia. Subsequently he taught at the University of Michigan and at Sarajevo University. His exposure to American values, however, did not seem to have instilled him with democratic values. An ardent Serb nationalist, he wrote an article advocating the formation of a Serb state to replace the multiethnic Yugoslavia, then under communist rule. For his temerity he was sentenced to two years in prison. In 1990, as Yugoslavia began to disintegrate, he founded the Radical Party (SRS) and joined a parliamentary alliance with Milošević's party. The alliance, however, quickly collapsed over Milošević's apparent readiness to withdraw military support to Bosnian Serbs who were fighting to create an independent state of their own. Milošević called his onetime ally "the personification of violence and primitivity," strong charges coming from a man who would later be charged by the ICTY with war crimes.

The two men, however, patched up their differences when the third Balkan war of the 1990s threatened to erupt in the province of Kosovo. Ethnic tensions had been brewing in the province between Serbs and the Albanians who made up the majority of the population. "Their country is Albania and they should live there," Seselj declared. "The only Albanians who should live here (Kosovo) are the ones who think of Serbia as their fatherland."

Imprisonment has not mellowed the former warlord. Even though he remains behind bars, he succeeded in winning a seat in the Yugoslav parliament in elections held in 2003, using a prison phone to communicate with a Belgrade radio station, which then broadcast his words to supporters. He has repudiated the UN-sponsored ICTY as an "American tool against Serbs," which he says he "will blast to pieces." Nor has he shown any deference to the judges, comparing them to Nazis and demanding that they change their red-and-black courtroom robes because they reminded him of the Roman Catholic Inquisition. Although other defendants facing trial at The Hague have shown intemperate behavior during the court proceedings—

Milošević in particular—none has proven quite so troublesome as Seselj. "Other accused have their ways of being difficult," said a tribunal spokesman, "but we have not seen such extreme verbal assaults before." His disruptive tactics have caused court officials to openly speculate whether a fair trial is even possible.

See also BOSNIA AND HERZEGOVINA, HUMAN RIGHTS VIOLATIONS IN; CROATIA, HUMAN RIGHTS VIOLATIONS IN; SERBIA, HUMAN RIGHTS VIOLATIONS IN; SLOVENIA, HUMAN RIGHTS VIOLATIONS IN.

Further Reading:
Hagan, John. *Justice in the Balkans: Prosecuting War Crimes in the Hague Tribunal.* Chicago Series in Law and Society. Chicago: University of Chicago Press, 2003.

Hazan, Pierre, and James Thomas Snyder. *Justice in a Time of War: The True Story behind the International Criminal Tribunal for the Former Yugoslavia.* Eugenia and Hugh M. Stewart Series on Eastern Europe. Austin: Texas A&M University Press, 2004.

Human Rights Watch. Serbia Human Rights. Available online. URL: http://www.hrw.org/europecentral-asia/serbia. Accessed March 20. 2010.

Kim, Julie. *War in the Former Yugoslavia: Chronology of Events August 16, 1992–May 30, 1993.* CRS report for Congress. Washington, D.C.: Foreign Affairs and National Defense Division, Congressional Research Service, the Library of Congress, 1993.

Kipp, Jacob W. *International Ramifications of Yugoslavia's Serial Wars: The Challenge of Ethno-national Conflicts for a Post-Cold-War, European order.* Fort Leavenworth, Kans.: European Military Studies Office, 1993.

Naimark, Norman, and Holly Case. *Yugoslavia and Its Historians: Understanding the Balkan Wars of the 1990s.* Stanford, Calif.: Stanford University Press, 2003.

OSCE.org. OSCE Mission to Serbia. Available online. URL: http://www.osce.org/serbia/13161.html. Accessed March 20, 2010.

Rogel, Carole. *The Breakup of Yugoslavia and the War in Bosnia.* Westport, Conn.: Greenwood Press, 1998.

Rossanet, Bertrand de. *War and Peace in the Former Yugoslavia.* Boston: Martinus Nijhoff, 1997.

Scharf, Michael P. *Balkan Justice: The Story behind the First International War Crimes Trial since Nuremberg.* Durham, N.C.: Carolina Academic Press, 1997.

Seyss-Inquart, Arthur (Arthur Zajtich) (1892–1946)
Nazi official

Arthur Seyss-Inquart served the Nazi regime during World War II as an official in Austria and occupied Poland before becoming *Reichskommissar* for the Occupied Netherlands. Under his rule nearly the entire Jewish population of the Netherlands was deported to CONCENTRATION CAMPS. After the war he was tried by the Allies at the NUREMBERG TRIALS, found guilty of war crimes, and sentenced to death.

The son of a teacher, Seyss-Inquart was born Arthur Zajtich in Stonarov, Moravia (then part of the Austro-Hungarian Empire), on July 22, 1892. He fought for the Austrian army in World War I and received several decorations for bravery in combat. He went on to obtain a degree in law from the University of Vienna and open a law practice in Austria. He soon became drawn to right-wing ideology and joined the Austrian National Socialist (Nazi) Party, which favored the union *(Anschluss)* of Austria and Germany. "The National Socialist Party in Austria never tried to hide its inclination for a greater Germany," he declared in a speech. "That Austria would one day return to the Reich was a matter of course for all National Socialists and for true Germans in Austria." Seyss-Inquart became state chancellor in the Austrian government of Kurt von Schuschnigg, but when Schushnigg was forced to resign after rejecting ADOLF HITLER's demands for a more pro-Nazi government, Seyss-Inquart replaced him as the head of a National Socialist cabinet; he later said that he had called on Hitler for armed assistance to save Austria from plunging into civil war. Seyss-Inquart subsequently drafted a law that reduced Austria to the level of a German province but continued to head the new Ostmark, as the province was known, answering to the chief minister ERNST KALTENBRUNNER. Seyss-Inquart was also given the honorary SS rank of *Gruppenführer*, which he held as well as minister without portfolio in Hitler's government.

In 1940 Seyss-Inquart was appointed deputy governor of Poland (occupied the year before) under Governor-General HANS FRANK. In his new capacity, he was involved with relocating Polish Jews into ghettoes (from which they would eventually be deported to extermination camps) and what was euphemistically called the "extraordinary pacification" of the remnants of Polish resistance. In May 1940, after the Germans had seized the Low Countries, Seyss-Inquart moved on to the Netherlands, charged with forging a closer economic relationship with Germany. As *Reichskommissar*, he was effectively in control of the Netherlands; to bolster his position he backed a right-wing party, the Dutch NSB, which formed a paramilitary unit known as the Landwacht. At the same time he locked up officials of other political parties that were banned. He extended his control into the cultural sphere "right down to the chess players' club" under a policy called the *Kulturkammer* and carried out orders to extract 50 million marks a month from the country to compensate Germany for the costs of occupation. He ruthlessly suppressed "terror," as he termed the

Adolf Hitler standing by Dr. Seyss-Inquart, the last chancellor of Austria, after Hitler's speech in the Heldenplatz, Vienna, announced that Germany would be taking over Austria *(Hulton/Archive)*

resistance, and directly ordered the execution of 800 people (although estimates range up to 3,500), among them political prisoners and Dutch men executed in reprisal killings, under the "Hostage Law." In addition, he supervised a FORCED LABOR recruitment campaign, drafting 530,000 Dutch civilians to work for the Germans; almost half of them were shipped to Germany to work in factories there. Ultimately insistent demands for more labor grew too much even for Seyss-Inquart, and when in 1944 Berlin asked for an additional 250,000 laborers, he was able to muster only 12,000.

An avowed anti-Semite, Seyss-Inquart had conducted a purge of all Jews in the government, the press, and the major professions shortly after arriving in the Netherlands. He then organized a registration campaign to document all Jews (about 140,000) in the country; by 1941 thousands of Jews had been herded into ghettoes in Amsterdam or camps at Westerbork and Vught. The first DEPORTATIONS occurred in February 1941, when 1,000 Dutch Jews were sent to the Buchenwald and Mauthausen concentration camps. Subsequently most Dutch Jews were deported to

Auschwitz. In September 1944, as the Allies were approaching the Netherlands, Jews were relocated from Westerbork and sent to their deaths at Theresienstadt in Czechoslovakia. Of the 140,000 Jews who were registered before the war, only 13,400 survived—5,400 who had returned from the camps and others who had emerged from hiding.

In the final months of the war, Seyss-Inquart helped carry out a brutal scorched earth policy to destroy Dutch harbor facilities and flood the country, devastating its agricultural industry and causing widespread famine, which is believed to have led to the deaths of 30,000 people. Seyss-Inquart remained head of the Netherlands until the bitter end. Captured by the Allies in May 1945, he was tried before the Nuremberg Tribunal on charges of conspiracy to commit crimes against peace; planning, initiating, and waging wars of aggression; war crimes; and CRIMES AGAINST HUMANITY. He was found guilty on all counts and hanged along with several other Nazi officials on October 16, 1946.

Further Reading:

Beigbeder, Yves, and Theo van Boven. *Judging War Criminals: The Politics of International Justice.* Sidney, Australia: Palgrave Macmillan, 1999.

Bloxham, Donald. *Genocide on Trial: War Crimes Trials and the Formation of Holocaust History and Memory.* Oxford: Oxford University Press, 2003.

Cooper, Belinda, and Richard Goldstone. *War Crimes: The Legacy of Nuremberg.* New York: TV Books Inc., 1999.

Dawidowicz, Lucy. *A Holocaust Reader.* Library of Jewish Studies. Chicago: Behrman House Publishing, 1976.

Dwork, Deborah, and Robert Jan Van Pelt. *Holocaust: A History.* New York: W. W. Norton & Company, 2003.

Gilbert, Martin. *The Holocaust: A History of the Jews of Europe during the Second World War.* New York: Owl Books, 1987.

Shattuck, John (1942–) *American diplomat and human rights advocate*

Former assistant secretary of state for democracy, human rights, and labor in the Clinton administration, John Shattuck has been an outspoken advocate for human rights. He deplored the failure of the United States to intervene and stop the GENOCIDE in Rwanda in 1994. In an interview for the PBS program *Frontline*, Shattuck blamed bureaucratic bungling and political concerns for Washington's inaction. Policy makers were already on "overload," he said, when the genocide broke out: "I discovered that [Secretary of State Warren] Christopher was totally preoccupied with China and the Middle East. . . . One of the untold stories about Rwanda is the terrible tragedy of the timing. . . . Had the genocide occurred a year and a half later, the response might well have been different." In another interview he

elaborated on the wisdom of intervention in humanitarian crises such as Rwanda's: "You want to save lives at first if genocide is under way, and there are instances in which intervention, including military intervention, is absolutely essential. It should have been done in Rwanda. It was belatedly done in Bosnia. It was done in Afghanistan. It was done in Kosovo. It was done the wrong way in Iraq, but it needed to be done. You also cannot assume that any model of democracy, certainly our own model, but even any other model, is necessarily going to work in another country. So you'd better listen closely to what you're hearing."

Shattuck, who later served as U.S. ambassador to the Czech Republic, is the author of the book *Freedom on Fire: Human Rights Wars and America's Response.* In 2000 he was named the chief executive officer of the John F. Kennedy Library and Foundation at Harvard University, where he has taught law. A graduate of Yale Law School with an M.A. in law from Cambridge University, he previously served as executive director of the American Civil Liberties Union Washington, D.C., office and national staff counsel from 1971 to 1984. Shattuck taught a course on diplomacy and foreign policy as a Senior Fellow at Tisch College at Tufts University in Massachusetts. In 2009 he was appointed president and rector of Central European University (CEU), an international European-American graduate school of social sciences, humanities, law, public policy, and business, based in Budapest.

See also RWANDA, GENOCIDE IN.

Further Reading:

Shattuck, John. *Freedom on Fire: Human Rights Wars and America's Response.* Cambridge, Mass.: Harvard University Press, 2003.

Shimada Shigetaro (1883–1976) *Japanese naval commander and militarist*

Admiral Shimada Shigetaro was a navy minister and a member of the Supreme War Council in Japan during World War II. Classified as a Class A war criminal, he was convicted by the International Military Tribunal for the Far East (the TOKYO TRIALS) for his actions during World War II.

Born in 1883, Shimada served as vice chief of the naval staff and commander of Japan's China Fleet before becoming minister of the navy, a position he held from 1941 to 1944. Naval forces under his command carried out massacres of Allied PRISONERS OF WAR and killed survivors of torpedoed Allied ships. Prisoners and civilians alike were also interned aboard ships—known as hell ships—under deplorable conditions. Ironically, Shimada and many other top naval officials had initially opposed Japan going to war with the United States. But in the interest of national unity, Shimada eventually acquiesced to the army, which was strongly in favor of war. He declared that the destruction of "harmony" between the army and navy was far worse than the prospect of war, which ultimately proved ruinous to Japan.

At the Tokyo Trials Shimada was one of several Class A war criminals who, the indictment charged, had "contemplated and carried out . . . murdering, maiming and ill-treating prisoners of war [and] civilian internees . . . forcing them to labor under inhumane conditions . . . plundering public and private property, wantonly destroying cities, towns and villages beyond any justification of military necessity; (perpetrating) mass murder, rape, PILLAGE, brigandage, TORTURE and other barbaric cruelties upon the helpless civilian population of the over-run countries." Shimada was found guilty on five counts and sentenced to prison. He was paroled in 1955 and died in 1976.

Further Reading:
Daws, Gavin. *Prisoners of the Japanese: POWs of World War II in the Pacific.* New York: Perennial, 1996.
Lamont-Brown, Raymond. *Ships from Hell: Japanese War Crimes on the High Seas.* Phoenix Mill, Stroud, U.K.: Sutton Publishing, 2002.

Shining Path (Sendero Luminoso)

The Shining Path (Sendero Luminoso in Spanish) was a radical Maoist insurgency that terrorized Peru throughout the 1980s. At its height the Shining Path was the most formidable guerrilla group in Latin America. Approximately 30,000 Peruvians, most of them civilians, were killed by both guerrillas and government forces in 15 years of conflict. The group, which was founded by a former philosophy professor, Abimael Guzmán Reynoso, in the late 1960s, grew out of the Peruvian Communist Party but eventually abandoned the facade of political legitimacy and turned to terrorism in 1980. Guzmán organized his guerrilla force for over a decade before he was prepared to launch its first strikes. The Shining Path's objective was to destroy the state, demolish all of its institutions, and install a communist peasant revolutionary regime in its place. Perhaps only Cambodia's Khmer Rouge rivaled the Shining Path in its drive to radicalize a nation. And like the Khmer Rouge, the Peruvian group adhered to a policy of self-reliance that led the group to shun all outside assistance, even from communist nations.

In 1980 the Shining Path signaled their forthcoming campaign of terror by stringing up dead dogs on lampposts in every city in Peru. The gruesome sight made a chilling impression on the population. By the mid-1980s, the guerrillas, who now numbered several thousand, had taken control over large parts of the Peruvian countryside. They then began to stage dramatic attacks in major cities, stirring

fears that the insurgents might be in a position to overrun the whole country. The worst single incident took place in July 1992, when two car bombs went off in the middle-class district of Miraflores in Lima, killing 20 people and injuring more than 250 others.

In 1992 then-president ALBERTO FUJIMORI declared martial law, setting the stage for a military crackdown that resulted in numerous human rights violations. The army began to score several successes. In 1992 Guzmán, who had practically become a mythical figure in the minds of many Peruvians due to his ability to elude detection, was captured. His arrest, together with the apprehension of most of the Shining Path's leaders, dealt a blow to the guerrillas from which they never recovered. Guzmán was tried and sentenced to life in prison. However, elements of the Shining Path have continued to wage war against the government on a lesser scale. There are reports that the rump faction, which is down to a few hundred members, has become involved in narcotrafficking and kidnapping for ransom to raise funds for its operations—a departure from earlier policy under Guzmán's leadership. Several of its members were taken captive as recently as 2003.

Although the Peruvian government declared victory over the Shining Path, the insurgent group has enjoyed something of a rebirth in recent years, albeit in a different form. Instead of espousing a Maoist ideology, the new incarnation of the Shining Path appears to have adopted the business model of FARC guerrillas in COLOMBIA, relying on cocaine profits to fuel their insurgency. Peru is second only to Colombia in producing cocaine (derived from the more or less legal cocoa plant). According to the United Nations, Peru's output of the drug increased 4 percent in 2007, the highest level in a decade, which translates to about 290 tons. "The guerrillas now operate with the efficiency and deadliness of an elite drug trafficking organization," observed a security analyst in Lima. It is believed that the Shining Path currently employs 500 laborers to produce and distribute the cocaine and some 350 armed combatants. The group operates in a remote region of the country, exploiting the cover of the jungle to elude the army. The group seems well disciplined and is more inclined to ensure the cooperation of the cocoa farmers than to terrorize them as the old Shining Path used to do, so long as they do not align themselves with the government. Twenty-two soldiers and police died at their hands in 2008, making it the most violent year in nearly a decade. Human rights organizations also accuse the security forces of committing atrocities in their anti-insurgency campaign, charges the army denies.

Further Reading:
Gorriti Ellenbogen, Gustavo. *The Shining Path: A History of the Millenarian War in Peru.* Translated by Robin

Kirle. Chapel Hill: University of North Carolina Press, 1999.

Palmer, David Scott, ed. *The Shining Path of Peru.* Sidney, Australia: Palgrave Macmillan, 1991.

Stern, Steve, ed. *Shining and Other Paths: War and Society in Peru 1980–1995.* Durham, N.C.: Duke University Press, 1998.

siege

As a military tactic, a siege of a city held by a belligerent force is not, at least in theory, explicitly outlawed by INTERNATIONAL HUMANITARIAN LAW: The capture of a city defended by an enemy could be considered a legitimate military objective. Sieges are generally employed to wear away the enemy's defenses while depriving the city's inhabitants of needed resources, including food, which will hasten its surrender. Until the end of World War II, sieges were justified under the doctrine of military necessity. The Regulations to the Hague Conventions of 1907, however, banned bombardment of "undefended" cities. Postwar treaties, notably the GENEVA CONVENTIONS of 1949 and the ADDITIONAL PROTOCOLS TO THE GENEVA CONVENTIONS of 1977, have imposed such restrictions on the infliction of harm on civilian populations "as a method of combat" that sieges are implicitly banned, though it should be noted that neither the conventions nor the additional protocols specifically mention sieges.

If in the past starvation was seen as a means of forcing the surrender of a besieged city, that practice is no longer considered acceptable. The Fourth Geneva Convention allows a force to bar food from reaching a civilian population if that food will also be used by enemy military forces. However, Additional Protocol I, which covers international conflicts, appears to negate that exception. It states that all efforts must be made to distinguish between military personnel and civilian populations, and military operations should be "directed only against military objectives." The protocol prohibits the starvation of civilians, even if some food delivered by relief agencies falls into the hands of troops defending the city. Moreover, a belligerent is barred from targeting property vital to civilian survival, such as electric plants, a further impediment to laying siege to a city. Protocol II, which covers internal conflicts, echoes this provision: "[T]he civilian population as such, as well as individual civilians, shall not be the object of attack."

In spite of these prohibitions, sieges continue to be employed as a method of warfare—for instance, in Iraq by U.S. forces and in Chechnya by Russian forces. But the true horror of a siege was driven home by the four-year siege of Sarajevo (1992–96) by Serb forces during the Bosnian War. Artillery attacks and snipers positioned in the mountains above Sarajevo killed 10,000–12,000 people and injured another 50,000, almost all of them civilians. Hardly a single building was left intact. During the siege, Serbs tried to starve the city out; only extraordinary efforts by UN relief agencies managed to prevent famine. The INTERNATIONAL CRIMINAL TRIBUNAL FOR THE FORMER YUGOSLAVIA found the commander of Bosnian Serb forces besieging the city guilty of deliberately targeting civilians, leaving little doubt that in most cases sieges are likely to violate the norms of international humanitarian law.

See also BOSNIA AND HERZEGOVINA, HUMAN RIGHTS VIOLATIONS IN; SARAJEVO, SIEGE OF; STARVATION AS A TACTIC OF WAR.

Further Reading:
Gutman, Roy, ed. *Crimes of War: What the Public Should Know.* New York: W. W. Norton & Company, 1999.

Hagan, John. *Justice in the Balkans: Prosecuting War Crimes in the Hague Tribunal.* Chicago Series in Law and Society. Chicago: University of Chicago Press, 2003.

Harris, Nathaniel. *The War in Former Yugoslavia.* London: Hodder & Stoughton, 1997.

Hazan, Pierre, and James Thomas Snyder. *Justice in a Time of War: The True Story behind the International Criminal Tribunal for the Former Yugoslavia.* Eugenia and Hugh M. Stewart Series on Eastern Europe. Austin: Texas A&M University Press, 2004.

United Nations War Crimes Commission. *Law Reports of Trials of War Criminals: Four Genocide Trials.* Boulder, Colo.: Lynne Rienner Publishers, 1992.

Sierra Leone, human rights violations in

Sierra Leone, a former British colony in West Africa, holds an especially grim distinction in the annals of war crimes and human rights violations. Once one of the most beautiful countries on the continent, Sierra Leone now lies in shambles as a result of a brutal civil war that engulfed the country over a 10-year period that spanned most of the 1990s. In a campaign of violence that shocked the world, rebels mutilated civilians, lopping off limbs and even lips to intimidate supporters of the government. It is believed that nearly 20,000 people were maimed in this way. The war cost the lives of 75,000 and displaced 2 million people. No one knows how many women were raped. An estimated 5,400 children were abducted by rebels and forced to become sexual slaves or pressed into combat.

By nearly every measure of civilization—health, mortality rates, sanitation, education, infrastructure, and so on—Sierra Leone now ranks almost dead last. Average life expectancy is only 38, infant mortality rate is 164 per thousand, and nearly two-thirds of the adult population is illiterate. The capital, Freetown, has been plundered, and most of the country's educated people have fled—a particularly bitter irony in a country that had boasted West Africa's first university. While rich in such natural resources as iron ore and bauxite, Sierra Leone is best known for its diamond reserves. These so-called CONFLICT DIAMONDS have turned out to be a curse, however: Without them the civil war might never have been fought or funded. (Legal exports of diamonds before the war were about $60 million annually.)

The war actually began in neighboring Liberia in 1991 and then proceeded to spill over the border when Liberian insurgents began to occupy parts of Sierra Leone. Although government troops succeeded in repelling these Liberian groups, they soon found themselves facing a Liberian-sponsored indigenous insurgency known as the Revolutionary United Front (RUF) under the leadership of FODAY SANKOH. Although a peace accord was reached between the warring factions in 1992, the country continued to be rocked by a series of coups and insurrections. In 1997, after a military coup toppled President Ahmed Kabbah, the stage was set for a second round of fighting. The crisis spurred the country's West African neighbors to intervene. In February 1998, Nigerian troops dispatched by ECOWAS MONITORING GROUP (ECOMOG) occupied Freetown and began an offensive against Sankoh and the RUF. A month later Kabbah was restored to power.

The presence of the peacekeepers failed to subdue the rebellion, however, and in January 1999 the RUF and other rebel factions launched an attack on the capital that left thousands of civilians dead. There is no more telling indication of the rebel intentions than the code name they assigned the offensive against Freetown: Operation No Living Thing. The assault lived up to its billing, taking the lives of 6,000 civilians in just two weeks. Many of the worst atrocities were committed by children soldiers, who burned homes and hacked limbs with casual savagery. One of the terrorists was a girl who proudly called herself Queen Cut Hands. Even though the rebels were eventually forced to retreat from the capital, they did not go far and continued to dominate the rural areas. They also maintained their control over the diamond mines, providing them a source of wealth to buy more arms.

By this time the Nigerians were running out of money to support the peacekeeping mission, forcing the hand of the British, the country's former colonial power, which was prepared to use force to restore order. The United States, however, opposed a military solution and called for negotiations. The Reverend Jesse Jackson was sent as a special envoy to broker a cease-fire agreement in late 1999 which became known as the Lome Peace Accords. By the terms of the accords, Sankoh—who had been condemned to death in 1998—was elevated to the vice presidency, effectively giving him control over the diamond mines. Even

more dismaying to human rights groups, the accord also provided for a blanket AMNESTY for all human rights abuses committed up to the date the agreement was signed.

International law—specifically Article 6 of Additional Protocol I to the GENEVA CONVENTIONS—encourages granting amnesty as a way of bringing about reconciliation after a conflict. However, legal experts disagree as to whether any amnesty can be applied to serious war crimes, such as those perpetuated by the RUF. This is the position taken by human rights organizations, and UN secretary general Kofi Annan declared that the United Nations would not be bound by the Lome accord.

In spite of the accord, peace did not hold in Sierra Leone. In spring 2000 RUF soldiers, many of them high on crack, marijuana, speed, and cheap gin, clashed with UN peacekeepers. The campaign of terror resumed. In May 2000, less than a year after the peace agreement, the RUF launched another assault on Freetown. Once again the capital descended into chaos. In the countryside, 500 UN peacekeepers were taken hostage by the rebels and were freed only because of an audacious rescue mission by British troops. Sankoh was caught as he attempted to flee Freetown.

In August 2000 the UN Security Council voted to establish a SPECIAL COURT FOR SIERRA LEONE under the joint jurisdiction of the Sierra Leone government and the United Nations to prosecute individuals charged with war crimes. Although the rebel groups were most culpable, all parties to the conflict, including soldiers of ECOMOG, the Nigerian-led peacekeeping mission, became implicated in human rights abuses. A second ceasefire in 2001 proved more enduring, and the United Nations was able to disarm 45,000 RUF fighters.

In February 2009 the Special Court for Sierra Leone meeting in Freetown found three Sierra Leone rebel commanders guilty of war crimes and crimes against humanity. It was the court's final trial. The judgments also set a new precedent, because it was the first time that an international tribunal found a defendant responsible for enforced marriage. (Many girls and young women were abducted from their villages and compelled to marry rebels or serve as sex slaves.) The RUF leaders Issa Sesay, Morris Kallon, and Augustine Gbao were convicted on several charges, including rape, mutilation, and murder of civilians during the 1991–2001 civil war. The indictment charged that the three had formed a criminal enterprise with the former Liberian dictator CHARLES GHANKAY TAYLOR in order to secure control over Sierra Leone's diamond fields. (The diamonds were used to fuel the war in both countries.) The RUF gained particular notoriety for its so-called Small Boys Units made up of forcibly recruited children who were known for their brutality toward civilians. As of early 2009, only one case technically remained on the Special

Court's docket, involving Charles Taylor, but his trial had been moved to The Hague for security reasons.

See also ADDITIONAL PROTOCOLS TO THE GENEVA CONVENTIONS; CHILDREN'S RIGHTS; LIBERIA, HUMAN RIGHTS VIOLATIONS IN.

Further Reading:
Abdullah, Ibrahim. *Between Democracy and Terror: The Sierra Leone Civil War.* Dakar: Codesria, 2000.

allAfrica.com. Sierra Leone Links. Available online. URL: http://allafrica.com/sierraleone/. Accessed March 20, 2010.

BBC.co.uk. *Country Profile: Sierra Leone.* Available online. URL: http://news.bbc.co.uk/2/hi/africa/country_profiles/1061561.stm. Accessed March 20, 2010.

Beah, Ishmael. *Long Way Gone: Memoirs of a Boy Soldier.* New York: Farrar, Straus and Giroux, 2008.

Ferme, Mariane C. *The Underneath of Things: Violence, History, and the Everyday in Sierra Leone.* Berkeley: University of California Press, 2001.

Gberie, Lansana. *A Dirty War in West Africa: The RUF and the Destruction of Sierra Leone.* Bloomington: Indiana University Press, 2005.

Jackson, Michael. *In Sierra Leone.* Durham, N.C.: Duke University Press, 2004.

Reno, William. *Corruption and State Politics in Sierra Leone.* Cambridge: Cambridge University Press, 2008.

Richards, Paul. *Fighting for the Rain Forest: War, Youth, and Resources in Sierra Leone.* African Issues Series. London: Heinemann, 1996.

Romano, Cesare, Andre Nollkaemper and Jann K. Kleffner, eds. *Internationalized Criminal Courts and Tribunals: Sierra Leone, East Timor, Kosovo, and Cambodia.* International Courts and Tribunals Series. Oxford: Oxford University Press, 2004.

The Special Court for Sierra Leone. Available online. URL: http://www.sc-sl.org/. Accessed March 20, 2010.

Voeten, Teun. *How de Body? One Man's Terrifying Journey through an African War.* New York: Thomas Dunne Books, 2002.

slavery

According to the United Nations *slavery* is a term that applies to a variety of human rights violations and is not limited to traditional slavery and the slave trade. The contemporary definition of slavery includes "the sale of children, child prostitution, child pornography, the exploitation of child labor, the sexual mutilation of female children, the use of children in armed conflicts, debt bondage, the traffic in persons and in the sale of human organs, the exploitation of prostitution, and certain practices under APARTHEID and colonial régimes." Though broad, this definition attempts to deal with the myriad ways that people are being exploited even if they receive a small amount of money. Debt bondage, for instance, is considered slavery since a person is not free to leave a job until money owed by the worker is repaid. Often slavery is practiced in secrecy, which makes it more difficult to uncover, punish, or put a stop to it. Not surprisingly, the people most likely to be enslaved are the poorest and most vulnerable.

In spite of its clandestine nature, the various forms of slavery are known to be widespread. For instance, according to the INTERNATIONAL LABOR ORGANIZATION (ILO), a United Nations body, as many as 100 million children alone are in FORCED LABOR. Modern attempts to abolish slavery extend back to the early 19th century: The British banned slavery throughout its empire in 1837. In the United States the LIEBER CODE, which governed the conduct of the Union Army during the Civil War, outlawed the enslavement of any prisoner. The Emancipation Proclamation, issued by President Abraham Lincoln on January 1, 1863, abolished slavery in the United States even though slavery persisted in Southern states until the Civil War ended in 1865.

The first treaty of the 20th century addressing the issue was the Slavery Convention of 1926, drawn up by the LEAGUE OF NATIONS. This convention broadened the definition of slavery to include the practices and institutions of debt bondage, servile forms of marriage, and the exploitation of children and adolescents. Article 1 states that enslavement "is the status or condition of a person over whom any or all of the powers attaching to the right of ownership are exercised." The slave trade is defined by the convention as "all acts involved in the capture, acquisition or disposal of a person with intent to reduce him to slavery; all acts involved in the acquisition of a slave with a view to selling or exchanging him; all acts of disposal by sale or exchange of a slave acquired with a view to being sold or exchanged and, in general, every act of trade or transport of slaves." The United Nations, the successor to the League, adopted the Slavery Convention in 1953. By 1993 some 86 states had ratified the convention, which obliges signatories to prevent and suppress the slave trade and to abolish slavery in all its forms.

There are other agreements that deal with various forms of slavery. The UNIVERSAL DECLARATION OF HUMAN RIGHTS of 1948 declares: "No one shall be held in slavery or servitude: slavery and the slave trade shall be prohibited in all their forms." The declaration is not a binding treaty, so over the next several years the United Nations enacted a series of agreements that banned various forms of slavery. For example, the 1949 Convention for the Suppression of the Traffic in Persons and of the Exploitation of the Prostitution of Others, targets the procurer and not the prostitute. This convention calls on parties to the accord to curb the traffic in persons of either sex for the purpose of prostitution. Other accords include the INTERNATIONAL COVENANT ON CIVIL AND POLITICAL RIGHTS, the International Covenant on Economic, Social and Cultural Rights, the Convention on the Elimination of All Forms of Discrimination against Women, and the CONVENTION ON THE RIGHTS OF THE CHILD. The latter, which entered into force in 1990, is considered potentially one of the most effective means of combating slavery because of the sheer number of children who are forced into slavery, prostitution, or combat around the world.

The 1977 Additional Protocol II to the GENEVA CONVENTIONS is the first accord explicitly banning slavery in internal armed conflict. Article 4 states: "Slavery and the slave trade in all their forms . . . are and shall remain prohibited at any time and in any place whatsoever." Although the United States and other countries did not ratify this protocol, the prohibition against slavery is considered binding nonetheless, based on CUSTOMARY LAW. Most recently, the 1998 ROME STATUTE OF THE INTERNATIONAL CRIMINAL COURT termed enslavement a crime against humanity when it is systematically directed at a civilian population. The statute uses the 1926 Slavery Convention in defining enslavement as "the exercise of any or all of the powers attaching to the right of ownership over a person and includes the exercise of such power in the course of TRAFFICKING IN PERSONS, in particular women and children."

See also ADDITIONAL PROTOCOLS TO THE GENEVA CONVENTIONS; CHILDREN'S RIGHTS.

Further Reading:
Dormann, Knut, and Louise Doswald-Beck. *Elements of War Crimes under the Rome Statute of the International Criminal Court: Sources and Commentary.* Cambridge: Cambridge University Press, 2003.
Meltzer, Milton. *Slavery: A World History.* New York: Da Capo Press, 1993.

Slovenia, human rights violations in

Of all the newly independent countries that once constituted the former Yugoslavia, Slovenia has emerged with the fewest scars. Slovenia was the first to formally break away from the federation in 1991, precipitating a brief war. After 10 days of fighting, the Yugoslav forces withdrew in defeat. Unlike Bosnia and Croatia, which also declared independence, Slovenia had a small Serb population, with the result that Belgrade did not envision it as an integral part of a "greater Serbia."

According to recent U.S. State Department reports, Slovenia receives fairly high marks for upholding human rights. There are some allegations of police brutality and self-censorship in the media because of political or economic pressure. The most serious human rights problems are a direct consequence of the war: More than 18,000 non-Slovenes lost their citizenship after Slovenia declared its independence. While ethnic Slovenes were automatically given citizenship, those people belonging to other ethnic groups had to apply for citizenship. Anyone who failed to do so within a year lost his citizenship, becoming in effect one of the "erased," who were deprived of their right to permanent residency, pensions, and health benefits. At least seven committed suicide in despair; thousands more were made homeless or were arrested for minor offenses, such as jaywalking, and then deported because they lacked proper papers. In 2004 a referendum was held to determine whether these legal "nonpersons" could be restored to citizenship. But the vast majority of Slovenes, responding to fears of illegal immigration and galvanized by nationalist sentiment, voted against restoring Slovene citizenship to nonpersons. "It is a shame that they were erased, but the country will go bankrupt if it has to pay compensation," said one voter. "We've come too far to let the country go down the drain just like that." A minority of Slovenes, however, viewed the vote as a manifestation of racism, intolerance, and xenophobia.

The problem of the "erased" remained a source of concern for human rights activists several years after Slovenia first revoked permanent residency status for inhabitants of the former Yugoslavia living in the country. In 2009 AMNESTY INTERNATIONAL (AI) declared in a report submitted to the UN that "'the erased' had been subject to violations of the principle of nondiscrimination, the right to work and social security, the right to the highest attainable standard of physical and mental health, and the right to education." In spite of rulings by the Slovenian Constitutional Court that the government's actions in regard to the "erased" were unconstitutional, AI said, this population was still being denied "restitution, compensation, rehabilitation, satisfaction and guarantees of non-repetition" of the discriminatory practices.

See also YUGOSLAVIA, WAR CRIMES IN.

Further Reading:
Glenny, Misha. *The Fall of Yugoslavia: The Third Balkan War.* New York: Penguin Books, 1996.
Kim, Julie. *War in the Former Yugoslavia: Chronology of Events August 16, 1992–May 30, 1993.* CRS report for Congress. Washington, D.C.: Foreign Affairs and National Defense Division, Congressional Research Service, the Library of Congress, 1993.

Solzhenitsyn, Aleksandr Isayevich (1918–2008)
Russian novelist and dissident
Aleksandr Solzhenitsyn, who won the Nobel Prize in literature in 1970, is probably as well known for his fearless

opposition to the now-defunct Soviet regime as he is for his large body of writing. His best-known works, the novels *One Day in the Life of Ivan Denisovich* and *The First Circle* and the nonfiction *The Gulag Archipelago,* are all based on his harrowing experiences as a prisoner in the Siberian GULAGS, the notorious Soviet prison camps where millions perished under the brutal dictatorship of JOSEPH STALIN.

Solzhenitsyn was born in 1918 into a Cossack intellectual family in the northern Caucasus Mountains. After receiving a degree in mathematics and physics from the University of Rostov-on-Don and taking correspondence courses in literature at Moscow State University, he joined the Red Army and fought in World War II, achieving the rank of captain of artillery and receiving two decorations for valor. But no sooner had the war ended than he was arrested in 1945 when it was discovered that he had written a letter critical of Stalin—"the man with the mustache." He spent the next eight years in the gulag and in labor prisons, but because of his advanced education he escaped having to endure hard labor.

In 1950 Solzhenitsyn was transferred to a political prison, where he performed manual labor. During this period he became ill with stomach cancer, which was successfully treated. His hospital experience formed the basis of his novel *The Cancer Ward.* Although he made a living as a teacher following his release, he continued to write in secret to avoid further problems with the regime. Stalin's death and the ascension to power of Premier Nikita Khrushchev ushered in a new, more open political era. In the more relaxed atmosphere, Solzhenitsyn published *One Day in the Life of Ivan Denisovich,* first in serial form in the literary journal *Novyi Mir,* then as a book in 1962. An immediate sensation, the novel was acclaimed not only because of its literary quality but also because of its subject matter: Until this point, writers had steered clear of the subject of the gulag and Stalinist repression. The book was published abroad and gained its author international acclaim. At the time Solzhenitsyn was 42. The thaw lasted only a few years, however, and it became increasingly difficult for him to get his words in print except by means of illegal samizdat—self-published writing surreptitiously passed from reader to reader. Between 1963 and 1966 he succeeded in publishing only four stories.

In 1965 many of Solzhenitsyn's manuscripts were confiscated by the KGB, but even so he managed to smuggle some of his work to the West. When he was awarded the Nobel Prize in 1970, he refused to go to Stockholm to accept the honor for fear that he would not be allowed to return home. In 1971 he published *August 1914,* a novel about czarist Russia during World War I. Two years later *The Gulag Archipelago,* the first book of his three-volume chronicle of the Soviet labor camps, appeared, earning its

author even wider recognition abroad. At home, though, he was viewed by the Communist regime as a dangerous dissident, and in 1974 he was detained on charges of treason, stripped of his citizenship, and then sent into exile. He lived first in Switzerland and later settled in Vermont, a state he found congenial because of its climate and relative isolation. He devoted himself to his work, turning out several new books, among them *The Red Wheel,* an epic about the Russian Revolution, which was part of a series that also included the earlier *August 1914* (which he revised), *October 1916, March 1917,* and *April 1917.*

In 1990 the new leader of the Soviet Union, Mikhail Gorbachev, offered to restore Solzhenitzyn's citizenship; a year later charges of treason against him were dropped. In 1994 Solzhenitsyn returned from exile and made a spectacular whistle-stop train tour through Siberia. No longer a pariah, he was greeted by President Boris Yeltsin, now the head of a new postcommunist Russia, and given the opportunity to deliver an address to the Russian Duma (parliament). But Solzhenitsyn did not fit into the new Russia anymore than he had the old Soviet Union or, for that matter, the United States. Calling for a revival of Holy Russia under the Russian Orthodox Church, he decried what he termed the "spiritual exhaustion" of Western culture, where "mediocrity triumphs under the guise of democratic restraints." In a controversial speech given to students at Harvard University in 1978, he declared, "We [Russians] have been through a spiritual training far in advance of Western experience. The complex and deadly crush of life has produced stronger, deeper, and more interesting personalities than those generated by standardized Western well-being." Solzhenitsyn saw in the ascension of then president (now prime minister) Vladimir Putin someone who would "restore" Russia to its earlier glory. He was incensed by the bombing of Belgrade by NATO warplanes during the war in KOSOVO, and in an interview with a German newspaper castigated the Western powers for advocating a form of democracy that "is not worth a brass farthing if it is installed by bayonet." He accepted a State Prize from Putin (after refusing similar prizes from Putin's predecessors Gorbachev and Yeltsin).

Further Reading:
Solzhenitsyn, Aleksandr. *August 1914.* New York: Farrar, Straus & Giroux, 2000.
———. *The Cancer Ward.* New York: Farrar, Straus & Giroux, 1991.
———. *The First Circle.* Evanston, Ill.: Northwestern University Press, 1997.
———. *The Gulag Archipelago.* New York: HarperCollins, 1978.
———. *One Day in the Life of Ivan Denisovich.* New York: Signet Classics, 1999.

Somalia, human rights violations in

Since the pullout of United Nations troops in March 1995 amid violence and chaos—an event made famous by the book and movie version of *Blackhawk Down*—Somalia has been largely abandoned by the international community. Whatever order exists in the country depends on Islamic law (sharia) and clan loyalty. However, as 2004 came to an end, negotiations conducted in Kenya among various elements of Somali civil society held out the promise of a restoration of a functioning government. Under the tumultuous conditions that have prevailed for the last decade, though, thousands of civilians have suffered from grave human rights abuses; according to a report by HUMAN RIGHTS WATCH, these abuses include "killings of civilians through the indiscriminate use of heavy weapons, the deliberate, targeted killing of civilians, execution-style killings of captives, rape and other cruel and degrading treatment, and forced displacement and controls on freedom of movement." The pattern of these abuses, the human rights group says, reflects clan rivalries that fueled and exacerbated a famine in 1991–92, leading to the intervention of United Nations (UN) forces, spearheaded by the United States. (President George H. W. Bush authorized the deployment of U.S. forces as part of the UN mission.)

Initially, after the UN withdrawal in 1995, the warlords defied expectations by cooperating with one another through a so-called Peace Committee, which administered the harbor and airport in the capital of Mogadishu. The accord broke down, but even so, the country never descended into the state of anarchy that existed before to the abortive UN mission. Traditional sources of authority—predominantly clan leaders—have managed to maintain a precarious peace ever since. But any calm is contingent on the willingness of warlords to refrain from resorting to violence.

The power of the warlords reaches into many parts of society, blurring the lines between nation and clan. Followers of these warlords, for example, also hold multiple positions—as militiamen, contract guards, or police officers, for example—while retaining their ultimate loyalty to the warlord. Human rights groups hope that a general weariness with perpetual conflict may have an ameliorative effect on the warlords and temper their readiness to use violence on a massive scale. Already civil war has led to hundreds of thousands of deaths from mass killings and the destruction of infrastructure vital to survival, including the water systems and the means of production. EXTRAJUDICIAL KILLINGS still characterize clan rivalries, and bodies are publicly displayed as a warning. When warnings go unheeded, warlords have killed clan elders and other traditional leaders who have sought to bring about reconciliation among factions that may threaten their power.

The clan rivalries have also resulted in whole communities being uprooted from their homes and threatened with death if they return. Women are especially at risk from these forced expulsions. Several hundred thousand Somalis have been forced to flee to neighboring countries where they have been settled temporarily in camps, while hundreds of thousands more have been internally displaced. It is only because of abundant rainfall and good harvests in recent years that thousands more have escaped starvation and death. According to Human Rights Watch, those civilians who are most at risk must rely for protection on application of sharia law in the absence of a national judicial system, although in their interpretation of Islamic law, Somali religious authorities mete out draconian punishments—known as *hudud*—that include summary executions and amputations. Compensation for victims of abuses often rests on clan identity. "The only human rights protection is the structure of the clan, in the sense that it is the clan that protects rights," noted a relief agency official.

Over the last several years elders, businessmen, women's groups, intellectuals, and religious leaders have gathered in Somalia and outside the country in an attempt to establish a new government and reach a political settlement. But these attempts at putting together a durable transitional government have largely failed. Ethiopian intervention in 2006, intended to put an end to Islamic rule over Mogadishu and other parts of the country, ended in an ignominious withdrawal two years later. Even peacekeepers from the African Union have been unsuccessful at bringing order to the Somali capital and, indeed, have been blamed for indiscriminate attacks on civilian areas and for other human rights abuses. By early 2009, with the withdrawal of Ethiopian troops, Islamic insurgents once again seemed in the ascendancy. The insurgents include a variety of Islamic groups as well as ethnic clans opposed to the transitional government; collectively they are called the *muqaawama* (resistance) by many Somalis. Yet even among those wishing to turn Somalia into an Islamic state there are divergent views, with some groups favoring a more moderate, and others a more fundamental, system of government. Militant groups such as al-Shabab and Hizb al-Islamiya oppose any talks with the fragile transitional government and have launched attacks against the African Union peace-support mission in Somalia (AMISOM). One suicide attack in February 2008 on an African Union base, purportedly carried out by a Shabab faction, killed 11 Burundian peacekeepers. Suspicion that Shabab might be sympathetic to or possibly allied with AL-QAEDA has raised concern that Somalia could become a base for radical Islamic elements. Throughout 2009 Shabab has gained power in much of the strife-torn country in contrast to the internationally supported transitional government, which could only claim a small portion of Mogadishu. (And, as audacious attacks and suicide bombings carried out by Shabab operatives demonstrate, including a bombing that killed three ministers, even that area is not secured.) Nonetheless, the ruthless imposition of sharia law in territory that has fallen under Shabab has alienated much of the population. In 2009, for instance, Shabab insurgents ordered the amputations of the hands and legs of four teenagers for the theft of mobile phones and people's belongings. AMNESTY INTERNATIONAL condemned the punishment, noting that the four did not even have a lawyer or a right to appeal. These are not exceptions. The Shabab has also conducted executions and public floggings of those who have run afoul of strict Islamic law. In effect, the government is under siege. Militants have even penetrated well-guarded facilities; in December 2009 a suicide bomber killed three ministers and several others (including the dean of a medical school) at a commencement ceremony for new medical school graduates.

The anarchic conditions prevailing in the country have also spawned a virulent outbreak of PIRACY that has prompted nations from around the world to mobilize to protect shipping off Somali waters. However, there is no question that it is the civilian population of Somalia that has suffered the most. It is difficult to accurately determine the numbers of civilians killed in the last few years, but it is certainly in the thousands. Many thousands more have been displaced. Even with the assistance of several international aid agencies, the survival of hundreds of thousands of Somalis remains at grave risk. Some United Nations officials now call Somalia "the forgotten crisis."

The violence is compounded by a variety of other urgent problems, including unemployment, drought, inflation, and tightening of global food supplies even as demand increases. As many as 3 million people require emergency rations to survive. In one instance, looters attacked a convoy of 35 UN-chartered food trucks and made off with 2 million pounds of food. Moreover, many aid workers have fled out of fear for their lives.

Clan warfare has played a significant part in the seemingly endless conflict, according to Amnesty International. Civilians have been singled out for murder, maiming, and rape because of their clan origins. Since early 2007, thousands of civilians have been killed by indiscriminate bombardment and heavy shelling in densely populated urban areas. Medical facilities are scarce and are often difficult to reach. According to Human Rights Watch, unlawful killings of civilians actually increased after Ethiopian troops entered Somalia at the end of 2006 to shore up the transitional government.

"Each of the parties to the armed conflict has committed serious violations of international humanitarian law," Human Rights Watch declared. "In some cases, where individuals knowingly or recklessly committed these viola-

tions, the violations amount to war crimes." Forces of the transitional government, while playing "a secondary role in much of the indiscriminate bombardment of Mogadishu" are nonetheless responsible for "widespread pillaging and looting of civilian property; rape; attacks on humanitarian workers; mass arbitrary arrests and mistreatment of detainees." The government has shown little appetite for going after or prosecuting those responsible. During their occupation, Ethiopian troops employed area bombardment in retaliation against insurgent attacks, killing and wounding hundreds of civilians. In some cases, hospitals were deliberately targeted. Civilians were gunned down by snipers or executed summarily in house-to-house searches. According to some accounts, recorded by Human Rights Watch, soldiers slit the throats of their victims—"slaughtering [them] like goats." Insurgent groups, too, have conducted repeated and indiscriminate attacks against civilians, using mortars, small arms, and remote-controlled explosive devices. They have also killed and mutilated captured combatants. Journalists, human rights defenders, and humanitarian aid workers have all come under attack. It is unclear in many cases which party is responsible. However, almost every party to the conflict appears willing to shut down (violently or otherwise) any voice that they deem contrary to their interests. The transitional government, for example, closed a number of media outlets and radio stations in Mogadishu on the grounds that they were inciting violence and detained journalists for extended periods. They were the lucky ones. In 2007, seven journalists were killed—the highest casualty rate for journalists since the collapse of a central Somali government in 1991.

Conditions continued to deteriorate through the first half of 2010. The transitional government's influence extended only to a small enclave of Mogadishu, even after receiving $200 million in U.S. aid to prop it up. Without African peacekeepers, most analysts expected that it would fall in a matter of days. In spite of sharp divisions within insurgent ranks that have led to internecine fighting, the Shabab has managed to extend its power in the capital and throughout the country. Even so, the Shabab has alienated large segments of the population by imposing its strict interpretation of Islam on people who fall under its control. Music, TV watching, and playing soccer have been banned, so have bras (the reasoning is that they were not worn in the time of Mohammed) and gold dental fillings. Thieves have been subject to public amputations. However, the government has also failed to make any gains, because its forces, along with peacekeepers, have killed scores of civilians by its habit of indiscriminately shelling crowded neighborhoods. In an alarming development, the Shabab expanded its campaign in July beyond Somali borders when it struck two restaurants in Kampala, UGANDA, killing 70 people who were watching the World Cup championship game. The Shabab apparently was retaliating against Uganda because it had deployed peacekeepers in Somalia. (The other major African contributor to the force is Burundi.) Noting the synchronized nature of the Kampala attacks, analysts believed that the Shabab could only have carried them out with the help of al-Qaeda. Nonetheless, a month later, Uganda announced that it would send more forces to Somalia in response to an African Union request for 2,000 additional troops to push the Shabab out of Mogadishu and help solidify the government's control. But the traditional resentment of the beleaguered Somali population against outsiders might hamper any effort to intervene on behalf of the fragile transitional regime.

See also INTERNALLY DISPLACED PERSONS.

Further Reading:
BBC.co.uk. *Somalia Country Profile.* Available online. URL: http://news.bbc.co.uk/2/hi/africa/country_profiles/1072592.stm. Accessed March 21, 2010.

CIA World Factbook. *Somalia* (March 3, 2010). Available online. URL: https://www.cia.gov/library/publications/the-world-factbook/geos/so.html. Accessed March 21, 2010.

Clarke, Walter, and Jeffrey Herbst, eds. *Learning from Somalia: The Lessons of Armed Humanitarian Intervention.* Boulder, Colo.: Westview Press, 1997.

Menkhaus, Ken. *Somalia: State Collapse and the Threat of Terrorism.* London: International Institute for Strategic Studies, 2004.

Osman, Abdulahi A. *Somalia at the Crossroads: Challenges and Perspectives in Reconstituting a Failed State.* London: Adonis & Abbey Publishers Ltd, 2007.

Peterson, Scott. *Me against My Brother: At War in Somalia, Sudan and Rwanda.* London: Routledge, 2001.

Razack, Sherene H. *Dark Threats and White Knights: The Somalia Affair, Peacekeeping, and the New Imperialism.* Toronto: University of Toronto Press, 2004.

Rutherford, Kenneth R. *Humanitarianism under Fire: The US and UN Intervention in Somalia.* Bloomfield, Conn.: Kumarian Press, 2008.

Shay, Shaul. *Somalia between Jihad and Restoration.* Edison, N.J.: Transaction Publishers, 2008.

Somoza Debayle, Anastasio (1925–1980)
Nicaraguan despot

The Nicaraguan dictator Anastasio Somoza Debayle was the third member of a political dynasty begun by his father, ANASTASIO SOMOZA GARCÍA. Born in 1925, he was educated in the United States, graduating from West Point in 1946. Somoza became the director of the National Guard in 1955, shortly after his father's assassination and the assumption of power by his older brother Luis Somoza Debayle as president. In his new position he led a bloody campaign against political opponents in revenge for his father's killing. Dissidents were tortured and imprisoned and civil liberties suspended. Somoza became president in 1967, shortly before his brother Luis succumbed to a heart attack. Although he did not run for the presidency in 1972 because of a law banning reelection of the president (which had been restored by Luis), he remained the dominant power behind the throne as head of the National Guard, using it as his base of power, like his father.

Known as "the vampire dictator," Somoza is reported to have made $12 million a year buying donated blood and selling it abroad at a 300 percent markup. An opportunist who became accustomed to outflanking his adversaries, he confronted growing opposition spearheaded by Pedro Joaquín Chamorro Cardenal, publisher of the newspaper *La Prensa,* as well as from outspoken prelates in the Catholic Church. Then in December 1972 the capital of Nicaragua, Managua, was hit by a devastating earthquake that killed an estimated 10,000 people and left 50,000 families homeless while destroying much of the city. The National Guard looted the ruins, and Somoza exploited the chaotic situation, declaring himself the country's leader again. It was later revealed that the Somozas embezzled much of the international aid—about $30 million in relief supplies—that poured into the country after the disaster.

Somoza imposed martial law and intensified political repression. In 1974, even in the face of opposition from his own party, he won election as president. A couple of months later an armed Marxist group known as the Sandinista National Liberation Front (FSLN) took several high government officials hostage, among them relatives of Somoza. After procuring a ransom of $1 million, the insurgents secured the release of political prisoners and flew with them to refuge in Cuba. Somoza responded to this humiliation with a further crackdown that included the TORTURE and murder of FSLN supporters. A state of siege was declared, and the country was plunged into civil war. Prodded by President Richard Nixon's administration, Somoza lifted the state of siege, which paved the way for a resumption of protests. An anti-Somoza alliance of businessmen and academics known as Los Doce (the Group of Twelve) sprang up and established ties with the Sandinistas.

The assassination in 1978 of the publisher Chamorro Cardenal triggered a public outcry and led to mass demonstrations against the Somoza regime. Characteristically, Somoza responded by a renewed crackdown, while boasting that he would remain in power until his term ended in 1981. In reaction, the Sandinistas carried out attacks throughout the country. The Somoza regime had outworn its welcome, and the United States washed its hands of the dictator, suspending all military aid. Somoza resorted to the number of human rights abuses, a move that was followed shortly by a UN resolution condemning the Nicaraguan government. By June 1979 virtually all of the country had fallen under the control of the Sandinistas, with the exception of the capital. Somoza tried to hang on to power—at one point he went so far as to bomb Managua—but he was finally forced to capitulate on July 17, bringing an end to the Somozas' 47-year rule. He fled to Miami and then to Paraguay; many members of the National Guard went into exile as well. In September 1980 Somoza was assassinated in Asunción, Paraguay's capital, reportedly by a leftist Argentine group. The civil war is thought to have cost as many as 50,000 lives; another 120,000 went into exile, and 600,000 were made homeless.

Further Reading:

Alegria, Claribel, and Darwin Flakoll. *Death of Somoza.* Willimantic, Conn.: Curbstone Press, 1996.

Diederich, Bernard. *Somoza and the Legacy of U.S. Involvement in Central America.* Princeton, N.J.: Marcus Wiener, 1989.

Walter, Knut. *The Regime of Anastasio Somoza, 1936–1956.* Chapel Hill: University of North Carolina Press, 1993.

Somoza García, Anastasio (1896–1956) *Nicaraguan dictator*

Anastasio Somoza García, the patriarch of the Somoza dynasty that dominated Nicaraguan political life for several decades, owed his presidency to the U.S. Marines, who had invaded Nicaragua in 1912 and stayed until 1933 to ensure political stability in the region under a pliable regime. The marines additionally formed the country's National Guard, which provided a base of support for three generations of Somoza rule. When the marines withdrew, they gave command of the National Guard to Somoza, who was characterized by General Smedley Butler, the marine commander, as "a high-class muscle man for big business, for Wall Street, and for the banks." It was President Franklin Delano Roosevelt who famously declared, "Somoza may be a son of a bitch, but he's our son of a bitch." The U.S. moves to install a government to its liking inspired armed resistance under the leadership of a Liberal Party general, Augusto César Sandino. Although he negotiated a peace agreement with the U.S.-backed government, he was still considered a threat, and in 1934 he was assassinated by National Guard officers. But for many Nicaraguans, Sandino remained a symbol of nationalism, and several years later his name was appropriated by a revitalized leftist movement, the Sandinistas.

Somoza used his post as a springboard to win the presidency; he then proceeded to use the power of patronage to employ several members of his family in top government and military positions. His party, the Liberal Nationalists,

Nicaraguan despot Anastasio Somoza Debayle *(Bettmann/ Corbis)*

international markets to buy the weapons he needed to fight the mounting insurgency. The country, which had never recovered from the earthquake, was practically bankrupt. Capital fled the country, inflation soared, and so did unemployment. More opposition groups joined Los Doce, forming what was called the Broad Opposition Front (FAO). The FAO then tried to resolve the crisis, but the Sandinistas were not about to wait: In August 1978 they seized the national palace and took nearly 2,000 officials and members of the Nicaraguan congress hostage for two days. The National Guard lost its nerve, and Somoza was forced to accede to most of the rebel demands, which included releasing 60 FSLN members from prison and providing safe passage for the hostage takers to Panama and Venezuela. Somoza was also compelled to allow the media to publish a Sandinista declaration.

At the end of 1978 the ORGANIZATION OF AMERICAN STATES Inter-American Commission on Human Rights issued a report charging the National Guard with a large enjoyed complete authority over the country, secure in the knowledge that it had the support of Washington. (Somoza García even had Roosevelt's birthday made a national holiday to curry favor with the United States.) Within a short time the National Guard was able to secure a virtual monopoly over most government-owned enterprises, including the national radio and telegraph networks, health services, and the national railroads. To solidify his power, Somoza had the constitutional ban on presidential reelection removed, allowing him to remain in office for as long as he chose.

As the country became a source of produce for the U.S. war effort, Nicaragua's economy flourished during World War II, though the Somozas managed to skim off most of the profits. During the war, Somoza confiscated German-owned property, which he then sold off at rock-bottom prices to cronies and members of his family. By the late 1940s he had become Nicaragua's largest landholder, giving him the right to most of the country's cattle ranches and coffee plantations. The Somoza family also either owned or controlled all the banks, the national airlines, a cement factory, textile plants, several large electric power companies, and extensive rental property in the cities. Somoza García's wealth during this period is thought to have been close to $60 million, which would probably run close to $1 billion today. It was the largest fortune ever amassed in the country's history.

Growing dissent to Somoza's rule caused him to step down and run Nicaragua through a number of proxies who served as nominal heads of state. His real power lay in the National Guard in any case. In 1950, though, he cut a deal with the opposition Conservatives to return to the presidency. Although he succeeded in bringing stability and a degree of prosperity to Nicaragua during the postwar years, his rule continued to be characterized by corruption and favoritism. When other elite families protested his authoritarian regime, he had them exiled. At the same time, to perpetuate his political dynasty, he groomed his two sons, Luis Somoza Debayle and ANASTASIO SOMOZA DEBAYLE, to take the reins of power, making the former director of the National Guard and the latter its commander. On September 21, 1956, Somoza García was fatally shot by a 27-year-old Nicaraguan poet. He died eight days later and was succeeded as president by his son Luis.

Further Reading:

Diederich, Bernard. *Somoza and the Legacy of U.S. Involvement in Central America.* Princeton, N.J.: Marcus Wiener, 1989.
Walter, Knut. *The Regime of Anastasio Somoza, 1936–1956.* Chapel Hill: University of North Carolina Press, 1993.

Souaidia, Habib (1972–) *Algerian dissident and writer*

Habib Souaidia, a former Algerian officer, was forced to flee to France after writing a book published in 2001 called *La Sale Guerre* (The dirty war), which exposed acts of TORTURE, EXTRAJUDICIAL KILLINGS, and other grave human rights abuses perpetrated by militias, security forces, and the army in the war against Islamic insurgents during the civil war in Algeria in the 1990s. Even after the violence abated, thousands of families still have no idea what became of family members who disappeared during the conflict. A parachute officer in the special forces, Souaida had been involved in fighting Islamic militant groups. He suffered from nightmares and flashbacks as a result of his experiences but was unable to obtain psychiatric help in Algeria because as a former officer he was not considered one of the "victims." Because his book revealed injustices committed by the government, he feared for his life. After living on the run, he finally managed to reach France in April 2000. "I was afraid of being turned away at the border," he told interviewers. "If I had been sent back it would have meant being killed or being sent back to prison." Even then he was compelled to wait for eight months before he was permitted to stay in France.

See also ALGERIA, HUMAN RIGHTS VIOLATIONS IN.

Further Reading:

Sammakia, Nejla. *Algeria, Elections in the Shadow of Violence and Repression.* New York: Human Rights Watch/Middle East, 1997.
Waltz, Susan Eileen. *Human Rights and Reform: Changing the Face of North African Politics.* Berkeley: University of California Press, 1995.
Whitley, Andrew. *Human Rights Abuses in Algeria: No One Is Spared.* New York: Human Rights Watch, 1994.

South Africa, human rights violations in *See* APARTHEID; BASSON, WOUTER; TRUTH AND RECONCILIATION COMMISSION; TUTU, DESMOND.

Soyinka, Wole (Akinwande Oluwole Soyinka) (1934–) *Nigerian writer and human rights advocate*

The Nigerian Nobel laureate Wole Soyinka is known in his native country as much for his human rights activism and political dissidence as he is for his books, poems, and plays. Born in 1934, he has been imprisoned or forced into exile because of his political views. He spent three years in prison (1969–70) as the Nigerian civil war raged, and during that time he wrote a prose work and several poems that were compiled in a collection called *Poems from Prison*. Soyinka won the Nobel Prize in literature in

1986 for plays and poems that depicted "the drama of existence," in the words of the Swedish Academy. His fame failed to protect him, however, and eight years later he was forced to flee the country, shortly after General Sani Abacha took power, introducing a brutal dictatorship. Soyinka was tried in absentia for treason in 1997. He returned to Nigeria only after Abacha's death and the collapse of his regime. Although democracy was restored, he continues to agitate for political rights. In a political demonstration in 2004, which turned violent, police briefly detained him as an instigator. He castigated the government for failing to uphold democratic principles. "We cannot claim we are running a democracy when we cannot assemble on the street," he said. In 2007 Soyinka called for the cancellation of the presidential elections in Nigeria because of widespread fraud and violence. His protest went unheeded, however. His 75th birthday on July 13, 2009, was celebrated by the publication of a book, *The Literary/Political Philosophy of Wole Soyinka,* by Yemi D. Ogunyemi.

See also NIGERIA, HUMAN RIGHTS VIOLATIONS IN.

Further Reading:
Soyinka, Wole. *Ake: The Years of Childhood.* New York: Vintage, 1989.
———. *Climate of Fear: The Quest for Dignity in a Dehumanized World.* Reith Lectures. New York: Random House Trade Paperbacks, 2005.
———. *Death and the King's Horseman.* New York: W. W. Norton & Company, 2002.

Special Court for Sierra Leone

In June 2000 the government of Sierra Leone asked the United Nations to set up an international tribunal for CRIMES AGAINST HUMANITY in order to try rebel leader Foday SANKOH and others implicated in atrocities committed during the civil war in that country. Unlike similar special UN tribunals for Rwanda and the former Yugoslavia, which are located in Tanzania and The Hague, respectively, the Special Court for Sierra Leone is based in the country where the crimes were committed. The Special Court is supposed to operate on a budget one-fifth of that for Rwanda and the former Yugoslavia—about $60 million for its first three years.

The Special Court is composed of lawyers and judges from Sierra Leone and abroad. Its mandate covers all the atrocities that occurred over 10 years of civil strife. It also covers the prosecution of leaders of the Revolutionary United Front (RUF), an insurgent movement responsible for killing and maiming thousands of civilians, as well as other actors in the war who had "the greatest responsibility" for war crimes, including government officials, members of the Sierra Leone military and police forces, and ECOWAS MONITORING GROUP (ECOMOG—the Nigerian-led peacekeeping force). However, a decision was made not to try any juveniles under the age of 15, although many children were pressed into combat by all parties to the conflict. Even children who had perpetrated atrocities, it was believed, should be considered victims and not perpetrators of crimes. The Geneva Conventions prohibit the use of children as soldiers.

Of the 12 men originally indicted, Sankoh was clearly the most important defendant but he cheated justice by dying of natural causes in prison in July 2003. As of September 2005, 11 persons associated with all three of the country's former warring factions had been indicted and charged with war crimes, crimes against humanity, and other serious violations of international humanitarian law. Specifically, the charges include murder, rape, extermination, acts of terror, enslavement, looting and burning, sexual slavery, conscription of children into an armed force, and attacks on United Nations peacekeepers and humanitarian workers, among others. By March 2010, the three cases heard in Freetown had been completed, including appeals. Those cases involved three former leaders of the Armed Forces Revolutionary Council (AFRC), two members of the Civil Defence Forces (CDF), and three former leaders of the RUF. The most important case, that of former Liberian President CHARLES TAYLOR, was taking place in The Hague for security reasons.

See also SIERRA LEONE, HUMAN RIGHTS VIOLATIONS IN.

Further Reading:
allAfrica.com. Sierra Leone Links. Available online. URL: http://allafrica.com/sierraleone/. Accessed March 20, 2010.
BBC.co.uk. *Country Profile: Sierra Leone.* Available online. URL: http://news.bbc.co.uk/2/hi/africa/country_profiles/1061561.stm. Accessed March 20, 2010.
Ferme, Mariane C. *The Underneath of Things: Violence, History, and the Everyday in Sierra Leone.* Berkeley: University of California Press, 2001.
Jackson, Michael. *In Sierra Leone.* Durham, N.C.: Duke University Press, 2004.
Richards, Paul. *Fighting for the Rain Forest: War, Youth, and Resources in Sierra Leone.* African Issues Series. London: Heinemann, 1996.
Romano, Cesare, Andre Nollkaemper, and Jann K. Kleffner, eds. *Internationalized Criminal Courts and Tribunals: Sierra Leone, East Timor, Kosovo, and Cambodia.* International Courts and Tribunals Series. Oxford: Oxford University Press, 2004.
The Special Court for Sierra Leone. Available online. URL: http://www.sc-sl.org/. Accessed March 20, 2010

Voeten, Teun. *How de Body? One Man's Terrifying Journey through an African War.* New York: Thomas Dunne Books, 2002.

Speer, Albert (1905–1981) *Nazi architect*

Albert Speer, ADOLF HITLER's principal architect and later the head of the Third Reich's armaments production, is one of the most complex and problematic Nazi war criminals to be tried at the NUREMBERG TRIALS. In contrast to other notorious Nazi officials such as JOSEPH GOEBBELS and HEINRICH HIMMLER, Speer freely acknowledged his guilt, although he contended that he was unaware of the Holocaust until his trial after the war. As one commentator put it, "Speer existed in what the Dutch Protestant theologian Willem Visser't Hooft has called 'a twilight between knowing and not knowing.'"

One of Speer's biographers called him a "frustrated romantic," emotionally crippled by an unhappy childhood. He was born in Mannheim, Germany, in 1905. While his was a life of privilege, the atmosphere at home was cold and distant. "Father and I never talked about our feelings," Speer recalled in one of his memoirs. "That was his way, and I have inherited from him." He initially hoped to become a mathematician but instead followed his father and grandfather's path and studied architecture. In 1931, shortly after completing his studies, he attended a Nazi Party rally where he first heard Hitler speak. He was mesmerized. Speer's intense attraction to Hitler has been characterized by biographers as "a sublimated, nonsexual but homoerotic devotion." "I am ashamed of it now," Speer acknowledged after the war, "but at the time, I found him deeply exciting." Hitler reciprocated his interest, seeing in the young architect a tabula rasa whom he could mold as he chose.

For his first commission, Speer was hired by Joseph Goebbels, the Nazi propaganda minister, to renovate the Propaganda Ministry. Goebbels found the results so impressive that he recommended him to Hitler, who put Speer to work renovating the Chancellery in Berlin, the official seat of power. By 1934, shortly after the Nazis had come to power, Speer was promoted to chief architect for the party. He then undertook one of his best-known commissions: the design of the parade grounds at Nuremberg where the Nazis orchestrated mass rallies. The grounds were inspired by ancient Greek temple architecture but constructed on a massive scale that was capable of holding 250,000 people. At a rally in 1934, to enhance the drama, he deployed 150 antiaircraft searchlights around the parade grounds, creating what one diplomat in attendance called "a cathedral of light." The rallies set against Speer's grandiose backdrop became known to the rest of the world thanks to Leni Riefenstahl's powerful propaganda film *Triumph of the Will.*

Strongly influenced by the legacy of classical Greek and Roman architecture, Speer derived a theory of his own that he called the theory of "ruin value." That is to say, every structure that was to be built to commemorate the Third Reich's glory should be so constructed that even after the passage of centuries it would produce aesthetically pleasing ruins. Hitler, who had declared that the Third Reich would endure for a thousand years, enthusiastically endorsed Speer's theory of built-in obsolescence. The führer decided to give Speer even more of an opportunity to put his theory into practice. Speer was now given the daunting assignment of reconstructing Berlin, which Hitler envisioned as the capital of a great state called Germania. The first step in carrying out this mammoth project was to design a new stadium that would play host to the 1936 Olympic games. He then went on to design a new Chancellery that, had it been built, would have contained a hall twice the size of the famous Hall of Mirrors in the Versailles palace. But the outbreak of World War II in 1939 put a halt to these grandiose plans. There were more pressing concerns for Germany, such as cranking out the tanks, planes, and guns to keep the war going.

In 1942 Hitler tapped Speer to take on a new responsibility, appointing him minister of armaments and war production. Speer proved that he could be just as capable and as diligent in his new capacity as he was as an architect. He displayed no compunction about using slave labor to increase production, even though he recognized that Germany had no chance of winning the war. "I'm not happy to face it," Speer recounted, "but in the context of my life then, these workers' only significance was what they could produce towards our war effort; I didn't see them as human beings, as individuals." If he objected to mistreatment of the slave laborers, it was not out of any humanitarian concerns. Rather, he was concerned that if his workers were abused, efficiency would suffer. Speer was an exemplary administrator; production levels at his factories continued to rise, reaching a peak in 1944 during the heaviest Allied bombing of the war. Historians believe that if Speer had not been quite so dedicated and proficient, Germany might not have been able to fight on as long as it did. Some experts estimate that Speer's efforts caused the war to last for a full year longer than it would otherwise, which also gave the Nazis more time to carry out mass exterminations.

But Speer's loyalty to Hitler had its limits. As the Allies encircled Berlin in 1945, Hitler gave an order to conduct a scorched-earth policy and raze every industrial facility so as to deny the victors the chance to gain any benefit. Speer recognized that if this order were carried out, it would impede any prospect for the country's postwar recovery, and he actively sought to undermine the führer's command. He went even further and plotted Hitler's assassination, though Hitler later saved him the trouble by taking his own life, apparently unaware that his former protégé had turned against him. In fact, he continued to look on Speer as a close friend, and the architect was one of the last people he spoke to before committing suicide.

Brought up on charges of war crimes before the International Military Tribunal at Nuremberg, Speer made no attempt to deny his culpability. He was, in fact, the only prominent member of the upper echelons of the Nazi Party to acknowledge carrying out Hitler's orders. Nonetheless, he denied that he had any knowledge of the mass extermination of Jews and other victims and said that until he heard testimony at the trial, he was unaware of the existence of the CONCENTRATION CAMPS. "Of the dreadful things, I knew nothing," he wrote to his daughter in 1952. Speer received special leniency from the court because of his reputation for incorruptibility and his willingness to take responsibility for his actions. He also had help from an unexpected source: His name had appeared in a list drawn up of future government officials by the July 20, 1944, conspirators who had tried unsuccessfully to assassinate Hitler and replace him with a de-Nazified government that could sue for peace. His inclusion on the list, Speer later said, might have saved his life.

The tribunal sentenced Speer to 20 years in Spandau prison in West Berlin, mainly on charges of having used slave labor. He resolved to use his imprisonment to transform himself into a "new man," an endeavor that was assisted by the prison chaplain, Georges Casalis. "When I met Speer," Casalis told Speer's biographer Gitta Sereny, "he was the most tortured man I had ever met. By the time I left Spandau (three years later), I saw him as the most repentant." Speer described Spandau as less a prison for him than "a refuge." He used the time to write, managing to turn out some 1,200 pages of a memoir, using toilet paper and cigarette papers. He later drew on these pages for two books published after he was released in 1966, *Inside the Third Reich* and *Spandau: The Secret Diaries*, which became international best-sellers. "You simply cannot understand what it is like to live in a dictatorship," he wrote in one account, "you can't understand the game of danger, but above all you cannot understand the fear on which the whole thing is based. Nor, I suppose, have you any concept of the charisma of a man such as Hitler." He claimed to have learned his lesson: "I am beginning to grasp that there is only one type of valid loyalty: toward morality." Critics charged, however, that his books were self-serving and that he downplayed his own role in Nazi atrocities.

Speer spent his remaining years trying to refurbish his image. "He worked hard at being penitent," as one writer put it. Albert Speer died in a London hospital on September 1, 1981—42 years to the day after Hitler's invasion of Poland marked the beginning of World War II.

Further Reading:

Sereny, Gitta. *Albert Speer: His Battle with Truth.* New York: Vintage, 1996.
Speer, Albert. *Inside the Third Reich.* New York: Simon & Schuster, 1997.
Van Der Vat, Dan. *The Good Nazi: The Life and Lies of Albert Speer.* Boston: Houghton Mifflin, 1997.

Srebrenica, massacre in

Srebrenica, a previously obscure town in eastern Bosnia and Herzegovina, became the site in 1995 of the worst atrocity in Europe since the end of World War II during the Bosnian War. The war was fought between Serbs, who made up the two remaining countries in the former Yugoslavia—Serbia and Montenegro on the one hand and Croatia and Bosnia on the other—both of which had declared their independence. Because of its large concentration of Muslims, the United Nations had declared the enclave of Srebrenica a safe haven that was guarded by a Dutch peacekeeping force. However, when confronted by Bosnian Serb forces in July 1995, the UN contingent withdrew: Women and young children were expelled from the area, and the occupiers proceeded to massacre as many as 7,800 Muslim men and boys between July 13 and 15.

Since the end of the war, some 1,200 of the victims have been identified by DNA analysis. Several Serbian officers involved in the killings have subsequently been tried and convicted by the INTERNATIONAL CRIMINAL TRIBUNAL FOR THE FORMER YUGOSLAVIA, sitting in The Hague. In a belated but welcome acknowledgment of responsibility, the Bosnian Serb government established after the war released a report in November 2004 that provided details of how the massacre was plotted and carried out. While the full contents of the report were not made public, it was said to contain the names of possible perpetrators. Srebrenica has also come to symbolize the failure of the international community to live up to its commitments to protect vulnerable populations in time of war. In the final months of 2005 the identities of thousands of Bosnian Serb soldiers, police officers, and officials involved in the massacres were revealed as a result of a two-year investigation by the Bosnian Serbian officials. A list of names of some 17,000 Bosnian Serbs who participated in the killings was made available to a war crimes tribunal in Bosnia and Herzegovina which said that based on the new evidence it would increase the number of its prosecutions. As many as 90 additional suspects were expected to be indicted. In a separate incident, five Serb paramilitaries were indicted for war crimes after a video surfaced that showed the men—members of the notorious Scorpions unit—executing six Srebrenica Muslim civilians. If convicted, they could face up to 50 years in prison. (Serb law does not permit the death penalty.)

See also Bosnia and Herzegovina, human rights violations in; safe havens; Yugoslavia, war crimes in.

Further Reading:
Glenny, Misha. *The Fall of Yugoslavia: The Third Balkan War.* New York: Penguin Books, 1996.
Honig, Jan Willem, and Norbert Both. *Srebrenica: Record of a War Crime.* New York: Penguin Books, 1997.
Mertus, Julie. *Former Yugoslavia: War Crimes Trials in the Former Yugoslavia.* Helsinki: Human Rights Watch/Helsinki, 1995.
Rhode, David. *Endgame: The Betrayal and Fall of Srebrenica.* New York: Farrar, Straus & Giroux, 1997.
Rossanet, Bertrand de. *War and Peace in the Former Yugoslavia.* Boston: Martinus Nijhoff, 1997.

Sri Lanka, human rights violations in

After decades of war, the Sri Lankan government succeeded in defeating the Liberation Tigers of Tamil Eelam (LTTE) by spring 2009. Thousands of civilians caught up in the final battles were targeted—intentionally or not—by both sides. Human rights organizations accused the Sri Lankan army of indiscriminate artillery attacks on civilians in the northern Vanni region and the separatists of prohibiting civilians from evacuating the conflict zone, sometimes shooting those who tried to flee. By forbidding journalists and human rights monitors from investigating, the government effectively cut off the flow of information about human rights violations in the final battle against the Tamil Tigers. In February alone, at the height of the fighting, Human Rights Watch estimated that 2,000 civilians were killed and another 5,000 were wounded. It is believed that about 7,000 civilians had been killed by the time the fighting ended. The Sri Lankan government regarded the fleeing Tamils as if they were supporters of the LTTE; according to Human Rights Watch, they were "treated as combatants, effectively sanctioning unlawful attacks." Even government "safe zones" were subject to shelling, as was the only functioning hospital in the conflict zone. A subsequent investigation by a leading Sri Lankan human rights group—the University Teachers for Human Rights (Jaffna) group, which has spent 21 years exposing abuses by both sides in the civil war—delivered a scathing criticism of elements of the army that had sunk to "the most depraved depths of humanity." It accused the government of authorizing a massacre of LTTE cadres after they had been persuaded to surrender. Citing sources inside the army, the report characterized it as a "politically ordered massacre of people who wanted to surrender or surrendered." Government forces were also accused of throwing grenades into bunkers where they knew civilians had taken refuge, and

they might have bulldozed wounded civilians into mass graves. The report did not spare the LTTE, which it accused of torture, murder, and the forced conscription of children and which was "probably responsible for most of the thousands of civilian casualties in the final days of the war." The war left an estimated 250,000 to 300,000 displaced people, who were consigned to government camps that were closed to NGOs or monitors, prompting an international outcry. The Sri Lankan authorities pressured the International Committee of the Red Cross, forcing the organization to close four offices in Sri Lanka's Eastern Province. What information that did leak out revealed that many refugees were not being provided with adequate food, shelter, or health care. At the same time, the government rejected demands for an international investigation into atrocities that might have been committed by both sides in the final battles of the war. In October 2009 the government promised to send the vast majority of the refugees back home by the end of January, although it said that it would first need to ensure that no Tamil Tigers were hiding among them. The government denied that the refugees were being held as prisoners. By fall 2009, however, fewer than 10 percent of the refugees had been allowed to return home. Human rights organizations expressed skepticism that the government intended to fulfill its commitment. A presidential commission of inquiry was established in 2007 to investigate claims of abuses prior to the final conflict on the Jaffna Peninsula. Of the 16 cases of abuses blamed on both sides, the commission had only reviewed a total of seven by the time its mandate expired in 2009.

In spite of the end of hostilities, a climate of fear persists in much of Sri Lanka. Several independent activists, lawyers, and journalists who criticized the government have been attacked or murdered.

The two major figures in the victory over the Tigers—President Mahinda Rajapaksa and General Sarath Fonseka, who commanded government forces in the conflict—were soon at loggerheads. Fonseka was embraced by a coalition of parties opposed to the president as the candidate most likely to defeat him in presidential elections early in 2010. Ironically, even many Tamils supported him, seeing him as more conciliatory than the president. In spite of reports of pervasive corruption and an increasingly autocratic style, Rajapaksa easily won reelection by 17 percent. But rather than savoring his victory, he ordered the arrest of his rival, whom he accused of plotting against him.

The source of the conflict stemmed in large part from ethnic tensions between the majority Singhalese (who mainly follow Buddhism) and the Tamil minority (who practice Hinduism). The conflict between the government and the LTTE, the major Tamil insurgent group, has resulted in the killing of more than 60,000 people. Both sides in the war were implicated in numerous human rights violations. Security forces were responsible for killing prisoners they took in addition to other EXTRAJUDICIAL KILLINGS, which they defend by claiming that the victims were Tiger guerrillas felled in combat. Military and police personnel also tortured detainees. Torture and arbitrary arrests and detentions became more frequent with the passage of New Emergency Regulations (ER) which, according to the U.S. State Department, further "eroded due process protections."

Even though the war has ended, the government has made little progress toward investigating past abuses or bringing those responsible for them to justice. Censorship has limited the ability of the media—domestic or foreign—to investigate or expose government culpability in abuses. Security forces have been known to harass journalists, although this situation, too, has eased since the cease-fire took hold. Many of the worst abuses have been blamed on proxy forces made up of defectors who have been recruited by the security forces to identify and hunt down their former comrades. These militias have been blamed for numerous extrajudicial killings and DISAPPEARANCES, although two of the groups were supposed to have been disarmed.

If anything, the Tigers were responsible for even more human rights violations, and the U.S. State Department has labeled them a terrorist group. According to HUMAN RIGHTS WATCH, the Tigers targeted and killed several people with links to Tamil political parties opposed to the LTTE even after the cease-fire took effect; many other Tamil opponents have been abducted without any indication as to their fate. In the past the Tigers staged spectacular terrorist acts, including suicide bombings—which the group introduced to the world as an innovative guerrilla tactic—killing 170 civilians in such bombings during a nine-month period at the height of the conflict.

Both the LTTE and the government recruited child soldiers—as young as 11—but the Tigers are probably more culpable in this respect. In one survey conducted in the 1990s, 40–60 percent of LTTE soldiers killed in battle were children under the age of 18. Children have also been used by the Tigers as suicide bombers. In 2002 UNICEF documented more than 3,500 cases of child recruitment after the cease-fire, and the total is likely to be much higher. In a number of instances families were threatened if they didn't surrender their children for "the cause" while in other cases they gave them up voluntarily because they were unable to care for them. Children have also been known to voluntarily join the LTTE because their families have suffered at the hands of government forces. The treatment of child recruits by LTTE is brutal, and those who try to escape are beaten in front of their peers as a warning. In June 2003 the LTTE signed an Action Plan for Children Affected by War that obliged it to cease its recruitment of child soldiers and free the children it held. Although LTTE did release 831 children, by November 2004 it had recruited or re-recruited 1,700 more.

See also CHILDREN'S RIGHTS, PRABHAKARAN, VELLUPILLAI.

Further Reading:

Amnesty International. Sri Lanka. Available online. URL: http://www.amnesty.org/en/region/sri-lanka. Accessed March 21, 2010.
CIA World Handbook. *Sri Lanka.* March 4, 2010. Available online. URL: https://www.cia.gov/library/publications/the-world-factbook/geos/ce.html. Accessed March 21, 2010.
Clarance, William. *Ethnic Warfare in Sri Lanka and the U.N. Crisis.* London: Pluto Press, 2006.
De Votta, Neil. *Blowback: Linguistic Nationalism, Institutional Decay, and Ethnic Conflict in Sri Lanka.* Contemporary Issues in Asia and the Pacific. Stanford, Calif.: Stanford University Press, 2004.
Human Rights Watch. Sri Lanka. Available online. URL: http://www.hrw.org/legacy/asia/srilanka. Accessed March 21, 2010.
Tambiah, Stanley Jeyaraja. *Buddhism Betrayed?: Religion, Politics, and Violence in Sri Lanka.* A Monograph of the World Institute for Development Economics Research. Chicago: University of Chicago Press, 1992.
———. *Ethnic Fratricide and the Dismantling of Democracy.* Chicago: University of Chicago Press, 1991.
Winslow, Deborah, and Michael Woost, eds. *Economy, Culture, and Civil War in Sri Lanka.* Bloomington: Indiana University Press, 2004.

SS (Schutzstaffel)

The SS was possibly the most feared security police force in the Nazi state terror apparatus. SS is the abbreviation for the German word *Schutzstaffel*, which means "defense corps." Initially, the SS served as an elite bodyguard for ADOLF HITLER, answerable to the SA (Sturmabteilung, or storm troops), the Nazi paramilitary unit. However, the SS began to expand in size and power, becoming both a police force and an army within the regular army; the Waffen SS, also took primary responsibility for manning the CONCENTRATION CAMPS.

The SS originated in Bavaria in the 1920s, a decade before the Nazis came to power. Under the direction of HEINRICH HIMMLER, the force developed into an efficient killing machine for the purpose of implementing Nazi racial policies. In June 1931 Himmler joined forces with REINHARD HEYDRICH. A year after Hitler came to power in 1933, the two men helped Hitler consolidate power in the SS by eliminating the rival SA as a viable force in a bloody purge known to history as the Night of the Long Knives. At the same time Himmler moved to infiltrate and reorganize the German police system and create a new security police. Under this scheme the political police—the GESTAPO (Geheime Staatspolize, or secret state police)— was put under Heydrich's control, and the Ordnungspolizei (or Orpo, the ordinary criminal police) was put under the charge of Kurt Dalugue. The SS proceeded to set up the first ghettoes in Poland and formed the EINSATZGRUPPEN, the extermination squads that followed the German army into occupied areas of Europe and the Soviet Union, killing Jews, Slavs, and others considered subhuman. There was, in addition, an economic component to the SS; under Obergruppenführer OSWALD POHL, the SS built up a vast network of enterprises based on slave labor, extortion, and murder.

Himmler selected Theodor Eicke to recruit personnel for the concentration camps. Eicke would prove more ruthless than the Bavarian police guards who were originally assigned to the camps. He formed the Totenkopfverbaende (SS Death's Head Battalion) by scouring the streets of Berlin, Hamburg, and Munich for unemployed thugs. He then dressed them in the black SS uniform but with the addition of a red fez with the design of a human skull beneath the swastika and a black silk tassel.

By 1939 the SS had been organized into four major branches: (1) the General SS, members of which served part-time on a voluntary basis; (2) the SD, or Security Service; (3) the Waffen SS; and (4) the Death's Head concentration-camp guard units. At the same time, the state police and Gestapo were merged into the Reich Main Security Office (Reichssicherheitshauptamt, or RSHA) under Heydrich's command.

At the NUREMBERG TRIALS the Allies took the unusual step of trying Nazi military and security bodies, indicting them as criminal organizations: the SS, the Gestapo, the SA, and the General Staff and High Command of the German armed forces. There were three cases that specifically focused on activities undertaken by SS personnel in which 56 "full-time" SS defendants were indicted. ("Full-time" SS officers were distinguished from "honorary" SS officers.) In the first (*United States v. Oswald Pohl et al.*), three of the defendants, including Pohl, were sentenced to death, with one sentence subsequently changed to a term of life imprisonment; 11 were given sentences ranging from 10 years to life; and three were acquitted. In the second case (*United States v. Ulrich Greifelt et al.*), eight of the defendants were sentenced to prison for periods ranging from life to 15 years, five were found guilty of membership in the SS, and one defendant was acquitted. In the third, known as the Einsatzgruppen Case, 14 were sentenced to death, two were sentenced to life imprisonment, and five others were

sentenced to imprisonment for terms ranging from 10 to 20 years.

Further Reading:
Browder, George C. *Hitler's Enforcers: The Gestapo and the SS Security Service in the Nazi Revolution.* Oxford: Oxford University Press, 1996.
Hohne, Heinz Zollen. *The Order of the Death's Head: The Story of Hitler's SS.* Classic Military History. New York: Penguin, 2001.
Whiting, Charles. *Heydrich: Henchman of Death.* Barnsley, U.K.: Leo Cooper, 1999.

Stalin, Joseph (Josif Vissarionovich Dzhugashvili)
(1879–1953) *Soviet dictator*

The future dictator of the Soviet Union was born Josif Vissarionovich Dzhugashvili to illiterate peasant parents in Georgia in the southern Caucuses. Some historians have attributed his tyrannical temperament to the frequent beatings he received from his father when he was growing up. His mother encouraged him to become a priest in the Russian Orthodox Church, and he studied for the priesthood until he was almost 20. However, he fell under the sway of Karl Marx rather than God, and he was expelled from the seminary in 1899. He then became involved in the socialist underground, distributing Marxist propaganda and serving as a labor agitator. Dzhugashvili was arrested by the czarist police in 1903 and sentenced to imprisonment in Siberia, but he was back in Georgia within a year. When the Social Democrats split into two factions (Mensheviks and Bolsheviks), he joined the more militant Bolsheviks under the leadership of Vladimir Lenin. In 1908 he was arrested again and sent into exile but managed to escape. The next several years were marked by other arrests, narrow escapes, and secret trips abroad on behalf of Lenin to raise support for the Bolsheviks. During this period Dzhugashvili assumed the pseudonym Stalin (meaning "man of steel") and was elevated by Lenin to the Central Committee, the highest body of the Bolshevik Party (later the Communist Party).

In 1913 Stalin was again arrested and again exiled to Siberia, to be freed only when the monarchy was toppled by revolution in 1917. He then established a base in Petrograd (now St. Petersburg) and became editor of *Pravda*, the Communist Party's mouthpiece. In 1919 he was elected a member of the Politburo, the Communist Party's most important decision-making body. He also became head of the Commissariat for Nationality Affairs, a position that was of crucial importance because the new Soviet regime was struggling to maintain control over the country's disparate ethnic groups and nationalities in the midst of civil war, which lasted from 1918 to 1921. Stalin was directly involved

Stalin (left) with top Soviet leader Sergey Kirov (later assassinated) *(Library of Congress)*

in planning military strategy against counterrevolutionary forces—the Whites—as well as against Polish forces in the war between Russia and Poland (1920–21). His decisions were disastrous and put him at loggerheads with Leon Trotsky, the commissar of war and heir apparent to Lenin.

After the Communist victory, Stalin quietly built up organizational strength. In 1923 he was elected general secretary of the Communist Party, a position he used as his power base. Lenin, who was seriously ill at this point, was beginning to harbor deep misgivings and wrote a "testament" in which he cautioned against allowing Stalin to succeed him. But Stalin continued his inexorable rise to power after Lenin's death in 1924. For the next few years he was obliged to outmaneuver a number of rivals, including Nikolai Bukharin, Lev Kamenev, and Grigory Zinovyev. But it was only after he had succeeded in marginalizing Trotsky, who was forced into exile, that he was able to secure uncontested power. (Trotsky was assassinated on Stalin's orders in Mexico City in 1940.) Thereafter, from 1928 until his death in 1953, Stalin was effectively in complete control over the party and the country.

With the economy in a state of decline, Stalin abandoned Lenin's New Economic Policy, which allowed some free-market commerce, in favor of a policy of collectivization of the agricultural sector to raise output and bolster efficiency. Although the policy was promoted as a boon to peasants, it was vigorously resisted by small farmers, known as kulaks, who were now being called upon to sacrifice their land and become members of a collective farm. The new policy threatened not only their livelihood but a traditional way of life that had endured for generations. Stalin

forcibly suppressed opposition, characterizing the kulaks as capitalist parasites and using special Shock Brigades to bring them to heel. The kulaks were either shot or sent to Siberia.

Between 1929 and 1933, as collectivization was being carried out, millions of people lost their lives—5 million in the Ukraine alone, according to some estimates—mostly on account of a famine that resulted from the massive disruption to agricultural production. At the same time, Stalin moved rapidly to industrialize Russia—regarded as one of the poorest nations in Europe before 1914—introducing a succession of five-year plans. The ramped-up production levels did yield extraordinary gains that exceeded Germany's pace of industrialization in the 19th century and Japan's earlier in the 20th century. To subsidize this ambitious program, Stalin relied to a great degree on wealth he appropriated from the people. However ruthless his regime, he is also credited with improving the health of the Soviet populace with aggressive immunization campaigns against typhus, cholera, and malaria and improving and expanding the educational system.

In the early 1930s Stalin consolidated absolute power by carrying out purges of political opponents, real or imagined—among them many old Bolsheviks. Between 1936 and 1937—a period known as the Great Terror—several once-powerful Communist Party officials were convicted in "show trials" and either shot or sent to the GULAG—the camps in Siberia and elsewhere. There were four major purge trials during these years: the Trial of the Sixteen; the Trial of the Seventeen; the Trial of the Red Army Generals; and finally, in March 1938, the Trial of the Twenty-One. The KGB, the successor to the NKVD (the Soviet secret police under Stalin), estimated that 681,692 people were shot between 1937 and 1938, although this figure might be an undercount. Millions of people were arrested, often in the dead of night, on the basis of trumped-up charges or none at all. (Historians are divided as to how many million victims there actually were, with estimates ranging from eight to 20 million; some put the number as high as 50 million.) Stalin is thought to have personally signed as many as 40,000 death warrants of political opponents.

For all his cunning, Stalin appears to have been taken in by ADOLF HITLER's assurances that the Germans had no territorial designs on the Soviet Union. In 1939 he agreed to a nonaggression pact with Nazi Germany (the Molotov-Ribbentrop Pact), which also contained a secret appendix that carved up Poland between the Soviet Union and Germany and allowed the USSR a free hand in the Baltic nations of Estonia, Latvia, and Lithuania. In 1940 Stalin effectively decapitated the Polish leadership, ordering the execution of thousands of Polish officers in Katyn Forest after they had been captured by the Red Army, which had seized its share of the country under the terms of the non-aggression pact. The Kremlin later tried to cover up responsibility and laid the blame on the Germans for the atrocity.

In 1941 the Germans, taking Stalin by surprise, launched Operation Barbarosa, the code name for their invasion of the Soviet Union. Initially Germany scored major gains. The Red Army was at a disadvantage because its leadership had been crippled by Stalin after he had purged so many of his top generals. There is no doubt that the Soviets suffered the most during World War II and yet were responsible in large part for Germany's ultimate defeat. Approximately 22 million people (13 percent of the Soviet population)—7 million of them civilians—were killed in the war. Ironically, German aggression united the Soviet people behind Stalin against a common invader, even after so many years of misrule. Stalin cleverly played the nationalist card, downplaying ideology, to mobilize resistance to the invader. The 1943 surrender of General von Paulus's Sixth Army to the Red Army at Stalingrad is generally considered the turning point of the war, making the German defeat inevitable.

Even before the end of the war, Stalin began to plan for the expansion of Soviet influence well beyond the borders of the USSR. As a vital wartime ally, he wrested concessions from an ailing President Franklin Roosevelt that allowed the Soviets to carve out a sphere of influence in Eastern Europe after the war. Between 1945 and 1948, the Soviets extended their influence over East Germany, Poland, Czechoslovakia, Hungary, Romania, and Bulgaria. (An independent communist regime under Josip Broz [Tito] was established in Yugoslavia.) These puppet "people's republics" formed a military alliance known as the Warsaw Pact, which was dominated by Moscow. In a famous speech in Fulton, Missouri, British prime minister Winston Churchill declared that an "iron curtain" had descended across Europe. The phrase stuck. What became known as the cold war between the Communist empire and the West had begun.

In the early 1950s Stalin increasingly showed signs of mental and physical disability. His megalomania was only matched by his paranoia. Those closest to him were fearful, never knowing when he would single them out for disloyalty, which could mean either imprisonment or execution. In early 1953 he ordered the arrests of several Kremlin doctors whom he accused of plotting against his life. As many of these doctors were Jewish, his action raised fears that he was about to initiate an anti-Semitic campaign throughout the country. But if he were planning such a pogrom, he never lived long enough to order it. On March 1, 1953, Stalin collapsed after an all-night dinner whose guests included Lavrenti Beria, head of the secret police, and Nikita Khrushchev, who would later become Soviet premier. He died four days later, having never regained consciousness. Officially the cause of death was a cerebral hemorrhage, but Vyacheslav Molotov, the foreign minister, claimed in his memoirs that Beria had poisoned Stalin.

Since Stalin's death, historians have quarreled about how he should be judged. For example, in his biography *Stalin: Breaker of Nations*, Robert Conquest found that there was "something in [Stalin's] character best thought of as an absence of life in its fullest sense." He characterized Stalin as a "vast, dark figure looming over the century," who was incapable of any sort of sympathetic human relationship. On the other hand, Robert Service in his portrait of the Soviet dictator, *Stalin: A Biography,* argues that while indeed Stalin was "as wicked a man as has ever lived" and someone who suffered from a "dangerously damaged" personality, he was nonetheless "hard-working," "capable of kindness to relatives," a "ruler of great assiduity," a "fluent and thoughtful writer," and "a delightful purveyor of jokes and mimicry." In addition, Service finds him "a thoughtful man" who "tried to make sense of the universe as he found it." Service allows that he could be guilty of trying to humanize Stalin but points out that "[i]f the likes of Stalin, Hitler, Mao and Pol Pot are represented as having been 'animals,' 'monsters' or 'killing machines,' we shall never be able to discern their successors."

In Russia, too, Stalin's reputation has undergone a resurrection of sorts. Denounced by Khrushchev for his excesses at a famous speech delivered in secret to the 20th Communist Party Congress, Stalin has enjoyed renewed popularity among some Russians who see him as a symbol of former Soviet glory. In 2005 the government announced a plan to erect a statue of Stalin in Moscow after a long period in which his once-ubiquitous image had been stripped from practically all public places. The backers of legislation to raise the statue maintained that Stalin should be honored for his leadership in World War II.

See also KATYN FOREST, MASSACRE IN.

Further Reading:

Applebaum, Anne. *Gulag: A History.* New York: Anchor, 2004.

Conquest, Robert. *Stalin: Breaker of Nations.* New York: Penguin Books, 1992.

Khlevniuk, Oleg. *The History of the Gulag: From Collectivization to the Great Terror.* Annals of Communism Series. Translated by Vadim A. Staklo. New Haven, Conn.: Yale University Press, 2004.

Kizny, Tomasz. *Gulag: Life and Death inside the Soviet Concentration Camps 1917–1990.* London: Firefly Books Ltd, 2004.

Montefiore, Simon Sebag. *Stalin: The Court of the Red Tsar.* New York: Knopf, 2004.

Radzinsky, Edvard. *Stalin: The First In-Depth Biography Based on Explosive New Documents from Russia's Secret Archives.* New York: Anchor, 1997.

Service, Robert. *Stalin: A Biography.* Cambridge, Mass.: Belknap Press, 2005.

Solzhenitsyn, Aleksandr. *The Gulag Archipelago.* New York: HarperCollins, 1978.

Ulam, Adam B. *Stalin: The Man and His Era.* Boston: Beacon Press, 1987.

starvation as a tactic of war

As a tool of war, starvation is prohibited under INTERNATIONAL HUMANITARIAN LAW. The ADDITIONAL PROTOCOLS TO THE GENEVA CONVENTIONS ban the starvation of civilian populations in both international and internal conflicts. However, the law also imposes no obligation on one party to a conflict to ensure the supply of food or other provisions to its adversary. How these two apparently opposing positions are to be reconciled has been an ongoing source of dispute among legal scholars and international bodies. The INTERNATIONAL COMMITTEE OF THE RED CROSS (ICRC) takes the unequivocal position that there is no justification for denying food to those who need it, regardless of the possibility that some of that food might be used by an enemy force. The ICRC's view, however, is a minority one. More specifically, the issue hinges on "the right of passage" through a battlefront. Article 23 of the Fourth Geneva Convention of 1949 refers to free passage for "children under fifteen, expectant mothers and maternity cases." Other civilians may also enjoy the right of free passage if the territory they inhabit is deemed "inadequately supplied."

Further limits on using starvation as a means of warfare are found in Additional Protocol I, covering international armed conflict, which prohibits the targeting or destruction of "objects indispensable to the survival of the civilian population," a provision applying to food and to the means of producing food—for example, a flour plant, reservoir, or farm. A belligerent is enjoined by the protocol from taking any action "which may be expected to leave the civilian population with such inadequate food or water as to cause starvation or force its movement." Protocol I also permits "relief actions which are humanitarian and impartial in character and conducted without any adverse distinction shall be undertaken," although this provision does add the qualification that both parties to the conflict must agree to it. Protocol II provides for similar protections for civilian in an internal armed conflict. Relief operations "which are of an exclusively humanitarian and impartial nature" can be undertaken when a civilian population is suffering "undue hardship" due to a lack of food or medical supplies "essential to its survival." Relief actions conducted "without any adverse distinction" shall be undertaken sub-

ject to the consent of the state involved. Even though the United States is not a party to either protocol, it subscribes to the prohibition of starvation as a military tactic.

See also GENEVA CONVENTIONS; SIEGE.

Further Reading:
Gutman, Roy, ed. *Crimes of War: What the Public Should Know.* New York: W. W. Norton & Company, 1999.

Stockholm Declaration on Genocide

The Stockholm Declaration on Genocide, announced on January 28, 2004, emerged from a three-day intergovernmental conference sponsored by the United Nations that was entitled "Preventing GENOCIDE: Threats and Responsibilities." Attended by delegates from 58 nations, it was the first major international conference on genocide since the United Nations adopted the GENOCIDE CONVENTION in 1948. The declaration called for collective efforts of the international community to prevent genocide, ethnic cleansing, and mass killings. The declaration also obliged state members to identify and report possible threats of genocide and take effective measures to stop it from happening.

This was the fourth conference held by the United Nations on genocide in recent years. The first conference, held in January 2000, called "The Holocaust", resulted in the Stockholm Declaration on Holocaust Education, Remembrance and Research. The second in 2001 was titled Combating Intolerance and the third, in 2002, the Conference on Truth, Justice and Reconciliation. The preamble from the Stockholm Declaration states: "Recalling our responsibility to fight the evils of genocide, ethnic cleansing, racism, anti-Semitism, Islamophobia and xenophobia, we, the participants of the Stockholm International Forum 2004: Preventing Genocide: Threats and Responsibilities, conscious of our obligations and responsibilities under international law including human rights and INTERNATIONAL HUMANITARIAN LAW, deeply concerned with the repeated occurrence of genocide, mass murder and ethnic cleansing in recent history as well as with the widespread occurrence of impunity for such crimes, are committed to doing our utmost for the prevention of these scourges in order to build a more secure future for us all."

St. Petersburg Declaration   *See* WEAPONS IN THE CONDUCT OF WAR.

Streicher, Julius (1885–1946) *Nazi propagandist*
Julius Streicher was a Nazi propagandist whose virulent anti-Semitic tirades earned him a reputation as Nazi

Julius Streicher (center) with other members of the Nazi Party during a rally in Nuremberg *(Library of Congress)*

Germany's most prominent Jew baiter. Although he was never charged with actively participating in Nazi killings, he was convicted for CRIMES AGAINST HUMANITY at the NUREMBERG TRIALS for his role in inciting hatred.

The son of a teacher, Streicher was born on February 12, 1885. He joined the German army during World War I and was awarded an Iron Cross for bravery. In 1919 he helped found an anti-Semitic organization called Wistrich, which was later integrated into the National Socialist German Workers Party (NSDAP), better known as the Nazis. ADOLF HITLER cited Streicher for turning the party over to him in his memoir *Mein Kampf.* In 1923 Streicher founded the anti-Semitic newspaper *Der Stürmer,* which would eventually have a circulation of 800,000. In 1933 he started another daily, *Fränkische Tageszeitung.* He also became a publisher of magazines and books, all of which carried the same racist message. Jews, he wrote, were responsible for all the problems that ailed Germany, including depression, unemployment, and inflation. He accused Jews of being heavily involved in prostitution as well. "We know that the Jew, whether he is baptized as a Protestant or as a Catholic, remains a Jew," he asserted. "Why cannot you realize, you Protestant clergymen, you Catholic priests, you who have scales before your eyes and serve the god of the

Jews who is not the God of Love but the God of Hate. Why do you not listen to Christ, who said to the Jews, 'You are children of the devil.'" In a speech he gave on another occasion, he asserted, "The Jew seeks domination not only among the German people but among all peoples. The communists pave the way for him. Do you not know that the God of the Old Testament orders the Jews to consume and enslave the peoples of the earth?" He credited Hitler for his commitment to target the Jews: "You may think about Adolf Hitler as you please, but one thing you must admit. He possessed the courage to attempt to free the German people from the Jew by a national revolution. That was action indeed."

Streicher did not only direct his anti-Semitic rants at adults; he also wanted to ensure that children too were inculcated in hatred against Jews. Accordingly, his publishing firm released an anti-Semitic children's book, *Der Giftpilz* (The poisonous mushroom). Even ardent Nazis had misgivings about Streicher's propaganda, not necessarily because of its anti-Semitism but because he also filled the pages of his papers with pornography and sensationalism. Because of his anti-Semitic credentials, Streicher was appointed chairman of the central committee directing the organization of a boycott against all Jewish-owned businesses in Germany. "Jewry will realize whom it has challenged," he declared on the eve of the boycott in late March 1933. He also published an article entitled "Defeat the Enemy of the World! by Julius Streicher, official leader of the central committee to combat the Jewish atrocity and boycott campaign," in which he stated, "Jewry wanted this battle. It shall have it until it realizes that the Germany of the brown battalions is not a country of cowardice and surrender. Jewry will have to fight until we have won victory." The "brown battalions" refers to the SA (Sturmabteilung), the Nazi paramilitaries who wore brown shirts and in fact were known as Brown Shirts. (The SS were known as Black Shirts for their characteristic uniforms.)

In spite of his prominence as a propagandist, Streicher held only a few official positions in the Nazi hierarchy—as a member of the Reichstag (parliament) from 1933 (the year the Nazis came to power) until 1945 and as *Obergruppenführer* in the SA. In 1940 Streicher finally went too far and defamed HERMANN GÖRING, Hitler's top deputy, in his papers, losing all of his party offices as a result. However, he did not fall out of favor entirely, because he remained on good terms with Hitler. After the war he was tried by the Nuremberg Military Tribunal and found guilty of crimes against humanity. Before he was hanged on October 16, 1946, his last words were "Heil Hitler."

Further Reading:
Bytwerk, Randell I. *Bending Spines: The Propagandas of Nazi Germany and the German Democratic Republic.* Rhetoric and Public Affairs Series. East Lansing: Michigan State University Press, 2004.
———. *Julius Streicher: Nazi Editor of the Notorious Anti-Semitic Newspaper Der Sturmer.* New York: Cooper Square Press, 2001.
Read, Anthony. *The Devil's Disciples: Hitler's Inner Circle.* New York: W. W. Norton, 2004.

Strössner, Alfredo (1912–2006) *Paraguayan dictator*
Alfredo Strössner was president of Paraguay from 1954 to 1989, one of the longest-lasting dictators in Latin American history. Born to a German Paraguayan family in 1912, he became a commissioned officer in 1932 and fought in the Chaco War between Paraguay and Bolivia over disputed territory (1932–35). He later participated in a civil war in 1947, which pitted the government against a leftist insurgency. In 1951 he was appointed commander in chief of the armed forces, and in 1954 he orchestrated the coup that brought him to power. He not only maintained control over the armed forces but went on to manipulate his "reelection" in the next seven presidential elections (1958, 1963, 1968, 1973, 1978, 1983, and 1988). An admirer of the Nazis, he opened his country's doors to wanted Nazi war criminals—among them the notorious Auschwitz doctor, JOSEF MENGELE, who was granted citizenship and allowed to practice as a doctor in the capital of Asunción. One correspondent described Strössner's administration as the "poor man's Nazi regime."

In the 1950s Strössner welcomed a delegation of TORTURE experts from Argentina who trained Paraguayans in their methods. Over the years he also played host to Croatian fascists and right-wing nationalists who gathered in the capital for the congress of the Anti-Communist League in 1971. The Paraguayan army carried out its own type of ethnic cleansing, targeting the indigenous Ache Indians, whom the dictator claimed were standing in the way of progress. "Progress" meant depriving the Ache of their land so that international corporations could exploit them for timber, mineral wealth, and grazing rights. Indians were killed and uprooted from their lands; some were sold into SLAVERY and others corralled on reservations under the supervision of American fundamentalist missionaries.

At the same time, Strössner brought a measure of economic stability to the country. In cooperation with Brazil, he built the Itaipú dam on the Paraná River; its power plant, the world's largest hydroelectric station, provided a new revenue source from the export of electricity. Yet prosperity came at the expense of the workers who saw their wages erode. Strössner kept a lid on political opposition (though he allowed greater dissent toward the end of his tenure). Nonetheless, his firm stance against communism won him many high-placed friends in Washington. President Richard Nixon described Paraguay as a "model of democracy for Latin America," and the U.S. House of Representatives passed a resolution authorizing U.S. troop movements to Paraguay in the event of a communist threat—which never materialized. The United States provided nearly $150 million in aid between 1962 and 1975 and trained more than 1,000 Paraguayan troops at U.S. installations.

Corruption flourished under Strössner's regime. In 1971 high-ranking officials in the government were implicated in a drug-smuggling scheme using Paraguay as a transit point. Yet in spite of Strössner's heavy-handed methods, he could not stifle all dissent. Beginning in the 1970s, leaders of the Catholic Church began to express misgivings about the regime's unsavory human rights record and called for social reform. Strössner responded by persecuting the church. His security forces stormed Catholic universities, arresting teachers and beating students. Church activists were arrested and Jesuits expelled from the country. Priests driven from their churches took up residence in impoverished neighborhoods where they continued to work for change, encouraging the poor to assert their rights.

By the 1980s, even the U.S. government no longer regarded Strössner as a valuable ally and began to openly repudiate his abuses of civil rights and habit of turning a blind eye to drug smuggling through Paraguayan territory. In 1989 a coup launched by a top general, Andres Rodriguez, toppled Strössner, who went into exile in Brazil. Strössner died on August 16, 2006, in Brasilia.

Further Reading:
BBC.co.uk. Obituary: Alfredo Stroessner. Available online. URL: http://news.bbc.co.uk/2/hi/americas/4792281. stm. Accessed March 20, 2010.
McKewen, Darren. *Transition from Stroessner: The 1989 Paraguayan Elections: Post-election Report.* CSIS Latin American Election Studies Series. Washington, D.C.: Center for Strategic & International Studies, 1989.
Sanders, Thomas Griffen. *The Fall of Stroessner: Continuity and Change in Paraguay.* Berkeley, Calif.: Universities Field Staff International, 1989.

Struger, Pavle   *See* WAR CRIMINALS OF THE FORMER YUGOSLAVIA.

Stuckart, Wilhelm (1902–1953) *drafter of the Nuremberg laws*

A member of the Nazi SS, Wilhelm Stuckart was responsible for drafting the notorious NUREMBERG LAWS (1936), which were designed to segregate Jews, deprive them of an ability to make a living, and prohibit them from intermarrying with Germans classified as Aryans. A lawyer by profession, Stuckart had previously served as a mayor of Stettin and as permanent secretary in the Prussian Ministry of Culture. After 1935 he was appointed state secretary (second in command) in the Reich Ministry of the Interior. A supporter of the FINAL SOLUTION—the Nazi policy to annihilate the entire Jewish population of Germany and occupied Europe—he represented the Reich Ministry of the Interior at the 1942 WANNSEE CONFERENCE, a gathering of high-ranking Nazi officials to determine how this policy should be implemented. Stuckart proved more moderate than many of his colleagues, arguing that those Jews who had some non-Jewish blood should be spared extermination. After the war, he was sentenced by the Allies to three years and 10 months in prison. He died in a traffic accident in 1953.

Further Reading:
Dawidowicz, Lucy. *A Holocaust Reader.* Library of Jewish Studies. Chicago: Behrman House Publishing, 1976.
Dwork, Deborah, and Robert Jan Van Pelt. *Holocaust: A History.* New York: W. W. Norton & Company, 2003.
Gilbert, Martin. *The Holocaust: A History of the Jews of Europe during the Second World War.* New York: Owl Books, 1987.
Roseman, Mark. *The Wannsee Conference and the Final Solution: A Reconsideration.* New York: Metropolitan Books, 2002.

Sudan, human rights violations in

Sudan, which formally became independent in 1956, has never been a truly unified state. The north is largely Arab and Muslim while the southern part of the country is dominated by animist and Christian populations. Power resides in the north, the location of the capital, Khartoum, but the country's wealth, mainly in the form of oil, is found in the south. Southerners believed that they were being unfairly treated by Khartoum, denied both the political and the economic power they were entitled to. In 1963 rebels in the south formed the Land Freedom Army and began to mount attacks against the central government, triggering a civil war. In 1969 a coup brought to power a pro-Soviet leader, Colonel Jaafar Nimeiry. Three years later Nimeiry agreed to end the civil war and allow the south more autonomy. Nimeiry, however, began to adopt a more pro-Arab policy and advocated the imposition of strict Islamic (sharia) law, stirring resentment in the south and setting the stage for a renewal of the conflict. Several guerrilla groups emerged in the south, led by the Sudanese People's Liberation Army (SPLA). In 1984 the Nimeiry regime, weakened by war, a severe food shortage and a debt crisis, was ousted in a coup by Brigadier OMAR AL-BASHIR. Bashir proceeded to set up a military government, clamped down on political opposition, and intensified efforts to bring the south to heel. The situation continued to deteriorate; in 1994, 100,000 refugees fled Sudan for temporary shelter in neighboring Uganda. To get food and other necessities to the peoples in beleaguered regions of the south, international aid groups negotiated with the government to create safety zones where aid could be airlifted in without risk of attack. By the mid-1990s the SPLA, led by John Garang, a former officer in the Sudanese army, controlled most of southern Sudan and a number of important towns. For its part, the government controlled Juba, the most important city in the south, as well as several strategically important southern towns along the Nile. Various international efforts to broker a halt to the fighting achieved little success until the parties to the conflict, meeting in Nairobi, finally agreed in 2004 to a peace accord, which included a power-sharing arrangement. In addition, the accord held out the prospect of eventual secession by the south if its inhabitants chose to go their own way. Garang's death in a helicopter accident in 2005 complicated, but did not derail, the peace accord. Ironically, the apparent resolution of the civil war between north and south took place at the same time a new civil war—in a region of western Sudan known as Darfur—was spiraling out of control. In Darfur government-backed Arab militias were pursuing a brutal campaign to drive out black African farmers from their lands, killing tens of thousands of people, burning villages, and stealing livestock. In spite of the crisis in Darfur the Bashir government and the SPLA began to implement the terms of the accord. Even the death only a few months later of the charismatic Garang in a helicopter crash—an apparent accident—failed to derail the agreement. By late summer 2005 top SPLA officials had joined Bashir's government.

Nonetheless, it will require a concerted effort on all sides—and there are serious policy differences among the various guerrilla groups in the south as well—to ensure that the accord takes firm hold. The cost of recovery from the long years of fighting is certain to be enormous and require a generous infusion of international aid. Moreover, it is unclear whether Khartoum would ever allow the south to secede in view of its oil resources.

In 2009 increasing clashes in southern Sudan, many of them involving tribal and ethnic disputes, put more strain on the 2005 peace accord that ended the civil war. More than 2,000 people have been killed in 2009 in these battles and several thousand displaced, but while local populations refer to "tribal war," southern Sudanese leaders and some UN diplomats suspect that they are being instigated by the regime in Khartoum as a way of preventing the possibility of secession in 2011, even though it is enshrined in the peace agreement. Observers have noted the flow of arms

into the south, evidence that the Bashir government might be supplying different factions, which is a policy that it has pursued in the past. Many of the ethnic clashes, whatever their origin, have proven lethal: Villages have been razed, children abducted, and thousands of people internally displaced. In one massacre on March 17, 2009, 700 people were killed. However, the meddling of Khartoum cannot be entirely to blame for the violence and deteriorating conditions. Political leaders in the south have mismanaged the region, failing to implement disarmament plans or addressing the needs of the 1 million displaced southern Sudanese people living in camps on the brink of starvation. Corruption among officials in the south is so rampant that the Finance Ministry is unable to account for what happened to $200 million in international food aid.

The war in the largest country in Africa, with a population of about 30 million, has claimed an estimated 2 million people—about 1 out of every 5—and uprooted 4 million others—almost one in five of the entire Sudanese population. Much of the population remains internally displaced, and hundreds of thousands have taken refuge in other countries. Under the terms of the peace accord, inhabitants of the south have the right to hold a referendum on independence within six years. However, there is no provision for accountability; those responsible for the worst atrocities will apparently face no charges. These atrocities have been committed by all sides in the conflict. The government in the north has systematically prevented food supplies from reaching civilian populations in the south in an effort to starve them, conducting a SCORCHED EARTH policy, displacing whole villages and forcing their inhabitants to take refuge in areas where it is impossible to survive. Those civilians in oil-rich regions have been singled out as targets and subjected to aerial bombardment, strafing of their villages by helicopter gunships, extrajudicial executions of male civilians, massacres, rapes, and abductions, according to AMNESTY INTERNATIONAL. Government troops have been accused of slitting the throats of women and children or nailing them to trees with iron spikes. Rebel forces of the Sudan People's Liberation Army have also been implicated in crimes including summary executions, rape, and the destruction of homes to terrorize civilian populations. The accord does not call for establishing a truth commission (as was the case in South Africa after APARTHEID), nor is there any mention of compensation for the victims. Human rights groups point out that having escaped punishment for past abuses, architects of the atrocities in the civil war are likely to believe that they can perpetuate more crimes in Darfur with the same sense of impunity. According to Amnesty International, the major difference between the results of the scorched earth policy pursued during the civil war and the ethnic cleansing going on in Darfur is only the rate at which the abuses are taking place. While in the north-south conflict it took 20 years to displace 4 million people, government troops and Arab militias needed only two years to push 1.6 million people out of their homes in Darfur.

Civilians have borne the brunt of the war between the army—the Popular Defense Force (PDF)—and the largest armed opposition force, the SPLA. (To replenish the ranks of the PDF, a government conscription law makes military training mandatory for university admission or gaining employment.) But another war was being waged simultaneously; the "other" war, which accounted for the majority of casualties in recent years, took place between various militias allied with the government or with the SPLA. What made the conflict more difficult to comprehend was the tendency of these militias to change sides depending on their interests, the prospect of acquiring more power, or simply because one side offered a more reliable source of arms. Amnesty International says that in the last years of the war, more civilians were being killed as a result of interfactional fighting among southerners than in clashes with government forces. More blame for civilian atrocities attaches to the government, however: Its forces have used helicopter gunships and high-altitude bombardment on populated areas in the south, causing thousands of villagers to abandon their homes. To ensure that the villagers would not return, the army regularly destroyed their crops and stole their livestock.

Race and religion only go so far in explaining why the civil war broke out or why it lasted so long. Oil plays a large role as well: Most of the oil lies in the south, and most of the refineries are located in the north. (Competition for resources also largely accounts for the Darfur conflict, where grazing land is at issue.) When the war began in 1984, one of the first attacks staged by the SPLA targeted Chevron workers. (The giant oil company was planning to build an oil pipeline from oil fields in the south to refineries in Port Sudan in the north.) According to Amnesty International, it is no coincidence that southerners living in oil-rich areas have suffered the worst excesses committed by government forces. A special brigade was even set up to protect oilfields; known as the oil brigade, its fighters are mujahideen—holy warriors—and they are promised martyrdom if they die in combat.

In 1999, Amnesty International says, fighting intensified in areas where foreign petroleum companies had staked exploitation rights. Amnesty and other human rights groups were denied access to the affected areas to investigate complaints of aerial bombardment and strafing of villages and the forcible displacement of populations. The army and allied militias have also perpetrated numerous other atrocities, including rape, mass murders, slitting children's throats, nailing women and children to trees with iron spikes, and crushing people to death with tanks.

Tensions intensified in advance of the national referendum, set for January 2011, which is intended to decide whether the south will secede. An overwhelming number of Sudanese in the south appear likely to vote for secession. Most observers do not expect that Khartoum will allow the south to go its own way without putting up a fight. Proposals to postpone the elections have, however, been rebuffed by the UN, which is to oversee the vote. The prospect of renewed civil war has stirred alarm in the international community. Belatedly, the United States has tried to head off a potential conflict by holding out an olive branch to Khartoum. In November 2010 the Obama administration offered to remove Sudan from its list of state sponsors of terrorism, which the country had been on since 1993, as part of a package of incentives (which also included debt relief, normalized diplomatic relations, and the lifting of sanctions) to allow the referendum to go forward and to honor the results.

See also DARFUR, WAR CRIMES IN; RELIGIOUS PERSECUTION.

Further Reading:
Amnesty International. Sudan Human Rights. Available online. URL: http://www.amnestyusa.org/all-countries/sudan/page.do?id=1011244. Accessed March 17, 2010.

Dodge, Cole P., and Magne Raundelen. *Reaching Children in War: Sudan Uganda and Mozambique.* London: Taylor & Francis, 1992.

Human Rights Today. Sudan Human Rights Violations News. Available online. URL: http://humanrights.einnews.com/news/human-rights-violations/sudan. Accessed March 21, 2010.

Johnson, Douglas Hamilton. *The Root Causes of Sudan's Civil Wars.* Bloomington: Indiana University Press, 2003.

Jok, Jok Madut. *Race, Religion and Violence.* London: Oneworld Publications, 2007.

———. *War and Slavery in Sudan.* Philadelphia: University of Pennsylvania Press, 2001.

Mamdani, Mahmood. *Saviors and Survivors: Darfur, Politics and the War on Terror.* New York: Pantheon, 2009.

Peterson, Scott. *Me against My Brother: At War in Somalia, Sudan and Rwanda.* London: Routledge, 2001.

Rone, Jemera. *Famine in Sudan, 1998: The Human Rights Causes.* New York: Human Rights Watch, 1999.

Salam, A. H. Abdel, and Alexander de Waal, eds. *The Phoenix State: Civil Society and the Future of Sudan.* London: Red Sea Press, 2000.

Sudan Human Rights Organization. Available online. URL: http://www.shro-cairo.org/. Accessed March 21, 2010.

Suharto (Soeharto) (1921–2008) *Indonesian dictator*
The second president of Indonesia, General Suharto was an authoritarian whose term extended for 32 years (1967–98). Under his rule the country became increasingly militarized

and nationalistic, and he used his domination of the country's levers of power to enrich both himself and his family. Suharto—like many Indonesians he uses only one name—was born on June 8, 1921. His parents were poor farmers in central Java, the main island of the sprawling Indonesian archipelago; at the time the country was under Dutch colonial rule. When Japan invaded and drove out the Dutch during World War II, Suharto joined the collaborationist Japanese "self defense corps" and became a battalion commander. When the war ended, the Dutch tried to restore their colonial rule, and armed resistance broke out. Suharto became actively involved in the struggle to throw off Dutch rule, and after Indonesia finally gained its independence in 1949, he rose in the ranks of the new Indonesian army.

In 1963 Suharto led Indonesian forces in a campaign to force the Dutch out of West Irian (now Papua Province). He was subsequently appointed head of a strategic command that was supposed to restore order in the event of a national emergency. The chance to respond to such an emergency arose in 1965 with the outbreak of a leftist uprising. Suharto put down the rebellion at the costs of thousands of lives and, exploiting the crisis, prevailed on Indonesia's first president, Sukarno, to transfer power to him. (Sukarno was placed under house arrest and died in 1970.) Suharto built a strong centralized government, with his political party, the New Order, providing his power base. He had grand designs for Indonesia—politically, economically, and territorially.

In 1975 Indonesian forces annexed East Timor after Portugal, the former colonial power, pulled out. Suharto encouraged Indonesians from Java to move to other parts of the country predominantly populated by ethnic minorities such as East Timor, in a policy of "transmigration" intended to assert centralized authority over the archipelago. He allowed the military free rein and permitted a climate of corruption. In doing so he set the stage for a wave of separatist uprisings that continued to bedevil Indonesia long after he left office.

A staunch anticommunist, Suharto formed close relations with the West and proceeded to develop Indonesia's economy, opening it up to foreign investment. While the economy flourished, the benefits were not distributed equally, and much of the population remained mired in poverty as Suharto's family and friends reaped much of the profits. Meanwhile Suharto used his power to build up his own financial empire. He began by acquiring several flour mills, but by the end of his reign he and his six children could claim the ownership of banks, automobile manufacturers, and cigarette companies. It is believed that he and his children took a considerable portion of an International Monetary Fund (IMF) loan of $43 billion for themselves.

At no point in his long rule did Suharto give any indication of when or if he planned to step down. In 1997 an economic crisis—the "Asian meltdown"—caused the Indonesian currency to plummet and food and fuel prices to rise. The crisis prompted calls for Suharto—about to begin his seventh term—to leave office, but he ignored them. The IMF concluded that no financial rescue package was likely to restore Indonesia's health so long as Suharto remained in power. In 1998 thousands of protesters, many of them university students, took to the streets. In May police fired on a demonstration, resulting in an estimated 500 deaths and setting off two days of rioting, looting, and arson. Even the president's supporters realized that the time had come for him to go, and on May 21 he submitted his resignation. Two years later, corruption charges were filed against the former dictator, but the courts ruled that Suharto's poor health—multiple strokes and digestive and respiratory disorders—prevented a trial. This resulted in violent protests throughout the capital, and the aged dictator was then sentenced to house arrest. Eventually, citing Suharto's failing health, the government dropped the charges that kept the former president under house arrest in 2006. However, in July 2007 another civil suit was filed, seeking $1.1 billion in embezzlement damages (Suharto was suspected of embezzling between $15 billion and $35 billion during his terms), and in December an investigation of human rights abuses was announced, mainly pertaining to 500,000 people who died in Indonesia during the 1960s. On January 27, 2008, Suharto died in a coma at the age of 86 after suffering multiple organ failure.

See also EAST TIMOR, HUMAN RIGHTS VIOLATIONS IN; INDONESIA, HUMAN RIGHTS VIOLATIONS IN.

Further Reading:

King, Peter. *West Papua and Indonesia since Suharto: Independence, Autonomy or Chaos?* Sydney, Australia: University of New South Wales Press, 2004.

Leith, Denise. *The Politics of Power: Freeport in Suharto's Indonesia.* Honolulu: University of Hawaii Press, 2002.

Schwarz, Adam. *A Nation in Waiting: Indonesia's Search for Stability.* Philadelphia: Westview Press, 1999.

Taylor, Jean. *Indonesia: Peoples and Histories.* New Haven, Conn.: Yale University Press, 2003.

Sullivan Principles (Global Sullivan Principles for Corporate Social Responsibility)

The Sullivan Principles, announced in 1977, were intended to put pressure on U.S. companies doing business in South Africa, then under APARTHEID rule, to treat African employees the same way they would American workers. Revised and "relaunched" in 1999, they were called the Global Sullivan Principles for Corporate Social Responsibility. The Sullivan Principles derive their name from the Reverend Leon Sullivan, who created them. In 1971

Sullivan had managed to secure a place on the board of directors at General Motors, which at the time was the largest employer of blacks in South Africa. Sullivan used his position to prod the board to bring pressure to bear on the South African government to reform its apartheid system based on strict segregation of the white minority and black majority. "Starting with the workplace, I tightened the screws step by step and raised the bar step by step," he told an interviewer. "Eventually I got to the point where I said that companies must practice corporate civil disobedience against the laws and I threatened South Africa and said in two years '[Nelson] Mandela must be freed, apartheid must end, and blacks must vote or else I'll bring every American company I can out of South Africa.'"

When Nelson Mandela, the imprisoned leader of the African National Congress, was not freed and apartheid did not end, Sullivan mounted a successful public-relations campaign to bring attention to the principles that bear his name. Thanks to his efforts, more than 100 foreign companies pulled out of South Africa, threatening its economy and hastening the end of the apartheid system. According to Sullivan, the revised 1999 Global Principles call on multinational companies to "encourage companies to support economic, social and political justice wherever they do business." The principles are meant to apply to companies of any size operating in any part of the world. They have been endorsed and implemented by about 100 companies that agree to make a commitment to the principles and demonstrate their compliance. Sullivan, who was awarded the Presidential Medal of Freedom by President George H. W. Bush, died in 2001 at the age of 78.

See also VOLUNTARY CODES OF CONDUCT.

Syria, human rights violations in

Since the death in 2000 of President Hafiz al-Assad, who dominated the country for 30 years, Syria has undergone a gradual loosening of restrictions but there is scant evidence that democratization will occur any time in the near future. After Assad died, the reins of power passed to his son Bashar, a London-trained ophthalmologist, who subsequently freed hundreds of political detainees and allowed political debates. This flirtation with liberalization did not last long, however; more recently the government has moved to suppress dissent. Nonetheless, opponents of autocratic rule, drawing encouragement from the example of SADDAM HUSSEIN's downfall in neighboring Iraq, have become more vocal. If their intention was to test the limits of freedom, these critics quickly found them. In April 2004 a Syrian military court sentenced 14 human rights advocates to three months in prison on the grounds that they belonged to an outlawed organization and had attended a lecture in which speakers called on the government to rescind its emergency law (which has been in effect since the country's revolution in 1963). AMNESTY INTERNATIONAL condemned the judgment, which was subject to appeal. Only a month before, on the 41st anniversary of the Baathist Party coming to power, 25 protesters against the emergency law audaciously demonstrated in front of the Parliament. Reformers said that they had collected 17,000 signatures in support of dismantling the emergency law. The police moved in on the demonstrators, shredding banners and destroying reporters' notebooks.

The Baathist Party, which has about 2 million members, constitutes a parallel or shadow government, but the younger Assad has taken some steps to strip the party of its power and consolidate it in the government. (Until the U.S.-led invasion of Iraq, that country had also been led by the Baathist Party, though the Iraqi and Syrian regimes seldom found common cause.) The regime has responded far more aggressively—and violently—to Kurdish dissent. The toppling of Saddam Hussein's regime has galvanized Syria's minority Kurdish population of 1.5 million (out of 17 million), spurring hopes of greater freedom. Some 200,000 Kurds have been denied Syrian citizenship, which means that they cannot vote or register their land. The government's repression of Kurdish rights stems from fears that Kurds may seek a state of their own. In late March 2004 Kurdish demonstrators in northeastern Syria were fired on by security forces. The riot was precipitated by events at a soccer match when some soccer fans began waving a Kurdish flag and held signs blessing President George W. Bush while chanting, "We will sacrifice our lives for Bush." Opposing fans responded with taunts, and soon fighting broke out. Police were summoned but their presence only exacerbated the unrest. According to Kurdish sources, 14 or 15 people were killed and 60 wounded in two days of rioting. The news set off more demonstrations by Kurds and students in the capital, Damascus. Riot police were deployed around the university and in a largely Kurdish suburb. Syrian human rights organizations rallied to support Kurdish protests, asserting that blame for the killings of unarmed demonstrators rested solely with the security forces. These organizations called for negotiations to ensure greater rights for the Kurdish people rather than resort to a violent crackdown.

The country's Supreme State Security Court has come under fire from human rights groups because of its special role in prosecuting activists, bloggers, and those individuals accused of "insulting the Syrian president" in private conversations. In a 2009 report HUMAN RIGHTS WATCH charged that the court "criminalizes freedom of expression" and restricts lawyers from providing the accused with an adequate defense. The court, which was reestablished in 1992, after a hiatus during the 1980s, has prosecuted thousands of dissidents, 237 of whom were hauled before the court between January 2007 and June 2008. The majority of cases involved Islamists accused of promoting radical ideas, although some were detained for "just being in possession of CDs and books by radical imams, and at the end of the spectrum those accused of being part of al-Qaeda." However, more than 150 bloggers were also put on trial by the court. In many of these cases, Human Rights Watch noted, confessions were elicited by torture, and the charges were frequently vague. The government dismissed the allegations, although rights activists in Damascus hailed the organization's recommendation to abolish the court. "This is not a court. This is just a means to legitimize the rulings of security apparatuses," said Mohammad Abdallah, a Syrian human rights activist living in exile who himself was once tried by the court on charges of distributing false information.

The assassination of former Lebanese prime minister Rafik Hariri in February 2005 precipitated widespread protest against Syria's hegemony over its neighbor. Hariri had been a longtime opponent of the Syrian military deployment in Lebanon, which was originally intended to impose peace after a decade of civil war. Although the Syrians had agreed in principle to withdraw the troops—numbering about 14,000 in 2005—Damascus has continued to stall. In addition to maintaining its troops on Lebanese soil, Syria has exercised political power over Beirut, securing a third term for the pro-Syrian president, which required a change in the constitution. A month after Hariri's slaying, investigators had yet to identify the perpetrators, although many Lebanese attributed the killing to Syria in light of Hariri's plans to run for office again. Unprecedented demonstrations against Syria erupted in Beirut, and both the French and the American governments called upon Syria to pull out its forces and intelligence agents. Even Saudi Arabia and other Arab governments, which traditionally might have been expected to back Damascus, urged Assad to leave Lebanon. Since Syria has reaped considerable economic benefits from Lebanon—some $4 billion annually in revenue from migrant laborers repatriating money as well as involvement in drug smuggling—Damascus is understandably reluctant to loosen its long-standing ties. The consequences of the Lebanese crisis were already being felt in Syria, however, as the Assad regime adopted a defensive posture, cracking down on hard-won freedoms. In late spring 2005 Syria bowed to international pressure and pulled its troops out of Lebanon, though it was believed that it had left many intelligence agents behind to monitor

developments. In September a United Nations inquiry into Hariri's assassination resulted in the arrests of four Lebanese security officials with close ties to Syria, further strengthening suspicions that Damascus was implicated in the slaying in spite of official denials. Speculation was rife in the Syrian capital that high-level figures in the regime, perhaps even Assad himself, might be named as suspects by the UN team, a possibility that might trigger a major political crisis.

The UN inquiry was still under way by the end of 2009, without any indictments having been made. The UN has, however, set up a court—formally known as The Special Tribunal for Lebanon, which is based in The Hague—in anticipation that indictments will be forthcoming. After a seven-day visit to Lebanon in December 2009, Daniel A. Bellemare, the UN prosecutor, announced that the investigation was "making progress and proceeding at full pace." However, by late 2010 the inquiry had become mired in controversy once rumors spread that Hezbollah operatives might be indicted in connection with the assassination. Hezbollah denounced the investigation and threatened retaliation if its members were named by the inquiry. Fears have intensified that any indictment implicating Syria and/or Hezbollah has the potential to cause a political crisis that could topple the fragile Lebanese government and lead to violence.

See also KURDISTAN, SUPPRESSION OF.

Further Reading:
George, Alan. *Syria: Neither Bread nor Freedom.* London: Zed Books, 2003.
Hinnebusch, Raymond. *Syria: Revolution from Above.* London: Routledge, 2002.
Human Rights Watch. Syria Human Rights. Available online. URL: http://www.hrw.org/middle-eastn-africa/syria. Accessed March 21, 2010.
Lesch, David W. *The New Lion of Damascus: Bashar al-Asad and Modern Syria.* New Haven, Conn.: Yale University Press, 2005.
Leverett, Flynt. *Inheriting Syria: Bashar's Trial by Fire.* Washington, D.C.: Brookings Institution Press, 2005.
Rubin, Barry M. *The Truth about Syria.* Basingstoke, U.K.: Palgrave Macmillan, 2007.
Seale, Patrick. *Asad: The Struggle for the Middle East.* Berkeley: University of California Press, 1990.
Syria Human Rights Committee. Available online. URL: http://www.shrc.org/. Accessed March 21, 2010.

T

Tachibana, Yoshio   *See* WAR CRIMINALS OF JAPAN.

Tadić, Dusan   *See* WAR CRIMINALS OF THE FORMER YUGOSLAVIA.

Taliban

The Taliban (derived from the Arabic for Students of Islamic Knowledge Movement) ruled Afghanistan from 1996 until 2001. After taking control of 90 percent of Afghan territory with the backing of neighboring Pakistan, the Taliban imposed a strict fundamentalist strain of Islam on the country. In 1996 Taliban leader MULLAH OMAR allowed the AL-QAEDA leader Osama bin Laden to establish camps in Afghanistan to train and arm Islamic militants. In December 2001 the Taliban was driven from power by American forces after Mullah Omar refused to hand over bin Laden, who had orchestrated the 9/11 (2001) attacks on New York and Washington, D.C.

Originally the Taliban were made up of mujahideen (holy warriors), who had fought the Soviet occupation of their country for 10 years. However, unlike other mujahideen who fought for various warlords, the Taliban drew their recruits from religious students, many of whom studied in the Islamic madrassas, or religious schools, in Pakistan. With arms clandestinely supplied by Pakistan, the Taliban overcame rival factions and seized power, taking the capital of Kabul in 1996. (Mullah Omar nonetheless continued to rule from his tribal stronghold in Kandahar.) Initially the Taliban enjoyed considerable popularity as it succeeded in restoring order to a country that had been plunged into near anarchy by factional and tribal fighting. But order came at a high cost: The Taliban introduced sharia, or Islamic, law, which banned television, the playing of music, the Internet, and even kite flying, which were denounced as frivolous or heretical. Women were forced to wear burkas—garments that covered them from head to toe—and were barred from public life. Girls could not attend school, and women were not permitted to work. Violators could be beaten, stoned to death, or shot by special vice police.

Throughout the years of Taliban rule, the country never knew peace. The Taliban were unable to dislodge their opposition, known as the Northern Alliance, nominally headed by the former president Burhanuddin Rabbani. In spite of successive Taliban offensives, the Northern Alliance managed to cling to about 10 percent of Afghan territory in the north. The Taliban were mainly Sunni Pashtuns (the largest of Afghanistan's several tribes), whereas the Northern Alliance was composed of Tajiks, Hazara, Uzbeks, and Turkmen. In its six years in power, the Taliban was only recognized by three countries—Saudi Arabia, Pakistan, and the United Arab Emirates. Nor did it win any friends by ordering the destruction of the 2000-year-old Buddhist statues of Bamian in March 2001, declaring that representations of the human figure were contrary to teachings of the Quran. (Many other precious Afghan antiquities were destroyed for the same reason.) Nevertheless, the Taliban might have remained in power longer if it had not been so quick to embrace bin Laden's terrorist organization. In addition to a common ideology, the Taliban was also beholden to bin Laden because they needed his money.

By the time the United States invaded Afghanistan, the Taliban had already split into opposing factions. Although most of the Taliban fighters surrendered or took flight across the border into Pakistan, its leaders retain an ability to make trouble for the new Afghan authorities. Taliban insurgents regularly stage guerrilla attacks, kidnapping and killing government officials, aid workers, and construction crews. Schools for girls have been bombed or forced to close because of threats. At the same time, the government of Hamid Karzai has made overtures to more moderate Taliban elements, raising the prospect that some former Taliban fighters could eventually be incorporated into the government and security forces.

The Taliban has proven more resilient and stronger than the United States had anticipated. Throughout 2008 and 2009, Taliban forces were able to launch attacks across the country, including the north, which had been relatively tranquil since the U.S. invasion in 2001. Taliban militants have repeatedly struck in the heart of Kabul too, attacking government institutions, hotels, and diplomatic residences. They have targeted aid agencies and NGOs, forcing many aid workers to evacuate the country. After eight years of war, U.S. forces found themselves on the defensive. The resurgence of the Taliban prompted President Obama to authorize deploying an additional 30,000 U.S. troops to Afghanistan, beginning in 2010, bringing the U.S. contingent in the country to about 100,000. NATO has also contributed several thousand forces (with the U.K., Germany, and Canada dispatching the largest contingents). However, many analysts do not believe that victory over the Taliban is possible. For one thing, they point out, the Taliban can move back and forth across the porous border with Pakistan practically at will. Because Pakistan is a nominal ally of the United States, Coalition forces are prohibited from engaging in hot pursuit. As a result, the United States has deployed unmanned drones in attempts to kill Taliban and al-Qaeda leaders. The Pakistanis have shown little willingness to suppress the Taliban, partly because of historical and ethnic ties (the Taliban came to power with the backing of the Pakistani military) and partly because of its usefulness as a proxy force to counter the influence of Pakistan's rival INDIA after the United States withdraws from Afghanistan. (The Taliban, which is mainly drawn from the Pashtun ethnic group, also enjoys support from Pashtun tribes in the Northwest Frontier Province of Pakistan near the Afghan border.) There is no indication that Pakistani intelligence or security forces have moved to shut down the so-called Quetta Shura, the Taliban base in the city of Quetta. By all accounts, Mullah Omar was still the leader of the group by the end of 2009. In Afghanistan the Taliban has established a kind of shadow government that imposes law and collects taxes in many regions of the country. This makes it difficult for the central government in Kabul to exercise much or any authority, especially in the absence of security. Moreover, the central government is considered so corrupt that it has squandered much of its goodwill. The disillusionment only intensified after Karzai

Under the Taliban, many women in Afghanistan were reduced to begging in the streets in order to survive. *(Shutterstock)*

supporters engaged in massive fraud to ensure his reelection. However, the Taliban has committed so many killings and human rights abuses as well that most Afghans are unlikely to welcome its return to power.

See also AFGHANISTAN, HUMAN RIGHTS VIOLATIONS IN; HAZARA, PERSECUTION OF; PAKISTAN, HUMAN RIGHTS VIOLATIONS IN; WAR ON TERROR.

Further Reading:

Anderson, J. L., and Thomas Dworzak. *Taliban.* London: Trolley, 2003.

Burke, Jason. *Al-Qaeda: Casting a Shadow of Terror.* London: I. B. Tauris, 2004.

———. *Al-Qaeda: The True Story of Radical Islam.* London: I. B. Tauris, 2004.

Council on Foreign Relations. *The Taliban in Afghanistan.* Available online. URL: http://www.cfr.org/publication/10551/. Accessed March 21, 2010.

CNN.com. The Taliban. Available online. URL: http://topics.edition.cnn.com/topics/the_taliban. Accessed March 21, 2010.

Guardian.co.uk. World News Taliban. Available online. URL: http://www.guardian.co.uk/world/taliban. Accessed March 21, 2010.

Rashid, Ahmed. *Jihad: The Rise of Militant Islam in Central Asia.* New York: Penguin Books, 2003.

———. *Taliban: Militant Islam, Oil and Fundamentalism in Central Asia.* New Haven, Conn.: Yale University Press, 2001.

Zayy-at, Montasser al-. *The Road to Al-Qaeda: The Story of bin Laden's Right-Hand Man.* Critical Studies on Islam. Translated by Ahmed Fekry. Edited by Sara Nimis. Ann Arbor, Mich.: Pluto Press, 2004.

Tamenori, Soto *See* WAR CRIMINALS OF JAPAN.

Tamil Tigers (Liberation Tigers of Tamil Eelam)

The long struggle by the Liberation Tigers of Tamil Eelam (LTTE) to gain independence for the ethnic Tamil region in the north of SRI LANKA came to a bloody end in 2009. The LTTE made a last stand in a sliver of territory in the Jaffna Peninsula before being crushed by Sri Lankan army forces. In the final battle, their leader VELLUPILLAI PRABHAKARAN was slain. The conflict was modern Asia's longest running war. The LTTE's losses came to some 3,000 dead; about 25,000 were wounded, many of them probably civilians. "We remain with one last choice—to remove the last weak excuse of the enemy for killing our people. We have decided to silence our guns," said a pro-rebel spokesperson. It was a departure for the Tigers, who were known to kill themselves rather than surrender. The group was condemned for having embraced a cult of suicide. (Some Tigers were said to wear cyanide capsules around their necks to use in the event of capture.) True to the ruthlessness that they had shown in the long years of warfare (broken briefly in 2005 by a cease-fire), the Tigers refused to permit the evacuation of 50,000–100,000 people trapped by the fighting and even killed some of those who tried to flee. (The Sri Lankan army was also widely criticized for indiscriminate firing into civilian zones.)

Founded in 1976, the Tigers sprang up in response to discrimination by the majority Sinhalese. The Tigers began a civil war with the Sri Lankan government in 1983, relying on guerrilla tactics characterized by acts of terror, atrocities, child recruitment, and numerous human rights abuses. The Tamil Tigers of Sri Lanka had a deserved reputation as one of the most organized and brutal terrorist groups in the world. At their peak, they could mobilize 5,000 to 10,000 guerrillas. They established a special unit known as the Black Tigers, which staged spectacular bombings of targets including public buildings, transportation hubs, and Buddhist temples. (The Tamils are mostly Hindu.) The Tigers introduced suicide bombing to the world years before it became a common form of terrorism in the Middle East. They also were the first to use female suicide bombers. Before their defeat, they could claim more than 200 such bombings, according to the Council on Foreign Relations. The Tamils also were able to deploy ground and sea forces armed with rockets and grenade launchers and could boast of assassinating one president of Sri Lanka and the prime minister of India (in retaliation for Indian intervention in the conflict). The Tamils relied on financing from drug smuggling and bank robberies as well as from ethnic Tamils in western Europe and Canada. Some analysts estimated that they were able to raise up to $200 million annually. But over a year after the war there was no indication that the insurgents had the will or ability to mount attacks. In July 2010, the UN refugee commission (UNHCR) declared that Sri Lanka had made substantial progress in resettling the refugees of the conflict, noting in its report that "the security situation in Sri Lanka had significantly stabilized, paving the way for a lasting solution for hundreds of thousands of internally displaced persons (IDPs) in the country's north and east." As of June 2010, the government had succeeded in returning 246,000 displaced persons to their homes out of nearly 270,000. Arrangements were being made to return the remainder as well. However, the resettlement effort was hamstrung by the presence of some 1.5 million antipersonnel mines planted in the north and east of the country, areas previously controlled by the Tamil Tigers, from which the refugees had fled.

See also SRI LANKA, HUMAN RIGHTS VIOLATIONS IN.

Further Reading:
BBC.co.uk. "Sri Lanka's Rebel Leader 'Killed.'" (May 19, 2009). Available online. URL: http://news.bbc.co.uk/2/hi/8055015.stm. Accessed March 20, 2010.

De Votta, Neil. *Blowback: Linguistic Nationalism, Institutional Decay, and Ethnic Conflict in Sri Lanka.* Contemporary Issues in Asia and the Pacific. Stanford, Calif.: Stanford University Press, 2004.

Tambiah, Stanley Jeyaraja. *Buddhism Betrayed?: Religion, Politics, and Violence in Sri Lanka.* A Monograph of the World Institute for Development Economics Research. Chicago: University Of Chicago Press, 1992.

Winslow, Deborah, and Michael Woost, eds. *Economy, Culture, and Civil War in Sri Lanka.* Bloomington: Indiana University Press, 2004.

Ta Mok   (Chhit Choeun) (1926–2006)   *Khmer Rouge leader*

Chhit Choeun was a leader of the Khmer Rouge, a fanatic communist insurgency that terrorized Cambodia—in and out of power—for decades. His reputation for savagery is underscored by his nom de guerre Ta Mok, which means "Grandfather Butcher." Ta Mok, a onetime Buddhist monk, played a critical role in the murder of between 1.5 and 2 million people who perished during the four years the Khmer Rouge ruled Cambodia. His power base lay with tribes in the southwestern part of Cambodia, and in 1975 he joined in an alliance with POL POT, the leader of the Khmer Rouge. He even supplied Pol Pot—otherwise known as "Brother No. 1"—with his bodyguards. (He also surrounded himself with bodyguards, all of whom were women.) Over the next two years, Ta Mok provided Pol Pot with the backing he needed to eliminate all internal opposition and enabled him to initiate a campaign of terror against the local population. Elements of Ta Mok's party fanned out from their base in the southwest into other parts of the country to carry out a purge of Pol Pot's enemies within the Khmer Rouge. In 1975 the guerrillas seized the capital, Phnom Penh, and proceeded to unleash a reign of terror. Ta Mok was given control over the army, and his chief lieutenant, Mit Deuch, was appointed head of the secret police.

In 1979 the Vietnamese invaded Cambodia and defeated the Khmer Rouge, which soon resumed guerrilla warfare from bases in the mountainous north. As commander of the northern zone, Ta Mok continued to exercise considerable influence in the Khmer Rouge insurgency. By 1997, though, internal dissension had erupted in the leadership. Ta Mok and two other top Khmer Rouge leaders, Nuon Chea and Khieu Samphan, turned against Pol Pot and placed him under house arrest. (Pol Pot died soon afterward.) But in 1998, other elements of the Khmer Rouge rebelled against Ta Mok, the last major Khmer Rouge leader still at large, and in March that year he was captured by the Cambodian army on the Thai border. Within two days he was charged under a 1994 law banning the Khmer Rouge. In February 2002 he was charged with crimes against humanity and placed in solitary confinement. Hun Sen, the Cambodian prime minister, warned that Ta Mok might implicate important political leaders who had had ties with the Khmer Rouge and in the process jeopardize moves toward national reconciliation. Hun Sen did, however, say that he supported a proposal for a tribunal to try former Khmer Rouge leaders with the assistance of the United Nations, but by 2004 efforts to organize such a tribunal were being hampered by the government's demands. Human rights organizations continued to voice concerns that without international involvement, the trial of Ta Mok and his colleagues would not be seen as fair. Cambodia "deserves better than a show trial," AMNESTY INTERNATIONAL declared. In an interview from prison, Ta Mok has said that he knew only "a fraction" of what went on during the years that the Khmer Rouge ruled the country. Then he went on to say, "Sometimes I think we are cursed. Everybody takes from this country. So few people give anything. Everybody betrays us in the end." Ta Mok died of natural causes on July 21, 2006, in a military hospital. His death ensured that he would never stand trial for his crimes.

See also CAMBODIA, WAR CRIMES IN.

Further Reading:
Hinton, Alexander Laban, and Robert Jay Lifton. *Why Did They Kill?: Cambodia in the Shadow of Genocide.* California Series in Public Anthropology, Vol. 11. Berkeley: University of California Press, 2004.

Kiernan, Ben. *How Pol Pot Came to Power: Colonialism, Nationalism, and Communism in Cambodia, 1930–1975.* New Haven, Conn.: Yale University Press, 2004.

———. *The Pol Pot Regime: Race, Power, and Genocide in Cambodia under the Khmer Rouge, 1975–79.* New Haven, Conn.: Yale University Press, 2002.

Pran, Dith, comp. *Children of Cambodia's Killing Fields: Memoirs by Survivors.* Edited by Kim DePaul. New Haven, Conn.: Yale University Press, 1999.

Short, Philip. *Pol Pot: Anatomy of a Nightmare.* New York: Holt Rinehart, 2005.

Ung, Loung. *First They Killed My Father: A Daughter of Cambodia Remembers.* New York: Perennial, 2001.

Tatoune, Jean   *See* HAITIAN HUMAN RIGHTS VIOLATORS.

Taylor, Charles "Chuckie" (1977–   ) *Liberian*
paramilitary leader

In January 2009 Charles "Chuckie" Taylor, the son of the former Liberian dictator, CHARLES GHANKAY TAYLOR, was convicted for killings and torture of his father's enemies during the civil war in LIBERIA in the late 1990s. Because the younger Taylor was born in the United States, it was possible to try him under a 14-year-old law holding U.S. citizens liable for crimes committed abroad. The atrocities he perpetrated were carried out while he was the commander of a paramilitary security force called the Antiterrorist Unit—known as the "Demon Forces"—that was set up to protect his father, who was then president of Liberia. He was convicted for a variety of crimes, which included applying electric shocks to the genitals of his victims; burning them with cigarettes, hot irons, and melting plastic; rubbing salt in their open wounds; throwing them naked into pits covered with iron bars, and subjecting them to stinging ants. He was also reported to have stopped a group of suspected rebels and choosing three of them for summary execution. In another incident, he ordered the beheading of a captive. "The acts of which he was convicted were horrific," the federal prosecutor said after Taylor was sentenced to 97 years in prison. "It's the first [case] of its kind but that doesn't mean it's the last of its kind." Taylor was born Charles Emmanuel in Boston in 1971 but is usually referred to by his nickname, Chuckie. He was arrested in Miami in 2006 and charged with lying about his father's identity on a passport application. "I am sorry, my brothers and sisters, for what has happened to you during the conflict," Taylor told victims and their families in the courtroom prior to his sentencing. Nonetheless, he continued to maintain his innocence.

Taylor, Charles Ghankay (Charles MacArthur
Dapkana Taylor) (1948–   ) *Liberian dictator*

Until he was unceremoniously sent into exile, Charles MacArthur Dapkana Taylor was one of Africa's most feared despots. Had he only terrorized his native Liberia—first as the leader of a savage insurgency and then as the country's president—he would have deserved his ignominious reputation. But he was also instrumental in instigating a reign of terror in the neighboring West African state of Sierra Leone.

The creation of former slaves sent to America in 1847, Liberia is the oldest black African republic. Unfortunately, its historic distinction has been overshadowed by corruption, exploitation, and repression. In the early 1990s Taylor was merely one of several warlords competing for power, but he proved more adept—and ruthless—than his rivals. The disintegration of the state had begun in 1980 with a coup led by an army master sergeant named Samuel Doe.

Until then Liberia had been dominated by the descendants of the freed African-American slaves. Taylor was born into one of these aristocratic families in 1948 but later, perhaps to make his name sound more "African," adopted Ghankay as his middle name. Following the example of other sons and daughters of the Liberian elite, he was sent to the United States to pursue his studies, returning home shortly after Doe's successful coup.

Doe saw in Charles Taylor a useful ally. Taylor, however, had no loyalties other than to himself. He was determined to back Doe only so long as it suited him. Unwisely, Doe put him in charge of the General Services Agency, which allowed Taylor to control—and plunder—much of the country's budget. Accused of stealing $1 million, he fled to the United States. But far from finding refuge, he was detained in the Plymouth County House of Correction in Massachusetts, under a Liberian extradition warrant. While he insisted on his innocence, he did not stick around to face charges. How he escaped prison is in dispute. There are stories that he managed to saw through the bars, but some conspiracy theorists maintain that his escape was abetted by Americans who were interested in using him to rid Liberia of Doe's corrupt regime.

On Christmas Eve, 1989, not long after his return, Taylor launched an insurrection intended to bring down his former patron. A shrewd tactician, he had already built up a vast and far-flung network of supporters and foreign allies. He counted among his friends the radical Colonel Muammar al-Gadhafi of Libya and the conservative Félix Houphouet-Boigny, then ruler of Ivory Coast, as well as a host of shady businessmen and arms dealers. Taylor was by no means alone in his quest to topple Doe. Other factions, equally as murderous, were also competing for power. Doe was finally abducted by elements of a rival force and executed.

Liberians who had hoped that Doe's death would restore order to the country were grievously mistaken. The next five years were marked by tribal and factional violence that brought ruin to the country. When a Nigerian-brokered peace accord was reached in 1995, Taylor had emerged as de facto ruler. Two years later he officially consolidated power, winning election for president though there is considerable evidence that he secured his victory only by intimidating his opponents. In the immediate aftermath of the elections, he made a show of instituting democratic government, bringing rival political leaders into his government. By 1999, however, with the withdrawal of Nigerian peacekeepers, he reverted to form, cracking down on opponents and shutting down independent newspapers and radio stations.

Taylor was not content simply to rule one country. He had designs on the diamond wealth of neighboring Sierra Leone as well. To this end he sponsored a civil war spearheaded by FODAY SANKOH, a former corporal and TV cameraman whose violent temperament matched his own. Diamond wealth fueled the conflict in Sierra Leone even as it allowed Taylor to maintain his grip on power in Liberia's capital, Monrovia.

Braggadocio has always been one of Taylor's most outstanding traits. In 1999 he went before a prayer meeting clad from head to toe in white to repudiate accusations by the United Nations that he was an arms dealer. A lay preacher in the Baptist Church, he prayed for forgiveness even as he continued to insist on his innocence. He freely gave interviews to the BBC, though he largely remained out of sight of his own people. When a BBC commentator pointed out that many people in the world considered him a murderer, he countered by saying that Jesus Christ had also been accused of being a murderer in his time.

Opposition to Taylor erupted into civil war. A rebel group called Liberians United for Reconciliation and Democracy (LURD) rose up in the countryside, and soon government forces were in retreat. By 2002 Taylor's control was reduced to the environs of Monrovia. He blamed Guinea, a neighboring state, for supporting the rebels and ordered retaliatory strikes aimed at Guinea border towns, widening the war and precipitating a refugee crisis.

In June 2003 Taylor was indicted on 17 violations of INTERNATIONAL HUMANITARIAN LAW, war crimes, and CRIMES AGAINST HUMANITY by the SPECIAL COURT FOR SIERRA LEONE. The charges stemmed from Taylor's involvement in the decade-long civil war in Sierra Leone, which ended in 2002. Specifically, the indictment found him in violation of Article 6.1 and 6.3 of the court's statute, which allows high-ranking officials to be held individually criminally responsible. Taylor was held accountable for attacks meant to terrorize civilian populations, which, according to the indictment, included "unlawful killings, physical and sexual violence against civilian men, women, and children, abductions and looting and destruction of civilian property." Taylor was also charged with several additional crimes, including sexual slavery, FORCED LABOR, forced combat training for children, and using physical mutilation as a form of intimidation.

Taylor ignored the indictments, but he could not ignore the mounting threat to his regime from rebel forces. Monrovia itself became engulfed in chaos as rebels moved on the capital. Under international pressure, he finally agreed to leave office but, fearing arrest, made his resignation contingent on an offer of sanctuary from another government. Although human rights organizations vehemently objected to any agreement that would allow him to go free, the Bush administration tacitly supported exile. Otherwise it was believed that he would make a last stand, subjecting the Liberian population to even more suffering. In August 2003, after days of hesitation, he finally stepped down, but he refused to climb aboard the plane waiting to spirit him into exile in Nigeria before holding a press conference. Declaring that he would one day return to reclaim power, he gave every indication that Liberians would welcome him back.

In 2006, three years after finding refuge in Nigeria, Taylor was arrested after then president of Nigeria, Olusegun Obasanjo, bowed to international pressure to turn him over to the Special Court for Sierra Leone. Taylor was outraged. "I stepped down as promised," he said, lamenting that he was "treated like a common criminal." He insisted that all pending war crimes charges against him had been annulled by an unwritten agreement with African leaders in exchange for his relinquishing office. Because he still had supporters in Liberia, he was transferred to The Hague in The Netherlands, becoming the first African head of state to be tried for war crimes. Among other charges, he was accused of murder, conscripting child soldiers, and terrorizing and mutilating civilians. (The latter charges related to his support of rebels in Sierra Leone.) When he finally took the stand in 2009 before a panel of four international judges, he immediately asserted his innocence and called himself a "democrat" and "a family man." Prosecutors called 91 witnesses, including victims of the wars in Liberia and Sierra Leone and child soldiers who had been forcibly recruited. The prosecution hoped to show that Taylor had shipped weapons to fuel the war in Sierra Leone and had enriched his regime using diamonds pillaged from that country. He denied that he bore responsibility for the atrocities committed by rebel groups in Sierra Leone, asserting that while he had heard about the amputations and rapes, he had found them "a little strange" and would "never, never, ever" have permitted such crimes. He similarly denied illicit traffic in diamonds, reportedly smuggled in mayonnaise jars. "Never, ever," Taylor said, "whether it's a mayonnaise or coffee or whatever jar." While the indictment only covered five years, his legal team said that they would need to bring up 15 years of events in order "to explain and refute allegations." Taylor withstood all attempts by prosecutors to admit wrongdoing, denying accusations that he looted his country's treasury—a covert $14 million bank account was established, he said, only to avoid outside scrutiny, not so he could enrich himself—or ran smuggling operations of weapons and diamonds. He insisted that he was not responsible for recruiting child soldiers or was involved in atrocities conducted by allies in neighboring Sierra Leone. On the contrary, he asserted that he had settled factional disputes and freed abducted UN peacekeepers. At the end of 2009, the prosecution rested. The fate of the tribunal hearing his case was uncertain because of budgetary concerns. The tribunal requires more than $18 million a year—Taylor's legal team alone costs the tribunal $1 million—and pledges from donor nations had still fallen short.

See also CONFLICT DIAMONDS; LIBERIA, HUMAN RIGHTS VIOLATIONS IN; SIERRA LEONE, HUMAN RIGHTS VIOLATIONS IN.

Further Reading:
Adebajo, Adekeye. *Building Peace in West Africa: Liberia, Sierra Leone, and Guinea-Bissau.* International Peace Academy Occasional Paper Series. Boulder, Colo.: Lynne Rienner Publishers, 2002.
———. *Liberia's Civil War: Nigeria, ECOMOG, and Regional Security in West Africa.* Boulder, Colo.: Lynne Rienner Publishers, 2002.
Ellils, Stephen. *The Mask of Anarchy: The Destruction of Liberia and the Religious Dimension of an African Civil War.* New York: New York University Press, 2001.
Kulah, Arthur F. *Liberia Will Rise Again: Reflections on the Liberian Civil Crisis.* Nashville, Tenn.: Abingdon Press, 1999.
Mohammed, Amos. *The Role of the Economic Community of the West African States: ECOWAS—Conflict Management in Liberia.* Bloomington, Ind.: Authorhouse, 2003.
Pham, John-Peter. *Liberia: Portrait of a Failed State.* London: Reed Press, 2004.

Taylor, Telford (1908–1998) *American prosecutor*
Telford Taylor achieved fame as a lead prosecutors of Nazi war criminals at the second round of NUREMBERG TRIALS after World War II. But Taylor, an army colonel at the time of the first trials, was more than a prosecutor since he also helped draft the rules for how such war criminals as HERMANN GÖRING and RUDOLF HESS were to be prosecuted. Until Nuremberg there was little precedent to rely upon for such proceedings.

Taylor was born on February 24, 1908, in Schenectady, New York. He showed promise as a jazz musician but found his true calling in government after graduating from Harvard Law School in 1932. It was not long before he entered government service, and over the next several years he held various legal posts in the Department of Interior, the Agricultural Adjustment Administration, the Senate Interstate Commerce Committee, the Department of Justice, and the Federal Communications Commission. When the United States entered World War II, he joined Army Intelligence. In 1943, promoted to lieutenant colonel, he became military attaché in the U.S. Embassy in London. He was a full colonel by 1944 at a time when Allied leaders were deliberating over how to deal with Nazi war criminals.

In the first group of Nuremberg Trials, Taylor served as assistant to ROBERT HOUGHWOUT JACKSON, the princi-

U.S. brigadier general Telford Taylor, who prosecuted top Nazis at the Nuremberg Trials *(Library of Congress)*

pal prosecutor for the Allies (Britain, France, the United States, and the Soviet Union). Before Nuremberg, some suspected war criminals were tried in national courts under a variety of laws. There was strong resistance among many Allied leaders to try Nazi officials in an international forum. British prime minister Winston Churchill was in favor of simply shooting Nazi leaders without a trial once they were caught and identified. JOSEPH STALIN, the Soviet dictator, also supported the idea of executing war criminals without troubling with legal formalities. Taylor, on the other hand, argued for an international trial, cautioning against holding "a scattering of small trials" because they would carry no weight "whereas the world's eyes and ears would be fastened on a big international trial." In the end, his was a view that prevailed. Both Taylor and Jackson also believed that it was possible to distinguish gradations of guilt even when confronted with suspects who had committed reprehensible acts. In other words, an industrialist who made profits off slave labor was not necessarily as culpable as a Nazi officer who had given the orders to execute thousands of civilians or a doctor who had performed MEDICAL

EXPERIMENTS on helpless children. Above all, the prosecutors—both Americans—were anxious that the trials not be considered a sham that allowed the victors to take revenge against the defeated. Taylor also believed that the trials could bring to an end a tragic chapter in Germany's history and pave the way for Germany to regain its former place in the international community. Germany would not be treated as a pariah state, Taylor believed, if there were not to be a recurrence of the same conditions that led to the Second World War.

Twenty-two top Nazi officials were brought to trial; 19 were convicted and 12 sentenced to death. (Göring escaped execution by committing suicide.) After the first round of trials ended in 1946, Jackson left his post and Taylor was promoted to brigadier general and appointed lead prosecutor in his place. In the second round of trials, Taylor indicted 23 German doctors and scientists—"infantile sadists" in his words; the only science they knew, he said, was the "science of inducing death." Taylor also prosecuted a number of Nazi officials and judges, industrialists, and SS officers. These trials ended in 1949—not entirely successfully from Taylor's point of view; ALFRED KRUPP, head of I. G. Farben Chemical, who was accused of using slave labor in his factories, won acquittal because of a lack of evidence. Nonetheless, Taylor did win several convictions of other defendants including 13 SS officers. Thirty-seven defendants were sentenced to death, and 64 others received prison sentences although some were subsequently commuted. Taylor later had cause to regret the longest sentence, which was given to Hess. Hess was held in Spandau Prison in Berlin for over 40 years—the only prisoner in the facility—until he killed himself at age 93. "Such long-continued incarceration," Taylor noted, was itself "a crime against humanity."

When he returned to the United States Taylor practiced law, but when the Korean War broke out he agreed to become administrator of the Small Defense Plants Administration at President Truman's behest. In the early 1950s he became an outspoken critic of Senator Joseph McCarthy, who conducted a vitriolic anticommunist campaign that Taylor denounced as "a vicious weapon of the extreme right against their political opponents." McCarthy, Taylor said at a speech at West Point in 1953, was "a dangerous adventurer." In response, McCarthy intimated that Taylor had somehow become linked with communists himself, an allegation that had no basis in fact. Taylor, undeterred, continued to criticize the senator.

In the late 1960s, Taylor, now a professor of law at Columbia University, proved to be just as vigorous in his opposition to U.S. policy in Vietnam. In 1971 he called for a national commission to investigate the origins and prosecution of the war. In 1972 he repudiated the bombing of Hanoi by American warplanes as "immoral and senseless."

A year later he joined a delegation (which included folk singer Joan Baez) that traveled to North Vietnam, where he visited prisoner-of-war camps. Not unexpectedly, he weighed in on the trial of Lieutenant William Calley, who was charged with ordering a massacre of unarmed Vietnamese civilians in My Lai. Taylor argued that Calley—the only individual convicted in the atrocity—had been made a scapegoat and that officials in the White House and Pentagon should also be held accountable. In the 1980s, in a departure from his usual assignments, Taylor's services were called upon by the National Basketball Association as a special master to resolve legal disputes.

Taylor was the author of several books that include *Grand Inquest: The Story of Congressional Investigations, Sword and Swastika, The March of Conquest, The Breaking Wave,* and *Munich: The Price of Peace.* A few years before his death on May 22, 1998, he commented on the war then raging in Bosnia, characterized by the worst atrocities in Europe since World War II. "We must never forget that the record on which we judge these defendants is the record on which history will judge us tomorrow," he declared. "To pass these defendants a poisoned chalice is to put it to our lips as well. . . . The wrongs which we seek to condemn and punish have been so calculated, so malignant, and so devastating, that civilization cannot tolerate their being ignored, because it cannot survive their being repeated. . . ."

See also MY LAI MASSACRE.

Further Reading:

Ferencz, Benjamin B., and Telford Taylor. *Less Than Slaves: Jewish Forced Labor and the Quest for Compensation.* Bloomington: Indiana University Press, 2002.
Taylor, Telford. *The Anatomy of the Nuremberg Trials: A Personal Memoir.* New York: Knopf, 1992.
———. *Munich: The Price of Peace.* New York: Random House, 1980.
———. *Nuremberg and Vietnam: An American Tragedy.* New York: Times Books, 1970.

terrorism and international humanitarian law

The September 11, 2001, terrorist attacks on the United States and the subsequent war on terror have confronted advocates of INTERNATIONAL HUMANITARIAN LAW (IHL) with a dilemma. How is it possible to justify applying the same laws to terrorists that govern the treatment of legitimate combatants and PRISONERS OF WAR (POWs)? On the one hand, the GENEVA CONVENTIONS and other relevant treaties establish rights for prisoners of war and the treatment of enemy combatants. On the other hand, terrorists and terrorist organizations are not parties to these agreements and willfully violate protections for civilians set out by many of these same accords. The Bush administration, for instance, has taken the view—disputed by many human rights advocates and called into question by several U.S. federal courts—that terrorists have no rights under the Geneva Conventions, the 1977 ADDITIONAL PROTOCOLS TO THE GENEVA CONVENTIONS, or the protections guaranteed to citizens under the U.S. Constitution. The U.S. Justice Department has even sought to treat American citizens suspected of supporting or participating in terrorist organizations as exempt from constitutional guarantees such as DUE PROCESS.

There are several explicit references to terrorism in IHL, even though it does not provide a definition of terrorism. The Fourth Geneva Convention of 1949 (Article 33) states that "Collective penalties and likewise all measures of intimidation or of terrorism are prohibited." Additional Protocol I (Article 51) states: "The civilian population as such, as well as individual civilians, shall not be the object of attack. Acts or threats of violence the primary purpose of which is to spread terror among the civilian population are prohibited." Additional Protocol II (Articles 4 and 13) prohibits "acts of terrorism" against persons not or no longer taking part in hostilities. Terrorism would also be classified as COLLECTIVE PUNISHMENT of civilians, a practice outlawed by IHL as well. (IHL does, however, include qualifications that permit attacks on military objectives or measures undertaken for military security that may have a negative impact on civilians.) The basic criterion relating to the treatment of civilians in combat is based on adherence to the "principle of distinction." This principle, considered the cornerstone of IHL, requires belligerents to distinguish between military and civilian objectives and protects civilians in wartime from deliberate targeting, deportation (with a few limited exceptions), and hostage taking, as well as protecting property vital to civilians from intentional destruction such as dams, power plants, and irrigation systems.

In peacetime, acts against a civilian population or civilian property would be classified as war crimes. Under the principle of UNIVERSAL JURISDICTION, war crimes can be prosecuted by any state even if its citizens were not directly involved and the act did not take place on its territory. In that respect, terrorism does not constitute a legally recognized armed conflict. IHL recognizes that there must be parties to a conflict. These parties may be states, but they can also be rebel groups if they meet certain criteria: They must have a military organization, for instance, and have a formal command structure. IHL applies equally to all parties to a conflict, whether aggressor or defender. It requires all belligerents to adhere to provisions protecting civilians. This implies parity between the adversaries and, in addition, makes a distinction between law enforcement and military action. Suppression of a violent protest by police and security forces, for instance, would not be covered by IHL because the protesters did not meet the criteria for an insurgent group.

The INTERNATIONAL COMMITTEE OF THE RED CROSS (ICRC) has weighed in on the application of IHL to the war on terrorism. It has issued a fact sheet (though not an institutional opinion), indicating that the war launched by the United States against Afghanistan in the wake of the 9/11 attacks was an armed conflict under the definition of IHL, specifically the Fourth Geneva Convention, as well as the rules of CUSTOMARY LAW. But waging a "war on terrorism," in the ICRC's assessment, does not necessarily meet the definition of an armed conflict because the element of parity is absent—that is, there are not two recognizable parties to the conflict. Most incidents of violence described as "terrorist," says the ICRC, are "perpetrated by loosely organized groups (networks), or individuals that, at best, share a common ideology." According to the ICRC, that makes it "doubtful" whether these groups and networks can be characterized as a "party" to a conflict within the meaning of IHL. This therefore suggests that such acts should be treated as crimes better addressed by either international or domestic law enforcement. In other words, the ICRC suggests, these acts are not covered by IHL because they do not take place in the context of armed conflict. By the same token, measures taken by states to combat or prevent terrorism do not amount to military actions in an armed conflict, but rather involve measures undertaken by the judiciary and police as well as policies and tactics adopted by international law-enforcement agencies such as Interpol. Many antiterrorism measures do not entail combat at all but instead focus on eliminating sources of financial support for terrorists or ensuring the security of computer networks. "'Terrorism' is a phenomenon," says the ICRC. "Both practically and legally, war cannot be waged against a phenomenon, but only against an identifiable party to an armed conflict."

In spite of the fact that terrorists and terrorist groups are not a party to an armed conflict under IHL, states nonetheless have the obligation to treat terrorists who are arrested or captured according to a national or international legal framework. In the view of the ICRC, those combatants who were captured during the war in Afghanistan, for instance, ought to be protected by IHL, meaning that they should be treated like prisoners of war in any armed conflict. This position is distinctly at odds with the one taken by the Bush administration, which views even fighters for the former TALIBAN regime taken in the war as "unlawful" combatants who are not entitled to rights and protections of prisoners of war. This policy considers the Taliban as allies of terrorists—specifically AL-QAEDA—and not as soldiers in the service of a legitimate government.

The U.S. military describes an unlawful combatant as an individual who is not authorized to take a direct part in hostilities but participates all the same and who, if captured, may be tried and punished. Such individuals could be civilians who engage in war without authorization; noncombat members of the military, such as medics or chaplains, who engage in combat; and soldiers who fight out of uniform. Under the policy promulgated by the United States, these captives may be detained indefinitely; thus, provisions of IHL calling for the repatriation of POWs after hostilities cease would not apply because it is impossible to determine when, if ever, a war on terrorism could be declared over.

If the status of a POW is in doubt, the Third Geneva Convention calls for a competent tribunal to be established to settle the question. The ICRC also notes that a POW can be tried for war crimes and may be held until the sentence is served regardless of whether hostilities have ended. The Fourth Geneva Convention does make a distinction between combatants and enemy nationals such as mercenaries or civilians who do not carry arms openly or wear a uniform (saboteurs, spies, etc.)—so-called unprivileged or unlawful belligerents. If arrested, these enemy nationals would not be considered prisoners of war but under IHL and would be tried for violations of domestic law and imprisoned until the sentence has been fulfilled. Nonetheless, individuals in this category are still entitled to a fair tiral.

ARTICLE 3 COMMON TO THE GENEVA CONVENTIONS and customary law also offer protections to individuals detained in noninternational armed conflicts, as was the case with Afghanistan after the Taliban was defeated in spring 2002. IHL and relevant criminal domestic laws apply to those detainees, who also have the right to a fair trial for any crimes of which they are accused. According to the ICRC, "no person captured in the fight against terrorism can be considered outside the law; there is no such thing as a 'black hole' in terms of legal protection." By the same token, under the Geneva Conventions, the ICRC must be granted access to persons detained in an international armed conflict, whether they are POWs or persons protected by the Fourth Geneva Convention. In that regard, the ICRC has called for a formal determination of the status of the individuals held at the U.S. base in Guantánamo Bay who are accused of terrorist activities.

See also GUANTÁNAMO DETAINEES; WAR ON TERROR.

Further Reading:
Burke, Jason. *Al-Qaeda: Casting a Shadow of Terror.* London: I. B. Tauris, 2004.
———. *Al-Qaeda: The True Story of Radical Islam.* London: I. B. Tauris, 2004.
Danner, Mark. *Torture and Truth: America, Abu Ghraib, and the War on Terror.* New York: New York Review Books, 2004.
Gunaratna, Rohan. *Inside al-Qaeda: Global Network of Terror.* New York: Berkley Publishing Group, 2003.
Hersh, Seymour M. *Chain of Command: The Road from 9/11 to Abu Ghraib.* New York: HarperCollins, 2004.
Micheletti, Eric. *Special Forces in Afghanistan 2001–2003: War against Terrorism.* Paris: Historie & Collections, 2003.
Scheuer, Michael. *Imperial Hubris: Why the West Is Losing the War on Terror.* Washington, D.C.: Potomac Books, 2004.
Zayy-at, Montasser al-. *The Road to Al-Qaeda: The Story of bin Laden's Right-Hand Man.* Critical Studies on Islam. Translated by Ahmed Fekry. Edited by Sara Nimis. Ann Arbor, Mich.: Pluto Press, 2004.

Thailand, human rights violations in

Although it is a democracy, Thailand's government still has a mixed record on human rights. There have been numerous cases of EXTRAJUDICIAL KILLINGS by police, especially in connection with an antidrug campaign. In the south of the country, the police and security forces have brutally suppressed dissent, killing about 650 Muslims in 2004, stirring widespread outrage in a region that is home to a large Muslim population. (The majority of Thais are Buddhists.) There is some question about the commitment of the government of Prime Minister Thaksin Shinawatra to freedom of the press in view of the fact that his family controls the Shin Corporation, the country's biggest media and communications company, which owns the major television channels and satellite and mobile phone network.

Probably no event in recent years has drawn attention to Thailand's human rights problems more than the deaths of 78 Muslim protesters who died in police custody in October 2004. The victims were suffocated or crushed to death while being transported to police headquarters after being arrested for taking part in a political demonstration. Eyewitnesses reported seeing the protesters being beaten after they were arrested and then thrown face down into military trucks and piled four or five high. Security forces shot and killed another seven protesters at the demonstration itself. (Another 1,200 were still being detained weeks later without access to legal representation.) This was by no means the first incident in which security forces used excessive force: The previous April they had killed some 110 Muslim militants armed only with machetes who had taken refuge in a mosque. Human rights groups decried the killings, insisting that lethal force was not necessary to subdue the insurgents, most of whom were in their teens or early 20s. Earlier, in March 2004, Somchai Neelapajit, a prominent human rights lawyer for Thai Muslims facing terrorism charges, was disappeared and, according to HUMAN RIGHTS WATCH, most likely to have been tortured and killed. "Each incident fostered the atmosphere of impunity in which security forces in Narithawit [southern Thailand] seemed to be operating," Human Rights Watch said in an open letter to the prime minister, demanding investigations into the incidents and the prosecutions of those found culpable.

The insurgency in the south of the country intensified through 2009, causing the government to double the size of security forces, including the army, the police, and militias, to about 60,000. Although the increase initially reduced the violence in 2008, it began to climb again the following year. By September 2009, more than 330 people had been killed, compared with 285 in the same period the previous year, for a total of approximately 3,500 since 2004. Civilians have suffered disproportionately; teachers, for example, have been increasingly singled out; nearly 100 have been killed between 2004 and 2009. Militants are believed to have adopted a more radical Islamic ideology in recent years, and their attacks have threatened to destabilize relations between majority Buddhist and Muslim communities in the region. The turmoil has also occurred at a particularly critical period in Thai politics, which has become increasingly polarized. Several governments have come and gone in Bangkok in recent years, but none of them has proven especially effective. In January 2009 AMNESTY INTERNATIONAL published a report accusing some members of the armed forces of human rights abuses, stating that they "systemically engage in torture" that included using electric shocks in their attempts to gather information and to force communities into withholding or withdrawing support for the rebels. Inappropriate behavior of soldiers—including drinking, dancing, and flirting—in the vicinity of mosques and Buddhist temples has also raised tensions in the area. The exact identities and agendas of these shadowy militant groups are still unclear, but experts believe that their aim is to drive Buddhists from the area, discredit the government, and impose strict Islamic laws.

The pattern of abuses by security forces also extends to the so-called war on drugs, which has accounted for at least 2,275 extrajudicial executions by security forces, according to Human Rights Watch. When he took office in February 2001, Prime Minister Thaksin Shinawatra declared the "prevention and suppression" of narcotic drugs as one of his top priorities. Two years later the antidrug campaign officially began, but it soon devolved into a spree of violence characterized by wholesale killings by security forces, arbitrary arrest, intimidation of human rights advocates, and the blacklisting of several thousand people. The government was quick to blame the killings on drug gangs, a claim that is belied by credible reports received by human rights organizations. The drug war also jeopardized Thailand's relatively successful fight against HIV/AIDS by creating such a climate of fear that drug users were driven underground rather than seeking help and risking imprisonment or worse. Some people taken into custody reported that drugs had been planted on them by police and that they were forced to make confessions in order for the police to fulfill arrest quotas.

Further Reading:

Amnesty International USA. Thailand Human Rights. Available online. URL: http://www.amnestyusa.org/all-countries/thailand/page.do?id=1011253. Accessed March 21, 2010.

Baker, Christopher, and Pasuk Phongpaichit. *A History of Thailand.* Cambridge: Cambridge University Press, 2005.

Human Rights Watch. Thailand Human Rights. Available online. URL: http://www.hrw.org/asia/thailand. Accessed March 21, 2010.

Slagter, Robert, and Harold Kerbo. *Modern Thailand.* Comparative Societies Series. Boston: McGraw-Hill, 2000.

U.S. Department of State. *2008 Human Rights Report Thailand.* Available online. URL: http://www.state.gov/g/drl/rls/hrrpt/2008/eap/119058.htm. Accessed March 21, 2010.

Tibet   *See* CHINA, HUMAN RIGHTS VIOLATIONS IN.

Tiger Force

U.S. involvement in Vietnam, which cost the lives of 50,000 Americans and as many as 2 million Vietnamese combatants and civilians, lasted from the early 1960s and ended in 1975. Because of the clandestine nature of the war, making it difficult to tell friend from foe, U.S. forces resorted to various strategies to combat an elusive enemy. Some of the methods relied on ambushes, booby traps, and strikes on suspected bases of guerrilla support—in other words, the same tactics that the Vietcong insurgents were using to attack U.S. and South Vietnamese forces. However, the result was that in certain instances, American troops committed illegal acts. Revelations of atrocities by American troops on a hitherto unknown scale, though, surfaced only in October 2003—30 years after the United States withdrew its troops from Indochina—thanks to a series of Pulitzer Prize–winning articles in the *Toledo Blade.* Until then most Americans believed that the 1968 massacre of approximately 400 Vietnamese civilians in the village of My Lai was an anomaly rather than part of a larger pattern.

A year before the MY LAI MASSACRE, the U.S. Army had set up a special task force to conduct operations against communist Vietcong insurgents in the Central Highlands, a region of South Vietnam that was the site of intense fighting at the time. One of the principal components of the task force was a platoon known as the Tiger Force, a 45-man unit detached from the 101st Airborne Division. In the short period of its existence, the Tiger Force was responsible for such atrocities as intentionally blowing up women and children in underground bunkers, shooting farmers while they were at work in their fields, and torturing and executing prisoners before lopping off their ears and scalps for souvenirs. It is believed that the Tiger Force might have killed several hundred people. One medic reported that 120 civilians had been killed in a single month. Attempts by two soldiers to halt the killings went ignored by the commanders. According to the *Toledo Blade*, the atrocities occurred over a period of seven months in 1967.

An internal army investigation into the atrocities went on for four and a half years (February 1971–June 1975)—the longest such probe related to the army's actions in Vietnam—and reached all the way to the White House. Although investigators found 18 soldiers culpable of 20 war crimes, including murder, assault, and dereliction of duty, no one was ever charged, nor was the public made aware of the investigation. The investigation suffered from delays and inaction: A year passed before witnesses were even interviewed, and five of the soldiers implicated were allowed to leave the army quietly. Although a March 2, 1973, White House memo described the case and referred to five "unidentified members of Tiger Force" under investigation for crimes ranging from murder to body mutilation, there was little interest in the administration of President Richard M. Nixon to follow up on the investigation, especially after American disengagement from the region. By the time the Ford administration took office, the climate had changed completely. "No one wanted to hear about war crimes then," said Dr. David Anderson, editor of a book about war crimes called *Facing My Lai*, adding, "It would have been embarrassing."

Altogether the U.S. Army conducted 242 war-crimes investigations stemming from the Vietnam War; 21 cases, or about a third of the total, were substantiated and led to convictions based on charges ranging from beating prisoners to murdering civilians. Ten soldiers received prison terms ranging from 30 days to 20 years, though many sentences were later reduced.

See also PHOENIX PROGRAM; VIETNAM, HUMAN RIGHTS VIOLATIONS IN.

Further Reading:
Anderson, David, ed. *Facing My Lai: Moving beyond the Massacre.* Lawrence: University Press of Kansas, 1998.
Bilton, Michael, and Kevin Sim. *Four Hours in My Lai.* New York: Penguin Books, 1993.
Hersh, Seymour. *My Lai 4: A Report on the Massacre and Its Aftermath.* New York: Random House, 1970.
Olson, James S., and Randy Roberts. *My Lai: A Brief History with Documents.* The Bedford Series in History and Culture. Sydney, Australia: Palgrave Macmillan, 1998.
Taylor, Telford. *Nuremberg and Vietnam: An American Tragedy.* New York: Times Books, 1970.
Vietnam Veterans against the War. *The Winter Soldier Investigation: An Inquiry into American War Crimes.* Boston: Beacon Press, 1972.

Togo, human rights violations in

Until recently human rights conditions in the West African state of Togo have been problematic. Until his death in February 2005, President Gnassingbé Eyadéma had led Togo for 38 years, since seizing power in a coup in January 1967. In principle, the country is democratic: Political parties were legalized in 1991, and a democratic constitution was adopted in 1992. Nonetheless the government has suppressed political dissent, and elections are not considered fair. Several hundred people were killed after disputed elections in 1998; an investigation into the affair by a joint United Nations–Organization of African Unity (now the African Union) committee found in 2001 that the government had systematically violated human rights. The press is similarly stifled: The one major television outlet is state-owned, and journalists working for independent publications are often harassed and threatened with legal action if they write articles opposed to government policies.

Ten years of economic sanctions by the European Union (EU) that began in the mid-1990s led Eyadéma to relax his grip on power and take some steps toward EU-demanded political reforms. In 2004 he announced an amnesty for more than 500 of the country's 3,200 prisoners, though most were common criminals. AMNESTY INTERNATIONAL identified seven of the released prisoners as members of the opposition party, the Union of Forces for Change (UFC), who were arrested after they had protested the barring of their candidate, Gilchrist Olympio, from taking part in presidential elections. Although the regime insists that it holds no political prisoners, the U.S. State Department in its annual *Country Report* has confirmed that political opponents are in fact incarcerated in Togolese prisons.

Trafficking in children represents another significant problem for the country. Child welfare groups say that Togo has failed to enact strict laws against the practice of exploiting children as prostitutes or as forced laborers. In the capital of Lomé, there is even an area known as the Child Market, where girls as young as nine are sold for sex, sometimes for as little as a dollar. Many of the children are abandoned, while others have been separated from their families. According to a report by HUMAN RIGHTS WATCH, the police do nothing to stop the trade.

Hopes that democracy would be restored to Togo after the death of Gnassingbé Eyadéma were shattered when the army announced that his 39-year-old son, Faure Gnassingbé, would assume power. The move was seen as a coup since it was in violation of the constitution, which calls for the speaker of the parliament as first in the line of succession. The African Union and other governments, including Washington, denounced this attempt to circumvent the law, and within days demonstrations broke out in the capital that led to three deaths. Togo was wracked by extreme violence following the death in February 2005 of President Eyadéma. Hundreds of people were killed and injured and tens of thousands forced into exile in neighboring Benin and Ghana. In April 2005 Eyadéma's son Faure Gnassingbé was declared the victor in presidential elections marked by what Amnesty International calls "irregularities." The Togolese League of Human Rights reported that 790 people had been killed and 4,345 hurt in the turmoil surrounding the election. Gnassingbé's rule has been characterized by egregious human rights violations, including extrajudicial executions of children, torture, rape, and arbitrary detentions. The situation has shown no sign of improvement in subsequent years. The Paris-based International Federation of Human Rights (FIDH) issued a report, documenting what it called "a picture of terror, with the use of blind and targeted violence by Togolese security forces against the civil population in general and the opposition in particular." Perpetrators of the violence were not held to account. Human rights activists have been intimidated, threatened, beaten up, and even poisoned. About 40,000 Togolese still remain in exile.

Tojo Hideki (1884–1948) *Japanese nationalist leader*
The best-known Japanese war criminal, Tojo Hideki served as Japan's minister of war and prime minister during World War II; for most of the war, he was for all practical purposes the country's dictator. As the official in command of Japanese occupation forces in China, he is responsible for the murder of almost 4 million Chinese. He also approved a secret program to conduct MEDICAL EXPERIMENTS on PRISONERS OF WAR and Chinese captives. After the war he was tried by the International Military Tribunal for the Far East—the TOKYO TRIALS—convicted, and condemned to death.

Tojo was born in Tokyo on December 30, 1884. After joining the Japanese army, he quickly rose in the ranks, becoming major general in 1933 and, in 1937, chief of staff of the Kwangtung Army in Manchuria, which Japan had

Former Japanese general and premier Tojo Hideki *(Bettmann/ Corbis)*

seized from China. After a brief six-month stint as vice minister of war in 1941, he rejoined the military, this time as the commander of the army's aviation division. A fervent right-wing nationalist, he was an admirer of Adolf HITLER and an advocate of preemptive air strikes on China and the Soviet Union, countries he saw as long-term threats to Japanese interests. He opposed efforts by the foreign minister, Shignori Togo, to withdraw Japanese troops from China and Korea, which Japan had ruled as a colonial power since 1905.

In 1941 Tojo was appointed prime minister by Emperor Hirohito; he was also given the position of war minister, which put him in charge of the Japanese army, and additionally held the positions of home minister and foreign minister. Within two months he approved the attack on U.S. forces in Hawaii. (The actual decision to attack Pearl Harbor was made by Admiral Isoroku Yamamoto.) Tojo personally took charge of the Battle of the Pacific against U.S. forces, but by July 1944, after Japan suffered the loss of the strategically important island of Saipan, he resigned and disgraced, made a failed attempt to commit suicide. The postwar military tribunal established by the Allies found him guilty of waging wars of aggression in violation of international law as well as waging unprovoked war against China, the United States, the British Commonwealth, the Netherlands, and France (the latter three were colonial powers in Asia). In addition, Tojo was convicted for ordering, authorizing, and permitting inhumane treatment of prisoners of war and civilians. He was sentenced to death on November 12, 1948, and executed by hanging.

Further Reading:

Browne, Courtney. *Tojo: The Last Banzai.* New York: Da Capo Press, 1998.

Daws, Gavin. *Prisoners of the Japanese: POWs of World War II in the Pacific.* New York: Perennial, 1996.

Harris, Sheldon. *Factories of Death: Japanese Biological Warfare 1932–45 and the American Cover-Up.* London: Routledge, 1995.

Hoyt, Edwin. *Warlord: Tojo against the World.* New York: Cooper Square Press, 2001.

Li, Peter. *Japanese War Crimes: The Search for Justice.* New Brunswick, N.J.: Transaction Publishers, 2003.

Maga, Timothy P. *Judgment at Tokyo: The Japanese War Crimes Trials.* Lexington: University Press of Kentucky, 2001.

Tokyo Trials   (International Military Tribunal for the Far East)

The International Military Tribunal for the Far East (IMTFE) began trying Japanese war criminals in Tokyo, Japan, on May 3, 1946, about half a year after the International Military Tribunal began trying Nazi war criminals in Germany (the NUREMBERG TRIALS). The tribunal held its final session on November 12, 1948. The trials of what were called Class A Japanese war criminals are known as the Tokyo Trials. The charges covered crimes committed by Japanese officials as far back as 1928 (involving the assassination of a Manchurian warlord) and up to the Japanese surrender to the Allies in August 1945. Judges from 11 nations served on the tribunal. The legal basis for the Tokyo Trials can be found in a number of agreements reached while the war was still in progress. These included the Cairo Conference, at which the United States, Great Britain, and China issued a declaration on December 1, 1943, that "the purpose of this war is to stop and punish Japanese aggression"; and the fifth article of the Potsdam Declaration of July 1945, signed by the same three Allies, which stated that "justice shall be meted out to all war criminals including those who have visited cruelties upon our prisoners." Specific provisions relating to the arrest and treatment of war criminals were enumerated in the Instrument of Japanese Surrender of September 2, 1945. The legal

framework for the tribunal itself stems from a recommendation by the new Commission of Crimes of the United Nations (established at London in summer 1943).

The Moscow Conference of foreign ministers of the "Big Four"—the United States, the Soviet Union, Great Britain, and China—decided to establish the tribunal in Tokyo. The Tokyo Trials drew upon the guiding principles of the Nuremberg Trials, which would make the accused liable to such charges as crimes against peace, CRIMES AGAINST HUMANITY, and war crimes and aggressive war, although there was to be no imposition of "collective guilt," which was the case regarding Nazi crimes. One judge was chosen from each of the 11 nations represented on the tribunal. Of the 70 Class A war criminal suspects arrested after 1945, 28 were brought to trial before the IMTFE; nine were political or civilian officials and 19 were military officials. They were charged with a military campaign that "contemplated and carried out . . . murdering, maiming and ill-treating prisoners of war (and) civilian internees . . . forcing them to labor under inhumane conditions . . . plundering public and private property, wantonly destroying cities, towns and villages beyond any justification of military necessity; (perpetrating) mass murder, rape, pillage, brigandage, TORTURE and other barbaric cruelties upon the helpless civilian population of the over-run countries." In a statement issued to the press, Joseph Keenan, the chief prosecutor representing the United States, declared that "war and treaty-breakers should be stripped of the glamour of national heroes and exposed as what they really are—plain, ordinary murderers."

The prosecutors presented evidence to prove that the Japanese had planned the war as early as 1931 and went on to show that many of the accused were responsible for (or were aware of) such atrocities as the rape of Nanjing (Nanking) in 1937, in which as many as 300,000 Chinese were killed by Japanese invaders and 20,000 women raped, and the 1942 Singapore massacre in which Japanese forces systematically killed at least 5,000 ethnic Chinese civilians (and perhaps several thousand more) in an avowed effort to hunt down guerrillas. American and British prosecutors were able to establish from documentary evidence that the Japanese had determined on attacks against both nations without any legal justification: No treaty had been broken, and Japan was not being threatened by either nation. In addition, prosecutors pressed the case that Japanese officials were instrumental in the trafficking of opium in occupied China with the purpose of weakening Chinese morale and providing revenues for the Japanese war machine.

When the trial finally drew to an end after two and a half years, the tribunal found 25 guilty, many on multiple counts. Seven were sentenced to death by hanging, the most prominent of whom was TOJO HIDEKI, the former prime minister, who was responsible for launching the attack on Pearl Harbor in 1941. Sixteen were sentenced to life in prison and two others to lesser terms. (Two of the original 28 died of natural causes during the trial, and one suffered a mental breakdown and was committed to a psychiatric institution before being released in 1948.) Three of those sentenced to life imprisonment died in prison; the remaining 13 were paroled between 1954 and 1956.

That still left more than 40 Class A criminals who remained in Tokyo's Sugamo prison awaiting trial. Many of these were other military and diplomatic officials as well as industrialists and financial figures who had helped finance the war and had engaged in munitions manufacture and drug trafficking. Most of these prisoners were released in 1947 and 1948 by General Douglas MacArthur, supreme commander of occupied Japan. Critics of the United States' handling of Japanese war criminals after the war are especially upset that so many were able to escape justice. Indeed, several of the accused who were never tried returned to politics in postwar Japan. Emperor Hirohito was removed from a list of war criminals and kept on the throne in the interest of reconciliation, even though former prime minister Tojo had admitted that he had consulted with the emperor about the sneak attack on Pearl Harbor, that the emperor "had consented, though reluctantly, to the war," and that "none of us would dare act against the Emperor's will."

See also MANCHURIA, JAPANESE WAR CRIMES IN; MATSUI IWANE; NANJING (NANKING), MASSACRE IN; OKAWA SHUMEI; SHIMADA SHIGETARO.

Further Reading:

Daws, Gavin. *Prisoners of the Japanese: POWs of World War II in the Pacific.* New York: Perennial, 1996.

Harris, Sheldon. *Factories of Death: Japanese Biological Warfare 1932–45 and the American Cover-Up.* London: Routledge, 1995.

Lamont-Brown, Raymond. *Ships from Hell: Japanese War Crimes on the High Seas.* Phoenix Mill, U.K.: Sutton Publishing, 2002.

Li, Peter. *Japanese War Crimes: The Search for Justice.* New Brunswick, N.J.: Transaction Publishers, 2003.

Maga, Timothy P. *Judgment at Tokyo: The Japanese War Crimes Trials.* Lexington: University Press of Kentucky, 2001.

Mendelsohn, John. *The Preservation of Japanese War Crimes Trials Records in the National Archives.* Washington, D.C.: National Archives and Records Administration, 1982.

Minear, Richard R. *Victors' Justice: The Tokyo War Crimes Trial.* Michigan Classics in Japanese Studies. Ann Arbor: University of Michigan Center for Japanese Studies, 2001.

Piccigallo, Philip R. *The Japanese on Trial: Allied War Crimes Operations in the East, 1945–1951.* Austin: University of Texas Press, 1980.

Rees, Laurence. *Horror in the East: Japan and the Atrocities of World War II.* New York: Da Capo Press, 2002.

Russell, of Liverpool, Edward Frederick Langley Russell, Baron. *Knights of the Bushido: A Short History of Japanese War Crimes.* London: Greenhill Books, 2005.

Tanaka, Yuki. *Hidden Horrors: Japanese War Crimes in World War II.* Philadelphia: Westview Press, 1998.

torture

Torture is universally prohibited under INTERNATIONAL HUMANITARIAN LAW. The 1984 Convention for the Prevention of Torture and Inhuman or Degrading Treatment or Punishment (known as the CONVENTION AGAINST TORTURE) states: "No exceptional circumstances whatsoever, whether a state of war or a threat of war, internal political instability or any other public emergency, may be invoked as a justification of torture." The convention defines torture as "any act by which severe pain or suffering, whether physical or mental, is intentionally inflicted on a person for such purposes as obtaining from him or a third person information or a confession." Torture may be "inflicted by or at the instigation of or acquiescence of a public official or other person acting in an official capacity." The legal definition of torture also includes the punishment of a detainee for an act he or another person committed as well as intimidation based on discrimination.

The Torture Convention is only one of several international agreements that address torture. Legal constraints against the practice can also be found in the INTERNATIONAL COVENANT ON CIVIL AND POLITICAL RIGHTS; the CONVENTION ON THE RIGHTS OF THE CHILD; and the European, African, and Inter-American Conventions on Human Rights. ARTICLE 3 COMMON TO THE GENEVA CONVENTIONS of 1949 emphasizes that torture is forbidden during internal or international conflicts. It outlaws "violence to life and person, in particular murder of all kinds, mutilation, cruel treatment and torture," and "outrages upon personal dignity, in particular humiliating and degrading treatment" are banned under any circumstances. The prohibition is especially applicable to PRISONERS OF WAR and civilians, but it extends even to common criminals. Torture is also banned by CUSTOMARY LAW—law that is based mainly on precedent and morality rather than on codified rules. Torture is specifically prohibited in armed conflict, whether international or internal. Article 44 of the Hague Regulations of 1907 on customs of war declares that "a belligerent is forbidden to force the inhabitants of territory occupied by it to furnish information about the army of the other belligerent, or about its means of defense."

International law does make some attempt to distinguish between torture and inhumane treatment; the former frequently makes use of force with the intent to inflict pain to extract information from a detainee, while the latter is aimed at robbing a detainee of his dignity. In practice, however, it is difficult to make such a determination, as the abuses by U.S. soldiers at the Iraqi prison of Abu Ghraib vividly demonstrate. In that case prisoners were often publicly humiliated; most legal experts reflected public opinion by labeling such abuses as torture even in the absence of overt physical force. Leaving a person naked, for instance, constitutes a form of torture although no force is employed. International law recognizes that in many instances torture is not used to elicit information but rather as a means of revenge to cause suffering. Individuals who engage in torture may also do so because they derive sadistic pleasure from it. Torture can also take the form of sexual assault. Article 27 of the Fourth Geneva Convention states that women must be protected against "rape, enforced prostitution, or any form of indecent assault" in conflict.

Although most nations have laws on their books forbidding torture, the practice is carried on routinely in many parts of the world. Security forces engaged in combating insurgencies or antiterrorism campaigns are particularly likely to resort to torture. To conceal evidence of their activities, police and security forces also torture suspects while holding them incommunicado, denying the detainee all contact with the outside world. Various means of torture can be employed without leaving marks, although the pain can be just as excruciating as the pain from methods that leave bruises and scars. In many countries—especially in Latin America during the "dirty wars" of the 1970s and early 1980s—political and military leaders engaged in widespread torture enact AMNESTY laws while they are still in power in an attempt (not always successful) to evade the legal consequences of their actions.

See also GENEVA CONVENTIONS; IRAQ, HUMAN RIGHTS VIOLATIONS IN POST-SADDAM; RAPE AS A TACTIC OF WAR.

Further Reading:

Greenberg, Karen J., and Johsua L. Dratel, eds. *The Torture Papers: The Road to Abu Ghraib.* Cambridge: Cambridge University Press, 2005.
Gutman, Roy, ed. *Crimes of War: What the Public Should Know.* New York: W. W. Norton & Company, 1999.
Jackson, Nyamuya Maogoto. *War Crimes and Realpolitik: International Justice from World War I to the 21st Century.* Boulder, Colo.: Lynne Rienner Publishers, 2004.
Jokie, Aleksander. *War Crimes and Collective Wrongdoing: A Reader.* London: Blackwell Publishers, 2001.
Levinson, Sanford, ed. *Torture: A Collection.* Oxford: Oxford University Press, 2004.

total war

The phrase *total war* has at least three different meanings. In one construction, total war entails the state's mobilization of all resources—political, military, and economic—to defeat an enemy. In a second interpretation, total war refers to the announced intent of a state to bring the conflict against the enemy to any part of the world, using any means at its disposal, which could mean resorting to illegal weapons of mass destruction (BIOLOGICAL WEAPONS, for instance) or engaging in a scorched-earth policy. In a third meaning, total war refers to a state's determination to conduct military operations on any part of an enemy's territory and incapacitate its industrial and agricultural base. World War II would meet the criteria for total war under any of these definitions. (Great Britain used the term to apply to both world wars.)

Total war is distinguished from LIMITED WAR; the latter is waged only to achieve objectives that are more circumscribed—taking back occupied territory, for example, or destroying an enemy's air force in a preemptive action—and is generally fought for only so long as needed to reach the objective. Total war, on the other hand, may go on for years if necessary to entirely destroy the enemy. This was the case with the Allied war against Germany in World War II: The Allied leaders had made the determination to settle for nothing less than unconditional surrender and occupation of all of Germany, ruling out any negotiated settlement.

INTERNATIONAL HUMANITARIAN LAW (IHL) does not necessarily outlaw total war under any of its three definitions, although it does ban specific practices in conducting any war such as the use of illegal weapons. These restrictions have the effect of making it more difficult for a belligerent to carry out a total war for which the goal is the complete destruction of an enemy's military and industrial infrastructure, for example. Similarly, IHL forbids targeting of civilian populations and calls for restraint in attacking military objectives if an attack is likely to cause wanton destruction of civilian property and a loss of civilian life disproportionate to the value of the military installation. In other words, total law does not give a belligerent license to employ whatever method it chooses to bring about an adversary's defeat. Any nation that announced it was prepared to take any measure to achieve a victory would be in grave breach of international law and subject to penalties by the United Nations Security Council that could range from sanctions to military action. Nor can total war be offered as an excuse for staging REPRISALS against civilians or civilian property that are banned by both the GENEVA CONVENTIONS of 1949 and Additional Protocol I of 1977.

See also ADDITIONAL PROTOCOLS TO THE GENEVA CONVENTIONS.

Further Reading:
Gutman, Roy, ed. *Crimes of War: What the Public Should Know.* New York: W. W. Norton & Company, 1999.
Marwick, Arthur, Wendy Simpson, and Clive Emsley, eds. *Total War and Historical Change: Europe, 1914–1955.* London: Open University Press, 2001.

Touvier, Paul (1915–1996) *French Nazi collaborator*
Paul Touvier has the dubious distinction of being the only Frenchman to be convicted of war CRIMES AGAINST HUMANITY. During World War II, while he was a member of a pro-Nazi militia established by the collaborationist regime of Vichy France, he had ordered the execution of seven Jews. Touvier was so loyal to his German superior, the notorious KLAUS BARBIE, the Lyon GESTAPO chief, that he became known as "the French Barbie" as well as "the hangman of Lyon." In addition to the executions of the seven Jews, there is evidence to suggest that he was responsible for many other crimes, including the killings of a prominent human rights advocate and his wife in 1944 and the deportation of 57 Spanish refugees who were rounded up in a Gestapo raid.

When the war ended, Touvier dropped out of sight. He was convicted in absentia of treason, collaboration, and helping TORTURE and execute members of the Resistance; he was sentenced to death. Relying on fake identity cards, Touvier survived under cover by passing counterfeit money and even selling bootleg chocolate to candy stores. In 1947 he was arrested while trying to rob a bakery but managed to escape once more. When the statute of limitations for the crimes with which he was charged expired, Touvier surfaced again. French president Georges Pompidou then granted him what amounted to a pardon, which allowed Touvier to return to Lyon and recover his property. The restoration of Touvier's legal status aroused a nationwide protest that only intensified when it was learned that the property he claimed had been seized from him had actually belonged to deported Jews. The protests led to an indictment in 1973 on charges of crimes against humanity, which are not liable to the statute of limitations. Touvier thereupon went into hiding again.

Aided by rightist Catholics, Touvier, remained elusive until he was captured on May 24, 1989, in a Catholic monastery in Nice that was operated by adherents of the excommunicated Marcel Lefebvre, a rabid conservative cleric. At the time of his arrest, Touvier declared, "I regret nothing." He later claimed at his trial that the Germans had demanded the lives of 100 Jews in retaliation for the assassination of the Vichy minister of information, but by bargaining with the Gestapo, Touvier had succeeded in sparing all but the seven he was charged with executing. The argument failed to persuade the jury. "I have never forgotten the victims . . ." he said when he was sentenced. "I think of them every day, every evening." He died in prison at age 81.

Further Reading:
Wexler, Leila Sadat. *The Trial of Vichy Collaborator Paul Touvier for Crimes against Humanity in France.* St. Louis: Washington University School of Law, 1994.

trafficking in persons

Trafficking in persons is a transnational criminal enterprise that is estimated to involve anywhere from 700,000 to 4 million people, primarily women and children. Many of the trafficked persons, whom criminal networks lure from their homes with the prospect of well-paying jobs, find themselves coerced into prostitution, domestic servitude, or farm or factory labor. Trafficking in persons is a crime under international law and the laws of most nations. It is characterized by the movement of people across or within borders; the use of threats, intimidation, or deception; and compelling victims into a situation against their will for the purposes of exploiting them. Traffickers ensure compliance with their demands even after the victim reaches his or her destination through a variety of means: debt-bondage, passport confiscation, physical and psychological abuse, rape, and TORTURE. The threat of arrest and deportation constantly hangs over the victim, who may also fear retaliation against his or her family. Trafficking of persons should not be confused with the smuggling of illegal migrants who, while often subject to exploitation, nonetheless undertake their journeys voluntarily.

In many respects, trafficking of persons is considered as a modern form of SLAVERY, and indeed it may result in putting its victims in situations that are indistinguishable from slavery. Trafficking in persons is often carried out by criminal networks and abetted by a climate of corruption. The practice also feeds into other types of criminal activity ranging from document fraud and bribery to child prostitution and indentured servitude. According to statistics compiled by the Congressional Research Service in 2000, the majority of victims originate in Asia: more than 225,000 from Southeast Asia and more than 150,000 from South Asia every year. About 100,000 trafficked persons come from states of the former Soviet Union, which provides the largest source of prostitution, and more than 75,000 come from Eastern Europe. An estimated 100,000 people are trafficked from Latin America and the Caribbean, and more than 50,000 are from Africa. The most common destinations for trafficked persons are large cities, tourist resorts, and military bases.

In spite of the fact that the U.S. Congress enacted a law in 2000 that imposed a life sentence on anyone engaged in human trafficking—defined as using fraud or force to exploit a person for sex or labor—the problem of trafficking in the United States has actually grown worse. In the decade since the law went into effect, the U.S. Department of Justice has brought charges in 196 cases and secured convictions against 419 people. (Thirty states have laws similar to the federal law.) However, those numbers are dwarfed by the estimates of the numbers of people who are trafficked in the country. According to the U.S. State Department, 14,500 to 17,500 people are believed to be brought into the United States each year for forced labor or sex.

Several misconceptions surround trafficking of persons. For one, traffickers include women as well as men. For another, not all women are trafficked for prostitution (many become domestic servants), and not all victims of trafficking are uneducated or from rural areas. On the contrary, many have had a secondary or postsecondary school education; many trafficked women from Russia and Eastern Europe hold college degrees and have lived in major cities. In Hong Kong a large number of Filipinas in domestic servitude were once teachers and nurses.

Trafficking of persons is increasingly recognized as an international problem requiring urgent action. In November 2000 the United Nations General Assembly adopted the Protocol to Prevent, Suppress and Punish Trafficking in Persons, Especially Women and Children, Supplementing the United Nations Convention Against Transnational Organized Crime; within a month the protocol was signed by 101 countries. Intended to "prevent and combat" trafficking in persons, the TRAFFICKING PROTOCOL, as it is called, covers specific criminal offenses and sets out measures that state parties are required to take to facilitate cooperation to stop the practice. It also sets out actions to protect and assist victims. The protocol is only the most recent of several other international human rights treaties to address trafficking, which include the United Nations Supplementary Convention on the Abolition of Slavery, the Slave Trade, and Institutions and Practices Similar to Slavery. In addition, the UN Convention on the Elimination of All Forms of Discrimination against Women calls for all parties to take measures "to suppress all forms of traffic in women and exploitation of prostitution of women." Many nations have become more aggressive about tackling the problem of trafficking as well. The U.S. Department of Justice prosecuted 76 traffickers in 2001 and 2002, three times as many as in the previous two years and by 2003 had opened another 125 trafficking investigations, nearly twice as many as in January 2001. In 2003 the United States Agency for International Development (USAID) provided over $15 million for specific antitrafficking activities in 36 countries, an increase of more than 50 percent over USAID antitrafficking funding for 2002.

See also CHILDREN'S RIGHTS; WOMEN'S RIGHTS, VIOLATIONS OF.

Further Reading:

Farley, Melissa, ed. *Prostitution, Trafficking, and Traumatic Stress.* Binghamton, N.Y.: Haworth Maltreatment & Trauma Press, 2004.

Powell, Colin, and Nancy Raphel, eds. *Trafficking in Persons Report, 2002.* Chicago: Diane Pub. Co., 2003.

Rijken, Conny. *Trafficking in Persons: Prosecution from a European Perspective.* Cambridge: Cambridge University Press, 2003.

Thomas, Dorothy Q., and Thomas Sidney Jones, eds. *A Modern Form of Slavery: Trafficking of Burmese Women and Girls into Brothels in Thailand.* New York: Human Rights Watch, 1994.

Trafficking in Persons. Available online. URL: http://www. traffickinginpersons.com/. Accessed March 21, 2010.

United Nations Office of the High Commissioner for Human Rights. *Special Rapporteur on the Trafficking of Persons, Especially Women and Children.* Available online. URL: http://www2.ohchr.org/english/issues/trafficking/index.htm. Accessed March 21, 2010.

U.S. Department of State. Office to Monitor and Combat Trafficking in Persons. Available online. URL: http://www.state.gov/g/tip/. Accessed March 21, 2010.

Trafficking Protocol

The United Nations' Trafficking Protocol, opened for signature in December 2000, is an international agreement that addresses all forms of TRAFFICKING IN PERSONS, FORCED LABOR, SLAVERY, and servitude. Its full title is Protocol to Prevent, Suppress and Punish Trafficking in Persons, Especially Women and Children, Supplementing the United Nations Convention against Transnational Organized Crime. *Trafficking* is taken to mean "recruitment, transportation, transfer, harboring or receipt of persons" by improper means (such as force, abduction, fraud, or coercion) for an improper purpose, which would include forced or coerced labor, servitude, slavery, or sexual exploitation.

One of three related agreements developed by the United Nations Crime Commission, the Trafficking Protocol contains the first definition of trafficking in international human rights law. The protocol is intended to "prevent and combat" trafficking in persons and calls for international cooperation against such trafficking. It provides for criminal offenses and control and cooperation measures against traffickers and also sets forth some measures to protect and assist the victims. The protocol covers a range of cases that must meet two criteria: that an element of duress is involved and that it must be international in nature. This means that a person must be taken across a national border against his or her will or that a transnational group—usually a criminal organization—is exploiting the person within a country's borders.

The protocol deliberately fails to clarify the meaning of such terms as *exploitation of the prostitution of others* and *sexual exploitation* so that even governments that legally tolerate prostitution would feel free to sign it. The two other related accords—the Convention Against Transnational Organized Crime and the Smuggling Protocol—are primarily meant as law-enforcement instruments designed to ensure cross-border cooperation and encourage all signatories—over 120 states—to put laws on their books that cover the crimes cited in the protocol if they have not already done so. Countries that have signed the protocol have taken different positions on its application, with some arguing that its major focus should be directed to women and children since they are most likely to be exploited and trafficked. Others contend that it should not discriminate among classes of victims since the protocol only refers to all "persons," even if it is taken to generally apply to women and children.

Another difficulty arises in determining the nature of force and coercion. Children cannot freely consent to participate in sexual activity or perform labor. But for adults the situation is much less clear: It is not always possible to distinguish between consensual acts and acts that are performed because of deception, fraud, abduction, force, or threat. It is also difficult to assess on the basis of the protocol what degree of international or organized crime involvement is required to invoke its provisions. It is thought that if there is only a marginal involvement, then the violation can be more efficiently dealt with by local or national law-enforcement authorities without recourse to the protocol. In cases where entirely domestic crimes are committed by a transnational crime group, however, it is more difficult to determine whether the protocol should or should not apply.

Further Reading:

Farley, Melissa, ed. *Prostitution, Trafficking, and Traumatic Stress.* Binghamton, N.Y.: Haworth Maltreatment and Trauma Press, 2004.

Powell, Colin, and Nancy Raphel, eds. *Trafficking in Persons Report, 2002.* Chicago: Diane Pub. Co., 2003.

Rijken, Conny. *Trafficking in Persons: Prosecution from a European Perspective.* Cambridge: Cambridge University Press, 2003.

Thomas, Dorothy Q., and Thomas Sidney Jones, eds. *A Modern Form of Slavery: Trafficking of Burmese Women and Girls into Brothels in Thailand.* New York: Human Rights Watch, 1994.

transfer of civilians

INTERNATIONAL HUMANITARIAN LAW (IHL) prohibits the forcible transfer of civilians by an OCCUPYING POWER under all but the most exigent circumstances. An occupier can relocate civilians if necessary for "imperative military reasons" under Article 17 of the 1977 Additional Protocol II to the GENEVA CONVENTIONS, which states: "Should such displacements have to be carried out, all possible measures shall be taken in order that the civilian population may be received under satisfactory conditions of shelter, hygiene, safety and nutrition." Nonetheless, the evacuation of the civilian population must be temporary, and those who have been relocated must be returned to their homes as soon as conditions permit. Individuals who are moved in this way are known as INTERNALLY DISPLACED PERSONS, or IDPs.

Following World War II, the forcible removal of civilians became an issue of particular importance for policy makers because of the Nazi practice of deporting civilians from occupied countries—whether to death camps or for work as forced laborers in German industry and agriculture—while settling Germans in the territory they had been uprooted from. The NUREMBERG TRIALS after the war indicted several Nazi officials for carrying out the forcible transfer of civilians, making it a crime against humanity. The final judgments, however, mentioned only the DEPORTATIONS and not the resettlement. The law regarding deportations of civilians has not, however, kept up with recent developments. For instance, it is difficult to find laws in IHL that cover a situation in which a state transfers its own nationals from refugee or IDP centers in parts of their territory that are relatively free from violence and puts them in harm's way by moving them closer to the front lines.

See also ADDITIONAL PROTOCOLS TO THE GENEVA CONVENTIONS.

Further Reading:

Feller, Erika, Volker Turk, and Frances Nicholson, eds. *Refugee Protection in International Law: UNHCR's Global Consultations on International Protection.* Cambridge: Cambridge University Press, 2003.

Gutman, Roy, ed. *Crimes of War: What the Public Should Know.* New York: W. W. Norton & Company, 1999.

Hyndman, Jennifer. *Managing Displacement: Refugees and the Politics of Humanitarianism.* Minneapolis: University of Minnesota Press, 2000.

Ingleby, David, ed. *Forced Migration and Mental Health: Rethinking the Care of Refugees and Displaced Persons.* New York: Plenum US, 2004.

Lischer, Sarah Kenyon. *Dangerous Sanctuaries: Refugee Camps, Civil War, and the Dilemmas of Humanitarian Aid.* Cornell Studies in Security Affairs. Ithaca, N.Y.: Cornell University Press, 2005.

Trujillo, Rafael Molino (1891–1961) *Dominican despot*

Rafael Trujillo controlled the Dominican Republic for three decades (1930–61) either as its president or as its military strongman. His long rule came to an end only by means of assassination. Trujillo was born into a poor, mixed-race family on October 24, 1891. His future course was set at the age of 18 when he joined the Dominican National Guard, a force established by the U.S. Marines, which had occupied the island in 1916 to protect American economic and political interests in the country. (The Dominican Republic shares the island of Hispaniola with Haiti.) Trujillo rose so rapidly in the ranks of the National Guard that when the marines pulled out in 1924, they left him in charge. He used his power base in the National Guard to run for president in 1930, in which he claimed—fraudulently—to have received 95 percent of the vote. He then set about suppressing all dissent, establishing a secret police force called SIM (Military Intelligence Service), and banishing political opponents. SIM was given a free hand to murder and TORTURE. In one particularly gruesome incident, Trujillo ordered the massacre of thousands of black Haitian migrant workers.

An admirer of the Spanish dictator Francisco Franco, Trujillo encouraged a cult of personality, renaming the capital Santo Domingo Ciudad Trujillo, which he rebuilt extensively after it was devastated by a hurricane. Neon signs greeted visitors to the city with the proclamation "God and Trujillo." He renamed the highest mountain of the country Pico Trujillo (Trujillo Peak). Even gestures that appeared selfless—such as permitting Jewish refugees from Nazi Germany to settle in the Dominican Republic when they were being barred from other nations—were seen as public relations stunts. In the meantime he went about enriching himself and his family, taking over plantations and businesses. By the late 1950s it was estimated that Trujillo's family controlled nearly all the wealth in the country. At the same time he made sure to ingratiate himself with Washington, welcoming American business investment and, after the end of World War II, embracing a staunch anticommunist policy.

From 1949 on, opponents of the Trujillo regime made several attempts to oust him. On June 14, 1949, exiled Dominicans launched an abortive strike—known as the Luperion invasion—using 14 seaplanes. The insurgency was crushed, and rebels who survived were rounded up, tortured, and executed at a military base. (Nonetheless, the invasion inspired the anti-Trujillo June 14th Movement.) Various anti-Trujillo conspiracies subsequently sprang up—some included Trujillo's relatives—but SIM agents usually succeeded in penetrating them before they had any chance of succeeding. Trujillo saw opposition everywhere and even took on the Catholic Church. SIM agents arrested five priests, accusing them of conspiracy and bomb making. The Catholic Church sent a pastoral letter to the dictator calling on him to halt the "excesses, dry the tears, heal the wounds."

Trujillo had no intention of stopping the excesses or healing any wounds, but in two cases, the secret police overplayed their hand. In the first they arrested two activists—Maria Teresa and Minerva Mirabel—and their husbands while they were driving home, then beat them and strangled them to death in a sugarcane patch. The brutal slayings of the Mirabel sisters provoked an international outcry, no doubt helped by the fact that they were both attractive and photogenic. In the second case, a critic of the regime, Jesús de Galíndez, disappeared in New York and was never seen again. The disappearance occurred only days before the publication of his book *The Age of Trujillo*, which exposed the inner workings of the regime based on his personal experience. There was strong suspicion that Trujillo's agents had kidnapped Galíndez, spiriting him away to the island before killing him.

When Trujillo received word that Venezuelan president Romulo Betancourt had lent support to Dominican rebels in exile, he tried to have Betancourt assassinated as well. The attempt failed, but it brought renewed attention to Trujillo's clumsy efforts to intervene in the affairs of other countries. In 1960 the ORGANIZATION OF AMERICAN STATES (OAS) imposed harsh sanctions against the country and severed diplomatic ties. By this time Washington had wearied of the Dominican dictator, and the CIA began to slip arms to rebels plotting Trujillo's assassination. On May 30, 1961, they succeeded: Trujillo was ambushed and killed while he was riding on a deserted highway. But his death did not bring about the immediate end of his regime. The next day his son, Ramfis Trujillo, took power, and within a month almost all of the assassins were apprehended. Some were tortured and committed suicide; others were dragged out of prison and taken to the younger Trujillo's hacienda, where they were tied to trees, shot, cut up, and fed to sharks at a nearby beach. By then, though, anti-Trujillo riots had broken out in the capital, forcing Ramfis Trujillo to flee the country under U.S. military protection. (Ramfis lived out his exile as an international socialite, dying in 1969 from injuries sustained in a car accident.) To keep the situation from descending into chaos, the U.S. Atlantic fleet put into Santo Domingo's harbor, reasserting Washington's interests on the island just as it had several decades before. Even in death, though, the Dominican Republic was a dangerous place for Rafael Trujillo. He was buried, not on Dominican soil, but in Père Lachaise Cemetery in Paris.

See also DOMINICAN REPUBLIC, HUMAN RIGHTS VIOLATIONS IN.

Further Reading:
Diederich, Bernard. *Trujillo: The Death of the Dictator.* Princeton, N.J.: Markus Wiener Pub., 1999.
Roorda, Eric Paul. *The Dictator Next Door: The Good Neighbor Policy and the Trujillo Regime in the Dominican Republic, 1930–1945.* Durham, N.C.: Duke University Press, 1998.

Truth and Reconciliation Commission

The Truth and Reconciliation Commission was established in South Africa to investigate human rights abuses that occurred under the defunct white supremacist APART-HEID regime between 1960 and 1994. The commission oversees three committees dealing with human rights violations, reparations, and AMNESTY. The commission was created by the 1995 Promotion of National Unity and Reconciliation Act with a mandate to investigate and provide "as complete a picture as possible of the nature, causes and extent of gross violations of human rights." The act allows the commission to provide amnesty "to those who make full disclosure of all the relevant facts relating to acts associated with a political objective committed in the course of the conflicts of the past." Applications for amnesty have come from police and rightist extremists active in the apartheid regime as well as from black militants who fought against it.

The apartheid government of South Africa, which was in power for 50 years, was based on a strict policy of racial separation. The major source of resistance came from the African National Congress (ANC), which was outlawed under apartheid; its leaders were either arrested or forced to go underground. Nonetheless, the regime was compelled to secure its power by increasingly brutal methods, including TORTURE and EXTRAJUDICIAL KILLINGS. The ANC and other black activists were also implicated in human rights abuses and terrorism, though to a lesser degree.

In the early 1990s the white leadership acknowledged that majority rule could not be put off indefinitely. ANC leader Nelson Mandela was released from prison after 27 years, and in 1994 he became president in the country's first free election. A number of black leaders called for a tribunal to try officials of the apartheid regime for their crimes, guided by the precedent of the International Military Tribunal set up by the Allies to try Nazi officials for war crimes (the NUREMBERG TRIALS). Mandela's government took the position, though, that such a tribunal would only aggravate existing tensions and deepen the racial divide. The government felt that the country's bitter wounds would have a better chance of healing if the priority was given to exposing the truth about abuses rather than punishing the perpetrators. The result was the Truth and Reconciliation

Commission, which opened its first sessions in April 1996. The commission was charged with identifying victims of gross human rights violations and ensuring that they received appropriate support and compensation. The commission's longtime chair was Archbishop DESMOND TUTU. In the two years of the commission's existence, it received more than 7,000 applications for amnesty; of these, 4,500 were rejected, and only about 125 have been granted. Some 21,000 victims of apartheid were willing to come forward to testify.

The Truth and Reconciliation Commission has not been without its critics: Many South Africans, including some ANC members, contended that the commission was too lenient in granting amnesty to white officials responsible for killing and torturing blacks. However, the commission has won wide support from human rights groups, and it has become a model for similar commissions in other countries that have recently thrown off tyrannical regimes.

See also GOLDSTONE, RICHARD J.

Further Reading:
Edelstein, Jillian. *Truth and Lies: Stories from the Truth and Reconciliation Commission in South Africa.* New York: New Press, 2002.
James, Wilmot Godfrey, and Linda van de Vijver, eds. *After the TRC: Reflections on Truth and Reconciliation in South Africa.* Athens: Ohio University Press, 2001.
Wilson, Richard A. *The Politics of Truth and Reconciliation in South Africa: Legitimizing the Post-Apartheid State.* Cambridge Studies in Law and Society. Cambridge: Cambridge University Press, 2001.

Tudjman, Franjo (1922–1999) *president of Croatia*

Franjo Tudjman, the autocratic president of Croatia during the war in Bosnia, liked to be known as "father of his country," but he was also a racist and anti-Semite with fascist inclinations. Under his rule, Croatian forces forced 400,000 Serbs out of Croatia during the Bosnian War in what amounted to ethnic cleansing.

Tudjman was born in the northern Croatian region of Zagorje on May 14, 1922. While attending secondary school in the Croatian capital of Zagreb from 1934 to 1941, he became an ardent nationalist and joined an antifascist movement, actions that led to his imprisonment. After the war he held top positions in the Ministry of National Defense and the Yugoslav People's Army (where he was the youngest major general in its history). In 1961 Tudjman left the military to establish the Institute for the History of the Labor Movement in Croatia. After earning a graduate degree in political science, he spent the next several years turning out several books on history, mythologizing the medieval origins of Croatia while downplaying the atrocities of the fascist organization USTACHE, which had been allied with the Nazis during World War II. In one book Tudjman wrote that 30,000 Serbs, Jews, Rom (Gypsies), and others had been killed in a Ustache camp when the true number was closer to 800,000. He characterized Ustache excesses as "positive achievements" that were "the expression of the historical efforts of the Croatian people." His distortion resulted in a brief prison sentence. No one could accuse him of a lack of industry, though: He found time to work as a senior lecturer on "Socialist Revolution and Contemporary National History of Croatia" at the Faculty of Political Sciences in Zagreb, serve as a representative in the Croatian Parliament, and edit a magazine as well as two encyclopedias.

In 1971 Tudjman was imprisoned for nine months for participating in a nationalist movement known as Croatian Spring, which advocated Croatian independence from Yugoslavia, of which it was then a part. By this time he had become a leading figure in the nationalist movement. In February 1981 the Communist government of Yugoslavia imprisoned him for giving interviews to Swedish, German, and French radio and television outlets advocating Croatian independence; he was released in May 1984 for health reasons. Three years later, after obtaining a passport for the first time in 17 years, he traveled throughout the United States and Canada, calling for Croatian independence. His vision of a free Croatia, however, also entailed the expulsion of Serb and Muslim minorities. Nor was Tudjman content to limit the state to its existing borders within the Yugoslav federation; Croatian territory, he believed, should be extended into part of Bosnia and Herzegovina (with Bosnian Serbs getting the rest), in effect depriving the Muslim majority there of any homeland at all. In his view, Catholic Croatia was the bulwark defending the West from the Orthodox Christian Serbs and Muslim Balkans.

In 1989 Tudjman established a political party called the Croatian Democratic Union (HDZ) and became its president. In 1991, after a referendum, Croatia declared itself independent in defiance of Belgrade. The Serbs reacted with predictable fury when they suddenly found themselves a beleaguered minority in Croatia and Bosnia and Herzegovina, which also broke away from the former Yugoslavian federation. Tudjman's party adopted some of the symbols of the Ustache, basing the design of its new flag on that of the Ustache flag and renaming streets and squares after Croatian nationalist "heroes."

The Bosnian War developed into a three-sided conflict among Croats, Serbs, and Muslims with so many shifting alliances that at one point Croats and Serbs were fighting together against Bosnian Muslims in one part of Bosnia, while in another Croats and Bosnians were lined up against Serb forces. In 1992 Croat forces initially targeted Muslims, massacring civilians in the Mostar region. Tudjman

extended Croatian influence in Bosnia by sponsoring and subsidizing the Croatian Defense Council (the HVO militia), which was responsible for killing Muslims and torching Serb churches. Two years later, however, the Croatian and Muslim forces formed an alliance against Serbs with the backing of the United States and Western European powers.

"Tudjman almost certainly did not care that he was a monster because, unlike Milošević, he was our monster," commented the author Misha Glenny, describing Tudjman's relationship with the Western powers. After all, for the West, the principal antagonist was the Serb dictator, SLOBODAN MILOŠEVIĆ, who had instigated the war. In 1995 the Croatians launched two offensives—dubbed "Lightning" and "Storm"—against the predominantly Serbian-inhabited regions of West Slavonia and Krajina, bombarding Knijn, the Serbian "capital" of Krajina. Approximately a quarter of a million Serbs were driven from their homes or murdered. A UN report described the carnage: "New evidence for the atrocities continues to emerge, on average, six corpses a day. . . . [T]he corpses, some fresh, others decayed, are predominantly old men. Many were shot in the back of the head or had their throats cut, others were mutilated. . . . The crimes were committed by the Croatian army, the Croatian police and Croatian civilians. No efforts were observed of them being ordered to stop, and everything points to a policy of scorched earth."

Before the war, Croatia's population had been about 12 percent Serb. After Tudjman's campaign, only a scattering of Serbs remained. With the military support of NATO, Croatian forces occupied large sections of northwest Bosnia as well, pushing out hundreds of thousands of Serbs who lived in that region. In 1994 the United States intervened to impose a cease-fire. Tudjman was pressured into participating in the American-sponsored Dayton, Ohio, talks that led to the DAYTON ACCORDS, ending the Bosnian War.

Throughout Tudjman's 10-year regime, Croatia suffered from economic devastation and corruption. Unemployment reached 20 percent. Members of Tudjman's family appropriated formerly state-owned property for themselves. Dissent was suppressed, and journalists who dared to openly challenge Tudjman were harassed. There were no fewer than nine different security agencies to ensure that people towed the line, including one directly under the control of Tudjman's son, Miroslav. As long as Tudjman remained in power, the European Union (EU) refused to consider Croatia for candidate status for EU membership. The Western powers became increasingly disillusioned with Tudjman, viewing with alarm his calls for the "independence" of a Croatian enclave in Bosnia and Herzegovina, which would threaten hard-won political stability throughout the region. Tudjman died after a long illness on December 11, 1999, opening the way for the creation of a truly democratic state.

See also BOSNIA AND HERZEGOVINA, HUMAN RIGHTS VIOLATIONS IN; CROATIA, HUMAN RIGHTS VIOLATIONS IN; YUGOSLAVIA, WAR CRIMES IN.

Further Reading:

Bassiouni, M. Cherif. *Sexual Violence: An Invisible Weapon of War in the Former Yugoslavia.* Chicago: International Human Rights Law Institute, DePaul University, 1996.

Clark, Wesley K. *Waging Modern War: Bosnia, Kosovo, and the Future of Combat.* New York: Public Affairs, 2001.

Glenny, Misha. *The Fall of Yugoslavia: The Third Balkan War.* New York: Penguin Books, 1996.

Harris, Nathaniel. *The War in Former Yugoslavia.* London: Hodder & Stoughton, 1997.

Kim, Julie. *War in the Former Yugoslavia: Chronology of Events August 16, 1992–May 30, 1993.* CRS Report for Congress. Washington, D.C.: Foreign Affairs and National Defense Division, Congressional Research Service, the Library of Congress, 1993.

Mertus, Julie. *Former Yugoslavia: War Crimes Trials in the Former Yugoslavia.* Helsinki: Human Rights Watch/Helsinki, 1995.

Rossanet, Bertrand de. *War and Peace in the Former Yugoslavia.* Boston: Martinus Nijhoff, 1997.

Tunisia, human rights violations in

Once considered among the freest and most open countries in the Middle East, Tunisia has in recent years become transformed into a quasi-police state, according to many human rights advocates. The North African nation won independence from France in 1956 and until 1987 enjoyed the relatively enlightened rule of Habib Bourguiba, an adherent of secularism who introduced compulsory education, encouraged the emancipation of women, and abolished polygamy. Nonetheless, he eventually became a dictator whose party dominated all political life in the country.

Seen as increasingly senile and unfit to rule, Bourguiba was ousted in a coup in 1987 by Zine El Abidine Ben Ali, who has retained the leadership of Tunisia ever since. Under Ben Ali's rule, practically all dissent has been crushed. The first targets were Islamic fundamentalists in the early 1990s, but the security forces soon moved on to human rights advocates, opposition leaders, and journalists who dared to criticize the regime. The media have been turned into a tool of government propaganda, and little dissent is allowed to be aired, even though the constitution calls for freedom of the press. Journalists are kept under surveillance and are at risk of harassment, imprisonment,

or exile. Editions of foreign papers are frequently seized if they carry stories critical of the government. Estimates of the number of political prisoners incarcerated in Tunisian jails range from 500 to 1,000. Most are Islamists who are labeled as terrorists without any evidence to support the accusation. Their trials—usually for charges relating to nonviolent political activities—are deplored by human rights organizations as unjust. "In Tunisia opponents or perceived opponents of the government are subjected to abuse within a justice system resembling one from a Kafka novel," an AMNESTY INTERNATIONAL representative declared. "Confessions are coerced out of detainees, at trial defendants' files are confiscated from lawyers or tampered with, and political prisoners are subjected to a harsh prison regime, including solitary confinement."

The Tunisian judiciary has little independence and is quick to convict political dissidents on the basis of dubious evidence and ignore allegations of torture by police. According to credible reports, some of the tortured prisoners are subjected to include "sleep deprivation for 8 consecutive days and nights; ice cold shower with the person bound hand and foot; needles stuck into the nape of the neck; beatings; suspension of the person and blows carried out with a stick to the soles of the feet; suspension from the ceiling, completely naked, hands tied in front or behind the back and the application of electric shocks to the sensitive parts of the body, including genital organs, often causing loss of consciousness, which is extremely dangerous in this suspended position; tightening of a cord placed around the testicles whilst the person is suspended, naked and tied-up." Another torture method is to plunge the prisoner "naked and tied up, into a bath of foul water and detergent, holding the head under the water until near suffocation, then quickly pulling the head out of water before plunging it straight back, and so on again. . . ." One especially gruesome type of torture is called "roasting," which entails "tying the person in an outstretched position by the hands and feet to an axle fastened between two tables, and then turning the person like a chicken on a spit in such a way that the head hits the floor with every turn, all the while drenching the person in ice cold water and slapping the back of the neck constantly, as if one were playing an instrument called the 'Darbouka,' applying high intensity electric shocks at rapid intervals."

In spite of the government's human rights violations, the United States has been reluctant to criticize the Ben Ali regime. In fact, Washington has praised the Tunisian president for his cooperation in combating terrorism. The United States has shown no indication of curtailing its modest military aid program to Tunisia, and the two countries have conducted joint military exercises. One member of a visiting congressional delegation called Ben Ali a statesman who has "done a tremendous job in Tunisia and who is well respected back home as well as here in the Arab world." On a December 2003 stopover in Tunis, the capital, Secretary of State Colin Powell acknowledged that the government might do more to bring about "more political pluralism and openness" but nonetheless expressed his support for Ben Ali's leadership.

Newspapers regularly refer to Ben Ali as the "Architect for Change," although any change that might bring about a relaxation of the president's grip on power appears remote. In a referendum that allowed him the right to stand for reelection to a fourth term in October 2004, he claimed to have received 99 percent of the vote. The same referendum also conferred on him immunity from prosecution for life. Not much had changed five years later in the run up to October 2009 elections. Although Ben Ali proclaimed that his government had "endeavored to provide for these elections all the guarantees of transparency and honesty," human rights groups begged to differ. HUMAN RIGHTS WATCH, for instance, said that the election process had been marred by "repressive acts and tight controls," citing laws that seemed designed to prevent candidates from some of the stronger opposition parties from running as well as placing severe constraints on freedoms of expression, assembly and the media to squelch opposition candidates from making their views known to the public. "Tunisian authorities are sadly no more inclined to tolerate criticism during elections than they are between them," observed Sarah Leah Whitson, Middle East and North Africa director at Human Rights Watch.

Further Reading:

Amnesty International. Human Rights in the Republic of Tunisia. Available online. URL: http://www.amnesty.org/en/region/tunisia. Accessed March 21, 2010.

Charrad, M. States and Women's Rights: The Making of Postcolonial Tunisia, Algeria, and Morocco. Berkeley: University of California Press, 2001.

King, Stephen J. Liberalization against Democracy: The Local Politics of Economic Reform in Tunisia. Bloomington: Indiana University Press, 2003.

Human Rights Watch. Tunisia Human Rights. Available online. URL: http://www.hrw.org/middle-eastn-africa/tunisia. Accessed March 21, 2010.

McNamara, Ronald J. Democracy and Human Rights in the Mediterranean Partner States of the Osce: Algeria, Egypt, Israel, Jordan, Morocco and Tunisia: Briefing of the Committee on Security and Cooperation in Europe. Chicago: Diane Pub. Co., 2004.

Perkins, Kenneth. A History of Modern Tunisia. Cambridge: Cambridge University Press, 2004.

U.S. Department of State. 2008 Human Rights Report Tunisia. Available online. URL: http://www.state.gov/g/drl/rls/hrrpt/2008/nea/119128.htm. Accessed March 21, 2010.

Tupamaros　　See URUGUAY, HUMAN RIGHTS VIOLATIONS IN.

Turkey, human rights violations in

In its quest for membership in the European Union (EU), Turkey has been obliged to undertake several major political reforms and put a troubling past behind it. By 2009, however, as opposition intensified in Europe against Turkey's accession, the prospect of the country joining the EU had appreciably dimmed. Some of that opposition stemmed from fears about the influence of a growing Muslim presence in Europe resulting from immigration. At the same time, the government of Recep Tayyip Erdogan appeared to be shifting Turkey's focus by making overtures to SYRIA and IRAN. Nonetheless, the progress Turkey has made in the sphere of human rights, partly as a result of pressure from the EU at a time when accession seemed more likely, should not be underestimated. In the early 1990s, for instance, state forces were still committing EXTRAJUDICIAL KILLINGS and DISAPPEARANCES, or political killings carried out by groups with ties to the military, on almost a daily basis. Deaths in police custody occurred on an average of one a week. Such abuses have been stopped for the most part.

According to human rights groups, two issues still require urgent action: failure to sufficiently curb TORTURE and mistreatment by police and the resolution of an insurgency by Turkish Kurds that has left hundreds of thousands of people internally displaced. According to HUMAN RIGHTS WATCH, torture is still practiced, although changes in the law have reduced its frequency. The system of detention and interrogation, the group says, "encouraged torture and protected the perpetrators." Over the last 20 years, more than 400 Turkish citizens died in custody, apparently as a result of torture, with 45 deaths in 1994 alone. However, there were no reports of deaths by torture in 2004. Legal reforms enacted since Turkey initiated its bid for EU candidacy now guarantee detainees the right to legal counsel, but there are reports that prisoners are still denied access to lawyers and suffer from beatings and intimidation in prison. Even as recently as 2004, Human Rights Watch reported that hundreds of Turkish citizens had complained of torture or ill-treatment to prosecutors, the official government human rights body, and independent human rights associations. Much of the abuse appears to stem from a lack of supervision at local police stations. A culture of impunity still persists, and there is no regular monitoring system in place to ensure that the rights of detainees are being upheld. The EU Commission summed up the situation in a report in 2004: "Although torture is no longer systematic, numerous cases of ill-treatment including torture still continue to occur and further efforts will be required to eradicate such practice."

A long-running bloody conflict with Kurdish insurgents fighting for independence has posed a challenge to a succession of Turkish civilian and military governments. The separatist movement—led by a guerrilla group known as the Kurdish Workers Party (PKK)—came into existence in the early 1990s, largely in reaction to the government's suppression of the rights of the country's 12 million Kurds, including banning of the use of the Kurdish language in national media or in Kurdish schools. In a decade of war, which was mostly concentrated in the southeast of the country near the Iraqi border, more than 380,000 Kurdish villagers were displaced. Turkish soldiers and security forces uprooted the villagers, destroying their homes, crops, and livestock. These operations also involved extrajudicial killings and disappearances. The military has deployed so many troops in the region that the rebellion has largely been brought to an end. But the PKK has been reported to be still operating out of bases in northern Iraq, beyond the control of U.S. occupation forces there.

Ankara cautiously begun to take some steps to improve relations with the Kurds. In 2003, for instance, state-run Turkish television for the first time aired a broadcast in Kurmandji, the most widely spoken Kurdish dialect. In addition, an appeals court ordered the release of four Kurdish dissidents who had spent nearly a decade in prison on charges of belonging to the PKK. The government also claims to have permitted the return of about a quarter of the displaced Kurds to their homes, though this report could not be independently substantiated. According to the BBC, Kurds are in fact being allowed to resettle near their old homes, but only if they promise to join a state-run village guard system. In spite of these gestures, Turkish and Kurdish intellectuals and lawyers continue to voice misgivings about the government's treatment of the Kurdish issue and charge that Ankara is trying to stifle dissent, citing the arrest of eight Kurdish MPs who were sentenced to 15 years on charges of promoting Kurdish separatism. In one case, prosecutors threatened to bring charges of separatism against Yasar Kemal, arguably the country's most important author, for writing an article accusing Turkey of oppressing its Kurdish population.

Although relations with the minority Kurdish population have improved in recent years, there were some signs that the government of Erdogan's Muslim Justice and Development Party (AKP) was taking a harder line. Promised reforms have been put on hold, and the AKP has assumed a more nationalist stance. The PKK launched repeated strikes against the Turkish military, prompting retaliatory attacks. However, there can be no doubt that the situation has dramatically improved. A scattering of Kurds sit in parliament, and public use of the Kurdish language is no longer banned, as the arrest in 2009 of a Turkish officer vividly demonstrated. That officer, Col. Cemal Temizoz, was arrested on charges of involvement with extrajudicial

killings of Kurds in the 1990s. The colonel had been stationed in the predominantly Kurdish southeast, about 40 miles from the Iraq border, between 1993 and 1996, a violent period when it is believed that security forces killed hundreds of Kurdish civilians and activists. Officials excavating in the vicinity of the town of Cizre uncovered bones and pieces of clothing belonging to some of the victims. The arrest of Temizoz and other military officers accused of plotting a coup in an unrelated case marks a break with precedent; prior to the ascension of the AKP in 2002, the military was practically immune from prosecution.

In the waning months of 2009 the government seemed to pursue a two-track policy toward the Kurds. On the one hand, it sought the liberalization of restrictive laws against the Kurds by enhancing Kurdish cultural and social rights and permitting the use of the Kurdish language in national broadcast media and political campaigns, but on the other it brought a court case that led to the disbanding of the Democratic Society Party, the only legal Kurdish party represented in parliament, on the grounds that it was linked to a "terrorist organization," meaning the PKK. Efforts at reconciliation have not been helped by sporadic attacks by the PKK that have claimed the lives of several Turkish soldiers. The conflict had already taken 40,000 lives on both sides in the quarter of a century that it has been raging.

The controversy over acknowledgment that Turkey (then under Ottoman control) was complicit in the ARMENIAN GENOCIDE during World War I appeared no closer to a resolution in 2009 than it had been for the last several decades. The government and judiciary have shown themselves willing to put human rights concerns aside when it comes to any mention of the country's role in driving out and killing Armenians during World War I. Twice a conference on the Armenian genocide was canceled under pressure from Turkish authorities. Justice Minister Cemil Cicek condemned the meeting as "treason" and a "stab in the back of the Turkish nation." However, when a court ordered the conference canceled a second time in September 2005 (it had done so in May), some members of the government reacted with dismay. "There's no one better at hurting themselves than us," Foreign Minister Abdullah Gul said, and Prime Minister Recep Tayyip Erdogan declared that the court decision was not worthy of a democratic country. Nonetheless, prosecutors continue to single out prominent individuals for speaking out about the events of a century earlier. The country's best-known writer, Orhan Pamuk, was charged in 2005 for remarks he made to a Swiss newspaper in which he said that "one million Armenians were killed in these lands and nobody but me dares to talk about it." He, too, was charged with committing "treason," and at least in one instance, a local official ordered his works seized and destroyed.

See also KURDISTAN (IRAQ), SUPPRESSION OF.

Further Reading:

Amnesty International. *Turkey: No Security without Human Rights.* London: Amnesty International, 1996.

Dalacoura, Katerina. *Engagement or Coercion?: Weighing Western Human Rights Policies towards Turkey, Iran, and Egypt.* London: Royal Institute of International Affairs, 2004.

europa.eu. Human Rights Turkey. Available online. URL: http://europa.eu/youth/your_rights/human_rights/index_tr_tr.html. Accessed March 21, 2010.

European Parliament Policy Dept. *Human Rights in Turkey.* Available online., URL: http://www.europarl.europa.eu/meetdocs/2004_2009/documents/fd/d-tr20060425_05/d-tr200 60425_05en.pdf. Accessed March 21, 2010.

Fuller, E. Graham. *New Turkish Republic: Turkey as a Pivotal State in the Muslim World.* Pivotal State Series. Washington, D.C.: United States Institute of Peace Press, 2007.

Kinzer, Stephen. *Crescent and Star: Turkey between Two Worlds.* New York: Farrar, Straus & Giroux, 2002.

Kurdish Human Rights Project. Available online. URL: http://www.khrp.org/component/page,shop.product_details/flypage,shop.flypage/product_id,1 35/category_id,19/manufacturer_id,0/option,com_virtuemart/Itemid,36/vmcchk,1/. Accessed March 21, 2010.

Mango, Andrew. *The Turks Today.* New York: Overlook TP, 2006.

Turkmenistan, human rights violations in

An independent central Asian republic, Turkmenistan was formerly a part of the Soviet Union until its breakup in 1991. From 1999 to 2006 the country was dominated by President Saparmyrat Niyazov, who gained power in flawed elections and fostered a cult of personality. His image was so ubiquitous that he appeared on the labels of vodka bottles and pop-ups in the top right corner on national television. The capital of Ashkhabad is dominated by a rotating 36-foot-tall, gold-leaf statue of the former president atop a 250-foot base. He had even renamed months of the year after himself, his mother, and his 2005 "inspirational" work *The Book of Spirit.* Niyazov seems to have used his office as a platform from which to promote his literary ambitions, giving readings of his poetry collections on national TV, even interrupting cabinet meetings to recite his poems.

Turkmenistan is a one-party state in which Niyazov's party—the Democratic Party of Turkmenistan (DPT)—enjoys absolute monopoly in the Majlis, or parliament. All other political activity is banned, and political opposition is stifled. The only individuals allowed to run for office had been chosen by Niyazov. The president also chooses judges for five-year terms without troubling with legislative review. He regularly dismisses cabinet members and other government officials on charges of corruption, has them tried in secret trials, and frequently imprisons or sentences them to internal exile. These actions, however, have little effect in reducing corruption, which is rampant. The economy is strictly regulated by the government, which limits access to opportunity and access to industry and services. The agricultural sector is also dominated by a state command-and-control system based on the old Soviet model. Citizens must carry internal passports, which indicate their place of residence and movements in and out of the country. There is no freedom of assembly. Freedom of the press exists only on paper but is prohibited in practice. All media are in the hands of the government. To prevent citizens from learning what is going on in the outside world, the government also restricts access to satellite television and foreign newspapers and magazines.

Freedom of religion, too, is guaranteed by the constitution, but that freedom is mainly enjoyed by members of the Sunni Islamic majority (89 percent of the population) and the Russian Orthodox Church. The government closely monitors any expression of religious faith, and even a religion that can claim only five adherents must register. However, in addition to the Sunnis and Russian Orthodox Church, only four minority faiths have registered successfully. Members of other religious congregations are prohibited from gathering publicly, proselytizing, or disseminating religious materials.

In November 2002 the president's motorcade came under armed attack. The abortive assassination attempt provided Niyazov with the pretext to launch a campaign against dissidents. According to the U.S. State Department, security forces committed numerous human rights abuses in carrying out their sweep of dissidents, including TORTURE and the punishment of suspects' families. Although the government denied charges of abuse, it refused to allow independent observers to attend the trials of the accused and denied access to members of a fact-finding mission of the ORGANIZATION FOR SECURITY AND COOPERATION IN EUROPE. Nor was the INTERNATIONAL COMMITTEE OF THE RED CROSS permitted to visit political prisoners.

In December 2006 President-for-Life Saparmyrat Niyazov died. While the human rights situation has improved to some degree under his successor, Gurbanguly Berdymukhamedov, the government continued to commit serious abuses with severe restrictions imposed on political and civil liberties. Detainees were still subject to torture and mistreatment; many were held incommunicado and in prolonged detention. The number of political prisoners is unknown. Members of religious minorities were still being persecuted, although harassment had diminished under the new regime. The U.S. State Department in its 2007 *Country Report* also cited "denial of due process and a fair trial; arbitrary interference with privacy, home, and correspondence; restrictions on freedom of speech, press, assembly, and association; restrictions on religious freedom; a government-maintained blacklist of individuals not permitted to travel abroad; violence against women; and restrictions on free association of workers." In some cases, however, the government showed more tolerance; two conscientious objectors were released without being sentenced, for example, and child labor is no longer as prevalent as it once was. Nonetheless, the French branch of HUMAN RIGHTS WATCH still considers Turkmenistan as "one of the most repressive countries in the world," noting that "independent civil society and media cannot operate openly, if at all." Turkmenistan remains closed to independent human rights monitors, including Human Rights Watch and the International Federation for Human Rights. A UN special rapporteur on freedom of religion was allowed to visit the country in September 2008, but this was a rare exception. Other UN monitors have been denied access. That Turkmenistan has escaped more widespread condemnation by Western countries such as France may be explained in part by the fact that it is rich in natural gas and, in addition, is considered an important strategic partner in a part of the world that is vital to European and U.S. interests.

Further Reading:

Amnesty International USA. Turkmenistan Human Rights. Available online. URL: http://www.amnestyusa.org/all-countries/turkmenistan/page.do?id=1011259. Accessed March 21, 2010.

Edgar, Adrienne Lynn. *Tribal Nation: The Making of Soviet Turkmenistan.* Princeton, N.J.: Princeton University Press, 2004.

Habeeb, William Mark. *Turkmenistan.* Philadelphia: Mason Crest Publishers, 2005.

Human Rights Watch. Turkmenistan Human Rights. Available online. URL: http://www.hrw.org/europecentral-asia/turkmenistan. Accessed March 21, 2010.

Tutu, Desmond (1931–) *South African antiapartheid activist and human rights defender*

The Anglican archbishop Desmond Tutu won the 1984 Nobel Peace Prize for his advocacy of human rights and racial justice in South Africa during the era of APARTHEID, the white supremacist system of government that ruled South Africa for half a century until 1994. In spite of arrests and intimidation, he continued to lead protests and draw attention to the inequalities in a country where the black majority was denied basic civil freedoms. For many years, while Nelson Mandela, the leader of the opposition African National Congress, was in prison, Archbishop Tutu was the most prominent foe of apartheid who did not take part in violent resistance. After South Africa's first free elections in which Mandela was elected president Tutu was appointed chair of the TRUTH AND RECONCILIATION COMMISSION, which provided a public forum for the disclosure of crimes committed by officials and military leaders as well as by black militants.

Tutu was born in 1931 in Klerksdorp, Transvaal, South Africa. He started out training to be a teacher but later turned to the study of theology. He was ordained as a priest in 1960 and obtained a Master of Theology in England in 1962. In 1975 he was appointed dean of St. Mary's Cathedral in Johannesburg, becoming the first black to hold that position. He was bishop of Lesotho from 1976 to 1978, and in 1978 he became the first black general secretary of the South African Council of Churches. In awarding the Peace Prize to Tutu, the Nobel Committee cited "the courage and heroism shown by black South Africans in their use of peaceful methods in the struggle against apartheid." In 1986 he was named archbishop of Cape Town, a position he gave up so that he could take over the chair of the Truth and Reconciliation Commission.

Tutu continues to speak out on issues such as poverty, AIDS, and oppressive governments in developing countries especially neighboring ZIMBABWE, whose government he condemned for its brutal repression of political opponents. (Mugabe countered by calling Tutu an "angry, evil and embittered little bishop.") He has also engaged in peacekeeping missions to Darfur and has denounced the Chinese for cracking down on protestors in TIBET before the Olympic Games in Beijing in 2008.

Further Reading:

Edelstein, Jillian. *Truth and Lies: Stories from the Truth and Reconciliation Commission in South Africa.* New York: New Press, 2002.

James, Wilmot Godfrey, and Linda van de Vijver, eds. *After the TRC: Reflections on Truth and Reconciliation in South Africa.* Athens: Ohio University Press, 2001.

Tutu, Desmond. *God Has a Dream: A Vision of Hope for Our Time.* New York: Doubleday, 2004.

Wilson, Richard A. *The Politics of Truth and Reconciliation in South Africa: Legitimizing the Post-Apartheid State.* Cambridge Studies in Law and Society. Cambridge: Cambridge University Press, 2001.

U

Uganda, human rights violations in

A former British colony, Uganda emerged relatively recently from decades of oppressive despotism. During nearly a decade in power (1971–79) IDI AMIN achieved a reputation for brutality and capriciousness on the international stage, distinguishing himself from other tyrants by his showmanship and outrageous remarks. Once, for instance, he praised ADOLF HITLER for killing Jews. He was finally ousted in 1980 by the former Ugandan leader MILTON OBOTE, whose regime turned out to be as corrupt and dictatorial as the one it had replaced. International human rights organizations estimate that up to half a million people were killed in state-sponsored killings during this period.

In July 1985 Obote, too, was forced from power by disaffected elements of the army. After a year of uncertainty, during which various factions contested for power, a former government official, Yoweri Museveni, assumed control of the country in 1986 as head of the National Resistance Party (NPR). Museveni introduced democratic and economic reforms that have brought Uganda relative stability and some degree of prosperity. Museveni has received high marks from international agencies for an aggressive campaign to halt the spread of HIV infection which has devastated many parts of Africa. He was elected to the presidency in 1996 in Uganda's first direct presidential election and reelected in 2001. Nonetheless, he has come in for criticism for maintaining what amounts to one-party rule and suppressing political opposition. He promulgated a form of one-party rule called the Movement, a system of government in which individual candidates could run for office on their own credentials but which effectively banned competing political parties. More recently he has announced a referendum in which voters will decide whether to support a multiparty system.

Museveni has also drawn the ire of the international community for intervening in neighboring Democratic Republic of the Congo in the late 1990s. Ugandan forces in the Congo were alleged to have stirred up ethnic strife between the Hema and Lendu peoples, whose bitter rivalry has led to the loss of over 7,000 lives and displaced 200,000. Ugandan security agencies in the Ituri region in eastern Congo have been implicated in TORTURE, illegal detention, and EXTRAJUDICIAL KILLINGS. Most of the Ugandan troops were later withdrawn under terms of a peace accord intended to bring a halt to fighting that at one time had involved nine African states and countless factions and armies within the Congo.

But the gravest threat to security and human rights within Uganda itself is posed by a cultlike insurgency in the north of the country—centered mainly in Acholiland—spearheaded by the Lord's Resistance Army (LRA). The rebellion by the shadowy group under JOSEPH KONY, which extends back to Museveni's rise to power in the mid-1980s, has accounted for the killings, kidnappings, and displacement of tens of thousands of people. The conflict is further complicated by tensions between Uganda and Sudan. The government in Kampala has supported rebels in Sudan, which in retaliation has supplied financing to the LRA in its campaign against Ugandan forces.

Considered the most brutal and effective guerrilla organization in Africa, the LRA claims that it is waging a war to overthrow Museveni's government and replace it with one based on the Ten Commandments. Although it purports to be a Christian fundamentalist group, Christian evangelicals have strongly denounced the LRA. The U.S. State Department has branded it a terrorist group that seeks to impose "a regime that will implement the group's brand of Christianity." The LRA is certainly well armed; it is said to have a formidable arsenal that includes shoulder-fired rocket launchers, making it, as one observer put it, "better equipped than many African armies." LRA guerrillas frequently conduct raids at night on villages, abducting children who then are either conscripted into their ranks or turned into sex slaves or forced laborers. Children who fail to obey orders are often executed—by other children.

According to UNICEF, about 30 children are abducted every day, often from boarding schools or their homes. Some 34,000 children have been abducted since 1994.

Aid agencies estimate that 23,000 people have been killed by both LRA and Ugandan forces in 18 years of civil war. The refugee population has swollen to over 1.2 million who have found temporary shelter in makeshift camps where health conditions are grim and children often suffer from malnutrition. In addition to the Ugandan refugee population, there are at least 24,000 Sudanese REFUGEES in the country who have been forcibly displaced by the conflict and several thousand more—the number is not known—who have been displaced inside the Sudan. In 2002 the LRA threatened to attack international aid agencies working with DISPLACED PERSON CAMPS. While relief agencies did scale back their staff and diminished their role, they did not close operations altogether. According to Médecins sans Frontières (DOCTORS WITHOUT BORDERS), "civilians are forced to choose between staying in insecure villages and towns, thereby risking another attack that could cost them their lives, or fleeing to urban areas that cannot offer them even the minimum conditions necessary to survive."

In March 2002 Kampala mounted a massive operation code-named Iron Fist to eliminate the LRA once and for all, sending 10,000 soldiers to the north. But the rebels put up stiff resistance, and the violence only escalated. "The rebels are all over," reported a local missionary. "I would say practically the whole countryside is in their hands." Just weeks after Museveni announced that they had "nearly defeated the LRA," guerrillas attacked a refugee camp in an unusual show of force, killing more than 50. "They don't usually attack in such a large group and they rarely use these big machine guns and mortar bombs," one witness said. "They must have amassed new supplies from somewhere." A government spokesman dismissed the strategic significance of the attack as "just a desperate attempt at getting publicity, because they know they are being crushed by our forces on the ground." But there is little evidence that the LRA has suffered a crippling blow in spite of Kampala's efforts. If anything, the number of kidnappings actually increased. In the two years since Operation Iron Fist, more than 10,000 children were abducted. As a result, families in the beleaguered region are sending their children into nearby towns in what amounts to a nightly exodus.

In February 2004 LRA insurgents raided a refugee camp, killing more than 200 before vanishing into the night. Just a month previously, the United Nations had decided to act. Luis Moreno-Ocampo, chief prosecutor of the INTERNATIONAL CRIMINAL COURT, announced that the court was considering an inquiry into rights abuses by the LRA in response to a request from Museveni, who appeared at a joint news conference with Moreno-Ocampo

at the time. The court charged the LRA with child abductions, summary executions, torture, rape and sexual assault, FORCED LABOR, and mutilation. Uganda thus became the first government to refer a case to the ICC since the court began its work. (The Ugandan parliament ratified the ICC treaty on June 14, 2002.) By referring the complaint to the ICC, the Ugandan government is committing itself to cooperating with the ICC "to investigate crimes, provide evidence, arrest and surrender persons sought by the court, and protect witnesses and victims. Such cooperation must extend to investigation by the prosecutor into UPDF [Ugandan People's Defense Forces] crimes."

In fact, many human rights groups, including HUMAN RIGHTS WATCH and AMNESTY INTERNATIONAL, expressed concern that any investigation by the court would concentrate wholly on crimes committed by the guerrilla group and ignore those carried out by Kampala. According to these groups, the UPDF, a government paramilitary force, is guilty of "extrajudicial killings, rape and sexual assault, forcible displacement of over one million civilians, and the recruitment of children under the age of 15 into government militias." "Human Rights Watch has documented many shocking abuses by the LRA in Uganda," said Richard Dicker, director of the International Justice program at Human Rights Watch. "But the ICC prosecutor cannot ignore the crimes that Ugandan government troops allegedly have committed."

The Ugandan government announced that it was removing one possible obstacle to an ICC investigation by exempting leaders of the LRA from an AMNESTY law that the parliament had passed that would have immunized individuals responsible for war crimes in the conflict. Some international organizations, however, objected on the grounds that removing a blanket amnesty would only fuel the conflict because the guerrilla leaders in effect had nothing left to lose. For instance, the Refugee Law Project, a Kampala-based advocacy group, asserted that LRA leader Joseph Kony would rebuff any effort to bring him to the negotiating table because he was "fighting for survival" and probably assumed that he would be killed if he tried to surrender or negotiate. In addition, many experts believe that without the cooperation of neighboring Sudan, which has backed the LRA, the ICC will make little progress. Sudanese cooperation, however, is likely only if Kampala ends its own support for rebels operating against Khartoum. "Nobody is winning this war," observed one missionary priest, "we are all losers."

The outrages perpetrated by the cultlike LRA have overshadowed alleged human rights violations by Ugandan forces that have been trying to suppress the group. Human rights groups charge Ugandan forces with a number of serious abuses, including extrajudicial execution, arbitrary detention, torture, rape, sexual assault, child recruitment, and the forcible relocation of civilians on the grounds that it was necessary for security. Under an order issued in 2002, for example, some 300,000 civilians were displaced. Altogether, it is estimated that 1.8 million people have been displaced because of armed conflict. In the United Nations Secretary-General's report to the Security Council on children in armed conflict, the UPDF was specifically cited for recruiting children. The Ugandan government's Joint Anti-Terrorist Task Force (JATF) has also been taken to task for committing abuses; in one case, four men detained on charges of terrorism were executed without trial. However, because of a culture of impunity, few soldiers or security officials have ever been punished for unlawful killings, sexual violence, and torture, according to Amnesty International. The 20-year war against the LRA has also left hundreds of thousands of people in northern Uganda—the former base of the group—physically and mentally traumatized, but the government has been cited for failing to put into place an effective program to treat them. "Thousands of Ugandans still bear the physical and mental scars of the abuses they suffered," stated Godfrey Odongo, Amnesty International's Uganda specialist. "They are unable to go forward with their lives. They desperately need government assistance to help them come to terms with the ordeals they survived and rebuild their lives—assistance that sadly has not been forthcoming."

In recent years a virulent anti-gay campaign has erupted in the country, influenced to some extent by fundamentalist Christian conservative groups in the United States. In 2010 the Ugandan legislature was considering a proposed Anti-Homosexuality Bill that would further criminalize homosexuality with harsh prison sentences. (Under international pressure, though, the government has retreated from proposals to impose the death penalty for certain types of homosexual behavior.) In a sign of how incendiary the anti-gay climate has become, a Ugandan tabloid (called *Rolling Stone*, unrelated to the U.S. publication of that name) carried an article that declared "100 Pictures of Uganda's Top Homos Leak" next to a banner headline which read: "Hang Them," inviting people to attack those pictured.

See also CHILDREN'S RIGHTS.

Further Reading:
Allen, Peter A. P. *Interesting Times: Life in Uganda under Idi Amin.* London: Book Guild, Limited, 2000.
Dodge, Cole P., and Magne Raundelen. *Reaching Children in War: Sudan, Uganda, and Mozambique.* London: Taylor & Francis, 1992.
Eichstaedt, Peter. *First Kill Your Family: Child Soldiers of Uganda and the Lord's Resistance Army.* Chicago: Lawrence Hill Books, 2009.

Finnström, Sverker. *Living with Bad Surroundings: War, History, and Everyday Moments in Northern Uganda.* The Cultures and Practice of Violence. Durham, N.C.: Duke University Press, 2008.
Human Rights Network Uganda. Available online. URL: http://www.hurinet.or.ug/. Accessed March 21, 2010.
Mutibwa, Phares. *Uganda since Independence: A Story of Unfulfilled Hopes.* London: Africa World Press, 1992.
NCADC. Uganda Human Rights. Available online. URL: http://ncadcworld.wordpress.com/2010/01/25/uganda-human-rights-2009-2010/. Accessed March 21, 2010.
Uganda Human Rights Commission. Available online. URL: http://www.uhrc.ug/. Accessed March 21, 2010.

Uighur, persecution of   *See* CAMBODIA, HUMAN RIGHTS VIOLATIONS IN; CHINA, HUMAN RIGHTS VIOLATIONS IN; WAR ON TERROR.

Ukraine, human rights violations in
The election of Viktor Yushchenko as Ukraine's president in December 2004 was hailed by human rights groups as a triumph of democracy that offered the prospect of political reform. The election that put Yushchenko into power only took place after an earlier disputed election in which his opponent, former prime minister Viktor Yanukovych, was declared the winner by the election commission. Until Yushchenko assumed the presidency in early 2005, Ukraine, the largest of the republics that formed the former Soviet Union, had been dominated by President Leonid Kuchma. Although Kuchma brought some measure of economic progress to Ukraine, he was dogged by allegations of corruption and human rights violations. During the first round of voting in October 2004, Kuchma's hand was seen in manipulating results to achieve Yanukovych's narrow win. According to the ORGANIZATION FOR SECURITY AND COOPERATION IN EUROPE (OSCE), state-owned media coverage was biased in favor of Kuchma's hand-picked candidate. The national television channels from which most Ukrainians get their news were either state-owned or controlled by persons close to Kuchma. The International Election Observation Mission reported that "State executive authorities and the Central Election Commission (CEC) displayed a lack of will to conduct a genuine democratic election process."

Thousands of demonstrators gathered in central Kiev, the capital, to protest the results of the first election. Over the next several days the pro-Yushchenko demonstrators remained in place until the election was annulled and new—and fair—elections were held. Fears of violence, however, were not realized as the army and security forces stayed in their barracks. According to news reports, several high-ranking officers in the security police sided with the demonstrators and warned against the use of force to crush the protest. In a surprising ruling, the Ukrainian Supreme Court determined that the election had been flawed and called for new elections. Perhaps just as surprisingly, Kuchma accepted the outcome and withdrew his support from Yanukovych. The former prime minister did, however, retain considerable support in the east of the country, a manufacturing and mining region, while Yushchenko's base of support rested mostly in the west. Yushchenko had managed to mobilize such popular support because he promised a dramatic departure from authoritarian rule.

Throughout his contentious campaign, Yushchenko called for respect of basic rights and the need for political reform. Upon assuming office, he named as prime minister Yulia Tymoshenko, whose pro-Western stance has aggravated the Kremlin. (Russian president Vladimir Putin had opposed a second round of voting and made no secret of his preference for Yanukovych.) The need for reform is unquestionable. Under Kuchma, suspects were frequently tortured and mistreated by police, and there were reports of deaths in custody. According to AMNESTY INTERNATIONAL, alleged mistreatment included beatings, the use of electric shocks, pistol whippings, and asphyxiation. Freedom of expression was hampered and the media stifled. The government also put restrictions on freedom of assembly. The controversial presidential election in 2004 was not without precedent. In the past, parliamentary elections have been marred by incidents of violence, intimidation, and "inappropriate influencing" of voters. In some cases, opposition figures have been slain under mysterious circumstances.

Journalists who have written about political corruption were also at risk under Kuchma's rule. In a five-year period (1998–2003), 10 journalists were killed in the country, according to Paris-based Reporters Sans Frontières; most of the murders were never solved. Taped telephone conversations—smuggled to the West by a former presidential bodyguard—allegedly linked Kuchma himself to the 2000 kidnapping and beheading of 31-year-old Internet journalist Georgy Gongadze, who had been a frequent critic of the government. Claiming that they were unable to identify the voice on the tape—apparently sanctioning the murder—as Kuchma's, prosecutors dropped the case. The new government has promised to look into such cases, and there has been widespread speculation that Kuchma—who had stepped down voluntarily—might be indicted for the murder and for other charges, although the ex-president declared that he was innocent of any wrongdoing.

Within months of taking office, Yushchenko's government was rocked by scandal and allegations of corruption,

forcing the president to fire his cabinet, including the popular but controversial Tymoshenko. Before he could win approval for a new government, though, he had to cut a deal with his old rival Yanukovych. One of the reported conditions was that any outstanding cases against partisans of Yanukovych would no longer go forward. Disappointed Yushchenko supporters viewed the agreement as an end to the reformist era ushered in by the Orange Revolution.

Five years later the country was still embroiled in political discord. The same three politicians who dominated during the Orange Revolution—Yushchenko, Yanukovych, and Prime Minister Yulia Tymoshenko (a former ally of the president who later broke with him)—were still engaged in rancorous feuding in 2009 in advance of general elections. The political upheaval and economic turmoil of recent years had left the public fatigued and disillusioned. In a turnabout from the outcome of the 2004 election, Yanukovych won the January 2010 vote, defeating his rivals Tymoshenko and Yushchenko, who came in third.

Further Reading:

European Union Agency for Fundamental Rights. Ukrainian Helsinki Rights Union. Available online. URL: http://infoportal.fra.europa.eu/InfoPortal/human OrganisationFrontEndAccess.do?id=11766. Accessed March 21, 2010.

Human Rights Watch. Ukraine Human Rights. Available online. URL: http://www.hrw.org/europecentral-asia/ukraine. Accessed March 21, 2010.

Lieven, Anatol. *Ukraine and Russia: A Fraternal Rivalry.* Washington, D.C.: United States Institute of Peace Press, 1999.

Wilson, Andrew. *Ukraine: Unexpected Nation.* New Haven, Conn.: Yale University Press, 2002.

Ulemek, Milorad   *See* WAR CRIMINALS OF THE FORMER YUGOSLAVIA.

United Arab Emirates, human rights violations in

The United Arab Emirates (UAE), composed of seven emirates on the Persian Gulf, is widely regarded as among the more advanced countries in the Middle East. However, according to the 2008 U.S. Department of State annual HUMAN RIGHTS REPORT, the UAE is woefully deficient when it comes to human rights. The emirates, which are mostly ruled by hereditary royal families, lack democratic institutions. According to the report, most emirates curtail political opposition, deny their citizens the right to a quick and fair trial, and mistreat detainees. (There are some exceptions; the Dubai police have opened special departments to protect the rights of people taken into custody.)

The U.S. report stated that arbitrary detention "remained a problem," the judiciary "lacked full independence," and officials "interfered with privacy and restricted civil liberties," including freedom of speech, press, association, and religion. In 2009 a new draft law was introduced to restrict the ability of the media to report on sensitive issues and give the governments the power to decide on whether a journalist is legitimate and which foreign media companies will be permitted to operate in the UAE. Freedoms of religion and assembly are similarly curtailed. On the other hand, the emirates have been slow to crack down on the trafficking of children, who are often pressed into service as camel jockeys. Significantly, the UAE has not signed most international human rights and labor rights treaties, including the International Covenant on Civil and Political Rights, the Convention on the Protection of the Rights of All Migrant Workers and Members of Their Families (especially important in view of the large numbers of migrant workers in the emirates), and the CONVENTION AGAINST TORTURE. While the Foreign Ministry has denied most of the allegations in the State Department report, asserting that it was filled with "various generalities and unsubstantiated statements," a videotape graphically showing torture by a member of the Abu Dhabi royal family, broadcast on network television in the United States, represented a grave setback to the UAE's efforts to burnish its human rights image. The 45-minute video, made in 2004, but only released in 2009, showed Sheik Issa bin Zayed al-Nahyan torturing an Afghan merchant, using whips, cattle prods, and a wooden plank with a nail, while relying on the assistance of police officers. (The sheik also used an SUV to run over the merchant, whom he believed had cheated him; the victim survived the ordeal with serious injuries.) It was reported that Sheik Issa had made previous torture videos—also depicting police cooperation—that he liked to watch in his palace. Initially, the government refused to act, saying that the incident was a matter between private parties, but spurred by international protests, took the step of detaining the sheik and putting him on trial. In spite of the graphic video evidence, Sheik Issa was acquitted. Although the judge did not explain his reasoning, Issa's lawyer insisted that his client had been drugged as part of an extortion attempt.

United Nations and the Geneva Conventions

The United Nations, which in 2004 had 191 members, is bound only by decisions of its Security Council and not necessarily by the GENEVA CONVENTIONS. This anomaly exists in spite of the fact that nearly all member states of the United Nations have also ratified the Geneva Conventions. The international body itself is not a party to the conventions. According to a representative of the UN Office of Legal Affairs (OLA) the role of the United Nations is "to carry out the will of the international community as expressed by it in the Security Council." In an essay for the CRIMES OF WAR PROJECT, Roy Gutman points out that citizens of a state bound by the conventions can "escape their legal obligations" by "donning the blue helmets"— that is, joining a UN peacekeeping force. That possibility arises because the force takes its orders directly from the Security Council, although in fact peacekeepers are equipped and supplied by their home countries. Resolutions by the Security Council responsible for deployment of UN peacekeepers do not invariably cite the applicability of provisions of the Geneva Conventions—for instance, the requirement of free passage for civilians through front lines even if they are citizens of the adversary.

The UN Charter defined the body's role as bringing peace to the world, and as a result the United Nations did not participate in the codification of rules of war that was the focus of the 1949 Geneva Conventions. "War having been outlawed, the regulation of its conduct has ceased to be relevant," stated the UN International Law Commission. In this view, the United Nations had no business becoming involved in drawing up an international accord to govern how conflict should be conducted. Instead, drafting of the conventions took place under the auspices of the INTERNATIONAL COMMITTEE OF THE RED CROSS (ICRC). Tensions between the two institutions periodically surfaces in conflict situations. In 1993, for example, UN forces involved in peacekeeping operations in Somalia detained hundreds of Somalis and then denied the ICRC access to the prisoners, causing the Red Cross to suspend its operations in protest.

The ICRC would prefer an explicit declaration "that UN troops are bound by INTERNATIONAL HUMANITARIAN LAW and that everyone under the UN flag will be informed, trained, and monitored," according to an ICRC representative quoted by Gutman. Discussions about drafting guidelines for UN deployments have in fact been ongoing between the ICRC and UN experts since 1993. The results of these negotiations did not satisfy the ICRC because the proposed drafts only held out the prospect of a UN soldier accused of a violation of the Geneva Conventions to be liable for trial in his own country. The concept of UNIVERSAL JURISDICTION—the right to try a human rights offender in any state with a competent and fair judiciary— was ruled out. Such a case is hardly theoretical; in late 2004 several UN peacekeepers in eastern Congo were implicated in rapes and other forms of sexual abuse of Congolese women and girls.

Further Reading:
Fasulo, Linda. *An Insider's Guide to the UN.* New Haven, Conn.: Yale University Press, 2003.

Gutman, Roy, ed. *Crimes of War: What the Public Should Know.* New York: W. W. Norton & Company, 1999.

Jinks, Derek. *The Rules of War: The Geneva Conventions in the Age of Terror.* Oxford: Oxford University Press, 2005.

Meisler, Stanley. *United Nations: The First Fifty Years.* New York: Atlantic Monthly Press, 1997.

Pilloud, Claude. *Commentary on the Additional Protocols of 8 June 1977 to the Geneva Conventions of 12 August 1949.* Boston: Brill Academic Publishers, 1987.

Roberts, Adam, and Richard Guelff. *Documents on the Laws of War.* Oxford: Oxford University Press, 2000.

Schlesigner, Stephen. *Act of Creation: The Founding of the United Nations: A Story of Superpowers, Secret Agents, Wartime Allies and Enemies, and Their Quest for a Peaceful World.* Westport, Conn.: Westview Press, 2003.

Trombly, Maria. *Journalist's Guide to the Geneva Conventions.* Indianapolis: Society of Professional Journalists, 2000.

Weiss, Thomas G., David P. Forsythe, and Roger A. Coate. *United Nations and Changing World Politics.* Westport, Conn.: Westview Press, 2004.

United Nations Commission on Human Rights   *See* UNITED NATIONS HUMAN RIGHTS COMMISSION.

United Nations Guiding Principles on Internal Displacement

The Guiding Principles on Internal Displacement were drafted by the United Nations to address the problems and needs of INTERNALLY DISPLACED PERSONS (IDPs) throughout the world. IDPs are defined by the United Nations as "persons or groups of persons who have been forced or obliged to flee or to leave their homes or places of habitual residence, in particular as a result of or in order to avoid the effects of armed conflict, situations of generalized violence, violations of human rights or natural or human-made disasters, and who have not crossed an internationally recognized State border." REFUGEES, by contrast, are people who are forced to flee across international borders. The Guiding Principles are designed to "identify rights and guarantees relevant to the protection of persons from forced displacement" and to ensure their protection and assistance while they remain displaced and when they are eventually returned to their home country or resettled in another country. Although the principles are not a binding legal instrument, they reflect and are consistent with international human rights and humanitarian law.

The creation of the Guiding Principles, which were issued in 1998, was impelled by a 1992 mandate by the UNITED NATIONS HUMAN RIGHTS COUNCIL (UNHRC) and reinforced by subsequent resolutions of both the UNHRC and the General Assembly. The United Nations was moved to act on the basis of a study that found that while existing law did provide for some needs of the internally displaced, there were significant gaps when it came to issues such as protecting and assisting displaced persons. The individual most responsible for laying the foundations for the Guiding Principles was the then Under-Secretary-General for Humanitarian Affairs SÉRGIO VIEIRA DE MELLO. He was tragically killed in a terrorist bombing of UN headquarters in Baghdad, Iraq, in 2003.

Further Reading:
Feller, Erika, Volker Turk, and Frances Nicholson, eds. *Refugee Protection in International Law: UNHCR's Global Consultations on International Protection.* Cambridge: Cambridge University Press, 2003.

Fritz, Mark. *Lost on Earth: Nomads of the New World.* New York: Routledge, 2000.

Groenewold, Julia, and Doctors Without Borders. *World in Crisis: The Politics of Survival at the End of the Twentieth Century.* London: Routledge, 1996.

Helton, Arthur C. *The Price of Indifference: Refugees and Humanitarian Action in the New Century.* A Council on Foreign Relations Book. Oxford: Oxford University Press, 2002.

Hyndman, Jennifer. *Managing Displacement: Refugees and the Politics of Humanitarianism.* Minneapolis: University of Minnesota Press, 2000.

Ingleby, David, ed. *Forced Migration and Mental Health: Rethinking the Care of Refugees and Displaced Persons.* New York: Plenum US, 2004.

Lischer, Sarah Kenyon. *Dangerous Sanctuaries: Refugee Camps, Civil War, and the Dilemmas of Humanitarian Aid.* Cornell Studies in Security Affairs. Ithaca, N.Y.: Cornell University Press, 2005.

Moorehead, Caroline. *Human Cargo: A Journey among Refugees.* New York: Henry Holt and Co., 2005.

United Nations High Commissioner for Human Rights

The United Nations High Commissioner for Human Rights, a post created in 1993, is the principal UN official with responsibility for human rights and is directly answerable to the secretary-general. The Office of the High Commissioner for Human Rights (OHCHR) is based in Geneva, Switzerland, with an office at United Nations Headquarters in New York.

Several human rights institutions and agencies exist within the United Nations, but they are all responsible for promoting and protecting human rights—civil, cultural, economic, political, and social—throughout the world based upon the principles affirmed by the UNIVERSAL DECLARATION OF HUMAN RIGHTS, adopted by the UN General Assembly in 1948. The High Commissioner is the public face of the UNITED NATIONS HUMAN RIGHTS COUNCIL and other human rights institutions; according to the UN job description, he or she serves as a "moral authority" and "voice for victims." The commissioner is also mandated to confer with governments, nongovernmental organizations (NGOs), academic institutions, and the private sector to ensure commitment to human rights. The commissioner has an educational role which he or she fulfills by promoting awareness of human rights issues and stimulating "thinking on prevention" of abuses. When new challenges arise—for example, TRAFFICKING IN PERSONS, HIV/AIDS, biotechnology, and the effects of globalization—it is the commissioner's role to address their human rights implications. The commissioner additionally supports other human rights agencies in the United Nations, providing expertise, research, advice, and administrative services.

Further Reading:
Brysk, Alison, ed. *Globalization and Human Rights.* Berkeley: University of California Press, 2002.
Fasulo, Linda. *An Insider's Guide to the UN.* New Haven, Conn.: Yale University Press, 2003.
Gutman, Roy, ed. *Crimes of War: What the Public Should Know.* New York: W. W. Norton & Company, 1999.
Trombly, Maria. *Journalist's Guide to the Geneva Conventions.* Indianapolis: Society of Professional Journalists, 2000.
United Nations Office of the High Commissioner for Human Rights. Available online. URL: http://www.ohchr.org/EN/Pages/WelcomePage.aspx. Accessed March 21, 2010.
Weiss, Thomas G., David P. Forsythe, Roger A. Coate. *United Nations and Changing World Politics.* Westport, Conn.: Westview Press, 2004.

United Nations High Commissioner for Refugees (UNHCR)

The position of the United Nations High Commissioner for Refugees (UNHCR) was established on December 14, 1950, by the UN General Assembly. The UNHCR was charged with leading and coordinating international action to protect refugees and resolve refugee problems worldwide. REFUGEES are legally defined "as people who are outside their countries because of a well-founded fear of persecution based on their race, religion, nationality, political opinion or membership in a particular social group, and who cannot or do not want to return home." The UNHCR has two primary purposes. The first is to protect the lives and rights of refugees, and the second is to ensure that refugees have the right to ASYLUM or are allowed to settle in the country where they have taken refuge or in third country if conditions at home make it impossible to return. The UNHCR also seeks to ensure that refugees are not repatriated against their will. In discharging its responsibility, the agency (the United Nations does not call it an "office") has assisted an estimated 50 million refugees over the last five decades; it is currently helping about 17 million people who meet the criteria of refugees. The agency has a staff of about 6,200 people based in more than 116 countries. The UNHCR's programs and policies are approved by an executive committee composed of 64 member states (which meets annually) and a "working group," or standing committee (which meets several times a year).

The office of High Commissioner for Refugees was one of the many attempts in the 20th century to provide protection and assistance to refugees. A similar position had been established by the LEAGUE OF NATIONS (the predecessor of the United Nations) in 1921. After World War II, two organizations—the United Nations Relief and Rehabilitation Administration and the International Refugee Organization—worked to address the refugee crisis created by the war. Initially the UNHCR was only supposed to exist for three years—sufficient time, it was thought, to resettle the 1.2 million European refugees that then remained from the war. But as continual conflicts around the world produced ever-greater populations of refugees, the mandate for the UNHCR was extended, and it is now a permanent institution within the United Nations. For its work the UNHCR has earned two Nobel Peace Prizes, in 1954 and 1981.

Further Reading:
Feller, Erika, Volker Turk, and Frances Nicholson, eds. *Refugee Protection in International Law: UNHCR's Global Consultations on International Protection.* Cambridge: Cambridge University Press, 2003.
Fritz, Mark. *Lost on Earth: Nomads of the New World.* New York: Routledge, 2000.
Groenewold, Julia, and Doctors Without Borders. *World in Crisis: The Politics of Survival at the End of the Twentieth Century.* London: Routledge, 1996.
Helton, Arthur C. *The Price of Indifference: Refugees and Humanitarian Action in the New Century.* A Council on Foreign Relations Book. Oxford: Oxford University Press, 2002.

Hyndman, Jennifer. *Managing Displacement: Refugees and the Politics of Humanitarianism.* Minneapolis: University of Minnesota Press, 2000.

Ingleby, David, ed. *Forced Migration and Mental Health: Rethinking the Care of Refugees and Displaced Persons.* New York: Plenum US, 2004.

Lischer, Sarah Kenyon. *Dangerous Sanctuaries: Refugee Camps, Civil War, and the Dilemmas of Humanitarian Aid.* Cornell Studies in Security Affairs. Ithaca, N.Y.: Cornell University Press, 2005.

Moorehead, Caroline. *Human Cargo: A Journey among Refugees.* New York: Henry Holt and Co., 2005.

United Nations High Commissioner for Refugees. Available online. URL: http://www.unhcr.org/cgi-bin/texis/vtx/home. Accessed March 21, 2010.

United Nations Human Rights Council (formerly United Nations Human Rights Commission)

Officially the United Nations Commission on Human Rights (UNCHR), the Human Rights Commission was established in 1946 to promote and protect human rights. It addresses such issues as arbitrary detention, the right to education, and INTERNALLY DISPLACED PERSONS and investigates reports of human rights abuses that may have occurred in any of the 53 states that are members of the UNCHR. (The representation is based on region; Western countries, for example, have three seats altogether.) The commission meets annually in the spring for six weeks in Geneva and may meet between sessions if the need arises. During its regular session, the UNCHR will adopt about 100 resolutions and decisions.

Founded after World War II, the UN was first chaired by Eleanor Roosevelt, the widow of U.S. president Franklin Delano Roosevelt. Under her leadership, in 1948 the Commission produced the UNIVERSAL DECLARATION OF HUMAN RIGHTS, a seminal document that called for the recognition of fundamental human rights for every man, woman, and child on the planet. For all its lofty goals, however, the UNHRC has repeatedly been mired in controversy over the half-century of its existence. It has condemned Israel for human rights violations by votes of 50-1, with the United States in lone opposition. In 2001 the commission actually expelled the United States even as Libya, Sudan, and Syria, none of them with good human rights records, were being offered seats on it. The ouster was regarded as a rebuke to policies of the Bush administration by delegates representing developing countries. (The United States rejoined a year later.) In another controversial move that called the body's credibility into question and sparked widespread criticism, Libya's representative was elected to chair the UNCHR in 2002. "Countries with dreadful rights records should never be in charge of chairing the Commission on Human Rights," Rory Mungoven, global advocacy director for HUMAN RIGHTS WATCH, said at the time. "Libya's long record of human rights abuses clearly does not merit such a reward."

Attempts to reform the Human Rights Commission or scrap it altogether and replace it with a new Human Rights Council with fewer—and more democratically responsive—members were still running into roadblocks in 2005. A document issued by the General Assembly after a summit in September attended by more than 150 world leaders said only that a Human Rights Council should be created. However, since the document left the details to the deeply divided General Assembly, it was uncertain whether any substantive change could be expected soon.

In 2006 the UN General Assembly voted to replace the UNCHR with the UN Human Rights Council. After years of shunning the earlier UN Human Rights Commission, the United States decided to seek a seat on the council in 2009, shortly after the Obama administration took office. The Bush administration, by contrast, had expressed strong misgivings about the composition of the previous 47-member commission, which was dominated by Asian and African nations (with 26 votes as of 2009). The Bush administration argued that the body was more likely to call for the investigation of alleged human rights abuses by ISRAEL than to seriously consider human rights violations committed by member states such as ZIMBABWE. By contrast, the Obama administration contended that the United States could exert far more influence on the newly constituted council if it were a member, rather than remaining on the sidelines. Although the reversal was welcomed by human rights organizations, some critics, such as former UN representative John Bolton, who served under the Bush administration, were dismissive, saying, "You don't show up at every ragtag little organization that comes into existence."

Further Reading:

Brysk, Alison, ed. *Globalization and Human Rights.* Berkeley: University of California Press, 2002.

Fasulo, Linda. *An Insider's Guide to the UN.* New Haven, Conn.: Yale University Press, 2003.

Gutman, Roy, ed. *Crimes of War: What the Public Should Know.* New York: W. W. Norton & Company, 1999.

Trombly, Maria. *Journalist's Guide to the Geneva Conventions.* Indianapolis: Society of Professional Journalists, 2000.

United Nations Human Rights Council. Available online. URL: http://www2.ohchr.org/english/bodies/hrcouncil/. Accessed March 21, 2010.

Weiss, Thomas G., David P. Forsythe, and Roger A. Coate. *United Nations and Changing World Politics.* Westport, Conn.: Westview Press, 2004.

United Nations Resolution 1368

United Nations Resolution 1368 was adopted by the UN Security Council on September 12, 2001, one day after the terrorist strikes on the World Trade Center and the Pentagon. In it the Security Council condemned "in the strongest possible terms" "the horrifying terrorist attacks which took place on 11 September 2001 in New York, Washington, D.C., and Pennsylvania and regards such acts, like any act of international terrorism, as a threat to international peace and security." The resolution called upon states to work together to bring to justice the "perpetrators, organizers and sponsors" of the attacks and warned that individuals or states who provided assistance or harbored those responsible would be held accountable. Two weeks later, on September 28, the Security Council adopted another resolution—1373—which invoked Chapter VII of the UN Charter, making the resolution binding upon UN member states, who were obliged to "ensure that any person who participates in the financing, planning, preparation or perpetration of terrorist acts or in supporting terrorist acts is brought to justice and ensure that, in addition to any other measures against them, such terrorist acts are established as serious criminal offences in domestic laws and regulations and that the punishment duly reflects the seriousness of such terrorist acts." The resolution also obliged member states to provide assistance to one another in connection with criminal investigations or legal proceedings related to the "financing or support of terrorist acts." States were also urged to take all necessary measures to prevent the free movement of terrorist groups through their territory.

Further Reading:

Burke, Jason. *Al-Qaeda: Casting a Shadow of Terror.* London: I. B. Tauris, 2004.
———. *Al-Qaeda: The True Story of Radical Islam.* London: I. B. Tauris, 2004.
Gunaratna, Rohan. *Inside Al Qaeda: Global Network of Terror.* New York: Berkley Publishing Group, 2003.
Scheuer, Michael. *Imperial Hubris: Why the West Is Losing the War on Terror.* Washington, D.C.: Potomac Books, 2004.
Zayy-at, Montasser al-. *The Road to Al-Qaeda: The Story of Bin Laden's Right-Hand Man.* Critical Studies on Islam. Translated by Ahmed Fekry. Edited by Sara Nimis. Ann Arbor, Mich.: Pluto Press, 2004.

United Nations Working Group on Enforced or Involuntary Disappearances

The Declaration on the Protection of All Persons from Enforced Disappearance, proclaimed by the United Nations General Assembly, defined a *disappearance* as a situation when "persons are arrested, detained or abducted against their will or otherwise deprived of their liberty by officials of different branches or levels of Government, or by organized groups, or private individuals acting on behalf of, or with the support, direct or indirect, consent or acquiescence of the Government, followed by a refusal to disclose the fate or whereabouts of the persons concerned or a refusal to acknowledge the deprivation of their liberty, which places such persons outside the protection of the law." The practice of DISAPPEARANCES has become increasingly frequent in recent years, especially in internal conflicts such as the Algerian civil war and the so-called dirty wars in Latin American countries during the 1970s.

In February 1980 the UNITED NATIONS HUMAN RIGHTS COUNCIL decided to "establish for a period of one year a working group consisting of five of its members, to serve as experts in their individual capacities, to examine questions relevant to enforced or involuntary disappearances of persons." The mandate for the working group has been renewed ever since. The Working Group on Enforced or Involuntary Disappearances deals with specific violations anywhere in the world. (Similar groups established previously were only mandated to address disappearances in a particular country.) The Working Group is charged with assisting the relatives of disappeared persons to ascertain the fate and whereabouts of their missing family members. The group then communicates reports of disappearances to the governments of the relevant countries (regardless of whether the government has ratified the Declaration on the Protection of All Persons from Enforced Disappearance).

The group "acts essentially as a channel of communication." Since its inception, some 50,000 individual cases in more than 70 countries have come to the attention of the group. Only a fraction of those cases have been "clarified" by the group, however, because the facts in many cases are still in doubt. The Working Group is credited with preventing further disappearances "through its patient and persistent contacts with the Governments concerned," according to the United Nations. The group has also been mandated by the Human Rights Commission to "take action in connection with acts of intimidation or reprisals against relatives of missing persons and private individuals or groups who seek to cooperate or have cooperated with United Nations." The group meets three times a year in New York and Geneva, although it has a mechanism to respond to urgent cases between sessions. The group then informs governments about the decisions it takes regarding cases in their countries. It also prods governments to take action about cases requiring additional clarification.

Further Reading:

Arditti, Rita. *Searching for Life: The Grandmothers of the Plaza De Mayo and the Disappeared Children of Argentina.* University of California Press, 1999.

Davis, William Columbus. *Warnings from the Far South: Democracy versus Dictatorship in Uruguay, Argentina, and Chile.* New York: Praeger Publishers, 1995.

Guest, Iain. *Behind the Disappearances: Argentina's Dirty War against Human Rights and the United Nations.* Pennsylvania Studies in Human Rights. Philadelphia: University of Pennsylvania Press, 2000.

Gutman, Roy, ed. *Crimes of War: What the Public Should Know.* New York: W. W. Norton & Company, 1999.

Kornbluh, Peter. *The Pinochet File: A Declassified Dossier on Atrocity and Accountability.* A National Security Archive Book. New York: New Press, 2003.

Politzer, Patricia, and Diane Wachtel. *Fear in Chile: Lives under Pinochet.* New York: New Press, 2001.

United Nations High Commissioner for Human Rights. *Working Group on Enforced or Involuntary Disappearances.* Available online. URL: http://www2.ohchr.org/english/issues/disappear/index.htm. Accessed March 21, 2010.

Unit 731 *See* MANCHURIA, JAPANESE WAR CRIMES IN.

Universal Declaration of Human Rights

The Universal Declaration of Human Rights, adopted by the United Nations on December 10, 1948, is an affirmation of the dignity and rights of all human beings based on principles expressed in the UN Charter. Adopted in 1945, the UN Charter set the goal of "promoting and encouraging respect for human rights and for fundamental freedoms of all without distinction as to race, sex, language, and religion." Article 1 of the Universal Declaration echoes these sentiments: "All human beings are born free and equal in dignity and human rights. They are endowed with reason and conscience and should act towards one another in a spirit of brotherhood."

The UN Charter, while giving new emphasis to human rights, was considered insufficient by many human rights advocates. What was needed, they believed, was an international equivalent of the United States Bill of Rights, which affirmed such liberties as freedom of the press, freedom of worship, and the right to DUE PROCESS. The declaration of 1948 is considered the first of a three-part international covenant addressing human rights. (The second part deals with civil and political rights and the third with economic, social, and cultural rights.) The Universal Declaration consists of 30 articles that set out such rights as life, liberty, and security of person; freedom of conscience, religion, opinion, expression, association, and assembly; freedom from arbitrary arrest; the right to a fair and impartial trial; the presumption of innocence; the right to privacy; the right to an adequate standard of living; the right to education; the right to marry and raise a family; the right to participate in government and in the social life of society; and the right to rest and leisure. In addition, all human beings are entitled to own property and enjoy the right to leave and return to their home country; they also have the right to work under acceptable conditions, receive equal pay for equal work, and join labor unions.

All signatories to the Universal Declaration were urged to publish—and publicize—it in their own countries. Provisions of some 90 national constitutions drafted since 1948 can be traced to the declaration, according to the Franklin and Eleanor Roosevelt Institute in New York. The actual work was carried out by the UNITED NATIONS HUMAN RIGHTS COUNCIL, which held its first session in January 1947 in New York; its first chair was Eleanor Roosevelt, the widow of President Franklin Roosevelt. What the commission intended to do was unprecedented: set forth a number of inalienable rights applicable to every man, woman, and child on the planet. In spite of the differences in cultures, ideologies, religions, and ethnicity, the commission delegates were all united by the wish never to see a recurrence of the horrors of World War II, which had concluded only two years previously. The delegates had some historical models to draw upon, including the 1941 Atlantic Charter, a joint U.S.-British accord establishing principles for implementing postwar policies, and Roosevelt's famous Four Freedoms speech, delivered earlier the same year to Congress, in which the president declared that all people were guaranteed freedom of speech and expression, freedom of worship, freedom from want, and freedom from fear. The delegates also took guidance from the principles set forth at the NUREMBERG TRIALS and TOKYO TRIALS, which the Allies conducted to try Nazi and Japanese war criminals, respectively. Both tribunals had made it clear that human rights violators should be punished for their individual actions and could not justify their abuses by claiming that they were only obeying orders. The delegates also realized that there was a need to forge treaties containing mechanisms to uphold human rights and punish offenders.

Governments were not the only players at the UN sessions; nongovernmental organizations (NGOs), especially human rights organizations, also had a significant input. In large measure, though, the groundwork for the Universal Declaration was laid by Eleanor Roosevelt, who, after her husband's death, became a leading exponent of human rights throughout the world. She was chosen as the U.S. representative to the commission, and because of her stature she was named chairperson. The drafting of the Universal Declaration did not proceed smoothly, however, since there was considerable disagreement about the nature and extent of the rights that should be accorded women, racial minorities, and religious liberty. There were disputes over the protections necessary for a free speech, the right to dissent, and what role social and economic rights should have. The most strident opposition came from the Soviet bloc, which held a conception of freedom totally at odds with that of the West. "The cult of individualism" so cherished by the West, declared the Soviet delegate, only led to economic exploitation. The communist regimes believed that economic rights should have priority over political rights. In one of the most famous exchanges, the British delegate countered, "This declaration must uphold as a model for all humanity the figure of free men, not well-fed slaves."

In an attempt to hamper the process of drafting the Universal Declaration, delegates from the communist countries would sometimes deliver speeches that went on as long as eight hours. Roosevelt was not about to allow Soviet tactics to impede the process forever, setting a deadline of Christmas 1948. "I drive hard, and when I get home I will be tired. The men on the commission will be also,"

she said. There was another rift, one between mostly smaller states, which wanted the declaration to include legally binding restraints, and larger states, including the United States, which preferred that the legal mechanisms wait for future treaties. Just to put together the declaration itself was difficult enough, the latter group argued; to try to add legally binding provisions would probably delay agreement for years. Their view prevailed, and the Universal Declaration of Human Rights, adopted as a resolution, has no force of law. The Human Rights Commission was, however, able to complete its work in time for the General Assembly to adopt the declaration on December 10, 1948, meeting Roosevelt's deadline. Of the 58 members represented at the General Assembly session, 48 voted in favor, none voted against, eight abstained, and two were absent. Most of the abstentions came from Soviet bloc delegates, but Saudi Arabia also abstained on the grounds that the declaration was too "Western-oriented," and South Africa

Eleanor Roosevelt, Chair, Commission on Human Rights *(UN Photo 23783)*

did the same because it believed that the declaration had taken too expansive a view of liberties. (South Africa's misgivings were understandable in light of APARTHEID, the white supremacist regime's suppression of black rights.)

After the vote, Roosevelt declared, "We stand today at the threshold of a great event both in the life of the United Nations and in the life of mankind. This Declaration may well become the international Magna Carta of all men everywhere. We hope its proclamation by the General Assembly will be an event comparable to the proclamation of the Rights of Man by the French people in 1789, the adoption of the Bill of Rights by the people of the United States, and the adoption of comparable declarations at different times in other countries." The UN Human Rights Commission meets annually in Geneva to assess how member states are complying with the declaration's provisions and determine how violators should be punished, although critics contend that enforcement mechanisms remain inadequate.

See also RELIGIOUS PERSECUTION.

Further Reading:
Brysk, Alison, ed. *Globalization and Human Rights.* Berkeley: University of California Press, 2002.
Fasulo, Linda. *An Insider's Guide to the UN.* New Haven, Conn.: Yale University Press, 2003.
Gutman, Roy, ed. *Crimes of War: What the Public Should Know.* New York: W. W. Norton, 1999.
Trombly, Maria. *Journalist's Guide to the Geneva Conventions.* Indianapolis: Society of Professional Journalists, 2000.
Weiss, Thomas G., David P. Forsythe, and Roger A. Coate. *United Nations and Changing World Politics.* Westport, Conn.: Westview Press, 2004.

universal jurisdiction
Universal jurisdiction is the principle holding that national courts have a right—and even the obligation—to prosecute crimes of GENOCIDE, CRIMES AGAINST HUMANITY, war crimes, TORTURE, EXTRAJUDICIAL KILLINGS, and DISAPPEARANCES regardless of where the crime took place or the country of the perpetrator's or victim's origin. Traditionally, national courts have only heard cases involving crimes committed in their territory. However, ever since World War II, national courts have begun to extend their jurisdiction to cover war crimes and human rights abuses that occurred elsewhere. More than a dozen states have conducted investigations or trials or at the very least arrested suspected war criminals wanted in other countries, including Australia, Austria, Belgium, Canada, Denmark, France, Germany, Israel, Mexico, Netherlands, Senegal, Spain, Switzerland, the United Kingdom, and the United States. A recent worldwide study of national laws by AMNESTY INTERNATIONAL found that more than 125 states had enacted laws that to one degree or another provided for universal jurisdiction over certain types of criminal conduct, though many of these laws are flawed. No state, however, has universal jurisdiction for all crimes involving human rights violations.

In one form of universal jurisdiction, national courts apply procedures ordinarily followed in domestic criminal cases to violations of human rights and war crimes, based on standards set out in United Nations conventions. This approach allows prosecutors in one country to seek offenders beyond their borders by means of demanding their extradition from third countries. This was the strategy that was taken to secure the arrest of RICARDO MIGUEL CAVALLO, an Argentine naval officer who was accused of state-sponsored murder and torture while Argentina was under the grip of military rule. Even though he was immune from prosecution in his native land because of AMNESTY laws and his residence in Mexico, he was ultimately extradited to Spain to answer an indictment issued by a Spanish judge.

The second approach to enforcing universal jurisdiction is by bringing offenders before the INTERNATIONAL CRIMINAL COURT (ICC), which is based on a treaty created by a conference in Rome in July 1998 and signed by 95 states, including most European countries. Presumably the ICC intends to follow the precedent established by special UN courts such as the INTERNATIONAL CRIMINAL TRIBUNAL FOR THE FORMER YUGOSLAVIA (ICTY), where former Yugoslav president SLOBODAN MILOŠEVIĆ was tried.

More far-reaching efforts to define the concept of universal jurisdiction have occurred in Belgium, where the government authorized its courts to prosecute perpetrators of crimes against humanity committed in any part of the world. Within a short time the Belgian courts were flooded with lawsuits alleging human rights violations against various U.S. officials and military leaders, including the American military commander in Iraq, General Tommy Franks; former president George H. W. Bush; former secretary of state Colin Powell; and Norman Schwarzkopf, who had led coalition forces in the 1991 Persian Gulf War. These cases were either dismissed or transferred to U.S. courts. Belgium later backed down under pressure from the United States. "By passing this law, Belgium has turned its legal system into a platform for divisive politicized lawsuits against her NATO allies," argued U.S. secretary of defense Donald Rumsfeld. The law was subsequently modified to make it more difficult to bring lawsuits before Belgian courts without first filing them in the defendant's own country, so long as that country's legal system is considered fair and functioning.

The very concept of universal jurisdiction is fairly recent, even if the philosophy underlying it dates back centuries. The sixth edition of *Black's Law Dictionary*, published in 1990, contains no entry for the term. Where universal justice was applied in practice, if not in name, was in cases where the crimes were committed outside any sovereignty—by pirates, hijackers, and terrorists, for instance. To critics of the concept, the idea that universal jurisdiction could cover high officials for crimes committed in other countries is both novel and alarming. One of the most ardent critics is former secretary of state and national security adviser Henry Kissinger. He traces the origin of universal jurisdiction to principles enshrined in the UNIVERSAL DECLARATION OF HUMAN RIGHTS of 1948, the GENOCIDE CONVENTION of 1948, and the CONVENTION AGAINST TORTURE of 1988. He also cites The Final Act of the Conference on Security and Cooperation in Europe, signed in Helsinki in 1975 by President Gerald Ford on behalf of the United States, which obligated the 35 signatory nations to observe certain stated human rights; violators would face international pressure to change their ways.

At the time the Helsinki agreement was signed, the Soviet Union was considered the principal offender, and the U.S. Congress passed several important pieces of legislation to punish the USSR for flouting the standards agreed upon in Helsinki. But in Kissinger's view, these accords were never intended to give individual nations the right to prosecute political leaders who might be in violation of these standards, even if their actions occurred in another country. In 1998, however, a Spanish court indicted AUGUSTO PINOCHET, the former Chilean president, for crimes against humanity; at the time Pinochet was in the United Kingdom on an unofficial visit. He was placed under house arrest until a British court refused to extradite him to Spain and he was freed to return to Chile. The danger in this approach, Kissinger warned in an article written for *Foreign Affairs*, "lies in pushing the effort to extremes that risk substituting the tyranny of judges for that of governments; historically, the dictatorship of the virtuous has often led to inquisitions and even witch-hunts. To be sure, human rights violations, war crimes, genocide, and torture have so disgraced the modern age and in such a variety of places that the effort to interpose legal norms to prevent or punish such outrages does credit to its advocates."

Kissinger and other critics of the concept of universal jurisdiction contend that these prosecutions, because they may be initiated in practically any country, are liable to be arbitrary and capricious. Kissinger pointed out some of the difficulties: "What legal norms are being applied? What are the rules of evidence? What safeguards exist for the defendant?" It is important to bring war criminals to account, say these critics, but it cannot be done without a system of checks and balances. Too much power is placed in the hands of individual magistrates who might act more from political or personal motives rather than in the interest of justice. In addition, a defendant might be forced to deal with a legal system with which he is unfamiliar. For that matter, what safeguards will be available to ensure the defendant's rights? Moreover, unlike domestic criminal cases, cases involving war criminals and human rights abusers are likely to have implications for the conduct of foreign policy and international relations. The arrest of Pinochet, for instance, heightened tensions between the United Kingdom and Chile. Kissinger also points out that such prosecutions may hamper reconciliation in countries where the crimes were committed; he goes on to assert that in many instances, coming to terms with the past is better left to the people in the country involved; in this view, a third country that seeks to redress historical grievances is butting in where it does not belong. Bringing charges against a suspect in a national court is quite different from prosecuting war criminals in international courts, Kissinger argues: "Such a system goes far beyond the explicit and limited mandates established by the UN Security Council for the tribunals covering war crimes in the former Yugoslavia and Rwanda as well as the one being negotiated for Cambodia."

But Kissinger is no more sanguine about the existence of the International Criminal Court, either. The goal of those who support the court, he says, "is to criminalize certain types of military and political actions and thereby bring about a more humane conduct of international relations." This is better than allowing individual states and magistrates to apply universal jurisdiction, but he contends that even so, "in its present form of assigning the ultimate dilemmas of international politics to unelected jurists—and to an international judiciary at that—it represents such a fundamental change in U.S. constitutional practice that a full national debate and the full participation of Congress are imperative." Many cases are fraught with ambiguity, and it is unclear as to what standards of law their actions are being held to by justices appointed to the ICC who may be operating under different guidelines than those followed by judges and juries in U.S. courts. As an example Kissinger worries that U.S. leaders could be put in the dock in a tribunal that might have been established for another purpose entirely, pointing to the ICTY, where judges briefly flirted with the idea of prosecuting NATO for crimes against humanity for its bombing campaign during the war in Kosovo.

Not surprisingly, advocates of the concept of universal jurisdiction take a distinctly different view of its validity and applicability. Far from being a relatively new idea, they say, universal jurisdiction has been exercised by U.S. courts (among others) for a considerable period of time. Hijackers and terrorists have often been extradited to face charges in the United States. MANUEL NORIEGA was toppled from power in Panama by U.S. forces and then forced to stand trial on drug-smuggling charges. Israeli agents were in effect operating under the principle of universal jurisdiction when they abducted ADOLF EICHMANN in 1961 from Buenos Aires and brought him to Israel to be tried for presiding over the extermination of 6 million Jews in Nazi-occupied Europe. Kenneth Roth, director of HUMAN RIGHTS WATCH, argued in a rebuttal to Kissinger (which also appeared in *Foreign Affairs*) that international agreements on human rights were fully intended by the signatories to have more teeth than he will acknowledge. "To the contrary," Roth writes, "the Torture Convention of 1984, ratified by 124 governments including the United States, requires states either to prosecute any suspected torturer found on their territory, regardless of where the torture took place, or to extradite the suspect to a country that will do so." He also points out that the Geneva convention of 1949 on the conduct of war, which was ratified by 189 countries including the United States, "require each participating state to 'search for' persons who have committed grave breaches of the conventions and to 'bring such persons, regardless of nationality, before its own courts'"—as succinct a definition of universal jurisdiction as it is possible to get. It is not the concept of extraterritorial jurisdiction that is so new, says Roth, but rather "the willingness of some governments to fulfill this duty against those in high places."

Increasingly, national courts are becoming more aggressive in pursuing war criminals and human rights abusers. In some cases, magistrates in third countries have launched prosecutions because the courts in countries where the crimes have been committed will not or cannot bring the criminals to justice themselves. That is what happened in Cavallo's case. Because of amnesty laws in place at the time in his own country, he would have escaped prosecution. It took a Spanish court to indict him and a Mexican court to extradite him to Madrid. This case, while important, is hardly unique. Were it not for the actions of national courts, it is likely that many Bosnian war criminals, Rwandan killers, and other Argentine torturers like Cavallo would still be at large and not be held to account for their crimes. In 2004 the U.S. Supreme Court affirmed the doctrine of universal jurisdiction—at least in civil cases—when it ruled that the ALIEN TORT CLAIMS ACT, an 18th-century statute, had broad application. Under the statute, for example, an individual can bring a civil suit in the United States against someone who tortured him in a third country.

Similarly, Roth challenges Kissinger's attack on the ICC because the crimes detailed in its establishing treaty are "vague and highly susceptible to politicized application." This is not the case at all, Roth asserts, pointing out that the treaty's definition of war crimes echoes that found in the Pentagon's own manuals. The definition is derived from the Genocide Convention of 1948 as well as the GENEVA CONVENTIONS and their ADDITIONAL PROTOCOLS TO THE GENEVA CONVENTIONS adopted in 1977. The United States itself is a signatory to all of these treaties. Moreover, the ICC borrowed the definition of crimes against humanity from the NUREMBERG CHARTER, which proscribes conduct that even Kissinger states is "self-evident[ly]" wrong. Nor does Roth envision much danger of an out-of-control prosecutor bringing capricious indictments since a simple majority of governments that ratified the treaty setting up the court can remove a prosecutor. A two-thirds vote of signatories can remove a judge. The absence of a jury system in the ICC is no reason to dispute its authority, Roth argues, citing martial-law courts in the United States that also do not use juries.

While it can be argued that the Belgian courts had overstepped their bounds by allowing lawsuits to be filed against high-profile political leaders and military officials in other countries, defenders of universal jurisdiction contend that there is little reason to fear courts routinely extraditing suspects simply out of political motives or a desire for retribution. Governments routinely deny extradition to courts, as British judges did in Pinochet's case. Foreign requests for extradition are also regularly denied by governments, especially when political concerns trump the prospect of prosecuting an individual.

In 2009 the British Foreign Secretary David Miliband announced that Britain would curb the ability of judges to use the concept of universal jurisdiction to try to detain Israeli or other political leaders from abroad. His action was prompted by the threat to arrest the former Israeli foreign minister Tzipi Livni prior to a scheduled visit to Britain. (She canceled the visit.) The British court that had ordered the arrest was acting on a complaint brought by a Palestinian activist group that accused Livni of being complicit in war crimes Israeli Defense Forces were accused of carrying out in the three-week war in GAZA in 2008–09. British judges had previously accepted petitions from anti-Israeli activists to arrest other top Israeli officials and military leaders, including defense minister Ehud Barak, who successfully claimed diplomatic immunity to avoid arrest. Miliband called for review of and changes to the British law permitting judges to issue arrest warrants against foreign dignitaries "without any prior knowledge or advice by a prosecutor." British legal experts have said that the law as it stands could allow for the arrest of any head of state who had presided over counterinsurgency operations, including President Barack Obama and Prime Minister Vladimir Putin of Russia.

See also BELGIAN WAR CRIMES TRIBUNAL; HELSINKI ACCORDS; ORGANIZATION FOR SECURITY AND COOPERATION IN EUROPE; ROME STATUTE OF THE INTERNATIONAL CRIMINAL COURT; WAR CRIMES, CATEGORIZATION OF.

Further Reading:

Ball, Howard. *Prosecuting War Crimes and Genocide: The Twentieth-Century Experience.* Lawrence: University Press of Kansas, 1999.

Beigbeder, Yves, and Theo van Boven. *Judging War Criminals: The Politics of International Justice.* Sidney, Australia: Palgrave Macmillan, 1999.

Bloxham, Donald. *Genocide on Trial: War Crimes Trials and the Formation of Holocaust History and Memory.* Oxford: Oxford University Press, 2003.

Brysk, Alison, ed. *Globalization and Human Rights.* Berkeley: University of California Press, 2002.

Cooper, Belinda, and Richard Goldstone. *War Crimes: The Legacy of Nuremberg.* New York: TV Books Inc., 1999.

Dormann, Knut, and Louise Doswald-Beck. *Elements of War Crimes under the Rome Statute of the International Criminal Court: Sources and Commentary.* Cambridge: Cambridge University Press, 2003.

Jinks, Derek. *The Rules of War: The Geneva Conventions in the Age of Terror.* Oxford: Oxford University Press, 2005.

Kissinger, Henry. *Does America Need a Foreign Policy?: Toward a Diplomacy for the 21st Century.* New York: Simon & Schuster; Touchstone edition, 2002.

Pilloud, Claude. *Commentary on the Additional Protocols of 8 June 1977 to the Geneva Conventions of 12 August 1949.* Boston: Brill Academic Publishers, 1987.

Roberts, Adam, and Richard Guelff. *Documents on the Laws of War.* Oxford: Oxford University Press, 2000.

Roth, Kenneth, ed. *Torture: A Human Rights Perspective.* New York: New Press, 2005.

Shelton, Dinah. *International Crimes, Peace, and Human Rights: The Role of the International Criminal Court.* Ardsley, N.Y.: Transnational Publishers, Inc., 2000.

Trombly, Maria. *Journalist's Guide to the Geneva Conventions.* Indianapolis: Society of Professional Journalists, 2000.

unlawful imprisonment

Unlawful imprisonment refers to the confinement of civilians during a conflict. INTERNATIONAL HUMANITARIAN LAW covers unlawful imprisonment in both international and internal conflicts. However, the law is much more explicit and extensive in its application to the former than it is to the latter. In general, the use of imprisonment as a form of persecution because of a person's nationality, religion, or ethnic group is banned. Under the Fourth Geneva Convention of 1949 unlawful confinement in an international conflict is considered a grave breach of the law. The INTERNATIONAL CRIMINAL TRIBUNAL FOR THE FORMER YUGOSLAVIA (ICTY), hearing cases involving the Balkan conflict of the 1990s, has ruled that unlawful confine-ment—which it defined as "seizure, collection, segregation, and forced transfer of civilians to camps"—is a crime against humanity. There is an exception under Article 42 of the Fourth Convention, which does allow a "detaining power" to intern people who pose a threat to its security—espionage, for instance, would constitute such a threat—if "absolutely necessary" or if the person has committed certain acts—such as sabotage or belonging to "organizations whose object is to cause disturbances"—against the detaining power. In addition, civilians may be temporarily relocated from their homes if it is required for security reasons or for their own safety, but the detaining power is obliged to treat them humanely; ensure that they have adequate food, medicine, and shelter in their new home; and make certain that they are returned home as soon as circumstances permit. Civilians may also be interned if "necessary, for imperative reasons of security, to take safety measures concerning protected persons." However, an individual cannot be interned simply because he or she is an enemy national. Detainees are permitted to keep personal possessions; seizure of personal articles or valuables by the detaining power is banned. A detaining power can arrest and intern a person for a criminal act but must guarantee that the suspect receives a fair trial.

The law is less explicit about when civilians may be interned during an internal armed conflict. ARTICLE 3 COMMON TO THE GENEVA CONVENTIONS, which applies to internal conflicts, states that "persons taking no active part in the hostilities . . . shall in all circumstances be treated humanely, without any adverse distinction founded on race, color, religion or faith, sex, birth or wealth, or any other similar criteria." Article 3 also prohibits "violence to life . . . in particular murder of all kinds, mutilation, cruel treatment and torture" and "the passing of sentences and the carrying out of executions without previous judgment pronounced by a regularly constituted court." Additional Protocol II of 1977 requires that any civilians who are confined in a conflict must be humanely treated. Prisoners must be protected from attack and provided with adequate resources including medicines and health care if required. Detainees cannot be held in close, unhealthy quarters unless it is necessary to "safeguard their health." In addition, they must be allowed to practice their faith without interference. The INTERNATIONAL COMMITTEE OF THE RED CROSS (ICRC) has a mandate to monitor conditions in any internment camps established by a detaining power during a conflict although the ICRC has been barred from making inspections in some conflicts, notably the Bosnian War when Serbs prevented any ICRC monitors from visiting internment camps where Muslims were being held.

See also ADDITIONAL PROTOCOLS TO THE GENEVA CONVENTIONS; GENEVA CONVENTIONS.

Further Reading:

Berry, Nicholas O. *War and the Red Cross: The Unspoken Mission.* New York: St. Martin's Press, 1997
Gutman, Roy, ed. *Crimes of War: What the Public Should Know.* New York: W. W. Norton & Company, 1999.
International Committee of the Red Cross. *International Law Concerning the Conduct of Hostilities: Collection of Hague Conventions and Some Other Treaties.* Geneva: International Committee of the Red Cross, 1989.

Uruguay, human rights violations in

A modern democracy today, Uruguay has yet to undertake a full investigation of grave human rights abuses that occurred in the "dirty war" of 1975–85, a period during which the country was run by a military dictatorship. As of 2004 the government had failed to investigate or prosecute any active or retired military official for torture or murder committed while the military held power. Like other dirty wars in Latin America (which also took place in Argentina, Bolivia, Chile, Brazil, and Paraguay), the one in Uruguay involved a confrontation between an authoritarian regime and leftist insurgents and their supporters. Legal action involving suspects was halted in 1986 under an AMNESTY law, which even its sponsors say was passed under pressure from the military. Nonetheless, Uruguayan voters approved the law in a national referendum.

One loophole remained in the law that allowed investigations into the fate of the estimated 160 people who were "disappeared" and whose cases have never been resolved; this loophole has been employed in Chile. Even so, neither the government of Uruguayan presidents Julio Sanguinetti (1985–90 and 1995–2000) and Luis Lacalle (1990–95) took any steps to initiate investigations. (Most of the disappeared were detained in Argentina, presumably in collaboration with the military regime in that country.) A peace commission was established in 2000 by President Jorge Batlle to fulfill Article 4 of the amnesty law, which covers DISAPPEARANCES. The commission did little more than state that 26 people had been tortured and killed in Uruguay and that their bodies were cremated and dumped into the sea. Not surprisingly, families of the victims were not satisfied. "We believe that now it is Uruguay's turn. We have high expectations and hopes, because of the new government," said a representative of Mothers and Relatives of Detained-Disappeared Uruguayans. The situation might change if Tabaré Vázquez, who was elected president in October 2004, fulfills his promise to emphasize human rights issues during his term, which ends in 2009.

Many of the officers responsible for the abuses have not shied away from public attention. They regularly gather on national holidays and commemorate comrades who were killed in what they call "the war on sedition," referring to the suppression of the Tupamaro National Liberation Movement (MLN), a leftist guerrilla movement that they blame for any human rights abuses. Founded in 1963, the guerrilla group emerged at a time when Uruguay's democratic welfare state was collapsing and a political stalemate had developed between the two major political parties. The Tupamaros took their name (as did a later Peruvian insurgency) from the legendary 18th-century Inca chief Tupac Amaru, who had resisted the Spanish invaders. Intent on transforming Uruguay into a Marxist state, the Tupamaros became the forerunner of and model for several similar Marxist guerrilla groups in Latin America. They initiated their insurgency with a series of bank robberies to fund their terrorist operations. In 1968 they launched their insurgency in earnest, carrying out a string of terrorist attacks, including assassinations, bombings, and spectacular kidnappings, taking hostage several British and United States citizens to gain international attention. In the late 1970s the Tupamaros briefly threatened to overrun the capital of Montevideo. In response the military cracked down, and over the next few years the army assassinated 300 guerrillas and locked up another 3,000. When democracy was restored in 1985, imprisoned Tupamoros were freed, and the former insurgent group became a legal political party.

Nevertheless, the majority of the human rights violations that took place in Uruguay occurred after the Tupamaros were defeated in 1972. The military crackdown occurred at a turbulent time characterized by labor strikes, student demonstrations, and militant street violence. The Tupamaros had attracted public attention by kidnapping prominent figures and trying them before special "People's Courts." "Unlike other Latin-American guerrilla groups," the *New York Times* stated in 1970, "the Tupamaros normally avoid bloodshed when possible. They try instead to create embarrassment for the Government and general disorder." As the government cracked down, the Tupamaros responded with increasing violence. The military had significant support from outside its borders—specifically from other states in Latin America and from the United States. Concerns about the spread of communist influence in Latin America had prompted Washington to provide assistance to several military regimes in the Southern Cone of South America. One of the men responsible for the secret U.S. effort in Montevideo was Dan Mitrione, nominally head of the Office of Public Safety (OPS), a division of the U.S. Agency for International Development (USAID). In an interview given to a leading Brazilian newspaper in 1970, the former Uruguayan chief of police intelligence, Alejandro Otero, credited Mitrione and other U.S. advisers for refining the practice of torture in Uruguay by introducing psychological methods. For example, the police would play a tape of women and children screaming in a room adjacent to the prisoner's cell and tell the prisoner that he was hearing his family being tortured. "The violent methods which were beginning to be employed," said Otero, "caused an escalation in Tupamaro activity. Before then their attitude showed that they would use violence only as a last resort." Mitrone was later killed, and in 1977 a Tupamoro adherent was sentenced to 30 years in prison for the assassination.

Torture by security forces became so common that the Uruguayan Senate launched an investigation. After a five-month study, the senate commission concluded unanimously that torture in Uruguay had become a "normal, frequent and habitual occurrence," which was not limited to the Tupamaros. The commission cited such methods as the use of electric shocks to the genitals, electric needles under the fingernails, burning with cigarettes, and use of psychological torture. Even pregnant women were brutalized. A death squad, composed largely of police officers, began to conduct operations marked by assassinations, kidnappings, and bombing of homes of suspected Tupamaro sympathizers. The restoration of democracy in the mid-1980s has fostered a spirit of reconciliation. Several former insurgents who have been released from prison now sit in the national legislature.

As a sign of how far Uruguay had come from the days of the dirty war, people went to the polls in 2009 to elect a former guerrilla to the presidency. The victor, José Mujica, 74, had spent 14 years in prison under the dictatorship. The former Tupamaro rebel pledged to use dialogue and diplomacy to unite the country and reassured businesses that he would work closely with them.

See also OPERATION CONDOR.

Further Reading:
Amnesty International. Uruguay Human Rights. Available online. URL: http://www.amnestyusa.org/all-countries/uruguay/page.do?id=1011264. Accessed March 21, 2010.

Davis, William Columbus. *Warnings from the Far South: Democracy versus Dictatorship in Uruguay, Argentina, and Chile.* New York: Praeger Publishers, 1995.

Gonzalez, Luis E. *Political Structures and Democracy in Uruguay.* Notre Dame, Ind.: University of Notre Dame Press, 1992.

Hampstein, Elizabeth. *Uruguay Nunca Mas: Human Rights Violations, 1972–1985.* Philadelphia: Temple University Press, 1993.

Human Rights Today. Uruguay Human Rights. March 21, 2010. Available online. URL: http://humanrights.einnews.com/uruguay/. Accessed March 21, 2010.

Human Rights Watch. Uruguay Human Rights. Available online. URL: http://www.hrw.org/americas/uruguay. Accessed March 21, 2010.

Ustache (Ustaše, Ustasha)

The Ustache was an extremist Croatian movement that began as a terrorist organization and later turned into a powerful fascist political party. Literally, *Ustache* means "rebellion." When World War II broke out and the Germans and Italians took over what was then the Kingdom of Yugoslavia, the Ustache aligned itself with the occupation forces and was installed as head of a puppet state. In their four years in power, they carried out a campaign of terror against Serbs, Muslims, Jews, Rom (Gypsies), and other minorities in Croatia and Bosnia and Herzegovina. It is estimated that the Ustache might have killed as many as 500,000 Serbs alone in what amounted to GENOCIDE. Executions were carried out by any means possible, including bullets, axes, knives, and chain saws. In addition to the killings, the Ustache were responsible for uprooting and expelling hundreds of thousands of minorities from their homes and the forcible conversion of Eastern Orthodox Serbs to Catholicism, the dominant faith of Croatia.

The reign of the Ustache was arguably the most barbaric of any regime collaborating with the Nazis. The group was founded in 1929 as a nationalist political movement. Its cofounder, ANTE PAVELIĆ, would later become the head of the Independent State of Croatia (which included parts of Bosnia and Herzegovina). To assert its authority, the Ustache also relied on military units—the Ustasha Army (Ustaška Vojnica)—which eventually could muster up to 76,000 men. In September 1944 Josef Broz (Marshal Tito), the leader of Yugoslav partisans fighting the German occupation, made a secret deal with JOSEPH STALIN that allowed the Red Army to enter Yugoslavia on the condition that the Soviet force help to eliminate the remnants of the German army and their Ustache allies. Seeing that the end was near, Ustache leaders, including Pavelić, fled the country, many taking refuge in Austria and later in South America. A number of Ustache members, however, were extradited and tried by the the postwar Yugoslav Communist government under Tito's rule.

See also CROATIA, HUMAN RIGHTS VIOLATIONS IN; TUDJMAN, FRANJO; YUGOSLAVIA, WAR CRIMES IN.

Further Reading:
Goldstein, Ivo. *Croatia: A History.* Montreal: McGill-Queen's University Press, 2000.

Muñoz, Antonio J. *For Croatia and Christ: The Croatian Army in World War II, 1941–1945.* Bayside, N.Y.: Europa Books Inc., 2004.

Tanner, Marcus. *Croatia: A Nation Forged in War.* New Haven, Conn.: Yale University Press, 2001.

Uzbekistan, human rights violations in

Uzbekistan gained its independence in the wake of the collapse of the former Soviet Union in 1991. With 25 million people, it is the most populous nation in the region. Uzbekistan also boasts the largest armed forces in central Asia, and in the aftermath of the terrorist attacks on September 11, 2001, has become an important strategic ally of the United States. It also has one of the worst human rights records of any of the former Soviet republics. Political opposition cannot freely function, the media are under state control, and religious and political dissension is dealt with severely by security forces. Poverty is endemic, and economic progress halting at best. A 2003 World Bank report observed that living standards were among the lowest in the former Soviet Union. Uzbekistan remains stubbornly independent as well, resisting cooperation with other central Asian republics even at the risk of heightened interregional tensions.

Since independence, Uzbekistan has been steered by the one-man rule of Islam Karimov, a onetime Communist Party leader. In 2000 he won the presidency in an election in which he ran unopposed; two years later he staged a referendum that extended his term two years beyond the initial five-year term. In 2003 the parliament granted him immunity from prosecution in the unlikely event that he leaves office voluntarily. The growth of militant Islamic groups has provided a pretext for Karimov to crack down on the opposition, with security forces targeting nonviolent Islamic movements in particular. There is some debate among political analysts as to just how serious a threat the Islamic terrorist groups actually pose to Uzbekistan's security. In 1999 more than a dozen people died in a series of bomb blasts in the capital of Tashkent that were blamed on "religious extremists." Karimov declared that these fundamentalists intended to destabilize the country and kill him.

Several thousand people have been thrown in jail because of their religious affiliation. Those Muslims who practice their faith outside state-approved mosques or other religious institutions are especially at risk of arrest. In the past year alone, HUMAN RIGHTS WATCH gathered materials on the trials of hundreds of individuals facing charges based on their religious practices and affiliations. In March 2004 Tashkent was again gripped by several days of bombings and gun battles between suspected Islamic militants and police. Scores were killed in the ensuing chaos, prompting human rights groups to fear that the government would use the incident to become even more repressive. Already an estimated 4,000 members of Hizb ut-Tahrir (Party of Liberation), which advocates the peaceful establishment of an Islamic state in Uzbekistan, have been detained on charges stemming from their affiliation with the group. Human rights groups and independent analysts estimate that Uzbek prisons hold as many as 7,000 political prisoners altogether.

Islamic groups are not the only ones to suffer from the crackdown. Political opposition groups and parties are also banned, and any expression of political dissent is ruthlessly suppressed. Members of outlawed political parties—Erk ("Freedom") Democratic Party and Birlik ("Unity")—are persecuted and harassed by police. Human rights advocates are also are routinely imprisoned or persecuted. The law requires that all independent political, religious, or human rights organizations register with the government. But the government makes it almost impossible for organizations it opposes to do so. The government has begun to impose onerous restrictions on the registration of international human rights groups, including Human Rights Watch, so as to minimize the possibility that abuses by the regime will be reported. The country's own media are hardly in a position to press for change. Although officially government censorship has been lifted, journalists practice self-censorship, saying nothing to criticize the government or its leader. Topics such as political opposition, corruption, or civil liberties are considered too sensitive to be raised. Those journalists who break the silence often find themselves in prison for their presumption.

According to both the United Nations and the U.S. State Department, the use of TORTURE in Uzbekistan is "systemic." In May 2003 alone, Human Rights Watch documented four new deaths in custody apparently due to torture. Judges regularly discount numerous allegations of torture by defendants charged with nonviolent crimes and convict them anyway. Few police officers or security agents have had to face trial for torture or killing prisoners. Even in the face of international pressure to investigate these abuses, the government has done little to investigate any allegations of torture.

Uzbekistan occupies a strategic position in the region because it shares a border with Afghanistan. Since the 9/11 terrorist attacks, the government has allowed the United States to establish a military presence on its territory. As a result, Washington has treated the Karimov regime with unusual delicacy. To placate the United States and ensure annual State Department certification—a necessary step if it is to receive continual assistance—Tashkent has responded with small gestures. The government, for instance, insisted that it had changed its legal definition of torture to bring it in line with the CONVENTION AGAINST TORTURE. Nonetheless, few concrete steps have been taken to actually do anything about putting a stop to it.

In another step aimed at defusing international criticism, the government stages well-publicized amnesties, releasing religious and political prisoners at regular intervals, although the releases are often provisional—the freed prisoners must abide by certain conditions—and the number of people released minimal. The government has also opened up the country for inspections of prison facilities by a UN special rapporteur and human rights groups, but these gestures have yet to result in any dramatic changes in policy, according to human rights advocates. The State Department formally acknowledged the lack of progress in correcting human rights abuses, and in January 2004 it decertified Uzbekistan for aid under a U.S. nonproliferation-assistance program, which is intended to help former Soviet republics get rid of nuclear, chemical, and BIOLOGICAL WEAPONS. Even though it received a waiver, allowing such assistance to continue, the decertification, it was hoped, would send a powerful message to the Karimov regime about the need to take concerted action.

The effectiveness of such diplomatic action was called into question after violence erupted in the southern city of Andijan in May 2005. Protests were triggered by the arrests of 23 businessmen, supposedly for supporting fundamentalist Islamic causes. Gunmen freed them and several other prisoners as well. In the crackdown that followed, security forces fired on thousands of protesters gathered in the main square, killing several. Reports of the dead varied from ten to two or three hundred, many of them reportedly civilians. The harsh response of the regime indicated how seriously the Karimov regime considered the uprising, which it blamed on Islamic militants. Since the violent suppression of protests in Andijon, the Karimov regime has taken a more conciliatory approach and released political prisoners and abolished the death penalty. In spite of some promising signs of democratization, political life is still tightly controlled, and opponents of the government still have little means of free expression. The ORGANIZATION FOR SECURITY AND COOPERATION IN EUROPE (OSCE) described the 2007 presidential election as having been "characterized by the absence of any real competition of ideas and political views" in light of the fact that Karimov's three opponents had all endorsed him. Two years later, the OSCE declined to send any observers to monitor parliamentary elections, on the grounds that "fundamental freedoms continue to be limited" and that Uzbekistan still "does not offer the electorate a genuine choice." While Karimov admitted that there had not been any political parties competing in the past, he insisted that more genuine competition could be seen in the races for parliament.

Further Reading:
Akbarzadeh, Shahram. *Uzbekistan and the United States: Authoritarianism, Islamism and Washington's New Security Agenda.* London: Zed Books, 2005.
Amnesty International. Uzbekistan Human Rights. Available online. URL: http://www.amnestyusa.org/all-countries/uzbekistan/page.do?id=1011265. Accessed March 21, 2010.
Human Rights Watch. Uzbekistan Human Rights. Available online. URL: http://www.hrw.org/en/europecentral-asia/uzbekistan. Accessed March 21, 2010.
Rashid, Ahmed. *Taliban: Militant Islam, Oil, and Fundamentalism in Central Asia.* New Haven, Conn.: Yale University Press, 2001.

V

Velpke Baby Farm

The Velpke Baby Farm—a home established in Velpke, Germany, for infant children of Polish female workers—achieved notoriety after the end of World War II when it was revealed that most of the children had sickened or died because of deliberate neglect on account of actions by Nazi officials. Several individuals associated with the baby farms—principally Heinrich Gerike—were tried for war crimes as a result, charged with "killing by willful neglect of a number of children."

The children had been compulsorily separated from their parents so that their parents—deported Poles—would not be distracted from their work on nearby farms to maintain the supply of food. In May 1944 Gerike, a high-ranking official (*Kreisleiter*) in nearby Helmstedt, was ordered to build a home to house the children. Gerike settled for a corrugated iron hut without running water, light, telephone, or a separate clinic. As a matron to run the home, he chose a former German teacher named Valentina Bilien, who had no experience caring for infants or children. Gerike ordered her not to return the children to their mothers or send any to the hospital if they took sick, although she was allowed to "call in a doctor if necessary." Bilien was assigned four helpers. At no time during the six months that the baby farm was in operation did Gerike express any interest in the deaths or trouble to visit the home to inspect conditions there. When Bilien realized that some children were dying because they needed their mothers' milk she relented and sent some back to their mothers, but once her action was discovered, she was admonished not to do so again in the future.

More than 80 Polish infants died from what was described in the indictment as "general weakness, dysentery, and what they called catarrh of the intestines." What made this case so unusual was that in contrast to most crimes of which Nazi war criminals were accused, this was a crime not of commission but rather of omission—that is, the children were mistreated and died because of neglect rather than because of violence done to them. Nonetheless, the prosecutor contended that the accused were in breach of Article 46 of the Regulations Annexed to the Hague Convention of 1907, which states: "Family honor and rights, individual life, and private property, as well as religious convictions and worship, must be respected. Private property may not be confiscated." In addition, he pointed out that international law forbids the killing of innocent or defenseless people in any conquered area "either in their own country or in the country of the occupying power." The prosecutor also made a novel case in which he maintained that the accused had also violated laws forbidding an OCCUPYING POWER to deport slave labor from the occupied country to its own territory in the first place. The Polish parents forced to work on the farms, he pointed out, fell into this category. Their status, he argued, should also apply to their children, who were born to them in captivity. Four of the defendants, including Gerike and Bilien, were found guilty while two others were acquitted. Bilien was sentenced to 15 years' imprisonment, and Gerike and another defendant were sentenced to death and hanged.

Venezuela, human rights violations in

Venezuela's controversial president Hugo Chávez has inspired supporters throughout the hemisphere and come under fire from Washington as well as from impartial human rights groups. Since taking power after winning a landslide election in 1998, Chávez has tightened his grip on power over the years, drawing increasing criticism. In May 2009, for instance, the Inter-American Human Rights Commission stated that Chávez had created "an environment hostile to political dissent and the increasing impunity in the country." The Venezuelan government sharply criticized the commission's conclusions. In 2010 Venezuela's top human rights official Ombudsman Gabriela Ramírez defended the government's human rights record, asserting that the data actually show improvement. That assessment is not shared by Human Rights Watch (HRW), which in a 2009 report titled "A Decade under Chavez" declared that government policies "have undercut the human rights protections established in the 1999 Constitution." HRW contends that Chávez exploited the failed 2002 coup against him by using it as a pretext to crack down on dissent, noting: "Discrimination on political grounds has been a defining feature of the Chávez presidency." The human rights group also assailed the Chávez administration for showing "an open disregard for the principle of separation of powers," threatening the independence of the judiciary. "In the absence of credible judicial oversight, the Chávez government has engaged in often discriminatory policies that have undercut journalists' freedom of expression, workers' freedom of association, and civil society's ability to promote human rights in Venezuela." Political opponents have been blacklisted and fired and in some cases arrested. In March 2010, for instance, an opposition politician, Oswaldo Álvarez Paz, was taken into custody for remarks he made on a television talk show, prompting a denunciation from a coalition of more than a dozen opposition parties, which said that he had been jailed for "the crime of opinion." In some way his case is unusual, because he was able to express his views on television despite the media having fallen increasingly under government control or having been shut down. In January 2010, the Chávez government threatened to take action against cable providers that aired channels that did not comply with Venezuelan regulations, which included a requirement to interrupt regular broadcasting to air presidential speeches. Cowed, cable providers immediately pulled the plug on seven channels. The move came three years after RCTV International, Venezuela's oldest television channel, known for its criticism of Chávez, had been taken off the air. Violence has sporadically flared amid protests against the regime. In one such incident in 2009, as noted by Amnesty International, security forces and armed civilian groups affiliated with the regime used excessive force on student demonstrators, injuring almost 600 and killing at least nine.

Further Reading:
Amnesty International. Human Rights in the Bolivarian Republic of Venezuela. Available online. URL: http://www.amnesty.org/en/region/venezuela. Accessed March 24, 2010.
Gott, Richard. Hugo Chavez: The Bolivarian Revolution in Venezuela. Brooklyn, N.Y.: Verso, 2005.
Human Rights Watch. A Decade under Chavez. Available online. URL: http://www.hrw.org/en/node/64174/section/2. Accessed March 24, 2010.
Iain, Bruce. The Real Venezuela: Making Socialism in the 21st Century. London: Pluto Press, 2009.
Inter-American Human Rights Commission. Colombia, Cuba, Haiti, and Venezuela with Severe Human Rights Problems. URL: http://internationallawobserver.eu/2009/05/10/inter-american-human-rights-commission-colo mbia-cuba-venezuela-and-haiti-with-severe-human-rights-problems/. Accessed March 24, 2010.
Wilpert, Gregory. Changing Venezuela by Taking Power: The History and Policies of the Chavez Government. Brooklyn, N.Y.: Verso, 2006.

Vergès, Jacques (1925–) *French lawyer*
The French lawyer Jacques Vergès, known as "the Devil's Advocate," has courted more than his share of controversy defending such notorious figures as Nazi war criminal Klaus Barbie and Carlos the Jackal, the Venezuelan-born terrorist. More recently Vergès announced that he was representing former Yugoslav dictator Slobodan Milošević (although Milošević begged to differ), and he has long claimed friendships with former Khmer Rouge leaders, including the late Pol Pot, who were responsible for the deaths of nearly a million Cambodians while they were in power. Even before trial dates had been set, Vergès declared that he had agreed to represent Saddam Hussein and Saddam's foreign minister, Tariq Aziz.

Born in Thailand and raised on Reunion Island, Vergès fought with the Free French Army under General Charles de Gaulle during World War II, but he later became a dedicated communist. He identified in particular with anticolonialist insurgents, and he took on several cases of Algerians charged with sabotage against French colonial rule. One of his clients was a woman named Djamila Bouhired, who was convicted and sentenced to death for planting bombs in cafés in Algiers. Vergès succeeded in getting her sentence commuted and later married her.

In spite of his communist leanings, Vergès was equally prepared to lend his legal expertise to radical rightists and fascists as well. It did not appear to matter what his defendants' politics were as long as they were sufficiently radical or militant in expressing them. He has defended Palestinians charged with attacks against Israeli civilians as well as neo-Nazi bombers. In 1987 he enthusiastically seized the opportunity to defend Klaus Barbie, the former Gestapo chief known as "the Butcher of Lyon," who was implicated in the torture and killing of hundreds of Jews. Barbie, Vergès told the court, was no worse than French soldiers who had committed atrocities in French colonial wars. In spite of his lawyer's spirited representation, Barbie was sentenced to life in prison on 341 charges.

Vergès had no better luck defending Illich Ramirez Sanchez, also known as Carlos the Jackal, who was convicted in 1997 of killing two French secret agents and a

Lebanese revolutionary, though the crimes attributed to him include a slew of bombings, kidnappings, and hijackings. "He is a fascist," one of Vergès's detractors told CBS, and went on to describe the lawyer as "anti-democrat, anti-liberal (and) anti-Jew. . . . But he's a clever man. You can be a fascist and be a clever man."

In 2008 Vergès undertook the defense of KHIEU SAMPHAN, the former Khmer Rouge leader, who was being tried by the Cambodian tribunal. Vergès maintained that while millions of people were killed under Khmer Rouge rule, his client should not be found guilty because he was not directly responsible.

Further Reading:

Bower, Tom. *Klaus Barbie, the Butcher of Lyons.* New York: Pantheon Books, 1984.
Dabringhaus, Erhard. *Klaus Barbie: The Shocking Story of How the U.S. Used This Nazi War Criminal as an Intelligence Agent.* New York: Acropolis Books, 1984.

victims, rights of

International law, as first spelled out in the Hague Convention of 1907, makes states liable for paying compensation to victims of violations of the convention on the grounds that the state is "responsible for all acts committed by persons forming part of its armed forces." In practice, however, victims seldom turn to the very state whose military abused them for restitution. It is more likely that in times of conflict victims will seek help from the INTERNATIONAL COMMITTEE OF THE RED CROSS (ICRC), which has the mandate under the GENEVA CONVENTIONS of ensuring the protection of civilians caught up in a conflict as well as PRISONERS OF WAR. The ICRC has the responsibility of monitoring the treatment of civilians and prisoners of war under an OCCUPYING POWER to ascertain their well-being; the ICRC is also charged with reuniting victims with their families as soon as circumstances permit.

The UNITED NATIONS HIGH COMMISSIONER FOR REFUGEES (UNHCR) assumes responsibility for both REFUGEES—civilians who are forced to seek refuge across international borders—and INTERNALLY DISPLACED PERSONS (IDPs) who are uprooted from their homes and are relocated within their own country. The problem of settling—or resettling—refugees and IDPs has grown exponentially in recent years because of the proliferation of internal conflicts throughout the world. Nongovernmental organizations (NGOs) such as the ICRC, DOCTORS WITHOUT BORDERS, OXFAM, Care, and so on, are coming under increasing pressure from belligerents in many conflicts who frequently ignore their neutrality and attack aid workers. In many cases NGOs have simply pulled out of a beleaguered country, as Doctors Without Borders did in

Afghanistan following attacks on its volunteers, further imperiling the conflicts victims. In the Bosnian War, the ICRC temporarily withdrew its workers after the head of the mission was deliberately killed in June 1992. In Burundi, three Red Cross workers were killed in 1996.

Even when international organizations such as the United Nations take an active role in the protection of civilians in conflicts, there is no guarantee that the victims will enjoy the safeguards to which they are entitled. This problem was vividly demonstrated in the Bosnian War when the United Nations declared certain parts of Bosnia and Herzegovina as SAFE HAVENS where Muslim civilians could seek sanctuary from Serb forces and enjoy UN protection. However, Serb forces overran one of these safe havens at Srebrinica without encountering any resistance from UN peacekeepers; they then proceeded to massacre some 7,000 Muslim men and boys.

Although in principle states have the obligation to prevent violations of international law or, failing that, to punish the offenders if violations do occur, in practice judicial institutions often refuse to address these cases. After the Bosnian War, for instance, Serbia and Croatia both resisted demands to try war criminals or hand them over to the INTERNATIONAL CRIMINAL TRIBUNAL FOR THE FORMER YUGOSLAVIA (ICTY) in The Hague. To many nationalists in both countries, the suspects were not regarded as criminals at all but rather as war heroes. Further, the law itself sometimes makes it difficult to determine whether a serious violation is occurring. The 1948 GENOCIDE CONVENTION, while requiring states to "prevent and to punish" GENOCIDE, provides no mechanism for assessing whether genocide is in fact taking place. Although tens of thousands of African Sudanese have been killed and driven from their homes in Darfur by Arab militias backed by the government, no consensus has emerged that the ethnic cleansing amounts to genocide. It should be noted that there is a provision in Additional Protocol I to the Geneva Conventions to establish a fact-finding commission to investigate charges of genocide. It also stipulates that both parties to a conflict agree before the commission can do anything at all, a situation that seldom arises, for obvious reasons.

The INTERNATIONAL CRIMINAL COURT (ICC) was established in 1998 under UN auspices in hope that it can rule on issues related to the rights of victims in the absence of action on the part of national governments. But because the United States and other countries have not recognized the authority of the court, it is unclear as to how much influence it will have. In the meantime the United Nations has set up other ad hoc courts to investigate war crimes committed in wars in the former Yugoslavia, Rwanda, and Sierra Leone while offering victims of those conflicts the satisfaction of seeing justice meted out to their oppressors. International law does allow victims to sue for violations of

INTERNATIONAL HUMANITARIAN LAW, but they rarely have recourse to courts that could hear their cases. There are some exceptions. After the end of World War II, the West German government paid hundreds of millions of dollars in reparations to the survivors and families of victims of the Holocaust. In the United States, the ALIEN TORT CLAIMS ACT allows a victim of a human rights abuse to sue the perpetrator even if the parties are foreign nationals and the crime in question occurred in another country.

See also ADDITIONAL PROTOCOLS TO THE GENEVA CONVENTIONS; HAGUE CONVENTIONS.

Further Reading:
Dubber, Markus Dirk. *Victims in the War on Crime: The Use and Abuse of Victims' Rights.* New York: New York University Press, 2002.
Rieff, David. *A Bed for the Night: Humanitarianism in Crisis.* New York: Simon & Schuster, 2002.
Vaux, Anthony. *The Selfish Altruist: Relief Work in Famine and War.* London: Earthscan Publications, 2001.
Weissman, Fabrice. *In the Shadow of "Just Wars": Violence, Politics, and Humanitarian Action.* Ithaca, N.Y.: Cornell University Press, 2004.

Victims Trust Fund

The Victims Trust Fund was established by the INTERNATIONAL CRIMINAL COURT (ICC) to provide compensation or restitution to victims of the most serious crimes covered by its mandate. Victims include child soldiers, women who have been raped during conflicts, and civilians who have lost their homes as a result of fighting or atrocities. According to Article 75 of the Rome Statute, which established the court, the ICC has the right to order a defendant found guilty of crime to directly compensate the victim. Funds can be distributed either to individuals or to a collective group; by the same token, funds may be directed to individuals or channeled to aid organizations on behalf of several victims. Because the defendants may not have the resources to comply with the order to pay compensation, the fund also relies on additional funding from governments, international organizations, or individuals. The Victims Trust Fund is supervised by an independent board of directors.

See also ROME STATUTE OF THE INTERNATIONAL CRIMINAL COURT.

Further Reading:
Coalition for the International Criminal Court. Victims' Trust Fund. Available online. URL: http://www.iccnow.org/?mod=trustfund. Accessed March 21, 2010.
Dormann, Knut, and Louise Doswald-Beck. *Elements of War Crimes under the Rome Statute of the International Criminal Court: Sources and Commentary.* Cambridge: Cambridge University Press, 2003.
Dubber, Markus Dirk. *Victims in the War on Crime: The Use and Abuse of Victims' Rights.* New York: New York University Press, 2002.
Gutman, Roy, ed. *Crimes of War: What the Public Should Know.* New York: W. W. Norton & Company, 1999.

Vieira de Mello, Sérgio (1948–2003) *UN envoy and human rights advocate*
A leading advocate of human rights, Sérgio Vieira de Mello served the UNITED NATIONS HIGH COMMISSIONER FOR REFUGEES (UNHCR) in several diplomatic posts over 33 years before his life was cut short by a bomb blast in Iraq. He was active in humanitarian and peace-keeping operations in BANGLADESH, SUDAN, CYPRUS, Mozambique, and PERU. In 2003 he was named by UN secretary general Kofi Annan to assume the post of UN representative in Iraq, which only a year before had been invaded by U.S.-backed coalition forces. He was killed in Baghdad during a terrorist bombing attack on August 19, 2003.

Known simply as Sérgio to his friends and colleagues, Vieira de Mello was born in Rio de Janeiro in 1948 and joined the United Nations in 1969 even as he continued to study philosophy and humanities at the University of Paris. His first major position was as senior political adviser to UN peacekeeping forces in Lebanon. Two years later he moved to UNHCR's headquarters in Geneva. From 1991 to 1996 he served in several top UN positions: as special envoy of the high commissioner for Cambodia, director of repatriation for the United Nations Transitional Authority in Cambodia (UNTAC), head of civil affairs of the United Nations Protection Force (UNPROFOR), and UN regional humanitarian coordinator for the Great Lakes Region of Africa. In 1996 Vieira de Mello was appointed UN assistant high commissioner for REFUGEES, and in January 1998 he became under secretary general for humanitarian affairs and emergency relief coordinator. He was instrumental in the creation of the UNITED NATIONS GUIDING PRINCIPLES ON INTERNAL DISPLACEMENT. Before assuming the post in Baghdad, he served as special representative of the UN secretary general in Kosovo and as UN transitional administrator in East timor.

In September 2002 Vieira de Mello was appointed UNITED NATIONS HIGH COMMISSIONER FOR HUMAN RIGHTS. In all of these many positions he proved himself a highly effective and pragmatic administrator and international civil servant. He is credited with instituting a program to protect and resettle Vietnamese refugees, overseeing the repatriation of 300,000 Cambodian refugees from Thailand, setting up a UN civil administration in Kosovo, and managing the political transition in East Timor.

Further Reading:
Feller, Erika, Volker Turk, and Frances Nicholson, eds. *Refugee Protection in International Law: UNHCR's Global Consultations on International Protection.* Cambridge: Cambridge University Press, 2003.
Groenewold, Julia, and Doctors Without Borders. *World in Crisis: The Politics of Survival at the End of the Twentieth Century.* London: Routledge, 1996.
Helton, Arthur C. *The Price of Indifference: Refugees and Humanitarian Action in the New Century.* A Council on Foreign Relations Book. Oxford: Oxford University Press, 2002.
Hyndman, Jennifer. *Managing Displacement: Refugees and the Politics of Humanitarianism.* Minneapolis: University of Minnesota Press, 2000.
Ogata, Sadako, and Kofi Annan. *The Turbulent Decade: Confronting the Refugee Crises of the 1990s.* New York: W. W. Norton & Company, 2005.

Vienna Convention on Diplomatic Relations

The Vienna Convention on Diplomatic Relations, adopted on April 14, 1961, is intended to establish the basis for diplomatic relations and privileges as well as the immunities of a diplomatic mission. The Vienna Convention, however, has a direct bearing on citizens as well as diplomatic personnel based on a decision of the INTERNATIONAL COURT OF JUSTICE (better known as the World Court). In December 2004 the United States Supreme Court agreed to hear a case involving a Mexican national who was scheduled for execution in Texas. The question at issue was whether the execution of the convicted Mexican would constitute a violation of international law, which requires that a diplomatic representative from the country of the accused be present during the trial and sentencing. On March 31, 2004, the World Court ordered the United States to undertake "an effective review" of the convictions and sentences of the convicted man, José Ernesto Medellín, and 50 other Mexicans on death row in nine states. (Medellín had been convicted for a gang-related murder.) The World Court made its determination on the basis of the Vienna Convention. The convention, ratified by the United States in 1969, also calls upon a government that is detaining a foreign citizen to notify the prisoner "without delay" of his right to request help from a consul from his home country. This did not occur in Medellín's case. Mexico sued the United States in the World Court on behalf of Medellín and the other Mexican nationals sentenced to death by U.S. courts. The United States opposed Mexico's suit on the grounds as "an unjustified, unwise and ultimately unacceptable intrusion in the United States criminal justice system." Nonetheless, the World Court ruled in Mexico's

favor. In 2005, after initially agreeing to accept the World Court's authority, the United States announced that it was withdrawing from the relevant protocol of the treaty on the grounds that the court was meddling in the U.S. legal system. The announcement, which seemed intended to placate foes of international institutions in the Bush White House and advocates of the death penalty, nonetheless represented a surprising about-face in view of the initial response from the White House. In its first response to the ruling, the Bush administration had acknowledged that the same provisions that guaranteed consular assistance to aliens on U.S. soil could apply to situations in foreign lands where American nationals were caught up in the legal system. Indeed, the United States had relied on the treaty when it took its case to the World Court demanding compensation for the Iranian authorities' taking of American diplomats as hostages in 1979–80.

Further Reading:
UN.org. *Vienna Convention on Diplomatic Relations.* Available online. URL: http://untreaty.un.org/ilc/texts/instruments/english/conventions/9_1_1961.pdf. Accessed March 21, 2010.

Vietnam, human rights violations in

The Communist Vietnamese authorities have violated human rights on a frequent basis, although some improvements have taken place as the country has opened itself up to the outside world. And while the civilian authorities largely maintain control over the security forces, there are some elements that appear to act on their own initiative, which may account for a number of the serious human rights violations. But the larger problem remains the fact that the country is under one-party communist rule that denies the right of citizens to change their government. Freedoms of the press, assembly, association, and religion are all restricted. There are numerous incidents of arbitrary arrests and detention and beatings of suspects by police. Some prisoners reportedly died because of abuse while in police custody. According to the U.S. State Department *Country Report* of 2004, some DISAPPEARANCES have occurred as well. People are still being arrested because of their political opinions or for having participated in religious demonstrations and political protests. Arrests of political prisoners do not, however, occur on the same scale as they did in the immediate aftermath of the fall of South Vietnam in 1975 when the Communist North took over the whole country. The judiciary is not independent, and suspects have difficulty receiving fair and expeditious trials. The government infringes on privacy rights and has taken steps to limit citizens' access to the Internet.

In recent years, human rights groups have raised concerns about the actions of security forces in the Central Highlands, where political unrest among the indigenous Montagnards has led to a harsh crackdown. The turmoil began in February 2001 when many Montagnards staged demonstrations calling for religious freedom and return of ancestral lands. The military deployed special units that restrict the free movement of citizens in the troubled area. These units enforce a system of household registration and rely on block monitors to maintain watch over their neighbors. Many Montagnard Christians, a minority in a traditionally Buddhist-oriented nation, have been rounded up and arrested without warrants or formal charges and detained for unconscionable lengths of time. Apparently the authorities are convinced that religious gatherings—even when they are simple Christmas ceremonies—might develop into a forum for political dissent. Pledges by officials to respect religious freedom do not seem to be matched by actions.

Although Vietnam began to loosen controls over the economy, emulating China's successful model, the government showed little inclination to lift restrictions on political dissent. Dissidents are regularly rounded up and tried. Arrests have increased in advance of the Communist Party Congress set for 2011. The outcome of these trials is usually a foregone conclusion, and the proceedings may last for only a few hours. In December 2009 Tran Anh Kim, a former army officer, was convicted of subversion for pro-democracy activities and sentenced to five and a half years in prison. He was one of five defendants charged with subversion, potentially a capital crime. Human rights advocates who have called for democratization and an end to Communist monopoly on power have also been arrested. In spite of the intimidation, some opponents of the regime have gone so far as to establish an illegal opposition party called the Democratic Party of Vietnam. In addition, a number of dissidents signed an April 2006 petition called Bloc 8406 that called for a multiparty state. The petition was spearheaded by Rev. Nguyen Van Ly, a Catholic priest who was sentenced to eight years in prison for "overtly revolutionary activities" and "conspiring with reactionary forces." Four others were convicted with him. On occasion, political dissent has boiled over into violence.

See also FREE-FIRE ZONES; MY LAI MASSACRE; PHOENIX PROGRAM; TIGER FORCE.

Further Reading:
Amnesty International. Viet Human Rights. Available online. URL: http://www.amnestyusa.org/all-countries/viet-nam/page.do?id=1011269. Accessed March 21, 2010.
Gettleman, Marvin, Jane Franklin, Marilyn B. Young, and Bruce Franklin, eds. *Vietnam and America: The Most Comprehensive Documented History of the Vietnam War.* New York: Grove Press, 1995.
Human Rights Watch. Vietnam Human Rights. Available online. URL: http://www.hrw.org/asia/vietnam. Accessed March 21, 2010.
Jamieson, Neil L. *Understanding Vietnam.* Berkeley: University of California Press, 1995.
Karnow, Stanley. *Vietnam: A History.* New York: Penguin Books, 1997.
Lamb, David. *Vietnam, Now: A Reporter Returns.* New York: PublicAffairs, 2003.
Langguth, A. J. *Our Vietnam: The War 1954–1975.* New York: Simon & Schuster, 2002.
SarDesai, D. R. *Vietnam Past and Present.* Boulder, Colo.: Westview Press, 2005.
Templer, Robert. *Shadows and Wind: A View of Modern Vietnam.* New York: Penguin, 1999.

voluntary codes of conduct

Until recently, multinational corporations regarded human rights issues as of little or no concern, but revelations of corporate malfeasance and complicity in environmental and human rights abuses have led to a degree of soul-searching in corporate boardrooms. Corporations are beginning to realize that human rights issues should enjoy more recognition and that adherence to human rights enhances a company's reputation, making it more attractive for customers and clients while bolstering employee recruitment and morale. Several manufacturers of footwear and apparel in Southeast Asia and elsewhere, for instance, have tried to eliminate sweatshop conditions, improve the workplace, institute more equitable wages, and eliminate child labor. However, as human rights groups point out, these voluntary codes of conduct have built-in limitations. For one thing, they are voluntary—that is to say, there are no mechanisms for enforcement and no provision for monitoring by neutral bodies to ensure compliance. Nor are there any uniform standards for assessing compliance, which is now left up to local labor groups or nongovernmental organizations (NGOs) on an ad hoc basis. (Some initiatives have been undertaken by the Fair Labor Association and governments and NGOs to draw up industry standards for upholding human rights in the workplace.)

Voluntary codes, say human rights advocates, are generally drafted without consulting employees; indeed, workers may not even be aware that their employer has a code. Moreover, while the language in these codes may express lofty principles, it is often so ambiguous that it obliges the company to very little. There is the additional problem of reconciling the principles of a voluntary code with the laws or policies of a host country that may, for instance, forbid workers from organizing unions. In July 2004 the United Nations tried to jump into the breach by launching a Global Compact of business, labor, and civil society to promote social responsibility in the global economy. The compact includes some reporting requirements intended to make member corporations more accountable for their conduct. The compact has the support of companies in Europe, Africa, Asia, and South America, which to some extent belies the assertions by some U.S. corporations that a commitment to human rights—which might include higher pay for workers, for example—puts them at a competitive disadvantage. However, enforcement remains a problem. Human rights groups contend that for all the improvement that voluntary codes represent, the only real solution lies in instituting binding codes.

See also SULLIVAN PRINCIPLES.

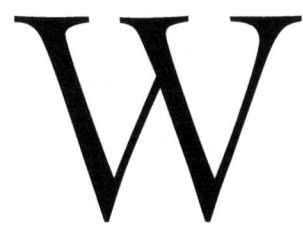

Waldheim, Kurt (1918–2007) *UN secretary-general*
Until his reputation was irrevocably tarnished by revelations about his activities during World War II, Kurt Waldheim was a highly regarded Austrian diplomat who had attained the top post of the United Nations as secretary-general from 1971 to 1981. Waldheim's service in a German army unit in Yugoslavia during the war was not well known when he was elected to his first five-year term at the United Nations' helm. He had already earned a distinguished record of diplomatic service as Austria's permanent representative to the United Nations and later as its foreign minister. During his tenure as secretary-general, he tried to put an end to a number of conflicts—the Iraq-Iran war and the China-Vietnam war among them—without appreciable success. After serving two terms, he ran for an unprecedented third term but opposition from China forced his withdrawal.

Shortly after Waldheim stepped down as secretary-general stories, appeared in the press that he had been an officer in a German army unit that had committed atrocities in Yugoslavia during World War II. He adamantly denied that he knew anything about the crimes, and an international commission set up to investigate the matter found him innocent of any complicity in the atrocities. Waldheim ran for and won the presidency of Austria in spite of the scandal, but he was treated as an international pariah and denied a visa to travel to the United States based on the allegations. He did not run for a second term in 1992. Waldheim died on June 14, 2007.

Further Reading:

Finger, Seymour Maxwell, and Arnold A. Saltzman. *Bending with the Winds: Kurt Waldheim and the United Nations.* New York: Praeger Publishers, 1990.
New York Times. "Kurt Waldheim, Former U.N. Chief, Is Dead at 88." Available online. URL: http://www.nytimes.com/2007/06/15/world/europe/15waldheim.html?pagewanted=1&_r=2. Accessed April 6, 2010.
Ryan, James Daniel. *The United Nations under Kurt Waldheim, 1972–1981.* Lanham, Md.: Scarecrow Press, 2001.

Walleyn, Luc (1949–) *Belgian human rights advocate*
A Belgian judge, lawyer, and human rights advocate, Luc Walleyn has taken advantage of Belgium's former policy of bringing legal suits against accused human rights violators in cases involving other countries. (That policy has since been modified under U.S. pressure.) In recent years Walleyn has initiated lawsuits against Belgian soldiers participating in the peacekeeping operation in Somalia for racist behavior and has undertaken the defense of Belgian victims of the former military regime in Guatemala. Perhaps he is best known, though, for representing some 23 Palestinian survivors of massacres by Christian Phalange militias at the Sabra and Shatilla refugee camps in Lebanon in 1982. Approximately 2,000 Palestinians were killed after Israeli forces invaded Lebanon and briefly occupied the capital of Beirut. Israel was then aligned with Christian forces fighting Muslim factions in the Lebanese civil war. In 2001 Defense Minister Ariel Sharon (by then Israel's prime minister) was accused by the plaintiffs of being responsible for the massacres since Israeli forces were thought to be in control of the area of the camps and yet failed to intervene to stop the massacres. (A subsequent Israeli investigation did assign some of the blame for the events to Sharon.) When the complaint was announced, Israel's Foreign Ministry denounced the charges, saying, "Israel views with the utmost gravity the distorted, unfair, and intentionally hostile nature of the Panorama program. The timing of the program, 19 years after the events in question, shows a lack of good faith and an attempt to tarnish Israel and its leader [Sharon]." The case was later dropped.

As a former member of Avocats Sans Frontières (Lawyers Without Borders, ASF), Walleyn participated in ASF programs in Rwanda, Burundi, and Kosovo and represented the organization at the 1998 UN conference in Rome that established the INTERNATIONAL CRIMINAL COURT. Walleyn specializes in immigration law as well as in human rights and humanitarian law and serves as a lecturer in the chair for immigration law at the University of Antwerp and as a guest professor at the Institut des Hautes Etudes Politiques in Paris.

In 2006 a team under Luc Walleyn undertook to represent 22 of the 103 victims participating in the Thomas Lubanga trial before the ICC. Lubanga, a former rebel leader from the DEMOCRATIC REPUBLIC OF THE CONGO, was the first person arrested under a warrant issued by the ICC on charges of war crimes, specifically conscripting child soldiers. His men are also blamed for ethnic massacres, murder, torture, rape, and mutilation. His trial began in January 2009.

See also BELGIAN WAR CRIMES TRIBUNAL; SABRA AND SHATILLA, MASSACRE IN.

Wannsee Conference

On January 20, 1942, 15 top Nazi officials met in the Berlin suburb of Wannsee to decide the fate of the 11 million Jews living in Europe (including 330,000 in England). The conference, held at a villa on the shores of Lake Wannsee owned by the SS, was chaired by REINHARD HEYDRICH, the chief of the Reich Main Security Office and head of the German secret police apparatus. The objective of the conference was described in the minutes: "At the beginning of the discussion Chief of the Security Police and of the SD, SS-Obergruppenführer Heydrich, reported that the Reich Marshal [HERMANN GÖRING] had appointed him delegate for the preparations for the FINAL SOLUTION of the Jewish question in Europe and pointed out that this discussion had been called for the purpose of clarifying fundamental questions. The wish of the Reich Marshal to have a draft sent to him concerning organizational, factual and material interests in relation to the final solution of the Jewish question in Europe makes necessary an initial common action of all central offices immediately concerned with these questions in order to bring their general activities into line."

By this point in the war, it was no longer thought feasible to eliminate so many people by the methods then in use—shooting and gassing using mobile vans. Although the EINSATZGRUPPEN—special death squads that operated behind advancing German forces—had killed over a million Jews and Slavs in conquered Soviet territory, they were not considered efficient or quick enough to meet the challenge.

Historians still debate when the Nazis determined on an official policy to annihilate European Jewry. ADOLF HITLER had called for the execution of Jews in his book *Mein Kampf (My Struggle)*, written in 1923, and in a speech delivered in Berlin the same year he had threatened the Jews with "total annihilation if a new world war should begin." Even if no explicit order was put in writing, there is general agreement that Hitler was responsible for putting the policy into effect. By late 1939 a special agency had been established under ADOLF EICHMANN to organize the DEPORTATIONS of Jews from the occupied territories. The first gassing of Jews at a concentration camp (Auschwitz) took place on September 3, 1941, and the first test gassing by van a few months later. That same month the commander of one mobile unit known as extermination group A reported the execution of over 130,000 Jews. So the killings of Jews were already well underway when the 15 SS officials gathered at the Wannsee villa.

The importance of the conference lay in the fact that it formalized as policy a systematic and massive extermination program. The participants also deliberated about how to distinguish the Jews subject to deportation to the death camps from those who were only partly Jewish. The minutes of the meeting were taken by Eichmann and edited by Heydrich, who carefully excised references to the intended extermination of Jews and substituted euphemisms in their place. Nonetheless, the document makes for chilling reading:

> The Reichsführer-SS and the Chief of the German Police [Chief of the Security Police and the SD] was entrusted with the official central handling of the final solution of the Jewish question without regard to geographic borders. The Chief of the Security Police and the SD then gave a short report of the struggle which has been carried on thus far against this enemy, the essential points being the following:
>
> a) the expulsion of the Jews from every sphere of life of the German people,
> b) the expulsion of the Jews from the living space of the German people.

The conferees weighed various "possible" solutions to the problem. Forced evacuations of Jews were considered only provisional, "but practical experience is already being collected which is of the greatest importance in relation to the future final solution of the Jewish question." Presumably, that "practical experience" referred to the experimentation with gassing Jews that was already occurring in Poland and the occupied parts of the Soviet Union. There were many impediments to putting the policy of extermination into effect, however: "The handling of the problem in the individual countries will meet with difficulties due to the attitude and outlook of the people there, especially in Hungary and Rumania. Thus, for example, even today the

Jew can buy documents in Rumania that will officially prove his foreign citizenship." The issue of slave labor was discussed: "Under proper guidance, in the course of the final solution the Jews are to be allocated for appropriate labor in the East. Able-bodied Jews, separated according to sex, will be taken in large work columns to these areas for work on roads, in the course of which action doubtless a large portion will be eliminated by natural causes."

WILHELM STUCKART, the lawyer responsible for drafting the 1935 NUREMBERG LAWS banning Jews from Germany's public and economic life, asked how much "Jewish blood was enough to taint German purity" when determining how many people of "mixed blood" (partly Jewish) should be "sent east"—to the death camps of Poland. But there was no question that once taken into custody, no Jews could be liberated. "The possible final remnant will, since it will undoubtedly consist of the most resistant portion, have to be treated accordingly, because it is the product of natural selection and would, if released, act as the seed of a new Jewish revival (see the experience of history)."

See also CONCENTRATION CAMPS.

Further Reading:
Dawidowicz, Lucy. *A Holocaust Reader.* Library of Jewish Studies. Chicago: Behrman House Publishing, 1976.
Dwork, Deborah, and Robert Jan Van Pelt. *Holocaust: A History.* New York: W. W. Norton & Company, 2003.
Gilbert, Martin. *The Holocaust: A History of the Jews of Europe during the Second World War.* New York: Owl Books, 1987.
Lagnado, Lucette Matalon, and Sheila Cohn Dekel. *Children of the Flames: Dr. Josef Mengele and the Untold Story of the Twins of Auschwitz.* New York: Penguin Books, 1992.
Rees, Laurence. *Auschwitz: A New History.* New York: PublicAffairs, 2005.
Roseman, Mark. *The Wannsee Conference and the Final Solution: A Reconsideration.* New York: Metropolitan Books, 2002.
Wistrich, Robert S. *Hitler and the Holocaust.* Modern Library Chronicles. New York: Modern Library, 2001.

War Child Project

The War Child Project consists of a network of several independent organizations throughout the world working to help children affected by war. The War Child Project is based on the philosophy that it is morally impermissible to ignore the most helpless victims and that the protection and well-being of children is vital to the future of society. The project had its genesis in Britain when two filmmakers, Bill Leeson and David Wilson, returned from reporting on

the plight of victims in the war in Bosnia in 1993. They were most appalled by the fact that civilians were at special risk of being made victims of the conflict. Even though they had no experience in philanthropy, they believed that they could be influential in gathering support for children using their contacts in media and entertainment. They received enough support to organize a convoy into the former Yugoslavia that was loaded with baking equipment to help feed REFUGEES in devastated parts of Bosnia and Herzegovina.

As the War Child Project grew, it received other sources of funding, including support from the UNITED NATIONS HIGH COMMISSIONER FOR REFUGEES and the European Union. It also had added support from celebrities such as the composer Brian Eno and the playwright Tom Stoppard. The War Child Project often works in partnership with local grassroots organizations, through both short-term emergency relief and long-term rehabilitation programs, to improve the living conditions of war-affected children. Branches of the War Child Project can be found in the United States, Italy, Canada, Ethiopia, Eritrea, and the Netherlands. Each organization is totally autonomous, with different trustees and financial structures.

See also CHILDREN'S RIGHTS.

Further Reading:
Apfel, Roberta, and Bennett Simon, eds. *Minefields in Their Hearts: The Mental Health of Children in War and Communal Violence.* New Haven, Conn.: Yale University Press, 1996.
Dodge, Cole P., and Magne Raundelen. *Reaching Children in War: Sudan Uganda and Mozambique.* London: Taylor & Francis, 1992.
Pran, Dith, comp. *Children of Cambodia's Killing Fields: Memoirs by Survivors.* Edited by Kim DePaul. New Haven, Conn.: Yale University Press, 1999.
Raymond, Alan. *Children in War.* New York: TV Books Inc., 2000.
Singer, P. W. *Children at War.* New York: Pantheon, 2005.
War Child. War Child Programs. Available online. URL: http://www.warchildusa.org/programs_int.aspx. Accessed March 21, 2010.
War Child International. Projects. Available online. URL: http://www.warchild.org/projects/projects.html. Accessed March 21, 2010.

war crimes, categorization of

Efforts to impose restrictions on behavior in conflict are not new. The writings of the sixth-century Chinese scholar and soldier Sun Tzu refer to limitations on conduct in war. Both the ancient Greeks and the Hindus believed that certain practices in war should be prohibited. Generally speaking, war crimes are considered violations of war or INTERNATIONAL HUMANITARIAN LAW (IHL). One of the fundamental criteria, established by the trials of Nazi war criminals at the NUREMBERG TRIALS, is that criminal responsibility inheres in the individual. A suspect therefore cannot seek exoneration by claiming that he or she was acting under orders to commit a crime.

As far as is known, in 1474 Sir Peter von Hagenbach became the first person actually tried for war crimes. An emissary of Charles the Bold, duke of Burgundy (also known to his critics as Charles the Terrible), Hagenbach was instructed to impose order on the town of Breisach, on the Upper Rhine in present-day Germany. He carried out his instructions by means of murder, rape, illegal taxation, and confiscation of property. When he was finally ousted after a SIEGE, he was not put to death—at least not at once—but was rather tried by a special court set up by the archduke of Austria, who chose judges from among the ranks of each member of the coalition that had defeated his forces. (Similarly, judges on the Nuremberg Tribunal represented each of the Allies responsible for the defeat of Nazi Germany.) Hagenbach was charged with "trampling the laws of God and man," including murder, rape, perjury, and other *malefacta*—evil deeds. He was also accused of ordering mercenaries to invade private residences, where they would kill the male members of the family, leaving the women and children at their mercy. Hagenbach resorted to a line of defense that has become familiar. "Is it not known that soldiers owe absolute obedience to their superiors?" his counsel asked, contending that in any case the accused did not recognize any authority apart from the duke of Burgundy. Neither defense worked; Hagenbach was found guilty and put to death.

The 19th century saw several innovative attempts to codify the laws of war, among then the First Geneva convention (1864) in Europe and the LIEBER CODE (1863) in the United States. Further initiatives were taken to ban certain types of warfare in the HAGUE CONVENTIONS of 1899 and 1907—for example, the bombardment of undefended cities. In 1945 the Allies established a set of principles that would form the basis of prosecutions of Nazi war criminals at Nuremberg. War crimes were defined by the NUREMBERG CHARTER of the International Military Tribunal as "violations of the laws or customs of war," including murder, ill-treatment, or deportation of civilians in occupied territory; murder or ill-treatment of PRISONERS OF WAR; killing of HOSTAGES; plunder of public or private property; wanton destruction of municipalities; and "devastation not militarily necessary." This document represented the first time that international humanitarian law had to be taken into account in judging culpability for war crimes. The four GENEVA CONVENTIONS of 1949 include as "grave breaches . . . any of the following acts, if committed against

persons or property protected by the Convention: willful killing, torture or inhuman treatment, including biological experiments, willfully causing great suffering or serious injury to body or health, and extensive destruction and appropriation of property, not justified by military necessity and carried out unlawfully and wantonly." The conventions also consider as grave breaches (1) compelling a prisoner of war or civilian to serve in the forces of the hostile power, (2) willfully depriving a prisoner of war or protected civilian of the rights of a fair and regular trial, (3) unlawful deportation or transfer of a protected civilian, (4) unlawful confinement of a protected civilian, and (5) taking of hostages. These grave breaches would constitute war crimes. The 1977 ADDITIONAL PROTOCOLS TO THE GENEVA CONVENTIONS add to and elaborate on the grave breaches of international law as defined in the Geneva Conventions. Among other provisions, Additional Protocol 1 forbids certain types of MEDICAL EXPERIMENTS, targeting nondefended localities and civilian populations, the forced transfer of civilians by an OCCUPYING POWER, attacks on cultural property, and depriving individuals of a fair trial. Protocol I also calls on member states to try individuals accused of grave breaches or else hand the suspect over to a state willing to do so.

Because Protocol 1 only applies to international conflicts, PROTECTED PERSONS are defined as the wounded and sick, combatants, prisoners of war, and civilians captured by an occupying power. Additional Protocol II, which applies only to internal conflicts, carries no criminal liability for grave breaches of the law. As Steven R. Ratner points out in his essay on the subject for the CRIMES OF WAR PROJECT, nongrave breaches are not necessarily war crimes. Failure of a captive power to maintain a record of prisoners of war as required by law, for example, would be a violation of the Third Geneva Convention, but it would not necessarily be defined as a grave breach or rise to the level of a war crime. Violations could be considered illegal acts and thus become prosecutable by the state in which the violation occurred, but it would not be an indictable offense under the Geneva Convention or Additional Protocol I. Such a violation would not require a state to try or extradite the suspect to be tried elsewhere. "Distinguishing among nongrave breaches to determine which are crimes is not an exact science," Ratner admits, "though it would seem that the more serious nongrave breaches do incur individual responsibility. Even if an atrocity is not explicitly banned by international law, it may still be considered a crime as a violation 'of the laws and customs of war.'"

What would appear to be a theoretical distinction has crucial ramifications in light of the fact that such atrocities as those perpetrated by JOSEPH STALIN in the Soviet Union, the Khmer Rouge in Cambodia, Hutu militants in Rwanda, and Serb and Croatian forces in the Bosnian War are not considered war crimes. There have been several attempts to fill this gap by making violations not specifically covered by the Geneva Conventions or Additional Protocol I subject to prosecution in international courts. The ROME STATUTE OF THE INTERNATIONAL CRIMINAL COURT expands the number and types of crimes it covers by 26 beyond the grave breaches specified by the Geneva Conventions. Where international law is more ambiguous is in its application to civil conflicts. The Rome Statute of the INTERNATIONAL CRIMINAL COURT (ICC) lists as war crimes for internal conflicts four serious violations of ARTICLE 3 COMMON TO THE GENEVA CONVENTIONS—violence to life and person, attacks on personal dignity, hostage taking, and summary executions—as well as 12 serious violations of the laws and customs of war that include attacks on civilians, PILLAGE, rape, or mutilation. Article 3 forbids "violence to life and person," and "outrages upon personal dignity" against "persons taking no part in the hostilities." However, Article 3, which can be applied to civilians in internal conflicts, does not carry the same force of law as the provisions of the Geneva Conventions themselves. Under the tribunal's mandate, an individual can be prosecuted for such crimes as murder, ill-treatment, torture, mutilation, corporal punishment, rape, enforced prostitution, summary executions, hostage taking, COLLECTIVE PUNISHMENT, and PILLAGE. Similarly, the Statute of the INTERNATIONAL CRIMINAL TRIBUNAL FOR THE FORMER YUGOSLAVIA (ICTY) includes "serious violations of Common Article 3 of the Geneva Conventions."

Whatever the reach of the law, though, the problem of enforcement remains. As Ratner acknowledges, the "creation of a body of law criminalizing certain violations of the laws of war does not mean that war criminals will actually be prosecuted." States may prosecute nationals for war crimes committed on its own territory; in certain instances, states may rely on the principle of UNIVERSAL JURISDICTION to prosecute noncitizens who committed crimes in another country. Spanish judges, for instance, have initiated criminal prosecutions against Argentine and Chilean officials for torture and murder committed in their respective countries. Frequently, though, when states do prosecute citizens for crimes not specifically addressed by the Geneva Conventions or Additional Protocol I, they do not punish the offender severely or else allow him or her to escape prosecution altogether. In an attempt to find a solution to this problem, the United Nations has established ad hoc courts—such as the ICTY as well as the INTERNATIONAL CRIMINAL TRIBUNAL FOR RWANDA and the SPECIAL COURT FOR SIERRA LEONE—which can try suspected war criminals for both grave breaches of the Geneva Conventions and Additional Protocol I and crimes covered only by the law of the states where the crimes took place.

Further Reading:
Bassiouni, M. Cherif. *Crimes against Humanity in International Criminal Law.* Boston: Martinus Nijhoff, 1999.
Benson, Bruce. *The Enterprise of Law: Justice without the State.* San Francisco: Pacific Research Institute for Public Policy, 1990.
Dormann, Knut, and Louise Doswald-Beck. *Elements of War Crimes under the Rome Statute of the International Criminal Court: Sources and Commentary.* Cambridge: Cambridge University Press, 2003.
Gutman, Roy, ed. *Crimes of War: What the Public Should Know.* New York: W. W. Norton & Company, 1999.
Hagan, John. *Justice in the Balkans: Prosecuting War Crimes in the Hague Tribunal.* Chicago Series in Law and Society. Chicago: University of Chicago Press, 2003.
Hazan, Pierre, and James Thomas Snyder. *Justice in a Time of War: The True Story behind the International Criminal Tribunal for the Former Yugoslavia.* Eugenia and Hugh M. Stewart Series on Eastern Europe. Austin: Texas A&M University Press, 2004.
Ratner, Steven. "War Crimes, Categories of," *Crimes of War: What the Public Should Know,* edited by Roy Guttman. New York: W. W. Norton & Co., 1999.
Romano, Cesare, Andre Nollkaemper, and Jann K. Kleffner, eds. *Internationalized Criminal Courts and Tribunals: Sierra Leone, East Timor, Kosovo, and Cambodia.* International Courts and Tribunals Series. Oxford: Oxford University Press, 2004.
Shelton, Dinah. *International Crimes, Peace, and Human Rights: The Role of the International Criminal Court.* Ardsley, N.Y.: Transnational Publishers, Inc., 2000.
United Nations War Crimes Commission. *Law Reports of Trials of War Criminals: Four Genocide Trials.* Boulder, Colo.: Lynne Rienner Publishers, 1992.

war criminals of Japan

With few exceptions—HIDEKI TOJO for one—most of those Japanese war criminals found guilty of war crimes, crimes against peace, and CRIMES AGAINST HUMANITY by the International Military Tribunal for the Far East (the TOKYO TRIALS) and by other courts in China and the Philippines are not as well known as the Nazi officials brought before the NUREMBERG TRIALS. However, some individuals are worth noting both because of the nature of the crimes they committed and because of the legal precedent that their cases established in war crimes tribunals.

Abe Koso

Admiral Abe Koso was responsible for the execution of several American PRISONERS OF WAR during the Pacific campaign in World War II, a crime for which he was subsequently convicted and hanged. The incident stemmed from an audacious raid in summer 1942 by U.S. Marines on Japanese-held Butaritari Island in the Gilbert Islands. The raid, launched on the night of August 16, was intended to destroy enemy installations, gain as much intelligence as possible, and divert Japanese attention from U.S. operations on Guadalcanal and Tulagi, but the operation was hampered by terrible weather. During the fighting 18 marines were slain, and nine members of the force were left behind when the marines retreated. The stranded marines were captured by the Japanese, who transferred them to the island of Kwajalein. There the prisoners came under the authority of Vice Admiral Abe, commander of Japanese naval forces in the Marshall Islands. Early in October 1942, he was told that as a result of a new government policy he had no obligation to send the marines to Tokyo for detention and that he could dispose of them as he chose. Abe therefore ordered the prisoners beheaded. After the war he was convicted of war crimes largely on the basis of the testimony of an islander who had witnessed the executions. He was hanged on the island of Guam.

Isayama Harukei

Lieutenant General Isayama Harukei was one of many Japanese military defendants tried for war crimes after the end of World War II for mistreatment of American prisoners of war on the occupied island of Formosa (now Taiwan). He was accused of "willfully, unlawfully and wrongfully" committing "cruel, inhuman and brutal atrocities and other offences against certain American prisoners of war by permitting and participating in an illegal and false trial and unlawful killing of said prisoners of war, in violation of the laws and customs of war" in spring 1945. The trial, conducted before a Japanese military tribunal, was considered "false" because Isayama (and others) gave an unlawful order to the tribunal to sentence the American POWs to death. He was also charged with authorizing the executions themselves. The failure to afford a prisoner of war a fair trial is a violation of the 1929 Geneva Convention. During the war Japan had adopted a policy that called for the execution of enemy airmen who had participated in bombing raids against Japanese territory. The policy led to several trials such as the one that Isayama participated in, which resulted in the executions of several captured U.S. airmen. Isayama was found guilty and sentenced to life imprisonment.

Kimura Heitaro

General Kimura Heitaro was the Japanese army commander in occupied Burma between 1944 and 1945. He was tried by the Allies after World War II on charges that he had helped plan wars in China and in the Pacific, including surprise attacks on the Allies. He was also indicted for having brutalized civilian and POW slave labor working on the Siam-Burma Railway. He was convicted by the International Tribunal for the Far East on six counts and sentenced to death by hanging.

Minami Jiro

Minami Jiro served as governor-general of Korea between 1936 and 1942 and is best known for enforcing an assimilation campaign that, in the words of one commentator, remains "notorious for its unmatched scope and extremity." A former minister of war and a member of the inner circle of army officers that dominated Japan in the 1930s and 1940s, Minami was the last of eight governors-general to preside over Japanese-occupied Korea. Under the banner of naisen ittai (Japan and Korea as one body) and kôminka (imperialization), Minami instituted an assimilation campaign that enshrined Shintoism as the state religion and forced Koreans to use Japanese names instead of their Korean ones. Minami exploited the media, educational system, and police to promote this campaign. But rather than achieve its objective of making the Koreans more Japanese, the campaign provoked intense opposition and ended up solidifying Korean nationalism. After being convicted at the Tokyo War Crimes trial, Minami was paroled.

Nagano Osami

As commander in chief of the Japanese Combined Fleet and a member of Supreme War Council, Admiral Nagano Osami was among the military officials involved in planning and carrying out the surprise attack on Pearl Harbor. He was charged with war crimes by the International Military Tribunal for the Far East but died of a heart attack before he could be sentenced. Born in 1884, Nagano was a graduate of Japan's Naval Academy and later studied at Harvard Law School. He became a naval attaché to the United States in the early 1920s and represented the Japanese navy at the London Naval Conference, which was established to place limits on naval power; he withdrew in protest in 1935 when Japan was denied naval parity with the United States and Great Britain. Subsequently Nagano was among the hard-liners who pushed for expansion of the Japanese navy. In 1936 he was appointed minister of the navy and a year later commander in chief of the fleet. In 1941, now chief of the Naval General Staff, Nagano became responsible for implementing a plan to attack the U.S. Pacific Fleet at Pearl Harbor drawn up by Admiral Isoroku Yamamoto. In December 1941, when negotiations between the United States and Japan collapsed, he approved the attack. He remained chief of the Naval General Staff through 1944. After the navy had suffered serious reverses, Nagano lost the support of Emperor Hirohito and Prime Minister Tojo Hideki, and he was removed from his post. Captured by the Allies in 1945, he was brought before the International Military Tribunal for the Far East, where he assumed responsibility for the attack on Pearl Harbor. He died in 1947 while the trials were still continuing.

Tachibana Yoshio

Vice Admiral Tachibana Yoshio was executed by the Allies in Guam for war crimes committed under his command on the Bonin Islands in the Pacific. He was implicated in participating in murders and atrocities involving U.S. pilots captured in 1944 and 1945. Among the grisliest crimes was having taken part in a "sake-fuelled feast" in which the flesh of the executed prisoners was consumed by Japanese officers. The details of the deaths of the nine "flyboys" were sealed in top-secret files in Washington for many years to spare their families distress.

Tamenori Sato

Major General Tamenori Sato was among several high-ranking Japanese officers convicted for war crimes; he was charged with killing and mistreating Burmese civilians under Japanese occupation during World War II. In July 1945 Japanese forces were stationed on the Andaman Islands off the coast of Burma when they captured a number of Burmese civilians—18 men, nine women, and 34 children—attempting to escape in a large boat. This information was reported to Tamenori, who approved the decision to have the civilians executed. After the Japanese surrender to the Allies in August, Tamenori ordered the bodies exhumed so that they could be burned in hope of concealing the evidence of the crime. Brought before a British court in Singapore, he admitted the charges against him but maintained that he was under orders to administer "severe punishment" to anyone trying to escape the islands. The Burmese were aware of the possible penalties for their actions, Tamenori contended, and so in effect they brought about their deaths. At the same time he acknowledged that he might have done something wrong and said that he took full responsibility in an attempt to shield his subordinates. Tamenori and one other defendant, Lieutenant Colonel Tazawa Keizo, were found guilty and executed; the other three officers involved in the massacre received relatively light sentences.

See also MATSUI IWANE; MATSUOKA YOSUKE; OKAWA SHUMEI; SAKAI TAKASHI; SHIMADA SHIGETARO; YAMASHITA TOMOYUKI.

Further Reading:
Daws, Gavin. *Prisoners of the Japanese: POWs of World War II in the Pacific.* New York: Perennial, 1996.
Li, Peter, ed. *Japanese War Crimes: The Search for Justice.* New Brunswick, N.J.: Transaction Publishers, 2003.

Maga, Timothy P. *Judgment at Tokyo: The Japanese War Crimes Trials.* Lexington: University Press of Kentucky, 2001.
Mendelsohn, John. *The Preservation of Japanese War Crimes Trials Records in the National Archives.* Washington, D.C.: National Archives and Records Administration, 1982.
Minear, Richard R. *Victors' Justice: The Tokyo War Crimes Trial.* Michigan Classics in Japanese Studies. Ann Arbor: University of Michigan, Center for Japanese Studies, 2001.
Piccigallo, Philip R. *The Japanese on Trial: Allied War Crimes Operations in the East, 1945–1951.* Austin: University of Texas Press, 1980.
Rees, Laurence. *Horror in the East: Japan and the Atrocities of World War II.* New York: Da Capo Press, 2002.
Russell of Liverpool, Edward Frederick Langley Russell, Baron. *Knights of the Bushido: A Short History of Japanese War Crimes.* London: Greenhill Books, 2005.
Tanaka, Yuki. *Hidden Horrors: Japanese War Crimes in World War II.* Philadelphia: Westview Press, 1998.

war criminals of the former Yugoslavia

Even while the war in the former Yugoslavia was still raging in the early 1990s, the United Nations was already drawing up plans to bring to justice perpetrators of war crimes, CRIMES AGAINST HUMANITY, and other atrocities before a special court. This was eventually established as the INTERNATIONAL CRIMINAL TRIBUNAL FOR THE FORMER YUGOSLAVIA (ICTY), sitting in The Hague, Netherlands. Those individuals indicted for participation in the war in Bosnia, Croatia, and Kosovo have included nationals from all sides in the conflict, although the majority of the accused have been Serbs. The most famous defendant is the former Yugoslav strongman SLOBODAN MILOŠEVIĆ. Several others—notably RATKO MLADIĆ, the former Serbian army commander, and the Bosnian Serb militant RADOVAN KARADŽIĆ—were still at large in early 2005, a decade after the end of the Bosnian War. Nonetheless, several lower-ranking and less well-known officers implicated in various atrocities have been handed over to The Hague or, in a few cases, have turned themselves in. More recently, under pressure from the United States and the European Union, Croatia and Serbia have begun to try suspects in their own courts, although in some instances men considered war criminals in the eyes of the world still enjoy a reputation as war heroes for nationalists in their own countries. The individuals described below represent only a small number of those who have been indicted or convicted for crimes committed in Bosnia, Croatia, or Kosovo from 1992 to 1999, but their cases are worth noting both for the nature of their crimes and for the legal precedent that they have established.

Beara, Ljubisa

A former Serbian colonel, Ljubisa Beara was arrested and turned over to the ICTY in The Hague for war crimes committed in the Bosnian War. Beara was implicated in the slaying of more than 7,000 Muslim men and boys in the town of Srebrenica in July 1995, which had been considered a UN-protected zone. The indictment accused Beara of having overseen the beheading of 800–1000 men and boys in the town. In addition, as the commander of an engineering unit, he was alleged to have taken charge of the digging of MASS GRAVES and making floodlights available so that firing squads could continue their work at night. Beara's arrest and extradition to The Hague by Serbia in October 2004 came as something of a surprise since Serbia had balked at cooperating with the tribunal in the past. Belgrade's action was believed to have been motivated by a desire to gain favor with the European Union and the United States, which has made financial assistance contingent on bringing war criminals to justice. Nonetheless, it is believed that several suspects wanted in The Hague are still being harbored in Serbia.

Blagojević, Vidoje

Colonel Vidoje Blagojević became the second defendant convicted of GENOCIDE by the ICTY. The tribunal handed down its verdict for the Bosnian Serb officer on January 17, 2005, in connection with his role in the 1995 massacre of more than 7,000 Muslim boys and men near the Bosnian town of Srebrenica. The ICTY found him guilty because he was aware that the massacre was being planned and then went ahead and helped transfer the captive men and boys to the site where it was to take place. He was convicted of complicity in genocide, one step below a finding of outright genocide, and sentenced to 18 years in prison. A codefendant, Major Dragan Jokić, was convicted on charges of murder, extermination, and persecution for having sent men and equipment to dig mass graves for the victims. He was sentenced to nine years in prison.

Blaskić, Tihomir

Tihomir Blaskić, a former general in the Croatian army, had already served eight years of a 45-year sentence for war crimes in the former Yugoslavia when an appeals court found his conviction flawed and freed him. The unprecedented ruling by the ICTY cleared Blaskić of charges that he was responsible for the April 1993 killings of Muslim civilians in half a dozen western Bosnian villages, which had fallen under Croatian control. In one incident in the village of Ahmici, Croatian forces had killed over 100 civilians, many of them elderly people who were burned in their own homes. The objective was to spread terror among the Muslim population and uproot them from a region the Croatians sought to take over as a part of a program of ethnic cleansing.

General Blaskić's trial was complicated and unusually long, lasting two years. The appeals court found that the lower court had made numerous errors and misinterpreted the law. Although it determined that the general had committed lesser war crimes, the court ruled that he had been sufficiently punished. The legal turnaround was also due to the discovery of previously hidden documents that had not been available when Blaskić was initially tried. These documents, which were in the possession of the Croatian intelligence agency, revealed that Blaskić's role in the atrocities was relatively minor; then-president of Croatia FRANJO TUDJMAN had refused to turn the material over to the ICTY. The new government, which took office after Tudjman's death in 1999, ordered the documents opened. Croatian attorneys examining the documents have concluded that they could have led to Tudjman's indictment for war crimes by the court.

Cesić, Rajko

Rajko Cesić, a Bosnian Serb officer, was convicted of war crimes in March 2004 by the ICTY in The Hague. In 1992, while the Balkan wars raged among Serbia, Croatia, and Bosnia, Cesić was stationed at the notorious Luka camp in Brcko, Bosnia, where Muslim prisoners were being held. A member of the Bosnian Serb reserve police corps, Cesić pleaded guilty to having personally committed 10 murders and two cases of sexual assault at the camp in May 1992. In one case he beat a Bosnian Muslim police officer to death, but not before first ordering him to shake the hands of his fellow inmates and say good-bye to them. He clubbed another to death and lined up eight other victims, whom he shot in two separate incidents. Cesić also admitted to holding a gun to two middle-aged Muslim brothers, both former neighbors, and forcing them to perform fellatio on each other while the other guards watched.

Cesić received an 18-year sentence even though he could have been sentenced to life. Defense lawyers asked the judges to take into account the fact that he was only 27 when he committed his crimes and that he was deprived as a child because he had been brought up by a single mother. In a novel defense, his lawyers also pointed out that since most of his victims had no idea that he would kill them, their executions were not quite as cruel as they would have been otherwise. His lawyers also claimed that Cesić had helped some inmates escape—those he had taken a liking to—and the judges agreed that the evidence supported this assertion. However, they were not terribly impressed. "These facts demonstrate that he was capable of some benevolence," said one judge, who observed that Cesić had demonstrated this characteristic only "on occasion" and that it should therefore not be given "undue weight." On the other hand, the judges did consider his cooperation a factor when determining his sentence and indicated that his expression of remorse appeared to be genuine.

Deronjić, Miroslav

Miroslav Deronjić is a former high Bosnian Serb official convicted for his actions in the Bosnian War; the ICTY sentenced him to 10 years in prison. Deronjić had pleaded guilty to a charge of ordering the burning and razing of a Bosnian Muslim village called Glogova in May 1992, which resulted in the deaths of at least 64 men, women, and children out of a population of almost 2,000. He admitted that the inhabitants had been assured that they would be safe if they handed over their weapons. Deronjić also cooperated with the tribunal as a prosecution witness in the trial of former Yugoslav strongman Slobodan Milošević. In that role he implicated the authorities in Belgrade for supplying arms and providing strategic advice to the Serbian forces in Bosnia, facilitating their ability to launch a war against the Muslim population. One of the judges sharply disagreed with Deronjić's sentence, saying that in view of the gravity of the offense it was much too light and violated the spirit and mandate of the tribunal. Some critics maintained that the verdict was part of a troubling pattern by the tribunal in its rush to render judgment on the suspects because of U.S. pressure to close down its investigations by the end of 2004 and conclude all trials by 2008. As a result, many cases involving low-ranking suspects may not be heard by the tribunal at all.

Galić, Stanislav

Stanislav Galić, commander of Serb forces besieging Sarajevo during the Bosnian War, was convicted by the ICTY in December 2003 for killing civilians. He was charged in the indictment with implementing a strategy of shelling and sniping intended to target civilians in the capital of Bosnia and Herzegovina. He was specifically cited for the killings of 66 and wounding of 140 in a mortar attack on a Sarajevo market in 1994. The indictment described his forces directing "shelling and sniping at civilians who were tending vegetable plots, queuing for bread, collecting water, attending funerals, shopping in markets, riding on trams, gathering wood or simply walking with their children and friends." One of the lead prosecutors described the siege of Sarajevo as "an episode of such notoriety that one must go back to World War II to find a parallel in European history." General Galić's superiors, General Ratko Mladić and the Bosnian Serb political leader, Radovan Karadžić, were also indicted but were still at large as of early 2005. Galić was sentenced to a prison term of 20 years.

Ganić, Ejup

Ejup Ganić, 63, was arrested in London in February 2010 on a Serbian warrant. Ganić was one of 19 Bosnian officials

Serbs accuse of conspiring to kill 40 injured Serb soldiers as they were withdrawing from the besieged city of Sarajevo during the Bosnian conflict. He was soon released on bail by a British court, based on the case made by his lawyers that the Serb warrant was politically motivated.

Glavas, Branimir

In 2009 Branimir Glavas became the first senior Croatian official to be convicted for the torture and murder of Serbian civilians between 1991 and 1995. Unlike many others charged with war crimes and other abuses during the Balkan wars of the nineties, Glavas, a deputy in parliament, was tried by a Croatian court and not the ITFY. During the war for Croatian independence, he commanded a unit that carried out the abduction, torture, and killings of Serbs in the eastern city of Osijek in 1991. He was sentenced to 10 years in prison.

Halilović, Sefer

Sefer Halilović was the highest-ranking Bosnian officer to be charged for criminal acts committed during the Bosnian War in the 1990s. As part of the command staff of the Bosnian military force in the region, Halilović was responsible for coordinating Operation Neretva aimed at lifting the siege of Mostar in 1993, according to the tribunal's indictment. He was charged with a single count of violating the laws or customs of war for the murder of 62 Bosnian Croats in the villages in September 1993. The indictment started then took no "effective measures to prevent killings of civilians" in both incidents nor take any action against the perpetrators. Halilović went on trial in January 2005. In November 2005 he was acquitted of all charges.

Haradinaj, Ramush

Just prior to his indictment by the ICTY in March 2005, Ramush Haradinaj had been prime minister of Kosovo, which, while officially still a part of Serbia, has gained a large measure of autonomy under the protection of UN peacekeepers. Before his ascension to the post, Haradinaj was a senior commander of the Kosovo Liberation Front (KLF), which had waged a long insurgency against Serbian forces, culminating in the war in Kosovo in 1998. The charges against Haradinaj stem from his involvement in the KLF; it is alleged that he took part in atrocities in which Serbian Kosovar civilians were targeted. Haradinaj denied culpability but resigned as prime minister and agreed to turn himself in to stand trial. He is the second KLF leader to have been indicted; the first, Fatmir Limaj, was indicted in 2003.

Janković, Gojko

A former Bosnian Serb police commander, Gojko Janković was indicted by the ICTY for crimes committed during the war in Bosnia between 1992 and 1995. In contrast to many other indicted individuals, he turned himself in after five years on the run. Janković was charged with torturing and raping Muslim women. What makes his case unusual was that according to reports (including an account by his own wife), Janković had sought refuge in Moscow and had enjoyed the protection of the Russian security services, although the government insists it had no knowledge of his whereabouts. (A Slavic country, Russia had been a political supporter of Serbia, another Slavic nation, during the conflict. Slobodan Milošević's wife, Mira Marković, also lives in Moscow.) Two other Serbian officers wanted in The Hague were also reportedly hiding out in Moscow under Russian protection.

Jelisić, Goran

As acting commander of Luka prison camp in the former Yugoslavia, Goran Jelisić reportedly used to introduce himself as "the Serb Adolf" before torturing and killing inmates, including children and the elderly. In 1995 the ICTY indicted him on seven charges, including genocide, crimes against humanity, and violations of CUSTOMARY LAW. The charges stem from acts committed by Jelisić during the Bosnian War. The Luka camp was established by Serb forces in 1992 in Bosnia and Herzegovina. The camp, also known as a collection center, was used to house Croat and Muslim REFUGEES who had been forced to flee their homes. Most of the detainees at Luka were men of military age, though there were also a number of women. According to the indictment, detainees were systematically killed at Luka over a period of two weeks in May 1992. Almost every day, guards entered the camp, singled out men for interrogation, then beat and killed them, usually by shooting them at close range. Victims were forced to place their heads on a metal grate that drained into a nearby river so that the guards would be spared the necessity of cleaning up after the executions. Before the camp was closed down in July 1992, hundreds of Muslims and Croats were killed.

The charge of genocide can only be brought if there is evidence that the accused intended to destroy a group based on its national origins, ethnic roots, or religious or political beliefs. Jelisić, the ICTY ruled, met this standard by announcing that he intended to kill Muslims and then systematically proceeded to do so. In October 1999 Jelisić was sentenced to 40 years' imprisonment, a sentence that was upheld on appeal. He was the 10th individual convicted by the ICTY to serve a sentence.

Krajisnik, Momcilo

Momcilo Krajisnik is one of the highest-ranking war criminals indicted for war crimes in the Bosnian War in 1991 and 1992. An aide to former Bosnian Serb leader Radovan Karadžić, Krajisnik was arrested by NATO peacekeepers in March 2004 and sent to The Hague to stand trial. Krajisnik

was indicted by the ICTY in connection with his activities between July 1, 1991, and December 31, 1992, during which time Serbian forces under his command secured control of several municipalities that had been proclaimed part of the Serbian Republic of Bosnia and Herzegovina. He was accused by the tribunal of "genocide, crimes against humanity, violations of the laws and customs of war, and grave breaches of the GENEVA CONVENTIONS, including murder, WILLFUL KILLING, extermination, complicity in genocide, deportation, and inhumane acts." According to a court spokesperson, Krajisnik was one of "the individuals who ran illegal operations that resulted in the deaths of thousands of Bosnians." He took part in decisions "that resulted in DEPORTATIONS, illegal arrests, ethnic cleansing and the deaths of thousands of Bosnians." Amor Masović, head of the Muslim commission for missing persons, described Krajisnik as "one of the masterminds of the genocide and ethnic cleansing in Bosnia."

Krajisnik had earlier served as speaker of the separatist Serb parliament; in that capacity he had repeatedly hindered efforts by international mediators to end the conflict. He had also participated in the Serb siege of Sarajevo that had killed hundreds of people and was responsible for ethnic-cleansing campaigns to expel Bosnian Muslim and Croatian populations from Serb-occupied territory. In addition, he was implicated in the massacre of thousands of Muslim men killed by Serb security forces after they had seized control of the UN safe haven of Srebrenica. He also controlled the municipal authorities and police in Serb-held territory, giving him a power base which he reportedly used for war profiteering. After the end of the war, Krajisnik briefly served as a member of Bosnia's first multiethnic collective government, a position he used to undermine any effort at reconciliation between the ethnic groups. He lost his seat after being defeated at the polls. Even after his arrest, Krajisnik still had his defenders among Serb radicals who described him as "conservative and pious." A widower and father of three, Krajisnik clung to the belief that separation based on ethnicity and religion was "natural."

Krstić, Radislav

The Bosnian Serb general Radislav Krstić was the first major Bosnian Serb officer to be put on trial at the ICTY. He was charged with eight counts of genocide, complicity to commit genocide, crimes against humanity, and violations of the laws and customs of war for actions he had taken in the Bosnian War. The most serious charges were based on Krstić's participation in the massacre of Muslim men and boys in the UN-protected enclave of Srebrenica in July 1995. At the time Krstić was a deputy commander of the Drina Corps. Known by his nickname "Krle," he became a valued ally of General Ratko Mladić, then the head of the Yugoslav forces who was also indicted by the ICTY for war crimes. Krstić maintained during his trial that he never discussed the fate of Bosnian Muslim civilians in Srebrenica with Mladić and insisted that he had nothing to do with organizing the deportation of women, children, or the elderly from the enclave. He further claimed that he had only heard about the executions of the Muslims a month or two after the fact. Nonetheless, the evidence indicated that Krstić was with Mladić in Srebrenica when Mladić announced that "the moment has finally come to take revenge on the Turks here"—a derogatory reference to the Muslims. Krstić was found guilty of genocide for the massacre at Srebrenica and was sentenced to 46 years' imprisonment, the longest sentence so far handed down by the ICTY. It was also the first time that the tribunal had found a defendant guilty of genocide. AMNESTY INTERNATIONAL hailed the verdict, saying that it represented "a significant contribution in achieving justice for the thousands of victims of summary executions in Srebrenica and their relatives."

Lazarević, Vladimir
Retired Serbian general Vladimir Lazarević possibly signaled a new spirit of cooperation by the Serbian government with the West when he agreed to surrender to the ICTY in January 2005. Lazarević was one of four generals indicted in absentia in connection with abuses committed by Serbian troops against ethnic Albanians in Kosovo. As commander of the Priština Corps in the breakaway Yugoslav province, Lazarević was responsible for actions of all subordinates, according to charges brought by the ICTY. Among the actions of Serbian troops cited in the indictment were the forcible relocation of Albanian villagers; the shelling of villages; the killings of civilians, including, in one case, 17 men whose bodies were thrown into wells; the burning of houses; and destruction of cultural property and mosques.

For years Serbia had adamantly resisted sending accused war criminals to The Hague in marked contrast to Bosnia and Croatia. Under intense pressure from the United States (which threatened to cut off financial assistance) and the European Union, however, Serbia began to show tentative signs of cooperation with the ICTY, and Lazarević's decision to turn himself in was taken as a further indication of Belgrade's changing attitude. However, the government was not prepared to repudiate its native son in spite of the crimes with which he was charged. An official statement stated that the Serbian government and the prime minister "personally, all appreciate and respect this patriotic, highly moral and honorable decision made by General Lazarević."

Martić, Milan
A former Croatian Serb police officer, Milan Martić was indicted by the ICTY for war crimes committed during the Bosnian War. As of late 2004 he was still at large, although he managed to get word out that there would be "many deaths" if UN peacekeepers attempted to arrest him. In 1995 he ordered two rocket attacks on Zagreb, the capital of Croatia; seven people were killed and 40 wounded. The attack made him one of the most reviled figures in Croatia. "I feel responsible in that I was the leader," Martić said. "But I do not feel ethically guilty. The charges made against me are ridiculous. How can I sit on the [court] bench for firing a few dozen rockets at military targets when [President] Tudjman [of Croatia, now deceased] ordered the bombing of Serb women and children as they fled for their lives?" When Croatian forces successfully counterattacked and drove out Serb forces, he took refuge in Republika Srpska, the Serbian enclave in Bosnia. He reportedly lives openly in the capital of Banja Luka within walking distance of the UN's International Police Task Force headquarters. He is said to live in high style as well, riding around the city in a Rolls Royce. To avoid capture, he is protected by a contingent of security men posing as gardeners. "I move with good security, at night or day," he once boasted.

Meakić, Željko
A former commander of a Serbian concentration camp in northern Bosnia and Herzegovina, Željko Meakić was charged with genocide for participating in the ethnic cleansing of Bosnian territory seized by Serb forces during the Bosnian War. From May 25, 1992, to August 30, 1992, Serb forces detained more than 3,000 Bosnian Muslims and Bosnian Croats in a mining complex in Omarska in the former Yugoslavia. Under Meakić's direction, prisoners were allegedly beaten, tortured, and killed. In February 1995 the ICTY indicted Meakić and 19 other individuals under his supervision with violations of the laws and customs of war and crimes against humanity. The indictment alleged that Omarska and another camp called Keraterm were the scenes of "severe beatings, killings as well as other forms of physical and psychological abuse, including sexual assault." Meakić was transferred to a detention center operated by the court in July 2003. In 2005, the Bosnian authorities requested Meakić's transfer to Bosnia for trial.

Nikolić, Ivan
A Serbian army reservist, Ivan Nikolić was the first person convicted by a Yugoslav court for crimes committed in the 1999 Kosovo War. Nikolić was implicated in the killing of an ethnic Albanian man and woman in a Kosovo village. "This was a war crime against the civilian population," observed the presiding judge who heard the case in 2002. The case was initially heard by a military court, which failed to render judgment. After he was given a sentence of eight years in prison, Nikolić claimed that he was innocent and a victim of a "show trial." However, representatives of the ICTY were heartened by the verdict, which they said was

568   war criminals of the former Yugoslavia

"a very important event for the judiciary in Serbia." Until Nikolić's trial, the Yugoslavs had tried only one other officer for war crimes committed in the Balkan wars of the 1990s.

Perisić, Momcilo

Former Serbian general Momcilo Perisić is one of the highest-profile suspects to go on trial before the ICTY. According to the indictment, he is alleged to have directed proxy Serbian forces fighting in Croatia and Bosnia from Belgrade, ensuring that these forces were supplied with personnel, equipment, provisions, and funding. Born in 1944, he became commander of Yugoslavia's Third Army in April 1993, shortly after the war in Bosnia had broken out. It was hoped that his trial would reveal the extent of the clandestine support extended by the Milošević regime to the forces of the Serbian Bosnian Army of the Republika Srpska, known as the VRS, and the Army of the Serbian Krajina (Croatia), known by its initials FRY. As the highest-ranking officer in the Yugoslav army, Perisić had overall command and authority over the operations conducted by these proxy forces, answerable only to President Slobodan Milošević himself. His involvement also implicated him in atrocities committed by these armies. The indictment also charges him with establishing elaborate covers to disguise the source of the logistical and funding support. The indictment noted that those individuals who received their pay and benefits from the coffers of the Yugoslav army under Perisić's command "reads like a who's who of indicted war criminals" including General Ratko Mladić and other generals who were responsible for the massacre of 7,000 Muslim men and boys at Srebrenica. In addition, Perisić is charged with providing personnel, weapons, and logistical support for the siege of Sarajevo and the shelling of the Croatian capital of Zagreb. The indictment specifically charges Perisić with "crimes against humanity for murder, inhumane acts, persecution and extermination and violations of the laws and customs of war for murder and attacks on civilians both the basis of his individual responsibility in aiding and abetting such crimes, and on the basis of command responsibility." Under pressure from the United States and the European Union and with the acquiescence of the new government in Belgrade, Perisić turned himself over to the tribunal's jurisdiction in May 2005.

Plavšić, Biljana

Biljana Plavšić, a former Serb president of Bosnia and known as the Serbian "Iron Lady," was convicted by the ICTY for crimes against humanity in 2002. She was originally indicted on charges of "persecution and terror tactics" and "liquidation" to drive non-Serbs out of Bosnia. Although she was also indicted on two counts of genocide and five counts of crimes against humanity as well as one count of violation of the laws or customs of war, she man-

aged to strike a plea bargain and was sentenced to 11 years in prison. She had served in a variety of positions in the Bosnian Serb regime, both during and after the war; she was one of the two acting presidents of the self-proclaimed "Serb Republic of Bosnia and Herzegovina" and later became president of the Republika Srpska between 1996 and 1998. Throughout her political career, she was known as an unstinting supporter of ethnic cleansing who declared that the deportations of non-Serbs were "a natural phenomenon" and not a war crime. Plavšić, the only woman and highest ranking Bosnian Serb official to have been convicted by the ICTY, subsequently expressed remorse for Serbian crimes during the war, although some observers believe that her show of contrition was designed to win a reduced sentence. Her appeals to secure an early release have repeatedly been rebuffed by the court.

Strugar, Pavle

A Serbian officer, Pavle Strugar was sentenced by the ICTY to eight years in prison for the destruction of cultural property during the Bosnian War. Struger, who was convicted in 2005, was specifically charged with allowing the shelling of the historic Croatian coastal town of Dubrovnik in 1991. Dubrovnik's Old Town, which was dominated by several medieval buildings, had been a United Nations World Heritage site since 1979. According to the indictment, "in the course of an unlawful attack" by the Yugoslav army on the Old Town in December 1991, two people were killed, three were seriously wounded, and "many buildings of historic and cultural significance in the Old Town, including institutions dedicated to . . . religion, and the arts and sciences, were damaged." The violations caused the ICTY to file six counts of violations of the laws or customs of war against the officer. Although the tribunal agreed that Strugar had not ordered the shelling, he was in a position to stop it "when he could have done so."

Šljivančanin, Veselin

A Serbian officer, Veselin Šljivančanin was originally convicted by the ITFY in 2007 for his role in indirectly allowing Serbian paramilitary units to carry out the massacre of Croatian prisoners of war in 1991. At the time, he was in charge of troops protecting wounded Croatian fighters and refugees in a hospital in Vukovar, a Croatian city seized by Serb forces (then known as the Yugoslav Army). In 2009, in an unusual move, the UN tribunal added several years to his sentence—for a total of 17 years—because of his failure to disobey illegal orders that called for him to withdraw troops protecting prisoners of war. By removing his troops, the indictment charged that Šljivančanin was effectively putting them at risk of Serbian paramilitary units that "would likely kill the prisoners." It was the first time that a UN war crimes tribunal made such a ruling based on the

Third Geneva Convention, which requires protection of prisoners of war by an occupying power.

Tadić, Dusan

Dusan Tadić was arrested in 1994 in Germany and charged with war crimes he was accused of committing as a member of Serb forces in the former Yugoslavia in June 1992. He was among the first defendants to be tried before the ICTY in The Hague, Netherlands. His conviction was considered a historical landmark in international law since it established the precedent that an individual can be found criminally responsible for serious violations of the laws or customs of war and crimes against humanity before an international criminal court. "International trials can work," declared former chief prosecutor Justice RICHARD J. GOLDSTONE when the guilty verdict was announced. The decision was also important because it marked the first judicial condemnation of ethnic cleansing by Serb forces. Tadić was charged for participating in the seizure, murder, and maltreatment of Bosnian Muslims and Croats in a region in Bosnia and Herzegovina taken by Serb forces. He was also indicted on 12 counts of grave breaches of the 1949 Geneva Conventions, torture or inhuman treatment, and abetting the commission of genocide. Some of the charges stemmed from his duties at the Omarska camp, one of several such camps set up to illegally detain thousands of Muslims and Croats. In his defense, Tadić argued that he had been elsewhere at the time the crimes attributed to him had occurred. The court found his defense implausible and pronounced him guilty on 11 counts, constituting both violations of the laws or customs of war and crimes against humanity.

Tolimir, Zdravko

A former Serbian general, Tolimir, 61, went on trial in early 2010 at the war crimes tribunal in The Hague on charges of genocide, crimes against humanity, and war crimes. Tolimir is accused of being the right-hand man of Gen. Ratko Mladić, the commander of Serb forces, the most notorious alleged war criminal still at large. Although Tolimir had been in custody since 2007, his trial had been delayed owing to his ill health.

Ulemek, Milorad

The *New York Times* dubbed Milorad Ulemek "Serbia's most infamous paramilitary soldier" who was responsible for innumerable atrocities during the Bosnian War of the 1990s. His nom de guerre Legija (which means "of the Legion") derives from the years he spent in the French foreign legion in the 1980s. In 1992, shortly after the outbreak of the war in his native country, he returned to Serbia and joined the Serb Volunteer Guard, a paramilitary group better known as ARKAN's Tigers. As a commander of the Tigers, Ulemek fought in both Croatia and Bosnia, which had declared their independence from Serb-dominated Yugoslavia. When the Tigers were disbanded, Ulemek then found employment with the Serb secret police, the Special Operations Unit, more popularly known as the Red Berets. In 1999, named as commander of the Red Berets, he fought in the war in the breakaway province of Kosovo. Ulemek is suspected in involvement in the killing of four political opposition figures (while President Slobodon Milošević was still in power) as well as an unsuccessful attempt on the life of Vuk Drašković, head of the opposition Serbian Renewal Movement. Although the Red Berets were considered to be Milošević's "praetorian guard," it is believed that Ulemek took part in secret negotiations with opposition leaders to arrange for Milošević to step down peacefully in exchange for a guarantee that he would not be prosecuted for his crimes during the wars. He has since been arrested in Yugoslavia on charges of participating in the assassination of Prime Minister Zoran Djindjić, who was shot and killed in March 2003. In spite of Ulemek's notoriety, a novel attributed to Ulemek, entitled *Iron Trench,* about his experiences in the Balkan wars, became an instant best seller when it went on sale in Yugoslavia in 2004.

See also BOSNIA AND HERZEGOVINA, HUMAN RIGHTS VIOLATIONS IN; CROATIA, HUMAN RIGHTS VIOLATIONS IN; KOSOVO, WAR CRIMES IN; SARAJEVO, SIEGE OF; SERBIA, HUMAN RIGHTS VIOLATIONS IN; SREBRENICA, MASSACRE IN; YUGOSLAVIA, WAR CRIMES IN.

Further Reading:
Askin, Kelly Dawn. *War Crimes against Women: Prosecution in International War Crimes Tribunals.* Leiden, Netherlands: Brill Academic Publishers, 1997.
Clark, Wesley K. *Waging Modern War: Bosnia, Kosovo, and the Future of Combat.* New York: Public Affairs, 2001.
Hagan, John. *Justice in the Balkans: Prosecuting War Crimes in the Hague Tribunal.* Chicago Series in Law and Society. Chicago: University of Chicago Press, 2003.
Harris, Nathaniel. *The War in Former Yugoslavia.* London: Hodder & Stoughton, 1997.
Hazan, Pierre, and James Thomas Snyder. *Justice in a Time of War: The True Story behind the International Criminal Tribunal for the Former Yugoslavia.* Eugenia and Hugh M. Stewart Series on Eastern Europe. Austin: Texas A&M University Press, 2004.
International Criminal Tribunal for the former Yugoslavia. Available online. URL: http://www.icty.org/. Accessed March 21, 2010.
Jurist. *Kosovo and Yugoslavia: Law in Crisis* (January 2000). Available online. URL: http://jurist.law.pitt.edu/kosovo.htm. Accessed March 21, 2010.

Mertus, Julie. *Former Yugoslavia: War Crimes Trials in the Former Yugoslavia.* Helsinki: Human Rights Watch/Helsinki, 1995.

Naimark, Norman, and Holly Case. *Yugoslavia and Its Historians: Understanding the Balkan Wars of the 1990s.* Stanford, Calif.: Stanford University Press, 2003.

Rhode, David. *Endgame: The Betrayal and Fall of Srebrenica.* New York: Farrar, Straus & Giroux, 1997.

Rogel, Carole. *The Breakup of Yugoslavia and the War in Bosnia.* Westport, Conn.: Greenwood Press, 1998.

Scharf, Michael P. *Balkan Justice: The Story behind the First International War Crimes Trial since Nuremberg.* Durham, N.C.: Carolina Academic Press, 1997.

warcriminals.com. War Crimes: Yugoslavia. Available online. URL: http://warcriminals.com/directory/Yugoslavia/index.html. Accessed March 21, 2010.

Whealey, Robert. *American Intervention in Yugoslavia: Civil War, 1991–1999.* Amherst, N.Y.: Humanity Books, 2005.

war dead, treatment of

The treatment of fatalities in war is rooted in religious tradition as much as it is in CUSTOMARY LAW. The inscription on the Tomb of the Unknown Soldier in Arlington Cemetery, Washington, D.C., underscores the respect in which the war dead are held: "Here Rests in Honored Glory an American Soldier Known But to God." Although the inscription refers to an unknown American soldier, it is a sentiment that is shared by people of almost every nationality, and indeed there are monuments to unknown soldiers in many countries of the world.

The proper disposal of the dead is considered an important responsibility of any party to a conflict, and this has been true since ancient times. Removing the dead from the battlefield and interring their bodies is not only a matter of showing respect but also serves a hygienic purpose. Allowing the corpses to decompose poses a grave risk of spreading disease to the living. Although the laws of war accept that death is an inherent part of war, they also recognize that the care of the living holds greater priority. The drafters of successive treaties dealing with conduct in war believed that the treatment of the war dead, however, could not depend on tradition alone but should be codified as well. Article 15 of the First Geneva Convention, adopted in 1864, provides that the parties must "at all times, and particularly after an engagement . . . search for the dead and prevent their being despoiled." The article also states that "whenever circumstances permit," an armistice should be concluded so as to facilitate the search for the wounded, which by implication means that in the process a search for the dead would also be undertaken. In its Commentary to the Geneva Convention, the INTERNATIONAL COMMITTEE OF THE RED CROSS (ICRC) specifically states that the dead must be brought back along with the wounded. The Red Cross offers two compelling justifications for this position. On the one hand, in light of the chaotic situation on the battlefield, it is often difficult to distinguish between the gravely injured and the dead. For another, the rules of war oblige the belligerents to properly—and promptly—dispose of the dead.

In an essay for the CRIMES OF WAR PROJECT, H. Wayne Elliott writes that the treatment of the war dead consists of two aspects. The first is a prohibition against mistreatment of the body, whether through failure to treat it with respect because of neglect or deliberate mutilation. The second is a prohibition against pillaging the body. These restrictions, he says, are as much enshrined in customary law—the moral principles and values that are universally accepted—as they are in international law. While mutilation of the dead is relatively rare, as long as disciplined armies are involved in the conflict, PILLAGE of the dead poses a more serious problem. Soldiers are permitted to search bodies—there is always a possibility information of intelligence value will be found—and may succumb to the temptation to take personal property off the dead in spite of legal prohibitions.

Article 16 of the First Geneva Convention sets out additional rules as to how a body is to be disposed of. If a body of an enemy soldier is discovered, the body is to be returned to the adversary, generally through a neutral party or the ICRC. The body should be accompanied by written evidence of death along with one half of the double identity disk and any personal effects found on the body.

In Article 17 there are specific instructions regarding the burial of war dead. First, a body should be examined, preferably by a person with the requisite medical skill, to ensure that the combatant is, in fact, deceased. Where possible, the body should be interred in an individual grave both because of the need to honor the dead and because it will make subsequent identification much easier. However, the First Geneva Convention makes clear that these obligations can sometimes be waived depending on other factors including climate, sanitation, or the exigencies of conflict. Cremation is in general prohibited, except where sanitary conditions make it imperative or where the tradition or the religious background of the diseased dictates otherwise. (Cremation, for instance, is a time-honored way of disposing of bodies in the Hindu tradition.) By the same token, the Geneva Convention also calls for the burial (or cremation) to be performed in accordance with the religious practices of the deceased; remains are to be interred by nationality and cemeteries mapped so that future identification can be expedited. Graves are also to be protected.

The laws pertaining to the treatment of the dead, first codified in the middle of the 19th century, were reaffirmed by the Fourth Geneva Convention of 1949, which requires parties to the conflict to protect the dead against pillage and ill-treatment and obliges them to ensure that the dead are honorably interred, their graves respected, and information pertaining to their identity provided to the ICRC. In war, of course, ascertaining who exactly is dead may be a problem. Almost invariably some of those who are later found to be dead are first reported missing. To take that situation into account, Protocol I to the 1949 Geneva Conventions states that, as a general principle, each party to the conflict shall search for the missing and report all relevant information to their adversary as soon as circumstances permit—at the latest at the end of hostilities.

Determining when a body is being mistreated and can therefore be classified as a war crime is a difficult proposition. Failure on the part of a warring party to meet the obligations under international law may not always mean that a violation has been committed—if, for instance, bodies of an enemy force remain on the battlefield for a prolonged period because of military necessity. A breach of law would be more clearly established, however, if bodies still have not been collected after hostilities have ceased. Further, putting bodies on display for propaganda purposes or as a means of humiliating an opponent—as was done in Mogadishu, Somalia, where the corpses of UN peacekeepers were dragged through the streets—can never be justified. In a more recent incident, U.S. forces in Iraq were widely criticized for displaying the bodies of Saddam HUSSEIN's two sons after they were killed in a firefight, especially in the Islamic world, where bodies are supposed to be interred as quickly as possible. Presumably U.S. military authorities had intended to prove to a skeptical Iraqi public that the two men—who were both feared figures while their father was in power—were truly dead, but in doing so they might have crossed a line that put them at risk of violating international law.

See also ADDITIONAL PROTOCOLS TO THE GENEVA CONVENTIONS; GENEVA CONVENTIONS.

Further Reading:
Berry, Nicholas O. *War and the Red Cross: The Unspoken Mission.* New York: St. Martin's Press, 1997.
Gutman, Roy, ed. *Crimes of War: What the Public Should Know.* New York: W. W. Norton & Company, 1999.
International Committee of the Red Cross. *International Law Concerning the Conduct of Hostilities: Collection of Hague Conventions and Some Other Treaties.* Geneva: International Committee of the Red Cross, 1989.

war on terror
The war on terrorism declared by the Bush administration shortly after the 9/11 attacks was based on the principle that countries were either allies or adversaries and that those countries that harbored or supported suspected terrorists were just as culpable as the militant groups themselves. This principle was, however, not so easy to put into practice; for one thing, it was impractical—it was impossible for U.S. and allied military and intelligence forces to pursue terrorists in every part of the globe. For another, the black-and-white formulation was flawed from the outset; the majority of the 19 terrorists participating in the attacks on New York and Washington, D.C., in 2001 were Saudis, but Saudi Arabia is an ally and the principal source of oil for the United States. Moreover, there are many different groups that have been labeled terrorist by the United States and the United Kingdom that are considered legitimate political entities, including Hamas in Gaza and Hezbollah in Lebanon. In addition, several critics of the Bush policy maintain that it is impossible to make war against a concept (which terrorism is) as opposed to individual practitioners of terrorism, such as AL-QAEDA. Other critics deride the idea that there should be a "war" at all and instead say that the problem is more criminal in nature, citing successful prosecutions of terrorists in cases such as the 1993 bombing of the World Trade Center. In early 2009 the International Commission of Jurists, a group of lawyers and justices, weighed in by adopting a report issued by a special panel that the "war on terror" had not only failed in its avowed objectives but had done "immense damage" to international law and human rights. The panel of legal experts, which included Mary Robinson, former Irish president and UNITED NATIONS HIGH COMMISSIONER FOR HUMAN RIGHTS, was especially concerned that democratic nations were increasingly resorting to secretive methods in the ongoing war, "introducing an array of measures which undermine cherished values as well as the international legal framework carefully developed since the Second World War." These measures, the panel declared, had resulted in human rights violations, including torture, enforced disappearances, secret and arbitrary detentions, and unfair trials. That there had been little accountability for these violations only made the situation more troubling. The panel warned that these so-called temporary counter-terrorism programs were becoming "permanent features of law and practice." Calling for a repudiation of the paradigm of a "war," the report additionally urged that the pursuit and prosecution of terrorism suspects should lie with the criminal justice system and not with secret intelligence agencies acting in the absence of adequate legal accountability. "We have seen intelligence services around the world acting with insufficient accountability and intelligence cooperation being undertaken outside the rule of law," said Hina Jilani, a lawyer of the Supreme Court of Pakistan and former UN Special Representative on Human Rights Defenders. "This

A New York City firefighter looks up at what remains of the World Trade Center after the terrorist attack of September 11, 2001. It was this incident that led to the invasion of Afghanistan that October. *(U.S. Navy)*

"enemy combatants" (making them exempt from PRIS-ONER-OF-WAR status) until the war was over. Given the nature of a shadowy global war, in which a definitive victory was impossible to declare, that essentially meant that detainees could be held indefinitely. Efforts to contrive a legal formula to try at least some of the suspects continued to hit stumbling blocks. Vehement objections were raised to the use of military tribunals or commissions by opponents of the Bush policy as well as by human rights groups. The effort to place detainees beyond the jurisdiction of U.S. courts by keeping them imprisoned under military guard offshore in Guantánamo, Cuba, did not succeed either. The Supreme Court ruled that in fact U.S. law applied to the base there as well. Guantánamo, which at one point held about 700 detainees, also became such a reviled symbol of U.S. unilateralism that upon taking office in January 2009 President Barack Obama vowed to shut it down within a year, a promise that remained unfulfilled two years later.

The case of the Uighurs, while a special case, raised important legal issues regarding the ability of U.S. courts to take jurisdiction of detainee cases. The Uighurs were captured in Afghanistan, but there was never any evidence that they had any aggressive intentions against the United States. Nonetheless, they ended up in Guantánamo. In 2009 a U.S. judge ruled that they posed no threat and should be freed. The U.S. government scrambled to find refuges for them—China demanded their repatriation on the ground that they were terrorists—rather than allow them on U.S. soil. The U.S. Supreme Court refused to decide the case of the Uighurs; in an unsigned opinion announced in March 2010, the Court vacated the decision of the appeals court and sent it back to the lower courts for reevaluation. A U.S. appeals court had already ruled that the lower court's decision freeing the Uighurs and allowing their resettlement in the United States was mistaken because the courts could not override executive authority when it came to setting immigration policy.

In November 2009, Attorney General Eric Holder announced that five top terrorist suspects, including Khalid Sheikh Mohammed, considered one of the masterminds of the 9/11 attacks, would be tried under the criminal justice system in New York. The decision was immediately denounced by many conservatives and some families of victims of the attacks who wanted to see the men dealt with by military commissions. However, the decision was also lauded by many human rights organizations and most Democrats in Congress, who pointed out that the criminal justice system had worked perfectly well in previous terrorist cases, including that of Sheikh Omar Abdel-Rahman (known as "the blind sheikh") who was convicted in the 1993 bombing of the World Trade Center. In 2009 about

intelligence is then used in various legal proceedings and cannot be contested. Secrecy is becoming a pervasive feature in our legal systems."

The war on terror did not begin after the attacks on the United States on 9/11, but most of the controversial laws intended to govern the way in which the war was conducted were enacted in their aftermath. The Bush administration was widely criticized for instituting and/or sanctioning questionable practices in a war that former vice president Dick Cheney admitted had to be conducted at least in part "on the dark side." One of the most contentious issues centered on the legal status of detainees accused of supporting or participating in terrorist activities. The Bush administration, while insisting that the detainees were being treated humanely (an assertion that itself was challenged), maintained that they could be held in a kind of legal limbo as

350 people convicted of terrorism were being held in prisons on U.S. soil.

At the same time, Holder also announced that another group of five suspects, detained in connection with the 2000 attack on the battleship USS *Cole* in YEMEN, would be tried under military commissions. About 40 terror suspects are scheduled for trial altogether in federal courts or before military commissions. (Some observers maintain that the evidence against the suspects in the latter case was more circumstantial and less likely to hold up in a civilian court.) Even as conservatives argued that all cases should be heard before military commissions, civil libertarians were denouncing what they called a two-tier system in which cases with less substantial evidence would be tried in forums where looser standards applied, heightening the chance of a conviction. Defense lawyers for the *Cole* defendants were expected to assert that their clients were entitled to the same protections as any criminal defendant, including those guaranteed by the Sixth Amendment, which entitles a defendant "to be confronted with the witnesses against him." How the Supreme Court would view this argument is unclear, and it might take years before the issue is resolved, potentially delaying the commissions or calling into question any guilty verdict they handed up. A military lawyer for one of the men accused of the *Cole* bombing filed a lawsuit in the U.S. Court of Appeals for the District of Columbia to stop any military commission from prosecuting his client.

In the months since Holder's announcement, opposition to trying Khalid Sheikh Mohammed and four other al-Qaeda suspects in civilian court only intensified. New York's mayor, Michael Bloomberg, who had previously supported the idea, changed his position, asserting that the costs of providing security for the trial would be prohibitive and would cause needless disruption to the people who lived and worked in Downtown Manhattan where the federal courthouses are located. Republicans in Congress threatened to withhold any funds for civilian trials. The political atmosphere became even more charged after the arrest in December 2009 of Umar Farouk Abdulmutallab, a 23-year-old Nigerian, after he attempted to blow up a plane bound for Detroit. He was read his rights and interrogated by the FBI. (It later emerged that he had been trained in Yemen.) Opponents of Obama's policy denounced the decision to treat him like a criminal rather than as an enemy combatant and remand him into military custody.

Military tribunals have not necessarily proven an effective way of disposing of detainee cases, mainly because of legal wrangling. By early 2010 only three detainees had been convicted since 9/11, two of whom were subsequently freed—SALIM AHMED HAMDAN, Osama bin Laden's former driver, and an Australian national arrested in Afghani-

stan named David Hicks. The third was given a life sentence. That small number stands in marked contrast to the nearly 200 terrorists convicted in federal criminal courts including JOSÉ PADILLA, accused of trying to set off a "dirty bomb" (but convicted on other charges), and the so-called "shoe bomber" Richard Reed. In fact, most suspected terrorists arrested during the Bush administration were tried and convicted in civilian courts.

Nonetheless, the political firestorm forced the Obama administration to consider reversing course, all but ruling out a civilian trial in New York, or anywhere else on American territory for that matter, if it was not at a military facility. It was even possible that when the dust settled the administration might try the five suspects in military tribunals (while permitting the participation of civilian lawyers), in exchange for the support of at least some key Republican senators for shutting down Guantánamo.

What evidence can be admitted into any criminal trial of the terrorist suspects remains one of the thorniest problems for prosecutors. The question boils down to whether sufficient evidence exists to persuade a jury that the suspects are guilty without compromising national security. There is also a related issue that involves the treatment or mistreatment of detainees. The CIA and elements of the U.S. military subjected many of the suspects to harsh interrogation techniques, including waterboarding (simulated drowning), which critics have characterized as torture. (The Obama administration promised to end these "enhanced interrogation techniques," as they have also been called.) The mistreatment of these prisoners might also taint their testimony and confessions, making them inadmissible in a federal court. It is also possible that some prisoners who have been mistreated in prison might be mentally unfit to stand trial. The issue of mental competence was raised in the case of Ahmed Khalfan Ghailani, a Tanzanian captured in 2004 in connection with plotting the bombings of U.S. embassies in Kenya and Tanzania in 1999. He was imprisoned for two years in secret CIA jails before being transferred to Guantánamo, where he was subjected to harsh interrogation techniques. Although he is one of the five terrorist suspects to go on trial in New York—he has pleaded not guilty—his lawyers have expressed concerns that "as a result of the residual aftereffects of the program that he was subjected to" while being incarcerated, he might not be able to assist in his own defense, regardless of whether it takes place in a criminal court or in a military tribunal.

In July 2010, a federal judge in Manhattan ruled that Ghailani could be tried on charges that included conspiracy, murder, bombing of a U.S. embassy, the use of weapons of mass destruction against U.S. nationals. That made him the first detainee from Cuba to face prosecution in the United States. The judge refused to dismiss the case, on the grounds that Ghailani, who had been held by the United States since 2004, had not received a speedy trial. The judge said that the federal government had not held him for such an extended period simply to gain advantage over him. (Ghailani had been held for part of the time in so-called "black sites," secret installations run by the CIA in different parts of the world.) Ghailani had been brought to the United States to face trial in June 2009 after being imprisoned for three years at Guantánamo. If he is found guilty, he would face a mandatory sentence of life imprisonment.

Some former counterterrorism officials have weighed in on the jurisdictional issue. John B. Bellinger III, a legal adviser to the National Security Council under President George W. Bush, expressed skepticism about relying exclusively on commissions. "This rush to military commissions is based on premises that are not true," he said, "I think it is neither appropriate nor necessary to limit terrorism cases to either military commissions alone or federal trials alone." He and other observers have cited several possible objections to favoring military tribunals at the expense of criminal courts. Some nations, for instance, might not be willing to extradite terrorism suspects if they will only be tried by the military. Moreover, federal courts can offer a variety of charges and possible sentences that could induce the cooperation of a defendant. In addition, critics of a one-size-fits-all policy say that the government would be tying their hands. "Denying yourself access to one system in favor of the other could be counterproductive," stated Kenneth Wainstein, an assistant attorney for national security in the Bush administration.

In February 2009 a United Nations (UN) human rights official issued a report after conducting an investigation at Guantánamo that concluded that evidence obtained from the interrogations at the prison was in fact tainted. He singled out foreign law enforcement and intelligence officials who were permitted to interrogate prisoners by U.S. authorities, contending that they were in violation of their legal obligation to reject the use of torture and arbitrary detention. (Officials and agents from such countries as France, Germany, Britain, Italy, Spain, and Jordan have provided U.S. interrogators with questions to ask detainees.) Martin Scheinin, the Special Rapporteur for the UN on the promotion and protection of human rights, while countering terrorism, reserved his harshest criticism for Western states, which, he said, had aided or been complicit in torture. "The active participation by a state through the sending of interrogators or questions, or even the mere presence of intelligence personnel at an interview with a person who is being held in places where he is tortured or subject to other inhuman treatment, can be reasonably understood as implicitly condoning torture."

In February 2010 the director general of Britain's MI5 security service denied that his agency had participated in torture in coordination with U.S. intelligence officers. His denial came after revelations emerged that MI5 was aware that a detained British resident had been subjected to torture in U.S. custody—shackled, threatened, and deprived of sleep. In another case involving a national of a U.S. ally, the Supreme Court of Canada ruled that Canadian agents violated the rights of Omar Khadr the only Canadian citizen held at Guantánamo when they interrogated him there. The court did not demand that the detainee be released, however.

In a potentially significant case related to foreign participation in interrogations at Guantánamo, a French appeals court overturned terrorist conspiracy convictions for five former inmates, all French citizens, who were tried and convicted in 2007, after they were returned to France. The court ruled in February 2009 that information acquired by French intelligence officials in interrogations at Guantánamo violated French rules for permissible evidence and that there was no other proof of wrongdoing.

Prosecutors in the Sheikh Khalid Mohammed case, however, insist that they will be able to convict him regardless of the fact that he was repeatedly waterboarded. There is some precedent for transferring such suspects to civilian courts. In March 2009 ALI SALEH KAHLAH AL-MARRI, accused of being a sleeper agent for al-Qaeda, but a legal resident of the United States, appeared before a criminal court after being held for almost six years in military detention. A native of Qatar, he was apprehended in Illinois in December 2001, originally on charges of financial fraud, although the government suspected that he was part of a broader attack to be carried out on 9/11. A year and a half later he was transferred to military custody. The government did not offer any evidence to support the allegations of conspiracy, however. His lawyers appealed to the Supreme Court in December 2008. As the date of his hearing neared, President Obama ordered his case transferred back to the Justice Department. He was subsequently indicted on two counts related to providing material support and resources to a terrorist organization. Six years after his arrest, al-Marri was back in a courthouse in Peoria, Illinois, where he was initially taken into custody. In March 2009 the Supreme Court nullified the ruling of the U.S. Court of Appeals for the Fourth Circuit, which had said that the president had the authority to order indefinite military detention of legal residents of the United States. The Court did not, however, indicate whether the military detention of a legal resident as an enemy combatant could ever be constitutional. In light of the fact that al-Marri was being tried in federal court, the Supreme Court did not weigh in on the merits of the case itself. The Supreme Court left a ruling of the Fourth Circuit stand in a similar case—that of José Padilla, a U.S. citizen who was also detained as an enemy combatant but who was eventually tried in federal court as well. In that case, the Fourth Circuit upheld the conviction of Padilla for participating in terrorist activities in Afghanistan. Each of these difficult terror cases seems to set its own precedent. So far, for instance, the Supreme Court has not shown much appetite for ruling on whether detainees held on suspicion of terrorism have a right to sue their captors for mistreatment. In December 2009 the Supreme Court refused to review an appeals court ruling that dismissed a lawsuit by four former detainees at Guantánamo—all British citizens—on the basis that U.S. officials enjoyed immunity.

The first case that was supposed to come to trial at Guantánamo under the Obama administration ended with a plea agreement in late 2010. That case involved Omar Khadr. The case was controversial for a number of reasons. For one thing, Khadr had been a teenager at the time he was alleged to have killed an American soldier on the battlefield in Afghanistan. Second, a military judge ruled that because he was not wearing a uniform, Khadr could not be considered a soldier under international law (which would exempt him from a charge of murder). Third, the military judge ruled that testimony obtained using coercive interrogation techniques could be admitted in his trial if it had gone ahead. In spite of the fact that he received a 40-year sentence under the terms of the plea agreement, most observers believed that Khadr was likely to be repatriated to Canada within a short time. The Canadian justice system indicated that it would not hold him in custody for more than two years.

Guantánamo is by no means the only facility where terrorist suspects have been taken into custody. Until the Bush administration moved to close them down, U.S. military and intelligence agencies were locking up suspects in secret prisons, known as "black sites," in places as diverse as Thailand and Poland. Many of these suspects were held incommunicado and denied access to lawyers, families or even the INTERNATIONAL COMMITTEE OF THE RED CROSS in contravention of the GENEVA CONVENTIONS. In addition, the CIA continued the practice of extraordinary rendition, which had been initiated under President Bill Clinton's administration. These renditions involved the abduction of terrorist suspects who were secretly transported to countries such as Egypt or Syria, where they were likely to be subject to torture, a crime under both U.S. and international law. In November 2009 an Italian court found 22 CIA agents and a Defense Department employee guilty in absentia in the rendition of an al-Qaeda sympathizer, Osama Moustafa Hassan Nasr, known as Abu Omar, who was kidnapped off a street in Rome in 2003 and sent to Egypt, where he was tortured by Egyptian security

personnel. The Italian court was the first to try a case involving rendition. (The verdict is under appeal.)

The policy of rendition has come under fire from civil libertarians, who cite two cases of apparent mistaken identity where men were abducted by intelligence agents and held under deplorable conditions before being released. In one case, a German citizen named Khalid El-Masri was kidnapped from Germany, flown to Afghanistan, and detained at a U.S. military base, where he was interrogated by the CIA. El-Masri alleges that he was subjected to torture over the months he was kept in captivity. (It is possible that he was apprehended because his name was similar to a suspected terrorist also named El-Masri.) But El-Masri's legal attempts to seek redress for his unlawful capture have gotten nowhere in U.S. courts. On May 18, 2006, a U.S. federal district judge dismissed his lawsuit against the CIA and three private companies allegedly involved with his transport on grounds that it would do injury to state secrets. The judge did, however, acknowledge that if El-Masri's allegations were true, he would be due compensation from the U.S. government. The American Civil Liberties Union, which took El-Masri's case, announced that it would appeal. The second disputed rendition case involves a Canadian citizen named Maher Arar, who was seized at an airport in New York in 2002 by U.S. intelligence agents and flown to Syria, where he was held and evidently tortured for 10 months. Again, it appears as if he was a victim of mistaken identity and that he was not the al-Qaeda operative U.S. intelligence believed him to be. Arar was subsequently exonerated by a Canadian public inquiry. The government apologized to him and awarded him a multimillion-dollar settlement. The Canadian government formally protested his treatment to Washington, and Canadian prime minister Stephen Harper insisted that "the United States government come clean with its version of events, to acknowledge . . . the deficiencies and inappropriate conduct that occurred in this case, particularly vis-à-vis its relationship with the Canadian government." However, the U.S. government has not admitted any wrongdoing in the case. Like El-Masri, Arar has made no headway in seeking redress in American courts. A U.S. federal court of appeals dismissed his suit (filed in 2004) against U.S. officials for their role in sending him to Syria. The court used similar reasoning to that of the judge in El-Masri's case, concluding that Arar's case raised too many sensitive foreign policy and secrecy issues to permit relief. The Center for Constitutional Rights, which took on Arar's case, announced that it would appeal.

To the disappointment of many liberals, the Obama administration has continued a number of policies instituted under the Bush administration. In a case argued before the Ninth Circuit Court in California in December

2009, for instance, the Justice Department tried to prevent a civil suit from going forward that had been brought by five people who claimed to have been subjected to "forced disappearance, torture and inhumane treatment" as part of the Bush administration's secret detention and interrogation program. The suit was brought against a Boeing subsidiary that is alleged to have helped arrange the rendition flights. Government attorneys contended that the suit should be blocked because otherwise it would risk the disclosure of "state secrets." The lead lawyer for the plaintiffs from the American Civil Liberties Union argued that courts dealt with sensitive information all the time without having to shut down a case entirely. Moreover, he pointed out, many of these "secrets" involving rendition and interrogation techniques had already been made public. To allow the executive branch to curtail the powers of the courts in such matters was to jeopardize the system of checks and balances and was subject to abuse. In September 2010 the Ninth Circuit Court of Appeals dismissed the lawsuit, upholding the Obama administration's argument that the rendition program constituted a state secret, so its legality could not be decided by courts. But in a ruling in another case before a three-judge panel from the same court, former Attorney John Ashcroft was found potentially liable for decisions that led to the detention of an American citizen as a material witness after the 9/11 attacks. The panel, which ruled in the case in September 2009, criticized the Bush administration's policy of detaining suspects without charging them, stating: "We find this to be repugnant to the Constitution, and a painful reminder of some of the most ignominious chapters of our national history." The lawsuit was brought in 2005 by Abdullah al-Kidd, a U.S. citizen, who was arrested in 2003 at Dulles Airport as he prepared to fly to Saudi Arabia for graduate work in Islamic studies. He was held for weeks under a law that allows the indefinite detention of material witnesses to a crime. According to a HUMAN RIGHTS WATCH report in 2005, about 70 people were detained improperly under the material witness law after 9/11. The power to detain material witnesses arose from a policy promulgated by President Bush, who asserted that the Military Commissions Act of 2006 stripped the federal courts of their habeas corpus review over al-Kidd's challenge to his detention.

Mistreatment of Terrorist Detainees

In December 2008 a bipartisan Senate report released by the Armed Services Committee asserted that policies established by former Defense Secretary Donald H. Rumsfeld and other top Bush administration officials were directly responsible for abuses of detainees at Guantánamo Bay as well as abuses of prisoners in U.S.-run prisons in IRAQ and elsewhere. The report accused Rumsfeld of fostering a climate of impunity for interrogators by sanctioning the use of harsh interrogation techniques on captured fighters and terrorism suspects. It rejected the position of the outgoing Bush administration that any abuses originated further down the chain of command. "The abuse of detainees in U.S. custody cannot simply be attributed to the actions of 'a few bad apples' acting on their own," the report concluded. "The fact is that senior officials in the United States government solicited information on how to use aggressive techniques, redefined the law to create the appearance of their legality, and authorized their use against detainees." The specific techniques employed on detainees included forced nudity, painful stress positions, sleep deprivation, extreme temperatures, and use of dogs. These techniques, according to the report, were first used in secret CIA prisons and then adapted for use on detainees at Bagram, the U.S. military base in AFGHANISTAN, as well at the Abu Ghraib prison in Iraq. (The abuses at Abu Ghraib aroused widespread indignation after photos taken of prisoners humiliated and tortured by U.S. soldiers were leaked to the press.) Senator John McCain, a former prisoner of war in Vietnam, issued a statement in which he condemned the policies that led to the abuses and said, "The Committee's report details the inexcusable link between abusive interrogation techniques used by our enemies who ignored the Geneva Conventions and interrogation policy for detainees in U.S. custody." Bush officials countered that the practices were instituted in response to demands from field officers who complained that traditional interrogation methods were ineffective on the hardcore prisoners.

The Memos Authorizing Coercive Techniques

The use of coercive techniques originated with a February 2002 memo signed by President Bush declaring that the Geneva Convention's standards did not apply to fighters for al-Qaeda and the Taliban captured in Afghanistan. The use of harsh interrogation tactics was discussed among top administration officials as early as the following spring. The techniques under consideration were basically reverse-engineered from a training program that was developed during the the Korean War and that was used by the U.S. military to prepare soldiers in the event that they were captured and tortured by Communist Chinese troops. The program was known as Survival, Evasion, Resistance and Escape, or SERE, and it included such techniques as waterboarding, putting detainees in stress positions, and depriving them of sleep. The CIA would make use of all 13 techniques in the program in the war on terrorism.

The legality of these techniques, however, was not so easily determined even after a legal opinion sought by top Bush officials concluded that such methods were lawful. The authorization for these coercive methods was based on a 1994 antitorture statute. The language of the 1994 law, however, was so narrow that it allowed attorneys to justify the harsh methods. "There's no doubt whatsoever that a great deal of coercive treatment that most people would call torture is not prohibited by the federal antitorture statute," observed Benjamin Wittes of the Brookings Institution in Washington, D.C., who studies interrogation techniques. Three Justice Department lawyers—John C. Yoo, Jay S. Bybee, and Steven G. Bradbury—were responsible for the original memos authorizing the techniques. One of the most notorious memos, drafted in 2002 (and withdrawn two years later), written by Yoo, asserted that only pain that caused organ failure or resulted in death could be categorized as torture. In reaching his conclusions, Yoo relied on the 1994 law. In October 2003 Jack Goldsmith, a former Harvard law professor who had served as an adviser to the Pentagon, was hired as head of the Office of Legal Counsel, the division of the Justice Department that advises the president on the limits of executive power. Goldsmith had previously written a memo for Defense Secretary Donald Rumsfeld warning that prosecutors from the INTERNATIONAL CRIMINAL COURT might indict American officials for their actions in the war on terror. Although Goldsmith withdrew the authorization for waterboarding—a move that unsettled the CIA, which was making use of it and feared that some agents might be exposed to legal liability—he left the authorizing legal memos in place. Nor did he do anything to prohibit other harsh techniques such as slamming detainees into walls. By April 2005 the legal opinion was in final form; it again reaffirmed the legality of the 13 techniques. The only major source of contention was the objection of a Justice Reportment lawyer, Jack Comey, to the use of multiple techniques during a single interrogation session. Comey raised the issue with then attorney general Alberto Gonzales, who informed him that he was "under great pressure" from Cheney to complete the two authorizing memos. Comey's concerns were not addressed. Although the Obama administration announced that it would no longer permit the use of harsh interrogation techniques—Holder in confirmation hearings called waterboarding "torture"—it tried to quash efforts by human rights groups, former detainees, and civil libertarians to use the courts to expose possible abuses and human rights violations under the Bush administration.

Although the Justice Department's internal watchdog office concluded in 2009 that Yoo and Bybee had committed "intentional professional misconduct" by advocating harsh interrogation techniques and recommended that they be disciplined by the relevant state bar associations, a senior department lawyer, David Margolis, overruled its findings in early 2010. Margolis found that the two lawyers might have exercised "poor judgment," but that there was no indication that they were guilty of misconduct.

In May 2010, in testimony before the House Judiciary Committee, Bybee maintained that he had never authorized several of the harsh interrogation tactics employed by the CIA, including prolonged shackling to a ceiling, repeated beatings, dousing with cold water, or using such humiliating procedures as forcing detainees to wear diapers. Bybee, who had become a federal judge since leaving the Bush administration, asserted that the CIA had never sought approval for such practices. "Those techniques were not authorized," he flatly declared. However, Bybee did admit to authorizing such controversial techniques as waterboarding and wall slamming, which he defended in his testimony. "We took a muscular view of presidential authority."

The Legality of Drones

The use of unmanned Predator drones to target terrorist suspects is well known, although U.S. intelligence officials routinely refuse to discuss the program in any detail. The United States has used drones to strike targets in Somalia, Afghanistan, and elsewhere, but nowhere more than in Pakistani tribal areas in the North-West Frontier Province, where many Islamic militant groups and elements of al-Qaeda are based. According to estimates by the New York Times, the United States has launched about 80 missile attacks from drones from 2007 to 2009 and killed "more than 400" enemy fighters, including some top al-Qaeda and Pakistani and Afghan Taliban figures. (The Pakistani Taliban is homegrown and emerged only in 2007; it is distinctly different from the Afghan Taliban.) However, U.S. officials have downplayed the number of civilian casualties, offering an estimate of about 20. Human rights groups and journalists believe that many more civilians have been killed in these strikes. Human rights groups are very skeptical of the use of drones altogether. "Anything that dehumanizes the process makes it easier to pull the trigger," observed a representative of Amnesty International.

While it is not illegal to target terror suspects—even civilians—under international law, certain standards do apply. First, a terrorist group has to be defined as one engaging in armed conflict. Second, the use of force must be a "military necessity." Third, no other reasonable alternative, such as capture, should be available to eliminate the threat of an adversary. Fourth, the target has to be directly participating in hostilities. Fifth, the use of force has to be "proportionate" to the threat. Finally, the attack cannot take place without permission from the country where it is going to take place. Lawyers who have examined the Predator program generally believe that it does meet most of these criteria. Whether the United States always complies with the last condition with respect to

Pakistan is unclear. However, there is some evidence that Pakistani security forces have collaborated surreptitiously with the CIA and U.S. military operatives, although officially Islamabad often denounces such attacks as infringements on Pakistani sovereignty. It is possible that the two nations, whose relations are on very shaky ground, have agreed on a quid pro quo arrangement whereby Pakistani intelligence officials choose many targets in exchange for extending their tacit cooperation. That may explain why in 2009 the CIA only targeted six of 41 strikes at al-Qaeda targets and three times that number at Pakistani militants who pose more of a threat to Pakistan than to Afghanistan; 14 strikes were aimed, for instance, at Baitullah Mehsud, one of the most notorious Pakistani militants. (He was finally killed in 2009.) The number of Predator attacks have significantly increased since President Obama came to office, and the number of targets has grown. According to an August 2009 report by the Senate Foreign Relations Committee, the Pentagon's list of approved terrorist targets, which had originally contained 367 names, was expanded to include about 50 Afghan drug lords suspected of financing the Taliban.

The policy of using Predators and Raptors to target terrorist suspects came under fire when the Obama administration announced that Anwar al-Awlaki, an Islamic cleric in hiding in Yemen, was a target for capture or assassination. Although critics had previously questioned the use of drones in conducting extrajudicial killings, al-Awlaki's case was different because he was a U.S. citizen. (He was born in New Mexico.) Al-Awlaki had been linked by U.S. intelligence to the bungled bombing of a U.S. airliner by Umar Farouk Abdulmutallab, a Nigerian national, on Christmas Day, 2009, and to the rampage by Army Major Nidal Hasan, who shot and killed 13 people at Fort Hood in Texas earlier that year. In spite of the inflammatory diatribes that the cleric has delivered over the Internet and his e-mail communication with Islamic radicals, no charges had been publicly filed against him. In August 2010, the American Civil Liberties Union, acting on behalf of al-Awlaki's father, announced that it wished to sue the U.S. government to curtail its practice of targeted assassinations. Targeting U.S. citizens outside of a war zone without due process, the ACLU charged, was unconstitutional. However, in order to challenge the constitutionality of the CIA's program, the ACLU, in addition to the Center for Constitutional Rights, another civil liberties organization, first had to obtain a license from the Treasury's Office of Foreign Assets Control. A license was required because the two groups could be held legally liable for assisting an individual designated by the Treasury Department as a "specially designated global terrorist," a restriction that the ACLU and the center contend is unconstitutional in itself. However, the Treasury Department quickly defused the

potential conflict by granting a license that would allow the groups to provide free legal counsel to Nasser al-Awlaki, the cleric's father. While expressing gratitude for the government's prompt response, the ACLU and the center said that they would not be deterred from attempting to invalidate the license requirement in the courts. At the same time, they announced that they would "pursue our litigation relating to the government's asserted authority to engage in targeted killings of American civilians without due process."

Further Reading:
Atwan, Abdel Bari. *The Secret History of al Qaeda.* Berkeley: University of California Press, 2008.
Federation of American Scientists. War on Terror. Available online. URL: http://www.fas.org/terrorism/. Accessed March 21, 2010.
Filkins, Douglas. *The Forever War.* New York: Vintage, 2009.
FindLaw.com. Special Coverage: War on Terrorism. Available online. URL: http://news.findlaw.com/legalnews/us/terrorism/cases/index.html. Accessed March 21, 2010.
Global Issues. War on Terror—Global Issues. Available online. URL: http://www.globalissues.org/issue/245/war-on-terror. Accessed March 21, 2010.
Gupta, Dipak K. *Understanding Terrorism and Political Violence.* New York: Routledge, 2008.
Meyer, Jane. *The Dark Side: The Inside Story of How the War on Terror Turned into a War on American Ideals.* New York: Doubleday, 2008.
Raymond, Ibrahim. *The Al-Qaeda Reader.* New York: Broadway, 2007.
Reidal, Bruce. *The Search for Al Qaeda: Its Leadership, Ideology and Future.* Washington, D.C.: Brookings Institution Press, 2008.
Rejali, Darius M. *Torture and Democracy.* Princeton, N.J.: Princeton University Press, 2009.
Sands, Philip. *Torture Team: Rumsfeld's Memo and the Betrayal of American Values.* Basingstoke, U.K.: Palgrave Macmillan, 2008.

weapons in the conduct of war

According to international CUSTOMARY LAW, weapons should not cause "unnecessary suffering" or "superfluous injury." The foundation of law regarding the use of weapons in international conflicts was established at an international conference held in St. Petersburg, Russia, in 1868. The treaty that emerged from that conference—the St. Petersburg Declaration—stated that the only "legitimate object" of any war was "to weaken the military forces of the enemy"; while this necessitated incapacitating "the greatest possible number of men," using arms to "aggravate the sufferings of disabled men, or render their death inevitable" amounted to a disproportionate use of force and would be "contrary to the laws of humanity." As customary law, this principle was considered binding on all nations regardless of whether they signed or ratified the treaty.

The St. Petersburg Declaration was used as a basis for provisions regarding the use of arms in the 1897 and 1907 HAGUE CONVENTIONS. Explosive projectiles filled with glass or other fragments were outlawed on the grounds that they caused excessive injuries. The objective, after all, was to remove the soldier from combat, which could be done by means of a serious wound. Riddling a body full of fragments—which might be too small to be detectable by X-ray—was therefore superfluous aside from causing unnecessary suffering. Dumdum and poisoned bullets were outlawed for the same reasons. But some weapons whose use is banned in one context might be legitimate in another. In World War I, as Burrus Carnahan points out in an essay in the CRIMES OF WAR PROJECT, British warplanes used machine guns on planes that fired incendiary bullets, which were banned on the battlefield. Initially the Germans asserted that any downed pilot who had used such weapons was in violation of the St. Petersburg Declaration and, as a result, should be treated as a war criminal. Later the German government reversed its position. The weapon in question was not being used to "cause unnecessary suffering" to the enemy pilot but rather to bring the enemy warplane down, which was a legitimate military objective.

Customary law also forbids the use of indiscriminate weapons, which are difficult or impossible to target. That is to say, the attackers would have no way of ascertaining whether the use of the weapon would be justified by the destruction of a military objective. Under this definition, the German V-2 rockets that were launched against London in World War II were indiscriminate because their purpose was simply to cause widespread destruction and demoralize the civilian population, not to damage British military capacity. SCUD missiles directed at Israel by Iraq during the 1991 Gulf War were also considered indiscriminate by the U.S. Defense Department for much the same reason. This is not to say that a weapon is necessarily indiscriminate simply because it has the potential of causing a great deal of destruction. Some legal scholars, for instance, believe that under certain circumstances, nuclear weapons could be used if a state believes that its existence is in peril, although other international law experts have disputed this assessment.

See also MILITARY NECESSITY; NUCLEAR ARMS AND INTERNATIONAL LAW; WEAPONS OF MASS DESTRUCTION.

Further Reading:
Cornish, Paul. *Anti-personnel Mines: Controlling the Plague of "Butterflies."* London: Royal Institute of International Affairs, 1994.
Feaver, Peter. *Guarding the Guardians: Civilian Control of Nuclear Weapons in the United States.* Cornell Studies in Security Affairs. Ithaca, N.Y.: Cornell University Press, 1992.
Gutman, Roy, ed. *Crimes of War: What the Public Should Know.* New York: W. W. Norton & Company, 1999.
International Committee of the Red Cross. *International Law Concerning the Conduct of Hostilities: Collection of Hague Conventions and Some Other Treaties.* Geneva: International Committee of the Red Cross, 1989.
Langford, R. Everett. *Introduction to Weapons of Mass Destruction: Radiological, Chemical, and Biological.* New York: Wiley-Interscience, 2004.
Nichols, Gary W., and Milton L. Boykin, eds. *Arms Control and Nuclear Weapons: U.S. Policies and the National Interest.* Contributions in Military Studies. Westport, Conn.: Greenwood Press, 1987.
Prokosch, Eric. *The Technology of Killing: A Military and Political History of Anti-personnel Weapons.* London: Zed Books, 1995.

weapons of mass destruction
Weapons of mass destruction (WMD) is a term that generally refers to nuclear, biological, and chemical weapons, or NBC for short. There is, however, no authoritative definition of WMD in either treaty law or international CUSTOMARY LAW. Its absence is explained by the fact that nations have historically used international law to address each category of weapons that falls under the WMD classification, using three different sets of rules for each technology. General rules of international law also have applications to WMD, but no law specifically applies to WMD. The issue of WMD is governed by various arms control treaties, which have three objectives: the deterrence of the use of WMD by states, exemplified by the accords governing nuclear proliferation, testing, and production between the United States and the former Soviet Union; the banning of WMD from certain areas (treaties preventing their deployment in space and on the ocean floor); and disarmament (treaties that outlaw the development and use of BIOLOGICAL WEAPONS and CHEMICAL WEAPONS).

The term *weapons of mass destruction* gained popular currency in the run-up to the 2003 U.S.-backed invasion of Iraq. The Bush administration had warned that SADDAM HUSSEIN was making every effort to acquire a nuclear capacity while retaining biological and chemical weapons. Indeed, precedent did argue in favor of this view since Iraq had used biological and chemical weapons in the past. An intensive search for such weapons after the occupation of Iraq turned up no WMD, however, leading many experts to believe that

Inspectors measuring the volume of nerve gas in a container *(United Nations)*

Saddam's stockpile of biological and chemical weapons had been destroyed or else had degraded significantly.

See also NUCLEAR ARMS AND INTERNATIONAL LAW.

Further Reading:

Alibek, Ken, and Stephen Handelman. *Biohazard: The Chilling True Story of the Largest Covert Biological Weapons Program in the World—Told from Inside by the Man Who Ran It.* New York: Delta, 2000.

Barnaby, Frank. *How to Build a Nuclear Bomb: And Other Weapons of Mass Destruction.* New York: Nation Books, 2004.

Feaver, Peter. *Guarding the Guardians: Civilian Control of Nuclear Weapons in the United States.* Cornell Studies in Security Affairs. Ithaca, N.Y.: Cornell University Press, 1992.

Guillemin, Jeanette. *Biological Weapons.* Columbia Contemporary Issues in National Security Policy. New York: Columbia University Press, 2005.

Krepon, Michael. *Strategic Stalemate: Nuclear Weapons and Arms Control in American Politics.* Sydney, Australia: Palgrave Macmillan, 1986.

Lederberg, Joshua, ed. *Biological Weapons: Limiting the Threat.* BCSIA Studies in International Security. Cambridge, Mass.: The MIT Press, 1999.

Mangold, Tom, and Jeff Goldberg. *Plague Wars: The Terrifying Reality of Biological Warfare.* New York: St. Martin's Press, 2001.

Nichols, Gary W., and Milton L. Boykin, eds. *Arms Control and Nuclear Weapons: U.S. Policies and the National Interest.* Contributions in Military Studies. Westport, Conn.: Greenwood Press, 1987.

Price, Richard M. *The Chemical Weapons Taboo.* Ithaca, N.Y.: Cornell University Press, 1997.

Tucker, Jonathan B., ed. *Toxic Terror: Assessing Terrorist Use of Chemical and Biological Weapons.* BCSIA Studies in International Security. Cambridge, Mass.: The MIT Press, 2000.

Wei Jingsheng **(Wei Ching-sheng)** (1950–   ) *Chinese human rights activist*

Wei Jingsheng is a leading Chinese activist whose opposition to the Communist government resulted in years of imprisonment and exile. Wei, an electrician by profession, first came to prominence in the late 1970s during a period of political relaxation when the Communist Party under Deng Xiaoping was flirting with reform. Probably nothing embodied the spirit of reform more than Beijing's Democracy Wall, where, for a few months in the winter of 1978–79, people could express their political views. In effect, the Democracy Wall became the first public forum for an open political debate. In his first contribution to this discussion, Wei, 28 at the time, criticized Deng's economic reforms because there was no provision in his program called "The Four Modernizations" to open the country to democracy. The Chinese people had to take matters into their own hands, he wrote, rather than count on the guidance of enlightened leaders.

Wei's poster, called "The Fifth Modernization," caused a sensation; even fellow activists were stunned that he had dared to scold the government so directly. They feared that such attacks would impel the authorities to take down the Democracy Wall. Wei was not moved by their arguments. Democracy, he contended, could only be assured if human rights were also guaranteed. Five months after the Democracy Wall had gone up, Wei posted his last broadside, entitled "Do We Want Democracy or New Autocracy?" In it he questioned whether Deng was seriously committed to democracy and concluded that he was not: "History tells us that there must be a limit to the trust placed in any one person."

An attack on China's supreme ruler was not allowed to go unanswered. A week later, on March 29, 1979, Wei was arrested. In October he was convinced on charges of "slandering the socialist system" and "plotting to overthrow the people's democratic dictatorship" and sentenced to 15 years in prison. Even during his trial, Wei remained defiant. "Criticism may not be beautiful or pleasant to hear, nor can it always be completely accurate," he told the court. "If one insists on criticism being pleasant to hear and demands its absolute accuracy on pain of punishment, this is as good as forbidding criticism and banning reforms."

During his imprisonment, much of it spent in solitary confinement, Wei's health deteriorated—he lost at least a dozen teeth and developed a heart condition—but he showed no sign of remorse for having voiced his opinions so openly. In spite of his isolation, his words began to resonate with other Chinese reformists, never more so than when the government launched a brutal repression of demonstrators gathered in Tiananmen Square in June 1989. "The repression of the 1989 movement," Wei said after his release in 1993, "taught the Chinese people a very bitter lesson: . . . that relying on the dictators to gradually move towards democracy was a vain hope."

Six and a half months before his term was up, Wei was freed, probably because China was seeking to burnish its image to win the 2000 Olympic Games for Beijing. Although the authorities insisted that he refrain from engaging in political activities or speaking to foreign journalists, Wei showed no hesitancy about resuming his campaign for human rights. He called for the release of thousands of political prisoners and even supported Tibetan independence, a position vehemently opposed by Beijing. He helped poverty-stricken dissidents with money awarded from his international prizes. Even though he was kept under police surveillance, he insisted on giving interviews to foreign correspondents and writing articles for publications outside of China. In 1994 he met with JOHN SHATTUCK, the U.S. assistant secretary of state for human rights and humanitarian affairs. He was again arrested and taken on what was said to be a "vacation"—which lasted for nearly five years. In November 1997, after spending cumulatively almost 18 years in prison, Wei was freed after an official visit to Washington by the Chinese president Jiang Zemin. He was forced to leave the country for the United States. Shortly after his arrival, he was received by President Bill Clinton, who acknowledged his long struggle for democracy and human rights.

In 2008 he was named as one of the 15 Champions of World Democracy by the Europe-based magazine *A Different View,* and in 2009 he was reportedly a contender for the Nobel Peace Prize.

See also CHINA, HUMAN RIGHTS VIOLATIONS IN.

Further Reading:

Foot, Rosemary. *Rights beyond Borders: The Global Community and the Struggle over Human Rights in China.* Oxford: Oxford University Press, 2001.

Kent, Ann. *Between Freedom and Subsistence: China and Human Rights.* Oxford: Oxford University Press, 1995.

Munro, R. *Punishment Season: Human Rights in China after Martial Law.* Asia Watch Report. New York: Human Rights Watch, 1990.

Santoro, Michael A. *Profits and Principles: Global Capitalism and Human Rights in China.* Ithaca, N.Y.: Cornell University Press, 2000.

Weatherley, Robert. *The Discourse of Human Rights in China: Historical and Ideological Perspectives.* Sydney, Australia: Palgrave Macmillan, 1999.

Wernich, Christián von (1938–   ) *Argentinean priest*

A Roman Catholic Argentine prelate, Father Christián von Wernich has been charged with 19 counts of murder and 33 of abduction and TORTURE in connection with his role as chaplain for the Buenos Aires police during Argentina's "dirty wars" in the 1970s. He was ordained a priest in 1976, the same year in which General Ramón Camps became head of the police of Buenos Aires. Camps chose Wernich as his personal confessor and made him police chaplain, allowing him access to secret prisons. He was also permitted to witness interrogations. It was in his capacity as police chaplain that Wernich was reported to have extorted money from the parents of seven left-wing youths who had been taken into custody. Once the money was paid, the prisoners, including a pregnant woman, were killed. According to an eyewitness, Wernich was present for three of the EXTRAJUDICIAL KILLINGS carried out by police. Afterward the priest attended a barbecue to celebrate. Although Wernich has admitted that he had frequently visited the secret police detention center, he refused to tell prosecutors what had ensued while he was there on the grounds that he would be violating "the secrecy of the confessional." The priest was discovered in Chile, where he was arrested and extradited to Argentina in 2003. In 2007 Wernich was convicted for involvement in seven murders, 42 abductions, and 31 cases of torture and received a term of life imprisonment.

See also ARGENTINA, HUMAN RIGHTS VIOLATIONS IN.

Further Reading:

Arditti, Rita. *Searching for Life: The Grandmothers of the Plaza de Mayo and the Disappeared Children of Argentina.* Berkeley: University of California Press, 1999.

Davis, William Columbus. *Warnings from the Far South: Democracy versus Dictatorship in Uruguay, Argentina, and Chile.* New York: Praeger Publishers, 1995.

Lewis, Paul H. *Guerrillas and Generals: The Dirty War in Argentina.* New York: Praeger, 2001.

Moyano, Maria. *Argentina's Lost Patrol: Armed Struggle, 1969–1979.* New Haven, Conn.: Yale University Press, 1995.

White Brigades

The White Brigades, a clandestine Mexican paramilitary group, has been linked by human rights groups to operations conducted by the Mexican army. It is thought that the brigades collaborated with the army and security forces in 1968 in carrying out the massacre of hundreds of student protesters in Mexico City. During the late 1960s and much of the 1970s—the period of Mexico's "dirty war"—hundreds of suspected leftists and other political opponents were abducted by the White Brigades. About 600 people have been "disappeared" in this way and never accounted for, although it is assumed that most were executed at military bases or police detention centers. On July 21, 1978, members of the White Brigades and the Mexican police, disguised as civilians, arrested over 150 striking workers, many of whom were tortured during the next two days. In 2000 retired general Alberto Quintanar Alvarez gave an interview to the Mexico City daily *La Jornada* in which he denied that any "dirty war" had occurred, contending that it was "a cleansing operation of Maoists, Trotskyists . . . students supported by trade unions and political parties who were destabilizing the country." Quintanar did acknowledge, however, that the White Brigades and other paramilitary groups were in fact created by and under the direction of the interior ministry. More recently, the White Brigades have been implicated in such crimes as executions, rapes, kidnappings, and TORTURE, according to an investigation conducted by the government of Vincente Fox. There are nonetheless reports that the White Brigades and other paramilitaries continue operations in rural parts of Oaxaca and Guerrero, suppressing insurgent activity in those states on behalf of landowners and local political bosses.

See also MEXICO, HUMAN RIGHTS VIOLATIONS IN.

Further Reading:

Amnesty International. *Mexico: Human Rights in Rural Areas.* London: Amnesty International, 1986.

Brysk, Alison, ed. *Globalization and Human Rights.* Berkeley: University of California Press, 2002.

Cartwright, William, ed. *Mexico: Facing the Challenges of Human Rights and Crime.* Ardsley, N.Y.: Transnational Pub., 1999.

Human Rights Watch. *Unceasing Abuses: Human Rights in Mexico One Year after the Introduction of Reform.* Americas Watch Report. New York: Human Rights Watch, 1991.

Wiesenthal, Simon (1908–2005) *Nazi hunter and Holocaust chronicler*

An architectural engineer by training, Simon Wiesenthal has become best known for disseminating information about the Holocaust to bring to account Nazi war criminals who escaped justice after World War II. He was born on December 31, 1908, in Buczacz, then in Austria-Hungary (now part of Ukraine). When World War II broke out, Wiesenthal was living with his wife, the former Cyla Mueller, in Lvov, Poland, managing his own architectural firm. They resided in a part of Poland that was seized by the Soviet Union under the terms of the nonaggression pact with Germany. During a purge of Jewish intellectuals, Wiesenthal's stepfather was arrested by the NKVD, the Soviet secret police, and eventually died in prison; in addition, Wiesenthal's stepbrother was shot. Wiesenthal was forced to close his business, and it was only by bribing an NKVD commissar that he was able to save himself, his wife, and his mother from deportation to Siberia.

In 1941, after the Germans pushed the Red Army out and took all Polish territory, Wiesenthal and his wife were imprisoned in a FORCED LABOR camp, where he worked in a repair shop for Lvov's Eastern Railroad. By September 1942, after the Germans had begun to implement the FINAL SOLUTION—the annihilation of all European Jewry—a total of 89 members of both his and his wife's families had been killed by the Nazis. Weisenthal survived by luck: His wife had blond hair and as a result could pass for an Aryan (a non-Jew). Wiesenthal worked for the Polish underground, supplying strategic information about the Lvov Railroad that the resistance used to plan acts of sabotage. In exchange, his wife received false papers that allowed her to live in Warsaw for two years. She was later sent to the Rhineland as a forced laborer, but even then her true identity—and Jewish origins—remained a secret. Wiesenthal himself escaped the work camp in 1943 just before the Germans began to exterminate its Jewish inmates. Recaptured in June 1944, he was interned in another concentration camp and would surely have been killed as well except for the fact that, with Germany's collapse inevitable, his SS guards decided to keep the remaining prisoners alive—34 out of an original 149,000—assuming that the Allies might give them lenient treatment.

Wiesenthal was barely alive when he was rescued by American forces in 1945. Once he recovered his health, he went to work for the U.S. Army's Office of Strategic Services and Counter-Intelligence Corps, gathering documentation for impending war-crimes trials. He also headed the Jewish Central Committee of the United States Zone of Austria, a relief and welfare organization. In late 1945 he was reunited with his wife, whom he had believed dead. In 1947 he founded the Jewish Documentation Center in Linz, Austria, with several other survivors. He persisted in gathering information about war criminals even after it became apparent that the United States and Soviet Union had lost interest in pursuing many more prosecutions. When the Linz office was closed, its files were transferred to YAD VASHEM, the Holocaust memorial and museum in Israel.

Throughout the 1950s Wiesenthal continued to hunt for the one war criminal he wanted to see brought to justice above all: ADOLF EICHMANN, the Nazi official who had been in charge of the Final Solution. Israeli agents eventually tracked Eichmann down in Argentina, where he was living under an alias. He was then abducted to Israel, where he was tried, found guilty of GENOCIDE, and executed in May 1961. Wiesenthal was also deeply involved in the apprehension of Karl Silberbauer, the GESTAPO officer responsible for the arrest of Anne Frank. His testimony helped debunk allegations that Frank's famous diary was a forgery. Her vivid account of life in hiding under the German occupation of Amsterdam gave a human face to the millions of Jewish victims of the Final Solution. Wiesenthal also helped find information responsible for tracking down nine of the 16 wanted SS officers who were put on trial in West Germany, including Franz Stangl, the commandant of the Treblinka and Sobibór extermination camps, and

Hermine Braunsteiner, who had supervised the murder of hundreds of children during the war. (When she was discovered, Braunsteiner was living as a seemingly ordinary housewife in Queens, New York.)

Wiesenthal operated out of the Jewish Documentation Center (JDC) in Vienna, which he had founded and is still in operation. Although it has only a small staff, it relies on a vast network of friends and sympathizers (and occasionally even former Nazis) for tips and documentation. Files have been gathered on 90,000 Nazi officials, most of whom have never been tried. The JDC is not only concerned with locating Nazi war criminals—whose numbers are shrinking because of old age—but also with monitoring right-wing extremist groups. In 1977 a Holocaust center opened in Los Angeles; it was named the Simon Wiesenthal Center in the Nazi hunter's honor. (There is a sister center in Jerusalem.)

Wiesenthal has received several honors for his work, including the French Legion of Honor, the United Nations League for the Help of Refugees Award, and the U.S. Congressional Gold Medal, which was presented to him by President Jimmy Carter in 1980. He has also been a consultant on documentaries about the Holocaust and the 1974 film thriller *The Odessa File*, and served as the model for the Laurence Olivier character, Herr Lieberman, in the 1977 movie *The Boys from Brazil*, based on the Ira Levin novel of the same name. Not surprisingly, Wiesenthal has received numerous death threats and once was the target of an abortive bomb attack by neo-Nazis in 1982. He announced his retirement in 2003 two years before his death. "I have survived them all. If there were any left, they'd be too old and weak to stand trial today," he said at the time. "My work is done."

Further Reading:
Levy, Alan. *Nazi Hunter: The Wiesenthal File.* New York: Carroll & Graf Publishers, 2002.
Wiesenthal, Simon. *Justice Not Vengeance: Recollections.* New York: Grove Press, 1990.
———. *The Sunflower: On the Possibilities and Limits of Forgiveness.* New York: Schocken, 1998.
Wiesenthal Center. Available online. URL: http://www.wiesenthal.com/site/pp.asp?c=lsKWLbPJLnF&b=4441251. Accessed March 21, 2010.

willful killing

International law prohibits the intentional killing of civilians and considers it a war crime. This does not mean that all killings of civilians in a conflict are war crimes; according to Additional Protocol I to the GENEVA CONVENTIONS, civilian deaths that occur because of MILITARY NECESSITY are not crimes even if the belligerent knows in advance that civilian casualties will ensue before launching an attack. Bombing a military installation—permissible under international law—may kill civilians in the vicinity without the assailant being found culpable of a war crime. The killing of a civilian by a sniper is not necessarily a war crime, either. On the other hand, the execution of HOSTAGES or PRISONERS OF WAR would be classified as a war crime under the Geneva Conventions and Additional Protocol I. By the same token, the bombing of a town or city that has as its aim the terrorizing of its civilian inhabitants would be illegal. In addition to civilians, prisoners of war, the sick or wounded, and soldiers who have surrendered (HORS DE COMBAT) are protected from willful killing, as are medical and religious personnel unless they have taken up arms as combatants. The Fourth Geneva Convention of 1949 forbids "grave breaches" by an OCCUPYING POWER regarding its treatment of a civilian population, including "willful killing, TORTURE or inhuman treatment."

The Geneva Conventions only deal with international conflicts. ARTICLE 3 COMMON TO THE GENEVA CONVENTIONS, though legally weaker than the provisions in the conventions, has been applied to the protection of civilians in internal conflicts as well. Additional Protocol I, while covering only international conflicts, does set forth the principle that all parties to a conflict must "distinguish between the civilian population and combatants . . . and accordingly shall direct their operations only against military objectives." The protocol also requires that "the civilian population as such, as well as individual civilians, shall not be the object of attack." Additional Protocol II, which covers internal as well as international conflicts, emphasizes that "the civilian population . . . shall enjoy general protection against the dangers arising from military operations." This establishes the principle of civilian inviolability, although in most cases protections of civilians have traditionally applied only in interstate conflicts. But more recently, various ad hoc courts, established by the United Nations to try crimes in such internal conflicts as the war in the former Yugoslavia, Rwanda, and Sierra Leone, have expanded the protections of civilians. In 1996 the Trial Chamber of the INTERNATIONAL CRIMINAL TRIBUNAL FOR THE FORMER YUGOSLAVIA (ICTY) stated: "The rule that the civilian population as such as well as individual citizens, shall not be the object of attack is a fundamental rule of international law applicable to all armed conflicts . . . irrespective of their characterization as international or non-international." In its rulings, the ICTY has followed through on its words and made no distinction between international and internal armed conflict. "(A)ttacks on [civilians and] civilian objects are prohibited as a matter of CUSTOMARY LAW in all conflicts," declared the senior legal advisor in the ICTY Office of the Prosecutor. Several defendants in ICTY trials, which are conducted in The Hague in the Netherlands, have been charged with acts of willful killings in the Bosnian War.

See also ADDITIONAL PROTOCOLS TO THE GENEVA CONVENTIONS; PROTECTED PERSONS.

Further Reading:

Gutman, Roy, ed. *Crimes of War: What the Public Should Know.* New York: W. W. Norton & Company, 1999.

Hagan, John. *Justice in the Balkans: Prosecuting War Crimes in the Hague Tribunal.* Chicago Series in Law and Society. Chicago: University of Chicago Press, 2003.

Hazan, Pierre, and James Thomas Snyder. *Justice in a Time of War: The True Story behind the International Criminal Tribunal for the Former Yugoslavia.* Eugenia and Hugh M. Stewart Series on Eastern Europe. Austin: Texas A&M University Press, 2004.

International Committee of the Red Cross. *International Law Concerning the Conduct of Hostilities: Collection of Hague Conventions and Some Other Treaties.* Geneva: International Committee of the Red Cross, 1989.

Mertus, Julie. *Former Yugoslavia: War Crimes Trials in the Former Yugoslavia.* Helsinki: Human Rights Watch/ Helsinki, 1995.

Wiranto (1947–) *Indonesian war criminal*

General Wiranto is one of Indonesia's most controversial military and political figures. Even as human rights advocates denounced him as a war criminal in connection with atrocities committed in East Timor, he was running for the presidency of his country. Specifically, he has been charged with the killings of more than 1,000 civilians in 1999 in East Timor while the province was in the process of obtaining its independence under UN supervision.

Until then Wiranto's career had proceeded on a fast track. Twenty years after graduating as a second lieutenant from the national military academy in 1968, he became an aide to former president SUHARTO, the undisputed ruler of Indonesia for decades. Wiranto (many Indonesians use only one name) became head of the military in 1998 as Suharto's regime was collapsing. (Wiranto is credited with prevailing on Suharto to relinquish his post voluntarily.) As commander of the Indonesian forces on East Timor, however, he was accused of failing to stop his soldiers or pro-Indonesian militias from committing serious human rights abuses and massacres. Although Wiranto initially suffered no consequences—on the contrary, he was appointed security minister—President Abdurrahman Wahid fired him in February 2000 when charges of human rights abuses failed to subside.

Wiranto has vigorously denied the charges and attributed the violence to long-simmering tensions between ethnic groups that had nothing to do with him. Indonesian security forces, he contended, "had an extraordinary difficult mission—I call it Mission Impossible." He maintained that his soldiers suffered from "psychological constraints" when faced with the prospect of acting against comrades who might have committed excesses. UN prosecutors were not swayed by his argument, and in February 2003 in East

Timor they charged him in absentia for CRIMES AGAINST HUMANITY. The indictment named six other senior military officers and a former governor as well. Wiranto and his fellow officers, the UN prosecutors said, had "effective control" over the militia groups, which implicated them in 280 documented murders. Wiranto and the others charged were also held responsible for forcibly deporting 200,000 East Timorese to West Timor, which was under Indonesian control, after the vote in which the vast majority of the East Timorese opted for independence.

The Indonesian record of bringing alleged either political or military officials to justice for such crimes is very poor, and there is little likelihood of Wiranto ever being tried. When the indictments were issued, the Indonesian foreign minister defiantly declared that his government would "simply ignore" them; even the East Timor government has not tried to pursue the case, fearing a rupture in diplomatic relations with Indonesia. The accusations against Wiranto did not deter his supporters in the powerful Golkar Party from nominating him as their presidential candidate in 2003. His popularity was not so huge, however, as to convince Indonesian voters to put him into office. He came in third.

After his failed bid Wiranto continued to remain politically active, joining former Presidents Wahid and Megawati and other former officials in an alliance opposing the Yudhoyono government. He subsequently founded a new political party, the People's Conscience Party. In 2009 he ran for vice president and lost again.

See also EAST TIMOR, HUMAN RIGHTS VIOLATIONS IN; INDONESIA, HUMAN RIGHTS VIOLATIONS IN.

Further Reading:

Dunn, James, and Xanana Gusmao. *East Timor: A Rough Passage to Independence.* Seattle: University of Washington Press, 2004.

Jardine, Matthew. *East Timor: Genocide in Paradise.* The Real Story Series. Monroe, Me.: Odonian Press, 2002.

Pinto, Constancio, and Matthew Jardine. *East Timor's Unfinished Struggle: Inside the Timorese Resistance.* Cambridge, Mass.: South End Press, 1996.

Romano, Cesare, Andre Nollkaemper, and Jann K. Kleffner, eds. *Internationalized Criminal Courts and Tribunals: Sierra Leone, East Timor, Kosovo, and Cambodia.* International Courts and Tribunals Series. Oxford: Oxford University Press, 2004.

women's rights, violations of

In principle, human rights have always been guaranteed to women in international law, but in practice women continue to be subjected to violence, rape, and other grave abuses as well as pervasive discrimination. Women and children are most likely to be victims of war; they are also more likely to be REFUGEES and INTERNALLY DISPLACED PERSONS. Women are not only discriminated against because of their sex; other factors such as race, ethnicity, caste, religion, class, and age may also play a role. In many regions of the world, violations of women's rights are defended as traditional or cultural practices, including honor killings, disenfranchisement, and genital mutilation. In North Africa, 6,000 women are genitally mutilated each day; each year more than 7,000 women in India are murdered by their families and in-laws in disputes over dowries. In countries such as Pakistan, South Africa, Peru, Russia, and Uzbekistan, women are beaten at home by their husbands at alarming rates. Annually it is estimated that 1,000 women are murdered in honor killings in Pakistan.

In recent conflicts in Sierra Leone, Kosovo, the Democratic Republic of the Congo, Afghanistan, and Rwanda, women have been raped as a deliberate tool of war. In Darfur in western Sudan, Arab militiamen known as *janjaweed* have raped black African women in order to stigmatize them, and women who bear children as a result are ostracized from their families and tribes. Governments often refuse to intervene, or else accuse the victim of being responsible. This phenomenon often occurs in cases where a rape victim is accused of infidelity or prostitution. According to a 2002 survey by the World Health Organization (WHO), nearly one in four women experiences sexual violence by an intimate partner during her life, and as many as one-third of all girls are forced into their first sexual experience. Abuses against women are hardly limited to the developing world. In the United States, for example, a woman is raped on the average of every six minutes, and a woman is battered every 15 seconds. In addition, millions of women throughout the world are forced to marry against their wishes. Women are also more vulnerable—socially and biologically—to infection from HIV/AIDS.

Women are also at higher risk of being trafficked for prostitution or enforced servitude because of inequalities in their native countries. Each year hundreds of thousands of women are trafficked from countries such as Nigeria, the Dominican Republic, Myanmar (Burma), Thailand, Ukraine, Moldova, Russia, Romania, and Poland. Probably more women are trafficked in and from Asia; about 15,000 women are sold into sexual SLAVERY in China alone every year.

Women in Arab countries frequently face discrimination that bars them from political, social, and cultural life. In Saudi Arabia, for instance, women cannot vote, take certain types of jobs, or even drive a car. In conservative Islamic countries they are required to wear chadors or burkas to conceal their faces and bodies. Legal restrictions in many countries prevent women from obtaining a divorce without their husband's consent, inheriting money or property, or retaining custody of children in the event of a divorce.

A woman wearing the traditional burka during the Taliban regime in Afghanistan *(Exile Images)*

The first major international recognition of women's rights is found in the 1945 United Nations Charter, which afforded to women and men alike equal economic, social, cultural, political, and civil rights. The UNIVERSAL DECLARATION OF HUMAN RIGHTS of 1948 stipulates that human rights apply to all people equally, "without distinction of any kind such as race, color, sex, language . . . or any other status." In 1979 the UN General Assembly adopted the Convention on the Elimination of All Form of Discrimination Against Women (CEDAW), or the International Women's Human Rights Treaty, which was the first international accord to comprehensively address women's rights within political, cultural, economic, social, and family spheres. In 1993 the UN General Assembly adopted the Declaration on the Elimination of Violence Against Women (DEVAW), which sets forth the means by which states should protect and defend women's rights. The declaration directs member states to "exercise due diligence to prevent, investigate and, in accordance with national legislation, punish acts of violence against women, whether those acts are perpetrated by the state or by private persons."

In 1995 the Beijing Platform for Action—an initiative that grew out of the Fourth World Conference on Women—called on governments to "condemn violence against women and refrain from invoking any custom, tradition or religious consideration to avoid their obligations with respect to its elimination as set out in the Declaration on the Elimination of Violence against Women. . . ." Further rec-

ognition of women's rights is found in the statutes establishing three special UN courts to try war crimes in the former Yugoslavia, Rwanda, and Sierra Leone as well as in the ROME STATUTE OF THE INTERNATIONAL CRIMINAL COURT, (1998). These statutes criminalize abuses of women's rights in times of conflict. Several states that have signed these accords have also enacted legislation providing for protection of women's rights in their own countries.

See also COMFORT WOMEN; RAPE AS A TACTIC OF WAR; TRAFFICKING IN PERSONS.

Further Reading:

Askin, Kelly Dawn. *War Crimes against Women: Prosecution in International War Crimes Tribunals.* Leiden, Netherlands: Brill Academic Publishers, 1997.

Bassiouni, M. Cherif. *Sexual Violence: An Invisible Weapon of War in the Former Yugoslavia.* Chicago: International Human Rights Law Institute, DePaul University, 1996.

Buergenthal, Thomas. *Religious Fundamentalisms and the Human Rights of Women.* Sydney, Australia: Palgrave Macmillan, 1999.

Charrad, M. *States and Women's Rights: The Making of Postcolonial Tunisia, Algeria, and Morocco.* Berkeley: University of California Press, 2001.

Cook, Rebecca J. *Human Rights of Women: National and International Perspectives.* Pennsylvania Studies in Human Rights. Philadelphia: University of Pennsylvania Press, 1994.

Dormann, Knut, and Louise Doswald-Beck. *Elements of War Crimes under the Rome Statute of the International Criminal Court: Sources and Commentary.* Cambridge: Cambridge University Press, 2003.

Global Issues. Women's Rights. Available online. URL: http://www.globalissues.org/article/166/womens-rights. Accessed March 21, 2010.

Human Rights Watch. Women's Rights. Available online. URL: http://www.hrw.org/en/category/topic/women. Accessed March 21, 2010.

Peters, Julie Stone, and Andrea Wolper. *Women's Rights, Human Rights: International Feminist Perspectives.* London: Routledge, 1995.

Thomas, Dorothy Q., and Thomas Sidney Jones, eds. *A Modern Form of Slavery: Trafficking of Burmese Women and Girls into Brothels in Thailand.* New York: Human Rights Watch, 1994.

UN.org. Women Watch. Available online. URL: http://www.un.org/womenwatch/. Accessed March 21, 2010.

World Court   *See* INTERNATIONAL COURT OF JUSTICE.

Y

Yad Vashem

Yad Vashem was established in 1953 as a memorial to the 6 million Jews who perished in the Nazi campaign of extermination during World War II while also serving as an archive of material related to the Holocaust. Formally known as the Holocaust Martyrs' and Heroes' Remembrance Authority, Yad Vashem was founded by an act of the Israeli Knesset (parliament) and entrusted with the documenting of the life of Jews who were swept up in the FINAL SOLUTION, better known as the Holocaust. Yad Vashem, which is located on Har Hazikaron (the Mount of Remembrance) in Jerusalem, is composed of several elements: museums, archives, a library, a school, exhibits, sculptures, and a memorial for the Righteous Among the Nations, which is dedicated to non-Jews who risked their lives by sheltering and aiding the escape of Jews fleeing Nazi persecution. Its archival collection is the largest and most comprehensive repository of material on the Holocaust in the world, boasting 62 million pages of documents and nearly 267,500 photographs, along with thousands of films and videotaped testimonies of survivors. Its library contains more than 90,000 books, thousands of periodicals, and a number of rare items from the period. By 2005 Yad Vashem had computerized 3.2 million names of Holocaust victims and relevant biographical data. Its International School for Holocaust Studies is the only school of its kind in the world—both a resource and a teaching center with a staff of over 100 educators. Its staff classes are attended by more than 100,000 students, 50,000 Israeli soldiers, and thousands of educators from Israel and around the world every year.

Further Reading:

Abells, Chana Byers. *The Children We Remember: Photographs from the Archives of Yad Vashem, the Holocaust Martyrs' and Heroes' Remembrance Authority, Jerusalem, Israel.* New York: HarperTrophy, 2002.

Dafni, Reuven, and Yehudit Kleiman, eds. *Final Letters: From Victims of the Holocaust (From the Yad Vashem Archive).* New York: Paragon House Publishers, 1991.
Yad Vashem. Available online. URL: http://www.yadvashem.org/. Accessed March 21, 2010.

Yamashita Tomoyuki (1885–1946) *Japanese general*

Yamashita Tomoyuki commanded Japanese forces in the Far East during World War II and was subsequently tried and convicted for war crimes even though there was little evidence indicating that he was personally involved in any atrocities. Born in 1885, he began his long army career at the age of 20. He rose quickly in the ranks, earning a promotion from captain to lieutenant colonel in just three years. In 1936 members of a rightist military faction rebelled against moderates in the government. When the coup failed, Yamashita was asked to serve as a mediator between the military and the political opposition. Yamashita managed to avoid being implicated in the uprising. Nonetheless, Emperor Hirohito suspected that he was more sympathetic to the mutineers than he had let on and sent him into quasi exile in Korea, which was then under Japanese colonial rule.

Yamashita managed to regain his previous status in spite of an adversarial relationship with War Minister HIDEKI TOJO. In October 1941 Tojo was asked to form a government, and within weeks he initiated plans to go to war. Yamashita was invited to a cabinet meeting at the Imperial Headquarters in Tokyo to discuss the war, which, in his view, was justified for economic reasons. With Japan's population expanding, he believed, the country needed to import more of its resources. "In order to buy or import her commodities she [Japan] had to pay ultimately in commodities," he wrote. "This effort on her part was prevented for one reason or another by other countries. Japan made attempts to solve the misunderstandings through peaceful methods, but when all her efforts were thwarted or negated she felt it necessary to engage in open warfare."

Yamashita was given command of the Twenty-fifth Army, which was assigned the mission of conquering the Malay Peninsula, then part of the British Empire. Yamashita developed a strategy tailored for jungle fighting that ensured a quick and decisive victory within 10 weeks. In February 1943 he was promoted to general and given the command of Japanese ground troops in the Philippines who were coming under increasing pressure from American forces. Yamashita moved his headquarters repeatedly—from Manila to Mindro and then to Luzon and Bangbang—to escape advancing American troops. He was in the process of organizing guerrilla resistance to a U.S. takeover of the Philippines when Japan surrendered unconditionally in August 1945.

Captured in early September and charged with violating "the laws of war," Yamashita was put on trial in Manila. The charges against him were based on atrocities committed by Japanese troops under his command, including the murder, TORTURE, rape, and maltreatment of thousands of Filipinos and of hundreds of Americans. The prosecution contended that he should have known of the excesses committed by his troops. He was defended by U.S. military officers who objected to the use of hearsay evidence—not allowed in a U.S. court of law—and the admission of diary entries by Japanese soldiers that could not be corroborated. No evidence or eyewitness testimony was ever presented to show that Yamashita either knew about or ordered his troops to violate the rules of war. Nonetheless, he was found guilty and condemned to death. His attorneys petitioned the U.S. Supreme Court on the grounds that his trial did not rise to the same standards of DUE PROCESS guaranteed by the U.S. Constitution. The Supreme Court turned down the petition after determining that the commission hearing the case was "lawfully constituted." The ruling stated that "the petitioner was charged with violation of the law of war and that the Commission had authority to proceed with the trial and in doing so, did not violate any statutory or Constitutional command." The Supreme Court decision (with two justices dissenting) meant that the execution could go ahead as planned. "The Tiger of Malaya," as Yamashita was known for his wartime exploits, was hanged in February 1946.

Further Reading:

Li, Peter, ed. *Japanese War Crimes: The Search for Justice.* New Brunswick, N.J.: Transaction Publishers, 2003.

Piccigallo, Philip R. *The Japanese on Trial: Allied War Crimes Operations in the East, 1945–1951.* Austin: Univ. of Texas Press, 1980.

Rees, Laurence. *Horror in the East: Japan and the Atrocities of World War II.* New York: Da Capo Press, 2002.

Russell of Liverpool, Edward Frederick Langley Russell, Baron. *Knights of the Bushido: A Short History of Japanese War Crimes.* London: Greenhill Books, 2005.

Yemen, human rights violations in

Yemen suffers from a multitude of problems, including poverty, corruption, terrorism (it is the home of Osama bin Laden), drug addiction, and a severe drought. The government has cracked down on dissent even as it tries to combat insurgencies and ethnic conflicts in various parts of the country. Foreigners—tourists as well as diplomats—have been kidnapped and in some cases put to death. Yemen only became a single country in 1990 with the union of its northern and southern regions. A civil war broke out between the two in 1994 in which the north prevailed. The legacy of that war persists; southern Yemenis maintain that they have been subject to discrimination and that the government has dismissed southerners from high-ranking jobs in the military and government. They also assert that they have been denied their fair share of national resources. In December 2009 HUMAN RIGHTS WATCH released a report that in many respects supported complaints by southerners, citing the government for mounting unprovoked attacks against the supporters of what is known as the Southern Movement as well as against journalists, academics, and other opinion makers. The report, based on 80 interviews, documented at least six occasions when security forces used lethal force against peaceful demonstrations, killing 11 and wounding dozens. The security forces have arbitrarily arrested thousands of people for exercising their right of peaceful assembly, according to the rights group. Journalists and writers critical of the government have been arrested on spurious charges. The Southern Movement was begun by retired military officers who had been fired from their jobs, but it soon grew as more people joined it and began to demand jobs, an end to corruption, and a share of the country's oil revenue. Yemini authorities have intensified their campaign to control the media. In 2009 the government suspended the distribution of several newspapers, although some were allowed to resume publication. In May security forces fought a battle with guards at the Aden compound of Al-Ayyam, Yemen's oldest and most widely circulated independent newspaper, killing one bystander and severely wounding another. Additional conflict has been escalating in the north of the country, which has embroiled Yemen's neighbor SAUDI ARABIA. The conflict, which began in August 2009, has pitted insurgents from the Huthi ethnic group and Yemini forces. In November Saudi forces became involved after border clashes with Huthi. Saudi forces were deployed across the border to fight the Huthi rebels, while Saudi warplanes bombed villages under their control. Thousands of people have been displaced by the violence, and the conflict has increasingly put civilians at risk. In early 2010 the government and Huthi leaders agreed to a cease-fire, although whether it would hold was in doubt.

See also QAEDA, AL; WAR ON TERROR.

Further Reading:
Amnesty International. *Human Rights in the Republic of Yemen.* Available online. URL: http://www.amnesty. org/en/region/yemen. Accessed March 21, 2010.
Derechos.org. *Human Rights in Yemen.* Available online. URL: http://www.derechos.org/human-rights/mena/ yemen/. Accessed March 21, 2010.
Human Rights Watch. *Yemen Human Rights.* Available online. URL: http://www.hrw.org/middle-eastn-africa/ yemen. Accessed March 21, 2010.
Phillips, Sarah. *Yemen's Democracy Experiment in Regional Perspective: Patronage and Pluralized Authoritarianism.* New York: Palgrave Macmillan, 2008.

Yugoslavia, war crimes in

The most devastating conflict in Europe since World War II broke out in 1991. The immediate cause was the violent dissolution of the Yugoslavian Federation, which at one point had consisted of six constituent republics. However, the origins of the Balkan conflict that would take a decade to play itself out can be traced to the efforts of SLOBODAN MILOŠEVIĆ, first as president of the Serbian Nationalist Party and later president of Serbia, to centralize power.

Until 1980 the federation had been kept together by one man, Josip Broz, Marshal Tito (1892–1980), who had dominated Yugoslavia for 37 years. It was largely through his efforts that bitter ethnic tensions among Serbs, Croats, and Muslims did not explode into violence. Although Yugoslavia was communist, Tito steered a course independently of the Soviet Union. However, he had made little provision for an orderly transition after his passing. For several years the federation was governed by a collective presidency, representing the different nationalities that composed Yugoslavia. Milošević, however, advocated a federation that would be dominated by the Serbs. As Serbian president, Milošević stripped two provinces—Kosovo (with an Albanian majority) and Vojvodina (largely Hungarian)—of their autonomy. These and other actions intended to extend Serb power stirred fears that he would interfere in other republics.

In 1990 elections nationalist parties scored gains in every republic. Negotiations to keep the federation from splintering apart failed. On June 25, 1991, both Croatia and Slovenia declared independence. Less than a year later, in April 1992, so did Bosnia and Herzegovina. Serb forces fought a brief war against Slovenia, but ultimately Slovenia was allowed to go its own way because it was home to relatively few Serbs. That was not the case, however, in Bosnia or Croatia, both of which had significant Serbian populations. (At the start of the war Bosnia's population consisted of 4.4 million people, 44 percent of whom were Muslim, 31 percent Serb, 17 percent Croat, and 8 percent other nationalities.) As a result, the war in those republics would be anything but brief.

From the outset the Bosnian Serbs made it clear that they had no intention of supporting a fledgling republic under Muslim leadership, rejecting the notion of a multiethnic nation. Their leader, RADOVAN KARADŽIĆ, mobilized the Serb nationalists and organized paramilitary units—the Bosnian Serb armed militia (BSA)—which collaborated with the Serb-dominated Yugoslav national army. The BSA initiated a campaign of terror to seize large areas of Bosnia and Croatia with the intention of linking up to Serbia to create a Greater Serbia. In the interim Karadžić declared the establishment of the Republika Srpska, or Serb Republic, in eastern Bosnia. The BSO engaged in what became known as ethnic cleansing, driving out the Muslim populations from eastern and northern Bosnia, razing their villages, laying SIEGE to towns and cities, and imprisoning thousands of others in CONCENTRATION CAMPS. In spite of international pressure and the imposition of sanctions on Belgrade, the BSA continued its incursions, laying siege to Sarajevo, Bosnia's capital, in 1992, and undertaking ethnic-cleansing campaigns in Banja Luka, later the capital of the Bosnian Serb Republic, and Bijeljina. Sarajevo came under Serbian shelling and sniper fire for months on end, resulting in the killings of 10,000–12,000 civilians. In 1993 the Serbian paramilitary forces struck several other towns. Attacks were not exclusively directed against ordinary Muslim civilians; the BSA carried out targeted killings as well against political and religious figures in an effort to destabilize and eliminate the leadership of Muslim society.

Croatia had its own agenda in the war, which frequently put it at odds with both Bosnia and Serbia. Initially Croatian and Bosnian forces were allies against Serbia. Then clashes occurred between Bosnian government forces and Bosnian Croatian militias known as the Croatian Defense Council (HVO) under the leadership of Mate Boban. Following the example of the Bosnian Serbs, Boban advocated the creation of a separate Bosnian Croat Republic of Herceg-Bosna, with Mostar as its capital. When the Bosnian government objected to Boban's plan, the HVO attacked Mostar and, according to a U.S. State Department report, "brutalized, confined, and raped its Muslim residents in an assault containing some of the most extreme human rights abuses in Bosnia and Herzegovina in 1993." Croatian forces subsequently broke with the Bosnian Muslims and sided with Boban. In central Bosnia the HVO went on a rampage; in one hamlet they massacred as many as 100 civilians and then razed it to the ground. In some cases the HVO collaborated with the BSA, creating "conditions of extreme deprivation" in Bosnian enclaves. By summer 1993 the HVO was involved in herding an estimated 20,000 Bosnians into so-called collection centers in Mostar and other parts of Bosnia predominantly populated by ethnic Croatians. There is evidence that many of the detainees were tortured and murdered or died as a result of brutal conditions in the camps. Representatives of Helsinki Watch, the human rights group, were denied access to the camps to find out what was going on, but reports of atrocities still reached the international press, causing an uproar and embarrassment for the Croatian government, the principal sponsor of HVO.

The Bosnian government forces perpetrated their share of atrocities and abuses, killing Croat civilians and driving thousands of Croats from their homes. In October 1993 Bosnian government forces rounded up 1,000 Bosnian Croat refugees trying to flee the town of Konjic, then robbed and beat them. Boban claimed that 150,000–190,000 Bosnian Croats had been displaced by fighting in central Bosnia or driven out by the government that same year. In March 1994 a Washington-mediated accord between Muslims and Croatians was reached that established a Muslim-Croat federation in Bosnia. With Bosnian Muslims and Croats once again allied, the Serb forces no longer could count on a decisive military advantage.

By the end of 1992, the Bosnian Serb army already had control of about two-thirds of Bosnia and Herzegovina. Most of the Muslims and Croats had taken refuge in government-held territory. Their sanctuary was precarious; Serb forces surrounded many of the enclaves, preventing relief agencies from gaining access to them and shutting off their electrical and water supply. By this time more than a million people had been internally displaced and were in desperate need of emergency food and shelter. Hundreds of thousands of REFUGEES had fled the country altogether in search of asylum in western European countries. At one point in the conflict there may have been up to 2 million refugees and displaced persons. Those who were not able to escape were frequently imprisoned in concentration camps. It is believed that 260 of these camps were set up by the three sides during the war. In January 1993 the U.S. government estimated that there were 135 Serb-run detention centers alone in Bosnia. There were also Muslim and HVO camps, though many of these were closed by 1993. How many people were held is unknown; the three sides defined all males between 16 and 65 as combatants, a classification that included many civilians. Outside observers were only sporadically permitted to inspect the camps, and in some cases, because the camps were unregistered, no international monitors ever visited.

In an attempt to rein in the belligerents, if not to stop the fighting, the UN Security Council authorized a mission known as the United Nations Protection Force (UNPRO-FOR). But the mission was dangerous; by 1993 over 60 UNPROFOR soldiers had been killed in outright attacks or by sniper fire. In spring 1993 the United Nations designated six besieged Bosnian towns as SAFE HAVENS deserving of international protection. But providing relief to the besieged areas was a major challenge; if food and other provisions were allowed to reach the enclaves, it would hamper the Serb ability to overrun them, suggesting that force might be required to get the aid to the populations in need. The UN Security Council recognized the need and adopted Resolution 770, ordering states to take "all necessary measures" to facilitate aid deliveries in Bosnia. On the ground, though, the United Nations failed to exert force when it was most needed. In July 1995, rather than resist the Serb takeover of Srebrinica—one of the six safe areas—UN peacekeepers withdrew. Serb forces proceeded to expel the women and children and murder more than 7,000 Muslim men and boys. International aid workers were not spared in the fighting and suffered several losses; several journalists were killed as well—34 in the first two years of the war.

Even as fighting raged in Bosnia, Serbs were also attacking Croatia, even shelling the historic Croatian coastal city of Dubrovnik. In the initial phase of the war, the Serbs had taken nearly a third of Croatian territory. As in Bosnia, Serbs relied on Croatian Serbs as proxies who were responsible for atrocities and abuses against Croats. In November 1991, for instance, Serbs from the Croatian region of Krajina removed several hundred wounded Croatian soldiers from a hospital in the eastern Slavonian town of Vukovar, shot them in a field, and buried them in a mass grave. Four years later, though, the tide had turned against the Serbs, and Croatians launched a campaign of ethnic cleansing of their own, retaking Serb-occupied western Slavonia and the Krajina region and sending thousands of Serb civilians fleeing from their homes.

The war in Bosnia and Croatia was also notable for the systematic violence directed against women. Bosnian Muslim women were separated from their families and held in Serbian detention camps where they were raped, tortured and subject to other degrading treatment as part of a genocidal campaign. (Bosnian men were not spared, either; many were raped and forced to commit sexual acts with other male prisoners.) According to Kelly Dawn Askin, author of *War Crimes against Women*, Serbs targeted Bosnian Muslim women in particular because of the patriarchal nature of Muslim society; unmarried women who lost their virginity were stigmatized, and married women who were "tarnished" by having had sexual relations with other men suffered disgrace. Thus rape became a form of assault against the family and Bosnian Muslim community. In the Bosnian town of Foca, the Yugoslav army set up a detention center at the Partizan Sports Complex in 1992 in which both Bosnian Muslim and Bosnian Croat women were held. The detainees were often raped every night and denied medical care for any injuries they sustained. (Rape, committed as an act of war rather than as a consequence of conflict, is an indictable offense under international law.) Young girls and old women who were raped often died as a result. Videotapes were also made of some of these incidents and sold as pornography. The BSO, which used RAPE AS A TACTIC OF WAR beginning in 1992, were not alone. Members of HVO, the Croatian paramilitary units, also were implicated in rape. According to the UNITED NATIONS HIGH COMMISSIONER FOR REFUGEES (UNHCR), HVO soldiers may have raped as many as 100 women in one incident.

In summer 1995 the Serbs began to suffer reverses as Bosnian and Croatian troops retook areas that had fallen under Serb control. Finally, bowing to pressure from Washington and the United Nations, the leaders of the three belligerent states—Bosnian president Alija Izetbegović, Serbian president Slobodan Milošević, and Croatian president FRANJO TUDJMAN—agreed to talks conducted under the auspices of the United States at an air force base near Dayton, Ohio. The three hammered out a comprehensive peace treaty known as the DAYTON ACCORDS, which was signed in Paris on December 1, 1995. Yet although the Bosnian war came to an end, the Balkans did not have much time to enjoy peace. In 1999 Milošević engineered another campaign of ethnic cleansing, this time against ethnic Albanians who made up the majority of the Yugoslav province of Kosovo. He launched his assault ostensibly to quell a separatist insurgency, but its real objective seemed to be a wholesale removal of Kosovo's Albanian population. That war was only halted because of an intensive bombing campaign carried out by NATO. A year later Milošević was forced to give up power.

Even while the Bosnian war was still going on, the United Nations recognized the need to address the atrocities and bring the perpetrators to account. In October l992 the UN Security Council approved an impartial international investigation to identify persons responsible for human rights abuses. The Commission of Experts, as the panel was known, was able to document thousands of crimes. By spring l993 the Security Council concluded that the atrocities that had taken place amounted to war crimes and had to be prosecuted. This determination led to the establishment of the INTERNATIONAL CRIMINAL TRIBUNAL FOR THE FORMER YUGOSLAVIA (ICTY). Three of the principal perpetrators were among the first to be indicted: Slobodan Milošević, Bosnian Serb leader Radovan Karadžić, and Bosnian Serb general RATKO MLADIĆ. Milošević was ousted from power in 2000 and handed over to the ICTY, which sits in The Hague, Netherlands. The former Serbian strongman was charged with 27 counts of war crimes and CRIMES AGAINST HUMANITY arising from the conflict in Bosnia and Herzegovina between 1992 and 1995. The charges were based on Milošević's "command responsibility" as president of Serbia and his alleged participation in a joint criminal enterprise. He was also charged in connection with the shelling of Sarajevo, the mass murder of thousands of Muslim men and boys at Srebrenica, and abuses committed at the Serbian-run Omarska detention camp. The indictment included one count of GENOCIDE and one count of complicity in genocide. He was also charged in connection with his role in organizing Serb attacks on Albanian civilians in the war in Kosovo in 1999.

In July 2008 Karadžić was arrested after a protracted manhunt and extradited to The Hague to stand trial, though Mladić has so far evaded capture. The ICTY also undertook the investigation of allegations of atrocities committed by the Bosnian Muslim forces as well as the HVO and Croatian armed forces on Bosnian territory. At first Croatia resisted demands of the ICTY to arrest and transfer suspected war criminals to The Hague, where the court sits. In 1997, however, Zlatko Aleksovski, a former chief of an HVO army internment camp in Bosnia, was sent to The Hague, an action hailed as demonstrating a willingness on Croatia's part to cooperate with the court. There is little question, however, that Croatia would not have acted if it were not for pressure from the West. The court later charged members of HVO with taking part in systematic attacks on Muslim villages and murdering civilians. In one case—the assault on the town of Ahmici—103 Muslims were killed by HVO militiamen. The court emphasized the link between the Croatian government and the HVO, charging the militia with committing grave breaches of the GENEVA CONVENTIONS of 1949: "[T]he Bosnian Croats can, for the purposes of these proceedings, be regarded as agents of Croatia in respect of discrete acts which are alleged to be violations of the grave breaches provisions of the Geneva Conventions. It appears that Croatia, in addition to assisting the Bosnian Croats . . . inserted its own armed forces into the conflict on the territory of Bosnia and exercised a high degree of control over both the military and political institutions of the Bosnian Croats." The ICTY found that then Croatian president Franjo Tudjman "was hoping to partition Bosnia and exercised such a degree of control over the Bosnian Croats and especially the HVO that it is justified to speak of overall control. [T]he close ties between Croatia and the Bosnian Croats did not cease with the establishment of the HVO."

See also BOSNIA AND HERZEGOVINA, HUMAN RIGHTS VIOLATIONS IN; CROATIA, HUMAN RIGHTS VIOLATIONS IN; KOSOVO, WAR CRIMES IN; ROM (ROMA, ROMANY, GYPSIES), PERSECUTION OF; SARAJEVO, SIEGE OF; SERBIA, HUMAN RIGHTS VIOLATIONS IN; SLOVENIA, HUMAN RIGHTS VIOLATIONS IN; SREBRENICA, MASSACRE IN; USTACHE; WOMEN'S RIGHTS, VIOLATIONS OF.

Further Reading:

Clark, Wesley K. *Waging Modern War: Bosnia, Kosovo, and the Future of Combat.* New York: Public Affairs, 2001.

Hagan, John. *Justice in the Balkans: Prosecuting War Crimes in the Hague Tribunal.* Chicago Series in Law and Society. Chicago: University of Chicago Press, 2003.

Harris, Nathaniel. *The War in Former Yugoslavia.* London: Hodder & Stoughton, 1997.

Hazan, Pierre, and James Thomas Snyder. *Justice in a Time of War: The True Story behind the International Criminal Tribunal for the Former Yugoslavia.* Eugenia and Hugh M. Stewart Series on Eastern Europe. Austin: Texas A&M University Press, 2004.

ICTY. Milosevic Trial Public Archive. Available online.URL: http://hague.bard.edu/. Accessed March 20, 2010.

International Criminal Tribunal for the former Yugoslavia. Available online. URL: http://www.icty.org/. Accessed March 21, 2010.

Jurist. Kosovo and Yugoslavia: Law in Crisis. January 2000. Available online. URL: http://jurist.law.pitt.edu/kosovo.htm. Accessed March 21, 2010.

Kim, Julie. *War in the Former Yugoslavia: Chronology of Events August 16, 1992–May 30, 1993.* CRS Report for Congress. Washington, D.C.: Foreign Affairs and National Defense Division, Congressional Research Service, the Library of Congress, 1993.

Kipp, Jacob W. *International Ramifications of Yugoslavia's Serial Wars: The Challenge of Ethno-national Conflicts for a Post-Cold-War, European Order.* Fort Leavenworth, Ka.: European Military Studies Office, 1993.

Mertus, Julie. *Former Yugoslavia: War Crimes Trials in the Former Yugoslavia.* Helsinki: Human Rights Watch/Helsinki, 1995.

Naimark, Norman, and Holly Case. *Yugoslavia and Its Historians: Understanding the Balkan Wars of the 1990s.* Stanford, Calif.: Stanford University Press, 2003.

Rossanet, Bertrand de. *War and Peace in the Former Yugoslavia.* Boston: Martinus Nijhoff, 1997.

Scharf, Michael P. *Balkan Justice: The Story behind the First International War Crimes Trial since Nuremberg.* Durham, N.C.: Carolina Academic Press, 1997.

Whealey, Robert. *American Intervention in Yugoslavia: Civil War, 1991–1999.* Portland, Me.: Humanity Books, 2005.

Z

Zimbabwe, human rights violations in

Since 1980, when majority rule came to Zimbabwe, President Robert Mugabe has kept a firm grip on the southern African nation. The mercurial former revolutionary has resorted to increasingly authoritarian methods to maintain control, even though, in theory, Zimbabwe is a parliamentary democracy. Although the political opposition came close to winning power in parliamentary and presidential elections in 2000 and 2002, the governing Zimbabwe African National Union–Patriotic Front, or ZANU-PF, has managed to manipulate the law to forestall the prospect of losing at the ballot box a third time. Mugabe has proven to be a consummate survivor. Although his country has suffered economic destitution (registering the highest inflation rate in the world), he has managed to maintain power through a combination of intimidation, violence, and nominal compromise. The country was plunged into a political crisis in the aftermath of parliamentary elections in March 2008 in which the ruling ZANU-PF lost its majority. Mugabe, however, had no intention of losing the presidential elections scheduled for June of 2009 and unleashed a violent campaign against supporters of the chief opposition party, the Movement for Democratic Change (MDC). In the months leading up to the presidential election, the MDC claimed that security forces had rounded up several thousands of its members and killed more than 80 of its supporters. ZANU-PF also relied on so-called war veterans, who had fought with Mugabe to overthrow British rule. These veterans established bases in both rural and urban areas from which they launched attacks against people considered backers of the MDC. Thousands were forced to attend "reeducation" sessions. Many were assaulted as "lessons" for others. ZANU-PF militias cordoned off entire villages of suspected MDC supporters and beat and tortured the people living in them, including women, children, and the elderly. Human rights activists and lawyers were also arbitrarily arrested. Suspects taken into custody were frequently denied bail. Violence fell off

markedly in the weeks prior to presidential elections, raising hopes that Mugabe might allow them to go ahead without trying to rig the results or intimidate the opposition. When, however, it appeared as if the MDC leader Morgan Tsvangirai had come out ahead in the balloting, election officials delayed releasing the vote for several weeks and then announced that neither candidate had won 50 percent of the vote, necessitating a runoff. Mugabe mobilized his police, military, and local ZANU-PF officials, as well as government-backed militia and war veterans, to terrorize MDC supporters, setting off a wave of torture, beatings, looting, and burning of property. According to HUMAN RIGHTS WATCH and other observers, at least 163 people were killed and some 5,000 were tortured or beaten. In the turmoil, tens of thousands of people were displaced. Ultimately, Tsvangirai felt he had no choice but to withdraw from the race rather than continue to put the lives of more supporters at risk. The international outrage that Mugabe's tactics aroused forced the government to enter into grudging negotiations with the opposition brokered by South African's then president Thabo Mbeki. Nonetheless, Mugabe continued to keep up pressure on the MDC, using violence and intimidation to achieve more gains at the bargaining table. Police arrested more than 100 presiding officers and election officials on trumped-up charges of electoral fraud and arrested hundreds of MDC supporters and officials on spurious charges of inciting violence. Meanwhile, ZANU-PF supporters were allowed to carry out abuses with almost absolute impunity. (Since 2000 the judiciary has been increasingly compromised by the government, although some independent judges continue to defy the regime; for example, the Supreme Court rejected terrorism charges brought against prominent human rights activist Jestina Mukoko and freed her.) Tsvangirai was forced to concede powerful ministries such as interior (which oversees the police and security services) and finance to ZANU-PF. Mugabe also made sure to keep his grip on the media. The two rivals finally signed a power-sharing agreement. Nonetheless, Mugabe continued to try to curtail the MDC's power at every turn; MDC members of parliament have been arrested on specious charges (one was arrested for stealing a cell phone), whittling away its majority. Roy Bennett, an MDC leader chosen as deputy agricultural minister, was arrested and imprisoned on charges of possessing arms for terrorist purposes, charges which human rights organizations assert were based on a confession extracted by torture. White farmers have been a frequent target and convenient scapegoat for the nation's ills; their farms have been seized and turned over to ZANU-PF supporters without any agricultural skills. Predictably, much of Zimbabwe's population has had to rely on international aid for food because the country can no longer afford to feed itself. Tsvangirai has undertaken an international campaign to raise funds and persuade Western governments to ease sanctions. But as of late 2009 relations between Mugabe and Tsvangirai were so tense that Tsvangirai announced a boycott of the cabinet in protest against strong-arm tactics of ZANU-PF, although he did not go so far as to withdraw from the government altogether. He accused Mugabe's party of using the law to punish his supporters while putting 16,000 members of his party's youth militia on the government payroll and remilitarizing the war veterans' bases used for attacks on MDC followers. In October 2009 the United Nations special rapporteur on torture who was scheduled to meet with Tsvangirai was turned away at the airport by police, underscoring Tsvangirai's relative impotence. When leaders of the National Association of Nongovernmental Organizations, which represents more than 1,000 civic groups, met in Victoria Falls for a three-day gathering they were charged with convening an illegal meeting without first getting police clearance. In December, at a conference of ZANU-PF, Mugabe called for new elections, threatening the fragile coalition. But his party is also torn by internal divisions, as rivals hoping to take Mugabe's place when he leaves the scene compete to be first in line to succeed him.

The changes in the composition of the government have not eased restrictions on freedoms of the press or assembly, which have been sharply curbed on the grounds of national security. The foreign media has been barred from the country. E-mail going in or out is censored, and the government has tried to ban cell phone calls anywhere outside Zimbabwe. Licenses are required from the government for domestic journalists. At the same time, the government has moved to place nongovernmental organizations (NGOs)—including churches and charities—under government control. The government can shut down NGOs at its discretion. To enforce its rule, the Mugabe government relies on a vast network of security forces and informers whose ranks have swelled in recent years; according to the *New York Times*, one out of every 60 Zimbabweans is on the payroll of the security services. (The population is about 11.3 million.) Apparently there is plenty of work for them to do. The Solidarity Peace Trust, an NGO made up of clerics, estimated that between 2000 and November 2004, 300,000 Zimbabweans (or one out of every 40 people) had suffered from abuses by government agents that included beatings, torture, being uprooted from their land, or denied food rations. The group also stated that another 300 people had died in politically motivated killings in the same period. Human rights groups say that Mugabe's government also rations food for political ends, distributing resources to its supporters while denying them to people who back the opposition. The desperation and destitution in the country have displaced from 3 million to 6 million people, according to a report carried on National Public Radio. Most of the displaced have taken refuge in neighboring South Africa. However, many of these refugees exist in legal limbo, unable to obtain visas or asylum, forced to live in squalid conditions, and vulnerable to abuse and harassment by South Africans who are also suffering from poverty and joblessness.

See also CONFLICT DIAMONDS.

Further Reading:

Amnesty International. Human Rights in the Republic of Zimbabwe. Available online. URL: http://www.amnesty.org/en/region/zimbabwe. Accessed March 21, 2010.

Blair, David. *Degrees in Violence: Robert Mugabe and the Struggle for Power in Zimbabwe.* London: Continuum International Publishing Group, 2003.

Bond, Patrick. *Zimbabwe's Plunge: Exhausted Nationalism, Neoliberalism, and the Search for Social Justice.* Durban, South Africa: University of Natal Press, 2003.

Hill, Geoff. *The Battle for Zimbabwe.* Hendon, U.K.: Struik Publishers, 2005.

Meredith, Martin. *Mugabe: Power, Plunder and the Struggle for Zimbabwe's Future.* New York: PublicAffairs, 2007.

———. *Our Votes, Our Guns: Robert Mugabe and the Tragedy of Zimbabwe.* New York: Public Affairs, 2003.

Smith, Ian Douglas. *Bitter Harvest: Zimbabwe and the Aftermath of Its Independence.* London: John Blake, 2008.

Zimbabwe Human Rights Forum NGO. Available online. URL: http://www.hrforumzim.com/. Accessed March 21, 2010.

Zimbabwe Lawyers for Human Rights. Available online. URL: http://www.zlhr.org.zw/. Accessed March 21, 2010.

List of Appendices

Primary Documents

Primary Documents

GENEVA CONVENTION RELATIVE TO THE TREATMENT OF PRISONERS OF WAR

*Adopted on 12 August 1949 by the Diplomatic Conference for the Establishment
of International Conventions for the Protection of Victims of War,
held in Geneva from 21 April to 12 August 1949;
entry into force: 21 October 1950*

Part I—General Provisions

Article 1

The High Contracting Parties undertake to respect and to ensure respect for the present Convention in all circumstances.

Article 2

In addition to the provisions which shall be implemented in peace time, the present Convention shall apply to all cases of declared war or of any other armed conflict which may arise between two or more of the High Contracting Parties, even if the state of war is not recognized by one of them.

The Convention shall also apply to all cases of partial or total occupation of the territory of a High Contracting Party, even if the said occupation meets with no armed resistance.

Although one of the Powers in conflict may not be a party to the present Convention, the Powers who are parties thereto shall remain bound by it in their mutual relations. They shall furthermore be bound by the Convention in relation to the said Power, if the latter accepts and applies the provisions thereof.

Article 3

In the case of armed conflict not of an international character occurring in the territory of one of the High Contracting Parties, each party to the conflict shall be bound to apply, as a minimum, the following provisions:

1. Persons taking no active part in the hostilities, including members of armed forces who have laid down their arms and those placed hors de combat by sickness, wounds, detention, or any other cause, shall in all circumstances be treated humanely, without any adverse distinction founded on race, colour, religion or faith, sex, birth or wealth, or any other similar criteria.

To this end the following acts are and shall remain prohibited at any time and in any place whatsoever with respect to the above-mentioned persons:

(a) Violence to life and person, in particular murder of all kinds, mutilation, cruel treatment and torture;

(b) Taking of hostages;

(c) Outrages upon personal dignity, in particular, humiliating and degrading treatment;

(d) The passing of sentences and the carrying out of executions without previous judgment pronounced by a regularly constituted court affording all the judicial guarantees which are recognized as indispensable by civilized peoples.

2. The wounded and sick shall be collected and cared for.

An impartial humanitarian body, such as the International Committee of the Red Cross, may offer its services to the Parties to the conflict.

The Parties to the conflict should further endeavour to bring into force, by means of special agreements, all or part of the other provisions of the present Convention.

The application of the preceding provisions shall not affect the legal status of the Parties to the conflict.

Article 4

A. Prisoners of war, in the sense of the present Convention, are persons belonging to one of the following categories, who have fallen into the power of the enemy:

1. Members of the armed forces of a Party to the conflict as well as members of militias or volunteer corps forming part of such armed forces.

2. Members of other militias and members of other volunteer corps, including those of organized resistance movements, belonging to a Party to the conflict and operating in or outside their own territory, even if this territory is occupied, provided that such militias or volunteer corps, including such organized resistance movements, fulfil the following conditions:

(a) That of being commanded by a person responsible for his subordinates;

(b) That of having a fixed distinctive sign recognizable at a distance;

(c) That of carrying arms openly;

(d) That of conducting their operations in accordance with the laws and customs of war.

3. Members of regular armed forces who profess allegiance to a government or an authority not recognized by the Detaining Power.

4. Persons who accompany the armed forces without actually being members thereof, such as civilian members of military aircraft crews, war correspondents, supply contractors, members of labour units or of services responsible for the welfare of the armed forces, provided that they have received authorization from the armed forces which they accompany, who shall provide them for that purpose with an identity card similar to the annexed model.

5. Members of crews, including masters, pilots and apprentices, of the merchant marine and the crews of civil aircraft of the Parties to the conflict, who do not benefit by more favourable treatment under any other provisions of international law.

6. Inhabitants of a non-occupied territory, who on the approach of the enemy spontaneously take up arms to resist the invading forces, without having had time to form themselves into regular armed units, provided they carry arms openly and respect the laws and customs of war.

B. The following shall likewise be treated as prisoners of war under the present Convention:

1. Persons belonging, or having belonged, to the armed forces of the occupied country, if the occupying Power considers it necessary by reason of such allegiance to intern them, even though it has originally liberated them while hostilities were going on outside the territory it occupies, in particular where such persons have made an unsuccessful attempt to rejoin the armed forces to which they belong and which are engaged in combat, or where they fail to comply with a summons made to them with a view to internment.

2. The persons belonging to one of the categories enumerated in the present Article, who have been received by neutral or non-belligerent Powers on their territory and whom these Powers are required to intern under international law, without prejudice to any more favourable treatment which these Powers may choose to give and with the exception of Articles 8, 10, 15, 30, fifth paragraph, 58–67, 92, 126 and, where diplomatic relations exist between the Parties to the conflict and the neutral or non-belligerent Power concerned, those Articles concerning the Protecting Power. Where such diplomatic relations exist, the Parties to a conflict on whom these persons depend shall be allowed to perform towards them the functions of a Protecting Power as provided in the present Convention, without prejudice to the functions which these Parties normally exercise in conformity with diplomatic and consular usage and treaties.

C. This Article shall in no way affect the status of medical personnel and chaplains as provided for in Article 33 of the present Convention.

Article 5

The present Convention shall apply to the persons referred to in Article 4 from the time they fall into the power of the enemy and until their final release and repatriation.

Should any doubt arise as to whether persons, having committed a belligerent act and having fallen into the hands of the enemy, belong to any of the categories enumerated in Article 4, such persons shall enjoy the protection of the present Convention until such time as their status has been determined by a competent tribunal.

Article 6

In addition to the agreements expressly provided for in Articles 10, 23, 28, 33, 60, 65, 66, 67, 72, 73, 75, 109, 110, 118, 119, 122 and 132, the High Contracting Parties may conclude other special agreements for all matters concerning which they may deem it suitable to make separate provision. No special agreement shall adversely affect the situation of prisoners of war, as defined by the present Convention, nor restrict the rights which it confers upon them.

Prisoners of war shall continue to have the benefit of such agreements as long as the Convention is applicable to them, except where express provisions to the contrary are contained in the aforesaid or in subsequent agreements, or where more favourable measures have been taken with regard to them by one or other of the Parties to the conflict.

Article 7

Prisoners of war may in no circumstances renounce in part or in entirety the rights secured to them by the present

Convention, and by the special agreements referred to in the foregoing Article, if such there be.

Article 8

The present Convention shall be applied with the cooperation and under the scrutiny of the Protecting Powers whose duty it is to safeguard the interests of the Parties to the conflict. For this purpose, the Protecting Powers may appoint, apart from their diplomatic or consular staff, delegates from amongst their own nationals or the nationals of other neutral Powers. The said delegates shall be subject to the approval of the Power with which they are to carry out their duties.

The Parties to the conflict shall facilitate to the greatest extent possible the task of the representatives or delegates of the Protecting Powers.

The representatives or delegates of the Protecting Powers shall not in any case exceed their mission under the present Convention. They shall, in particular, take account of the imperative necessities of security of the State wherein they carry out their duties.

Article 9

The provisions of the present Convention constitute no obstacle to the humanitarian activities which the International Committee of the Red Cross or any other impartial humanitarian organization may, subject to the consent of the Parties to the conflict concerned, undertake for the protection of prisoners of war and for their relief.

Article 10

The High Contracting Parties may at any time agree to entrust to an organization which offers all guarantees of impartiality and efficacy the duties incumbent on the Protecting Powers by virtue of the present Convention.

When prisoners of war do not benefit or cease to benefit, no matter for what reason, by the activities of a Protecting Power or of an organization provided for in the first paragraph above, the Detaining Power shall request a neutral State, or such an organization, to undertake the functions performed under the present Convention by a Protecting Power designated by the Parties to a conflict.

If protection cannot be arranged accordingly, the Detaining Power shall request or shall accept, subject to the provisions of this Article, the offer of the services of a humanitarian organization, such as the International Committee of the Red Cross, to assume the humanitarian functions performed by Protecting Powers under the present Convention.

Any neutral Power or any organization invited by the Power concerned or offering itself for these purposes, shall be required to act with a sense of responsibility towards the Party to the conflict on which persons protected by the present Convention depend, and shall be required to furnish sufficient assurances that it is in a position to undertake the appropriate functions and to discharge them impartially.

No derogation from the preceding provisions shall be made by special agreements between Powers one of which is restricted, even temporarily, in its freedom to negotiate with the other Power or its allies by reason of military events, more particularly where the whole, or a substantial part, of the territory of the said Power is occupied.

Whenever in the present Convention mention is made of a Protecting Power, such mention applies to substitute organizations in the sense of the present Article.

Article 11

In cases where they deem it advisable in the interest of protected persons, particularly in cases of disagreement between the Parties to the conflict as to the application or interpretation of the provisions of the present Convention, the Protecting Powers shall lend their good offices with a view to settling the disagreement.

For this purpose, each of the Protecting Powers may, either at the invitation of one Party or on its own initiative, propose to the Parties to the conflict a meeting of their representatives, and in particular of the authorities responsible for prisoners of war, possibly on neutral territory suitably chosen. The Parties to the conflict shall be bound to give effect to the proposals made to them for this purpose. The Protecting Powers may, if necessary, propose for approval by the Parties to the conflict a person belonging to a neutral Power, or delegated by the International Committee of the Red Cross, who shall be invited to take part in such a meeting.

Part II—General Protection of Prisoners of War

Article 12

Prisoners of war are in the hands of the enemy Power, but not of the individuals or military units who have captured them. Irrespective of the individual responsibilities that may exist, the Detaining Power is responsible for the treatment given them.

Prisoners of war may only be transferred by the Detaining Power to a Power which is a party to the Convention and after the Detaining Power has satisfied itself of the willingness and ability of such transferee Power to apply the Convention. When prisoners of war are transferred under such circumstances, responsibility for the application of the Convention rests on the Power accepting them while they are in its custody.

Nevertheless if that Power fails to carry out the provisions of the Convention in any important respect, the Power by whom the prisoners of war were transferred shall, upon being notified by the Protecting Power, take effective measures to correct the situation or shall request the return of the prisoners of war. Such requests must be complied with.

Article 13

Prisoners of war must at all times be humanely treated. Any unlawful act or omission by the Detaining Power causing death or seriously endangering the health of a prisoner of war in its custody is prohibited, and will be regarded as a serious breach of the present Convention. In particular, no prisoner of war may be subjected to physical mutilation or to medical or scientific experiments of any kind which are not justified by the medical, dental or hospital treatment of the prisoner concerned and carried out in his interest.

Likewise, prisoners of war must at all times be protected, particularly against acts of violence or intimidation and against insults and public curiosity.

Measures of reprisal against prisoners of war are prohibited.

Article 14

Prisoners of war are entitled in all circumstances to respect for their persons and their honour. Women shall be treated with all the regard due to their sex and shall in all cases benefit by treatment as favourable as that granted to men. Prisoners of war shall retain the full civil capacity which they enjoyed at the time of their capture. The Detaining Power may not restrict the exercise, either within or without its own territory, of the rights such capacity confers except in so far as the captivity requires.

Article 15

The Power detaining prisoners of war shall be bound to provide free of charge for their maintenance and for the medical attention required by their state of health.

Article 16

Taking into consideration the provisions of the present Convention relating to rank and sex, and subject to any privileged treatment which may be accorded to them by reason of their state of health, age or professional qualifications, all prisoners of war shall be treated alike by the Detaining Power, without any adverse distinction based on race, nationality, religious belief or political opinions, or any other distinction founded on similar criteria.

Part III—Captivity

SECTION I: BEGINNING OF CAPTIVITY

Article 17

Every prisoner of war, when questioned on the subject, is bound to give only his surname, first names and rank, date of birth, and army, regimental, personal or serial number, or failing this, equivalent information. If he wilfully infringes this rule, he may render himself liable to a restriction of the privileges accorded to his rank or status.

Each Party to a conflict is required to furnish the persons under its jurisdiction who are liable to become prisoners of war, with an identity card showing the owner's surname, first names, rank, army, regimental, personal or serial number or equivalent information, and date of birth. The identity card may, furthermore, bear the signature or the fingerprints, or both, of the owner, and may bear, as well, any other information the Party to the conflict may wish to add concerning persons belonging to its armed forces. As far as possible the card shall measure 6.5 x 10 cm. and shall be issued in duplicate. The identity card shall be shown by the prisoner of war upon demand, but may in no case be taken away from him.

No physical or mental torture, nor any other form of coercion, may be inflicted on prisoners of war to secure from them information of any kind whatever. Prisoners of war who refuse to answer may not be threatened, insulted, or exposed to any unpleasant or disadvantageous treatment of any kind.

Prisoners of war who, owing to their physical or mental condition, are unable to state their identity, shall be handed over to the medical service. The identity of such prisoners shall be established by all possible means, subject to the provisions of the preceding paragraph.

The questioning of prisoners of war shall be carried out in a language which they understand.

Article 18

All effects and articles of personal use, except arms, horses, military equipment and military documents shall remain in the possession of prisoners of war, likewise their metal helmets and gas masks and like articles issued for personal protection. Effects and articles used for their clothing or feeding shall likewise remain in their possession, even if such effects and articles belong to their regulation military equipment.

At no time should prisoners of war be without identity documents. The Detaining Power shall supply such documents to prisoners of war who possess none.

Badges of rank and nationality, decorations and articles having above all a personal or sentimental value may not be taken from prisoners of war.

Sums of money carried by prisoners of war may not be taken away from them except by order of an officer, and after the amount and particulars of the owner have been recorded in a special register and an itemized receipt has been given, legibly inscribed with the name, rank and unit of the person issuing the said receipt. Sums in the currency of the Detaining Power, or which are changed into such currency at the prisoner's request, shall be placed to the credit of the prisoner's account as provided in Article 64.

The Detaining Power may withdraw articles of value from prisoners of war only for reasons of security; when such articles are withdrawn, the procedure laid down for sums of money impounded shall apply.

Such objects, likewise the sums taken away in any currency other than that of the Detaining Power and the conversion of which has not been asked for by the owners, shall be kept in the custody of the Detaining Power and shall be returned in their initial shape to prisoners of war at the end of their captivity.

Article 19

Prisoners of war shall be evacuated, as soon as possible after their capture, to camps situated in an area far enough from the combat zone for them to be out of danger.

Only those prisoners of war who, owing to wounds or sickness, would run greater risks by being evacuated than by remaining where they are, may be temporarily kept back in a danger zone.

Prisoners of war shall not be unnecessarily exposed to danger while awaiting evacuation from a fighting zone.

Article 20

The evacuation of prisoners of war shall always be effected humanely and in conditions similar to those for the forces of the Detaining Power in their changes of station.

The Detaining Power shall supply prisoners of war who are being evacuated with sufficient food and potable water, and with the necessary clothing and medical attention. The Detaining Power shall take all suitable precautions to ensure their safety during evacuation, and shall establish as soon as possible a list of the prisoners of war who are evacuated.

If prisoners of war must, during evacuation, pass through transit camps, their stay in such camps shall be as brief as possible.

SECTION II: INTERNMENT OF PRISONERS OF WAR

Chapter I—General Observations

Article 21

The Detaining Power may subject prisoners of war to internment. It may impose on them the obligation of not leaving, beyond certain limits, the camp where they are interned, or if the said camp is fenced in, of not going outside its perimeter. Subject to the provisions of the present Convention relative to penal and disciplinary sanctions, prisoners of war may not be held in close confinement except where necessary to safeguard their health and then only during the continuation of the circumstances which make such confinement necessary.

Prisoners of war may be partially or wholly released on parole or promise, in so far as is allowed by the laws of the Power on which they depend. Such measures shall be taken particularly in cases where this may contribute to the improvement of their state of health. No prisoner of war shall be compelled to accept liberty on parole or promise.

Upon the outbreak of hostilities, each Party to the conflict shall notify the adverse Party of the laws and regulations allowing or forbidding its own nationals to accept liberty on parole or promise. Prisoners of war who are paroled or who have given their promise in conformity with the laws and regulations so notified, are bound on their personal honour scrupulously to fulfil, both towards the Power on which they depend and towards the Power which has captured them, the engagements of their paroles or promises. In such cases, the Power on which they depend is bound neither to require nor to accept from them any service incompatible with the parole or promise given.

Article 22

Prisoners of war may be interned only in premises located on land and affording every guarantee of hygiene and healthfulness. Except in particular cases which are justified by the interest of the prisoners themselves, they shall not be interned in penitentiaries.

Prisoners of war interned in unhealthy areas, or where the climate is injurious for them, shall be removed as soon as possible to a more favourable climate.

The Detaining Power shall assemble prisoners of war in camps or camp compounds according to their nationality, language and customs, provided that such prisoners shall not be separated from prisoners of war belonging to the armed forces with which they were serving at the time of their capture, except with their consent.

Article 23

No prisoner of war may at any time be sent to or detained in areas where he may be exposed to the fire of the combat zone, nor may his presence be used to render certain points or areas immune from military operations.

Prisoners of war shall have shelters against air bombardment and other hazards of war, to the same extent as the local civilian population. With the exception of those engaged in the protection of their quarters against the aforesaid hazards, they may enter such shelters as soon as possible after the giving of the alarm. Any other protective measure taken in favour of the population shall also apply to them.

Detaining Powers shall give the Powers concerned, through the intermediary of the Protecting Powers, all useful information regarding the geographical location of prisoner of war camps.

Whenever military considerations permit, prisoner of war camps shall be indicated in the day-time by the letters PW or PG, placed so as to be clearly visible from the air. The Powers concerned may, however, agree upon any other system of marking. Only prisoner of war camps shall be marked as such.

Article 24

Transit or screening camps of a permanent kind shall be fitted out under conditions similar to those described in the present Section, and the prisoners therein shall have the same treatment as in other camps.

Chapter II—Quarters, Food and Clothing of Prisoners of War

Article 25

Prisoners of war shall be quartered under conditions as favourable as those for the forces of the Detaining Power who are billeted in the same area. The said conditions shall make allowance for the habits and customs of the prisoners and shall in no case be prejudicial to their health.

The foregoing provisions shall apply in particular to the dormitories of prisoners of war as regards both total surface and minimum cubic space, and the general installations, bedding and blankets.

The premises provided for the use of prisoners of war individually or collectively, shall be entirely protected from dampness and adequately heated and lighted, in particular between dusk and lights out. All precautions must be taken against the danger of fire.

In any camps in which women prisoners of war, as well as men, are accommodated, separate dormitories shall be provided for them.

Article 26

The basic daily food rations shall be sufficient in quantity, quality and variety to keep prisoners of war in good health and to prevent loss of weight or the development of nutritional deficiencies. Account shall also be taken of the habitual diet of the prisoners.

The Detaining Power shall supply prisoners of war who work with such additional rations as are necessary for the labour on which they are employed.

Sufficient drinking water shall be supplied to prisoners of war. The use of tobacco shall be permitted.

Prisoners of war shall, as far as possible, be associated with the preparation of their meals; they may be employed for that purpose in the kitchens. Furthermore, they shall be given the means of preparing, themselves, the additional food in their possession.

Adequate premises shall be provided for messing.

Collective disciplinary measures affecting food are prohibited.

Article 27

Clothing, underwear and footwear shall be supplied to prisoners of war in sufficient quantities by the Detaining Power, which shall make allowance for the climate of the region where the prisoners are detained. Uniforms of enemy armed forces captured by the Detaining Power should, if suitable for the climate, be made available to clothe prisoners of war.

The regular replacement and repair of the above articles shall be assured by the Detaining Power. In addition, prisoners of war who work shall receive appropriate clothing, wherever the nature of the work demands.

Article 28

Canteens shall be installed in all camps, where prisoners of war may procure foodstuffs, soap and tobacco and ordinary articles in daily use. The tariff shall never be in excess of local market prices. The profits made by camp canteens shall be used for the benefit of the prisoners; a special fund shall be created for this purpose. The prisoners' representative shall have the right to collaborate in the management of the canteen and of this fund.

When a camp is closed down, the credit balance of the special fund shall be handed to an international welfare organization, to be employed for the benefit of prisoners of war of the same nationality as those who have contributed to the fund. In case of a general repatriation, such profits shall be kept by the Detaining Power, subject to any agreement to the contrary between the Powers concerned.

Chapter III—Hygiene and Medical Attention

Article 29

The Detaining Power shall be bound to take all sanitary measures necessary to ensure the cleanliness and healthfulness of camps and to prevent epidemics.

Prisoners of war shall have for their use, day and night, conveniences which conform to the rules of hygiene and are maintained in a constant state of cleanliness. In any camps in which women prisoners of war are accommodated, separate conveniences shall be provided for them.

Also, apart from the baths and showers with which the camps shall be furnished, prisoners of war shall be provided with sufficient water and soap for their personal toilet and for washing their personal laundry; the necessary installations, facilities and time shall be granted them for that purpose.

Article 30

Every camp shall have an adequate infirmary where prisoners of war may have the attention they require, as well as appropriate diet. Isolation wards shall, if necessary, be set aside for cases of contagious or mental disease.

Prisoners of war suffering from serious disease, or whose condition necessitates special treatment, a surgical operation or hospital care, must be admitted to any military or civilian medical unit where such treatment can be given, even if their repatriation is contemplated in the near future. Special facilities shall be afforded for the care to be given to the disabled, in particular to the blind, and for their rehabilitation, pending repatriation.

Prisoners of war shall have the attention, preferably, of medical personnel of the Power on which they depend and, if possible, of their nationality.

Prisoners of war may not be prevented from presenting themselves to the medical authorities for examination. The detaining authorities shall, upon request, issue to every prisoner who has undergone treatment, an official certificate indicating the nature of his illness or injury, and the duration and kind of treatment received. A duplicate of this certificate shall be forwarded to the Central Prisoners of War Agency.

The costs of treatment, including those of any apparatus necessary for the maintenance of prisoners of war in good health, particularly dentures and other artificial appliances, and spectacles, shall be borne by the Detaining Power.

Article 31

Medical inspections of prisoners of war shall be held at least once a month. They shall include the checking and the recording of the weight of each prisoner of war. Their purpose shall be, in particular, to supervise the general state of health, nutrition and cleanliness of prisoners and to detect contagious diseases, especially tuberculosis, malaria and venereal disease. For this purpose the most efficient methods available shall be employed, e.g. periodic mass miniature radiography for the early detection of tuberculosis.

Article 32

Prisoners of war who, though not attached to the medical service of their armed forces, are physicians, surgeons, dentists, nurses or medical orderlies, may be required by the Detaining Power to exercise their medical functions in the interests of prisoners of war dependent on the same Power. In that case they shall continue to be prisoners of war, but shall receive the same treatment as corresponding medical personnel retained by the Detaining Power. They shall be exempted from any other work under Article 49.

Chapter IV—Medical Personnel and Chaplains Retained to Assist Prisoners of War

Article 33

Members of the medical personnel and chaplains while retained by the Detaining Power with a view to assisting prisoners of war, shall not be considered as prisoners of war. They shall, however, receive as a minimum the benefits and protection of the present Convention, and shall also be granted all facilities necessary to provide for the medical care of, and religious ministration to, prisoners of war.

They shall continue to exercise their medical and spiritual functions for the benefit of prisoners of war, preferably those belonging to the armed forces upon which they depend, within the scope of the military laws and regulations of the Detaining Power and under the control of its competent services, in accordance with their professional etiquette. They shall also benefit by the following facilities in the exercise of their medical or spiritual functions:

(a) They shall be authorized to visit periodically prisoners of war situated in working detachments or in hospitals outside the camp. For this purpose, the Detaining Power shall place at their disposal the necessary means of transport.

(b) The senior medical officer in each camp shall be responsible to the camp military authorities for everything connected with the activities of retained medical personnel. For this purpose, Parties to the conflict shall agree at the outbreak of hostilities on the subject of the corresponding ranks of the medical personnel, including that of societies mentioned in Article 26 of the Geneva Convention for the Amelioration of the Condition of the Wounded and Sick in Armed Forces in the Field of August 12, 1949. This senior medical officer, as well as chaplains, shall have the right to deal with the competent authorities of the camp on all questions relating to their duties. Such authorities shall afford them all necessary facilities for correspondence relating to these questions.

(c) Although they shall be subject to the internal discipline of the camp in which they are retained, such personnel may not be compelled to carry out any work other than that concerned with their medical or religious duties.

During hostilities, the Parties to the conflict shall agree concerning the possible relief of retained personnel and shall settle the procedure to be followed.

None of the preceding provisions shall relieve the Detaining Power of its obligations with regard to prisoners of war from the medical or spiritual point of view.

Chapter V—Religious, Intellectual and Physical Activities

Article 34

Prisoners of war shall enjoy complete latitude in the exercise of their religious duties, including attendance at the service of their faith, on condition that they comply with the disciplinary routine prescribed by the military authorities.

Adequate premises shall be provided where religious services may be held.

Article 35

Chaplains who fall into the hands of the enemy Power and who remain or are retained with a view to assisting prisoners of war, shall be allowed to minister to them and to exercise freely their ministry amongst prisoners of war of the same religion, in accordance with their religious conscience. They shall be allocated among the various camps and labour detachments containing prisoners of war belonging to the same forces, speaking the same language or practising the same religion. They shall enjoy the necessary facilities, including the means of transport provided for in Article 33, for visiting the prisoners of war outside their camp. They shall be free to correspond, subject to censorship, on matters concerning their religious duties with the ecclesiastical authorities in the country of detention and with international religious organizations. Letters and cards which they may send for this purpose shall be in addition to the quota provided for in Article 71.

Article 36

Prisoners of war who are ministers of religion, without having officiated as chaplains to their own forces, shall be at liberty, whatever their denomination, to minister freely to the members of their community. For this purpose, they shall receive the same treatment as the chaplains retained by the Detaining Power. They shall not be obliged to do any other work.

Article 37

When prisoners of war have not the assistance of a retained chaplain or of a prisoner of war minister of their faith, a minister belonging to the prisoners' or a similar denomination, or in his absence a qualified layman, if such a course is feasible from a confessional point of view, shall be appointed, at the request of the prisoners concerned, to fill this office. This appointment, subject to the approval of the Detaining Power, shall take place with the agreement of the community of prisoners concerned and, wherever necessary, with the approval of the local religious authorities of the same faith. The person thus appointed shall comply with all regulations established by the Detaining Power in the interests of discipline and military security.

Article 38

While respecting the individual preferences of every prisoner, the Detaining Power shall encourage the practice of intellectual, educational, and recreational pursuits, sports and games amongst prisoners, and shall take the measures necessary to ensure the exercise thereof by providing them with adequate premises and necessary equipment.

Prisoners shall have opportunities for taking physical exercise, including sports and games, and for being out of doors. Sufficient open spaces shall be provided for this purpose in all camps.

Chapter VI—Discipline

Article 39

Every prisoner of war camp shall be put under the immediate authority of a responsible commissioned officer belonging to the regular armed forces of the Detaining Power. Such officer shall have in his possession a copy of the present Convention; he shall ensure that its provisions are known to the camp staff and the guard and shall be responsible, under the direction of his government, for its application.

Prisoners of war, with the exception of officers, must salute and show to all officers of the Detaining Power the external marks of respect provided for by the regulations applying in their own forces.

Officer prisoners of war are bound to salute only officers of a higher rank of the Detaining Power; they must, however, salute the camp commander regardless of his rank.

Article 40

The wearing of badges of rank and nationality, as well as of decorations, shall be permitted.

Article 41

In every camp the text of the present Convention and its Annexes and the contents of any special agreement provided for in Article 6, shall be posted, in the prisoners' own language, at places where all may read them. Copies shall be supplied, on request, to the prisoners who cannot have access to the copy which has been posted.

Regulations, orders, notices and publications of every kind relating to the conduct of prisoners of war shall be issued to them in a language which they understand. Such regulations, orders and publications shall be posted in the manner described above and copies shall be handed to the prisoners' representative. Every order and command addressed to prisoners of war individually must likewise be given in a language which they understand.

Article 42

The use of weapons against prisoners of war, especially against those who are escaping or attempting to escape, shall constitute an extreme measure, which shall always be preceded by warnings appropriate to the circumstances.

Chapter VII—Rank of Prisoners of War

Article 43

Upon the outbreak of hostilities, the Parties to the conflict shall communicate to one another the titles and ranks of all the persons mentioned in Article 4 of the present Convention, in order to ensure equality of treatment between prisoners of equivalent rank. Titles and ranks which are subsequently created shall form the subject of similar communications.

The Detaining Power shall recognize promotions in rank which have been accorded to prisoners of war and which have been duly notified by the Power on which these prisoners depend.

Article 44

Officers and prisoners of equivalent status shall be treated with the regard due to their rank and age.

In order to ensure service in officers' camps, other ranks of the same armed forces who, as far as possible, speak the same language, shall be assigned in sufficient numbers, account being taken of the rank of officers and prisoners of equivalent status. Such orderlies shall not be required to perform any other work.

Supervision of the mess by the officers themselves shall be facilitated in every way.

Article 45

Prisoners of war other than officers and prisoners of equivalent status shall be treated with the regard due to their rank and age.

Supervision of the mess by the prisoners themselves shall be facilitated in every way.

Chapter VIII—Transfer of Prisoners of War after Their Arrival in Camp

Article 46

The Detaining Power, when deciding upon the transfer of prisoners of war, shall take into account the interests of the prisoners themselves, more especially so as not to increase the difficulty of their repatriation.

The transfer of prisoners of war shall always be effected humanely and in conditions not less favourable than those under which the forces of the Detaining Power are transferred. Account shall always be taken of the climatic conditions to which the prisoners of war are accustomed and the conditions of transfer shall in no case be prejudicial to their health.

The Detaining Power shall supply prisoners of war during transfer with sufficient food and drinking water to keep them in good health, likewise with the necessary clothing, shelter and medical attention. The Detaining Power shall take adequate precautions especially in case of transport by sea or by air, to ensure their safety during transfer, and shall draw up a complete list of all transferred prisoners before their departure.

Article 47

Sick or wounded prisoners of war shall not be transferred as long as their recovery may be endangered by the journey, unless their safety imperatively demands it.

If the combat zone draws closer to a camp, the prisoners of war in the said camp shall not be transferred unless their transfer can be carried out in adequate conditions of safety, or if they are exposed to greater risks by remaining on the spot than by being transferred.

Article 48

In the event of transfer, prisoners of war shall be officially advised of their departure and of their new postal address. Such notifications shall be given in time for them to pack their luggage and inform their next of kin.

They shall be allowed to take with them their personal effects, and the correspondence and parcels which have arrived for them. The weight of such baggage may be limited, if the conditions of transfer so require, to what each prisoner can reasonably carry, which shall in no case be more than twenty-five kilograms per head.

Mail and parcels addressed to their former camp shall be forwarded to them without delay. The camp commander shall take, in agreement with the prisoners' representative, any measures needed to ensure the transport of the prisoners' community property and of the luggage they are unable to take with them in consequence of restrictions imposed by virtue of the second paragraph of this Article.

The costs of transfers shall be borne by the Detaining Power.

SECTION III: LABOUR OF PRISONERS OF WAR

Article 49

The Detaining Power may utilize the labour of prisoners of war who are physically fit, taking into account their age, sex, rank and physical aptitude, and with a view particularly to maintaining them in a good state of physical and mental health.

Non-commissioned officers who are prisoners of war shall only be required to do supervisory work. Those not so required may ask for other suitable work which shall, so far as possible, be found for them.

If officers or persons of equivalent status ask for suitable work, it shall be found for them, so far as possible, but they may in no circumstances be compelled to work.

Article 50

Besides work connected with camp administration, installation or maintenance, prisoners of war may be compelled to do only such work as is included in the following classes:

(a) Agriculture;

(b) Industries connected with the production or the extraction of raw materials, and manufacturing industries, with the exception of metallurgical, machinery and chemical industries; public works and building operations which have no military character or purpose;

(c) Transport and handling of stores which are not military in character or purpose;

(d) Commercial business, and arts and crafts;

(e) Domestic service;

(f) Public utility services having no military character or purpose.

Should the above provisions be infringed, prisoners of war shall be allowed to exercise their right of complaint, in conformity with Article 78.

Article 51

Prisoners of war must be granted suitable working conditions, especially as regards accommodation, food, clothing and equipment; such conditions shall not be inferior to those enjoyed by nationals of the Detaining Power employed in similar work; account shall also be taken of climatic conditions.

The Detaining Power, in utilizing the labour of prisoners of war, shall ensure that in areas in which prisoners are employed, the national legislation concerning the protection of labour, and, more particularly, the regulations for the safety of workers, are duly applied.

Prisoners of war shall receive training and be provided with the means of protection suitable to the work they will have to do and similar to those accorded to the nationals of the Detaining Power. Subject to the provisions of Article 52, prisoners may be submitted to the normal risks run by these civilian workers.

Conditions of labour shall in no case be rendered more arduous by disciplinary measures.

Article 52

Unless he be a volunteer, no prisoner of war may be employed on labour which is of an unhealthy or dangerous nature.

No prisoner of war shall be assigned to labour which would be looked upon as humiliating for a member of the Detaining Power's own forces.

The removal of mines or similar devices shall be considered as dangerous labour.

Article 53

The duration of the daily labour of prisoners of war, including the time of the journey to and fro, shall not be excessive, and must in no case exceed that permitted for civilian workers in the district, who are nationals of the Detaining Power and employed on the same work.

Prisoners of war must be allowed, in the middle of the day's work, a rest of not less than one hour. This rest will be the same as that to which workers of the Detaining Power are entitled, if the latter is of longer duration. They shall be allowed in addition a rest of twenty-four consecutive hours every week, preferably on Sunday or the day of rest in their country of origin. Furthermore, every prisoner who has worked for one year shall be granted a rest of eight consecutive days, during which his working pay shall be paid him.

If methods of labour such as piece-work are employed, the length of the working period shall not be rendered excessive thereby.

Article 54

The working pay due to prisoners of war shall be fixed in accordance with the provisions of Article 62 of the present Convention.

Prisoners of war who sustain accidents in connection with work, or who contract a disease in the course, or in consequence of their work, shall receive all the care their condition may require. The Detaining Power shall furthermore deliver to such prisoners of war a medical certificate enabling them to submit their claims to the Power on which they depend, and shall send a duplicate to the Central Prisoners of War Agency provided for in Article 123.

Article 55

The fitness of prisoners of war for work shall be periodically verified by medical examinations at least once a month. The examinations shall have particular regard to the nature of the work which prisoners of war are required to do.

If any prisoner of war considers himself incapable of working, he shall be permitted to appear before the medical authorities of his camp. Physicians or surgeons may recommend that the prisoners who are, in their opinion, unfit for work, be exempted therefrom.

Article 56

The organization and administration of labour detachments shall be similar to those of prisoner of war camps.

Every labour detachment shall remain under the control of and administratively part of a prisoner of war camp. The military authorities and the commander of the said camp shall be responsible, under the direction of their government, for the observance of the provisions of the present Convention in labour detachments.

The camp commander shall keep an up-to-date record of the labour detachments dependent on his camp, and shall communicate it to the delegates of the Protecting Power, of the International Committee of the Red Cross, or of other agencies giving relief to prisoners of war, who may visit the camp.

Article 57

The treatment of prisoners of war who work for private persons, even if the latter are responsible for guarding and protecting them, shall not be inferior to that which is provided for by the present Convention. The Detaining Power, the military authorities and the commander of the camp to which such prisoners belong shall be entirely responsible for the maintenance, care, treatment, and payment of the working pay of such prisoners of war.

Such prisoners of war shall have the right to remain in communication with the prisoners' representatives in the camps on which they depend.

SECTION IV: FINANCIAL RESOURCES OF PRISONERS OF WAR

Article 58

Upon the outbreak of hostilities, and pending an arrangement on this matter with the Protecting Power, the Detaining Power may determine the maximum amount of money in cash or in any similar form, that prisoners may have in their possession. Any amount in excess, which was properly in their possession and which has been taken or withheld from them, shall be placed to their account, together with any monies deposited by them, and shall not be converted into any other currency without their consent.

If prisoners of war are permitted to purchase services or commodities outside the camp against payment in cash, such payments shall be made by the prisoner himself or by the camp administration who will charge them to the accounts of the prisoners concerned. The Detaining Power will establish the necessary rules in this respect.

Article 59

Cash which was taken from prisoners of war, in accordance with Article 18, at the time of their capture, and which is in the currency of the Detaining Power, shall be placed to their separate accounts, in accordance with the provisions of Article 64 of the present Section.

The amounts, in the currency of the Detaining Power, due to the conversion of sums in other currencies that are taken from the prisoners of war at the same time, shall also be credited to their separate accounts.

Article 60

The Detaining Power shall grant all prisoners of war a monthly advance of pay, the amount of which shall be fixed by conversion, into the currency of the said Power, of the following amounts:

Category I: Prisoners ranking below sergeant: eight Swiss francs.

Category II: Sergeants and other non-commissioned officers, or prisoners of equivalent rank: twelve Swiss francs.

Category III: Warrant officers and commissioned officers below the rank of major or prisoners of equivalent rank: fifty Swiss francs.

Category IV: Majors, lieutenant-colonels, colonels or prisoners of equivalent rank: sixty Swiss francs.

Category V: General officers or prisoners of equivalent rank: seventy-five Swiss francs.

However, the Parties to the conflict concerned may by special agreement modify the amount of advances of pay due to prisoners of the preceding categories.

Furthermore, if the amounts indicated in the first paragraph above would be unduly high compared with the pay of the Detaining Power's armed forces or would, for any reason, seriously embarrass the Detaining Power, then, pending the conclusion of a special agreement with the Power on which the prisoners depend to vary the amounts indicated above, the Detaining Power:

(a) Shall continue to credit the accounts of the prisoners with the amounts indicated in the first paragraph above;

(b) May temporarily limit the amount made available from these advances of pay to prisoners of war for their own use, to sums which are reasonable, but which, for Category I, shall never be inferior to the amount that the Detaining Power gives to the members of its own armed forces.

The reasons for any limitations will be given without delay to the Protecting Power.

Article 61

The Detaining Power shall accept for distribution as supplementary pay to prisoners of war sums which the Power on which the prisoners depend may forward to them, on condition that the sums to be paid shall be the same for each prisoner of the same category, shall be payable to all prisoners of that category depending on that Power, and shall be placed in their separate accounts, at the earliest opportunity, in accordance with the provisions of Article 64. Such supplementary pay shall not relieve the Detaining Power of any obligation under this Convention.

Article 62

Prisoners of war shall be paid a fair working rate of pay by the detaining authorities direct. The rate shall be fixed by the said authorities, but shall at no time be less than one-fourth of one Swiss franc for a full working day. The Detaining Power shall inform prisoners of war, as well as the Power on which they depend, through the intermediary of the Protecting Power, of the rate of daily working pay that it has fixed.

Working pay shall likewise be paid by the detaining authorities to prisoners of war permanently detailed to duties or to a skilled or semi-skilled occupation in connection with the administration, installation or maintenance of camps, and to the prisoners who are required to carry out spiritual or medical duties on behalf of their comrades.

The working pay of the prisoners' representative, of his advisers, if any, and of his assistants, shall be paid out of the fund maintained by canteen profits. The scale of this working pay shall be fixed by the prisoners' representative and approved by the camp commander. If there is no such fund, the detaining authorities shall pay these prisoners a fair working rate of pay.

Article 63

Prisoners of war shall be permitted to receive remittances of money addressed to them individually or collectively.

Every prisoner of war shall have at his disposal the credit balance of his account as provided for in the following Article, within the limits fixed by the Detaining Power, which shall make such payments as are requested. Subject to financial or monetary restrictions which the Detaining Power regards as essential, prisoners of war may also have payments made abroad. In this case payments addressed by prisoners of war to dependants shall be given priority.

In any event, and subject to the consent of the Power on which they depend, prisoners may have payments made in their own country, as follows: the Detaining Power shall send to the aforesaid Power through the Protecting Power a notification giving all the necessary particulars concerning the prisoners of war, the beneficiaries of the payments, and the amount of the sums to be paid, expressed in the Detaining Power's currency. The said notification shall be signed by the prisoners and countersigned by the camp commander. The Detaining Power shall debit the prisoners' account by a corresponding amount; the sums thus debited shall be placed by it to the credit of the Power on which the prisoners depend.

To apply the foregoing provisions, the Detaining Power may usefully consult the Model Regulations in Annex V of the present Convention.

Article 64

The Detaining Power shall hold an account for each prisoner of war, showing at least the following:

1. The amounts due to the prisoner or received by him as advances of pay, as working pay or derived from any other source; the sums in the currency of the Detaining Power which were taken from him; the sums taken from him and converted at his request into the currency of the said Power.

2. The payments made to the prisoner in cash, or in any other similar form; the payments made on his behalf and at his request; the sums transferred under Article 63, third paragraph.

Article 65

Every item entered in the account of a prisoner of war shall be countersigned or initialled by him, or by the prisoners' representative acting on his behalf.

Prisoners of war shall at all times be afforded reasonable facilities for consulting and obtaining copies of their accounts, which may likewise be inspected by the representatives of the Protecting Powers at the time of visits to the camp.

When prisoners of war are transferred from one camp to another, their personal accounts will follow them. In case of transfer from one Detaining Power to another, the monies which are their property and are not in the currency of the Detaining Power will follow them. They shall be given certificates for any other monies standing to the credit of their accounts.

The Parties to the conflict concerned may agree to notify to each other at specific intervals through the Protecting Power, the amount of the accounts of the prisoners of war.

Article 66

On the termination of captivity, through the release of a prisoner of war or his repatriation, the Detaining Power shall give him a statement, signed by an authorized officer of that Power, showing the credit balance then due to him. The Detaining Power shall also send through the Protecting Power to the government upon which the prisoner of war depends, lists giving all appropriate particulars of all prisoners of war whose captivity has been terminated by repatriation, release, escape, death or any other means, and showing the amount of their credit balances. Such lists shall be certified on each sheet by an authorized representative of the Detaining Power.

Any of the above provisions of this Article may be varied by mutual agreement between any two Parties to the conflict.

The Power on which the prisoner of war depends shall be responsible for settling with him any credit balance due to him from the Detaining Power on the termination of his captivity.

Article 67

Advances of pay, issued to prisoners of war in conformity with Article 60, shall be considered as made on behalf of the Power on which they depend. Such advances of pay, as well as all payments made by the said Power under Article 63, third paragraph, and Article 68, shall form the subject of arrangements between the Powers concerned, at the close of hostilities.

Article 68

Any claim by a prisoner of war for compensation in respect of any injury or other disability arising out of work shall be referred to the Power on which he depends, through the Protecting Power. In accordance with Article 54, the Detaining Power will, in all cases, provide the prisoner of war concerned with a statement showing the nature of the injury or disability, the circumstances in which it arose and particulars of medical or hospital treatment given for it. This statement will be signed by a responsible officer of the Detaining Power and the medical particulars certified by a medical officer.

Any claim by a prisoner of war for compensation in respect of personal effects, monies or valuables impounded by the Detaining Power under Article 18 and not forthcoming on his repatriation, or in respect of loss alleged to be due to the fault of the Detaining Power or any of its servants, shall likewise be referred to the Power on which he depends. Nevertheless, any such personal effects required for use by the prisoners of war whilst in captivity shall be replaced at the expense of the Detaining Power. The Detaining Power will, in all cases, provide the prisoner of war with a statement, signed by a responsible officer, showing all available information regarding the reasons why such effects, monies or valuables have not been restored to him. A copy of this statement will be forwarded to the Power on which he depends through the Central Prisoners of War Agency provided for in Article 123.

SECTION V: RELATIONS OF PRISONERS OF WAR WITH THE EXTERIOR

Article 69

Immediately upon prisoners of war falling into its power, the Detaining Power shall inform them and the Powers on which they depend, through the Protecting Power, of the measures taken to carry out the provisions of the present Section. They shall likewise inform the parties concerned of any subsequent modifications of such measures.

Article 70

Immediately upon capture, or not more than one week after arrival at a camp, even if it is a transit camp, likewise in case of sickness or transfer to hospital or another camp, every prisoner of war shall be enabled to write direct to his family, on the one hand, and to the Central Prisoners of War Agency provided for in Article 123, on the other hand, a card similar, if possible, to the model annexed to the present Convention, informing his relatives of his capture, address and state of health. The said cards shall be forwarded as rapidly as possible and may not be delayed in any manner.

Article 71

Prisoners of war shall be allowed to send and receive letters and cards. If the Detaining Power deems it necessary to limit the number of letters and cards sent by each prisoner of war, the said number shall not be less than two letters and four cards monthly, exclusive of the capture cards provided for in Article 70, and conforming as closely as possible to the models annexed to the present Convention. Further limitations may be imposed only if the Protecting Power is satisfied that it would be in the interests of the prisoners of war concerned to do so owing to difficulties of translation caused by the Detaining Power's inability to find sufficient qualified linguists to carry out the necessary censorship. If limitations must be placed on the correspondence addressed to prisoners of war, they may be ordered only by the Power on which the prisoners depend, possibly at the request of the Detaining Power. Such letters and cards must be conveyed by the most rapid method at the disposal of the Detaining Power; they may not be delayed or retained for disciplinary reasons.

Prisoners of war who have been without news for a long period, or who are unable to receive news from their next of kin or to give them news by the ordinary postal route, as well as those who are at a great distance from their homes, shall be permitted to send telegrams, the fees being charged against the prisoners of war's accounts with the Detaining Power or paid in the currency at their disposal. They shall likewise benefit by this measure in cases of urgency.

As a general rule, the correspondence of prisoners of war shall be written in their native language. The Parties to the conflict may allow correspondence in other languages.

Sacks containing prisoner of war mail must be securely sealed and labelled so as clearly to indicate their contents, and must be addressed to offices of destination.

Article 72

Prisoners of war shall be allowed to receive by post or by any other means individual parcels or collective shipments containing, in particular, foodstuffs, clothing, medical supplies and articles of a religious, educational or recreational character which may meet their needs, including books, devotional articles, scientific equipment, examination papers, musical instruments, sports outfits and materials allowing prisoners of war to pursue their studies or their cultural activities.

Such shipments shall in no way free the Detaining Power from the obligations imposed upon it by virtue of the present Convention.

The only limits which may be placed on these shipments shall be those proposed by the Protecting Power in the interest of the prisoners themselves, or by the International Committee of the Red Cross or any other organization giving assistance to the prisoners, in respect of their own shipments only, on account of exceptional strain on transport or communications.

The conditions for the sending of individual parcels and collective relief shall, if necessary, be the subject of special agreements between the Powers concerned, which may in no case delay the receipt by the prisoners of relief supplies. Books may not be included in parcels of clothing and foodstuffs. Medical supplies shall, as a rule, be sent in collective parcels.

Article 73

In the absence of special agreements between the Powers concerned on the conditions for the receipt and distribution of collective relief shipments, the rules and regulations concerning collective shipments, which are annexed to the present Convention, shall be applied.

The special agreements referred to above shall in no case restrict the right of prisoners' representatives to take possession of collective relief shipments intended for prisoners of war, to proceed to their distribution or to dispose of them in the interest of the prisoners.

Nor shall such agreements restrict the right of representatives of the Protecting Power, the International Committee of the Red Cross or any other organization giving assistance to prisoners of war and responsible for the forwarding of collective shipments, to supervise their distribution to the recipients.

Article 74

All relief shipments for prisoners of war shall be exempt from import, customs and other dues.

Correspondence, relief shipments and authorized remittances of money addressed to prisoners of war or despatched by them through the post office, either direct or through the Information Bureaux provided for in Article 122 and the Central Prisoners of War Agency provided for in Article 123, shall be exempt from any postal dues, both in the countries of origin and destination, and in intermediate countries.

If relief shipments intended for prisoners of war cannot be sent through the post office by reason of weight or for any other cause, the cost of transportation shall be borne by the Detaining Power in all the territories under its control. The other Powers party to the Convention shall bear the cost of transport in their respective territories.

In the absence of special agreements between the Parties concerned, the costs connected with transport of such shipments, other than costs covered by the above exemption, shall be charged to the senders.

The High Contracting Parties shall endeavour to reduce, so far as possible, the rates charged for telegrams sent by prisoners of war, or addressed to them.

Article 75

Should military operations prevent the Powers concerned from fulfilling their obligation to assure the transport of the shipments referred to in Articles 70, 71, 72 and 77, the Protecting Powers concerned, the International Committee of the Red Cross or any other organization duly approved by the Parties to the conflict may undertake to ensure the conveyance of such shipments by suitable means (railway wagons, motor vehicles, vessels or aircraft, etc.). For this purpose, the High Contracting Parties shall endeavour to supply them with such transport and to allow its circulation, especially by granting the necessary safe-conducts.

Such transport may also be used to convey:

(a) Correspondence, lists and reports exchanged between the Central Information Agency referred to in Article 123 and the National Bureaux referred to in Article 122;

(b) Correspondence and reports relating to prisoners of war which the Protecting Powers, the International Committee of the Red Cross or any other body assisting the prisoners, exchange either with their own delegates or with the Parties to the conflict.

These provisions in no way detract from the right of any Party to the conflict to arrange other means of transport, if it should so prefer, nor preclude the granting of safe-conducts, under mutually agreed conditions, to such means of transport.

In the absence of special agreements, the costs occasioned by the use of such means of transport shall be borne proportionally by the Parties to the conflict whose nationals are benefited thereby.

Article 76

The censoring of correspondence addressed to prisoners of war or despatched by them shall be done as quickly as possible. Mail shall be censored only by the despatching State and the receiving State, and once only by each.

The examination of consignments intended for prisoners of war shall not be carried out under conditions that will expose the goods contained in them to deterioration; except in the case of written or printed matter, it shall be done in the presence of the addressee, or of a fellow-prisoner duly delegated by him. The delivery to prisoners of individual or collective consignments shall not be delayed under the pretext of difficulties of censorship.

Any prohibition of correspondence ordered by Parties to the conflict, either for military or political reasons, shall be only temporary and its duration shall be as short as possible.

Article 77

The Detaining Powers shall provide all facilities for the transmission, through the Protecting Power or the Central Prisoners of War Agency provided for in Article 123, of instruments, papers or documents intended for prisoners of war or despatched by them, especially powers of attorney and wills.

In all cases they shall facilitate the preparation and execution of such documents on behalf of prisoners of war; in particular, they shall allow them to consult a lawyer and shall take what measures are necessary for the authentication of their signatures.

SECTION VI: RELATIONS BETWEEN PRISONERS OF WAR AND THE AUTHORITIES

Chapter I—Complaints of Prisoners of War Respecting the Conditions of Captivity

Article 78

Prisoners of war shall have the right to make known to the military authorities in whose power they are, their requests regarding the conditions of captivity to which they are subjected.

They shall also have the unrestricted right to apply to the representatives of the Protecting Powers either through their prisoners' representative or, if they consider it necessary, direct, in order to draw their attention to any points on which they may have complaints to make regarding their conditions of captivity.

These requests and complaints shall not be limited nor considered to be a part of the correspondence quota referred to in Article 71. They must be transmitted immediately. Even if they are recognized to be unfounded, they may not give rise to any punishment.

Prisoners' representatives may send periodic reports on the situation in the camps and the needs of the prisoners of war to the representatives of the Protecting Powers.

Chapter II—Prisoner of War Representatives

Article 79

In all places where there are prisoners of war, except in those where there are officers, the prisoners shall freely elect by secret ballot, every six months, and also in case of vacancies, prisoners' representatives entrusted with representing them before the military authorities, the Protecting Powers, the International Committee of the Red Cross and any other organization which may assist them. These prisoners' representatives shall be eligible for re-election.

In camps for officers and persons of equivalent status or in mixed camps, the senior officer among the prisoners of war shall be recognized as the camp prisoners' representative. In camps for officers, he shall be assisted by one or more advisers chosen by the officers; in mixed camps, his assistants shall be chosen from among the prisoners of war who are not officers and shall be elected by them.

Officer prisoners of war of the same nationality shall be stationed in labour camps for prisoners of war, for the purpose of carrying out the camp administration duties for which the prisoners of war are responsible. These officers may be elected as prisoners' representatives under the first paragraph of this Article. In such a case the assistants to the prisoners' representatives shall be chosen from among those prisoners of war who are not officers.

Every representative elected must be approved by the Detaining Power before he has the right to commence his duties. Where the Detaining Power refuses to approve a prisoner of war elected by his fellow prisoners of war, it must inform the Protecting Power of the reason for such refusal.

In all cases the prisoners' representative must have the same nationality, language and customs as the prisoners of war whom he represents. Thus, prisoners of war distributed in different sections of a camp, according to their nationality, language or customs, shall have for each section their own prisoners' representative, in accordance with the foregoing paragraphs.

Article 80

Prisoners' representatives shall further the physical, spiritual and intellectual well-being of prisoners of war.

In particular, where the prisoners decide to organize amongst themselves a system of mutual assistance, this organization will be within the province of the prisoners' representative, in addition to the special duties entrusted to him by other provisions of the present Convention.

Prisoners' representatives shall not be held responsible, simply by reason of their duties, for any offences committed by prisoners of war.

Article 81

Prisoners' representatives shall not be required to perform any other work, if the accomplishment of their duties is thereby made more difficult.

Prisoners' representatives may appoint from amongst the prisoners such assistants as they may require. All material facilities shall be granted them, particularly a certain freedom of movement necessary for the accomplishment of their duties (inspection of labour detachments, receipt of supplies, etc.).

Prisoners' representatives shall be permitted to visit premises where prisoners of war are detained, and every prisoner of war shall have the right to consult freely his prisoners' representative.

All facilities shall likewise be accorded to the prisoners' representatives for communication by post and telegraph with the detaining authorities, the Protecting Powers, the International Committee of the Red Cross and their delegates, the Mixed Medical Commissions and with the bodies which give assistance to prisoners of war. Prisoners' representatives of labour detachments shall enjoy the same facilities for communication with the prisoners' representatives of the principal camp. Such communications shall not be restricted, nor considered as forming a part of the quota mentioned in Article 71.

Prisoners' representatives who are transferred shall be allowed a reasonable time to acquaint their successors with current affairs.

In case of dismissal, the reasons therefore shall be communicated to the Protecting Power.

Chapter III—Penal and Disciplinary Sanctions

I. General provisions

Article 82

A prisoner of war shall be subject to the laws, regulations and orders in force in the armed forces of the Detaining Power; the Detaining Power shall be justified in taking judicial or disciplinary measures in respect of any offence committed by a prisoner of war against such laws, regulations or orders. However, no proceedings or punishments contrary to the provisions of this Chapter shall be allowed.

If any law, regulation or order of the Detaining Power shall declare acts committed by a prisoner of war to be punishable, whereas the same acts would not be punishable if committed by a member of the forces of the Detaining Power, such acts shall entail disciplinary punishments only.

Article 83

In deciding whether proceedings in respect of an offence alleged to have been committed by a prisoner of war shall be judicial or disciplinary, the Detaining Power shall ensure that the competent authorities exercise the greatest leniency and adopt, wherever possible, disciplinary rather than judicial measures.

Article 84

A prisoner of war shall be tried only by a military court, unless the existing laws of the Detaining Power expressly permit the civil courts to try a member of the armed forces of the Detaining Power in respect of the particular offence alleged to have been committed by the prisoner of war.

In no circumstances whatever shall a prisoner of war be tried by a court of any kind which does not offer the essential guarantees of independence and impartiality as generally recognized, and, in particular, the procedure of which does not afford the accused the rights and means of defence provided for in Article 105.

Article 85

Prisoners of war prosecuted under the laws of the Detaining Power for acts committed prior to capture shall retain, even if convicted, the benefits of the present Convention.

Article 86

No prisoner of war may be punished more than once for the same act, or on the same charge.

Article 87

Prisoners of war may not be sentenced by the military authorities and courts of the Detaining Power to any penalties except those provided for in respect of members of the armed forces of the said Power who have committed the same acts.

When fixing the penalty, the courts or authorities of the Detaining Power shall take into consideration, to the widest extent possible, the fact that the accused, not being a national of the Detaining Power, is not bound to it by any duty of allegiance, and that he is in its power as the result of circumstances independent of his own will. The said courts or authorities shall be at liberty to reduce the penalty provided for the violation of which the prisoner of war is accused, and shall therefore not be bound to apply the minimum penalty prescribed.

Collective punishment for individual acts, corporal punishments, imprisonment in premises without daylight and, in general, any form of torture or cruelty, are forbidden.

No prisoner of war may be deprived of his rank by the Detaining Power, or prevented from wearing his badges.

Article 88

Officers, non-commissioned officers and men who are prisoners of war undergoing a disciplinary or judicial punishment, shall not be subjected to more severe treatment than that applied in respect of the same punishment to members of the armed forces of the Detaining Power of equivalent rank.

A woman prisoner of war shall not be awarded or sentenced to a punishment more severe, or treated whilst undergoing punishment more severely, than a woman member of the armed forces of the Detaining Power dealt with for a similar offence.

In no case may a woman prisoner of war be awarded or sentenced to a punishment more severe, or treated whilst undergoing punishment more severely, than a male member of the armed forces of the Detaining Power dealt with for a similar offence.

Prisoners of war who have served disciplinary or judicial sentences may not be treated differently from other prisoners of war.

II. Disciplinary sanctions

Article 89

The disciplinary punishments applicable to prisoners of war are the following:

1. A fine which shall not exceed 50 per cent of the advances of pay and working pay which the prisoner of war would otherwise receive under the provisions of Articles 60 and 62 during a period of not more than thirty days.

2. Discontinuance of privileges granted over and above the treatment provided for by the present Convention.

3. Fatigue duties not exceeding two hours daily.

4. Confinement.

The punishment referred to under (3) shall not be applied to officers.

In no case shall disciplinary punishments be inhuman, brutal or dangerous to the health of prisoners of war.

Article 90

The duration of any single punishment shall in no case exceed thirty days. Any period of confinement awaiting the hearing of a disciplinary offence or the award of disciplinary punishment shall be deducted from an award pronounced against a prisoner of war.

The maximum of thirty days provided above may not be exceeded, even if the prisoner of war is answerable for several acts at the same time when he is awarded punishment, whether such acts are related or not.

The period between the pronouncing of an award of disciplinary punishment and its execution shall not exceed one month.

When a prisoner of war is awarded a further disciplinary punishment, a period of at least three days shall elapse between the execution of any two of the punishments, if the duration of one of these is ten days or more.

Article 91

The escape of a prisoner of war shall be deemed to have succeeded when:

1. He has joined the armed forces of the Power on which he depends, or those of an allied Power;

2. He has left the territory under the control of the Detaining Power, or of an ally of the said Power;

3. He has joined a ship flying the flag of the Power on which he depends, or of an allied Power, in the territorial waters of the Detaining Power, the said ship not being under the control of the last-named Power.

Prisoners of war who have made good their escape in the sense of this Article and who are recaptured, shall not be liable to any punishment in respect of their previous escape.

Article 92

A prisoner of war who attempts to escape and is recaptured before having made good his escape in the sense of Article 91 shall be liable only to a disciplinary punishment in respect of this act, even if it is a repeated offence.

A prisoner of war who is recaptured shall be handed over without delay to the competent military authority.

Article 88, fourth paragraph, notwithstanding, prisoners of war punished as a result of an unsuccessful escape may be subjected to special surveillance. Such surveillance must not affect the state of their health, must be undergone in a prisoner of war camp, and must not entail the suppression of any of the safeguards granted them by the present Convention.

Article 93

Escape or attempt to escape, even if it is a repeated offence, shall not be deemed an aggravating circumstance if the prisoner of war is subjected to trial by judicial proceedings in respect of an offence committed during his escape or attempt to escape.

In conformity with the principle stated in Article 83, offences committed by prisoners of war with the sole intention of facilitating their escape and which do not entail any violence against life or limb, such as offences against public property, theft without intention of self-enrichment, the drawing up or use of false papers, the wearing of civilian clothing, shall occasion disciplinary punishment only.

Prisoners of war who aid or abet an escape or an attempt to escape shall be liable on this count to disciplinary punishment only.

Article 94

If an escaped prisoner of war is recaptured, the Power on which he depends shall be notified thereof in the manner defined in Article 122, provided notification of his escape has been made.

Article 95

A prisoner of war accused of an offence against discipline shall not be kept in confinement pending the hearing unless a member of the armed forces of the Detaining Power would be so kept if he were accused of a similar offence, or if it is essential in the interests of camp order and discipline.

Any period spent by a prisoner of war in confinement awaiting the disposal of an offence against discipline shall be reduced to an absolute minimum and shall not exceed fourteen days.

The provisions of Articles 97 and 98 of this Chapter shall apply to prisoners of war who are in confinement awaiting the disposal of offences against discipline.

Article 96

Acts which constitute offences against discipline shall be investigated immediately.

Without prejudice to the competence of courts and superior military authorities, disciplinary punishment may be ordered only by an officer having disciplinary powers in his capacity as camp commander, or by a responsible officer who replaces him or to whom he has delegated his disciplinary powers.

In no case may such powers be delegated to a prisoner of war or be exercised by a prisoner of war.

Before any disciplinary award is pronounced, the accused shall be given precise information regarding the offences of which he is accused, and given an opportunity of explaining his conduct and of defending himself. He shall be permitted, in particular, to call witnesses and to have recourse, if necessary, to the services of a qualified interpreter. The decision shall be announced to the accused prisoner of war and to the prisoners' representative.

A record of disciplinary punishments shall be maintained by the camp commander and shall be open to inspection by representatives of the Protecting Power.

Article 97

Prisoners of war shall not in any case be transferred to penitentiary establishments (prisons, penitentiaries, convict prisons, etc.) to undergo disciplinary punishment therein.

All premises in which disciplinary punishments are undergone shall conform to the sanitary requirements set forth in Article 25. A prisoner of war undergoing punishment shall be enabled to keep himself in a state of cleanliness, in conformity with Article 29.

Officers and persons of equivalent status shall not be lodged in the same quarters as non-commissioned officers or men.

Women prisoners of war undergoing disciplinary punishment shall be confined in separate quarters from male prisoners of war and shall be under the immediate supervision of women

Article 98

A prisoner of war undergoing confinement as a disciplinary punishment, shall continue to enjoy the benefits of the provisions of this Convention except in so far as these are necessarily rendered inapplicable by the mere fact that he is confined. In no case may he be deprived of the benefits of the provisions of Articles 78 and 126.

A prisoner of war awarded disciplinary punishment may not be deprived of the prerogatives attached to his rank.

Prisoners of war awarded disciplinary punishment shall be allowed to exercise and to stay in the open air at least two hours daily.

They shall be allowed, on their request, to be present at the daily medical inspections. They shall receive the attention which their state of health requires and, if necessary, shall be removed to the camp infirmary or to a hospital.

They shall have permission to read and write, likewise to send and receive letters. Parcels and remittances of money, however, may be withheld from them until the completion of the punishment; they shall meanwhile be entrusted to the prisoners' representative, who will hand over to the infirmary the perishable goods contained in such parcels.

III. Judicial proceedings

Article 99

No prisoner of war may be tried or sentenced for an act which is not forbidden by the law of the Detaining Power or by international law, in force at the time the said act was committed.

No moral or physical coercion may be exerted on a prisoner of war in order to induce him to admit himself guilty of the act of which he is accused.

No prisoner of war may be convicted without having had an opportunity to present his defence and the assistance of a qualified advocate or counsel.

Article 100

Prisoners of war and the Protecting Powers shall be informed as soon as possible of the offences which are punishable by the death sentence under the laws of the Detaining Power.

Other offences shall not thereafter be made punishable by the death penalty without the concurrence of the Power upon which the prisoners of war depend.

The death sentence cannot be pronounced on a prisoner of war unless the attention of the court has, in accordance with Article 87, second paragraph, been particularly called to the fact that since the accused is not a national of the Detaining Power, he is not bound to it by any duty of allegiance, and that he is in its power as the result of circumstances independent of his own will.

Article 101

If the death penalty is pronounced on a prisoner of war, the sentence shall not be executed before the expiration of a period of at least six months from the date when the Protecting Power receives, at an indicated address, the detailed communication provided for in Article 107.

Article 102

A prisoner of war can be validly sentenced only if the sentence has been pronounced by the same courts according to the same procedure as in the case of members of the armed forces of the Detaining Power, and if, furthermore, the provisions of the present Chapter have been observed.

Article 103

Judicial investigations relating to a prisoner of war shall be conducted as rapidly as circumstances permit and so that his trial shall take place as soon as possible. A prisoner of war shall not be confined while awaiting trial unless a member of the armed forces of the Detaining Power would be so confined if he were accused of a similar offence, or if it is essential to do so in the interests of national security. In no circumstances shall this confinement exceed three months.

Any period spent by a prisoner of war in confinement awaiting trial shall be deducted from any sentence of imprisonment passed upon him and taken into account in fixing any penalty.

The provisions of Articles 97 and 98 of this Chapter shall apply to a prisoner of war whilst in confinement awaiting trial.

Article 104

In any case in which the Detaining Power has decided to institute judicial proceedings against a prisoner of war, it shall notify the Protecting Power as soon as possible and at least three weeks before the opening of the trial. This period of three weeks shall run as from the day on which such notification reaches the Protecting Power at the address previously indicated by the latter to the Detaining Power.

The said notification shall contain the following information:

1. Surname and first names of the prisoner of war, his rank, his army, regimental, personal or serial number, his date of birth, and his profession or trade, if any;

2. Place of internment or confinement;

3. Specification of the charge or charges on which the prisoner of war is to be arraigned, giving the legal provisions applicable;

4. Designation of the court which will try the case, likewise the date and place fixed for the opening of the trial.

The same communication shall be made by the Detaining Power to the prisoners' representative.

If no evidence is submitted, at the opening of a trial, that the notification referred to above was received by the Protecting Power, by the prisoner of war and by the prisoners' representative concerned, at least three weeks before the opening of the trial, then the latter cannot take place and must be adjourned.

Article 105

The prisoner of war shall be entitled to assistance by one of his prisoner comrades, to defence by a qualified advocate or counsel of his own choice, to the calling of witnesses and, if he deems necessary, to the services of a competent interpreter. He shall be advised of these rights by the Detaining Power in due time before the trial.

Failing a choice by the prisoner of war, the Protecting Power shall find him an advocate or counsel, and shall have at least one week at its disposal for the purpose. The Detaining Power shall deliver to the said Power, on request, a list of persons qualified to present the defence. Failing a choice of an advocate or counsel by the prisoner of war or the Protecting Power, the Detaining Power shall appoint a competent advocate or counsel to conduct the defence.

The advocate or counsel conducting the defence on behalf of the prisoner of war shall have at his disposal a period of two weeks at least before the opening of the trial, as well as the necessary facilities to prepare the defence of the accused. He may, in particular, freely visit the accused and interview him in private. He may also confer with any witnesses for the defence, including prisoners of war. He shall have the benefit of these facilities until the term of appeal or petition has expired.

Particulars of the charge or charges on which the prisoner of war is to be arraigned, as well as the documents which are generally communicated to the accused by virtue of the laws in force in the armed forces of the Detaining Power, shall be communicated to the accused prisoner of war in a language which he understands, and in good time before the opening of the trial. The same communication in the same circumstances shall be made to the advocate or counsel conducting the defence on behalf of the prisoner of war.

The representatives of the Protecting Power shall be entitled to attend the trial of the case, unless, exceptionally, this is held in camera in the interest of State security. In such a case the Detaining Power shall advise the Protecting Power accordingly.

Article 106

Every prisoner of war shall have, in the same manner as the members of the armed forces of the Detaining Power, the right of appeal or petition from any sentence pronounced upon him, with a view to the quashing or revising of the sentence or the reopening of the trial. He shall be fully informed of his right to appeal or petition and of the time limit within which he may do so.

Article 107

Any judgment and sentence pronounced upon a prisoner of war shall be immediately reported to the Protecting Power in the form of a summary communication, which shall also indicate whether he has the right of appeal with a view to the quashing of the sentence or the reopening of the trial. This communication shall likewise be sent to the prisoners' representative concerned. It shall also be sent to the accused prisoner of war in a language he understands, if the sentence was not pronounced in his presence. The Detaining Power shall also immediately communicate to the Protecting Power the decision of the prisoner of war to use or to waive his right of appeal.

Furthermore, if a prisoner of war is finally convicted or if a sentence pronounced on a prisoner of war in the first instance is a death sentence, the Detaining Power shall as soon as possible address to the Protecting Power a detailed communication containing:

1. The precise wording of the finding and sentence;

2. A summarized report of any preliminary investigation and of the trial, emphasizing in particular the elements of the prosecution and the defence;

3. Notification, where applicable, of the establishment where the sentence will be served.

The communications provided for in the foregoing subparagraphs shall be sent to the Protecting Power at the address previously made known to the Detaining Power.

Article 108

Sentences pronounced on prisoners of war after a conviction has become duly enforceable, shall be served in the same establishments and under the same conditions as in the case of members of the armed forces of the Detaining Power. These conditions shall in all cases conform to the requirements of health and humanity.

A woman prisoner of war on whom such a sentence has been pronounced shall be confined in separate quarters and shall be under the supervision of women.

In any case, prisoners of war sentenced to a penalty depriving them of their liberty shall retain the benefit of the provisions of Articles 78 and 126 of the present Convention. Furthermore, they shall be entitled to receive and despatch correspondence, to receive at least one relief parcel monthly, to take regular exercise in the open air, to have the medical care required by their state of health, and the spiritual assistance they may desire. Penalties to which they may be subjected shall be in accordance with the provisions of Article 87, third paragraph.

Part IV—Termination of Captivity

SECTION I: DIRECT REPATRIATION AND ACCOMMODATION IN NEUTRAL COUNTRIES

Article 109

Subject to the provisions of the third paragraph of this Article, Parties to the conflict are bound to send back to their own country, regardless of number or rank, seriously wounded and seriously sick prisoners of war, after having cared for them until they are fit to travel, in accordance with the first paragraph of the following Article.

Throughout the duration of hostilities, Parties to the conflict shall endeavour, with the cooperation of the neutral Powers concerned, to make arrangements for the accommodation in neutral countries of the sick and wounded prisoners of war referred to in the second paragraph of the following Article. They may, in addition, conclude agreements with a view to the direct repatriation or internment in a neutral country of able-bodied prisoners of war who have undergone a long period of captivity.

No sick or injured prisoner of war who is eligible for repatriation under the first paragraph of this Article, may be repatriated against his will during hostilities.

Article 110

The following shall be repatriated direct:

1. Incurably wounded and sick whose mental or physical fitness seems to have been gravely diminished.

2. Wounded and sick who, according to medical opinion, are not likely to recover within one year, whose condition requires treatment and whose mental or physical fitness seems to have been gravely diminished.

3. Wounded and sick who have recovered, but whose mental or physical fitness seems to have been gravely and permanently diminished.

The following may be accommodated in a neutral country:

1. Wounded and sick whose recovery may be expected within one year of the date of the wound or the beginning of the illness, if treatment in a neutral country might increase the prospects of a more certain and speedy recovery.

2. Prisoners of war whose mental or physical health, according to medical opinion, is seriously threatened by continued captivity, but whose accommodation in a neutral country might remove such a threat.

The conditions which prisoners of war accommodated in a neutral country must fulfil in order to permit their repatriation shall be fixed, as shall likewise their status, by agreement between the Powers concerned. In general, prisoners of war who have been accommodated in a neutral country, and who belong to the following categories, should be repatriated:

1. Those whose state of health has deteriorated so as to fulfil the conditions laid down for direct repatriation;

2. Those whose mental or physical powers remain, even after treatment, considerably impaired.

If no special agreements are concluded between the Parties to the conflict concerned, to determine the cases of disablement or sickness entailing direct repatriation or accommodation in a neutral country, such cases shall be settled in accordance with the principles laid down in the Model Agreement concerning direct repatriation and accommodation in neutral countries of wounded and sick prisoners of war and in the Regulations concerning Mixed Medical Commissions annexed to the present Convention.

Article 111

The Detaining Power, the Power on which the prisoners of war depend, and a neutral Power agreed upon by these two Powers, shall endeavour to conclude agreements which will enable prisoners of war to be interned in the territory of the said neutral Power until the close of hostilities.

Article 112

Upon the outbreak of hostilities, Mixed Medical Commissions shall be appointed to examine sick and wounded prisoners of war, and to make all appropriate decisions regarding them. The appointment, duties and functioning of these Commissions shall be in conformity with the provisions of the Regulations annexed to the present Convention.

However, prisoners of war who, in the opinion of the medical authorities of the Detaining Power, are manifestly seriously injured or seriously sick, may be repatriated without having to be examined by a Mixed Medical Commission.

Article 113

Besides those who are designated by the medical authorities of the Detaining Power, wounded or sick prisoners of war belonging to the categories listed below shall be entitled to present themselves for examination by the Mixed Medical Commissions provided for in the foregoing Article:

1. Wounded and sick proposed by a physician or surgeon who is of the same nationality, or a national of a Party to the conflict allied with the Power on which the said prisoners depend, and who exercises his functions in the camp.

2. Wounded and sick proposed by their prisoners' representative.

3. Wounded and sick proposed by the Power on which they depend, or by an organization duly recognized by the said Power and giving assistance to the prisoners.

Prisoners of war who do not belong to one of the three foregoing categories may nevertheless present themselves for examination by Mixed Medical Commissions, but shall be examined only after those belonging to the said categories.

The physician or surgeon of the same nationality as the prisoners who present themselves for examination by the Mixed Medical Commission, likewise the prisoners' representative of the said prisoners, shall have permission to be present at the examination.

Article 114

Prisoners of war who meet with accidents shall, unless the injury is self-inflicted, have the benefit of the provisions of this Convention as regards repatriation or accommodation in a neutral country.

Article 115

No prisoner of war on whom a disciplinary punishment has been imposed and who is eligible for repatriation or for accommodation in a neutral country, may be kept back on the plea that he has not undergone his punishment.

Prisoners of war detained in connection with a judicial prosecution or conviction and who are designated for repatriation or accommodation in a neutral country, may benefit by such measures before the end of the proceedings or the completion of the punishment, if the Detaining Power consents.

Parties to the conflict shall communicate to each other the names of those who will be detained until the end of the proceedings or the completion of the punishment.

Article 116

The costs of repatriating prisoners of war or of transporting them to a neutral country shall be borne, from the frontiers of the Detaining Power, by the Power on which the said prisoners depend.

Article 117

No repatriated person may be employed on active military service.

SECTION II: RELEASE AND REPATRIATION OF PRISONERS OF WAR AT THE CLOSE OF HOSTILITIES

Article 118

Prisoners of war shall be released and repatriated without delay after the cessation of active hostilities.

In the absence of stipulations to the above effect in any agreement concluded between the Parties to the conflict with a view to the cessation of hostilities, or failing any such agreement, each of the Detaining Powers shall itself establish and execute without delay a plan of repatriation in conformity with the principle laid down in the foregoing paragraph.

In either case, the measures adopted shall be brought to the knowledge of the prisoners of war.

The costs of repatriation of prisoners of war shall in all cases be equitably apportioned between the Detaining Power and the Power on which the prisoners depend. This apportionment shall be carried out on the following basis:

(a) If the two Powers are contiguous, the Power on which the prisoners of war depend shall bear the costs of repatriation from the frontiers of the Detaining Power.

(b) If the two Powers are not contiguous, the Detaining Power shall bear the costs of transport of prisoners of war over its own territory as far as its frontier or its port of embarkation nearest to the territory of the Power on which the prisoners of war depend. The Parties concerned shall agree between themselves as to the equitable apportionment of the remaining costs of the repatriation. The conclusion of this agreement shall in no circumstances justify any delay in the repatriation of the prisoners of war.

Article 119

Repatriation shall be effected in conditions similar to those laid down in Articles 46 to 48 inclusive of the present Convention for the transfer of prisoners of war, having regard to the provisions of Article 118 and to those of the following paragraphs.

On repatriation, any articles of value impounded from prisoners of war under Article 18, and any foreign currency which has not been converted into the currency of the Detaining Power, shall be restored to them. Articles of value and foreign currency which, for any reason whatever, are not restored to prisoners of war on repatriation, shall be despatched to the Information Bureau set up under Article 122.

Prisoners of war shall be allowed to take with them their personal effects, and any correspondence and parcels which have arrived for them. The weight of such baggage may be limited, if the conditions of repatriation so require, to what each prisoner can reasonably carry. Each prisoner shall in all cases be authorized to carry at least twenty-five kilograms.

The other personal effects of the repatriated prisoner shall be left in the charge of the Detaining Power which shall have them forwarded to him as soon as it has concluded an agreement to this effect, regulating the conditions of transport and the payment of the costs involved, with the Power on which the prisoner depends.

Prisoners of war against whom criminal proceedings for an indictable offence are pending may be detained until the end of such proceedings, and, if necessary, until the completion of the punishment. The same shall apply to prisoners of war already convicted for an indictable offence.

Parties to the conflict shall communicate to each other the names of any prisoners of war who are detained until the end of the proceedings or until punishment has been completed.

By agreement between the Parties to the conflict, commissions shall be established for the purpose of searching for dispersed prisoners of war and of assuring their repatriation with the least possible delay.

SECTION III: DEATH OF PRISONERS OF WAR

Article 120

Wills of prisoners of war shall be drawn up so as to satisfy the conditions of validity required by the legislation of their country of origin, which will take steps to inform the Detaining Power of its requirements in this respect. At the request of the prisoner of war and, in all cases, after death, the will shall be transmitted without delay to the Protecting Power; a certified copy shall be sent to the Central Agency.

Death certificates in the form annexed to the present Convention, or lists certified by a responsible officer, of all persons who die as prisoners of war shall be forwarded as rapidly as possible to the Prisoner of War Information Bureau established in accordance with Article 122. The death certificates or certified lists shall show particulars of identity as set out in the third paragraph of Article 17, and also the date and place of death, the cause of death, the date and place of burial and all particulars necessary to identify the graves.

The burial or cremation of a prisoner of war shall be preceded by a medical examination of the body with a view to confirming death and enabling a report to be made and, where necessary, establishing identity.

The detaining authorities shall ensure that prisoners of war who have died in captivity are honourably buried, if possible according to the rites of the religion to which they belonged, and that their graves are respected, suitably maintained and marked so as to be found at any time. Wherever possible, deceased prisoners of war who depended on the same Power shall be interred in the same place.

Deceased prisoners of war shall be buried in individual graves unless unavoidable circumstances require the use of collective graves. Bodies may be cremated only for imperative reasons of hygiene, on account of the religion of the deceased or in accordance with his express wish to this effect. In case of cremation, the fact shall be stated and the reasons given in the death certificate of the deceased.

In order that graves may always be found, all particulars of burials and graves shall be recorded with a Graves Registration Service established by the Detaining Power. Lists of graves and particulars of the prisoners of war interred in cemeteries and elsewhere shall be transmitted to the Power on which such prisoners of war depended. Responsibility for the care of these graves and for records of any subsequent moves of the bodies shall rest on the Power controlling the territory, if a Party to the present Convention. These provisions shall also apply to the ashes, which shall be kept by the Graves Registration Service until proper disposal thereof in accordance with the wishes of the home country.

Article 121

Every death or serious injury of a prisoner of war caused or suspected to have been caused by a sentry, another prisoner of war, or any other person, as well as any death the cause of which is unknown, shall be immediately followed by an official enquiry by the Detaining Power.

A communication on this subject shall be sent immediately to the Protecting Power. Statements shall be taken from witnesses, especially from those who are prisoners of war, and a report including such statements shall be forwarded to the Protecting Power.

If the enquiry indicates the guilt of one or more persons, the Detaining Power shall take all measures for the prosecution of the person or persons responsible.

Part V—Information Bureaux and Relief Societies for Prisoners of War

Article 122

Upon the outbreak of a conflict and in all cases of occupation, each of the Parties to the conflict shall institute an official Information Bureau for prisoners of war who are in its power. Neutral or non-belligerent Powers who may have received within their territory persons belonging to one of the categories referred to in Article 4, shall take the same action with respect to such persons. The Power concerned shall ensure that the Prisoners of War Information Bureau is provided with the necessary accommodation, equipment and staff to ensure its efficient working. It shall be at liberty to employ prisoners of war in such a Bureau under the conditions laid down in the Section of the present Convention dealing with work by prisoners of war.

Within the shortest possible period, each of the Parties to the conflict shall give its Bureau the information referred to in the fourth, fifth and sixth paragraphs of this Article regarding any enemy person belonging to one of the categories referred to in Article 4, who has fallen into its power. Neutral or non-belligerent Powers shall take the same action with regard to persons belonging to such categories whom they have received within their territory.

The Bureau shall immediately forward such information by the most rapid means to the Powers concerned, through the intermediary of the Protecting Powers and likewise of the Central Agency provided for in Article 123.

This information shall make it possible quickly to advise the next of kin concerned. Subject to the provisions of Article 17, the information shall include, in so far as available to the Information Bureau, in respect of each prisoner of war, his surname, first names, rank, army, regimental, personal or serial number, place and full date of birth, indication of the Power on which he depends, first name of the father and maiden name of the mother, name and address of the person to be informed and the address to which correspondence for the prisoner may be sent.

The Information Bureau shall receive from the various departments concerned information regarding transfers, releases, repatriations, escapes, admissions to hospital, and deaths, and shall transmit such information in the manner described in the third paragraph above.

Likewise, information regarding the state of health of prisoners of war who are seriously ill or seriously wounded shall be supplied regularly, every week if possible.

The Information Bureau shall also be responsible for replying to all enquiries sent to it concerning prisoners of war, including those who have died in captivity; it will make any enquiries necessary to obtain the information which is asked for if this is not in its possession.

All written communications made by the Bureau shall be authenticated by a signature or a seal.

The Information Bureau shall furthermore be charged with collecting all personal valuables, including sums in currencies other than that of the Detaining Power and documents of importance to the next of kin, left by prisoners of war who have been repatriated or released, or who have escaped or died, and shall forward the said valuables to the Powers concerned. Such articles shall be sent by the Bureau in sealed packets which shall be accompanied by statements giving clear and full particulars of the identity of the person to whom the articles belonged, and by a complete list of the contents of the parcel. Other personal effects of such prisoners of war shall be transmitted under arrangements agreed upon between the Parties to the conflict concerned.

Article 123

A Central Prisoners of War Information Agency shall be created in a neutral country. The International Committee of the Red Cross shall, if it deems necessary, propose to the Powers concerned the organization of such an Agency.

The function of the Agency shall be to collect all the information it may obtain through official or private channels respecting prisoners of war, and to transmit it as rapidly as possible to the country of origin of the prisoners of war or to the Power on which they depend. It shall receive from the Parties to the conflict all facilities for effecting such transmissions.

The High Contracting Parties, and in particular those whose nationals benefit by the services of the Central Agency, are requested to give the said Agency the financial aid it may require.

The foregoing provisions shall in no way be interpreted as restricting the humanitarian activities of the International Committee of the Red Cross, or of the relief Societies provided for in Article 125.

Article 124

The national Information Bureaux and the Central Information Agency shall enjoy free postage for mail, likewise all the exemptions provided for in Article 74, and further, so far as possible, exemption from telegraphic charges or, at least, greatly reduced rates.

Article 125

Subject to the measures which the Detaining Powers may consider essential to ensure their security or to meet any other reasonable need, the representatives of religious organizations, relief societies, or any other organization assisting prisoners of war, shall receive from the said Powers, for themselves and their duly accredited agents, all necessary facilities for visiting the prisoners, distributing relief supplies and material, from any source, intended for religious, educational or recreative purposes, and for assisting them in organizing their leisure time within the camps. Such societies or organizations may be constituted in the territory of the Detaining Power or in any other country, or they may have an international character.

The Detaining Power may limit the number of societies and organizations whose delegates are allowed to carry out their activities in its territory and under its supervision, on condition, however, that such limitation shall not hinder the effective operation of adequate relief to all prisoners of war.

The special position of the International Committee of the Red Cross in this field shall be recognized and respected at all times.

As soon as relief supplies or material intended for the above-mentioned purposes are handed over to prisoners of war, or very shortly afterwards, receipts for each consignment, signed by the prisoners' representative, shall be forwarded to the relief society or organization making the shipment. At the same time, receipts for these consignments shall be supplied by the administrative authorities responsible for guarding the prisoners.

Part VI—Execution of the Convention

SECTION I: GENERAL PROVISIONS

Article 126

Representatives or delegates of the Protecting Powers shall have permission to go to all places where prisoners of war may be, particularly to places of internment, imprisonment and labour, and shall have access to all premises occupied by prisoners of war; they shall also be allowed to go to the places of departure, passage and arrival of prisoners who are being transferred. They shall be able to interview the prisoners, and in particular the prisoners' representatives, without witnesses, either personally or through an interpreter.

Representatives and delegates of the Protecting Powers shall have full liberty to select the places they wish to visit. The duration and frequency of these visits shall not be restricted. Visits may not be prohibited except for reasons of imperative military necessity, and then only as an exceptional and temporary measure.

The Detaining Power and the Power on which the said prisoners of war depend may agree, if necessary, that compatriots of these prisoners of war be permitted to participate in the visits.

The delegates of the International Committee of the Red Cross shall enjoy the same prerogatives. The appointment of such delegates shall be submitted to the approval of the Power detaining the prisoners of war to be visited.

Article 127

The High Contracting Parties undertake, in time of peace as in time of war, to disseminate the text of the present Convention as widely as possible in their respective countries, and, in particular, to include the study thereof in their programmes of military and, if possible, civil instruction, so that the principles thereof may become known to all their armed forces and to the entire population.

Any military or other authorities, who in time of war assume responsibilities in respect of prisoners of war, must possess the text of the Convention and be specially instructed as to its provisions.

Article 128

The High Contracting Parties shall communicate to one another through the Swiss Federal Council and, during hostilities, through the Protecting Powers, the official translations of the present Convention, as well as the laws and regulations which they may adopt to ensure the application thereof.

Article 129

The High Contracting Parties undertake to enact any legislation necessary to provide effective penal sanctions for persons committing, or ordering to be committed, any of the grave breaches of the present Convention defined in the following Article.

Each High Contracting Party shall be under the obligation to search for persons alleged to have committed, or to have ordered to be committed, such grave breaches, and shall bring such persons, regardless of their nationality, before its own courts. It may also, if it prefers, and in accordance with the provisions of its own legislation, hand such persons over for trial to another High Contracting Party concerned, provided such High Contracting Party has made out a prima facie case.

Each High Contracting Party shall take measures necessary for the suppression of all acts contrary to the provisions of the present Convention other than the grave breaches defined in the following Article.

In all circumstances, the accused persons shall benefit by safeguards of proper trial and defence, which shall not be less favourable than those provided by Article 105 and those following of the present Convention.

Article 130

Grave breaches to which the preceding Article relates shall be those involving any of the following acts, if committed against persons or property protected by the Convention: wilful killing, torture or inhuman treatment, including biological experiments, wilfully causing great suffering or serious injury to body or health, compelling a prisoner of war to serve in the forces of the hostile Power, or wilfully depriving a prisoner of war of the rights of fair and regular trial prescribed in this Convention.

Article 131

No High Contracting Party shall be allowed to absolve itself or any other High Contracting Party of any liability incurred by itself or by another High Contracting Party in respect of breaches referred to in the preceding Article.

Article 132

At the request of a Party to the conflict, an enquiry shall be instituted, in a manner to be decided between the interested Parties, concerning any alleged violation of the Convention.

If agreement has not been reached concerning the procedure for the enquiry, the Parties should agree on the choice of an umpire who will decide upon the procedure to be followed.

Once the violation has been established, the Parties to the conflict shall put an end to it and shall repress it with the least possible delay.

SECTION 11: FINAL PROVISIONS

Article 133

The present Convention is established in English and in French. Both texts are equally authentic. The Swiss Federal Council shall arrange for official translations of the Convention to be made in the Russian and Spanish languages.

Article 134

The present Convention replaces the Convention of 27 July 1929, in relations between the High Contracting Parties.

Article 135

In the relations between the Powers which are bound by The Hague Convention respecting the Laws and Customs of War on Land, whether that of July 29, 1899, or that of October 18, 1907, and which are parties to the present Convention, this last Convention shall be complementary to Chapter II of the Regulations annexed to the above-mentioned Conventions of The Hague.

Article 136

The present Convention, which bears the date of this day, is open to signature until February 12, 1950, in the name of the Powers represented at the Conference which opened at Geneva on April 21, 1949; furthermore, by Powers not represented at that Conference, but which are parties to the Convention of July 27, 1929.

Article 137

The present Convention shall be ratified as soon as possible and the ratifications shall be deposited at Berne.

A record shall be drawn up of the deposit of each instrument of ratification and certified copies of this record shall be transmitted by the Swiss Federal Council to all the Powers in whose name the Convention has been signed, or whose accession has been notified.

Article 138

The present Convention shall come into force six months after not less than two instruments of ratification have been deposited.

Thereafter, it shall come into force for each High Contracting Party six months after the deposit of the instrument of ratification.

Article 139

From the date of its coming into force, it shall be open to any Power in whose name the present Convention has not been signed, to accede to this Convention.

Article 140

Accessions shall be notified in writing to the Swiss Federal Council, and shall take effect six months after the date on which they are received.

The Swiss Federal Council shall communicate the accessions to all the Powers in whose name the Convention has been signed, or whose accession has been notified.

Article 141

The situations provided for in Articles 2 and 3 shall give immediate effect to ratifications deposited and accessions notified by the Parties to the conflict before or after the beginning of hostilities or occupation. The Swiss Federal Council shall communicate by the quickest method any ratifications or accessions received from Parties to the conflict.

Article 142

Each of the High Contracting Parties shall be at liberty to denounce the present Convention.

The denunciation shall be notified in writing to the Swiss Federal Council, which shall transmit it to the Governments of all the High Contracting Parties.

The denunciation shall take effect one year after the notification thereof has been made to the Swiss Federal Council. However, a denunciation of which notification has been made at a time when the denouncing Power is involved in a conflict shall not take effect until peace has been concluded, and until after operations connected with the release and repatriation of the persons protected by the present Convention have been terminated.

The denunciation shall have effect only in respect of the denouncing Power. It shall in no way impair the obligations which the Parties to the conflict shall remain bound to fulfil by virtue of the principles of the law of nations, as they result from the usages established among civilized peoples, from the laws of humanity and the dictates of the public conscience.

Article 143

The Swiss Federal Council shall register the present Convention with the Secretariat of the United Nations. The Swiss Federal Council shall also inform the Secretariat of the United Nations of all ratifications, accessions and denunciations received by it with respect to the present Convention.

IN WITNESS WHEREOF the undersigned, having deposited their respective full powers, have signed the present Convention.

DONE at Geneva this twelfth day of August 1949, in the English and French languages. The original shall be deposited in the Archives of the Swiss Confederation. The Swiss Federal Council shall transmit certified copies thereof to each of the signatory and acceding States.

Annex I

Model agreement concerning direct repatriation and accommodation in neutral countries of wounded and sick prisoners of war (see Article 110)

I. Principles for Direct Repatriation and Accommodation in Neutral Countries

A. Direct Repatriation

The following shall be repatriated direct:

1. All prisoners of war suffering from the following disabilities as the result of trauma: loss of limb, paralysis, articular or other disabilities, when this disability is at least the loss of a hand or a foot, or the equivalent of the loss of a hand or a foot.

Without prejudice to a more generous interpretation, the following shall be considered as equivalent to the loss of a hand or a foot:

(a) Loss of a hand or of all the fingers, or of the thumb and forefinger of one hand; loss of a foot, or of all the toes and metatarsals of one foot.

(b) Ankylosis, loss of osseous tissue, cicatricial contracture preventing the functioning of one of the large articulations or of all the digital joints of one hand.

(c) Pseudarthrosis of the long bones.

(d) Deformities due to fracture or other injury which seriously interfere with function and weight-bearing power.

2. All wounded prisoners of war whose condition has become chronic, to the extent that prognosis appears to exclude recovery-in spite of treatment-within one year from the date of the injury, as for example, in case of:

(a) Projectile in the heart, even if the Mixed Medical Commission should fail, at the time of their examination, to detect any serious disorders.

(b) Metallic splinter in the brain or the lungs, even if the Mixed Medical Commission cannot, at the time of examination, detect any local or general reaction.

(c) Osteomyelitis, when recovery cannot be foreseen in the course of the year following the injury, and which seems likely to result in ankylosis of a joint, or other impairments equivalent to the loss of a hand or a foot.

(d) Perforating and suppurating injury to the large joints.

(e) Injury to the skull, with loss or shifting of bony tissue.

(f) Injury or burning of the face with loss of tissue and functional lesions.

(g) Injury to the spinal cord.

(h) Lesion of the peripheral nerves, the sequelae of which are equivalent to the loss of a hand or foot, and the cure of which requires more than a year from the date of injury, for example: injury to the brachial or lumbosacral plexus, the median or sciatic nerves, likewise combined injury to the radial and cubital nerves or to the lateral popliteal nerve (*N. peroneus communes*) and medial popliteal nerve (*N. tibialis*); etc. The separate injury of the radial (musculo-spiral), cubital. lateral or medial popliteal nerves shall not, however, warrant repatriation except in case of contractures or of serious neurotrophic disturbance.

(i) Injury to the urinary system, with incapacitating results.

3. All sick prisoners of war whose condition has become chronic to the extent that prognosis seems to exclude recovery—in spite of treatment—within one year from the inception of the disease, as, for example, in case of:

(a) Progressive tuberculosis of any organ which, according to medical prognosis, cannot be cured, or at least considerably improved, by treatment in a neutral country.

(b) Exudate pleurisy.

(c) Serious diseases of the respiratory organs of non-tubercular etiology, presumed incurable, for example: serious pulmonary emphysema, with or without bronchitis, chronic asthma:° chronic bronchitis° lasting more than one year in captivity; bronchiectasis,° etc.

(d) Serious chronic affections of the circulatory system, for example: valvular lesions and myocarditis° which have shown signs of circulatory failure during captivity, even though the Mixed Medical Commission cannot detect any such signs at the time of examination; affections of the pericardium and the vessels (Buerger's disease, aneurism of the large vessels); etc.

(e) Serious chronic affections of the digestive organs, for example: gastric or duodenal ulcer-, sequelae of gastric operations performed in captivity; chronic gastritis, enteritis or colitis, having lasted more than one year and seriously affecting the general condition: cirrhosis of the liver, chronic cholecystopathy;° etc.

(f) Serious chronic affections of the genito-urinary organs, for example: chronic diseases of the kidney with consequent disorders; nephrectomy because of a tubercular kidney; chronic pyelitis or chronic cystitis: hydronephrosis or pyonephrosis; chronic grave gynaecological conditions, normal pregnancy, and obstetrical disorder, where it is impossible to accommodate in a neutral country; etc.

(g) Serious chronic diseases of the central and peripheral nervous system, for example: all obvious psychoses and psychoneuroses, such as serious hysteria, serious captivity psychoneurosis, etc., duly verified by a specialist;° any epilepsy duly verified by the camp physicians, cerebral arteriosclerosis, chronic neuritis lasting more than one year, etc.

(h) Serious chronic disease of the neuro-vegetative system, with considerable diminution of mental or physical fitness, noticeable loss of weight and general asthenia.

(i) Blindness of both eyes, or of one eye when the vision of the other is less than I in spite of the use of corrective glasses; diminution of visual acuity in cases where it is impossible to restore it by correction to an acuity of 1/2 in at least one eye;° other grave ocular affections, for example: glaucoma, iritis, choroiditis; trachoma, etc.

(k) Auditive disorders, such as total unilateral deafness, if the other ear does not discern the ordinary spoken word at a distance of one metre;° etc.

(l) Serious affections of metabolism, for example: diabetes mellitus requiring insulin treatment; etc.

(m) Serious disorders of the endocrine glands, for example: thyrotoxicosis; hypothyrosis; Addison's disease; Simmonds' cachexia; tetany; etc.

(n) Grave and chronic disorders of the blood-forming organs.

(o) Serious cases of chronic intoxication, for example: lead poisoning, mercury poisoning, morphinism, cocainism, alcoholism; gas or radiation poisoning; etc.

(p) Chronic affections of locomotion, with obvious functional disorders, for example: arthritis deformans, primary and secondary progressive chronic polyarthritis; rheumatism with serious clinical symptoms; etc.

(q) Serious chronic skin diseases, not amenable to treatment.

(r) Any malignant growth.

(s) Serious chronic infectious diseases, persisting for one year after their inception, for example: malaria with decided organic impairment, amoebic or bacillary dysentery with grave disorders; tertiary visceral syphilis resistant to treatment; leprosy; etc.

(t) Serious avitaminosis or serious inanition.

B. Accommodation in Neutral Countries
The following shall be eligible for accommodation in a neutral country:

1. All wounded prisoners of war who are not likely to recover in captivity, but who might be cured or whose condition might be considerably improved by accommodation in a neutral country.

2. Prisoners of war suffering from any form of tuberculosis, of whatever organ, and whose treatment in a neutral country would be likely to lead to recovery or at least to considerable improvement, with the exception of primary tuberculosis cured before captivity.

3. Prisoners of war suffering from affections requiring treatment of the respiratory, circulatory, digestive, nervous, sensory, genito-urinary, cutaneous locomotive organs, etc., if such treatment would clearly have better results in a neutral country than in captivity.

4. Prisoners of war who have undergone a nephrectomy in captivity for a nontubercular renal affection; cases of osteomyelitis, on the way to recovery or latent; diabetes mellitus not requiring insulin treatment; etc.

5. Prisoners of war suffering from war or captivity neuroses.

Cases of captivity neurosis which are not cured after three months of accommodation in a neutral country, or which after that length of time are not clearly on the way to complete cure, shall be repatriated.

6. All prisoners of war suffering from chronic intoxication (gases, metals, alkaloids, etc.), for whom the prospects of cure in a neutral country are especially favourable.

7. All women prisoners of war who are pregnant or mothers with infants and small children.

The following cases shall not be eligible for accommodation in a neutral country:

1. All duly verified chronic psychoses.

2. All organic or functional nervous affections considered to be incurable.

3. All contagious diseases during the period in which they are transmissible, with the exception of tuberculosis.

°The decision of the Mixed Medical Commission shall be based to a great extent on the records kept by camp physicians and surgeons of the same nationality as the prisoners of war, or on an examination by medical specialists of the Detaining Power.

II. General Observations

1. The conditions given shall, in a general way, be interpreted and applied in as broad a spirit as possible.

Neuropathic and psychopathic conditions caused by war or captivity, as well as cases of tuberculosis in all stages, shall above all benefit by such liberal interpretation. Prisoners of war who have sustained several wounds, none of which, considered by itself, justifies repatriation, shall be examined in the same spirit, with due regard for the psychic traumatism due to the number of their wounds.

2. All unquestionable cases giving the right to direct repatriation (amputation, total blindness or deafness. open pulmonary tuberculosis, mental disorder. malignant growth, etc.) shall be examined and repatriated as soon as possible by the camp physicians or by military medical commissions appointed by the Detaining Power.

3. Injuries and diseases which existed before the war and which have not become worse. as well as war injuries which have not prevented subsequent military service, shall not entitle to direct repatriation.

4. The provisions of this Annex shall be interpreted and applied in a similar manner in all countries party to the conflict. The Powers and authorities concerned shall grant to Mixed Medical Commissions all the facilities necessary for the accomplishment of their task.

5. The examples quoted under (1) above represent only typical cases. Cases which do not correspond exactly to these provisions shall be judged in the spirit of the provisions of Article I 10 of the present Convention, and of the principles embodied in the present Agreement.

Annex II

Regulations concerning Mixed Medical Commissions (see Article 112)

Article 1

The Mixed Medical Commissions provided for in Article 112 of the Convention shall be composed of three members, two of whom shall belong to a neutral country. the third being appointed by the Detaining Power. One of the neutral members shall take the chair.

Article 2

The two neutral members shall be appointed by the International Committee of the Red Cross, acting in agreement with the Protecting Power, at the request of the Detaining Power. They may be domiciled either in their country of origin, in any other neutral country, or in the territory of the Detaining Power.

Article 3

The neutral members shall be approved by the Parties to the conflict concerned, who notify their approval to the International Committee of the Red Cross and to the Protecting Power. Upon such notification, the neutral members shall be considered as effectively appointed.

Article 4

Deputy members shall also be appointed in sufficient number to replace the regular members in case of need. They shall be appointed at the same time as the regular members or, at least, as soon as possible.

Article 5

If for any reason the International Committee of the Red Cross cannot arrange for the appointment of the neutral members, this shall be done by the Power protecting the interests of the prisoners of war to be examined.

Article 6

So far as possible, one of the two neutral members shall be a surgeon and the other a physician.

Article 7

The neutral members shall be entirely independent of the Parties to the conflict, which shall grant them all facilities in the accomplishment of their duties.

Article 8

By agreement with the Detaining Power, the International Committee of the Red Cross, when making the appointments provided for in Articles 2 and 4 of the present Regulations, shall settle the terms of service of the nominees.

Article 9

The Mixed Medical Commissions shall begin their work as soon as possible after the neutral members have been approved, and in any case within a period of three months from the date of such approval.

Article 10

The Mixed Medical Commissions shall examine all the prisoners designated in Article 113 of the Convention. They shall propose repatriation, rejection, or reference to a later examination. Their decisions shall be made by a majority vote.

Article 11

The decisions made by the Mixed Medical Commissions in each specific case shall be communicated, during the month following their visit, to the Detaining Power, the Protecting Power and the International Committee of the

Red Cross. The Mixed Medical Commissions shall also inform each prisoner of war examined of the decision made, and shall issue to those whose repatriation has been proposed, certificates similar to the model appended to the present Convention.

Article 12
The Detaining Power shall be required to carry out the decisions of the Mixed Medical Commissions within three months of the time when it receives due notification of such decisions.

Article 13
If there is no neutral physician in a country where the services of a Mixed Medical Commission seem to be required, and if it is for any reason impossible to appoint neutral doctors who are resident in another country, the Detaining Power, acting in agreement with the Protecting Power, shall set up a Medical Commission which shall undertake the same duties as a Mixed Medical Commission, subject to the provisions of Articles 1, 2, 3, 4, 5 and 8 of the Present Regulations.

Article 14
Mixed Medical Commissions shall function permanently and shall visit each camp at intervals of not more than six months.

Annex III
Regulations concerning collective relief (see Article 73)

Article 1
Prisoners' representatives shall be allowed to distribute collective relief shipments for which they are responsible, to all prisoners of war administered by their camp, including those who are in hospitals or in prisons or other penal establishments.

Article 2
The distribution of collective relief shipments shall be effected in accordance with the instructions of the donors and with a plan drawn up by the prisoners' representatives. The issue of medical stores shall, however, be made for preference in agreement with the senior medical officers, and the latter may. In hospitals and infirmaries, waive the said instructions, if the needs of their patients so demand. Within the limits thus defined, the distribution shall always be carried out equitably.

Article 3
The said prisoners' representatives or their assistants shall be allowed to go to the points of arrival of relief supplies near their camps, so as to enable the prisoners' representatives or their assistants to verify the quality as well as the quantity of the goods received, and to make out detailed reports thereon for the donors.

Article 4
Prisoners' representatives shall be given the facilities necessary for verifying whether the distribution of collective relief in all sub-divisions and annexes of their camps has been carried out in accordance with their instructions.

Article 5
Prisoners' representatives shall be allowed to fill up, and cause to be filled up by the prisoners' representatives of labour detachments or by the senior medical officers of infirmaries and hospitals, forms or questionnaires intended for the donors, relating to collective relief supplies (distribution, requirements, quantities, etc.). Such forms and questionnaires, duly completed, shall be forwarded to the donors without delay.

Article 6
In order to secure the regular issue of collective relief to the prisoners of war in their camp, and to meet any needs that may arise from the arrival of new contingents of prisoners, prisoners' representatives shall be allowed to build up and maintain adequate reserve stocks of collective relief. For this purpose, they shall have suitable warehouses at their disposal; each warehouse shall be provided with two locks, the prisoners' representative holding the keys of one lock and the camp commander the keys of the other.

Article 7
When collective consignments of clothing are available each prisoner of war shall retain in his possession at least one complete set of clothes. If a prisoner has more than one set of clothes, the prisoners' representative shall be permitted to withdraw excess clothing from those with the largest number of sets, or particular articles in excess of one, if this is necessary in order to supply prisoners who are less well provided. He shall not, however, withdraw second sets of underclothing, socks or footwear, unless this is the only means of providing for prisoners of war with none.

Article 8
The High Contracting Parties, and the Detaining Powers in particular, shall authorize, as far as possible and subject to the regulations governing the supply of the population, all purchases of goods made in their territories for the distribution of collective relief to prisoners of war. They shall

similarly facilitate the transfer of funds and other financial measures of a technical or administrative nature taken for the purpose of making such purchases.

Article 9

The foregoing provisions shall not constitute an obstacle to the right of prisoners of war to receive collective relief before their arrival in a camp or in the course of transfer, nor to the possibility of representatives of the Protecting Power, the International Committee of the Red Cross, or any other body which may be responsible for the forwarding of such supplies, giving assistance to prisoners ensuring the distribution thereof to the addressees by any other means that they may deem useful.

GENEVA CONVENTION RELATIVE TO THE PROTECTION OF CIVILIAN PERSONS IN TIME OF WAR

★

Adopted on 12 August 1949 by the Diplomatic Conference for the Establishment of International Conventions for the Protection of Victims of War, held in Geneva from 21 April to 12 August 1949; entry into force: 21 October 1950

Part I—General Provisions

Article 1

The High Contracting Parties undertake to respect and to ensure respect for the present Convention in all circumstances.

Article 2

In addition to the provisions which shall be implemented in peacetime, the present Convention shall apply to all cases of declared war or of any other armed conflict which may arise between two or more of the High Contracting Parties, even if the state of war is not recognized by one of them.

The Convention shall also apply to all cases of partial or total occupation of the territory of a High Contracting Party, even if the said occupation meets with no armed resistance.

Although one of the Powers in conflict may not be a party to the present Convention, the Powers who are parties thereto shall remain bound by it in their mutual relations. They shall furthermore be bound by the Convention in relation to the said Power, if the latter accepts and applies the provisions thereof.

Article 3

In the case of armed conflict not of an international character occurring in the territory of one of the High Contracting Parties, each Party to the conflict shall be bound to apply, as a minimum, the following provisions:

1. Persons taking no active part in the hostilities, including members of armed forces who have laid down their arms and those placed hors de combat by sickness, wounds, detention, or any other cause, shall in all circumstances be treated humanely, without any adverse distinction founded on race, colour, religion or faith, sex, birth or wealth, or any other similar criteria.

To this end, the following acts are and shall remain prohibited at any time and in any place whatsoever with respect to the above-mentioned persons:

(a) Violence to life and person, in particular murder of all kinds, mutilation, cruel treatment and torture;

(b) Taking of hostages;

(c) Outrages upon personal dignity, in particular humiliating and degrading treatment;

(d) The passing of sentences and the carrying out of executions without previous judgment pronounced by a regularly constituted court, affording all the judicial guarantees which are recognized as indispensable by civilized peoples.

2. The wounded and sick shall be collected and cared for.

An impartial humanitarian body, such as the International Committee of the Red Cross, may offer its services to the Parties to the conflict.

The Parties to the conflict should further endeavour to bring into force, by means of special agreements, all or part of the other provisions of the present Convention.

The application of the preceding provisions shall not affect the legal status of the Parties to the conflict.

Article 4

Persons protected by the Convention are those who, at a given moment and in any manner whatsoever, find themselves, in case of a conflict or occupation, in the hands of a Party to the conflict or Occupying Power of which they are not nationals.

Nationals of a State which is not bound by the Convention are not protected by it. Nationals of a neutral State who find themselves in the territory of a belligerent State, and nationals of a co-belligerent State, shall not be regarded as protected persons while the State of which they are nationals has normal diplomatic representation in the State in whose hands they are.

The provisions of Part II are, however, wider in application, as defined in Article 13.

Persons protected by the Geneva Convention for the Amelioration of the Condition of the Wounded and Sick in Armed Forces in the Field of August 12, 1949, or by the Geneva Convention for the Amelioration of the Condition of Wounded, Sick and Shipwrecked Members of Armed Forces at Sea of August 12, 1949, or by the Geneva Convention relative to the Treatment of Prisoners of War of August 12, 1949, shall not be considered as protected persons within the meaning of the present Convention.

Article 5

Where, in the territory of a Party to the conflict, the latter is satisfied that an individual protected person is definitely suspected of or engaged in activities hostile to the security of the State, such individual person shall not be entitled to claim such rights and privileges under the present Convention as would, if exercised in the favour of such individual person, be prejudicial to the security of such State.

Where in occupied territory an individual protected person is detained as a spy or saboteur, or as a person under definite suspicion of activity hostile to the security of the Occupying Power, such person shall, in those cases where absolute military security so requires, be regarded as having forfeited rights of communication under the present Convention.

In each case, such persons shall nevertheless be treated with humanity, and in case of trial, shall not be deprived of the rights of fair and regular trial prescribed by the present Convention. They shall also be granted the full rights and privileges of a protected person under the present Convention at the earliest date consistent with the security of the State or Occupying Power, as the case may be.

Article 6

The present Convention shall apply from the outset of any conflict or occupation mentioned in Article 2.

In the territory of Parties to the conflict, the application of the present Convention shall cease on the general close of military operations.

In the case of occupied territory, the application of the present Convention shall cease one year after the general close of military operations; however, the Occupying Power shall be bound, for the duration of the occupation, to the extent that such Power exercises the functions of government in such territory, by the provisions of the following Articles of the present Convention: I to 12, 27, 29 to 34, 47, 49, 51, 52, 53, 59, 61 to 77, and 143.

Protected persons whose release, repatriation or re-establishment may take place after such dates shall meanwhile continue to benefit by the present Convention.

Article 7

In addition to the agreements expressly provided for in Articles 11, 14, 15, 17, 36, 108, 109, 132, 133 and 149, the High Contracting Parties may conclude other special agreements for all matters concerning which they may deem it suitable to make separate provision. No special agreement shall adversely affect the situation of protected persons, as defined by the present Convention, nor restrict the rights which it confers upon them.

Protected persons shall continue to have the benefit of such agreements as long as the Convention is applicable to them, except where express provisions to the contrary are contained in the aforesaid or in subsequent agreements, or where more favourable measures have been taken with regard to them by one or other of the Parties to the conflict.

Article 8

Protected persons may in no circumstances renounce in part or in entirety the rights secured to them by the present Convention, and by the special agreements referred to in the foregoing Article, if such there be.

Article 9

The present Convention shall be applied with the cooperation and under the scrutiny of the Protecting Powers whose duty it is to safeguard the interests of the Parties to the conflict. For this purpose, the Protecting Powers may appoint, apart from their diplomatic or consular staff, delegates from amongst their own nationals or the nationals of other neutral Powers. The said delegates shall be subject to the approval of the Power with which they are to carry out their duties.

The Parties to the conflict shall facilitate to the greatest extent possible the task of the representatives or delegates of the Protecting Powers.

The representatives or delegates of the Protecting Powers shall not in any case exceed their mission under the present Convention. They shall, in particular, take account of the imperative necessities of security of the State wherein they carry out their duties.

Article 10

The provisions of the present Convention constitute no obstacle to the humanitarian activities which the International Committee of the Red Cross or any other impartial humanitarian organization may, subject to the consent of the Parties to the conflict concerned, undertake for the protection of civilian persons and for their relief.

Article 11

The High Contracting Parties may at any time agree to entrust to an organization which offers all guarantees of impartiality and efficacy the duties incumbent on the Protecting Powers by virtue of the present Convention.

When persons protected by the present Convention do not benefit or cease to benefit, no matter for what reason, by the activities of a Protecting Power or of an organization provided for in the first paragraph above, the Detaining Power shall request a neutral State, or such an organization, to undertake the functions performed under the present Convention by a Protecting Power designated by the Parties to a conflict.

If protection cannot be arranged accordingly, the Detaining Power shall request or shall accept, subject to the provisions of this Article, the offer of the services of a humanitarian organization, such as the International Committee of the Red Cross, to assume the humanitarian functions performed by Protecting Powers under the present Convention.

Any neutral Power, or any organization invited by the Power concerned or offering itself for these purposes, shall be required to act with a sense of responsibility towards the Party to the conflict on which persons protected by the present Convention depend, and shall be required to furnish sufficient assurances that it is in a position to undertake the appropriate functions and to discharge them impartially.

No derogation from the preceding provisions shall be made by special agreements between Powers one of which is restricted, even temporarily, in its freedom to negotiate with the other Power or its allies by reason of military events, more particularly where the whole, or a substantial part, of the territory of the said Power is occupied.

Whenever in the present Convention mention is made of a Protecting Power, such mention applies to substitute organizations in the sense of the present Article.

The provisions of this Article shall extend and be adapted to cases of nationals of a neutral State who are in occupied territory or who find themselves in the territory of a belligerent State with which the State of which they are nationals has not normal diplomatic representation.

Article 12

In cases where they deem it advisable in the interest of protected persons, particularly in cases of disagreement between the Parties to the conflict as to the application or interpretation of the provisions of the present Convention, the Protecting Powers shall lend their good offices with a view to settling the disagreement. For this purpose, each of the Protecting Powers may, either at the invitation of one Party or on its own initiative, propose to the Parties to the conflict a meeting of their representatives, and in particular of the authorities responsible for protected person, possibly on neutral territory suitably chosen. The Parties to the conflict shall be bound to give effect to the proposals made to them for this purpose. The Protecting Powers may, if necessary, propose for approval by the Parties to the conflict, a person belonging to a neutral Power or delegated by the International Committee of the Red Cross who shall be invited to take part in such a meeting.

Part II—General Protection of Populations against Certain Consequences of War

Article 13

The provisions of Part II cover the whole of the populations of the countries in conflict, without any adverse distinction based, in particular, on race, nationality, religion or political opinion, and are intended to alleviate the sufferings caused by war.

Article 14

In time of peace, the High Contracting Parties and, after the outbreak of hostilities, the Parties thereto, may establish in their own territory and, if the need arises, in occupied areas, hospital and safety zones and localities so organized as to protect from the effects of war, wounded, sick and aged persons, children under fifteen, expectant mothers and mothers of children under seven.

Upon the outbreak and during the course of hostilities, the Parties concerned may conclude agreements on mutual recognition of the zones and localities they have created. They may for this purpose implement the provisions of the Draft Agreement annexed to the present Convention, with such amendments as they may consider necessary.

The Protecting Powers and the International Committee of the Red Cross are invited to lend their good offices in order to facilitate the institution and recognition of these hospital and safety zones and localities.

Article 15

Any Party to the conflict may, either directly or through a neutral State or some humanitarian organization, propose to the adverse Party to establish, in the regions where fighting is taking place, neutralized zones intended to shelter from the effects of war the following persons, without distinction:

(a) Wounded and sick combatants or non-combatants;

(b) Civilian persons who take no part in hostilities, and who, while they reside in the zones, perform no work of a military character.

When the Parties concerned have agreed upon the geographical position, administration, food supply and supervision of the proposed neutralized zone, a written agreement shall be concluded and signed by the representatives of the Parties to the conflict. The agreement shall fix the beginning and the duration of the neutralization of the zone.

Article 16

The wounded and sick, as well as the infirm, and expectant mothers, shall be the object of particular protection and respect.

As far as military considerations allow, each Party to the conflict shall facilitate the steps taken to search for the killed and wounded, to assist the shipwrecked and other persons exposed to grave danger, and to protect them against pillage and ill-treatment.

Article 17

The Parties to the conflict shall endeavour to conclude local agreements for the removal from besieged or encircled areas, of wounded, sick, infirm, and aged persons, children and maternity cases, and for the passage of ministers of all religions, medical personnel and medical equipment on their way to such areas.

Article 18

Civilian hospitals organized to give care to the wounded and sick, the infirm and maternity cases, may in no circumstances be the object of attack, but shall at all times be respected and protected by the Parties to the conflict.

States which are Parties to a conflict shall provide all civilian hospitals with certificates showing that they are civilian hospitals and that the buildings which they occupy are not used for any purpose which would deprive these hospitals of protection in accordance with Article 19.

Civilian hospitals shall be marked by means of the emblem provided for in Article 38 of the Geneva

Convention for the Amelioration of the Condition of the Wounded and Sick in Armed Forces in the Field of August 12, 1949, but only if so authorized by the State.

The Parties to the conflict shall, in so far as military considerations permit, take the necessary steps to make the distinctive emblems indicating civilian hospitals clearly visible to the enemy land, air and naval forces in order to obviate the possibility of any hostile action.

In view of the dangers to which hospitals may be exposed by being close to military objectives, it is recommended that such hospitals be situated as far as possible from such objectives.

Article 19

The protection to which civilian hospitals are entitled shall not cease unless they are used to commit, outside their humanitarian duties, acts harmful to the enemy. Protection may, however, cease only after due warning has been given, naming, in all appropriate cases, a reasonable time limit, and after such warning has remained unheeded.

The fact that sick or wounded members of the armed forces are nursed in these hospitals, or the presence of small arms and ammunition taken from such combatants which have not yet been handed to the proper service, shall not be considered to be acts harmful to the enemy.

Article 20

Persons regularly and solely engaged in the operation and administration of civilian hospitals, including the personnel engaged in the search for, removal and transporting of and caring for wounded and sick civilians, the infirm and maternity cases, shall be respected and protected.

In occupied territory and in zones of military operations, the above personnel shall be recognizable by means of an identity card certifying their status, bearing the photograph of the holder and embossed with the stamp of the responsible authority, and also by means of a stamped, water-resistant armlet which they shall wear on the left arm while carrying out their duties. This armlet shall be issued by the State and shall bear the emblem provided for in Article 38 of the Geneva Convention for the Amelioration of the Condition of the Wounded and Sick in Armed Forces in the Field of August 12, 1949.

Other personnel who are engaged in the operation and administration of civilian hospitals shall be entitled to respect and protection and to wear the armlet, as provided in and under the conditions prescribed in this Article, while they are employed on such duties. The identity card shall state the duties on which they are employed.

The management of each hospital shall at all times hold at the disposal of the competent national or occupying authorities an up-to-date list of such personnel.

Article 21

Convoys of vehicles or hospital trains on land or specially provided vessels on sea, conveying wounded and sick civilians, the infirm and maternity cases, shall be respected and protected in the same manner as the hospitals provided for in Article 18, and shall be marked, with the consent of the State, by the display of the distinctive emblem provided for in Article 38 of the Geneva Convention for the Amelioration of the Condition of the Wounded and Sick in Armed Forces in the Field of August 12, 1949.

Article 22

Aircraft exclusively employed for the removal of wounded and sick civilians, the infirm and maternity cases, or for the transport of medical personnel and equipment, shall not be attacked, but shall be respected while flying at heights, times and on routes specifically agreed upon between all the Parties to the conflict concerned.

They may be marked with the distinctive emblem provided for in Article 38 of the Geneva Convention for the Amelioration of the Condition of the Wounded and Sick in Armed Forces in the Field of August 12, 1949.

Unless agreed otherwise, flights over enemy or enemy-occupied territory are prohibited.

Such aircraft shall obey every summons to land. In the event of a landing thus imposed, the aircraft with its occupants may continue its flight after examination, if any.

Article 23

Each High Contracting Party shall allow the free passage of all consignments of medical and hospital stores and objects necessary for religious worship intended only for civilians of another High Contracting Party, even if the latter is its adversary. It shall likewise permit the free passage of all consignments of essential foodstuffs, clothing and tonics intended for children under fifteen, expectant mothers and maternity cases.

The obligation of a High Contracting Party to allow the free passage of the consignments indicated in the preceding paragraph is subject to the condition that this Party is satisfied that there are no serious reasons for fearing:

(a) That the consignments may be diverted from their destination;

(b) That the control may not be effective; or

(c) That a definite advantage may accrue to the military efforts or economy of the enemy through the substitution of the above-mentioned consignments for goods which would otherwise be provided or produced by the enemy or through the release of such material, services or facilities as would otherwise be required for the production of such goods.

The Power which allows the passage of the consignments indicated in the first paragraph of this Article may make such permission conditional on the distribution to the persons benefited there by being made under the local supervision of the Protecting Powers.

Such consignments shall be forwarded as rapidly as possible, and the Power which permits their free passage shall have the right to prescribe the technical arrangements under which such passage is allowed.

Article 24

The Parties to the conflict shall take the necessary measures to ensure that children under fifteen, who are orphaned or are separated from their families as a result of the war, are not left to their own resources, and that their maintenance, the exercise of their religion and their education are facilitated in all circumstances. Their education shall, as far as possible, be entrusted to persons of a similar cultural tradition.

The Parties to the conflict shall facilitate the reception of such children in a neutral country for the duration of the conflict with the consent of the Protecting Power, if any, and under due safeguards for the observance of the principles stated in the first paragraph.

They shall, furthermore, endeavour to arrange for all children under twelve to be identified by the wearing of identity discs, or by some other means.

Article 25

All persons in the territory of a Party to the conflict, or in a territory occupied by it, shall be enabled to give news of a strictly personal nature to members of their families, wherever they may be, and to receive news from them. This correspondence shall be forwarded speedily and without undue delay.

If, as a result of circumstances, it becomes difficult or impossible to exchange family correspondence by the ordinary post, the Parties to the conflict concerned shall apply to a neutral intermediary, such as the Central Agency provided for in Article 140, and shall decide in consultation with it how to ensure the fulfilment of their obligations under the best possible conditions, in particular with the cooperation of the National Red Cross (Red Crescent, Red Lion and Sun) Societies.

If the Parties to the conflict deem it necessary to restrict family correspondence, such restrictions shall be confined to the compulsory use of standard forms containing twenty-five freely chosen words, and to the limitation of the number of these forms dispatched to one each month.

CONVENTION ON THE PREVENTION AND PUNISHMENT OF THE CRIME OF GENOCIDE

Adopted by Resolution 260 (III) A of the United Nations General Assembly on 9 December 1948

Article 1

The Contracting Parties confirm that genocide, whether committed in time of peace or in time of war, is a crime under international law which they undertake to prevent and to punish.

Article 2

In the present Convention, genocide means any of the following acts committed with intent to destroy, in whole or in part, a national, ethnical, racial or religious group, as such:

(a) Killing members of the group;

(b) Causing serious bodily or mental harm to members of the group;

(c) Deliberately inflicting on the group conditions of life calculated to bring about its physical destruction in whole or in part;

(d) Imposing measures intended to prevent births within the group;

(e) Forcibly transferring children of the group to another group.

Article 3

The following acts shall be punishable:

(a) Genocide;

(b) Conspiracy to commit genocide;

(c) Direct and public incitement to commit genocide;

(d) Attempt to commit genocide;

(e) Complicity in genocide.

Article 4

Persons committing genocide or any of the other acts enumerated in Article 3 shall be punished, whether they are constitutionally responsible rulers, public officials or private individuals.

Article 5

The Contracting Parties undertake to enact, in accordance with their respective Constitutions, the necessary legislation to give effect to the provisions of the present Convention and, in particular, to provide effective penalties for persons guilty of genocide or any of the other acts enumerated in Article 3.

Article 6

Persons charged with genocide or any of the other acts enumerated in Article 3 shall be tried by a competent tribunal of the State in the territory of which the act was committed, or by such international penal tribunal as may have jurisdiction with respect to those Contracting Parties which shall have accepted its jurisdiction.

Article 7

Genocide and the other acts enumerated in Article 3 shall not be considered as political crimes for the purpose of extradition.

The Contracting Parties pledge themselves in such cases to grant extradition in accordance with their laws and treaties in force.

Article 8

Any Contracting Party may call upon the competent organs of the United Nations to take such action under the Charter of the United Nations as they consider appropriate for the prevention and suppression of acts of genocide or any of the other acts enumerated in Article 3.

Article 9

Disputes between the Contracting Parties relating to the interpretation, application or fulfilment of the present Convention, including those relating to the responsibility of a State for genocide or any of the other acts enumerated in Article 3, shall be submitted to the International Court of Justice at the request of any of the parties to the dispute.

Article 10

The present Convention, of which the Chinese, English, French, Russian and Spanish texts are equally authentic, shall bear the date of 9 December 1948.

Article 11

The present Convention shall be open until 31 December 1949 for signature on behalf of any Member of the United Nations and of any non-member State to which an invitation to sign has been addressed by the General Assembly.

The present Convention shall be ratified, and the instruments of ratification shall be deposited with the Secretary-General of the United Nations.

After 1 January 1950, the present Convention may be acceded to on behalf of any Member of the United Nations and of any non-member State which has received an invitation as aforesaid.

Instruments of accession shall be deposited with the Secretary-General of the United Nations.

Article 12

Any Contracting Party may at any time, by notification addressed to the Secretary-General of the United Nations, extend the application of the present Convention to all or any of the territories for the conduct of whose foreign relations that Contracting Party is responsible.

Article 13

On the day when the first twenty instruments of ratification or accession have been deposited, the Secretary-General shall draw up a proces-verbal and transmit a copy of it to each Member of the United Nations and to each of the non-member States contemplated in Article 11.

The present Convention shall come into force on the ninetieth day following the date of deposit of the twentieth instrument of ratification or accession.

Any ratification or accession effected subsequent to the latter date shall become effective on the ninetieth day following the deposit of the instrument of ratification or accession.

Article 14

The present Convention shall remain in effect for a period of ten years as from the date of its coming into force.

It shall thereafter remain in force for successive periods of five years for such Contracting Parties as have not denounced it at least six months before the expiration of the current period.

Denunciation shall be effected by a written notification addressed to the Secretary-General of the United Nations.

Article 15

If, as a result of denunciations, the number of Parties to the present Convention should become less than sixteen, the Convention shall cease to be in force as from the date on which the last of these denunciations shall become effective.

Article 16

A request for the revision of the present Convention may be made at any time by any Contracting Party by means of a notification in writing addressed to the Secretary-General.

The General Assembly shall decide upon the steps, if any, to be taken in respect of such request.

Article 17

The Secretary-General of the United Nations shall notify all Members of the United Nations and the non-member States contemplated in Article 11 of the following:

(a) Signatures, ratifications and accessions received in accordance with Article 11;

(b) Notifications received in accordance with Article 12;

(c) The date upon which the present Convention comes into force in accordance with Article 13;

(d) Denunciations received in accordance with Article 14;

(e) The abrogation of the Convention in accordance with Article 15;

(f) Notifications received in accordance with Article 16.

Article 18

The original of the present Convention shall be deposited in the archives of the United Nations.

A certified copy of the Convention shall be transmitted to all Members of the United Nations and to the non-member States contemplated in Article 11.

Article 19

The present Convention shall be registered by the Secretary-General of the United Nations on the date of its coming into force.

UNIVERSAL DECLARATION OF HUMAN RIGHTS

Adopted and proclaimed by General Assembly Resolution 217 A (III) of 10 December 1948

On December 10, 1948 the General Assembly of the United Nations adopted and proclaimed the Universal Declaration of Human Rights the full text of which appears in the following pages. Following this historic act the Assembly called upon all Member countries to publicize the text of the Declaration and "to cause it to be disseminated, displayed, read and expounded principally in schools and other educational institutions, without distinction based on the political status of countries or territories."

Preamble

Whereas recognition of the inherent dignity and of the equal and inalienable rights of all members of the human family is the foundation of freedom, justice and peace in the world,

Whereas disregard and contempt for human rights have resulted in barbarous acts which have outraged the conscience of mankind, and the advent of a world in which human beings shall enjoy freedom of speech and belief and freedom from fear and want has been proclaimed as the highest aspiration of the common people,

Whereas it is essential, if man is not to be compelled to have recourse, as a last resort, to rebellion against tyranny and oppression, that human rights should be protected by the rule of law,

Whereas it is essential to promote the development of friendly relations between nations,

Whereas the peoples of the United Nations have in the Charter reaffirmed their faith in fundamental human rights, in the dignity and worth of the human person and in the equal rights of men and women and have determined to promote social progress and better standards of life in larger freedom,

Whereas Member States have pledged themselves to achieve, in co-operation with the United Nations, the promotion of universal respect for and observance of human rights and fundamental freedoms,

Whereas a common understanding of these rights and freedoms is of the greatest importance for the full realization of this pledge,

Now, Therefore THE GENERAL ASSEMBLY proclaims THIS UNIVERSAL DECLARATION OF HUMAN RIGHTS as a common standard of achievement for all peoples and all nations, to the end that every individual and every organ of society, keeping this Declaration constantly in mind, shall strive by teaching and education to promote respect for these rights and freedoms and by progressive measures, national and international, to secure their universal and effective recognition and observance, both among the peoples of Member States themselves and among the peoples of territories under their jurisdiction.

Article 1.

All human beings are born free and equal in dignity and rights. They are endowed with reason and conscience and should act towards one another in a spirit of brotherhood.

Article 2.
Everyone is entitled to all the rights and freedoms set forth in this Declaration, without distinction of any kind, such as race, colour, sex, language, religion, political or other opinion, national or social origin, property, birth or other status. Furthermore, no distinction shall be made on the basis of the political, jurisdictional or international status of the country or territory to which a person belongs, whether it be independent, trust, non-self-governing or under any other limitation of sovereignty.

Article 3.
Everyone has the right to life, liberty and security of person.

Article 4.
No one shall be held in slavery or servitude; slavery and the slave trade shall be prohibited in all their forms.

Article 5.
No one shall be subjected to torture or to cruel, inhuman or degrading treatment or punishment.

Article 6.
Everyone has the right to recognition everywhere as a person before the law.

Article 7.
All are equal before the law and are entitled without any discrimination to equal protection of the law. All are entitled to equal protection against any discrimination in violation of this Declaration and against any incitement to such discrimination.

Article 8.
Everyone has the right to an effective remedy by the competent national tribunals for acts violating the fundamental rights granted him by the constitution or by law.

Article 9.
No one shall be subjected to arbitrary arrest, detention or exile.

Article 10.
Everyone is entitled in full equality to a fair and public hearing by an independent and impartial tribunal, in the determination of his rights and obligations and of any criminal charge against him.

Article 11.
(1) Everyone charged with a penal offence has the right to be presumed innocent until proved guilty according to law in a public trial at which he has had all the guarantees necessary for his defence.

(2) No one shall be held guilty of any penal offence on account of any act or omission which did not constitute a penal offence, under national or international law, at the time when it was committed. Nor shall a heavier penalty be imposed than the one that was applicable at the time the penal offence was committed.

Article 12.
No one shall be subjected to arbitrary interference with his privacy, family, home or correspondence, nor to attacks upon his honour and reputation. Everyone has the right to the protection of the law against such interference or attacks.

Article 13.
(1) Everyone has the right to freedom of movement and residence within the borders of each state.

(2) Everyone has the right to leave any country, including his own, and to return to his country.

Article 14.
(1) Everyone has the right to seek and to enjoy in other countries asylum from persecution.

(2) This right may not be invoked in the case of prosecutions genuinely arising from non-political crimes or from acts contrary to the purposes and principles of the United Nations.

Article 15.
(1) Everyone has the right to a nationality.

(2) No one shall be arbitrarily deprived of his nationality nor denied the right to change his nationality.

Article 16.
(1) Men and women of full age, without any limitation due to race, nationality or religion, have the right to marry and to found a family. They are entitled to equal rights as to marriage, during marriage and at its dissolution.

(2) Marriage shall be entered into only with the free and full consent of the intending spouses.

(3) The family is the natural and fundamental group unit of society and is entitled to protection by society and the State.

Article 17.
(1) Everyone has the right to own property alone as well as in association with others.

(2) No one shall be arbitrarily deprived of his property.

Article 18.
Everyone has the right to freedom of thought, conscience and religion; this right includes freedom to change his religion or belief, and freedom, either alone or in community with others and in public or private, to manifest his religion or belief in teaching, practice, worship and observance.

Article 19.
Everyone has the right to freedom of opinion and expression; this right includes freedom to hold opinions without interference and to seek, receive and impart information and ideas through any media and regardless of frontiers.

Article 20.
(1) Everyone has the right to freedom of peaceful assembly and association.

(2) No one may be compelled to belong to an association.

Article 21.
(1) Everyone has the right to take part in the government of his country, directly or through freely chosen representatives.

(2) Everyone has the right of equal access to public service in his country.

(3) The will of the people shall be the basis of the authority of government; this will shall be expressed in periodic and genuine elections which shall be by universal and equal suffrage and shall be held by secret vote or by equivalent free voting procedures.

Article 22.
Everyone, as a member of society, has the right to social security and is entitled to realization, through national effort and international co-operation and in accordance with the organization and resources of each State, of the economic, social and cultural rights indispensable for his dignity and the free development of his personality.

Article 23.
(1) Everyone has the right to work, to free choice of employment, to just and favourable conditions of work and to protection against unemployment.

(2) Everyone, without any discrimination, has the right to equal pay for equal work.

(3) Everyone who works has the right to just and favourable remuneration ensuring for himself and his family an existence worthy of human dignity, and supplemented, if necessary, by other means of social protection.

(4) Everyone has the right to form and to join trade unions for the protection of his interests.

Article 24.
Everyone has the right to rest and leisure, including reasonable limitation of working hours and periodic holidays with pay.

Article 25.
(1) Everyone has the right to a standard of living adequate for the health and well-being of himself and of his family, including food, clothing, housing and medical care and necessary social services, and the right to security in the event of unemployment, sickness, disability, widowhood, old age or other lack of livelihood in circumstances beyond his control.

(2) Motherhood and childhood are entitled to special care and assistance. All children, whether born in or out of wedlock, shall enjoy the same social protection.

Article 26.
(1) Everyone has the right to education. Education shall be free, at least in the elementary and fundamental stages. Elementary education shall be compulsory. Technical and professional education shall be made generally available and higher education shall be equally accessible to all on the basis of merit.

(2) Education shall be directed to the full development of the human personality and to the strengthening of respect for human rights and fundamental freedoms. It shall promote understanding, tolerance and friendship among all nations, racial or religious groups, and shall further the activities of the United Nations for the maintenance of peace.

(3) Parents have a prior right to choose the kind of education that shall be given to their children.

Article 27.
(1) Everyone has the right freely to participate in the cultural life of the community, to enjoy the arts and to share in scientific advancement and its benefits.

(2) Everyone has the right to the protection of the moral and material interests resulting from any scientific, literary or artistic production of which he is the author.

Article 28.
Everyone is entitled to a social and international order in which the rights and freedoms set forth in this Declaration can be fully realized.

Article 29.
(1) Everyone has duties to the community in which alone the free and full development of his personality is possible.

(2) In the exercise of his rights and freedoms, everyone shall be subject only to such limitations as are determined by law solely for the purpose of securing due recognition and respect for the rights and freedoms of others and of meeting the just requirements of morality, public order and the general welfare in a democratic society.

(3) These rights and freedoms may in no case be exercised contrary to the purposes and principles of the United Nations.

Article 30.
Nothing in this Declaration may be interpreted as implying for any State, group or person any right to engage in any activity or to perform any act aimed at the destruction of any of the rights and freedoms set forth herein.

United Nations Convention against Torture and Other Cruel, Inhuman or Degrading Treatment or Punishment

★

The States Parties to this Convention,

Considering that, in accordance with the principles proclaimed in the Charter of the United Nations, recognition of the equal and inalienable rights of all members of the human family is the foundation of freedom, justice and peace in the world,

Recognizing that those rights derive from the inherent dignity of the human person,

Considering the obligation of States under the Charter, in particular Article 55, to promote universal respect for, and observance of, human rights and fundamental freedoms,

Having regard to article 5 of the Universal Declaration of Human Rights and article 7 of the International Covenant on Civil and Political Rights, both of which provide that no one may be subjected to torture or to cruel, inhuman or degrading treatment or punishment,

Having regard also to the Declaration on the Protection of All Persons from Being Subjected to Torture and Other Cruel, Inhuman or Degrading Treatment or Punishment, adopted by the General Assembly on 9 December 1975 (resolution 3452 (XXX)),

Desiring to make more effective the struggle against torture and other cruel, inhuman or degrading treatment or punishment throughout the world,

Have agreed as follows:

Part I

Article 1

1. For the purposes of this Convention, torture means any act by which severe pain or suffering, whether physical or men-

tal, is intentionally inflicted on a person for such purposes as obtaining from him or a third person information or a confession, punishing him for an act he or a third person has committed or is suspected of having committed, or intimidating or coercing him or a third person, or for any reason based on discrimination of any kind, when such pain or suffering is inflicted by or at the instigation of or with the consent or acquiescence of a public official or other person acting in an official capacity. It does not include pain or suffering arising only from, inherent in or incidental to lawful sanctions.

2. This article is without prejudice to any international instrument or national legislation which does or may contain provisions of wider application.

Article 2

1. Each State Party shall take effective legislative, administrative, judicial or other measures to prevent acts of torture in any territory under its jurisdiction.

2. No exceptional circumstances whatsoever, whether a state of war or a threat or war, internal political instability or any other public emergency, may be invoked as a justification of torture.

3. An order from a superior officer or a public authority may not be invoked as a justification of torture.

Article 3

1. No State Party shall expel, return ("refouler") or extradite a person to another State where there are substantial grounds for believing that he would be in danger of being subjected to torture.

2. For the purpose of determining whether there are such grounds, the competent authorities shall take into

account all relevant considerations including, where applicable, the existence in the State concerned of a consistent pattern of gross, flagrant or mass violations of human rights.

Article 4

1. Each State Party shall ensure that all acts of torture are offences under its criminal law. The same shall apply to an attempt to commit torture and to an act by any person which constitutes complicity or participation in torture.

2. Each State Party shall make these offences punishable by appropriate penalties which take into account their grave nature.

Article 5

1. Each State Party shall take such measures as may be necessary to establish its jurisdiction over the offences referred to in article 4 in the following cases:

   1. When the offences are committed in any territory under its jurisdiction or on board a ship or aircraft registered in that State;
   2. When the alleged offender is a national of that State;
   3. When the victim was a national of that State if that State considers it appropriate.

2. Each State Party shall likewise take such measures as may be necessary to establish its jurisdiction over such offences in cases where the alleged offender is present in any territory under its jurisdiction and it does not extradite him pursuant to article 8 to any of the States mentioned in Paragraph 1 of this article.

3. This Convention does not exclude any criminal jurisdiction exercised in accordance with internal law.

Article 6

1. Upon being satisfied, after an examination of information available to it, that the circumstances so warrant, any State Party in whose territory a person alleged to have committed any offence referred to in article 4 is present, shall take him into custody or take other legal measures to ensure his presence. The custody and other legal measures shall be as provided in the law of that State but may be continued only for such time as is necessary to enable any criminal or extradition proceedings to be instituted.

2. Such State shall immediately make a preliminary inquiry into the facts.

3. Any person in custody pursuant to paragraph 1 of this article shall be assisted in communicating immediately with the nearest appropriate representative of the State of which he is a national, or, if he is a stateless person, to the representative of the State where he usually resides.

4. When a State, pursuant to this article, has taken a person into custody, it shall immediately notify the States referred to in article 5, paragraph 1, of the fact that such person is in custody and of the circumstances which warrant his detention. The State which makes the preliminary inquiry contemplated in paragraph 2 of this article shall promptly report its findings to the said State and shall indicate whether it intends to exercise jurisdiction.

Article 7

1. The State Party in territory under whose jurisdiction a person alleged to have committed any offence referred to in article 4 is found, shall in the cases contemplated in article 5, if it does not extradite him, submit the case to its competent authorities for the purpose of prosecution.

2. These authorities shall take their decision in the same manner as in the case of any ordinary offence of a serious nature under the law of that State. In the cases referred to in article 5, paragraph 2, the standards of evidence required for prosecution and conviction shall in no way be less stringent than those which apply in the cases referred to in article 5, paragraph 1.

3. Any person regarding whom proceedings are brought in connection with any of the offences referred to in article 4 shall be guaranteed fair treatment at all stages of the proceedings.

Article 8

1. The offences referred to in article 4 shall be deemed to be included as extraditable offences in any extradition treaty existing between States Parties. States Parties undertake to include such offences as extraditable offences in every extradition treaty to be concluded between them.

2. If a State Party which makes extradition conditional on the existence of a treaty receives a request for extradition from another State Party with which it has no extradition treaty, it may consider this Convention as the legal basis for extradition in respect of such offenses. Extradition shall be subject to the other conditions provided by the law of the requested State.

3. States Parties which do not make extradition conditional on the existence of a treaty shall recognize such offences as extraditable offences between themselves subject to the conditions provided by the law of the requested state.

4. Such offences shall be treated, for the purpose of extradition between States Parties, as if they had been committed not only in the place in which they occurred but also in the territories of the States required to establish their jurisdiction in accordance with article 5, paragraph 1.

Article 9

1. States Parties shall afford one another the greatest measure of assistance in connection with civil proceedings brought in respect of any of the offences referred to in

article 4, including the supply of all evidence at their disposal necessary for the proceedings.

2. States Parties shall carry out their obligations under paragraph 1 of this article in conformity with any treaties on mutual judicial assistance that may exist between them.

Article 10

1. Each State Party shall ensure that education and information regarding the prohibition against torture are fully included in the training of law enforcement personnel, civil or military, medical personnel, public officials and other persons who may be involved in the custody, interrogation or treatment of any individual subjected to any form of arrest, detention or imprisonment.

2. Each State Party shall include this prohibition in the rules or instructions issued in regard to the duties and functions of any such persons.

Article 11

Each State Party shall keep under systematic review interrogation rules, instructions, methods and practices as well as arrangements for the custody and treatment of persons subjected to any form of arrest, detention or imprisonment in any territory under its jurisdiction, with a view to preventing any cases of torture.

Article 12

Each State Party shall ensure that its competent authorities proceed to a prompt and impartial investigation, wherever there is reasonable ground to believe that an act of torture has been committed in any territory under its jurisdiction.

Article 13

Each State Party shall ensure that any individual who alleges he has been subjected to torture in any territory under its jurisdiction has the right to complain to and to have his case promptly and impartially examined its competent authorities. Steps shall be taken to ensure that the complainant and witnesses are protected against all ill-treatment or intimidation as a consequence of his complaint or any evidence given.

Article 14

1. Each State Party shall ensure in its legal system that the victim of an act of torture obtains redress and has an enforceable right to fair and adequate compensation including the means for as full rehabilitation as possible. In the event of the death of the victim as a result of an act of torture, his dependents shall be entitled to compensation.

2. Nothing in this article shall affect any right of the victim or other person to compensation which may exist under national law.

Article 15

Each State Party shall ensure that any statement which is established to have been made as a result of torture shall not be invoked as evidence in any proceedings, except against a person accused of torture as evidence that the statement was made.

Article 16

1. Each State Party shall undertake to prevent in any territory under its jurisdiction other acts of cruel, inhuman or degrading treatment or punishment which do not amount to torture as defined in article 1, when such acts are committed by or at the instigation of or with the consent or acquiescence of a public official or other person acting in an official capacity. In particular, the obligations contained in articles 10, 11, 12 and 13 shall apply with the substitution for references to torture or references to other forms of cruel, inhuman or degrading treatment or punishment.

2. The provisions of this Convention are without prejudice to the provisions of any other international instrument or national law which prohibit cruel, inhuman or degrading treatment or punishment or which relate to extradition or expulsion.

Article 17

1. There shall be established a Committee against Torture (hereinafter referred to as the Committee) which shall carry out the functions hereinafter provided. The Committee shall consist of 10 experts of high moral standing and recognized competence in the field of human rights, who shall serve in their personal capacity. The experts shall be elected by the States Parties, consideration being given to equitable geographical distribution and to the usefulness of the participation of some persons having legal experience.

2. The members of the Committee shall be elected by secret ballot from a list of persons nominated by States Parties. Each State Party may nominate one person from among its own nationals. States Parties shall bear in mind the usefulness of nominating persons who are also members of the Human Rights Committee established under the International Covenant on Civil and Political Rights and are willing to serve on the Committee against Torture.

3. Elections of the members of the Committee shall be held at biennial meetings of States Parties convened by the Secretary-General of the United Nations. At those meetings, for which two thirds of the States Parties shall constitute a quorum, the persons elected to the Committee shall be those who obtain the largest number of votes and an absolute majority of the votes of the representatives of States Parties present and voting.

4. The initial election shall be held no later than six months after the date of the entry into force of this

Convention. At least four months before the date of each election, the Secretary-General of the United Nations shall address a letter to the States Parties inviting them to submit their nominations within three months. The Secretary-General shall prepare a list in alphabetical order of all persons thus nominated, indicating the States Parties which have nominated them, and shall submit it to the States Parties.

5. The members of the Committee shall be elected for a term of four years. They shall be eligible for re-election if renominated. However, the term of five of the members elected at the first election shall expire at the end of two years; immediately after the first election the names of these five members shall be chosen by lot by the chairman of the meeting referred to in paragraph 3.

6. If a member of the Committee dies or resigns or for any other cause can no longer perform his Committee duties, the State Party which nominated him shall appoint another expert from among its nationals to serve for the remainder of his term, subject to the approval of the majority of the States Parties. The approval shall be considered given unless half or more of the States Parties respond negatively within six weeks after having been informed by the Secretary-General of the United Nations of the proposed appointment.

7. States Parties shall be responsible for the expenses of the members of the Committee while they are in performance of Committee duties.

Article 18

1. The Committee shall elect its officers for a term of two years. They may be re-elected.

2. The Committee shall establish its own rules of procedure, but these rules shall provide, inter alia, that

1. Six members shall constitute a quorum;
2. Decisions of the Committee shall be made by a majority vote of the members present.

3. The Secretary-General of the United Nations shall provide the necessary staff and facilities for the effective performance of the functions of the Committee under this Convention.

4. The Secretary-General of the United Nations shall convene the initial meeting of the Committee. After its initial meeting, the Committee shall meet at such times as shall be provided in its rules of procedure.

5. The State Parties shall be responsible for expenses incurred in connection with the holding of meetings of the States Parties and of the Committee, including reimbursement of the United Nations for any expenses, such as the cost of staff and facilities, incurred by the United Nations pursuant to paragraph 3 above.

Article 19

1. The States Parties shall submit to the Committee, through the Secretary-General of the United Nations,

reports on the measures they have taken to give effect to their undertakings under this Convention, within one year after the entry into force of this Convention for the State Party concerned. Thereafter the States Parties shall submit supplementary reports every four years on any new measures taken, and such other reports as the Committee may request.

2. The Secretary-General shall transmit the reports to all States Parties.

3. [Each report shall be considered by the Committee which may make such comments or suggestions on the report as it considers appropriate, and shall forward these to the State Party concerned. That State Party may respond with any observations it chooses to the Committee.

4. The Committee may, at its discretion, decide to include any comments or suggestions made by it in accordance with paragraph 3, together with the observations thereon received from the State Party concerned, in its annual report made in accordance with article 24. If so requested by the State Party concerned, the Committee may also include a copy of the report submitted under paragraph 1.]

Article 20

1. If the Committee receives reliable information which appears to it to contain well-founded indications that torture is being systematically practised in the territory of a State Party, the Committee shall invite that State Party to co-operate in the examination of the information and to this end to submit observations with regard to the information concerned.

2. Taking into account any observations which may have been submitted by the State Party concerned as well as any other relevant information available to it, the Committee may, if it decides that this is warranted, designate one or more of its members to make a confidential inquiry and to report to the Committee urgently.

3. If an inquiry is made in accordance with paragraph 2, the Committee shall seek the co-operation of the State Party concerned. In agreement with that State Party, such an inquiry may include a visit to its territory.

4. After examining the findings of its member or members submitted in accordance with paragraph 2, the Committee shall transmit these findings to the State Party concerned together with any comments or suggestions which seem appropriate in view of the situation.

5. All the proceedings of the Committee referred to in paragraphs 1 to 4 of this article shall be confidential, and at all stages of the proceedings the co-operation of the State Party shall be sought. After such proceedings have been completed with regard to an inquiry made in accordance with paragraph 2, the Committee may, after consultations with the State Party concerned, decide to include a

summary account of the results of the proceedings in its annual report made in accordance with article 24.

Article 21

1. A State Party to this Convention may at any time declare under this article 3 that it recognizes the competence of the Committee to receive and consider communications to the effect that a State Party claims that another State Party is not fulfilling its obligations under this Convention. Such communications may be received and considered according to the procedures laid down in this article only if submitted by a State Party which has made a declaration recognizing in regard to itself the competence of the Committee. No communication shall be dealt with by the Committee under this article if it concerns a State Party which has not made such a declaration. Communications received under this article shall be dealt with in accordance with the following procedure:

1. If a State Party considers that another State Party is not giving effect to the provisions of this Convention, it may, by written communication, bring the matter to the attention of that State Party. Within three months after the receipt of the communication the receiving State shall afford the State which sent the communication an explanation or any other statement in writing clarifying the matter which should include, to the extent possible and pertinent, references to domestic procedures and remedies taken, pending, or available in the matter.

2. If the matter is not adjusted to the satisfaction of both States Parties concerned within six months after the receipt by the receiving State of the initial communication, either State shall have the right to refer the matter to the Committee by notice given to the Committee and to the other State.

3. The Committee shall deal with a matter referred to it under this article only after it has ascertained that all domestic remedies have been invoked and exhausted in the matter, in conformity with the generally recognized principles of international law. This shall not be the rule where the application of the remedies is unreasonably prolonged or is unlikely to bring effective relief to the person who is the victim of the violation of this Convention.

4. The Committee shall hold closed meetings when examining communications under this article.

5. Subject to the provisions of subparagraph (c), the Committee shall make available its good offices to the States Parties concerned with a view to a friendly solution of the matter on the basis of respect for the obligations provided for in the present Convention. For this purpose, the Committee may, when appropriate, set up an ad hoc conciliation commission.

6. In any matter referred to it under this article, the Committee may call upon the States Parties concerned, referred to in subparagraph (b), to supply any relevant information.

7. The States Parties concerned, referred to in subparagraph (b), shall have the right to be represented when the matter is being considered by the Committee and to make submissions orally and/or in writing.

8. The Committee shall, within 12 months after the date of receipt of notice under subparagraph (b), submit a report.

   1. If a solution within the terms of subparagraph (e) is reached, the Committee shall confine its report to a brief statement of the facts and of the solution reached.

   2. If a solution within the terms of subparagraph (e) is not reached, the Committee shall confine its report to a brief statement of the facts; the written submissions and record of the oral submissions made by the States Parties concerned shall be attached to the report.

In every matter, the report shall be communicated to the States Parties concerned.

2. The provisions of this article shall come into force when five States Parties to this Convention have made declarations under paragraph 1 of this article. Such declarations shall be deposited by the States Parties with the Secretary-General of the United Nations, who shall transmit copies thereof to the other States Parties. A declaration may be withdrawn at any time by notification to the Secretary-General. Such a withdrawal shall not prejudice the consideration of any matter which is the subject of a communication already transmitted under this article; no further communication by any State Party shall be received under this article after the notification of withdrawal of the declaration has been received by the Secretary-General, unless the State Party concerned has made a new declaration.

Article 22

1. A State Party to this Convention may at any time declare under this article that it recognizes the competence of the Committee to receive and consider communications from or on behalf of individuals subject to its jurisdiction who claim to be victims of a violation by a State Party of the provisions of the Convention. No communication shall be received by the Committee if it concerns a State Party to the Convention which has not made such a declaration.

2. The Committee shall consider inadmissible any communication under this article which is anonymous, or

which it considers to be an abuse of the right of submission of such communications or to be incompatible with the provisions of this Convention.

3. Subject to the provisions of paragraph 2, the Committee shall bring any communication submitted to it under this article to the attention of the State Party to this Convention which has made a declaration under paragraph 1 and is alleged to be violating any provisions of the Convention. Within six months, the receiving State shall submit to the Committee written explanations or statements clarifying the matter and the remedy, if any, that may have been taken by that State.

4. The Committee shall consider communications received under this article in the light of all information made available to it by or on behalf of the individual and by the State Party concerned.

5. The Committee shall not consider any communication from an individual under this article unless it has ascertained that:

1. The same matter has not been, and is not being examined under another procedure of international investigation or settlement;
2. The individual has exhausted all available domestic remedies; this shall not be the rule where the application of the remedies is unreasonably prolonged or is unlikely to bring effective relief to the person who is the victim of the violation of this Convention.

6. The Committee shall hold closed meetings when examining communications under this article.

7. The Committee shall forward its views to the State Party concerned and to the individual.

8. The provisions of this article shall come into force when five States Parties to this Convention have made declarations under paragraph 1 of this article. Such declarations shall be deposited by the States Parties with the Secretary-General of the United Nations, who shall transmit parties thereof to the other States Parties. A declaration may be withdrawn at any time by notification to the Secretary-General. Such a withdrawal shall not prejudice the consideration of any matter which is the subject of a communication already transmitted under this article; no further communication by or on behalf of an individual shall be received under this article after the notification of withdrawal of the declaration has been received by the Secretary-General, unless the State Party concerned has made a new declaration.

Article 23

The members of the Committee, and of the ad hoc conciliation commissions which may be appointed under article 21, paragraph 1 (e), shall be entitled to the facilities, privileges and immunities of experts on missions for the United Nations as laid down in the relevant sections of the Convention on the Privileges and Immunities of the United Nations.

Article 24

The Committee shall submit an annual report on its activities under this Convention to the States Parties and to the General Assembly of the United Nations.

Part III

Article 25

1. This Convention is open for signature by all States.

2. This Convention is subject to ratification. Instruments of ratification shall be deposited with the Secretary-General of the United Nations.

Article 26

This Convention is open to accession by all States. Accession shall be effected by the deposit of an instrument of accession with the Secretary-General of the United Nations.

Article 27

1. This Convention shall enter into force on the thirtieth day after the date of the deposit with the Secretary-General of the United Nations of the twentieth instrument of ratification or accession.

2. For each State ratifying this Convention or acceding to it after the deposit of the twentieth instrument of ratification or accession, the Convention shall enter into force on the thirtieth day after the date of the deposit of its own instrument of ratification or accession.

Article 28

1. Each State may, at the time of signature or ratification of this Convention or accession thereto, declare that it does not recognize the competence of the Committee provided for in article 20.

2. Any State Party having made a reservation in accordance with paragraph 1 of this article may, at any time, withdraw this reservation by notification to the Secretary-General of the United Nations.

Article 29

1. Any State Party to this Convention may propose an amendment and file it with the Secretary-General of the United Nations. The Secretary-General shall thereupon communicate the proposed amendment to the States Parties to this Convention with a request that they notify him whether they favour a conference of States Parties for the purpose of considering and voting upon the proposal. In the event that within four months from the date of such communication at least one third of the State Parties favours

such a conference, the Secretary-General shall convene the conference under the auspices of the United Nations. Any amendment adopted by a majority of the States Parties present and voting at the conference shall be submitted by the Secretary-General to all the States Parties for acceptance.

2. An amendment adopted in accordance with paragraph 1 shall enter into force when two thirds of the States Parties to this Convention have notified the Secretary-General of the United Nations that they have accepted it in accordance with their respective constitutional processes.

3. When amendments enter into force, they shall be binding on those States Parties which have accepted them, other States Parties still being bound by the provisions of this Convention and any earlier amendments which they have accepted.

Article 30

1. Any dispute between two or more States Parties concerning the interpretation or application of this Convention which cannot be settled through negotiation, shall, at the request of one of them, be submitted to arbitration. If within six months from the date of the request for arbitration the Parties are unable to agree on the organization of the arbitration, any one of those Parties may refer the dispute to the International Court of Justice by request in conformity with the Statute of the Court.

2. Each State may at the time of signature or ratification of this Convention or accession thereto, declare that it does not consider itself bound by the preceding paragraph. The other States Parties shall not be bound by the preceding paragraph with respect to any State Party having made such a reservation.

3. Any State Party having made a reservation in accordance with the preceding paragraph may at any time withdraw this reservation by notification to the Secretary-General of the United Nations.

Article 31

1. A State Party may denounce this Convention by written notification to the Secretary-General of the United Nations. Denunciation becomes effective one year after the date of receipt of the notification by the Secretary-General.

2. Such a denunciation shall not have the effect of releasing the State Party from its obligations under this Convention in regard to any act or omission which occurs prior to the date at which the denunciation becomes effective. Nor shall denunciation prejudice in any way the continued consideration of any matter which is already under consideration by the Committee prior to the date at which the denunciation becomes effective.

3. Following the date at which the denunciation of a State Party becomes effective, the Committee shall not commence consideration of any new matter regarding that State.

Article 32

The Secretary-General of the United Nations shall inform all members of the United Nations and all States which have signed this Convention or acceded to it, or the following particulars:

1. Signatures, ratifications and accessions under articles 25 and 26;

2. The date of entry into force of this Convention under article 27, and the date of the entry into force of any amendments under article 29;

3. Denunciations under article 31.

CHARTER OF THE NUREMBERG INTERNATIONAL MILITARY TRIBUNAL

Article 1.

In pursuance of the Agreement signed on the 8th day of August 1945 by the Government of the United States of America, the Provisional Government of the French Republic, the Government of the United Kingdom of Great Britain and Northern Ireland and the Government of the Union of Soviet Socialist Republics, there shall be established an International Military Tribunal (hereinafter called "the Tribunal") for the just and prompt trial and punishment of the major war criminals of the European Axis.

Article 2.

The Tribunal shall consist of four members, each with an alternate. One member and one alternate shall be appointed by each of the Signatories. The alternates shall, so far as they are able, be present at all sessions of the Tribunal. In case of illness of any member of the Tribunal or his incapacity for some other reason to fulfill his functions, his alternate shall take his place.

Article 3.

Neither the Tribunal, its members nor their alternates can be challenged by the prosecution, or by the Defendants or their Counsel. Each Signatory may replace its members of the Tribunal or his alternate for reasons of health or for other good reasons, except that no replacement may take place during a Trial, other than by an alternate.

Article 4

(a) The presence of all four members of the Tribunal or the alternate for any absent member shall be necessary to constitute the quorum.

(b) The members of the Tribunal shall, before any trial begins, agree among themselves upon the selection from their number of a President, and the President shall hold office during the trial, or as may otherwise be agreed by a vote of not less than three members. The principle of rotation of presidency for successive trials is agreed. If, however, a session of the Tribunal takes place on the territory of one of the four Signatories, the representative of that Signatory on the Tribunal shall preside.

(c) Save as aforesaid the Tribunal shall take decisions by a majority vote and in case the votes are evenly divided, the vote of the President shall be decisive: provided always that convictions and sentences shall only be imposed by affirmative votes of at least three members of the Tribunal.

Article 5.

In case of need and depending on the number of the matters to be tried, other Tribunals may be set up; and the establishment, functions, and procedure of each Tribunal shall be identical, and shall be governed by this Charter.

II. Jurisdiction and General Principles

Article 6.

The Tribunal established by the Agreement referred to Article 1 hereof for the trial and punishment of the major war criminals of the European Axis countries shall have the power to try and punish persons who, acting in the interests of the European Axis countries, whether as individuals or as members of organizations, committed any of the following crimes.

The following acts, or any of them, are crimes coming within the jurisdiction of the Tribunal for which there shall be individual responsibility:

(a) CRIMES AGAINST PEACE: namely, planning, preparation, initiation or waging of a war of aggression, or a war in violation of international treaties, agreements or assurances, or participation in a common plan or conspiracy for the accomplishment of any of the foregoing;

(b) WAR CRIMES: namely, violations of the laws or customs of war. Such violations shall include, but not be limited to, murder, ill-treatment or deportation to slave labor or for any other purpose of civilian population of or in occupied territory, murder or ill-treatment of prisoners of war or persons on the seas, killing of hostages, plunder of public or private property, wanton destruction of cities, towns or villages, or devastation not justified by military necessity;

(c) CRIMES AGAINST HUMANITY: namely, murder, extermination, enslavement, deportation, and other inhumane acts committed against any civilian population, before or during the war; or persecutions on political, racial or religious grounds in execution of or in connection with any crime within the jurisdiction of the Tribunal, whether or not in violation of the domestic law of the country where perpetrated.

Leaders, organizers, instigators and accomplices participating in the formulation or execution of a common plan or conspiracy to commit any of the foregoing crimes are responsible for all acts performed by any persons in execution of such plan.

Article 7.
The official position of defendants, whether as Heads of State or responsible officials in Government Departments, shall not be considered as freeing them from responsibility or mitigating punishment.

Article 8.
The fact that the Defendant acted pursuant to order of his Government or of a superior shall not free him from responsibility, but may be considered in mitigation of punishment if the Tribunal determines that justice so requires.

Article 9.
At the trial of any individual member of any group or organization the Tribunal may declare (in connection with any act of which the individual may be convicted) that the group or organization of which the individual was a member was a criminal organization.

After the receipt of the Indictment the Tribunal shall give such notice as it thinks fit that the prosecution intends to ask the Tribunal to make such declaration and any member of the organization will be entitled to apply to the

Tribunal for leave to be heard by the Tribunal upon the question of the criminal character of the organization. The Tribunal shall have power to allow or reject the application. If the application is allowed, the Tribunal may direct in what manner the applicants shall be represented and heard.

Article 10.
In cases where a group or organization is declared criminal by the Tribunal, the competent national authority of any Signatory shall have the right to bring individual to trial for membership therein before national, military or occupation courts. In any such case the criminal nature of the group or organization is considered proved and shall not be questioned.

Article 11.
Any person convicted by the Tribunal may be charged before a national, military or occupation court, referred to in Article 10 of this Charter, with a crime other than of membership in a criminal group or organization and such court may, after convicting him, impose upon him punishment independent of and additional to the punishment imposed by the Tribunal for participation in the criminal activities of such group or organization.

Article 12.
The Tribunal shall have the right to take proceedings against a person charged with crimes set out in Article 6 of this Charter in his absence, if he has not been found or if the Tribunal, for any reason, finds it necessary, in the interests of justice, to conduct the hearing in his absence.

Article 13.
The Tribunal shall draw up rules for its procedure. These rules shall not be inconsistent with the provisions of this Charter.

III. Committee for the Investigation and Prosecution of Major War Criminals

Article 14.
Each Signatory shall appoint a Chief Prosecutor for the investigation of the charges against and the prosecution of major war criminals.

The Chief Prosecutors shall act as a committee for the following purposes:

(a) to agree upon a plan of the individual work of each of the Chief Prosecutors and his staff,

(b) to settle the final designation of major war criminals to be tried by the Tribunal,

(c) to approve the Indictment and the documents to be submitted therewith,

(d) to lodge the Indictment and the accompany documents with the Tribunal,

(e) to draw up and recommend to the Tribunal for its approval draft rules of procedure, contemplated by Article 13 of this Charter. The Tribunal shall have the power to accept, with or without amendments, or to reject, the rules so recommended.

The Committee shall act in all the above matters by a majority vote and shall appoint a Chairman as may be convenient and in accordance with the principle of rotation: provided that if there is an equal division of vote concerning the designation of a Defendant to be tried by the Tribunal, or the crimes with which he shall be charged, that proposal will be adopted which was made by the party which proposed that the particular Defendant be tried, or the particular charges be preferred against him.

Article 15.

The Chief Prosecutors shall individually, and acting in collaboration with one another, also undertake the following duties:

(a) investigation, collection and production before or at the Trial of all necessary evidence,

(b) the preparation of the Indictment for approval by the Committee in accordance with paragraph (c) of Article 14 hereof,

(c) the preliminary examination of all necessary witnesses and of all Defendants,

(d) to act as prosecutor at the Trial,

(e) to appoint representatives to carry out such duties as may be assigned them,

(f) to undertake such other matters as may appear necessary to them for the purposes of the preparation for and conduct of the Trial.

It is understood that no witness or Defendant detained by the Signatory shall be taken out of the possession of that Signatory without its assent.

IV. Fair Trial for Defendants

Article 16.

In order to ensure fair trial for the Defendants, the following procedure shall be followed:

(a) The Indictment shall include full particulars specifying in detail the charges against the Defendants. A copy of the Indictment and of all the documents lodged with the Indictment, translated into a language which he understands, shall be furnished to the Defendant at reasonable time before the Trial.

(b) During any preliminary examination or trial of a Defendant he will have the right to give any explanation relevant to the charges made against him.

(c) A preliminary examination of a Defendant and his Trial shall be conducted in, or translated into, a language which the Defendant understands.

(d) A Defendant shall have the right to conduct his own defense before the Tribunal or to have the assistance of Counsel.

(e) A Defendant shall have the right through himself or through his Counsel to present evidence at the Trial in support of his defense, and to cross-examine any witness called by the Prosecution.

V. Powers of the Tribunal and Conduct of the Trial

Article 17.

The Tribunal shall have the power

(a) to summon witnesses to the Trial and to require their attendance and testimony and to put questions to them

(b) to interrogate any Defendant,

(c) to require the production of documents and other evidentiary material,

(d) to administer oaths to witnesses,

(e) to appoint officers for the carrying out of any task designated by the Tribunal including the power to have evidence taken on commission.

Article 18.

The Tribunal shall

(a) confine the Trial strictly to an expeditious hearing of the cases raised by the charges,

(b) take strict measures to prevent any action which will cause reasonable delay, and rule out irrelevant issues and statements of any kind whatsoever,

(c) deal summarily with any contumacy, imposing appropriate punishment, including exclusion of any Defendant or his Counsel from some or all further proceedings, but without prejudice to the determination of the charges.

Article 19.

The Tribunal shall not be bound by technical rules of evidence. It shall adopt and apply to the greatest possible extent expeditious and nontechnical procedure, and shall admit any evidence which it deems to be of probative value.

Article 20.

The Tribunal may require to be informed of the nature of any evidence before it is entered so that it may rule upon the relevance thereof.

Article 21.

The Tribunal shall not require proof of facts of common knowledge but shall take judicial notice thereof. It shall also take judicial notice of official governmental documents and reports of the United Nations, including the acts and documents of the committees set up in the various allied countries for the investigation of war crimes, and of records and findings of military or other Tribunals of any of the United Nations.

Article 22.

The permanent seat of the Tribunal shall be in Berlin. The first meetings of the members of the Tribunal and of the Chief Prosecutors shall be held at Berlin in a place to be designated by the Control Council for Germany. The first trial shall be held at Nuremberg, and any subsequent trials shall be held at such places as the Tribunal may decide.

Article 23.

One or more of the Chief Prosecutors may take part in the prosecution at each Trial. The function of any Chief Prosecutor may be discharged by him personally, or by any person or persons authorized by him.

The function of Counsel for a Defendant may be discharged at the Defendant's request by any Counsel professionally qualified to conduct cases before the Courts of his own country, or by any other person who may be specially authorized thereto by the Tribunal.

Article 24.

The proceedings at the Trial shall take the following course:

(a) The Indictment shall be read in court.

(b) The Tribunal shall ask each Defendant whether he pleads "guilty" or "not guilty."

(c) The prosecution shall make an opening statement.

(d) The Tribunal shall ask the prosecution and the defense what evidence (if any) they wish to submit to the Tribunal, and the Tribunal shall rule upon the admissibility of any such evidence.

(e) The witnesses for the Prosecution shall be examined and after that the witnesses for the Defense. Thereafter such rebutting evidence as may be held by the Tribunal to be admissible shall be called by either the Prosecution or the Defense.

(f) The Tribunal may put any question to any witness and to any defendant, at any time.

(g) The Prosecution and the Defense shall interrogate and may crossexamine any witnesses and any Defendant who gives testimony.

(h) The Defense shall address the court.

(i) The Prosecution shall address the court.

(j) Each Defendant may make a statement to the Tribunal.

(k) The Tribunal shall deliver judgment and pronounce sentence.

Article 25.

All official documents shall be produced, and all court proceedings conducted, in English, French and Russian, and in the language of the Defendant. So much of the record and of the proceedings may also be translated into the language of any country in which the Tribunal is sitting, as the Tribunal is sitting, as the Tribunal considers desirable in the interests of the justice and public opinion.

VI. Judgment and Sentence

Article 26.

The judgment of the Tribunal as to the guilt or the innocence of any Defendant shall give the reasons on which it is based, and shall be final and not subject to review.

Article 27.

The Tribunal shall have the right to impose upon a Defendant, on conviction, death or such other punishment as shall be determined by it to be just.

Article 28.

In addition to any punishment imposed by it, the Tribunal shall have the right to deprive the convicted person of any stolen property and order its delivery to the Control Council for Germany.

Article 29.

In case of guilt, sentences shall be carried out in accordance with the orders of the Control Council for Germany, which may at any time reduce or otherwise alter the sentences, but may not increase the severity thereof. If the Control Council for Germany, after any Defendant has been convicted and sentenced, discovers fresh evidence which, in its opinion, would found a fresh charge against him, the Council shall report accordingly to the Committee established under Article 14 hereof, for such action as they may consider proper, having regard to the interests of justice.

VII. Expenses

Article 30.

The expenses of the Tribunal and of the Trials, shall be charged by the Signatories against the funds allotted for maintenance of the Control Council of Germany.

Law for the Protection of Hereditary Health: The Attempt to Improve the German Aryan Breed, July 14, 1933

★

Article I.

(1.) Anyone who suffers from an inheritable disease may be surgically sterilized if, in the judgement of medical science, it could be expected that his decendants will suffer from serious inherited mental or physical defects. (2.) Anyone who suffers from one of the following is to be regarded as inheritably diseased within the meaning of this law:

    1. congenital feeble-mindedness
    2. schizophrenia
    3. manic-depression
    4. congenital epilepsy
    5. inheritable St. Vitus dance (Huntington's Chorea)
    6. hereditary blindness
    7. hereditary deafness
    8. serious inheritable malformations (3.) In addition, anyone suffering from chronic alcoholism may also be sterilized.

Article II.

(1.) Anyone who requests sterilization is entitled to it. If he be incapacitated or under a guardian because of low state of mental health or not yet 18 years of age, his legal guardian is empowered to make the request. In other cases of limited capacity the request must receive the approval of the legal representative. If a person be of age and has a nurse, the latter's consent is required. (2.) The request must be accompanied by a certificate from a citizen who is accredited by the German Reich stating that the person to be sterilized has been informed about the nature and consequence of sterilization. (3.) The request for sterilization can be recalled.

Article III.

Sterilization may also be recommended by: (1.) the official physician (2.) the official in charge of a hospital, sanitarium, or prison.

Article IV.

The request for sterilization must be presented in writing to, or placed in writing by the office of the Health Inheritance Court. The statement concerning the request must be certified by a medical document or authenticated in some other way. The business office of the court must notify the official physician.

Article VII.

The proceedings of the Health Inheritance Court are secret.

Article X.

The Supreme Health Insurance Court retains final jurisdiction.

THE NUREMBERG LAWS ON CITIZENSHIP AND RACE: SEPTEMBER 15, 1935

THE REICH CITIZENSHIP LAW OF SEPTEMBER 15, 1935

THE REICHSTAG HAS ADOPTED by unanimous vote the following law which is herewith promulgated.

Article 1.

(1) A subject of the state is one who belongs to the protective union of the German Reich, and who, therefore, has specific obligations to the Reich. (2) The status of subject is to be acquired in accordance with the provisions of the Reich and the state Citizenship Law.

Article 2.

(1) A citizen of the Reich may be only one who is of German or kindred blood, and who, through his behavior, shows that he is both desirous and personally fit to serve loyally the German people and the Reich. (2) The right to citizenship is obtained by the grant of Reich citizenship papers. (3) Only the citizen of the Reich may enjoy full political rights in consonance with the provisions of the laws.

Article 3.

The Reich Minister of the Interior, in conjunction with the Deputy to the *Fuehrer,* will issue the required legal and administrative decrees for the implementation and amplification of this law.
Promulgated: September 16, 1935. *In force:* September 30, 1935.

FIRST SUPPLEMENTARY DECREE OF NOVEMBER 14, 1935

On the basis of Article III of the Reich Citizenship Law of September 15, 1935, the following is hereby decreed:

Article 1.

(1) Until further provisions concerning citizenship papers, all subjects of German or kindred blood who possessed the right to vote in the *Reichstag* elections when the Citizenship Law came into effect, shall, for the present, possess the rights of Reich citizens. The same shall be true of those upon whom the Reich Minister of the Interior, in conjunction with the Deputy to the *Fuehrer* shall confer citizenship. (2) The Reich Minister of the Interior, in conjunction with the Deputy to the *Fuehrer,* may revoke citizenship.

Article 2.

(1) The provisions of Article I shall apply also to subjects who are of mixed Jewish blood. (2) An individual of mixed Jewish blood is one who is descended from one or two grandparents who, racially, were full Jews, insofar that he is not a Jew according to Section 2 of Article 5. Full-blooded Jewish grandparents are those who belonged to the Jewish religious community.

Article 3.

Only citizens of the Reich, as bearers of full political rights, can exercise the right of voting in political matters, and have the right to hold public office. The Reich Minister of the Interior, or any agency he empowers, can make exceptions during the transition period on the matter of holding public office. The measures do not apply to matters concerning religious organizations.

Article 4.

(1) A Jew cannot be a citizen of the Reich. He cannot exercise the right to vote; he cannot hold public office. (2)

Jewish officials will be retired as of December 31, 1935. In the event that such officials served at the front in the World War either for Germany or her allies, they shall receive as pension, until they reach the age limit, the full salary last received, on the basis of which their pension would have been computed. They shall not, however, be promoted according to their seniority in rank. When they reach the age limit, their pension will be computed again, according to the salary last received on which their pension was to be calculated. (3) These provisions do not concern the affairs of religious organizations. (4) The conditions regarding service of teachers in public Jewish schools remains unchanged until the promulgation of new laws on the Jewish school system.

Article 5.
(1) A Jew is an individual who is descended from at least three grandparents who were, racially, full Jews . . . (2) A Jew is also an individual who is descended from two full-Jewish grandparents if: (a) he was a member of the Jewish religious community when this law was issued, or joined the community later; (b) when the law was issued, he was married to a person who was a Jew, or was subsequently married to a Jew; (c) he is the issue from a marriage with a Jew, in the sense of Section I, which was contracted after the coming into effect of the Law for the Protection of German Blood and Honor of September 15, 1935; (d) he is the issue of an extramarital relationship with a Jew, in the sense of Section I, and was born out of wedlock after July 31, 1936.

Article 6.
(1) Insofar as there are, in the laws of the Reich or in the decrees of the National Socialist German Workers' Party and its affiliates, certain requirements for the purity of German blood which extend beyond Article 5, the same remain untouched. . . .

Article 7.
The *Fuehrer* and Chancellor of the Reich is empowered to release anyone from the provisions of these administrative decrees.

LAW FOR THE PROTECTION OF GERMAN BLOOD AND GERMAN HONOR SEPTEMBER 15, 1935
Thoroughly convinced by the knowledge that the purity of German blood is essential for the further existence of the German people and animated by the inflexible will to safe-guard the German nation for the entire future, the Reichstag has resolved upon the following law unanimously, which is promulgated herewith:

Section 1
1. Marriages between Jews and nationals of German or kindred blood are forbidden. Marriages concluded in defiance of this law are void, even if, for the purpose of evading this law, they are concluded abroad. 2. Proceedings for annulment may be initiated only by the Public Prosecutor.

Section 2
Relation outside marriage between Jews and nationals of German or kindred blood are forbidden.

Section 3
Jews will not be permitted to employ female nationals of German or kindred blood in their households.

Section 4
1. Jews are forbidden to hoist the Reich and national flag and to present the colors of the Reich. 2. On the other hand they are permitted to present the Jewish colors. The exercise of this authority is protected by the State.

Section 5
1. A person who acts contrary to the prohibition of section 1 will be punished with hard labor. 2. A person who acts contrary to the prohibition of section 2 will be punished with imprisonment or with hard labor. 3. A person who acts contrary to the provisions of section 3 or 4 will be punished with imprisonment up to a year and with a fine or with one of these penalties.

Section 6
The Reich Minister of the Interior in agreement with the Deputy of the Fuehrer will issue the legal and administrative regulations which are required from the implementation and supplementation of this law.

Section 7
The law will become effective on the day after the promulgation, section 3 however only on 1 January, 1936.
Nuremberg, the 15th day of September 1935 at the Reich Party Rally of Freedom.
The Fuehrer and Reich Chancellor Adolf Hitler
The Reich Minister of the Interior Frick
The Reich Minister of Justice Dr. Goertner
The Deputy of the Fuehrer R. Hess

Resources

★

Amnesty International

"A worldwide campaigning movement that works to promote all the human rights enshrined in the Universal Declaration of Human Rights and other international standards. In particular, Amnesty International campaigns to free all prisoners of conscience; ensure fair and prompt trials for political prisoners; abolish the death penalty, torture and other cruel treatment of prisoners; end political killings and 'disappearances'; and oppose human rights abuses by opposition groups."

5 Penn Plaza, 16th Floor
New York, NY 10001
Tel: (212) 807-8400
Fax: (212) 463-9193 or (212) 627-1451
http://www.amnesty.org/

Carter Center

"Every day in countries all over the world, people live under difficult, life-threatening circumstances caused by war, disease, famine, and poverty. The non-profit Carter Center strives to relieve this suffering by advancing peace and health in neighborhoods and nations around the globe. The Center, in partnership with Emory University, is guided by a fundamental commitment to human rights, wages peace by bringing warring parties to the negotiating table, monitoring elections, safeguarding human rights, and building strong democracies through economic development."

One Copenhill
453 Freedom Parkway
Atlanta, GA 30307
Tel: (404) 420-5100
http://www.cartercenter.org/default.asp

Derechos Human Rights

"Derechos Human Rights, together with our sister organization Equipo Nizkor, work for the respect and promotion of human rights throughout the world. Our work includes the socialization of human rights related information and analysis through the internet and other media, the promotion of prosecutions of human rights violators and the support of local human rights NGOs and activists."

Equipo Nizkor
(Derechos Representative in Spain)
Apartado de Correo 156037
Madrid, Spain
Tel: +34 91 526 7502
Fax: +34 91 526 7515
E-mail: nizkor@derechos.org
http://www.derechos.org

Doctors Without Borders (Médecins Sans Frontières)

"Médecins Sans Frontières (also known as Doctors Without Borders or MSF) delivers emergency aid to victims of armed conflict, epidemics, and natural and man-made disasters, and to others who lack health care due to social or geographical isolation."

333 7th Avenue, 2nd Floor
New York, NY 10001-5004
Tel: (212) 679-6800
Fax: (212) 679-7016

2525 Main Street, Suite 110
Santa Monica, CA 90405
Tel: (310) 399-0049
Fax: (310) 399-8177
http://www.doctorswithoutborders.org/

François-Xavier Bagnoud Center for Health and Human Rights

"The François-Xavier Bagnoud Center for Health and Human Rights is the first academic center to focus exclusively on health and human rights. The Center combines the academic strengths of research and teaching with a strong commitment to service and policy development."

Harvard School of Public Health
651 Huntington Avenue, 7th Floor
Boston, MA 02115
Tel: (617) 432-0656
Fax: (617) 432-4310
http://www.hsph.harvard.edu/fxbcenter/

Freedom House

"Freedom House, a nonprofit, nonpartisan organization, is a clear voice for democracy and freedom around the world. Through a vast array of international programs and publications, Freedom House is working to advance the remarkable worldwide expansion of political and economic freedom."

Washington, DC Office
1301 Connecticut Avenue NW
Washington, DC 20036
Tel: (202) 296-5101
Fax: (202) 296-5078

New York, NY Office
120 Wall Street, Floor 26
New York, NY 10005
Tel: (212) 514-8040
Fax: (212) 514-8055
http://www.freedomhouse.org/

Gendercide Watch

"Gendercide Watch is working to raise awareness, conduct research, and produce educational resources on gendercide. In particular, we seek to dispel stereotypes that blame victims and survivors for their own suffering. Among our activities is the maintenance of this website, which represents our major means of outreach and public education. This site includes a constantly growing database of case-studies and other research materials on gendercide."

GIEF/Gendercide Watch
Ste. #501, 10011—116th Street
Edmonton, Alberta T5K 1V4
Canada
http://www.gendercide.org

Global Exchange

"A human rights organization dedicated to promoting environmental, political, and social justice around the world. Since our founding in 1988, we have been striving to increase global awareness among the US public while building international partnerships around the world."

2017 Mission Street, #303
San Francisco, CA 94110
Tel: (415) 255-7296
Fax: (415) 255-7498
http://www.globalexchange.org/

The Human Rights Internet

"Founded in 1976, Human Rights Internet (HRI) is a world leader in the exchange of information within the worldwide human rights community. Launched in the U.S., HRI has its headquarters in Ottawa, Canada. From Ottawa, HRI communicates by phone, fax, mail and the information highway with more than 5,000 organizations and individuals around the world working for the advancement of human rights. A key objective of the organization is to support the work of the global non-governmental community in its struggle to obtain human rights for all. To this end, HRI promotes human rights education, stimulates research, encourages the sharing of information, and builds international solidarity among those committed to the principles enshrined in the International Bill of Human Rights."

One Nicholas Street, Suite 1105
Ottawa, Ontario K1N 7B7
Canada
Tel: (613) 789-7407
Fax: (613) 789-7414
E-mail: hri@hri.ca
http://www.hri.ca

Human Rights Library

"Located at the University of Minnesota, this comprehensive web-site offers access to documents, reports, legislation, and reports from national and international organizations."

Human Rights Center
University of Minnesota
Mondale Hall, N-120
229 19th Avenue South
Minneapolis, MN 55455
Tel: (612) 626-0041 or 1-888-HREDUC8
Fax: (612) 625-2011
http://www1.umn.edu/humanrts/

Human Rights Watch

"Dedicated to protecting the human rights of people around the world. We stand with victims and activists to prevent discrimination, to uphold political freedom, to protect people from inhumane conduct in wartime, and to bring offenders to justice. We investigate and expose human rights violations and hold abusers accountable. We challenge governments and those who hold power to end abusive practices and respect international human rights law. We enlist the public and the international community to support the cause of human rights for all."

http://www.hrw.org/

New York Office
350 Fifth Avenue, 34th Floor
New York, NY 10118-3299
Tel: (212) 290-4700
Fax: (212) 736-1300
E-mail: hrwnyc@hrw.org

Washington, DC, Office
1630 Connecticut Avenue NW, Suite 500
Washington, DC 20009
Tel: (202) 612-4321
Fax: (202) 612-4333
E-mail: hrwdc@hrw.org

Los Angeles Office
11500 W. Olympic Boulevard, Suite 441
Los Angeles, CA 90064
Tel: (310) 477-5540
Fax: (310) 477-4622
E-mail: hrwla@hrw.org

San Francisco Office
100 Bush Street, Suite 1812
San Francisco, CA 94104
Tel: (415) 362-3250
Fax: (415) 362-3255
E-mail: hrw-sf@hrw.org

Toronto Office
2300 Yonge Street
Suite 803, Box 2376
Toronto, Ontario M4P 1E4
Canada
E-mail: toronto@hrw.org

International Commission on Missing Persons

"As a political transition unfolds after a period of armed conflict, violence or repression, a society is confronted with a difficult legacy of human rights abuses that often include large numbers disappearances of persons never to be heard from again. Resolving their fate is important."

ICMP Headquarters
Alipašina 45 A
71000 Sarajevo
Bosnia and Herzegovina
Tel: +387 33 218 660
Fax: +387 33 203 297
http://www.ic-mp.org

International Committee of the Red Cross

"Whether through formal dissemination sessions or spontaneously at military checkpoints, reminding actual and potential warring parties of their rights and obligations under international humanitarian law is one of the ICRC's major activities worldwide."

ICRC Regional Delegation
1100 Connecticut Avenue NW
Suite 500
Washington, DC 20036
Tel: (202) 587-4600 (General)
Fax: (202) 587-4696 (General)
E-mail: washington.was@icrc.org
http://www.icrc.org

International Criminal Court

"The International Criminal Court (ICC) is the first ever permanent, treaty based, international criminal court established to promote the rule of law and ensure that the gravest international crimes do not go unpunished."

P.O. Box 19519
2500 CM, The Hague
The Netherlands
Tel: +31 (0)70 515-8515
Fax: +31 (0)70 515-8555
http://www.icc-cpi.int/

International Criminal Tribunal for the Former Yugoslavia

"Spearheading the shift from impunity to accountability, establishing the facts, bringing justice to thousands of victims and giving them a voice, the accomplishments in international law, strengthening the Rule of Law."

P.O. Box 13888
2501 EW The Hague
The Netherlands
Press Tel: +31 (70) 512-5343 or 512-5356 or 512-8752
Fax: +31 (70) 512-5355
http://www.icty.org/

International Humanitarian Fact-Finding Commission

"A major objective of the two Additional Protocols to the 1949 Geneva Conventions, which were drafted at the Diplomatic Conference held from 1974 to 1977, is to improve implementation of the Conventions and Protocols. The first of the Protocols addresses international armed conflicts, the second non-international armed conflicts. To help ensure the protection afforded to the victims of armed conflicts, Article 90 of the First Protocol provides for the establishment of a permanent International Fact-Finding Commission. The Commission is empowered to enquire into allegations of breaches of international humanitarian law and to restore compliance with it by providing good offices."

Federal Palace (North)
CH—3003 Berne
Switzerland
Tel: +41 31 32 50768
Fax: +41 31 32 50767
http://www.ihffc.org/

International Labor Organization (ILO)

"The International Labour Organization is the UN specialized agency which seeks the promotion of social justice and internationally recognized human and labour rights. It was founded in 1919 and is the only surviving major creation of the Treaty of Versailles which brought the League of Nations into being and it became the first specialized agency of the UN in 1946."

International Labour Office
4, route des Morillons
CH-1211 Geneva 22
Switzerland
Tel: +41 22 799 6111
http://www.ilo.org/

International Physicians for the Prevention of Nuclear War (IPPNW)

"A non-partisan global federation of medical organizations dedicated to research, education, and advocacy relevant to the prevention of nuclear war. To this end, IPPNW seeks to prevent all wars, to promote non-violent conflict resolution, and to minimize the effects of war and preparations for war on health, development, and the environment."

66–70 Union Square, #204
Somerville, MA 02143
Tel: (617) 440-1733
Fax: (617) 440-1734
http://www.ippnw.org/

Lawyers Without Borders

"Lawyers Without Borders is a US-based non-profit organization whose goal is to engage the legal profession, on a global basis supporting capacity building of NGOs worldwide, advancing Rule of Law, protecting the integrity of legal process through neutral observation, offering support to lawyers in the field and serving as a law oriented clearinghouse linking needs with the legal resources to meet them."

750 Main Street
Hartford, CT 06103
Tel: (860) 541-2288
Fax: (860) 525-0287
http://www.judgeswithoutborders.org/

National Center for Human Rights Education (USA)

"Founded in 1996, the National Order is the first human rights education organization in the United States that focuses primarily on domestic human rights violations. CHRE works to build a domestic human rights movement by training community leaders and student activists to apply human rights standards to issues of injustice in the United States. As an information clearinghouse and technical assistance provider, CHRE seeks to increase human rights understanding, improve cooperation among progressive social change movements, and use human rights education as a catalyst for social transformation."

P.O. Box 311020
Atlanta, GA 31131
Tel: (404) 344-9629
Fax: (404) 346-7517
http://www.nchre.org/

Office of Special Investigations

"The Office of Special Investigations detects and investigates individuals who took part in Nazi-sponsored acts of persecution abroad before and during World War II, and who subsequently entered, or seek to enter, the United States illegally and/or fraudulently. It then takes appropriate legal action seeking their exclusion, denaturalization and/or deportation. The unit also detects, investigates and takes legal action to denaturalize persons who participated abroad in acts of genocide or in acts of torture or extrajudicial killings committed under color of foreign law. OSI also handles emerging war crimes issues."

Department of Justice
Criminal Division
950 Pennsylvania Avenue
Washington, DC 20530-0001
http://www.justice.gov/criminal/osi.html

Organization for Security and Co-operation in Europe

"The Organization for Security and Co-operation in Europe (OSCE) is the largest regional security organization in the world with 55 participating States from Europe, Central Asia and North America. It is active in early warning, conflict prevention, crisis management and post-conflict rehabilitation."

OSCE Secretariat Press and Public Information Section
Walnerstrasse 6, 1010
Vienna, Austria
Tel: +43-1 514 36 180
Fax: +43-1 514 36 105
http://www.osce.org/

Organization of American States

"The Organization of American States (OAS) brings together the countries of the Western Hemisphere to strengthen cooperation and advance common interests. It is the region's premier forum for multilateral dialogue and concerted action."

Headquarters:
17th Street & Constitution Avenue NW
Washington, DC 20006
Tel: (202) 458-3000
http://www.oas.org/

Oxfam

"Oxfam believes that in a world rich in resources, poverty isn't a fact of life but an injustice which must be overcome. We believe that everyone is entitled to a life of dignity and opportunity; and we work with poor communities, local partner organisations, volunteers, and supporters to make this a reality."

Oxfam House
John Smith Drive, Cowley
Oxford
OX4 2JY
England
Tel: +44 1865 47 2602
http://www.oxfam.org.uk/

Peoples' Decade of Human Rights Education

"Founded in 1988, the People's Decade of Human Rights Education (PDHRE-International) is a non-profit, international service organization that works directly and indirectly with its network of affiliates primarily women's and social justice organizations to develop and advance pedagogies for human rights education relevant to people's daily lives in the context of their struggles for social and economic justice and democracy."

The People's Movement for Human Rights Learning (PDHRE)
New York Office
526 West 111th Street
New York, NY 10025
Tel: (212) 749-3156
Fax: (212) 666-6325
http://www.pdhre.org/

Physicians for Human Rights

"An organization of health professionals, scientists, and concerned citizens that uses the knowledge and skills of the medical and forensic sciences to investigate and prevent violations of international human rights and humanitarian law."

Two Arrow Street, Suite 301
Cambridge, MA 02138
Tel: (617) 301-4200
Fax: (617) 301-4250
http://www.physiciansforhumanrights.org/

Physicians for Social Responsibility

"Physicians for Social Responsibility combines the power of an active and concerned citizenry with the credibility of physicians and other health professionals to promote public policies that protect human health from the threats of nuclear war and other weapons of mass destruction, global environmental degradation, and the epidemic of gun violence in our society today."

1875 Connecticut Avenue NW, Suite 1012
Washington, DC 20009
Tel: (202) 667-4260
Fax: (202) 667-4201
http://www.psr.org/

Refugees International

"Refugees International generates lifesaving humanitarian assistance and protection for displaced people around the world and works to end the conditions that create displacement."

2001 S Street NW, Suite 700
Washington, DC 20009
Tel: (202) 828-0110 or 800-REFUGEE (800-733-8433)
Fax: (202) 828-0819
http://www.refugeesinternational.org/

Reporters Without Borders

"Reporters Without Borders works constantly to restore their right to be informed. Forty-two media professionals lost their lives in 2003 for doing what they were paid to do—keeping us informed. Today, more than 130 journalists around the world are in prison simply for doing their job. In Nepal, Eritrea and China, they can spend years in jail just for using the "wrong" word or photo. Reporters Without Borders believes imprisoning or killing a journalist is like eliminating a key witness and threatens everyone's right to be informed. It has been fighting such practices for more than 18 years."

United States Office
1500 K Street NW, Suite 600
Washington, DC 20005
Tel: (202) 256-5613
E-mail: clc@rsf.org
http://www.rsf.org

Simon Wiesenthal Center

"The Simon Wiesenthal Center is an international Jewish human rights organization dedicated to preserving the memory of the Holocaust by fostering tolerance and understanding through community involvement, educational outreach and social action. The Center confronts important contemporary issues including racism, antisemitism, terrorism and genocide and is accredited as an NGO both at the United Nations and UNESCO. With a membership of over 400,000 families, the Center is headquartered in Los Angeles and maintains offices in New York, Toronto, Miami, Jerusalem, Paris and Buenos Aires."

International Headquarters
1399 South Roxbury Drive
Los Angeles, CA 90035
Tel: (310) 553-9036 or Tel: (800) 900-9036
Fax: (310) 553-4521
http://www.wiesenthal.com

Union of Concerned Scientists

"UCS is an independent nonprofit alliance of more than 100,000 concerned citizens and scientists. We augment rigorous scientific analysis with innovative thinking and committed citizen advocacy to build a cleaner, healthier environment and a safer world."

National Headquarters
2 Brattle Square
Cambridge, MA 02238-9105
Tel: (617) 547-5552
Fax: (617) 864-9405

Washington, DC, Office
1707 H Street NW, Suite 600
Washington, DC 20006-3962
Tel: (202) 223-6133
Fax: (202) 223-6162

West Coast Office
2397 Shattuck Avenue, Suite 203
Berkeley, CA 94704-1567
Tel: (510) 843-1872
Fax: (510) 843-3785
http://www.ucsusa.org/

United Nations High Commissioner for Human Rights

"The United Nations vision is of a world in which the human rights of all are fully respected and enjoyed in conditions of global peace. The High Commissioner works to keep that vision to the forefront through constant encouragement of the international community and its member States to uphold universally agreed human rights standards."

Case Postale 2500
CH-1211 Genève 2 Dépôt
Switzerland
Tel: +41 22 739 8111
http://www.unhcr.ch

United States Department of State

"The protection of fundamental human rights was a foundation stone in the establishment of the United States over 200 years ago. Since then, a central goal of U.S. foreign policy has been the promotion of respect for human rights, as embodied in the Universal Declaration of Human Rights. The United States understands that the existence of human rights helps secure the peace, deter aggression, promote the rule of law, combat crime and corruption, strengthen democracies, and prevent humanitarian crises."

2201 C Street NW
Washington, DC 20520
Tel: (202) 647-4000
(800) 877-8339 (Federal Relay Service)
http://contact-us.state.gov/

Universal Rights Network

"A meeting place for the peoples of the world to share their stories of the importance of universal human rights and fundamental freedom to us all."
http://www.universalrights.net/

WITNESS

"A pioneer in the use of video and technology to fight for human rights. WITNESS gives human rights activists video cameras and help them to expose the crimes, right the wrongs, and end impunity for human rights violators. WITNESS partners with human rights organizations throughout the world, and trains grassroots activists in video and investigative techniques. WITNESS equips them with the latest technology, provides assistance in field video productions, and ensures that the evidence generated gets an international audience."

80 Hanson Place, 5th Floor
Brooklyn, NY 11217
Tel: (718) 783-2000
Fax: (718) 783-1593
http://www.witness.org/

Selected Bibliography

Aall, Pamela R., Daniel Miltenberger, and George Weiss. *IGOs, NGOs, and the Military in Peace and Relief Operations.* Washington, D.C.: United States Institute of Peace Press, 2000.

Aburish, Saïd K. *Saddam Hussein: The Politics of Revenge.* London: Bloomsbury Publishing, 2000.

Adebajo, Adekeye. *Building Peace in West Africa: Liberia, Sierra Leone, and Guinea-Bissau.* International Peace Academy Occasional Paper Series. Boulder, Colo.: Lynne Rienner Publishers, 2002.

————. *Liberia's Civil War: Nigeria, ECOMOG, and Regional Security in West Africa.* Boulder, Colo.: Lynne Rienner Publishers, 2002.

AkCam, Taner. *From Empire to Republic: Turkish Nationalism and the Armenian Genocide.* London: Zed Books, 2004.

Alibek, Ken, and Stephen Handelman. *Biohazard: The Chilling True Story of the Largest Covert Biological Weapons Program in the World—Told from Inside by the Man Who Ran It.* New York: Delta, 2000.

Allen, John. *Idi Amin. History's Villains.* San Diego: Blackbirch Press, 2003.

Allen, Peter A. P. *Interesting Times: Life in Uganda under Idi Amin.* London: Book Guild, Limited, 2000.

Andreopoulous, George J., and Richard Pierre Claude, eds. *Human Rights Education for the Twenty-First Century.* Pennsylvania Studies in Human Rights. Philadelphia: University of Pennsylvania Press, 1997.

Applebaum, Anne. *Gulag: A History.* New York: Anchor, 2004.

Arditti, Rita. *Searching for Life: The Grandmothers of the Plaza De Mayo and the Disappeared Children of Argentina.* Berkeley: University of California Press, 1999.

Armstrong, Robert. *El Salvador: The Face of Revolution.* Boston: South End Press, 1982.

Arthur, Charles. *Haiti: A Guide to the People, Politics, and Culture.* New York: Interlink Publishing Group, 2002.

Aspinall, Edward. *The Aceh Peace Process: Why It Failed.* Washington, D.C.: East-West Center, 2003.

Atwan, Abdel Bari. *The Secret History of al Qaeda.* Berkeley: University of California Press, 2008.

Balakian, Peter. *The Burning Tigris: The Armenian Genocide and America's Response.* New York: HarperCollins, 2003.

Ball, Howard. *Prosecuting War Crimes and Genocide: The Twentieth-Century Experience.* Lawrence: University Press of Kansas, 1999.

Barnaby, Frank. *How to Build a Nuclear Bomb: And Other Weapons of Mass Destruction.* New York: Nation Books, 2004.

Barnett, Michael. *Eyewitness to a Genocide: The United Nations and Rwanda.* Ithaca, N.Y.: Cornell University Press, 2003.

Bass, Gary Jonathan. *Stay the Hand of Vengeance: The Politics of War Crimes Tribunals.* Princeton, N.J.: Princeton University Press, 2001.

Bassiouni, M. Cherif. *Crimes against Humanity in International Criminal Law.* Boston: Martinus Nijhoff, 1999.

————. *Sexual Violence: An Invisible Weapon of War in the Former Yugoslavia.* Chicago: International Human Rights Law Institute, DePaul University, 1996.

Beah, Ishmael, *Long Way Gone: Memoirs of a Boy Soldier.* New York: Farrar, Straus & Giroux, 2008.

Beigbeder, Yves, and Theo van Boven. *Judging War Criminals: The Politics of International Justice.* Sidney, Australia: Palgrave Macmillan, 1999.

Benenson, Peter. *Persecution.* London: Penguin Books, 1961.

Benson, Bruce. *The Enterprise of Law: Justice without the State.* San Francisco: Pacific Research Institute for Public Policy, 1990.

Bergquist, Charles, Ricardo Penaranda, and Gonzalo Sanchez, eds. *Violence in Colombia 1990–2000: Waging War and Negotiating Peace.* Wilmington, Del.: Scholarly Resources Inc., 2001.

Berkhoff, Karel C. *Harvest of Despair: Life and Death in Ukraine under Nazi Rule.* Cambridge, Mass.: Belknap Press of Harvard University, 2004.

Berry, Nicholas O. *War and the Red Cross: The Unspoken Mission.* New York: St. Martin's Press, 1997.

Bertrand, Jacques, and John Ravenhill. *Nationalism and Ethnic Conflict in Indonesia.* Cambridge: Cambridge University Press, 2003.

Bilton, Michael, and Kevin Sim. *Four Hours in My Lai.* New York: Penguin Books, 1993.

Bloxham, Donald. *Genocide on Trial: War Crimes Trials and the Formation of Holocaust History and Memory.* Oxford: Oxford University Press, 2003.

Bodansky, Yossef. *The Secret History of the Iraq War.* New York: Regan Books, 2004.

Bortolotti, Dan. *Hope in Hell: Inside the World of Doctors Without Borders.* Richmond Hill, Ontario: Firefly Books Ltd., 2004.

Bose, Sumanira. *Kashmir: Roots of Conflict, Paths to Peace.* Cambridge, Mass.: Harvard University Press, 2003.

Bower, Tom. *Klaus Barbie, the Butcher of Lyons.* New York: Pantheon Books, 1984.

Broome, Richard. *Aboriginal Australians.* London: Allen & Unwin, 2002.

Browder, George C. *Hitler's Enforcers: The Gestapo and the Ss Security Service in the Nazi Revolution.* Oxford: Oxford University Press, 1996.

Brysk, Alison, ed. *Globalization and Human Rights.* Berkeley: University of California Press, 2002.

Buergenthal, Thomas. *Religious Fundamentalisms and the Human Rights of Women.* Sidney, Australia: Palgrave Macmillan, 1999.

Burke, Jason. *Al-Qaeda: Casting a Shadow of Terror.* London: I. B. Tauris, 2004.

———. *Al-Qaeda: The True Story of Radical Islam.* London: I. B. Tauris, 2004.

Buscher, Frank M. *The U.S. War Crimes Trial Program in Germany, 1946–1955.* Contributions in Military Studies. Westport, Conn.: Greenwood Press, 1989.

Butler, Rupert. *The Gestapo: A History of Hitler's Secret Police 1933–45.* Havertown, Pa.: Casemate Publishers and Book Distributors, 2004.

Byman, Daniel, Ian Lesser, Bruce Pirnie, Cheryl Benard, and Matthew Waxman. *Strengthening the Partnership: Improving Military Coordination with Relief Agencies and Allies in Humanitarian Operations.* Santa Monica, Calif.: Rand Corporation (NBN), 2000.

Campbell, Greg. *Blood Diamonds: Tracing the Deadly Path of the World's Most Precious Stones.* New York: Perseus Books Group, 2002.

Carrion, Julio F. *The Fujimori Legacy: The Rise of Electoral Authoritarianism in Peru.* University Park: Pennsylvania State University Press, 2006.

Carter, Jimmy. *The Personal Beliefs of Jimmy Carter: Winner of the 2002 Nobel Peace Prize.* New York: Three Rivers Press, 2002.

Chandler, David. *A History of Cambodia.* Philadelphia: Westview Press, 2000.

———. *The Tragedy of Cambodian History: Politics, War, and Revolution since 1945.* New Haven, Conn.: Yale University Press, 1993.

Charrad, M. *States and Women's Rights: The Making of Postcolonial Tunisia, Algeria, and Morocco.* Berkeley: University of California Press, 2001.

Chinnery, Philip D. *Korean Atrocity!: Forgotten War Crimes, 1950–1953.* Annapolis, Md.: United States Naval Institute, 2001.

Clark, Wesley K. *Waging Modern War: Bosnia, Kosovo, and the Future of Combat.* New York: Public Affairs, 2001.

Clarke, Walter, and Jeffrey Herbst, eds. *Learning from Somalia: The Lessons of Armed Humanitarian Intervention.* Boulder, Colo.: Westview Press, 1997.

Claude, Richard Pierre, and Burns H. Weston. *Human Rights in the World Community: Issues and Action.* Philadelphia: University of Pennsylvania Press, 1992.

Coates, Karen J. *Cambodia Now: Life in the Wake of War.* Jefferson, N.C.: McFarland & Company, 2005.

Cockburn, Andrew, and Patrick Cockburn. *Out of the Ashes: The Resurrection of Saddam Hussein.* New York: Perennial.

Coll, Steve. *Ghost Wars: The Secret History of the CIA, Afghanistan, and Bin Laden, from the Soviet Invasion to September 10, 2001.* New York: Penguin, 2004.

Conquest, Robert. *Stalin: Breaker of Nations.* New York: Penguin Books, 1992.

Constable, Pamela. *A Nation of Enemies: Chile under Pinochet.* New York: W. W. Norton & Company, 1993.

Cook, Rebecca J. *Human Rights of Women: National and International Perspectives.* Pennsylvania Studies in Human Rights. Philadelphia: University of Pennsylvania Press, 1994.

Cooper, Belinda, and Richard Goldstone. *War Crimes: The Legacy of Nuremberg.* New York: TV Books Inc., 1999.

Cornish, Paul. *Anti-personnel Mines: Controlling the Plague of "Butterflies."* London: Royal Institute of International Affairs, 1994.

Coughlin, Con. *Saddam: King of Terror.* New York: Ecco, 2002.

Cox, Margaret, and Jon Sterenberg. *Forensic Archaeology, Anthropology and the Investigation of Mass Graves.* London: CRC Press, 2006.

Dabringhaus, Erhard. *Klaus Barbie: The Shocking Story of How the U.S. Used This Nazi War Criminal as an Intelligence Agent.* New York: Acropolis Books, 1984.

Dalacoura, Katerina. *Engagement or Coercion?: Weighing Western Human Rights Policies towards Turkey, Iran, and Egypt.* London: Royal Institute of International Affairs, 2004.

Dallaire, Romeo, and Brent Beardsley. *Shake Hands with the Devil: The Failure of Humanity in Rwanda.* New York: Carroll & Graf, 2004.

Danner, Mark. *The Massacre at El Mozote.* New York: Vintage, 1994.

———. *Torture and Truth: America, Abu Ghraib, and the War on Terror.* New York: New York Review of Books, 2004.

Davis, William Columbus. *Warnings from the Far South: Democracy versus Dictatorship in Uruguay, Argentina, and Chile.* New York: Praeger Publishers, 1995.

Dawidowicz, Lucy. *A Holocaust Reader.* Library of Jewish Studies. Chicago: Behrman House Publishing, 1976.

Daws, Gavin. *Prisoners of the Japanese: POWs of World War II in the Pacific.* New York: Perennial, 1996.

Del Ponte, Carla, and Chuck Sudetic. *Madame Prosecutor: Confrontation with the World's Worst Criminals and the Culture of Impunity.* New York: Other Press, 2009.

de Waal, Alexander. *Famine That Kills: Darfur, Sudan.* Oxford Studies in African Affairs. Oxford: Oxford University Press, 2004.

Dinges, John. *The Condor Years: How Pinochet and His Allies Brought Terrorism to Three Continents.* New York: New Press, 2004.

Dodge, Cole P., and Magne Raundelen. *Reaching Children in War: Sudan, Uganda and Mozambique.* London: Taylor & Francis, 1992.

Dodge, Toby. *Inventing Iraq: The Failure of Nation-Building and a History Denied.* New York: Columbia University Press, 2003.

Dorfman, Ariel. *Exorcising Terror: The Incredible Unending Trial of Augusto Pinochet.* New York: Seven Stories Press, 2002.

Dormann, Knut, and Louise Doswald-Beck. *Elements of War Crimes under the Rome Statute of the International Criminal Court: Sources and Commentary.* Cambridge: Cambridge University Press, 2003.

Dubber, Markus Dirk. *Victims in the War on Crime: The Use and Abuse of Victims' Rights.* New York: New York University Press, 2002.

Dudley, Steven S. *Walking Ghosts: Murder and Guerrilla Politics in Colombia.* New York: Routledge, 2006.

Dunn, James, and Xanana Gusmão. *East Timor: A Rough Passage to Independence.* Seattle: University of Washington Press, 2004.

Dwork, Deborah, and Robert Jan Van Pelt. *Holocaust: A History.* New York: W. W. Norton & Company, 2003.

Edgerton, Robert. *The Troubled Heart of Africa: A History of the Congo.* New York: St. Martin's Press, 2002.

Eichstaedt, Peter. *First Kill Your Family: Child Soldiers of Uganda and the Lord's Resistance Army.* Chicago: Lawrence Hill Books, 2009.

Ekwe-Ekwe, Herbert. *The Biafra War: Nigeria and the Aftermath.* African Studies, Vol. 17. Philadelphia: Edwin Mellen Press, 1990.

El-Kikhia, Mansour O. *Libya's Qaddafi: The Politics of Contradiction.* Gainsville: University Press of Florida, 1998.

Ellils, Stephen. *The Mask of Anarchy: The Destruction of Liberia and the Religious Dimension of an African Civil War.* New York: New York University Press, 2001.

Erskins, Toni. *Can Institutions Have Responsibilities: Collective Moral Agency and International Relations.* Global Issues Series. Sydney, Australia: Palgrave Macmillan, 2004.

Ewans, Martin. *Afghanistan: A Short History of Its People and Politics.* New York: Perennial, 2002.

Falk, Richard A. *Human Rights Horizons: The Pursuit of Justice in a Globalizing World.* London: Routledge, 2000.

Farmer, Paul. *The Uses of Haiti.* 2d ed. Monroe, Me.: Common Courage Press, 2003.

Fasulo, Linda. *An Insider's Guide to the UN.* New Haven, Conn.: Yale University Press, 2003.

Feaver, Peter. *Guarding the Guardians: Civilian Control of Nuclear Weapons in the United States.* Cornell Studies in Security Affairs. Ithaca, N.Y.: Cornell University Press, 1992.

Feller, Erika, Volker Turk, and Frances Nicholson, eds. *Refugee Protection in International Law: UNHCR's Global Consultations on International Protection.* Cambridge: Cambridge University Press, 2003.

Ferme, Mariane C. *The Underneath of Things: Violence, History, and the Everyday in Sierra Leone.* Berkeley: University of California Press, 2001.

Foot, Rosemary. *Rights beyond Borders: The Global Community and the Struggle over Human Rights in China.* Oxford: Oxford University Press, 2001.

Forsythe, David P. *Human Rights in International Relations.* Themes in International Relations. Cambridge: Cambridge University Press, 2000.

Fritz, Mark. *Lost on Earth: Nomads of the New World.* New York: Routledge, 2000.

Ganguly, Sumit. *Conflict Unending.* New York: Columbia University Press, 2002.

Gerlach, Allen. *Indians, Oil, and Politics: A Recent History of Ecuador.* Wilmington, Del.: Scholarly Resources, 2003.

Giblin, James Cross. *The Life and Death of Adolf Hitler.* New York: Clarion Books, 2002.

Gibney, Matthew J. *The Ethics and Politics of Asylum: Liberal Democracy and the Response to Refugees.* Cambridge: Cambridge University Press, 2004.

Gilbert, Martin. *The Holocaust: A History of the Jews of Europe during the Second World War.* New York: Owl Books, 1987.

Glenny, Misha. *The Fall of Yugoslavia: The Third Balkan War.* New York: Penguin Books, 1996.

Goldstone, Richard. *For Humanity: Reflections of a War Crimes Investigator.* Castle Lectures Series. New Haven, Conn.: Yale University Press, 2000.

Goni, Uki. *The Real Odessa: How Peron Brought the Nazi War Criminals to Argentina.* London: Granta Books, 2003.

Gottesman, Evan. *Cambodia after the Khmer Rouge: Inside the Politics of Nation Building.* New Haven, Conn.: Yale University Press, 2004.

Gourevich, Philip. *We Wish to Inform You That Tomorrow We Will Be Killed with Our Families: Stories from Rwanda.* New York, Picador, 1999.

Groenewold, Julia, and Doctors Without Borders. *World in Crisis: The Politics of Survival at the End of the Twentieth Century.* London: Routledge, 1996.

Grotius, Hugo. *On the Law of War and Peace.* Kila: Kessinger Publishing, 2004.

Guillemin, Jeanette. *Biological Weapons.* Columbia Contemporary Issues in National Security Policy. New York: Columbia University Press, 2005.

Guimaraes, Fernando Andresen. *The Origins of the Angolan Civil War: Foreign Intervention and Domestic Political Conflict.* Sydney, Australia: Palgrave Macmillan, 2001.

Gunaratna, Rohan. *Inside Al Qaeda: Global Network of Terror.* New York: Berkley Publishing Group, 2003.

Gupta, Dipak K. *Understanding Terrorism and Political Violence.* New York: Routledge, 2008.

Gutierrez, Alberto Ostria. *The Tragedy of Bolivia: A People Crucified.* Westport, Conn.: Greenwood Press, 1981.

Gutman, Roy, ed. *Crimes of War: What the Public Should Know.* New York: W. W. Norton & Company, 1999.

Hagan, John. *Justice in the Balkans: Prosecuting War Crimes in the Hague Tribunal.* Chicago Series in Law and Society. Chicago: University of Chicago Press, 2003.

Hampstein, Elizabeth. *Uruguay Nunca Mas: Human Rights Violations, 1972–1985.* Philadelphia: Temple University Press, 1993.

Harpviken, Kristian Berg, ed. *The Future of Humanitarian Mine Action (Third Worlds).* Sydney, Australia: Palgrave Macmillan, 2004.

Harris, Mark Edward. *Inside North Korea.* San Francisco: Chronicle Books, 2007.

Harris, Nathaniel. *The War in Former Yugoslavia.* London: Hodder & Stoughton, 1997.

Harris, Sheldon. *Factories of Death: Japanese Biological Warfare 1932–45 and the American Cover-Up.* London: Routledge, 1995.

Hazan, Pierre, and James Thomas Snyder. *Justice in a Time of War: The True Story behind the International Criminal Tribunal for the Former Yugoslavia.* Eugenia and Hugh M. Stewart Series on Eastern Europe. Austin: Texas A&M University Press, 2004.

Helton, Arthur C. *The Price of Indifference: Refugees and Humanitarian Action in the New Century.* Oxford: Oxford University Press, 2002.

Hersh, Seymour M. *Chain of Command: The Road from 9/11 to Abu Ghraib.* New York: HarperCollins, 2004.

———. *My Lai 4: A Report on the Massacre and Its Aftermath.* New York: Random House Trade, 1970.

Hicks, George. *The Comfort Women: Japans Brutal Regime of Enforced Prostitution in the Second World War.* New York: W. W. Norton & Company, 1997.

Hicks, Neil. *Escalating Attacks on Human Rights Protection in Egypt: A Report of the Lawyers Committee for Human Rights.* New York: Lawyers Committee for Human Rights, 1995.

Hinton, Alexander Laban, and Robert Jay Lifton. *Why Did They Kill?: Cambodia in the Shadow of Genocide.* California Series in Public Anthropology, Vol. 11. Berkeley: University of California Press, 2004.

Hitler, Adolf. *Mein Kampf.* New York: Mariner Books, 1998.

Hochschild, Adam. *King Leopold's Ghost.* Boston: Mariner Books, 1999.

Hodges, Tony. *Angola from Afro-Stalinism to Petro-Diamond Capitalism.* Bloomington: Indiana University Press, 2001.

Hohne, Heinz Zollen. *The Order of the Death's Head: The Story of Hitler's SS.* Classic Military History. New York: Penguin, 2001.

Holzgrefe, J. L., and Robert O. Keohane, eds. *Humanitarian Intervention: Ethical, Legal and Political Dilemmas.* Cambridge: Cambridge University Press, 2003.

Honda, Katsuichi, and Frank Gibney, eds. *The Nanjing Massacre: A Japanese Journalist Confronts Japan's National Shame.* Studies of the Pacific Basin Institute. Armonk, N.Y.: East Gate Book, 1999.

Honig, Jan Willem, and Norbert Both. *Srebrenica: Record of a War Crime.* New York: Penguin Books, 1997.

Hufbauer, Gary Clyde, and Nicholas K. Mitrokostas. *Awakening Monster: The Alien Tort Statute of 1789.* Policy Analyses in International Economics. Washington, D.C.: Institute for International Economics, 2003.

Hyndman, Jennifer. *Managing Displacement: Refugees and the Politics of Humanitarianism.* Minneapolis: University of Minnesota Press, 2000.

Ignatieff, Michael. *Virtual War: Kosovo and Beyond.* New York: Picador, 2001.

Ingleby, David, ed. *Forced Migration and Mental Health: Rethinking the Care of Refugees and Displaced Persons.* New York: Plenum US, 2004.

International Committee of the Red Cross. *International Law Concerning the Conduct of Hostilities: Collection of Hague Conventions and Some Other Treaties.* Geneva, Switzerland: International Committee of the Red Cross, 1989.

Ishay, Micheline R., ed. *The Human Rights Reader: Major Political Writings, Essays, Speeches, and Documents from the Bible to the Present.* London: Routledge, 1997.

Jackson, Michael. *In Sierra Leone.* Durham, N.C.: Duke University Press, 2004.

Jackson, Nyamuya Maogoto. *War Crimes and Realpolitik: International Justice from World War I to the 21st Century.* Boulder, Colo.: Lynne Rienner Publishers, 2004.

Jacques, Martin. *When China Rules the World: The End of the Western World and the Birth of a New Global Order.* New York: Penguin, 2009.

Jacquin-Berdal, Dominique. *Unfinished Business: Ethiopia and Eritrea at War.* London: Red Sea Press, 2004.

Jardine, Matthew. *East Timor: Genocide in Paradise.* The Real Story Series. Monroe, Me.: Odonian Press, 2002.

Jaskof, Paul B. *The Architecture of Oppression: The SS, Forced Labor and the Nazi Monumental Building Economy.* London: Routledge, 2000.

Jinks, Derek. *The Rules of War: The Geneva Conventions in the Age of Terror.* Oxford: Oxford University Press, 2005.

Johnson, Douglas Hamilton. *The Root Causes of Sudan's Civil Wars.* Bloomington: Indiana University Press, 2003.

Jok, Madut Jok. *Race, Religion and Violence.* London: Oneworld Publications, 2007.

———. *War and Slavery in Sudan.* Philadelphia: University of Pennsylvania Press, 2001.

Jokie, Aleksandar, ed. *War Crimes and Collective Wrongdoing: A Reader.* London: Blackwell Publishers, 2001.

Jones, Adam, ed. *Genocide, War Crimes and the West: History and Complicity.* London: Zed Books, 2004.

Jones, Seth G. *In the Graveyard of Empires: America's War in Afghanistan.* New York: W. W. Norton & Company, 2009.

Judah, Tim. *Kosovo: War and Revenge.* New Haven, Conn.: Yale University Press, 2002.

Karsh, Efraim. *The Iran-Iraq War 1980–1988.* London: Osprey Publishing, 2002.

Karsh, Efraim, and Inari Rautsi. *Saddam Hussein: A Political Biography.* New York: Grove Press, 2003.

Kavass, Igor I., ed. *Human Rights, European Politics, and the Helsinki Accord: The Documentary Evolution of the Conference on Security and Co-operation in Europe 1973–1975.* Buffalo, N.Y.: William S. Hein & Co., 1981.

Keddie, Nikki R. *Modern Iran: Roots and Results of Revolution.* New Haven, Conn.: Yale University Press, 2003.

Keegan, John. *The Iraq War.* New York: Knopf, 2004.

Kennedy, David. *The Dark Sides of Virtue: Reassessing International Humanitarianism.* Princeton, N.J.: Princeton University Press, 2004.

Kenney, Charles D. *Fujimori's Coup and the Breakdown of Democracy in Latin America.* Notre Dame, Ind.: University of Notre Dame Press, 2004.

Kent, Ann. *Between Freedom and Subsistence: China and Human Rights.* Oxford: Oxford University Press, 1995.

Khlevnink, Oleg. *The History of the Gulag: From Collectivization to the Great Terror.* Translated by Vadim A. Staklo. *Annals of Communism Series.* New Haven, Conn.: Yale University Press, 2004.

Kiernan, Ben. *How Pol Pot Came to Power: Colonialism, Nationalism, and Communism in Cambodia, 1930–1975.* New Haven, Conn.: Yale University Press, 2004.

———. *The Pol Pot Regime: Race, Power, and Genocide in Cambodia under the Khmer Rouge, 1975–79.* New Haven, Conn.: Yale University Press, 2002.

Kim, Julie. *War in the Former Yugoslavia: Chronology of Events August 16, 1992–May 30, 1993.* CRS report for Congress. Washington, D.C.: Foreign Affairs and National Defense Division, Congressional Research Service, the Library of Congress, 1993.

Kimura, Rei. *Alberto Fujimori of Peru: The President Who Dared to Dream.* Woodstock, N.Y.: Beekman Books Inc., 1998.

King, Charles. *The Ghost of Freedom: A History of the Caucasus.* New York: Oxford University Press, 2009.

King, Peter. *West Papua and Indonesia since Suharto: Independence, Autonomy or Chaos?* Sydney, Australia: University of New South Wales Press, 2004.

Kipp, Jacob W. *International Ramifications of Yugoslavia's Serial Wars: The Challenge of Ethno-national Conflicts for a post-Cold-War, European Order.* Fort Leavenworth, Kans.: European Military Studies Office, 1993.

Kissinger, Henry. *Does America Need a Foreign Policy?: Toward a Diplomacy for the 21st Century.* New York: Simon & Schuster; Touchstone edition, 2002.

Kizny, Tomasz. *Gulag: Life and Death Inside the Soviet Concentration Camps 1917–1990.* London: Firefly Books Ltd, 2004.

Knock, Thomas J. *To End All Wars: Woodrow Wilson and the Quest for a New World Order.* Princeton, N.J.: Princeton University Press, 1995.

Korey, William. *Human Rights and the Helsinki Accord: Focus on U.S. Policy.* New York: Foreign Policy Assn., 1983.

Kornbluh, Peter. *The Pinochet File: A Declassified Dossier on Atrocity and Accountability. A National Security Archive Book.* New York: New Press, 2003.

Krepon, Michael. *Strategic Stalemate: Nuclear Weapons and Arms Control in American Politics.* Sydney, Australia: Palgrave Macmillan, 1986.

Kulah, Arthur F. *Liberia Will Rise Again: Reflections on the Liberian Civil Crisis.* Nashville, Tenn.: Abingdon Press, 1999.

Lagnado, Lucette Matalon, and Sheila Cohn Dekel. *Children of the Flames: Dr. Josef Mengele and the Untold Story of the Twins of Auschwitz.* New York: Penguin Books, 1992.

Lamont-Brown, Raymond. *Ships from Hell: Japanese War Crimes on the High Seas.* Phoenix Mill, U.K.: Sutton Publishing, 2002.

Lang, Anthony F., Jr., ed. *Just Intervention.* Washington, D.C.: Georgetown University Press, 2003.

Langford, R. Everett. *Introduction to Weapons of Mass Destruction: Radiological, Chemical, and Biological.* New York: Wiley-Interscience, 2004.

Latell, Brian. *After Fidel, Updated Edition: Raul Castro and the Future of Cuba's Revolution.* Basingstoke, U.K.: Palgrave Macmillan, 2007.

Lauren, Paul Gordon. *The Evolution of International Human Rights: Visions Seen. Pennsylvania Studies in Human Rights.* Philadelphia: University of Pennsylvania Press, 2003.

Lederberg, Joshua, ed. *Biological Weapons: Limiting the Threat. BCSIA Studies in International Security.* Cambridge, Mass.: MIT Press, 1999.

Legge, John D. *Sukarno: A Political Biography.* Burlington, Vt.: Butterworth-Heinemann, 2003.

Lehr, Peter. *Violence at Sea: Piracy in the Age of Global Terrorism.* New York: Routledge, 2006.

Leith, Denise. *The Politics of Power: Freeport in Suharto's Indonesia.* Honolulu: University of Hawaii Press, 2002.

Lemarchand, Reni, and Lee H. Hamilton. *Burundi: Ethnic Conflict and Genocide.* Cambridge: Cambridge University Press, 1996.

Lewis, Paul H. *Guerrillas and Generals: The Dirty War in Argentina.* New York: Praeger, 2001.

Leyton, Elliot. *Touched by Fire: Doctors Without Borders in a Third World Crisis.* Toronto: McClelland & Stewart, 1998.

Li, Peter, ed. *Japanese War Crimes: The Search for Justice.* New Brunswick, N.J.: Transaction Publishers, 2003.

Lifton, Robert. *The Nazi Doctors: Medical Killing and the Psychology of Genocide.* New York: Basic Books, 2000.

Lischer, Sarah Kenyon. *Dangerous Sanctuaries: Refugee Camps, Civil War, and the Dilemmas of Humanitarian Aid. Cornell Studies in Security Affairs.* Ithaca, N.Y.: Cornell University Press, 2005.

MacDonald, C. A. *The Killing of Reinhard Heydrich: The SS "Butcher of Prague."* New York: Da Capo Press, 1998.

MacKey, Sandra. *The Reckoning: Iraq and the Legacy of Saddam Hussein.* New York: W. W. Norton & Company, 2003.

Maga, Timothy P. *Judgment at Tokyo: The Japanese War Crimes Trials.* Lexington: University Press of Kentucky, 2001.

Malcolm, Noel. *Kosovo: A Short History.* New York: HarperPerennial, 1999.

Mamdani, Mahmood. *Saviors and Survivors: Darfur, Politics and the War on Terror.* New York: Pantheon, 2009.

———. *When Victims Become Killers: Colonialism, Nativism, and the Genocide in Rwanda.* Princeton, N.J.: Princeton University Press, 2002.

Mangold, Tom, and Jeff Goldberg. *Plague Wars: The Terrifying Reality of Biological Warfare.* New York: St. Martin's Press, 2001.

Marrus, Michael R. *The Nuremberg War Crimes Trial of 1945–46: A Documentary History. Bedford Series in History and Culture.* Sydney, Australia: Palgrave Macmillan, 1997.

Matar, Khalil I., and Robert W. Thabit. *Lockerbie and Libya: A Study in International Relations.* Jefferson, N.C.: McFarland & Company, 2003.

May, Larry, and Gerald Postema. *Crimes against Humanity: A Normative Account. Cambridge Studies in Philosophy and Law.* Cambridge: Cambridge University Press, 2004.

Mayer, Ann Elizabeth. *Islam and Human Rights: Tradition and Politics.* Philadelphia: Westview Press, 1998.

McNamara, Ronald J. *Democracy and Human Rights in the Mediterranean Partner States of the Osce: Algeria, Egypt, Israel, Jordan, Morocco and Tunisia: Briefing of the Committee on Security and Cooperation in Europe.* Chicago: Diane Pub. Co., 2004.

Meisler, Stanley. *United Nations: The First Fifty Years.* New York: Atlantic Monthly Press, 1997.

Melvern, Linda. *A People Betrayed: The Role of the West in Rwanda's Genocide.* London: Zed Books, 2000.

Mendelsohn, John. *The Preservation of Japanese War Crimes Trials Records in the National Archives.* Washington, D.C.: National Archives and Records Administration, 1982.

Menkhaus, Ken. *Somalia: State Collapse and the Threat of Terrorism.* London: International Institute for Strategic Studies, 2004.

Meron, Theodor. *War Crimes Law Comes of Age: Essays.* Oxford: Oxford University Press, 1999.

Mertus, Julie. *Former Yugoslavia: War Crimes Trials in the Former Yugoslavia.* Helsinki: Human Rights Watch/Helsinki, 1995.

———. *Kosovo: How Myths and Truths Started a War.* Berkeley: University of California Press, 1999.

Meyer, Jane. *The Dark Side: The Inside Story of How the War on Terror Turned into a War on American Ideals.* New York: Doubleday, 2008.

Micheletti, Eric. *Special Forces in Afghanistan 2001–2003: War against Terrorism.* Translated by Cyril Lombardini. Paris: Historie & Collections, 2003.

Miller, Donald E., and Lorna Touryan Miller. *Survivors: An Oral History of the Armenian Genocide.* Berkeley: University of California Press, 1999.

Miller, John, and Aaron Kenedi. *Inside Iraq: The History, the People, and the Modern Conflicts of the World's Least Understood Land.* New York: Marlowe & Company, 2003.

Minear, Richard R. *Victors' Justice: The Tokyo War Crimes Trial.* Michigan Classics in Japanese Studies. Ann Arbor: University of Michigan, Center for Japanese Studies, 2001.

Montefiore, Simon Sebag. *Stalin: The Court of the Red Tsar.* New York: Knopf, 2004.

Moorehead, Caroline. *Dunant's Dream: War, Switzerland, and the History of the Red Cross.* New York: Carroll & Graf Publishers, 1999.

———. *Human Cargo: A Journey among Refugees.* New York: Henry Holt and Co., 2005.

Mosley, Leonard. *The Reich Marshal: A Biography of Hermann Göring.* London: Weidenfeld and Nicolson, 1974.

Moyano, Maria. *Argentina's Lost Patrol: Armed Struggle, 1969–1979.* New Haven, Conn.: Yale University Press, 1995.

Munro, R. *Punishment Season: Human Rights in China After Martial Law.* Asia Watch Report. New York: Human Rights Watch, 1990.

Naimark, Norman, and Holly Case. *Yugoslavia and Its Historians: Understanding the Balkan Wars of the 1990s.* Stanford, Calif.: Stanford University Press, 2003.

Neier, Aryeh. *War Crimes: Brutality, Genocide, Terror, and the Struggle for Justice.* New York: Crown, 1998.

Nevins, Joseph. *A Not-So-Distant Horror: Mass Violence in East Timor.* Ithaca, N.Y.: Cornell University Press, 2005.

Nichols, Gary W., and Milton L. Boykin, eds. *Arms Control and Nuclear Weapons: U.S. Policies and the National Interest.* Contributions in Military Studies. Westport, Conn.: Greenwood Press, 1987.

Njoku, H. *Tragedy without Heroes: The Nigeria-Biafra War.* Chicago: Fourth Dimension Publications Ltd., 1987.

Ogata, Sadako, and Kofi Annan. *The Turbulent Decade: Confronting the Refugee Crises of the 1990s.* New York: W. W. Norton & Company, 2005.

Okonta, Ike. *Where Vultures Feast: Shell, Human Rights and Oil.* New York: Verso, 2003.

Olson, James S., and Randy Roberts, eds. *My Lai: A Brief History with Documents. The Bedford Series in History and Culture.* Sydney, Australia: Palgrave Macmillan, 1998.

Orford, Anne, James Crawford, and John Bell, eds. *Reading Humanitarian Intervention: Human Rights and the Use of Force in International Law.* Cambridge Studies in International and Comparative Law. Cambridge: Cambridge University Press, 2003.

Overbey, Fern. *The Dachau Defendants: Life Stories from Testimony and Documents of the War Crimes Prosecutions.* Jefferson, N.C.: McFarland & Company, 2004.

Paul, Wolfgang. *Hermann Göring: Hitler Paladin or Puppet?* Translated by Helmet Bogler. New York: Arms & Armour, 1998.

Pausewang, Siegfried, Kjetil Tronvoll, and Lovise Aaeln, eds. *Ethiopia since the Derg: A Decade of Democratic Pretension and Performance.* London: Zed Books, 2003.

Pearce, Jenny. *Inside Colombia: Drugs, Democracy, and War.* New Brunswick, N.J.: Rutgers University Press, 2004.

Peterson, Merrill D. *Starving Armenians: America and the Armenian Genocide, 1915–1930 and After.* Charlottesville: University Press of Virginia, 2004.

Peterson, Scott. *Me against My Brother: At War in Somalia, Sudan and Rwanda.* London: Routledge, 2001.

Pham, John-Peter. *Liberia: Portrait of a Failed State.* London: Reed Press, 2004.

Piccigallo, Philip R. *The Japanese on Trial: Allied War Crimes Operations in the East, 1945–1951.* Austin: University of Texas Press, 1980.

Pilloud, Claude. *Commentary on the Additional Protocols of 8 June 1977 to the Geneva Conventions of 12 August 1949*. Boston: Brill Academic Publishers, 1987.

Pinto, Constancio, and Jardine Matthew. *East Timor's Unfinished Struggle: Inside the Timorese Resistance*. Boston: South End Press, 1996.

Politzer, Patricia, and Diane Wachtel. *Fear in Chile: Lives under Pinochet*. New York: New Press, 2001.

Power, Samantha. *A Problem from Hell*. New York: Perennial, 2003.

Pran, Dith, comp. *Children of Cambodia's Killing Fields: Memoirs by Survivors*. Edited by Kim DePaul. New Haven, Conn.: Yale University Press, 1999.

Price, Monroe, and Mark Thompson, eds. *Forging Peace: Intervention, Human Rights, and the Management of Media Space*. Bloomington: Indiana University Press, 2002.

Price, Richard M. *The Chemical Weapons Taboo*. Ithaca, N.Y.: Cornell University Press, 1997.

Prokosch, Eric. *The Technology of Killing: A Military and Political History of Anti-personnel Weapons*. London: Zed Books, 1995.

Prunier, Gérard. *Darfur: A 21st Century Genocide*. 3d ed. Crises in World Politics. Ithaca, N.Y.: Cornell University Press, 2008.

Rabasa, Angel, and Peter Chalk. *Colombian Labyrinth: The Synergy of Drugs and Insurgency and Its Implications for Regional Stability*. Santa Monica, Calif.: Rand Corporation (NBN), 2001.

Radzinsky, Edvard. *Stalin: The First In-Depth Biography Based on Explosive New Documents from Russia's Secret Archives*. New York: Anchor, 1997.

Rashid, Ahmed. *Taliban: Militant Islam, Oil and Fundamentalism in Central Asia*. New Haven, Conn.: Yale University Press, 2001.

Razack, Sherene H. *Dark Threats and White Knights: The Somalia Affair, Peacekeeping, and the New Imperialism*. Toronto: University of Toronto Press, 2004.

Read, Anthony. *The Devil's Disciples: Hitler's Inner Circle*. New York: W. W. Norton & Company, 2004.

Rees, Laurence. *Horror in the East: Japan and the Atrocities of World War II*. New York: Da Capo Press, 2002.

Reidal, Bruce, *The Search for Al Qaeda: Its Leadership, Ideology and Future*. Washington: Brookings Institution Press, 2008.

Rejali, Darius M. *Torture and Democracy*. Princeton, N.J.: Princeton University Press, 2009.

Rhode, David. *Endgame: The Betrayal and Fall of Srebrenica*. New York: Farrar, Straus & Giroux, 1997.

Ricks, Thomas. *Fiasco: The American Adventure in Iraq*. New York: Penguin Press, 2006.

Rieff, David. *A Bed for the Night: Humanitarianism in Crisis*. New York: Simon & Schuster, 2002.

Roberts, Adam, and Richard Guelff. *Documents on the Laws of War*. Oxford: Oxford University Press, 2000.

Roberts, Jeremy. *Joseph Goebbels: Nazi Propaganda Minister*. Holocaust Biographies. New York: Rosen Publishing Group, 2000.

Robertson, Geoffrey. *Crimes against Humanity: The Struggle for Global Justice*. New York: New Press, 2003.

Rogel, Carole. *The Breakup of Yugoslavia and the War in Bosnia*. Westport, Conn.: Greenwood Press, 1998.

Romano, Cesare, Andre Nollkaemper, and Jann K. Kleffner, eds. *Internationalized Criminal Courts and Tribunals: Sierra Leone, East Timor, Kosovo, and Cambodia*. International Courts and Tribunals Series. Oxford: Oxford University Press, 2004.

Rone, Jemera. *Famine in Sudan, 1998: The Human Rights Causes*. New York: Human Rights Watch, 1999.

Roseman, Mark. *The Wannsee Conference and the Final Solution: A Reconsideration*. New York: Metropolitan Books, 2002.

Ross, James D. *Human Rights in Burma (Myanmar) since the May 1990 National Election*. New York: Lawyers Committee for Human Rights, 1991.

Rossanet, Bertrand de. *War and Peace in the Former Yugoslavia*. Boston: Martinus Nijhoff, 1997.

Roth, Kenneth, ed. *Torture: A Human Rights Perspective*. New York: New Press, 2005.

Russell of Liverpool, Edward Frederick Langley Russell, Baron. *Knights of the Bushido: A Short History of Japanese War Crimes*. London: Greenhill Books, 2005.

———. *The Scourge of the Swastika: A Short History of Nazi War Crimes*. London: Greenhill Books/Lionel Leventhal, 2002.

Sammakia, Nejla. *Algeria, Elections in the Shadow of Violence and Repression*. New York: Human Rights Watch/ Middle East, 1997.

Sanford, Victoria. *Buried Secrets: The Truth and Human Rights in Guatemala*. Basingstoke, U.K.: Palgrave Macmillan, 2004.

Santoro, Michael A. *Profits and Principles: Global Capitalism and Human Rights in China*. Ithaca, N.Y.: Cornell University Press, 2000.

Saracin, Philip. *Blood Diamonds*. Victoria, Canada: BookSurge Publishing, 2002.

Scharf, Michael P. *Balkan Justice: The Story behind the First International War Crimes Trial since Nuremberg*. Durham, N.C.: Carolina Academic Press, 1997.

Scheuer, Michael. *Imperial Hubris: Why the West Is Losing the War on Terror*. Washington, D.C.: Potomac Books, 2004.

Schlesigner, Stephen. *Act of Creation: The Founding of the United Nations: A Story of Superpowers, Secret Agents, Wartime Allies and Enemies, and Their Quest for a Peaceful World.* Boulder, Colo.: Westview Press, 2003.

Schofield, Victoria. *Kashmir in Conflict: India, Pakistan and the Unending War.* London: I. B. Tauris, 2002.

Schultz, William. *Tainted Legacy: 9/11 and the Ruin of Human Rights.* New York: Nation Books, 2003.

Schulze, Kirsten E. *The Free Aceh Movement (GAM): Anatomy of a Separatist Organization.* Washington, D.C.: East-West Center, 2004.

Schwarz, Adam. *A Nation in Waiting: Indonesia's Search for Stability.* Philadelphia: Westview Press, 1999.

Sciolino, Elaine. *Persian Mirrors: The Elusive Face of Iran.* New York: Free Press, 2001.

Shelton, Dinah. *International Crimes, Peace, and Human Rights: The Role of the International Criminal Court.* Ardsley, N.Y.: Transnational Publishers, Inc., 2000.

———. *Remedies in International Human Rights Law.* Oxford: Oxford University Press, 2001.

Sherry, Virginia N. *Cleaning the Face of Morocco: Human Rights Abuses and Recent Developments/North Africa.* New York: Human Rights First, 1990.

Short, Philip. *Pol Pot: Anatomy of a Nightmare.* New York: Holt Rinehart, 2005.

Siegel, James T. *The Rope of God.* Ann Arbor: University of Michigan Press, 2000.

Simons, Geoff. *Libya and the West: From Independence to Lockerbie.* London: I. B. Tauris, 2004.

Sjamsuddin, Nazaruddin. *The Republican Revolt: A Study of the Acehnese Rebellion.* Singapore: Institute of Southeast Asian Studies, 1988.

Slyomovics, Susan. *The Performance of Human Rights in Morocco.* Pennsylvania Studies in Human Rights. Philadelphia: University of Pennsylvania Press, 2005.

Smith, Sebastian. *Allah's Mountain: The Battle for Chechnya.* London: Tauris Parke Paperbacks, 2005.

Solzhenitsyn, Aleksandr. *The Gulag Archipelago.* New York: Harpercollins, 1978.

Southall, Roger, and Kristina Bentley. *African Peace Process: Mandela, South Africa, and Burundi.* Pretoria, South Africa: Human Sciences Research Council, 2005.

Steiner, Henry J., and Philip Alston. *International Human Rights in Context: Law, Politics, Morals.* Oxford: Oxford University Press, 2000.

Steinhardt, Ralph G., and Anthony A. D'Amato. *The Alien Tort Claims Act: An Analytical Anthology.* Ardsley, N.Y.: Transnational Publishers, 1999.

Straus, Scott. *The Order of Genocide: Race, Power, and War in Rwanda.* Ithaca, N.Y.: Cornell University Press, 2008.

Sukma, Rizal. *Security Operations in Aceh: Goals, Consequences, and Lessons.* Washington: East-West Center, 2004.

Takeyh, Ray. *Guardians of the Revolution: Iran and the World in the Age of the Ayatollahs.* New York: Oxford University Press, 2009.

Talbott, Strobe. *Engaging India: Diplomacy, Democracy, and the Bomb.* Washington, D.C.: Brookings Institution Press, 2004.

Tambiah, Stanley Jeyaraja. *Ethnic Fratricide and the Dismantling of Democracy.* Chicago: University of Chicago Press, 1991.

Tamm, Ingrid J. *Diamonds in Peace and War: Severing the Conflict Diamond Connection.* WPF Report #30. Cambridge, Mass.: World Peace Foundation, 2002.

Tanaka, Toshiyuki. *Hidden Horrors: Japanese War Crimes in World War II.* Boulder, Colo.: Westview Press, 1998.

Taylor, David. *The Wars of Former Yugoslavia.* Bloomington, Ind.: Raintree, 2003.

Taylor, Telford. *Nuremberg and Vietnam: An American Tragedy.* New York: Times Books, 1970.

Temple-Rason, Dina. *Justice on the Grass: Three Rwandan Journalists, Their Trial for War Crimes and a Nation's Quest for Redemption.* New York: Free Press, 2005.

Thompson, Joseph E. *American Policy and African Famine: The Nigeria-Biafra War, 1966–1970.* Contributions in Afro-American and African Studies. Westport, Conn.: Greenwood Press, 1990.

Toland, John. *Adolf Hitler: The Definitive Biography.* New York: Anchor, 1991.

Trombly, Maria. *Journalist's Guide to the Geneva Conventions.* Indianapolis: Society of Professional Journalists, 2000.

Tuck, Richard. *The Rights of War and Peace: Political Thought and the International Order from Grotius to Kant.* Oxford: Oxford University Press, 2001.

Tucker, Jonathan B., ed. *Toxic Terror: Assessing Terrorist Use of Chemical and Biological Weapons.* BCSIA Studies in International Security. Cambridge, Mass.: MIT Press, 2000.

Tutorow, Norman E. *War Crimes, War Criminals, and War Crimes Trials: An Annotated Bibliography and Source Book. Bibliographies and Indexes in World History.* Westport, Conn.: Greenwood Publishing Group, 1986.

Ulam, Adam B. *Stalin: The Man and His Era.* Boston: Beacon Press, 1987.

United Nations War Crimes Commission. *Law Reports of Trials of War Criminals: Four Genocide Trials.* Boulder, Colo.: Lynne Rienner Publishers, 1992.

Vargas Llosa, Álvaro. *The Madness of Things Peruvian: Democracy under Siege.* New Brunswick, N.J.: Transaction Publishers, 1994.

Vatikiotis, Michael R. *Indonesian Politics under Suharto: The Rise and Fall of the New Order.* London: Routledge, 1999.

Vaux, Anthony. *The Selfish Altruist: Relief Work in Famine and War.* London: Earthscan Publications, 2001.

Veloso, Caetano. *Tropical Truth: A Story of Music and Revolution in Brazil.* New York: Knopf, 2002.

Vietnam Veterans against the War. *The Winter Soldier Investigation: An Inquiry into American War Crimes.* Boston: Beacon Press, 1972.

Vyver, Johan D. van der, and John Witte, Jr., eds. *Religious Human Rights in Global Perspective: Legal Perspectives.* 2d ed. Grand Rapids, Mich.: Wm. B. Eerdmans Publishing Company, 2000.

Waltz, Susan Eileen. *Human Rights and Reform: Changing the Face of North African Politics.* Berkeley: University of California Press, 1995.

Weatherley, Robert. *The Discourse of Human Rights in China: Historical and Ideological Perspectives.* Sydney, Australia: Palgrave Macmillan, 1999.

Weiss, Thomas G., David P. Forsythe, and Roger A. Coate. *United Nations and Changing World Politics.* Westport, Conn.: Westview Press, 2004.

Weissman, Fabrice. *In the Shadow of "Just Wars": Violence, Politics, and Humanitarian Action.* Ithaca, N.Y.: Cornell University Press, 2004.

Welch, Claude E., Jr. *Ngos and Human Rights: Promise and Performance.* Pennsylvania Studies in Human Rights. Philadelphia: University of Pennsylvania Press, 2000.

Welsh, Jennifer M. *Humanitarian Intervention and International Relations.* Oxford: Oxford University Press, 2004.

Whealey, Robert. *American Intervention in the Yugoslavia: Civil War, 1991–1999.* Amherst, N.Y.: Humanity Books, 2005.

Wheeler, Nicholas J. *Saving Strangers: Humanitarian Intervention in International Society.* Oxford: Oxford University Press, 2003.

Whitley, Andrew. *Human Rights Abuses in Algeria: No One Is Spared.* New York: Human Rights Watch, 1994.

Wiendling, Paul Julian. *Nazi Medicine and the Nuremberg Trials: From Medical War Crimes to Informed Consent.* Sydney, Australia: Palgrave Macmillan, 2005.

Wilkinson, Daniel. *Silence on the Mountain: Stories of Terror, Betrayal, and Forgetting in Guatemala.* Boston: Houghton Mifflin, 2002.

Winner, David. *Peter Benenson: Taking a Stand against Injustice—Amnesty International (People Who Have Helped the World).* Milwaukee: Gareth Stevens Pub., 1992.

Winslow, Philip C. *Sowing the Dragon's Teeth: Land Mines and the Global Legacy of War.* Boston: Beacon Press, 1998.

Wistrich, Robert S. *Hitler and the Holocaust. Modern Library Chronicles.* New York: Modern Library, 2001.

Wood, Elisabeth Jean, Peter Lange et al., eds. *Insurgent Collective Action and Civil War in El Salvador.* Cambridge Studies in Comparative Politics. Cambridge: Cambridge University Press, 2003,

Wrong, Michela. *In the Footsteps of Mr. Kurtz: Living on the Brink of Disaster in Mobutu's Congo.* New York: HarperCollins Publishers, 2001.

Zayy-at, Montasser al-. *The Road to Al-Qaeda: The Story of Bin Laden's Right-Hand Man.* Critical Studies on Islam. Translated by Ahmed Fekry. Edited by Sara Nimis. Ann Arbor, Mich.: Pluto Press, 2004.

Encyclopedias, Guides, and Handbooks

Encyclopedia of Human Rights. Edited by David P. Forsythe. Comprehensive coverage of all aspects of human rights theory, practice, law, and history.

Encyclopedia of Human Rights. 2d ed. E. Lawson. Comprehensive compendium including texts of 200 instruments, descriptions of human rights organizations, status of human rights in countries, etc.

Encyclopedia of Human Rights Issues since 1945. W. Langley.

Encyclopedia of the United Nations. 3d ed. 4 vols. Useful background information on human rights and the relevant conventions, including texts of the major instruments.

Great Events from History II: Human Rights Series. 5 vols. Articles covering over 460 topics in the history of human rights arranged chronologically from 1900 to 1991. Each essay provides a summary of the event and its impact along with a bibliography and cross-references.

Historical Dictionary of Human Rights and Humanitarian Organizations. R. Gorman.

Human Rights Encyclopedia. J. Lewis, ed. 3 vols.

Human Rights: The Essential Reference. C. Devine et al.

International Encyclopedia of Human Rights: Freedoms, Abuses, and Remedies. R. Maddex.

United Nations and Human Rights, 1945–1995. UN Blue Book Series, Vol. 7.

United Nations Reference Guide in the Field of Human Rights.

Guides to Research

Guide to Human Rights Research. J. Tobin. Comprehensive guide to the literature

Guide to International Human Rights Practice. 2d ed., 1992. H. Hannum.

Human Rights: A Reference Handbook. 2d ed. N. Redman and L. Whalen.

Document Sources
Basic Documents on Human Rights. 3d ed. I. Brownlie.
Human Rights: A Compilation of International Instruments. 7th ed. United Nations.
Human Rights Documents: Compilation of Documents Pertaining to Human Rights: US Laws on Human Rights; Basic UN Human Rights.

Annuals
Amnesty International Report.
Country Reports on Human Rights Practices. Dept. of State. (also on Dept. of State Web site)
European Union Annual Report on Human Rights.
For the Record: The UN Human Rights System 1997–.
Freedom in the World: Political Rights and Civil Liberties. Freedom House.
Human Rights in Developing Countries.
Human Rights Watch World Report.
Nations in Transit: Civil Society, Democracy and Markets in East Central Europe and the Newly Independent States. 1997– .
World Refugee Survey.
Yearbook of the United Nations.

Periodicals Indexes/Databases

Bibliographic Databases and Online Catalogs
Human rights law and related commentaries are growing at an amazing rate. The two major bibliographic databases in the United States are RLG and OCLC.

A guide is available about how to research human rights on the Internet. The Concise Guide to Human Rights on the Internet can be found at http://www.derechos.org/humanrights/manual.htm.

Alternative Press Index
http://www.altpress.org/
Index to more than 380 alternative, radical, and left publications from 1991 to present

CIAO (Columbia International Affairs Online).
http://www.ciaonet.org/
Provides full text of working papers, conferences, abstracts of journal articles, web links, etc.

CLC (the Online Computer Library Center)
http://www.oclc.org/home
This data bank includes the records of many academic institutions, law firm libraries, and smaller libraries in the U.S. Some large libraries have their holdings on both systems. Most bibliographic databases and online catalogs use standard Library of Congress Subject Headings (LCSH).

EUREKA (Eureka Guide to UN Information)
http://www.library.yale.edu:80/un/un2a5.htm
The Dag Hammarskjöld Library (United Nations Library) has allowed their records to be included.

Expanded Academic ASAP
http://www.galegroup.com/tlist/sb5019.html
Indexes 1,600 popular and scholarly journals from 1988 to present.

Human Rights and Humanitarian Affairs: Information Resources
http://www.columbia.edu/cu/lweb/indiv/lehman/guides/human.html
This is a selective guide to resources at Columbia University Libraries and on the Internet, for conducting research on international human rights issues.

PAIS International
http://www.pais.org/
Indexes books, articles, government documents and working papers from around the world.

ProQuest
http://www.proquestk12.com/
Index to general interest and academic periodicals with full text for most, 1986 to present.

RLG Union Catalog (the Research Libraries Group)
http://www.rlg.org/
The RLGU contains the holdings of some of the major academic institutions such as University of California at Berkeley, Columbia University, Harvard University, and Yale University. This is a database from 1979 to the present with quarterly updates.

Worldwide Political Science Abstracts
http://www.asu.edu/lib/resources/db/polscbib.htm
Indexes and abstracts journals from political science and related fields.

Periodicals
Columbia Human Rights Law Review
CSCE Digest (Commission on Security and Cooperation in Europe)
http://www.law.columbia.edu/current_student/student_service/Law_Journals/human_rights
Harvard Human Rights Journal
http://www.law.harvard.edu/students/orgs/hrj/
Human Rights: A Quarterly Review of the Office of UNHCHR
Human Rights Internet Reporter
http://www.osa.ceu.hu/lpe?id=1380
Human Rights Law Journal
Human Rights Quarterly: A Comparative and International Journal of the Social Sciences, Philosophy, and Law

Human Rights Tribune [Human Rights Internet]
http://www.hrtribune.com/
Human Rights Watch [reports] (also available on HRW Web site)
http://www.hrw.org/
Brief reports documenting current human rights abuses in countries/regions around the world
Index on Censorship [Writers and Scholars International] Presents issues on censorship of writers worldwide
International Human Rights Reports
International Journal of Human Rights
Netherlands Quarterly of Human Rights
South African Journal on Human Rights
Yale Human Rights and Development Law Journal
http://islandia.law.yale.edu/yhrdlj/

News Sources

America's Newspapers
Full text of over 200 U.S. newspapers on political, economic, and social events at the local, state, national and international levels.

Global NewsBank 1996–
Full-text international news from 1,500 newspapers, wire services, radio, and TV broadcasts and periodicals. All sources translated to English.
http://www.newsbank.com/academic/global.html

Lexis/Nexis Academic
http://www.lexisnexis.com/
Full-text database of news, legal, and business sources.

Indexes

Access UN
http://www.newsbank.com/un/
1948–
Indexes United Nations documents with links to online text where available; documents also available on fiche, 1983 to present as well as in paper. Check for periodic reports by states parties to various international human rights agreements and reports of the special rapporteurs on the status of human rights in particular countries.

Lexis/Nexis Legislative
http://www.lexisnexis.com/academic/3cis/cisl/
LegislativePublications.asp
Indexes congressional publications from 1970 to present and provides full text of bills, laws, regulations, testimony, and other congressional sources.

Lexis/Nexis Statistical
Indexes federal, state, and international statistical sources and provides links to online text where available.
http://www.lexisnexis.com/academic/1univ/stat/default.asp

UNBISnet
http://www.un.org.pk/library/biblo-ref-data.htm
Compilation of 10 databases providing bibliographic access to UN and non-UN publications. Includes full text of resolutions, voting records, and citations to speeches and agendas.

UN Documents Sources

UN High Commissioner for Human Rights
http://www.ohchr.org/english/

UN Human Rights Reports
For a guide to the documents issued by the various human rights committees see http://www.un.org/Depts/dhl/resguide/spechr.htm.
The most comprehensive source for UN human rights documentation is the home page of the United Nations. This site provides electronic text of the human rights treaty and charter-based bodies and periodic reports by states, press releases, etc.
Additionally, UN-I-QUE, a reference database of the Dag Hammarskjöld (UN) Library, indexes selected UN documents from 1946 to present.

Internet Sources

Council of Europe Human Rights
http://www.hri.org/docs/ECHR50.html
Provides access to the European Court of Human Rights and other relevant human rights instruments for Europe.

Derechos Human Rights
http://www.derechos.org
The first Internet-based human rights organization. It works with human rights situations in countries.

Human Rights Internet
http://www.hri.ca/index.aspx
International NGO, documentation center, and publishing house in Canada. See section: UN Processes and Documentation and click on "For the Record: The UN Human Rights System" which provides an annual country-by-country overview of human rights issues with links to relevant UN documents. Reports are available from 1997 to present.

University of Minnesota Human Rights Library
http://www1.umn.edu/humanrts/
A joint project of Yale Law School, University of Toronto Law School and the University of Minnesota. Each site has different information—Yale focuses on human rights legal cases and documents, and Toronto on women's human rights resources.

Index

religious persecution **445–446**
   in Azerbaijan 41
   in Bhutan 53
   in Bulgaria 66
   in China 99, 101, 445–446
   in Cuba 137
   in Egypt 169
   in India 228, 272
   in Iran 293
   in Iraq 297
   in Ivory Coast 300, 301
   in Laos 335
   in Nigeria 386–387
   in Russia 453, 454
   in Uzbekistan 548
   in Vietnam 554, 555
relocation centers. *See*
   concentration camps
*Remaining Documents of Talat
   Pasha, The* (Bardakci) 31–32
Remer, Otto 214
Renzaho, Tharcisse 460
reparations 173, **446–447,** 470
Reporters Without Borders 295,
   332, 534
reprisal 253, **447,** 519
Republika Srpska (RS) 59, 61, 567,
   568, 589
requisitioning 421
resistance killings, in Brazil 65
Responsibility to Protect **447–
   448**
retributive genocide 205
Revolutionary Armed Forces of
   Colombia. *See* FARC
Revolutionary Front for Haitian
   Advancement and Progress
   (FRAPH) 233, 234, 235,
   236–237
Revolutionary Guards 293, 294,
   295
Revolutionary United Front (RUF)
   121, 465, 478, 487
Reyes, Arturo Lona 363
Reyes, Raúl 167
Rhee, Syngman 388
Rhodesia 54, 108. *See also*
   Zimbabwe
Ribbentrop, Joachim von 243, 384,
   396, **448,** 451
Rice, Susan 448
Richardson, Sophie 97
Ridenhour, Ron 379
Rights and Democracy 90
Ríos Montt, José Efraín 225, 226,
   448–449
Robinson, Mary 571
Rodriguez, Andres 498
Rodriguez, Eduardo 58
Rohingya people 378
Rohm, Ernst 247
Rom (Roma, Romany, Gypsies),
   persecution of **449–451**
   in Bulgaria 66
   in Croatia 416, 417, 547
   in Macedonia 348
   in Nazi Germany 62, 105, 119,
      180, 186, 358, 398, 449–450
   in Russia 453
Romania, human rights violations
   in 80–82
Romero, Oscar 147, 175, 467

Rome Statute of the International
   Criminal Court **451**
   on genocide 205, 207
   ICC established by 283, 284,
      440, 451
   on medical experiments 356,
      431
   on public property 433
   on rape 440
   on slavery 480
   on war crimes 561
Roosevelt, Eleanor 191, 538,
   540–542, *541*
Roosevelt, Franklin D. 55, 66, 303,
   336, 470, 485, 494
Roosevelt, Theodore 232
Rosenbaum, Eli M. 403, 404
Rosenberg, Alfred 249, **451–452**
Rossi, Luiz Basilio 21
Roth, Kenneth 544
Roxas, Melissa 418
Royal Dutch Shell 16
Royal Institute for Amazigh Culture
   53
RS. *See* Republika Srpska
RSS. *See* National Volunteer Corps
Rúa, Fernando de la 27
Rudd, Kevin 2
Rudolph, Arthur 403, 404
RUF. *See* Revolutionary United
   Front
Rukundo, Emmanuel 460
Rumsfeld, Donald 50, 221, 409,
   542, 576, 577
Russia. *See also* Soviet Union
   arms sales by 33
   and Belarus 49
   and Chechnya 83–88, *84,* 453
   children in 86–87, 94
   and Georgia 209, 447
   human rights violations in
      452–454
   pogrom in 426
   refugees in 86, 443
   scorched earth tactic used by
      471
   and Serbia 566
   and Sudan 47–48
Rwanda
   arms trafficking in 32–33
   and Congo, Democratic
      Republic of the 124, 125, 126,
      128, 456–457
   humanitarian aid barred in 254
   refugees from 442, 454, 455–
      456, 457, 462
   refugees in 68
   sanctions on 34, 463
   and United States 256, 456, 475
Rwanda, genocide in 180, **454–
   457,** *455. See also* International
   Criminal Tribunal for Rwanda
   arms trafficking and 33
   Belgian war crimes tribunal
      on 50
   Burundi and 68, 69–70
   combatant identification in 267
   and humanitarian intervention
      256
   Human Rights Watch on 260
   incitement to 270, 286, 459
   intent of 206

   mass graves 353
   Elizaphan Ntakirutimana 105
   rape 285, 455, 458, 459, 460
   as retributive genocide 205
   safe havens in 462
   UN on 144, 454–457
Rwandan human rights violators
   457–460
Rwandan Patriotic Front 454, 455
Ryle, John 189

S

SA (Sturm Abteilung) 58, 62, 358,
   396, 397, 399, 491
Saakashvili, Mikhail 208–209
Sabra and Shatilla, massacre in
   461, 557
Saca, Antonio 175
Sachsenhausen concentration camp
   240, 244, 450
Sadat, Anwar 436
safe havens **461–462,** 466, 489,
   552, 590
Sainović, Nikola 24
Saipov, Alisher 333
Sakai Takashi **462–463**
Salinas, Carlos 149, 363
Salinas, Raúl 149
Saloth Sar. *See* Pol Pot
Salsinha, Gastão 165
Sánchez de Lozada, Gonzalo 57
sanctions 34, 138, 290, 341, 343,
   463–464, 515
Sandinista National Liberation
   Front (FSLN) 484, 485
Sandino, Augusto César 485
Sanguinetti, Julio 546
Sankoh, Foday 121, 340, 342,
   464–465, 478, 487, 509
Sant'Anna di Stazzema, massacre in
   465–466
Santebal 77
Santos, Jose dos 22
Santos, Juan Manuel 115
Sarajevo, siege of 368, **466–467**
   as attack on safe haven 466
   civilians killed in 269, 466, 589
   ICTY on 312, 477, 565, 566
   as indiscriminate attack 103
   Ratko Mladić 370
Saravia, Álvaro 175, **467**
sarin 88, 90
Sarkozy, Nicolas 450
Saro-Wiwa, Ken 16
Sauckel, Fritz **467**
Saudi Arabia
   Idi Amin in 19
   Amnesty International on 21,
      468–469
   executions in 182, 468–469
   human rights violations in **467–
      469,** 585
   and Yemen 588–589
Savimbi, Joseph 22
Sawoniuk, Anthony **469**
Scalia, Anthony 15
Schabas, William 207
Schacht, Hjalmar Horace Greeley
   415, **469–470**
Schakowsky, Jan 361
Scheinin, Martin 574

Schellenberg, Walter 243,
   470–471
Schickelgruber, Alois. *See* Hitler,
   Adolf
Schirach, Baldur von **471**
Schlesinger, James 298
Schutzstaffel. *See* SS
Schwarzkopf, Norman 542
Scilingo, Adolfo 198
scorched earth 180, 401, **471,** 475,
   488, 499
SD (Sicherheitsdienst) 44, 170,
   186, 211, 243, 245, 310
seawater experiments 154
Securitate 81, 82
security zones. *See* safe havens
Sejested, Francis 38
Sendero Luminoso. *See* Shining Path
SENDET. *See* National Prisoners
   Service
Senegal 231
Seng, Theary C. 71
September 11, 2001, terrorist
   attacks 572. *See also* war on terror
   as act of war 5
   Balthasar Garzón investigating
      199
   ghost prisoners after 212
   mastermind of 222, 375, 437
   refugee admissions after 36
   rights of combatants 115–116
   "20th hijacker" in 437–438
   United Nations Resolution 1368
      on 539
Serbia
   Martti Ahtisaari 12
   human rights violations in
      471–472. *See also* Balkan wars;
      Milošević, Slobodan
   sanctions on 464
Serb Volunteer Guard (SDG) 28,
   569
Sereny, Gitta 489
Serrano Elias, Jorge 224
Sesay, Issa 478
Seselj, Vojislav **472–473**
Severe Acute Respiratory
   Syndrome (SARS) 101, 306
sex slaves 22, 90, 91, 116–117. *See
   also* prostitution (forced)
Seyss-Inquart, Arthur **473–475,**
   474
SFOR. *See* Stabilization Force
Shabab, al- 437, 482–483, 484
Shah, Abdullah 9
Shahroudi, Mahmoud 293
Shalikashvili, John 89
sharia law 46, 47, 386, 468, 482,
   483, 504
Sharon, Ariel 50, 412, 414, 461,
   557
Shattuck, John **475,** 581
Shell Oil 16
Shevardnadze, Eduard 208
Shiite Muslims
   in Afghanistan 239
   Martti Ahtisaari 12
   in Bahrain 42
   in Iran 293
   in Iraq 263, 264, 296, 297
   in Pakistan 411
   in Saudi Arabia 468